an introduction to philosophy

ENCOUNTER

edited by

RAMONA CORMIER
bowling green state university

EWING CHINN
trinity university

RICHARD H. LINEBACK
bowling green state university

academic editor
WILLIAM K. FRANKENA
university of michigan

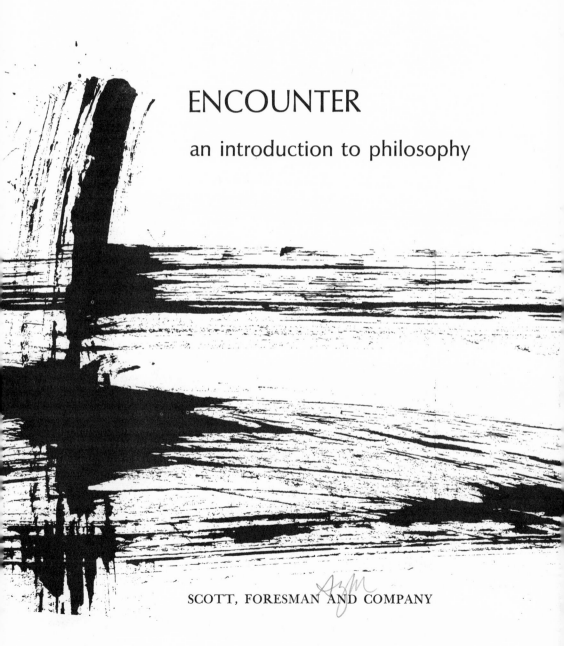

ENCOUNTER

an introduction to philosophy

SCOTT, FORESMAN AND COMPANY

preface

The philosophy that prevails in a given time and place may include, among its very foundations, the rejection of rival modes of thought. In fact, since those who call themselves "Philosophers" are empowered by their profession to define the nature and scope of philosophy itself, they may, without hindrance, do so in such a way that others who have also claimed the title "Philosopher" are left beyond the pale. Thus, the body of writings constituting "real" philosophy is reduced and "purified."

It is the conviction of the editors of this volume that such an approach—whatever its virtues—is inappropriate to an introductory text. We have assumed that a first encounter with philosophy should involve exposure to basic traditional and contemporary approaches to the major problems, that it should allow the reader to see each position in the context of its alternatives. Consequently, although the book provides considerable representation of dominant trends in contemporary Anglo-American philosophy, these are somewhat counterpoised with a fair sampling of traditional writing—including metaphysical speculation—and more recent Continental trends such as existentialism, phenomenology, and Bergson's intuitive metaphysics of duration. It is hoped that the arrangement of the selections in a sequence of contrasting positions will evoke critical scrutiny of each approach and allow the reader to arrive at his own conclusions by choice rather than by dint of editorial decisions.

Encounter is a joint venture of the three editors who conceived it and arranged the readings. However, Ramona Cormier was primarily responsible for Parts II, III, and IV, Ewing Chinn for Parts I and VI, and Richard H. Lineback for Parts V and VII.

The editors wish to thank Paul Rohe and Oscar Kenshur of Scott, Foresman and Company for their cooperation and guidance. We also wish to thank Professor William K. Frankena for his valuable suggestions.

R.C.
E.C.
R.H.L.

CONTENTS

part III   MINDS, BODIES, AND SELVES

part   I

perception
and the
external world

INTRODUCTION

Common sense dictates that there exists an external world of (at least) material or physical objects and events. To reject this dictate is tantamount to consistently denying obvious facts—such as the presence of a large ferocious dog blocking one's path—which should not be treated as figments of the imagination. We could scarcely cope with the exigencies of everyday life if we were to maintain uncompromisingly an incredulous attitude toward every ordinary object or occurrence. Surely no one could be so foolish as to oppose the voice of common sense in so radical a manner, no one *except the philosopher*.

It has been said (usually, but not always, by the uninitiated) that the philosopher, unlike the common man, is uniquely inseminated with the insight that whatever *appears* to be real cannot *be* real. Consequently he must doubt the veracity of observations and judgments yielded by anyone's experience, including much of his own. In short, contrary to man's natural disposition, the philosopher is the unmitigated and insatiable sceptic, resolved to question the most commonplace and seemingly inescapable features of human experience. But how can anyone actually take this stance of total scepticism with utter seriousness? Surely if one is truly convinced that the objects and events of our experiential world are unreal, then in the light of the simple demands of normal existence he must be either a benign fool or completely irrational. If he is neither, and only plays at disbelieving, then what could be more pointless?

Moreover, a vexing problem suddenly arises as a result of philosophic doubt, a problem which, some say, has been the source of countless protracted and inconclusive debates between competing philosophic points of view. The problem is that of finding some viable substitute for what the common man had so innocently believed to be the real world. If the world of our senses is not real, what is real? Where can we go for some evidence that would help to determine which theory of reality is true, or, at the very least, more acceptable than any other? Once we leave or reject the solid ground of "ordinary experience," are we not cut off from knowledge? Or do philosophers possess a unique *vision* that allows them to see what normal men are unable to see? Unfortunately, such an audacious claim of a special philosophic "sense" requires independent validation and actually compounds the problem rather than solving it. Must we, then, conclude that no good grounds exist for believing anything to be real, or that the "real world," if there is one, cannot be known?

The philosophic posture of inexorable scepticism that we have drawn is, no doubt, absurd in the context of common experience; and its implications are extraordinarily problematic. Fortunately, however, this picture is, in the main, a misleading interpretation of the philosopher's critical attitude toward common sense. Certainly the philosopher does not deny that we are, at every conscious moment, confronted with events and objects that are (experienced as) distinct from the experiencer. There is no denying that, in this sense, there is an *experienced* reality of some kind that exists as the totality of all the objects of our consciousness. That which we experience exists *for us* as a world external to, or "outside of," our acts of perceiving or sensing. If this is what it means to say that an external world exists, the proposition is incontestable. In fact, it may be said that the gist of this claim is merely a characterization, albeit a trivial one, of what is most basic and indisputable in any perceptual experience.

However, what we have construed as an obviously harmless assertion concerning the status of things that we perceive is usually imbued with additional meaning and taken to express or imply a number of other propositions. What it is taken to mean, in addition to the trivial claim that there is something, some phenomenon, that is real for us *insofar as we do perceive it or have perceived it,* is (1) that this phenomenon is *independently real* and (2) that it inherently has all of the characteristics and properties that we perceive it to have. The first proposition, that the perceived world is not just the phenomenal world (those objects which are perceived) but the independently real, physical world, leads us to two natural corollaries: The external world will continue to exist whether or not anyone is perceiving it; and all of us, under normal conditions, will perceive the *same* world and the same constitutents of that world. The second proposition, that, through perception, we have *direct knowledge* of the objectively real nature of the external world and not just of the nature that the world *represent*s to our experience, presumably involves no argument or thought. To ascertain that this object has this or that property, we merely have to *see* what kind of properties it, in fact, has. What is crucial is the contention that perceptual experience is inherently the one-and-only unerring, totally dependable basis of our knowledge of the external world, the basis, that is, of *objective knowledge*.

These conclusions, which we have set forth as implications of the original claim that we perceive an external world, comprise the view called *naïve realism*—"realism" because of the contention that the things perceived exist independent of and unaffected by the perceiver, and have just those qualities that they are perceived as having; and "naïve" because these beliefs are generally accepted uncritically, that is, without examination.

It is the soundness of this common-sense view of perception and the external world that is at issue, and *not* whether or not we should question the "objectivity" of our perceptual experiences (e.g., whether we should dispute the fact that there is a large dog in front of us). It is, then, the complacent, uncritical acceptance of naïve realism that has been a target of philosophic criticism and doubt; and the consideration of this position has provided the stimulus for the endeavor to gain a better understanding of the nature of perception and to propose more enlightened theories on this matter.

To begin with, it becomes apparent, upon close examination, that most individuals do not, in practice, subscribe to naïve realism with any consistency. For example, a reasonably intelligent person would not maintain that everything contained in his experience of an object belongs to, or is a part of, that object. He would often make a distinction between those properties that make the object what it is (its intrinsic properties) and those properties ascribed to the object that actually result from the interaction of the object with the perceiver and with external, environmental conditions. The ringing sound of a bell that one hears is not conceived to be an intrinsic or primary property of the bell, but only as having its physical, causal source partly in the bell. The sound would not exist without a medium through which the sound waves could travel and without auditory organs to receive these waves. In other words, naïve realism is not even accurate as a description of what everyone believes; no one is totally naïve in his realism.

The highly dubious nature of the assumption that we can always perceive things as they really are is further revealed by the occurrence of such deceptive phenomena as illusions and hallucinations. Everyone agrees that experiences of, for example, mirages, double images, and mirror reflections either do not represent anything in the external world (pink elephants do not physically exist even though they seem to), or present to us a distortion of what is real (the stick that appears bent in the water is not really bent at all). Although, in most cases, the explanation of *how* such experiences occur is satisfactory to us, the illusions and hallucinations introduce a problem that is not easily disposed of. They suggest that perhaps there is no essential difference, in fact, between the *nature* of a veridical perception and the nature of a deceptive perception. Of course, the veridical perception, unlike the deceptive one, is said to correspond to a real object (or, more simply, the object perceived is said to be real). Nevertheless this claim is not to be simply taken for granted, especially in light of two considerations with regard to the nature of perceptual experience, considerations which cannot be ignored.

First of all, can we detect any *qualitative* difference between the experience, for example, of seeing a pink elephant that is not there and that of seeing a large dog that is? Can we explain what this difference is and isolate it in our experience? Or is it, rather, not the case that instead of *seeing* that the pink elephant is not real, we *infer* its unreality and its illusory nature from certain independent facts or beliefs that we have previously accepted? The perceiver cannot distinguish between veridical and non-veridical experiences merely on the basis of the experiences themselves. If the naïve realist admits this point and, nevertheless, persists in maintaining his position, can he avoid accepting such implications as, that the pink elephant is as real as the large dog, or that the stick is bent when immersed in a body of water and straight when taken out of the water, or that the very same coin is both round and elliptical in shape? Can he account for the difference between a veridical perception and a non-veridical perception in terms of his position? It is doubtful that he can.

Secondly, it seems difficult to deny—what is impressed upon us, in part, by psychological and physiological studies—that perception is a *mediated* affair. We do not yet (and may never) know precisely how our perceptual experiences are affected by the mediating agencies interposed between the conscious mind of the observer and the alleged object-in-itself; but that there is *some* influence on what we actually perceive appears to be an inescapable conclusion, a conclusion that is typically presupposed in scientific investigations. Whereas the previous argument merely rendered naïve realism problematic, the acceptance of this perceptual mediacy would lead to the conclusion that the naïve position is simply *false*. Accepting this conclusion would entail rejecting the notion that perception brings us into immediate and direct contact with independently existing objects "out there." Although we may *behave* as if perception were direct and, moreover, *believe* that we are capable of distinguishing between veridical and non-veridical experiences (real objects and illusions), it remains to be philosophically demonstrated that men are not merely accepting the persuasive and habitual convictions (useful as they may be) of common sense.

While the foregoing analysis does seem to reveal the inadequacy of the naïve realism that most people embrace, it cannot be said to have refuted the fundamental claim of common sense that we do perceive (with whatever variation or inaccuracy) objects and events in the external world. The rejection of naïve realism does not *necessarily* require the acceptance of a theory alleging that we perceive not external objects, in any sense of the word "perceive," but instead some kind of mental or nonphysical phenomena. However, many philosophers of otherwise conflicting viewpoints have held that one version of this alternative is far more tenable than the claims of common sense. This position, generally known as the sense-datum theory of sense perception, usually distinguishes three factors within the perceptual experience (or involved in perceptual knowledge): (1) There is, first, the act of conscious awareness, the act of sensing, or simply the sensation; (2) there is, next, the object of which we are directly aware (modern philosophers speak of "sense impressions," "sense-data," "sensa," or "percepts"), which is distinct from the subjective act of awareness; and (3) there is the ordinary physical object that can only be known through the mediation of the information or data given to our senses, or (as some philosophers prefer) through the objects that are actually sensed or perceived.

The working out of a philosophical theory of perception based on this position is not a simple, mechanical task, for one must deal with a number of controversial issues that naturally arise. What the sense-datum position maintains is that our perceptual knowledge or experience of things in the external world is not what we normally tend to believe it is. It is not a *direct* apprehension of the nature of the physical world and of all that exists in it. This position does not deny that we have perceptual knowledge of the external world, but merely asserts that the perception of physical objects is far more complex than we naturally suppose. But if the sense-datum advocate claims that our knowledge of the external world is based upon a sensory experience (the seeing, hearing, feeling of a sense-datum) whose content or object is distinct from anything in the external world, but which is nevertheless related in some way to such ordinary objects, several problems arise. What is the status of sense-data? Since they appear only when there is an act of sensing, in what way are they *distinct from* the subjective event of sensing? Can they be real, independent entities if they are the contents of hallucinatory and illusory experiences as well as of veridical experiences? An even more difficult problem concerns the relationship between sense-data and physical objects. Some of the solutions to this problem require a radical reinterpretation of the nature and status of the physical objects that populate our common-sense world.

Despite the complexities of the sense-datum position, there is an alluring quality about it; for, certainly, it is a view that avoids being entrapped by the paradoxes and puzzles to which naïve realism is susceptible, and it preserves sense perception's status as the only direct means of knowledge. We cannot be mistaken about how an object appears to us, no matter how its appearance may differ from its real nature. We can be mistaken, of course, about what *caused* the sensible experience of a sense-datum or about the nature of its physical correlate, but such errors, we say, are errors of *inference* or of *judgment* and not of sense perception.

The presentation and defense of the sense-datum position are found in the selections by John Locke, a classical exponent of seventeenth-century empiricistic philosophy, and A. J. Ayer, a contemporary philosopher of that same basic persuasion.

The Lockean theory of perception is based upon the conviction that the senses are passive, but that, nevertheless, they are the only source of objective knowledge. The passivity of the senses means, for Locke, that we are *caused* to perceive certain sense impressions which he called "ideas" by the physical objects that exist independently in the external world and outside of our consciousness. Locke maintains that we can have knowledge of these physical substances through the given ideas, because *some* of these ideas correspond to *similar* qualities (called *primary qualities*) in the objects. We can determine the size, shape, motion, and weight of an external object because our experiences (sensory ideas) of these qualities represent the objective qualities themselves. There are other ideas of alleged qualities (*secondary qualities*) which do not represent properties of the object at all, but only the *effects* of the object upon us—these would be ideas of color, sound, heat, and wetness, for example. Locke may thus be called a "selective" realist because of his theory of primary and secondary qualities, and because he postulated the existence of material substances which endure through changes in sensory perception.

A. J. Ayer is a contemporary exponent of the sense-datum theory of perception, but differs from, and advances beyond, Locke in several respects. The two major differences lie, perhaps, in Ayer's rejection of the distinction between primary and secondary qualities (in the eighteenth century, Locke's theory had suffered some devastating criticism) and his reinterpretation of the concept of material object (in a way which avoids many of the objections leveled against Locke). Ayer also gives us an assessment of the principal arguments for regarding sense-data as the immediate objects of perception and the basis of our knowledge of the external world.

Gilbert Ryle recognizes that, on the one hand, it is difficult not to accept the existence of sense-data (or at least to use the sense-datum concept in our explanation of how we are able to have perceptual knowledge) and yet, on the other hand, that it is even more difficult to construct a fully acceptable and intelligible sense-datum theory. Ryle proceeds to examine some of the problems involved in the notion of sense-data, with a view to trying to understand what drives one to postulate their existence and exposing certain confusions in the arguments for their existence.

In a more positive vein, Brand Blanshard introduces the point of view that perception is the *active judgment,* or act of mind, concerning what is before us in experience, rather than the passive reception of sense-data. That is to say, any conscious experience of objects already involves more than the mere consciousness of sensation that is, of course, present in the act of perceiving. By itself, the sensation can only function as a *cue* for the perceiver. It is Blanshard's contention that by treating perception as basically an act of judgment, we would have a proper basis for a theory of knowledge.

Finally, Maurice Merleau-Ponty also recognizes the need to reestablish the "world of perception," the need, that is, to try to restore perception to its proper primary status in the achievement of knowledge, and to understand the nature of the perceived world. He contends that only through perception do we have communication with "things," and that we do live in a world of perception. Merleau-Ponty opposes the sense-datum approach to perception because it artificially severs the relationship between the perceiver and the world of objects. He would be far more sympathetic to Blanshard, but would not accept his basic assertion that perception is an act of judgment. He would say that it is primarily a relationship of the *person*, a composite of body and mind, to the so-called "life-world" of immediate experience. It is through the action or behavior of the person, prior to any reflective thought, that this world is constituted for human consciousness. While Merleau-Ponty's development of these themes is quite difficult to follow, it is well worth our effort.

What we have in this section is but a sampling from an immense corpus of writings on the problem of perception. But these selections will convey a sense of the problem's nature and importance.

THE SENSORY BASIS OF KNOWLEDGE

john locke

Of ideas in general and their original

. . .

All ideas come from sensation or reflection.—Let us then suppose the mind to be, as we say, white paper, void of all characters, without any ideas; how comes it to be furnished? Whence comes it by that vast store, which the busy and boundless fancy of man has painted on it with an almost endless variety? Whence has it all the materials of reason and knowledge? To this I answer, in one word, from EXPERI-ENCE; in that all our knowledge is founded, and from that it ultimately derives itself. Our observation, employed either about external sensible objects, or about the internal operations of our minds, perceived and reflected on by ourselves, is that which supplies our understandings with all the materials of thinking. These two are the fountains of knowledge, from whence all the ideas we have, or can naturally have, do spring.

The objects of sensation one source of ideas.—First, our senses, conversant about particular sensible objects, do convey into the mind several distinct perceptions of things, according to those various ways wherein those objects do affect them; and thus we come by those *ideas* we have of yellow, white, heat, cold, soft, hard, bitter, sweet, and all those which we call sensible qualities; which when I say the senses convey into the mind, I mean, they from external objects convey into the mind what produces there those perceptions. This great source of most of the ideas we have, depend-ing wholly upon our senses, and derived by them to the understanding, I call, SENSATION.

The operations of our minds the other source of them.—Secondly, the other fountain, from which experience furnisheth the understanding with ideas, is the perception of the operations of our own minds within us, as it is employed about the ideas it has got; which operations, when the soul comes to reflect on and consider, do furnish the understanding with another set of ideas which could not be had from

From John Locke, *An Essay Concerning Human Understanding*, A. S. Pringle-Pattison, Ed. (Oxford: The Clarendon Press, 1924), Book II, Chap. I, Secs. 2–4 (pp. 42–44), Chap. VIII, Secs. 7–13, 23–25 (pp. 66–73), Chap. IX, Secs. 1–10 (pp. 73–77); Book IV, Chap. XI, Secs. 1–9 (pp. 321–326). Reprinted by permission of The Clarendon Press.

things without: and such are perception, thinking, doubting, believing, reasoning, knowing, willing, and all the different actings of our own minds; which we being conscious of, and observing in ourselves, do from these receive into our understanding as distinct ideas, as we do from bodies affecting our senses. This source of ideas every man has wholly in himself: and though it be not sense, as having nothing to do with external objects, yet it is very like it, and might properly enough be called internal sense. But as I call the other Sensation, so I call this REFLECTION, the ideas it affords being such only as the mind gets by reflecting on its own operations within itself. By Reflection, then, in the following part of this discourse, I would be understood to mean that notice which the mind takes of its own operations, and the manner of them, by reason whereof there come to be ideas of these operations in the understanding. These two, I say, viz., external material things as the objects of Sensation, and the operations of our own minds within as the objects of Reflection, are, to me, the only originals from whence all our ideas take their beginnings. The term *operations* here, I use in a large sense, as comprehending not barely the actions of the mind about its ideas, but some sort of passions arising sometimes from them, such as is the satisfaction or uneasiness arising from any thought.

. . .

Simple ideas of sensation

. . .

Ideas in the mind, qualities in bodies.—To discover the nature of our ideas the better, and to discourse of them intelligibly, it will be convenient to distinguish them, as they are ideas or perceptions in our minds, and as they are modifications of matter in the bodies that cause such perceptions in us; that so we may not think (as perhaps usually is done) that they are exactly the images and resemblances of something inherent in the subject; most of those of sensation being in the mind no more the likeness of something existing without us than the names that stand for them are the likeness of our ideas, which yet upon hearing they are apt to excite in us.

Whatsoever the mind perceives in itself, or is the immediate object of perception, thought, or understanding, that I call *idea*; and the power to produce any idea in our mind, I call *quality* of the subject wherein that power is. Thus a snowball having the power to produce in us the ideas of white, cold, and round, the powers to produce those ideas in us as they are in the snowball, I call qualities; and as they are sensations or perceptions in our understandings, I call them ideas; which ideas, if I speak of them sometimes as in the things themselves, I would be understood to mean those qualities in the objects which produce them in us.

Primary qualities of bodies.—Qualities thus considered in bodies are, First, such as are utterly inseparable from the body, in what estate soever it be; such as, in all the alterations and changes it suffers, all the force can be used upon it, it constantly keeps; and such as sense constantly finds in every particle of matter which has bulk enough to be perceived, and the mind finds inseparable from every particle of matter, though less than to make itself singly be perceived by our senses: v.g., take a grain of wheat, divide it into two parts, each part has still solidity, extension, figure, and mobility; divide it again, and it retains still the same qualities: and so divide it on, till the parts become insensible; they must retain still each of them all those qualities. [These I call *original* or *primary qualities* of body, which I think we may observe to produce simple ideas in us, viz., solidity, extension, figure, motion or rest, and number.

Secondary qualities of bodies.—Secondly, Such qualities, which in truth are nothing in the objects themselves, but powers to produce various sensations in us by their primary qualities, i.e., by the bulk, figure, texture, and motion of their insensible parts, as colours, sounds, tastes, &c.; these I call *secondary qualities*. To these might be added a third sort, which are allowed to be barely powers, though they are as much real qualities in the subject as those which I, to comply with the common way of speaking, call qualities, but, for distinction, secondary qualities. For the power in fire to produce a new colour or consistence in wax or clay by its primary qualities, is as much a quality in fire as the power it has to produce in *me* a new idea or sensation of warmth or burning, which I felt not before, by the same primary qualities, viz., the bulk, texture, and motion of its insensible parts.]

How primary qualities produce their ideas.—The next thing to be considered is, how bodies produce ideas in us; and that is manifestly by impulse, the only way which we can conceive bodies operate in.

If, then, external objects be not united to our minds when they produce ideas in it, and yet we perceive these original qualities in such of them as singly fall under our senses, it is evident that some motion must be thence continued by our nerves or animal spirits, by some parts of our bodies, to the brains or the seat of sensation, there to produce in our minds the particular ideas we have of them. And since the extension, figure, number, and motion of bodies of an observable bigness, may be perceived at a distance by the sight, it is evident some singly imperceptible bodies must come from them to the eyes, and thereby convey to the brain some motion which produces these ideas which we have of them in us.

How secondary.—After the same manner that the ideas of these original qualities are produced in us, we may conceive that the ideas of secondary qualities are also produced, viz., by the operation of insensible particles on our senses. The different motions and figures, bulk and number of such particles, affecting the several organs of our senses, produce in us those different sensations which we have from the colours and smells of bodies; v.g., that a violet, by the impulse of such insensible particles of matter of peculiar figures and bulks, and in different degrees and modifications of their motions, causes the ideas of the blue colour and sweet scent of that flower to be produced in our minds. It being no more impossible to conceive that God should annex such ideas to such motions with which they have no similitude, than that he should annex the idea of pain to the motion of a piece of steel dividing our flesh, with which that idea hath no resemblance.

•   •   •

Three sorts of qualities in bodies.—The qualities then that are in bodies, rightly considered, are of three sorts:

First, the bulk, figure, number, situation, and motion or rest of their solid parts. Those are in them, whether we perceive them or no; and when they are of that size that we can discover them, we have by these an idea of the thing as it is in itself, as is plain in artificial things. These I call *primary qualities*.

Secondly, the power that is in any body, by reason of its insensible primary qualities, to operate after a peculiar manner on any of our senses, and thereby produce in *us* the different ideas of several colours, sounds, smells, tastes, &c. These are usually called *sensible qualities*.

Thirdly, the power that is in any body, by reason of the particular constitution of its primary qualities, to make such a change in the bulk, figure, texture, and motion of another body, as to make it operate on our senses differently from what it did before. Thus the sun has a power to make wax white, and fire, to make lead fluid. These are usually called *powers*.

The first of these, as has been said, I think may be properly called real, original, or primary qualities, because they are in the things themselves, whether they are perceived or no: and upon their different modifications it is that the secondary qualities depend.

The other two are only powers to act differently upon other things, which powers result from the different modifications of those primary qualities.

The first are resemblances; the second thought resemblances, but are not; the third neither are, nor are thought so.—But though these two latter sorts of qualities are powers barely, and nothing but powers, relating to several other bodies, and resulting from the different modifications of the original qualities, yet they are generally otherwise thought of. V.g., the idea of heat or light which we receive by our eyes or touch from the sun, are commonly thought real qualities existing in the sun, and something more than mere powers in it. But when we consider the sun in reference to wax, which it melts or blanches, we look upon the whiteness and softness produced in the wax, not as qualities in the sun, but effects produced by powers in it: whereas, if rightly considered, these qualities of light and warmth, which are perceptions in me when I am warmed or enlightened by the sun, are no otherwise in the sun than the changes made in the wax, when it is blanched or melted, are in the sun. They are all of them equally powers in the sun, depending on its primary qualities.

The reason why the one are ordinarily taken for real qualities, and the other only for bare powers, seems to be because the ideas we have of distinct colours, sounds, &c., containing nothing at all in them of bulk, figure, or motion, we are not apt to think them the effects of these primary qualities which appear not to our senses to operate in their production, and with which they have not any apparent congruity, or conceivable connexion. Hence it is that we are so forward to imagine that those ideas are the resemblances of something really existing in the objects themselves. But, in the other case, in the operations of bodies changing the qualities one of another, we plainly discover that the quality produced hath commonly no resemblance with anything in the thing producing it; wherefore we look on it as a bare effect of power. The former, I think, may be called secondary qualities immediately perceivable, the latter secondary qualities mediately perceivable.

Of perception

It is the first simple idea of reflection.—Perception, as it is the first faculty of the mind exercised about our ideas, so it is the first and simplest idea we have from reflection, and is by some called thinking in general. Though thinking, in the propriety of the English tongue, signifies that sort of operation of the mind about its ideas wherein the mind is active; where it, with some degree of voluntary attention, considers anything. For in bare, naked perception, the mind is, for the most part, only passive; and what it perceives, it cannot avoid perceiving.

Is only when the mind receives the impression.—What perception is, every one will know better by reflecting on what he does himself, when he sees, hears, feels, &c., or thinks, than by any discourse of mine. Whoever reflects on what passes in his own mind, cannot miss it: and if he does not reflect, all the words in the world cannot make him have any notion of it. This is certain, that whatever alterations are made in the body, if they reach not the mind; whatever impressions are made on the outward parts, if they are not taken notice of within, there is no perception. Fire may burn our bodies with no other effect than it does a billet, unless the motion be continued to the brain, and there the sense of heat or idea of pain be produced in the mind, wherein consists actual perception. How often may a man observe in himself, that whilst his mind is intently employed in the contemplation of some objects, and curiously surveying some ideas that are there, it takes no notice of impressions of sounding bodies made upon the organ of hearing with the same alteration that uses to be for the producing the idea of sound? Want of sensation in this case is not through any defect in the organ, or that the man's ears are less affected than at other times when he does hear; but that which uses to produce the idea, though conveyed in by the usual organ, not being taken notice of in the understanding, and so imprinting no idea on the mind, there follows no sensation.

Children, though they have ideas in the womb, have none innate.—Therefore, I doubt not but children, by the exercise of their senses about objects that affect them in the womb, receive some few ideas before they are born, as the unavoidable effects either of the bodies that environ them, or else of those wants or diseases they suffer; amongst which (if one may conjecture concerning things not very capable of examination) I think the ideas of hunger and warmth are two, which probably are some of the first that children have, and which they scarce ever part with again. Yet these simple ideas are far from those innate principles which some contend for, and we above have rejected, being the effects of sensation, and no otherwise differing in their manner of production from other ideas derived from sense, but only in the precedency of time. So, after they are born, those ideas are the earliest imprinted which happen to be the sensible qualities which first occur to them: amongst which, light is not the least considerable, nor of the weakest efficacy. And how covetous the mind is to be furnished with all such ideas as have no pain accompanying them, may be a little guessed by what is observable in children new born, who always turn their eyes to that part from whence the light comes, lay them how you please.

Ideas of sensation often changed by the judgment.—We are farther to consider concerning perception, that the ideas we receive by sensation are often in grown people altered by the judgment without our taking notice of it. When we set before our eyes a round globe of any uniform colour, v.g., gold, alabaster, or jet, it is certain that the idea thereby imprinted in our mind is of a flat circle variously shadowed, with several degrees of light and brightness coming to our eyes. But we having by use been accustomed to perceive what kind of appearance convex bodies are wont to make in us, what alterations are made in the reflections of light by the difference of the sensible figures of bodies, the judgment presently, by an habitual custom, alters the appearances into their causes: so that, from that which truly is variety of shadow or colour collecting the figure, it makes it pass for a mark of figure, and frames to itself the perception of a convex figure and an uniform colour; when the idea we receive from thence is only a plane variously coloured, as is evident in painting. [To which purpose I shall here insert a problem of that very ingenious and studious promoter of real knowledge, the learned and worthy Mr. Molineux, which he was pleased to send me in a letter some months since; and it is this: "Suppose a man born blind, and now adult, and taught by his touch to distinguish between a cube and a sphere of the same metal, and nighly of the same bigness, so as to tell, when he felt one and the other, which is the cube, which the sphere. Suppose then the cube and sphere placed on a table, and the blind man to be made to see; *quaere*, Whether by his sight, before he touched them, he could now distinguish and tell which is the globe, which the cube?" To which the acute and judicious proposer answers: "Not. For though he has obtained the experience of how a globe, how a cube, affects his touch; yet he has not yet attained the experience, that what affects his touch so or so, must affect his sight so or so; or that a protuberant angle in the cube, that pressed his hand unequally, shall appear to his eye as it does in the cube." I agree with this thinking gentleman, whom I am proud to call my friend, in his answer to this his problem; and am of opinion, that the blind man, at first sight, would not be able with certainty to say which was the globe, which the cube, whilst he only saw them; though he could unerringly name them by his touch, and certainly distinguish them by the difference of their figures felt. This I have set down, and leave with my reader, as an occasion for him to consider how much he may be beholden to experience, improvement, and acquired notions, where he thinks he has not the least use of, or help from them; and the rather, because this observing gentleman farther adds, that having upon the occasion of my book proposed this to divers very ingenious men, he hardly ever met with one that at first gave the answer to it which he thinks true, till by hearing his reasons they were convinced.]

But this is not, I think, usual in any of our ideas but those received by sight; because sight, the most comprehensive of all our senses, conveying to our minds the ideas of light and colours which are peculiar only to that sense; and also the far different ideas of space, figure, and motion, the several varieties whereof change the appearances of its proper object, viz., light and colours; we bring ourselves by use to judge of the one by the other. This, in many cases, by a settled habit, in things whereof we have frequent experience, is performed so constantly and so quick, that we take that for the perception of our sensation which is an idea formed by our judgment; so that one, viz., that of sensation, serves only to excite the other, and is scarce taken notice of itself; as a man who reads or hears with attention and understanding, takes little notice of the characters or sounds, but of the ideas that are excited in him by them.

Nor need we wonder that this is done with so little notice, if we consider how very quick the actions of the mind are performed: for as itself is thought to take up no space, to have no extension, so its actions seem to require no time, but many of them seem to be crowded into an instant. I speak this in comparison to the actions of the body. Any one may easily observe this in his own thoughts who will take the pains to reflect on them. How, as it were in an instant, do our minds with one glance see all the parts of a demonstration, which may very well be called a long one, if we consider the time it will require to put it into words, and step by step show it another? Secondly, we shall not be so much surprised that this is done in us with so little notice, if we consider how the facility which we get of doing things, by a custom of doing, makes them often pass in us without our notice. Habits, especially such as are begun very early, come at last to produce actions in us which often escape our observation. How frequently do we in a day cover our eyes with our eyelids, without perceiving that we are at all in the dark? Men, that by custom have got the use of a byword, do almost in every sentence pronounce sounds which, though taken notice of by others, they themselves neither hear nor observe. And therefore it is not so strange that our mind should often change the idea of its sensation into that of its judgment, and make one serve only to excite the other, without our taking notice of it.

·   ·   ·

Of our knowledge of the existence of other things

It is to be had only by sensation.—The knowledge of our own being we have by intuition. The existence of a God reason clearly makes known to us, as has been shown.

The knowledge of the existence of any other thing we can have only by sensation: for there being no necessary connexion of real existence with any idea a man hath in his memory; nor of any other existence but that of God with the existence of any particular man: no particular man can know the existence of any other being, but only when, by actual operating upon him, it makes itself perceived by him. For the having the idea of anything in our mind no more proves the existence of that thing than the picture of a man evidences his being in the world, or the visions of a dream make thereby a true history.

It is therefore the actual receiving of ideas from without that gives us notice of the existence of other things, and makes us know that something doth exist at that time without us which causes that idea in us, though perhaps we neither know nor consider how it does it. For it takes not from the certainty of our senses, and the ideas we receive by them, that we know not the manner wherein they are produced: v.g., whilst I write this, I have, by the paper affecting my eyes, that idea produced in my mind, which whatever object causes, I call white; by which I know that that quality or accident (i.e., whose appearance before my eyes always causes that idea) doth really exist, and hath a being without me. And of this, the greatest assurance I can possibly have, and to which my faculties can attain, is the testimony of my eyes, which are the proper and sole judges of this thing; whose testimony I have reason to rely on as so certain, that I can no more doubt, whilst I write this, that I see white and black, and that something really exists that causes that sensation in me, than that I write or move my hand; which is a certainty as great as human nature is capable of, concerning the existence of anything but a man's self alone, and of God.

This, though not so certain as demonstration, yet may be called knowledge, and proves the existence of things without us.—The notice we have by our senses of the existing of things without us, though it be not altogether so certain as our intuitive knowledge, or the deductions of our reason employed about the clear abstract ideas of our own minds; yet it is an assurance that deserves the name of *knowledge*. If we persuade ourselves that our faculties act and inform us right concerning the existence of those objects that affect them, it cannot pass for an ill-grounded confidence: for I think nobody can, in earnest, be so sceptical as to be uncertain of the existence of those things which he sees and feels. At least, he that can doubt so far (whatever he may have with his own thoughts) will never have any controversy with me; since he can never be sure I say anything contrary to his opinion. As to myself, I think God has given me assurance enough of the existence of things without me; since by their different application I can produce in myself both pleasure and pain, which is one great concernment of my present state. This is certain, the confidence that our faculties do not herein deceive us is the greatest assurance we are capable of concerning the existence of material beings. For we cannot act anything but by our faculties, nor talk of knowledge itself, but by the help of those faculties which are fitted to apprehend even what knowledge is. But besides the assurance we have from our senses themselves, that they do not err in the information they give us of the existence of things without us, when they are affected by them, we are farther confirmed in this assurance by other concurrent reasons.

Because we cannot have them but by the inlet of the senses.—First, It is plain those perceptions are produced in us by exterior causes affecting our senses, because those that want the organs of any sense never can have the ideas belonging to that sense produced in their minds. The organs themselves, it is plain, do not produce them; for then the eyes of a man in the dark would produce colours, and his nose smell roses in the winter: but we see nobody gets the relish of a pineapple till he goes to the Indies where it is, and tastes it.

Because an idea from actual sensation and another from memory are very distinct perceptions.—Secondly, Because sometimes I find that I cannot avoid the having those ideas produced in my mind. For though when my eyes are shut, or windows fast, I can at pleasure recall to my mind the ideas of light or the sun, which former sensations had lodged in my memory; so I can at pleasure lay by that idea, and take into my view that of the smell of a rose, or taste of sugar. But if I turn my eyes at noon towards the sun, I cannot avoid the ideas which the light or sun then produces in me. So that there is a manifest difference between the ideas laid up in my memory, and those which force themselves upon me, and I cannot avoid having. And therefore it must needs be some exterior cause, and the brisk acting of some objects without me, whose efficacy I cannot resist, that produces those ideas in my mind, whether I will or no. Besides, there is nobody who doth not perceive the difference in himself between contemplating the sun as he hath the idea of it in his memory, and actually looking upon it: of which two, his perception is so distinct, that few of his ideas are more distinguishable one from another. And therefore he hath certain knowledge that they are not both memory, or the actions of his mind, and fancies only within him; but that actual seeing hath a cause without.

Pleasure or pain, which accompanies actual sensation, accompanies not the returning of those ideas without the external objects.—Thirdly, Add to this, that many of those ideas are produced in us with pain, which afterwards we remember without the least offence. Thus the pain of heat or cold, when the idea of it is revived in our minds, gives us no disturbance; which, when felt, was very troublesome, and is again, when actually repeated: which is occasioned by the disorder the external object causes in our bodies when applied to it. And we remember the pain of hunger, thirst, or the headache, without any pain at all; which would either never disturb us, or else constantly do it as often as we thought of it, were there nothing more but ideas floating in our minds, and appearances entertaining our fancies, without the real existence of things affecting us from abroad. The same may be said of pleasure accompanying several actual sensations; and though mathematical demonstration depends not upon sense, yet the examining them by diagrams gives great credit to the evidence of our sight, and seems to give it a certainty approaching to that of the demonstration itself. For it would be very strange that a man should allow it for an undeniable truth, that two angles of a figure which he measures by lines and angles of a diagram, should be bigger one than the other, and yet doubt of the existence of those lines and angles which, by looking on, he makes use of to measure that by.

Our senses assist one another's testimony of the existence of outward things.— Fourthly, Our senses, in many cases, bear witness to the truth of each other's report concerning the existence of sensible things without us. He that sees a fire may, if he doubt whether it be anything more than a bare fancy, feel it too, and be convinced by putting his hand in it; which certainly could never be put into such exquisite pain by a bare idea or phantom, unless that the pain be a fancy too; which yet he cannot, when the burn is well, by raising the idea of it, bring upon himself again.

Thus I see, whilst I write this, I can change the appearance of the paper; and by designing the letters, tell beforehand what new idea it shall exhibit the very next moment, barely by drawing my pen over it: which will neither appear (let me fancy as much as I will) if my hand stand still, or though I move my pen, if my eyes be shut; nor, when those characters are once made on the paper, can I choose afterwards but see them as they are; that is, have the ideas of such letters as I have made. Whence it is manifest that they are not barely the sport and play of my own imagination, when I find that the characters that were made at the pleasure of my own thoughts do not obey them; nor yet cease to be, whenever I shall fancy it, but continue to affect my senses constantly and regularly, according to the figures I made them. To which if we will add, that the sight of those shall, from another man, draw such sounds as I beforehand design they shall stand for, there will be little reason left to doubt that those words I write do really exist without me, when they cause a long series of regular sounds to affect my ears, which could not be the effect of my imagination, nor could my memory retain them in that order.

This certainty is as great as our condition needs.—But yet, if after all this any one will be so sceptical as to distrust his senses, and to affirm that all we see and hear, feel and taste, think and do, during our whole being, is but the series and deluding appearances of a long dream whereof there is no reality; and therefore will question the existence of all things or our knowledge of anything: I must desire him to consider, that if all be a dream, then he doth but dream that he makes the question; and so it is not much matter that a waking man should answer him. But yet, if he pleases, he may dream that I make him this answer, that the certainty of things existing *in rerum natura,* when we have the testimony of our senses for it, is not only as great as our frame can attain to, but as our condition needs. For our faculties being suited not to the full extent of being, nor to a perfect, clear, comprehensive knowledge of things free from all doubt and scruple; but to the preservation of us, in whom they are; and accommodated to the use of life: they serve to our purpose well enough, if they will but give us certain notice of those things which are convenient or inconvenient to us. For he that sees a candle burning, and hath experimented the force of its flame by putting his finger in it, will little doubt that this is something existing without him, which does him harm and puts him to great pain. And if our dreamer pleases to try whether the glowing heat of a glass furnace be barely a wandering imagination in a drowsy man's fancy, by putting his hand into it, he may perhaps be awakened into a certainty, greater than he could wish, that it is something more than bare imagination. So that this evidence is as great as we can desire, being as certain to us as our pleasure or pain, i.e., happiness or misery; beyond which we have no concernment, either of knowing or being. Such an assurance of the existence of things without us is sufficient to direct us in the attaining the good and avoiding the evil which is caused by them, which is the important concernment we have of being made acquainted with them.

But reaches no farther than actual sensation.—In fine, then, when our senses do actually convey into our understandings any idea, we cannot but be satisfied that there doth something at that time really exist without us, which doth affect our senses, and by them give notice of itself to our apprehensive faculties, and actually produce that idea which we then perceive: and we cannot so far distrust their testimony as to doubt that such collections of simple ideas as we have observed by our senses to be united together, do really exist together. But this knowledge extends as far as the present testimony of our senses, employed about particular objects that do then affect them, and no farther. For if I saw such a collection of simple ideas as is wont to be called man, existing together one minute since, and am now alone, I cannot be certain that the same man exists now, since there is no necessary connexion of his existence a minute since with his existence now: by a thousand ways he may cease to be, since I had the testimony of my senses for his existence. And if I cannot be certain that the man I saw last today is now in being, I can less be certain that he is so who hath been longer removed from my senses, and I have not seen since yesterday, or since the last year; and much less can I be certain of the existence of men that I never saw. And therefore, though it be highly probable that millions of men do now exist, yet whilst I am alone writing this, I have not that certainty of it which we strictly call knowledge; though the great likelihood of it puts me past doubt, and it be reasonable for me to do several things upon the confidence that there are men (and men also of my acquaintance, with whom I have to do) now in the world: but this is but probability, but knowledge.

·   ·   ·

PERCEPTION

a. j. ayer

1 Are physical objects directly perceived?

The problem of perception, as the sceptic poses it, is that of justifying our belief in the existence of the physical objects which it is commonly taken for granted that we perceive. In this, as in other cases, it is maintained that there is a gap, of a logically perplexing kind, between the evidence with which we start and the conclusions that we reach. If the conclusions are suspect, it is because of the way in which they seem to go beyond the evidence on which they depend. The starting-point of the argument is, as we have seen, that our access to the objects whose existence is in question must be indirect.

In the case of perception, however, it may well be doubted whether this premise is acceptable. There appears to be no harm in saying that our belief in the existence of such things as chairs and tables is founded on the evidence of our senses; but if this talk of evidence is meant to imply that such a belief is always an inference from something else, it begs a disputed question. And even allowing that this is a case in which one can separate evidence and conclusion, it has yet to be shown that there is a difference of level between them. It is certainly not obvious that there is any question here of a passage from one type of object to another.

Nevertheless, a great many philosophers have held that this was so. From John Locke onwards, those who have sought to erect an edifice of knowledge on the basis of what Bertrand Russell, himself an exponent of this method, has called "hard data," have commonly agreed that such data were yielded by sense perception; but they have also agreed that they did not include physical objects. Taking the hard data to be securely known, they have regarded the existence of physical objects as being relatively problematic.

This point may be obscured by the fact that philosophers of this way of thinking have allowed themselves to refer to their hard data by the use of words which are normally taken to stand for physical objects. Thus Berkeley claimed to follow common sense in holding that such things as trees and stones and houses were

From A. J. Ayer, *The Problem of Knowledge* (London: Macmillan & Co. Ltd., 1956), Chap. III, pp. 91–106, 115–125. Reprinted by permission of St. Martin's Press, Inc., The Macmillan Company of Canada, Ltd., and Macmillan & Co. Ltd.

directly perceived. But if we consider what is ordinarily meant by a physical object of this kind, I think that we must admit that the class comprises only such things as are accessible, at least in theory, to more than one sense and to more than one observer. Various other properties are requisite, including that of occupying space and of having more than a momentary duration, but for the purpose of our argument it is the feature of publicity that is the most important. If anything perceptible is properly to be called a physical object, it must at least make sense to say of it that it is perceived by different people and that it is, for example, touched as well as seen. But these conditions are not satisfied by the objects which Berkeley, and most other philosophers, have regarded as hard data. What, according to them, is immediately given in perception is an evanescent object called an idea, or an impression, or a presentation, or a sense-datum, which is not only private to a single observer but private to a single sense.

This contention that we directly perceive sense-data, rather than physical objects, is not easy to interpret. The first thing to be noted is that, whether true or false, it is not an empirical statement of fact. A philosopher who thinks that he directly perceives physical objects does not for that reason expect anything different to happen from what is expected by one who believes that he directly perceives sense-data. Each is claiming to give an account of all perceptual experience, whatever form it may take, so that no experiment can settle the issue between them. Neither can the statement that only sense-data are directly perceived be interpreted as a reflection on the ordinary usage of sensory verbs like "hear" and "touch" and "see." Or rather, if it were so interpreted, it would be obviously false. It is true that there is a familiar use of words like "hear" and "taste" and "smell," according to which the objects that are heard or tasted or smelled are private to a single sense. We commonly talk of hearing sounds, as well as of hearing the things that make the sounds, and whereas the things that make the sounds can be perceived in other ways besides, the sounds themselves can only be heard. But neither sounds nor tastes nor smells are ordinarily regarded as being private to a single observer; it makes perfectly good sense to speak of two different persons hearing the same sound or smelling the same smell. The only sounds that are by nature private to a single observer are those that he hears in his mind's ear, those, in fact, that make no sound at all. And when we come to the most important senses, those of sight and touch, we find that ordinary usage does not provide them with accusatives on the analogy of sound and hearing. One may speak indifferently of hearing a clock or of hearing its tick, but one does not speak of touching the feel of a clock or of seeing its look. What one is ordinarily said to touch and see is the clock itself. And the clock which is seen is the very same object as the clock which is touched. There are objects such as mirror-images which are private to the sense of sight, but they again are not private to a single observer. It is only the things that one sees in one's mind's eye that are exclusively one's own.

Thus it appears that those who would have us say that the only immediate objects of perception are sense-data are making a considerable departure from ordinary usage. They are assimilating all forms of perception to the possession of mental images; thereby achieving the paradoxical result of taking as the standard case of sense perception something that is ordinarily contrasted with it. We can say, if we like, that they are making a linguistic recommendation. By giving them new accusatives they are introducing a special usage of sensory words like "hear" and "touch" and "see." But this is not for them a mere matter of caprice. If they make the recommendation, it is because they feel bound to make it; they feel that the introduction of these accusatives is somehow forced upon them by the facts, that it alone permits them to give an adequate account of what perception is. The question is why it should be thought that this is so.

2   The argument from illusion

If we examine the reasons which philosophers have in fact given in favor of the view that only sense-data are directly perceived, we find that they mainly rest upon what is known as the argument from illusion. The starting-point of this argument is that objects appear differently to different observers, or differently to the same observer under different conditions, and further, that the way in which they appear is causally dependent upon extraneous factors such as the presence of light, the position of the observer, or the state of his nervous system. These premises themselves are not likely to be questioned. The difficulty is to see how they can lead to the desired result.

Now considering first the fact that appearances vary, we may argue that this proves at least that people sometimes do not perceive things as they really are. If, to take a familiar example, a coin looks at the same time round to one person and, from a different angle, elliptical to another, it follows that it is to one of them at least presenting a deceptive appearance. The coin may in fact be neither round nor elliptical; it cannot in any case be both. So that if each of these persons judges that he is perceiving the coin as it really is, at least one of them will be undergoing an illusion. It is not, however, necessary to the argument that anyone should ever actually be deceived by an experience of this kind. It is not necessary to it even that the appearance of a physical object should ever actually vary. All that is required is that it be possible that it should. It is enough that it makes sense to say of the coin that it looks at the same time round to one person and elliptical to another, whether or not this ever occurs in fact. Perhaps if such things never did occur, we should not have this usage; but that is irrelevant. The point is that we do have it, and that thereby we admit the possibility that physical objects may appear to people otherwise than as they really are.

But to say that an object may sometimes appear to be what it is not does not imply that we never perceive it as it really is, still less that what we directly perceive is never the object itself but something else. To obtain this last result one has to make the ruling that in every case in which an object seems to be perceived there is something which is directly perceived, and also that what is directly perceived cannot appear otherwise than as it is. One will then be able to conclude that whenever a physical object appears differently from what it is, something other than it is being directly perceived. Even so, it will not follow that a physical object cannot ever be directly perceived; for there is nothing in the argument, so far developed, to show that we never do, or can, perceive the object as it really is: all that has been established is that we sometimes may not. At this point, however, we are invited to take notice of the similarity which obtains between the cases, if there are any, in which the object appears in its true guise and those in which it does not. From different angles the coin may appear a variety of different shapes: let it be assumed that one of them is the shape that it really is. There will be nothing to mark off this appearance from the others except a difference of aspect which may be extremely slight. There will in any case be no such difference between the way in which the coin is perceived in this instance and the way in which it is perceived in all the others as to render it at all plausible to say that they are generically distinct; that the object which is directly perceived in this instance is of a different kind altogether from that which is directly perceived in all the others. But, since only one of the appearances can fail to be deceptive, we must allow that in all but one of the instances it is not the physical object itself that is directly perceived. And if we are willing to admit that the instances are all sufficiently alike for it to be reasonable to hold that an object of the same type is directly perceived in every case, it will follow that the physical object is not directly perceived in the remaining instance either. In this way we are brought to the conclusion that, even granting that physical objects may sometimes be perceived as they really are, what is directly perceived is always something else.

This argument is plainly not conclusive, but I think that it has much persuasive force, provided always that we accept the ruling that when a physical object appears in any way other than it is, it is not itself directly perceived. But why should we accept this ruling? It makes perfectly good sense to talk of perceiving things which look in some way different from what they are, and there is at least no obvious reason why we should here feel bound to add that these things are not perceived directly. It is not clear even what "direct perception" is supposed to mean, if I do not directly perceive the things at which I am directly looking, however deceptive their appearances may be. The suggestion seems to be that the object interposes its appearance, like a sheet of glass, between itself and the observer. The glass may be so frosted that we are left in doubt as to the character, or even the existence, of what lies behind it: or it may be so transparent that we hardly realize that it is there at all. We are to think of physical objects as detachable from their looks, or from their tactual qualities, in the way that they are detachable from the sounds that they may make. Even this, as we have seen, does not bring in sense-data, but it takes a large step toward them. It is, I think, a move that can be made; but if all we had to go upon were the fact that physical objects may appear otherwise than as they are, there would seem to be little reason for our making it.

A further motive is provided by the possibility of complete hallucinations. The case which we have so far been considering is that in which a physical object looks to have some quality that it does not really have: there has been no question of its not being really there to be perceived. But it may also happen that one "perceives" a physical object which is not there at all. Let us take as an example Macbeth's visionary dagger: since we are concerned only with what is possible, the fact that this episode may be fictitious does not matter. There is an obvious sense in which Macbeth did not see a dagger; he did not see a dagger for the sufficient reason that there was no dagger there for him to see. There is another sense, however, in which it may quite properly be said that he did see a dagger; to say that he saw a dagger is quite a natural way of describing his experience. But still not a real dagger; not a physical object; not even the look of a physical object, if looks are open to all to see. If we are to say that he saw anything, it must have been something that was accessible to him alone, something that existed only so long as this particular experience lasted; in short, a sense-datum. But then, it is argued, there would not have been anything in the character of the experience, considered simply in itself, to differentiate it from one that was not delusive. It is because an experience of this sort is like the experience of seeing a real physical object that hallucinations are possible. But in so far as the experiences are alike, their analysis should follow the same pattern. So if we are bound in one case to say that what is seen is a sense-datum, it is reasonable to hold that this is so in all.

But the fact is that in giving an account of such hallucinations we are not bound to say that anything is seen. It would be perfectly legitimate to describe Macbeth's experience by saying that he thought he was seeing a dagger, whereas in fact he was not seeing anything. It is just as natural a way of putting it as the other. And even if we insist on saying that he was seeing something, though not of course a physical object, we are not bound to infer from this that there *was* something which he saw; any more than we are bound to infer that ghosts exist from the fact that people see them. In general, we do use words like "see" in such a way that from the fact that something is seen it follows that it exists. For this reason, if one does not believe in ghosts, one will be more inclined, in reporting a ghost story, to say that the victim thought he saw a ghost than that he did see one. But the other usage is not incorrect. One can describe someone as having seen a ghost without being committed to asserting that there was a ghost which he saw. And the same applies to Macbeth's visionary dagger or to any other example of this sort. It is only if we artificially combine the decision to say that the victim of a hallucination is seeing something with the ruling that what is seen must exist, that we secure the introduction of sense-data. But once again there seems to be no good reason why we should do this.

The position may be thought to change, however, when one brings in the causal aspect of the argument from illusion. For this is taken to prove that we never come near to perceiving a physical object as it really is, or at least that we have no reason to suppose that we ever do. And if this were so, our inclination to say that what we perceive does often have the properties that it appears to have might lead us to conclude that physical objects themselves were not perceived. But this would conflict with our very strong inclination to say that they are. An attempt, therefore, may be made to resolve the difficulty by saying that physical objects are indeed perceived, but only indirectly. What is directly perceived, being dependent for its existence on the state of the observer's nervous system, may then be held to be a sense-datum.

This causal argument has been charged with inconsistency on the ground that the physiological facts, which it relies on, are facts about physical objects; and our knowledge of these facts is gained through perception. But the question is not, at this stage, *whether* we know anything about the character of physical objects but *how* we know it; and to say that we know it through perceiving them does not commit us to saying that this perception of them is direct. It is true that the assumption that it is indirect raises problems of its own, which we shall consider when we come to deal with the causal theory of perception; and it is true also that the scientific information, on which the causal argument draws, has its source in the naïve realism of common sense. But even if it could be shown that these scientific theories were not merely historically but logically based upon naïve realism, this would not protect it from them. On the contrary, as Russell has succinctly put it: "Naïve realism leads to physics, and physics, if true, shows that naïve realism is false. Therefore naïve realism, if true, is false; therefore it is false." [1]

But is it the case that "physics, if true, shows that naïve realism is false"? What physics shows, if it is true, is that the way in which things appear to us is causally

[1] Bertrand Russell, *An Inquiry into Meaning and Truth*, p. 15.

conditioned by a number of factors which are extraneous to the thing itself. If, for example, this carpet now looks blue to me it is because light of a certain wavelength is being transmitted from it to my eyes, from which impulses pass along the appropriate nerve fibers to my brain. In a different light, or if my eyes or brain were injured, it might appear to me a different color, or no identifiable color at all. But to infer from this that we do not perceive things as they really are, that, for example, the physical object which I refer to as "this carpet" is not really blue, is to make the assumption that if a thing's appearing to have a certain property is caused, in part, by outside factors, then it does not really have it. Stated generally, this assumption is obviously false. Thus, part of the cause of the carpet's now appearing blue to me may be that it has been dyed: but no one would regard this causal dependence on the performance of the dyeing machine as a reason for concluding that the carpet was not really blue. It may be thought, however, that the assumption does hold in the special case where the outside factors are to be found in the condition of the observer. The idea at work is that if the object owes its properties to us, they are not legally its own. But what it owes, or partly owes, to the observer is its appearing to him in the way it does: and if, to revert to our example, this does not lead us to deny that the carpet really *looks* blue, it is not clear why it should lead us to deny that the carpet really *is* blue. There are criteria for deciding what color things "really" are; it is mainly a question of the color they appear to be under what are regarded as normal conditions. The fact that the causal explanation of these appearances brings in the observer does not prevent these criteria from being satisfied; neither, therefore, does it prevent things from really having the colors that we ascribe to them. And the same would apply to any of the other properties with which things are credited by common sense. It would seem, therefore, that physics does not refute naïve realism, in the sense that it shows it to be false. Physics does not prove that we do not perceive physical objects as they really are. We shall see presently, however, that it does undermine naïve realism by casting doubt upon the adequacy of the picture which the naïve realist forms of the external world. The tendency is then to substitute the picture which is associated with the causal theory of perception: but this, as we shall also see, is hardly an improvement.

A variant of the causal argument, which has impressed some philosophers, adduces the fact that light takes time to travel. From this it is inferred that we do not see physical objects as they really are at the time at which we see them, but only, at best, as they were some time before. In the case of objects which are close at hand this difference in time is negligibly small, so small that it is doubtful if it warrants the conclusion that we do not see these objects in the state in which they are, but there are other cases in which it is appreciable. An instance which Russell often cites is that of the sun which we see only as it was eight minutes before: when it comes to remote stars the difference may amount to thousands of years. It may even happen that by the time we see it the star has ceased to exist. But if the star no longer exists, we cannot, so it is argued, now be seeing it; and since in every case in which the light has had an appreciable distance to travel it is possible that the object which we think that we are seeing has gone out of existence in the interval, we cannot ever identify it with what we see: for our present experience will be the same, whether the object still exists or not. But if, in these cases, we are not to say that we see the physical object, then we should not say it even in the cases where the time interval is negligibly small; for the comparative length of the interval makes no difference to the character of our experience: there would be no justification for maintaining that we saw an object of one kind when the interval was very short, and an object of an entirely different kind when it was somewhat longer. At what point in the continuous series of possible time intervals would this fundamental change take place? Once more, however, it seems too paradoxical to deny that we see physical objects in any sense at all. So again the solution offered is that we see them only indirectly: what we directly see is something else.

This argument draws its strength from the fact that one tends to think of seeing as concerned only with the present. It is assumed that, unlike our memories or our imaginations, our eyes cannot range into the past: whatever it is that we see must exist here and now if it exists at all. But this assumption is not unassailable. Why should it not be admitted that our eyes can range into the past, if all that is meant by this is that the time at which we see things may be later than the time when they are in the states in which we see them? And having admitted this, why then should we not also admit that it is possible to see things which no longer exist? Such ideas might never have occurred to us were it not for the discoveries of physics; but once these physical facts are recognized, it does not seem too hard to adapt our way of speaking to them. We have to balance the oddity of saying that we can see what is past against the oddity of saying that we do not see physical objects; and to give our eyes access to the past may well seem the more reasonable course.

The result of this discussion is that the arguments so far put forward do not make it excessively uncomfortable to hold the position of naïve realism. It will, how- ever, need a little sophistication. We must be prepared to say that we do not always perceive things as they are; that sometimes we see them only as they were, and some- times as they neither are nor were; that what we see, or otherwise perceive, may not exist, or else that we may think that we are perceiving something when we are not in fact perceiving anything at all; and that the physical objects which we do perceive may owe some of their properties in part to the conditions which attend our percep- tion of them. Of these admissions the last is perhaps the most difficult to make; but not so difficult that, even when combined with the others, it should drive us, without further argument, into putting up a screen of sense-data between ourselves and the physical world.

3   A method of introducing sense-data

The argument from illusion may, however, be developed in a simpler, but also more effective, way. We have already remarked, in the course of discussing the question whether any statements are incorrigible, that the ordinary way of describing what one perceives appears to make a stronger claim than the perception itself can cover. This follows indeed from the fact that illusions are possible. If I can be undergoing an illusion when, on the basis of my present experience, I judge, for example, that my cigarette case is lying on the table in front of me, I may, in saying that I see the cigarette case, be claiming more than the experience strictly warrants: it is logically consistent with my having just this experience that there should not really be a cigarette case there, or indeed any physical object at all. It may be suggested, there- fore, that if I wish to give a strict account of my present visual experience, I must make a more cautious statement. I must say not that I see the cigarette case, if this is to carry the implication that there is a cigarette case there, but only that it seems to me that I am seeing it. We are not here concerned with the question whether such statements are incorrigible; we have already found reason to hold that they are not. Their point is not that they give us complete security from error; it is that, if they are true, they serve as descriptions of the contents of our sense experiences, irrespective of any larger claims that these experiences may normally induce us to make.

Because of the possibility of illusion, it will not necessarily be true that whenever it seems to me that I am perceiving something, I really am perceiving it. On the other hand, the converse is intended to hold. From the statement that I see the cigarette case it is supposed to follow that it seems to me that I see it. Or, if this cannot be maintained, it is at least supposed to follow that it seems to me that I see something or other. It is to be a necessary fact that whenever anything is perceived something must, in this sense, seem to be perceived. But whether this entailment really holds is a question which we shall have presently to examine.

The next step, continuing with our example, is to convert the sentence "It now seems to me that I see a cigarette case" into "I am now seeing a seeming-cigarette case." And this seeming-cigarette case, which lives only in my present experience, is an example of a sense-datum. Applying this procedure to all cases of perception, whether veridical or delusive, one obtains the result that whenever anyone perceives, or thinks that he perceives, a physical object, he must at least be, in the appropriate sense, perceiving a seeming-object. These seeming-objects are sense-data; and the conclusion may be more simply expressed by saying that it is always sense-data that are directly perceived.

.   .   .

4   Concerning the legitimacy of sense-data

What appears most dubious of all is the final step by which we are to pass from "it seems to me that I perceive x" to "I perceive a seeming-x," with the implication that there is a seeming-x which I perceive. Since the existence and character of these seeming-things is not affected by the question whether the perception is veridical or delusive, or whether they are or are not perceived by any other person, or in any other conditions, or at any other time, they cannot be physical objects. They are momentary, private entities, created, it may well seem, only by a stroke of the pen, yet threatening to imprison the observer within a circle of his own consciousness. They may, therefore, fairly be regarded as a nuisance, but this, as we have seen, is not a justification for ignoring them. The question which has now to be decided is whether their introduction is legitimate.

Again, many philosophers would say that it was not. Professor Ryle once more may serve as an example. His view about sense-data, with which, as we have remarked, our seeming-things may be identified, is that "this whole theory rests upon a logical howler, the howler, namely, of assimilating the concept of sensation to the concept of observation." [2] His reason for thinking that this is a howler is that if observing something entails having a sensation, then having a sensation cannot itself be a form of observation; for if it were, it would in its turn entail having a further sensation and

2 G. Ryle, *The Concept of Mind*, p. 213.

we should be involved in an infinite regress. Moreover, the sort of thing that can be said about observation, or perception, cannot significantly be said about sensation. "When a person has been watching a horse race, it is proper to ask whether he had a good or a bad view of it, whether he watched it carefully or carelessly and whether he tried to see as much of it as he could." But no one asks questions of this sort about sensations, "any more than any one asks how the first letter in 'London' is spelled." [3] Sensations, although they can be noticed and attended to, are not "objects of observation," and "having a sensation cannot itself be a species of perceiving, finding or espying." [4] This last statement is based on the assumption that it is impossible to perceive anything without having the appropriate sensation, that to speak of someone's seeing something without having any visual sensations, or of his hearing something without having any auditory sensations, would be self-contradictory. But Ryle himself subsequently decides that this assumption is false. His reconsidered view is that the "primary concept of sensation," the concept which we employ when, for example, we speak of sensation returning to a numbed part of the body, "is not a component of the generic concept of perception, since it is just a species of that genus." [5] To have a sensation of this sort is just to feel something, and since one can see and hear without feeling anything, seeing and hearing do not in this sense entail having sensations. They may be accompanied by sensations, such as a sense of strain in the eyes, or a tingling in the ears, but these sensations are not representatives of what is seen or heard. Thus when philosophers speak, in the way they do, of visual and auditory sensations, they must be using the word "sensation" in some more sophisticated sense. There might be no harm in this if they still made the word apply to something, but that, according to Ryle, is just what they fail to do. The "impressions," to which they wish to make it apply, do not exist. They are invented by philosophers in the mistaken belief that something is required to mediate between external objects and the mind. "Impressions are ghostly impulses, postulated for the ends of a para-mechanical theory." [6]

These arguments have commanded a fairly widespread assent, but I do not myself think that they show the introduction of sense-data to be illegitimate. In the first place, it may be answered that even if it were correct to say that the advocates of sense-data treat sensation as a form of observation, what must here be meant by observation is not something which itself entails sensation. It therefore does not follow that they are committed to an infinite regress. They have special reasons, as I have tried to show, for analyzing the perception of physical objects into the "sensing" of seeming-objects: but these reasons do not apply in turn to the sensing of seeming-objects. One is not obliged to analyze this into an awareness of seeming-seeming-objects; there is no question of one's having to adopt the general rule that no object is approachable except through an intermediary. Ryle has indeed considered the possibility of some such defense; and his rejoinder is that it "in effect explains the having of sensations as the *not* having any sensations," [7] on the ground that if having a sensation is construed as an awareness of a sensible object, then one may have sensations without being sensitively affected. But this rejoinder seems to me very weak.

3 *Ibid.,* p. 207.
4 *Ibid.,* p. 214.
5 *Ibid.,* p. 242.
6 *Ibid.,* p. 243.
7 *Ibid.,* p. 215.

For to talk of someone's sensing a sense-datum is intended to be another way of saying that he is sensitively affected; the manner in which he is affected reappears as a property of the sense-datum: to demand that provision should also be made for his having a sensation is to require that the same thing should be said twice over.

But let us suppose that Ryle is right, and that sensing a sense-data cannot be made to do duty for having a sensation. This will still not be a decisive objection to the sense-datum theory. For the theory does not in fact require that the two should be identified: it does not have to be interpreted as referring to sensations at all. To talk of sense-data is to talk of the way things seem, in the special sense of "seeming" that I have been trying to explain. And if it be granted that people can seem to perceive things, in this sense, the question whether this coincides with what is ordinarily meant by their having sensations may be treated as irrelevant. Neither is there any need for sense-datum theorists to hold that the sensing of sense-datum is a form of observation, if calling it a form of observation is to be taken to imply that everything that can significantly be said about seeing, hearing, and the rest, in the more familiar uses of these words, can also be said about it. Accordingly, Ryle's comments on the everyday vocabulary of sensation and perception need not trouble them. It is not as if they were trying to give an account of the ways in which this vocabulary is commonly made to work. They need not even be suggesting that it is in any way inadequate for the ordinary purposes of communication. Their own talk of sense-data, assuming it to be legitimate, is obviously far less practical. What they are doing is to redescribe the facts in a way that is supposed to bring to light distinctions, of philosophical interest, which the ordinary methods of description tend to conceal. In pursuing this course they may in some cases have been guilty of the confusions which Ryle attributes to them. But I do not think that he has succeeded in showing that these confusions are an essential ingredient in their theory.

The view that sense-data are mythical is sometimes upheld on psychological grounds. The experiments made by gestalt psychologists are adduced to show that Locke, who with his conception of "simple ideas" may fairly be regarded as the principal ancestor of the sense-datum theorists, was mistaken in supposing either that the mind is actually supplied with unitary impressions or that it is a merely passive receptor.[8] But the answer to this is that the advocates of sense-data need not commit themselves to any special psychological theory about the character, or genesis, of what is sensibly given. Their interest lies only in establishing that there are seeming-objects, in the sense we have explained: it does not matter to them what particular features these seeming-objects are empirically found to have, or how they come to have them. Psychology cannot be used to refute them: for their concept of sense-data is intended to be so general that everything that the psychologists may discover about the machinery of perception is describable by its means.

Even so, there is something suspect about their procedure. The transition from "It now seems to me that I see x" to "There is a seeming-x which I now see" may be defended on the ground that the second sentence is merely a reformulation of the first, a reformulation which it is convenient to make because it is simpler and neater in the contexts for which such sentences might be required to make nouns do the work of verbs, to talk of sense-data rather than of how things seem to people. But, if this is allowed, one must be careful to say nothing about sense-data that cannot be

8 *An Essay Concerning Human Understanding*, Book II.

translated back into the terminology of seeming. The danger is that these private objects, which have been brought into existence as a matter of literary convenience, become independent of their origin. Questions arise about the criteria for the self-identity of these objects, the means of distinguishing one of them from another, the possibility of their changing, the duration of their existence; and one may think that mere inspection of them will provide the answers. But the position is rather that until such questions have been answered there are no objects to inspect. It is from the way in which we *decide* to answer them that the term "sense-datum" acquires a more definite use. But how are these decisions to be reached? How, for example, are we to determine what is to count as one sense-datum? At the present moment it seems to me that I see the walls of a house, covered with Virginia creeper, and a rose tree climbing to an open window, and two dogs asleep upon a terrace, and a lawn bespeckled with buttercups and clover, and many other things besides; and it seems to me that I hear, among other things, the buzzing of insects and the chirruping of birds. How many visual or auditory sense-data am I sensing? And at what point are they replaced by others? If one of the dogs seems to stir in its sleep does this create a new sense-datum for me or merely transform an old one? And if it is to be new, do all the others remain the same? Clearly the answers to these questions will be arbitrary; the appearance of the whole frontage of the house may be treated as one sense-datum, or it may be divided into almost any number. The difficulty is to find a rule that would be generally applicable. It might be suggested, for example, that we should say that there were, for a given observer at any given moment, as many visual sense-data as there were features that he could visually discriminate: but this again raises the question of what is to count as a single feature. And similar objections may be made to any other ruling that I can think of. The correct reply may, therefore, be that these questions do not admit of a definite answer, any more than there is a definite answer to the question how many parts a thing can have, or how much it can change without altering its identity. That is to say, there are no general rules from which the answers to such questions can be derived; but this does not mean that they cannot be given answers in particular cases. In the present instance, I can choose to speak of there being a sense-datum of the rose tree, or a sense-datum of one of its roses, or of one of the petals of the rose, or even just a sense-datum of something red; the only condition is that I in every case refer to something which it now seems to me that I see. And if it be asked whether my present contemplation of the rose tree yields me one sense-datum of it, or a series, and if it is a series, how many members it has, the answer once again is that there can be as many as I choose to distinguish. No single sense-datum can outlast the experience of which it helps to make up the content; but then it is not clear what is to count as one experience. I can distinguish the experience I am having now from those that I have had at different times in the past, but if I were asked how many experiences I had had, for example, during the last five minutes, I should not know what to answer: I should not know how to set about counting. The question would appear to have no meaning. It does not follow, however, that I cannot at any given moment delimit some experience which I am then having: the boundaries may be fluid, but I can say confidently of certain things that they fall within the experience, and of others that they do not. And for our present purposes this may be all that is required.

It must then be admitted that the notion of a sense-datum is not precise. Moreover, it appears to borrow what little precision it has from the way in which we talk about physical objects. If I can pick out my present sense-datum of a rose it is because roses are things for which there are established criteria of identity. It is, in fact, only by the use of expressions which refer to the perception of physical objects that we have given any meaning to talking of sense-data at all. And it is hard to see how else we could have proceeded if we were to have any hope of being intelligible. This seems to me, however, to be a matter of psychology rather than of logic. If one has to describe the use of an unfamiliar terminology, the description, in order to be informative, must be given in terms of what is already understood; and we are all brought up to understand a form of language in which the perception of physical objects is treated as the standard case. But this is a contingent fact: it is surely not inconceivable that there should be a language in which sense experiences were described by the use of purely qualitative expressions which carried no reference to the appearances of physical objects. Such a language would not be very useful, but it could be adequate for the description of any given experience. Neither do I see any reason *a priori* why someone who had devised it as a means of recording his own experiences should not succeed in teaching it to others. But even if I am mistaken on this point, it would not follow, as has sometimes been suggested, that the so-called language of sense-data had no function to fulfil. If it derives its meaning only from the use of sentences which refer to the perception of physical objects, then it cannot, indeed, be made the vehicle of an argument which would seek to prove that sentences which purport to refer to physical objects are themselves devoid of meaning. But no such argument is here being considered: the fact that it is meaningful to talk of physical objects is not in question. What is in question is the truth of statements which imply that physical objects are perceived, or rather the strength of the reasons that we can have for believing that such statements are true. And even if all talk about sense-data derived its meaning from talk about the perception of physical objects, it would not follow that the truth of a statement which implied that some physical object was perceived was, in any given instance, a logical condition of the truth of a statement which was merely descriptive of some sense-datum. Logically, the sense-datum statement might be true even though any given claim to perceive a physical object were false.

This question of the admissibility of sense-data is, I think, still worth discussing both for its own sake and because of the important part which it has played in the history of modern philosophy. It is, however, to be remarked that they are not strictly needed for the formulation of the sceptic's problem. Even if one refuses to take the final step of transforming "seeming to perceive an object" into " 'perceiving' a seeming-object," and inferring from this that there is a seeming-object which is directly perceived, there will still be the gap between evidence and conclusion which the sceptic requires. It is the gap between things as they seem and things as they are; and the problem consists in our having to justify our claims to know how physical objects are on the basis of knowing only how they seem. In another aspect, it is the problem of setting out the relationship between perceiving a physical object and seeming to perceive it, in the sense we have explained. A problem of this sort must arise once it is admitted that our ordinary judgments of perception claim more than is strictly contained in the experiences on which they are based. We have seen that this assumption can be challenged, but the tendency of our discussion has been to show that it should be upheld.

.   .   .

3

SENSATION

gilbert ryle

One of the things that worry me most is the notion of sensations or sense impressions. It seems, on the one hand, very hard to avoid saying that hearing, seeing, and tasting could not happen unless appropriate sense impressions were received; and yet also very hard to give a coherent account of what such sense impressions are, or how the having of sense impressions is connected with, say, our hearing a conversation or our seeing a tree.

There seem to be some very good reasons for saying that sense impressions can occur in abnormal situations, when no perceiving occurs. For example, after looking at a bright light I have an afterimage; or if I knock my head I seem to see stars or lightning flashes; or when I have a bad cold I have a singing noise in my head. One seems bound to say that in these situations I have optical or acoustic sensations or sense impressions, and that it is just in the presence of these that the similarity consists between merely having an afterimage and genuinely seeing a tree, or between merely having a singing in my head and genuinely hearing the choir singing in the concert hall. In cases of genuine perception, we are inclined to say, we both have sense impressions, produced or stimulated in the normal ways, and also contribute something of our own, namely, to put it too picturesquely, the interpretation or significance, without which we should not have perceived, say, an oak tree. Yet the moment we start to press this tempting idea we are landed in familiar difficulties. Colors as we see them and sounds as we hear them seem at once to collapse into internal reactions or states of ourselves. The oak tree is not really green and the tenor's voice is not literally shrill. The sense impressions which were supposed to make perception of trees and choirs possible finish by becoming screens between ourselves and trees or choirs. The sensible qualities of things in the world cease to be qualities of those things and become, instead, momentary states of our own minds or nervous systems. They come to have the status of stomach aches, caused, indeed, fairly indirectly by mechanical and chemical properties of external things, of the intervening medium, and of our own nervous systems, but no more to be equated with attributes of external things than my stomach ache is an attribute of the uncooked beans which indirectly caused my stomach to ache.

Reprinted from *Contemporary British Philosophy*, H. D. Lewis, ed. (London: George Allen & Unwin Ltd., 1956), pp. 427–443, by permission of the publisher.

There are further difficulties. First, the notion of sense impression seems to be a technical or specialist notion. People without special theories or technical knowledge of physiology, optics, chemistry, or psychology know well how to use the concepts of seeing, hearing, and smelling, though not the concept of *sense impression*. They have to be introduced to this notion by being introduced to the outlines of special theories about the physics and physiology of perception. Only after having heard a bit about the propagation of waves and the like, and then about the transmission of impulses up the nerves, and then perhaps also something about the psychology of stimuli and responses—only then can they begin to use the notion of *sense impressions*. Consequently, in the ordinary contexts in which we talk about seeing, hearing, and the rest, no mention is made of sense impressions, any more than in ordinary contexts in which meat, vegetables, and fruit are discussed, any mention is made of calories or vitamins. As I might put it, the concept of *perception* is on a more elementary or less technical level than that of *sense impression*. We can know all that is a part of common knowledge about seeing and hearing, without knowing anything about these impressions. But from this it follows directly that the concept of sense impression is not any sort of component of the concept of perception, any more than the concept of *vitamin* is any sort of component of the concept of *dinner*.

Unfortunately, however, the logical situation is a confused one. For we are perfectly familiar with not one, but at least two quite different nontechnical notions of *sensation*—and philosophers and psychologists have nearly always tried to equate their technical notion of *sense impression* with one, or more often with both of these nontechnical notions of *sensation*. They pass without apology from saying that without optical or auditory sense impressions there is no seeing or hearing, to saying that seeing and hearing involve the having of sensations, as if the one assertion were a mere paraphrase of the other.

To get this point a bit clearer, let me examine in some detail the two nontechnical notions of sensation.

First, there is the sense of the word "sensation" or the word "feeling," in which sensations or feelings are such things as pains, tickles, feelings of nausea, suffocation, thirst, and the like. A pain is what anodynes and anaesthetics exist to relieve or prevent. Sensations of this sort can be more or less acute or intense; they can be short-lived or protracted, and they are, in general, localizable in particular parts of the body. Most sensations, in this sense of the word, if not all of them, are in some degree distressing. Some philosophers, like Bishop Berkeley, have argued, quite fallaciously it seems to me, that the family which includes such things as pains, tickles, and feelings of suffocation also includes such things as our sensations of temperature. When I bring my hand nearer and nearer to the fire, I begin by feeling increases in the heat, but at a certain point the heat is intense enough to hurt. Berkeley argues that therefore a feeling of warmth differs only in degree from the feeling of pain. So the feeling of warmth is a state of myself in the way in which a pain is.

But this will not do at all. For one thing, some weight must be attached to the fact that no one does suppose that painfulness characterizes the fire, in the way in which they do suppose that warmth does. A child will say that the fire is so hot that it hurts his hand, and thus is already distinguishing between an effect which the fire has upon him from a property which the fire has, without which it would not hurt him. Moreover, feeling, say with one's hand, that the fire is hotter than it was, is finding the answer to a question. The owner of the hand is discriminating something, finding out a difference. In some cases he would admit to having made a mistake. He had not been careful enough. But in having a pain there is no finding anything out, no discerning of similarities or differences, no place, even, for mistakes and so no room for carefulness or lack of carefulness. Feeling, in the sense of finding out or discerning, the warmth of things is a kind of perception, and a kind at which some people, like bakers and laundrygirls, become better than other people; it is the product of an acquired skill; but feeling, in the sense of suffering pains, is not a kind of perception, and there is no question of one victim being better or worse than another at feeling toothaches. In this sense of "feeling" or "sensation," pains are not things the feeling of which is the product of an acquired skill. So far from the feeling of warmth being merely a lower degree of the feeling of pain, the two things are "felt" only in quite different senses of the word. They are not even species of the one genus, as perhaps seeing and tasting are species of the one genus, perception. They belong to different categories from one another. The attempt to classify felt temperatures with pains, and so to show that felt warmth is a state or reaction in ourselves, as pain in some way is, was a logical mistake.

We need, therefore, to distinguish the sense of "feeling" or "sensation" in which we call pains and tickles "feelings" or "sensations" from the entirely different sense in which we say that we perceive some things not by seeing, hearing, smelling, or tasting, but by feeling—the sense in which we say that a person whose feet or fingers are numb with cold has lost sensation or the power of feeling things with his fingers and toes. Let me just remind you of some of the properties of external things which are perceived by feeling, as opposed to seeing, hearing, smelling, or tasting. First, to detect how hot or cold something is, we have to feel it with the hands, or lips, or tongue, or, less efficiently, with other parts of our bodies. We cannot see, hear, or smell how cold things are. Next, to detect the roughness, smoothness, slipperiness, or stickiness of the surfaces of things, we normally have to handle them or finger them. Next, to detect whether something is vibrating, stiff, resilient, loose in its socket, and so on, we usually have to touch it, and very likely also muscularly to manipulate it. Some people are much better than others at discrimination-tasks of these kinds. Doctors can feel the pulses of patients which are too faint for you or me to detect and the trained driver can feel the car going into a skid long before the novice could have done so.

We should notice that tactual and kinesthetic detection is unlike seeing, hearing, tasting, and smelling in one important respect. What I detect by seeing, hearing, tasting, and smelling are with extremely few exceptions, properties or features of things and happenings outside me. What I detect tactually and kinesthetically *may* be properties or features of external though contiguous things and events; but they may be and quite often are properties or features of anatomically internal things and events. I can detect, sometimes, the beating of my own heart, the distension of my own stomach, the straining or relaxing of my own muscles, the creaking of my own joints, and the fishbone in my own throat. A doctor, I imagine, learns to detect by feeling the congestion of his own lungs.

In this sense of "feeling," feeling is a species of perception or perceptual discrimination. We have to learn to do it; we may be better or worse than other people at doing it. There is room for care and carelessness in doing it; and there is always the possibility of making mistakes. To be able to feel things, in this sense, is to have got a certain amount of a specific skill or family of skills, just as to be able to detect and discriminate things by seeing, hearing, tasting, and smelling is to have got a certain amount of a specific skill or family of skills. In all cases alike there can be trained or untrained observers. To detect or discriminate something, whether by sight or touch, is to achieve something, namely, to find something out by the exercise of an acquired and perhaps deliberately trained skill. This shows how enormously different is the sense of the verb "feel" when used to denote detection by touch, from the sense of the verb "feel" when used to denote the suffering of a pain or other discomfort.

But different though these two concepts of "feeling" or "sensation" are, still both are quite untechnical concepts. The child has learned to use both long before he has heard of any physiological, neurological, or psychological theories.

So now we can ask whether it is true that all perceiving involves the having of sensations or the feeling of anything, in either of these senses. Well, to begin with, it is perfectly clear that usually when I see, hear, taste, or smell anything, or detect something by touch, I do not suffer any discomfort or pain in my eyes, ears, tongue, nose, or finger tips. Seeing a tree does not hurt my eyes; and hearing a bird singing does not set up the slightest sort of tickling feeling in my ears. Sometimes, certainly, looking at things, like the headlights of motor cars, or listening to things, like the whistle of a railway engine a few yards away, does hurt my eyes and ears. But not only is this exceptional, but still more important, these disagreeable sensations do not help, they hinder perception. I see much better when I am not being dazzled than when I am. Sensations, in this sense, are not usually present when perception occurs; and when they are present, they tend to impair perception. They are not *sine qua nons* of perception.

But nor is it true that when I see, hear, or smell things I feel anything with my eyes, ears, and nose, in the sense of detecting something tactually or kinesthetically. When I see a green tree, I do not concomitantly detect, with my eyes, the warmth or coldness, the smoothness or roughness, the vibrations or the resilience of anything. My eyes are very inferior organs with which to detect things tactually and kinesthetically. My ears and nose are even worse. But whether they are good or bad, when I see things with my eyes, I do not therewith have to detect something else tactually or kinesthetically with those eyes or mine and usually I do not; and similarly with my ears and nose. With my tongue the situation is slightly different. Usually when I taste things, I do also detect with my tongue the temperature and some of the tactually and kinesthetically discoverable properties of the food or the drink in my mouth. But even this is a case of concomitance and not dependence. I can taste the taste of onions, when there is no longer anything in my mouth with a temperature of its own or with any shape or consistency of its own. In tasting, I often do in fact, but I do not in logic have also to feel anything with my tongue, in the sense of "feel" in which I feel the roughness of the nutshell or the smoothness of the eggshell with my fingers or, sometimes, with my tongue. My tongue is, so to speak, a double sense organ. I can both feel things with it and taste things with it. But I can feel the shape and surfaces of things like spoons without tasting anything; and I can taste, e.g., onions or pepper, without feeling anything.

So when philosophers and psychologists assert that all perceiving involves the having of sensations or the feeling of something, either they are dead wrong, or else they are using a third, quite different notion of feeling or sensation. In particular, the notion of sensing or having sense impressions which, they assert, is a component of the notion of perceiving, must be a notion quite different both from the notion of feelings like pains and tickles, and from the notion of tactual and kinesthetic detection or discrimination.

But at this point there arises something of a crux. When a person has a pain we think that he must, in some sense of the word, be conscious or aware of the pain; and when a person detects or discriminates something by touch, his perceiving what he perceives must also be, in some sense of the word, conscious. A person cannot require to be told by someone else that he is in pain or that he has just perceived something. Well then, what of the sense impressions which, we are told, enter into perceiving? Are we conscious of them or do we have to be told of their existence by others, or, perhaps, infer to them ourselves in accordance with some more or less technical theory of optics or neurology or psychology? It is generally maintained that our sense impressions are certainly and necessarily things that we are conscious of and cannot be unconscious of, as we cannot, with certain reservations, be unconscious of our pains and tickles and as we cannot see, hear, or taste things unconsciously. Indeed it is apt to be maintained that if sense impressions were things of which we were unconscious, then they could not do their proper business, namely, that of providing the basic *given* elements in seeing, hearing, and the rest. Well then, are we conscious of having sense impressions? Do people ever say, whether to themselves or to anyone else, "I am having" or "I have just had a sense impression of such and such a description"? Or rather, since the actual term "sense impression" is obviously a somewhat technical, classificatory term, do people ever say, to themselves or others, "I am having" or "I have just had a so and so," where the concrete filling of the vacancy "so and so" would be something which properly fell under the technical, classificatory term "sense impression"? Certainly people say that they see trees or have just heard some birds singing; but these verbs of perception carry too much luggage to be what is wanted. Certainly too, people sometimes say, more noncommittally, "I see something green," or "I have just heard a twittering noise." But these expressions also carry too much luggage. A person who said "I see something green" might then learn that there was a tree in front of him, and say "Then what I saw was a green tree, though I did not at the time know that the green thing I saw was a tree." What is wanted, apparently, is some family of expressions, in constant and familiar use by everyone, in which they report, without inference of external information, the occurrence of a conscious experience unencumbered, as yet, with any beliefs or knowledge about the existence or properties of any external object.

Sometimes it is suggested that we do report such basic experiences in such utterances as "I seem to smell onions" or "I thought I heard birds singing" or "It looks as if there is a green tree over there." In reporting mere appearances, without committing ourselves to their veracity, we are, it is suggested, reporting the having of sense impressions without the addition of any perceptual claims about the external world. But this will not do. We use such tentative, guarded or noncommittal expressions in all sorts of fields or departments, in most of which there is no question of there being any appropriate sense impressions to isolate. I can say, after a rapid piece of calculation in my head "15 × 16 appears to make 220"; I can say, after a cursory glance "It looks as if the river here is about twice the width of the road in front of my house"; I can say "She appeared to be half angry and half amused"; and I can say "The period of general inflation seems to be coming to an end."

Now all these are guarded statements of what I am tempted or inclined to judge to be the case, though I do not yet commit myself to their being the case. Yet no one supposes that in saying such things I am reporting the occurrence of any sense impressions. Statements of the form "it looks as if"—"there seems to be"—"apparently, . . . " are not *ex officio* dedicated to the wanted reports of the experiences alleged to be basic ingredients in sense perception. So we cannot, unless provided with some extra restrictions which are not in fact provided, adduce idioms of these patterns as being the untutored, uninferential deliverances of our consciousness of the postulated sense impressions. We have, in fact, no special way of reporting the occurrence of these postulated impressions; we are, therefore, without the needed marks of our being conscious of such things at all. For there is surely something absurd in maintaining that we are constantly conscious of some things in the way in which we are conscious of pains, and yet have no way of telling ourselves or other people anything whatsoever about them.

We must acknowledge, therefore, that the view of some epistemologists and psychologists that there are sense impressions is not arrived at at all in the way in which everyone comes to know that pains and tickles occur, or in the way in which everyone comes to know that we sometimes detect things by sight, hearing, taste, and touch. The view that sense impressions occur is arrived at as a deduction from a theory, or perhaps from two or more seemingly interlocking theories.

I want to separate out two quite different theoretical allegiances which, in their different ways, drive people to postulate sense impressions.

(1) If a child and a man are looking at the first word of the first line of a page, the man may say that he sees the word "Edinburgh" misprinted, where the child may not detect the misprint but say only that he sees the word "Edinburgh." The child's eyesight is as good as the man's, but because he is worse at spelling, he fails to see the misprint that the man sees. If now an illiterate Eskimo looks at the same part of the page, though his eyesight is excellent, he will not see a word at all, but only some black marks.

Or if a countryman and a townsman, with equally good sight, are looking at the same field, the one may say that he sees a field of young wheat, while the other may say only that he sees a field of green stuff. In these and countless other such cases, the one observer claims to discern much more than the other, though admitting that their eyesight is equally good. It is natural and tempting to say that the observer whose eyes, somehow, tell him more is putting more into his report of what he sees or that he is giving to it a fuller "interpretation" than the other can do. He has learned more spelling or more agriculture than the other, so he includes in his report of what he sees the extra information which his previous experience and education had equipped him with. His report of what he sees is inflated with knowledge or beliefs which the other man does not possess; in short it carries a mass of ideas or thoughts which are absent from the other observer's report of what *he* sees. In detecting a misprint or a field of young wheat he seems, therefore, to be combining the piece of seeing, which, presumably, contains only what the townsman's seeing contains, with a piece of thinking, which the townsman is unable to supply. What is more, this extra thought-luggage may be right or wrong. The countryman may have misidentified the green crop.

Now there exists a view, which is accepted almost as an axiom, that all thinking, or anyhow all thinking which is intended to result in the discovery or establishment of truths, is inferring; and therewith that all errors and mistakes issue from fallacious reasoning. Accordingly, when philosophers and psychologists consider things like the detection of misprints or the identification of the green crop with young wheat, they automatically describe the thinking element in this detection and identification with reasoning. The question at once arises, Whence then do we get the initial premises of our perceptual conclusions? On this view, the premises must be ascertained at a level prior to any thinking, and prior therefore to any exploitation of knowledge or beliefs previously acquired. There must be a totally non-cogitative acceptance of some basic premises for us to be able to move from these initial data to our correct or incorrect perceptual conclusions about misprints or young wheat. It is, I think, with this idea in mind that many thinkers use the expression "sense-data" for the postulated sense impressions which must be there to inaugurate our perceptual inferrings. For "datum" ordinarily has the force of "evidence" or "reasons." A datum is something that we reason from and does not itself have to be reasoned to.

This reason for postulating the existence of sense impressions seems to me a bad reason, and bad on two scores. First, if it is not true that all thinking is inferring, then it need not be true that the thinking which enters into perceptual recognition, identification, comparison, etc., is inferring, and if it is not, then the search for its fund of premises is a search for nothing. In multiplying we think out the answers to questions, but our results are not conclusions and our mistakes are not fallacies. This thinking does not start from any data or premises; and the same might be true of the thinking that is supposed to go on in perceptual recognition, identification, etc. But second, it seems to me false or at least highly misleading to say that a man who detects a misprint or a farmer who identifies the green crop with growing wheat is necessarily *thinking* at all.

For one thing, the misprint and the nature of the crop might be discerned at sight or in a flash. As soon as his eye falls on the misprinted word, the man might start to pencil in the correction. There might be no moment, however short, in which he could be described as pondering, reflecting, or putting two and two together. He might say, quite truly, that he saw the misprint the moment his eye fell on the word, and that he did not have time to think or even that he did not need to think.

To meet this sort of objection, epistemologists and psychologists sometimes say that though he does not remember doing any thinking, and though the time available for thinking seemed to be wanting, still he must have thought, and so his thinking must have been done at lightning speed—and this might be the reason why he cannot remember doing any thinking afterwards. But we should mistrust these "musts." Why must he have done any pondering, considering, or putting two and two together? All that the argument up to date has shown is that if he had not previously learned to spell, he could not now recognize misprints at sight. But why must the exploitation of knowledge previously acquired take the form of pondering? We ponder when things are not obvious to us. But when previous training results in things being obvious at sight, which would not have been obvious without that training, why should we have to postulate a present piece of pondering to explain the immediate obviousness of the misprint? Ordinarily we account for someone needing to stop to think by showing how something was, at the start, unobvious to him. But here, apparently, the fact that the misprint is immediately obvious to him is supposed to need to be explained not just by reference to his prior education, but also by the postulation of the performance by him of a piece of thinking, with the queer property of not requiring any time for its performance.

So I maintain not only that perceptual recognition, identification, etc., need not embody any inferential thinking, but that they need not embody any thinking at all. They involve the possession and exploitation of knowledge previously acquired. But this exploitation is not thinking. So the argument for the occurrence of sense impressions to be the data or premises for the inferential thinking embodied is doubly broken-backed.

(2) There is another theoretical allegiance which helps to drive philosophers, psychologists, physiologists, and physicists into postulating the existence of sense impressions. This is their natural and up to a point proper allegiance to causal theories of perception. We learn from optics and acoustics about the transmission of light and sound; we learn from physiology the structure of the eye and ear; we are learning from neurophysiology about the transmission of impulses along the nerve fibres. When we ask what makes seeing and hearing possible, and what makes them impossible or inefficient, we derive our answers, quite properly, from the relevant stretches of these scientific theories.

We trace the propagation of light from a light-giving source to the surface of a light-reflecting object and thence to the lens and the retina of the human eye; we then trace the nervous impulses set up at the retina to the right place in the brain. Some further transformation may then be supposed, such that the terminal neural impulse sets up, somehow, a psychic or mental reaction, and thus seeing takes place— or rather, since seeing a misprint requires a special education and maybe also, as is often supposed, a special act of lightning-speed thinking, we should perhaps say that the last neural impulse sets up a mental reaction which is the necessary spur or stimulus to seeing, though seeing consists not only in this stimulus but also in some part of our immediate response to it. This sort of account of perception operates naturally with the notions of propagation, transmission, impulse, stimulus, and response, rather than with the notions of *data*, premises, evidence, and conclusions. Sense impressions are now thought of not as steps in a lightning-swift argument but as links in a causal chain. They are indeed often spoken of as "given," but they are "given," now, in the sense in which electric shocks are given, not in the sense in which Euclid's axioms are given, i.e., are the uninferred premises for inferred consequences. "Given" now means "inflicted," not, as before, "accepted without argument." Sense impressions are now thought of as things impressed on us, impulses transmitted through us, not as things found by us by some sort of pre-cogitative finding.

Now there can be no quarrelling with this sort of account, whether we are thinking of the stages covered by optics and acoustics, or whether we are thinking of the stages covered by physiology and neurophysiology. The final stage, covering a supposed jump from neural impulses in the body to mental experiences, or sense impressions is, however, quite a different matter. It presupposes the Cartesian, body-mind view which I have found fault with at some length in my book. But, apart from this general objection, there remains the specific objection, that the existence of these sense impressions is something postulated; they are not things which anyone reports who has not been convinced by the whole story of the chain of physical, neural, and psychic impulses. Even if the Cartesian view were true, yet still we should be without the Cartesian grounds for asserting the existence of sense impressions which we possess for pains and tickles.

What has gone wrong? It seems to me that this is what has gone wrong. The perfectly proper and necessary research into the physics of light and sound, and into the physiology of seeing and hearing came to be misrepresented as an enquiry which when completed would "explain" seeing and hearing—explain it, that is to say, in the sense of "explain" in which an earthquake is explained by seismological theory or diabetes is explained by a certain branch of pathology. The idea, then, is that what we need to know about seeing and hearing is the various physical and physiological conditions from modifications in which we could infer to the cessation or alteration of our seeing and hearing; in short, that our questions about perception are merely causal questions.

Now of course we have causal questions to ask about perception, and the sciences of optics and acoustics, ophthalmology and neurology have either already provided us with the answers to these causal questions, or can confidently be expected to provide them in the fairly near future. But not all our questions about perception are causal questions; and the proffering of causal answers to non-causal questions leads to inevitable dissatisfaction, which cannot be relieved by promises of yet more advanced causal answers still to be discovered.

Perceiving, as I have pointed out earlier, is exercising an acquired skill; or rather it embodies the exercise of an acquired skill. Seeing a misprint is an impossibility for someone who has not learned to spell. Now about the exercises of any acquired skills there are, of course, causal questions to be asked. If a tightrope walker succeeds in walking along the stretched wire, we can, of course, ask and fairly easily find out the answers to all sorts of causal questions about his performance—mechanical questions about his equilibrium, physiological questions about his muscles and nerves, and pedagogic questions about the training he had received, and so on. But quite different from these causal questions are technical questions, questions, that is, about the nature of the task of tightrope walking, about the various kinds of mistakes that are to be avoided, and the various kinds of attentiveness, courage, and ingenuity which make for success—all the things which the tightrope walker must either have been taught by his trainers or found out for himself. Lessons of this sort need not include much, if any, of the information which might be provided by the physicist, the physiologist, or the psychologist. Nor does the chess player need to know anything about the physiology of his muscular system, despite the fact that he could not be good or even bad at chess if he could not move his fingers and hands where he wished.

In the same sort of way, I am arguing that some questions about perceiving, and particularly those which are of interest in epistemology, are not causal questions—though there are such questions, and many of them have been answered—but questions about, so to speak, the *crafts* or *arts* of finding things out by seeing and hearing—including questions about the nature of mistakes and failures in perception and their relations with mistakes and failures in thinking, spelling, counting, and the like.

It is not that hearing and smelling are queer happenings which are exempt from causal conditions, but that not all questions about hearing and smelling are questions about these causal conditions. Checkmating an opponent at chess is certainly a happening, and a happening conditioned by all sorts of known and unknown causes. But the chess player's interest is not in these causes, but in the tactics or strategy or sometimes just the luck of which the checkmating was the outcome. It is not the dull physical fact of the arrival of the Queen at a particular square, it is the fact that this arrival constituted the success or victory of the player, which is what is significant for the players and spectators of the game. Similarly, finding out something by seeing or hearing is, so to speak, a success or victory in the game of exploring the world.

This seeing or hearing is of course susceptible of a complete and very complex causal explanation, given in terms of optics or acoustics, physiology, neurology, and the rest; but the player's interest is not primarily in the contents of this explanation, but in the exploratory task itself and its accomplishment.

In other words, verbs like "see" and "hear" do not merely denote special experiences or mental happenings, with special causal antecedents; they denote achievements of tasks, or successes in undertakings. There are questions of technique to be asked about them as well as questions of causal conditioning, and questions of technique are not answerable by any multiplication of answers to questions of causal conditioning; they are questions of quite different types.

So I want to suggest that the postulation of sense impressions as causal antecedent of seeing and hearing, only an antecedent not of a physical or physiological, but of a psychological kind arose from two sources, (1) a proper realization of the fact that physical and physiological causal accounts of perception cannot answer technical questions about perceptual successes and failures; (2) an improper, non-realization of the fact that what was lacking to such causal accounts was not that they needed an extra, psychological link in the causal chain; but that they were answers to causal questions and not to questions of technique. When we want to describe the differences between hearing, mishearing, and non-hearing, no discovery or postulation of causal links can give us what we want. Sense impressions were postulated as the missing causal links which would solve a problem which was not a causal problem.

However, after all this has been said, I confess to a residual embarrassment. There is something in common between having an afterimage and seeing a misprint. Both are visual affairs. How ought we to describe their affinity with one another, without falling back on to some account very much like a part of the orthodox theories of sense impressions? To this I am stumped for an answer.

PERCEPTION IS JUDGMENTAL

brand blanshard

. . .

. . . Perception is that experience in which, on the warrant of something given in sensation at the time, we unreflectingly take some object to be before us. The terms "object," "unreflectingly," and "sensation" call for comment. "Object" is a wide term here; it may mean a certain *thing*, a certain *kind* of thing, or what is not properly a thing at all, but a quality or relation. We are obviously perceiving, for example, when we happen to recognize our typewriter or our dog. We are also perceiving when we take something to be *a* typewriter or *a* dog. But we are no less perceiving when we listen to music or conversation, when we relish the taste of a plum pudding, when we observe one car to be going faster than another, or when we stop before a shop window to admire the blue in a new dress. In all these cases we are perceiving, because, with what is given in sense as our cue, we go on without reflection to take some object as presented. And it is evident that perception in this sense is an experience we have every hour of our waking lives. Unfortunately such extreme familiarity does not make it easier to analyze. It is so completely automatic and effortless that we seldom have occasion to think of it, and its parts are so cemented by habit that we are hardly able, even ideally, to take them apart.

It is the more satisfactory, therefore, to find that the comments naturally called for on "sensation" and "unreflectingly" serve to define perception for us in a new way. They mark its limits in a course of evolution, so that we may see it as a segment or stage in a continuous growth. Perception is not perception unless it supplies us a ground in sensation for something that goes beyond this. But if sensation is present alone, we are below the perceptual level; judgment, or something like judgment, must be present also. If, for example, when we looked at the dress we were aware of nothing but blue, we should not in strictness be perceiving; perceiving proper would appear when we took the blue *as* something—as the color of the dress, or as one of the series of colors, or even merely as blue. Sensation is the nether limit of perception. Explicit judgment is the upper limit. We are clearly be-

From Brand Blanshard, *The Nature of Thought* (New York: The Macmillan Company, 1941), I:52–54, 60–75, 81–83. Reprinted by permission of George Allen & Unwin Ltd. and Humanities Press.

yond mere perceiving when judgment is made reflectively, when what we assert is no longer taken as simply presented, but is recognized as a venture of our own that may be mistaken. For example, if the light raised doubts about the color and we said "That is a darker blue than it looks," we should have passed beyond mere perception into the region of explicit judgment. Thus the territory we are first to explore lies between two well-marked boundaries, pure sensation on the one hand and explicit judgment on the other. But while differing from both of its neighbors, perception has something in common with each. It plainly involves sensation, though sensation molded and "interpreted"; it involves judgment, but judgment that is still in the implicit stage.

.   .   .

We must now try to describe the experience out of which perception arises. Our tools must be imagination and inference. We cannot fall back on experiment, for there is no experiment that will show how it feels to be an infant; we must beware of filling the mind of innocence with logical simples and acquired meanings; we must beware, finally, of making it a prison from which the child could never escape. With these warnings in mind, we proceed.

"The baby," says [William] James in a well-known passage, "assailed by eyes, ears, nose, skin, and entrails at once, feels it all as one great blooming, buzzing confusion." [1] Probably all the major types of sensation—sights and sounds, smells and tastes, hots, colds, pains, and the rest—form ingredients in the brew. And probably within any of these the range is considerable. The baby who cries at a loud noise but not at a low one, or cries harder at a bad than at a mild digestive attack, is feeling various intensities of sound and pain. But does he perceive the loud sound *as* loud, or as a sound, or even as distinct from the pain? These questions raise a different issue, and they must all, I think, be met with a No. You cannot perceive loud as loud without placing it in a scale where it is opposed to the less loud, and at the beginning there are no less louds. Not that the mere experience of loudness depends on experiencing other loudnesses, for then the first sound could have had no loudness at all; but rather that loudness is not perceived *as* loudness till it is set off against something else. Indeed, at the start, no sound is perceived as a sound, nor anything as what it is. This is not merely because materials for distinction are absent; the required differences may be there in plenty if only we knew how to use them. It is because there is absent a root condition on which depend alike our power to perceive these differences and the power to perceive anything as itself, a condition, therefore, which lies at the root of intelligence generally. This is the power to see in things the embodiment of universals. To perceive a sound *as* a sound, you must perceive it *as* a sound, as an example of what might be embodied in other sounds. And at the start this perception must be supposed absent. Why? Because it is only as other sounds are given that it could dawn on us that they are cases of one kind, only then that each could be seen in the light of the common nature of all. One could hardly ask that upon hearing the first sound, the mind should at once seize it as a revelation of what might be embodied otherwise. The approach to sound is through sounds, the road to the universal, through particulars.[2] So far, the empiricists are right. If our first sound is a

---

1 *Principles of Psychology*, I., 488.
2 The transition from particulars to universals is gradual, unbroken and even unproblematic, according to Blanshard. It would be problematic if a "particular" is conceived as a distinct entity essentially unrelated to any other entity or property and thus devoid

sound at all, it must be so in virtue of a nature that is realized also in other sounds, though not in smells or colors, and we must suppose this nature present whether it is apprehended as such or not. The history of perception is a history of the gradually improving grasp of the universal.

"Do you mean to say," we may be asked, "that from the moment of his first perception, a child has dealings with universals? Is he not to be allowed to perceive a sound without getting involved with timeless logical essences? If any such doctrine is true, why should it not carry on down to dogs and cats? And shall we not be compelled next to hear of barnyard fowls who are in commerce with Platonic εἰδή?" Now it is easier to satirize this view than to produce another that will work. Any theory that is to work must, as we have seen, provide a passage to later experience. This later experience involves perceiving things *as* things of a kind, and it leads on continuously to the judgment of recognition, "this is what I have seen before." Now what would critics have? If they start with sensations of the purely particular, or transient "moods of the self," they will either end where they began, or, like Lotze, retrace their steps and insert, from later necessity, the universals omitted at first. For if we are really confined to transient particulars, then every judgment of recognition, every identification of anything, and in the last resort every perception, is a snare and a delusion. For the claim of all these experiences is to take us beyond the moment's impression, not merely to give us a "this" but to tell us something about it. And this they cannot do if impressions are the whole story. But if impressions are not the whole story, and we do in perceiving go beyond bare sensation, what is it that we first reach? It is clearly a universal. And when we begin to realize its presence on coming to our second sound or perhaps our hundredth, there is no reason to think that it only then began to exist. What has a history is not *it* but our perceiving of it. And if this implies that dogs and cats in perceiving are grasping universals, our answer is not, "So much the worse for universals," but, "So much the better for dogs and cats."

Indeed we may say confidently that there is no stage in experience, not even pure sensation, if such a stage exists, in which universals are not present. Much depends here, of course, on what is meant by universals. It would be absurd to say that at the beginning a child has general ideas, such ideas as we employ ourselves when we use the word "color" or "man." It would be absurd also to credit him with abstract ideas, such as the thought of the redness of this ball in distinction from its other qualities. But this special shade of redness is not necessarily confined to this context; it may be given in various contexts; and if so, it is, in an important sense of the word, a universal. Now there is every reason to believe that from the very earliest moment when visual sensation is possible the child is apprehending this shade, and therefore that he is apprehending universals from the very inception of

of universal characteristics. But Blanshard maintains that, if "particularity . . . is the uniqueness achieved by *exhausting* a thing's relations," then *particulars do not exist.* In Chapter XVII of *The Nature of Thought*, Blanshard rejects, after a lengthy analysis, the major attempts to render the existence of particulars intelligible. When Blanshard uses the term "particulars" then, he is referring to *specific universals*, which differ only in degree of generality and coherence from more general universals (for which he has several names). Consequently it makes sense to speak of a particular patch of white, but it must be kept in mind that two patches of white are not essentially distinct, separate realities. They are two instances of the same whiteness. [Eds.]

his sentient life. If it is intolerable to say that the child is *sensing* a universal, then we must deny that there has ever been a time when he was confined to mere sensation. What must not be done is to say that we begin with the sensing of bare particulars in which nothing is identical with anything else, and that we somehow find identities as we go on. Identities that are not there cannot be found. We shall not argue this matter, because one of the decisive battles of modern philosophy was fought over it. The reader who is interested will find an arsenal of what we believe to be unanswerable argument in Green's account of the British empiricists.[3] In that classic criticism the old bridge from acquaintance with sense particulars to knowledge of actual things was damaged beyond repair.

But of course to say that we begin with universals does not mean that we begin by knowing them as universals. It is only very gradually and with the help of processes still to be examined that this knowledge is achieved. Much of the confusion here is due to the assumption that our only contact with universals is through general ideas, and hence that to say universals are apprehended from the beginning is equivalent to saying that general ideas are used from the beginning. But the assumption is a mistake.

To return now to describing. We saw that when we open our eyes on the world, we experience sights and smells, sounds and pains, though all in an undistinguished jumble. But we do not perceive the loudness of the sound *as* loudness, nor the sound *as* sound, nor therefore, by the same reasoning, anything for what it is. But it may be said that the mixture is at any rate not a blend. Even at the beginning a pain and a sound differ widely, and, as different, must be distinct. But this again is scarcely correct. It is true that sounds and pains, every shade of color and every degree of heat that enter into experience has a character of its own which sets it off from everything else. But to be different and to be distinguished are not the same. We must believe that in the experience of the infant, however dim and undiscriminated its sensations may be, those sensations are still different. But they are certainly not distinct, in the sense of being distinguished. One cannot distinguish anything until one has perceived it *as* this rather than that (for otherwise *what* is distinct?), and in this first experience no "whats" have yet been recognized. Distinctness of characters from each other and the use of universals as universals have their beginning together. However, it would be still another error to suppose, in line with James's phrase about the "blooming, buzzing confusion," that because our first experience is undifferentiated it is therefore confused. Confusion is not mere absence of distinction. It takes two things that are recognizably distinct to be confounded, and where differentiation has not begun, this twoness has not yet been arrived at. Some sophistication is necessary before one can be really confused.

When we spoke a moment ago of perceiving a character as such, the phrase we used was "perceive it as this rather than that." This is the natural form of expression, and it is significant. It suggests that the recognition of the universal and the placing it in relation to other universals are aspects of the same process. To *be* for thought at all is to be distinct, and to be distinct is to be related to something else through space, time, degree, or otherwise. And this "something else," in turn,

___

[3] In the General Introduction to *David Hume: Philosophical Works,* vol. I., T. H. Green and T. N. Grose, eds. (London, 1886). [Eds.]

receives and maintains its character for thought only through distinction from the
first thing. Here is the first intimation of a truth which, as it recurs over and over
again in the study that follows, will gain an increasing significance, namely, that to
think involves the relating of the object thought of to something else within a system.
Abstract thinking, in the sense of dealing with any character quite alone and apart
is not only an impossibility; it is a self-contradiction.

The process of distinction could hardly get under weigh, as we have admitted,
unless it had differences to start with, and such differences we must suppose to subsist
even within the immediate experience from which we start. But now a doubt suggests itself. Is there any reason to suppose that the universals that emerge into explicitness through this joint recognition and distinction are the same as those present in
the initial experience? There is no conceivable experiment that could settle this
question, since anyone who could apply experiment would have left his first immediacy far behind, and the mind that was still immersed in this would be incapable
of reports. It is a question that has to be settled by resort to some general principle,
and unfortunately what this principle should be is one of the most disputed points in
contemporary thought. The issue is whether or not the nature of a thing is affected by
being placed in new relations. This very difficult question is more appropriately
considered later, but we may perhaps say at once that we believe the nature of a
term is thus affected. And if so, the conclusion will follow that the emergence of the
mind from immediacy is its emergence into a world in some degree new. How new
we cannot tell. But if the above principle is accepted, we may be confident of two
things: first, that some change in the content of initial experience is made by its
explicit ordering; and, second, that this change is not a total transformation. Complete breaks in continuity are not the way of the mind. For example, while it seems
reasonable to suppose that human pain is made different from animal pain by its
relations to a remembered past and a foreseen future, still the man who should
presume on such differences to the extent of denying, like certain Cartesians, that
animals suffered at all would be absurd. In like manner we are entitled to speak of
sensations, pleasures, etc., as components of initial experience, but if we spoke quite
strictly, we should have to say, not that they are simply identical with those we are
now familiar with, but rather that they are the same *sort* of thing.

To proceed, then, with our somewhat conjectural description: Is our first experience simply a mass of undistinguished sensations? No, it is undoubtedly more;
there is no reason to exclude other elements. It certainly includes both varieties of
affection, pleasure and displeasure; and it would be hard to deny that emotion also
is there. Again, if these different elements are present, they are not present as unconnected fragments, but are united by relations, spatial, temporal, and other. Such
relations must be there from the start, though they are no more perceived *as* relations
than [are] qualities as qualities. The child's mind has its bony framework as truly
as his body, and it is interesting to note that growth follows similar lines in both.
As the fleshy volume increases, the bony framework extends and strengthens. Similarly,
as the mass of experience widens, the framework of inner relations gains greater
explicitness and gives greater definition to the parts. Indeed, we shall see that the
ordering of the mass of experience into a special kind of structure or system is at
once the principal aim of thought and the measure of its advance.

In the experience with which we start, then, sensation is present, and relations, and pleasure, and displeasure, and emotion. On the other hand, there is no proper perception, no memory, nor even recognition. There are no ideas of any kind, no images, no judgments, no desires, no anticipations, nothing that we should now call hopes or fears, no wishes or regrets, no sense of right or wrong, beautiful or ugly, true or false. Nor is there yet any sense of self and not-self, for it is only gradually that experience comes to be split up and apportioned, part to me, and part to the world of external things.

Is it possible to go beyond such summaries and get a notion through example of what this primitive state is like? It does seem that, in some present states of mind and in certain areas of our conscious field, we even now approach it. In the drowsiness that precedes full waking and in the dullness of extreme fatigue, the meanings that we usually attach to things may almost vanish, and we may be sunk in a state that is not far from mere sensation. Indeed, something like such a state we carry about with us always. On the margins of our field of vision there is a region where we can neither quite deny that we are sensing something nor be sure that we perceive. And then there is what the psychologists call coenesthesia, or what [F. H.] Bradley called the "felt surplus in our undistinguished core." [4] At any moment of our waking life, one part of our experience is a mass of obscure sensation connected with breathing and digestion, the pressure of clothes, vague hungers and fatigues, our bodily fitness or unfitness. We seldom think of these feelings, but they are there undoubtedly; if they are disordered, as they often are in illness, we may become painfully conscious of them, while if, as apparently happens in some extreme cases, they vanish wholly, the foundations of sanity are threatened. It is true that if we were asked to furnish *proof* that these states exist, we might find the question awkward. The reply that we can introspect them directly will hardly pass, for once such feelings are dragged into the limelight of attention they are no longer the twilight creatures we wanted. But we need not discuss the technique of our knowledge of immediacy, since our interest is less in the state itself than in our way of escaping from it. It is enough if the reader agrees that it exists or has existed, and that from its morass of indistinctness our thought does in fact arise.

How do we make our way out? It is by finding in the bog piers or stepping-stones that will give footholds for our escape. The level waste is, after all, not quite level. There are minor mounds in it, pushed up by subterranean forces that are very imperfectly understood. These come to stand out for our notice, to attain some clearness of outline, and at last to set themselves before us as objects. How do they do this? There are three chief factors involved.

(1) Even in the primitive state of indistinctness there is a great difference in the *force* or *intensity* with which sensations come to us. It would be absurd to say that because a child cannot identify lights or pains they are all felt on the same level of vividness. The range of intensity of some sensations, particularly pains, in minds in which perception has scarcely begun is probably enormous. There are few persons who can have known the minds of lowly animals better than Darwin did, and he tells us how, convinced that even earthworms have reached the dignity of pain, he used to administer a homemade anesthetic before he used them in his fishing.[5]

4 *Appearance and Reality*, p. 293.
5 *Life and Letters*, I., 30.

He was certainly nearer the truth than the Cartesians above mentioned. Sensations may be very intense before there is any power to say, or even to think, what they are sensations of. To be sure we must beware of a fallacy here. The intensity of a sensation is not the same thing as the perception of it, and in theory the intensity could be increased to infinity without producing the smallest recognition, or even what we now call notice. When we notice anything we always invest it with significance drawn from past experience, and it is usually in virtue of this significance that we come to single it out. And such significance at the first is wanting. Nevertheless, just as in later life it is the vivid experiences that remain in memory and not the faint ones, so here at the beginning it is the vivid sensations that are most likely to leave the traces needed in identifying them later on.

(2) Again, some sensations, from the beginning, have an *interest* that others lack. This is what is meant when it is said that we "instinctively notice" some things rather than others. It obviously holds of both animal and human infants. An early observer, Douglas Spalding, hooded some chicks the instant they left their shell and kept them hooded for periods of one to three days, but on taking the hoods off, found them, sometimes within two minutes, following clearly with their eyes the movements of crawling insects.[6] The same inquirer, immediately after working with puppies, put his hands into a basket of three-day-old kittens, still with their eyes unopened, and produced a storm of spitting and puffing, owing, he thought, to the puppy smell.[7] Through practically the whole animal scale we find this instinctive favoritism, a curious and unlearned selection of certain qualities for special attention. Strings and straws that have hitherto been beneath notice become interesting to the bird at mating time; the fresh meat to which the young horse or cow is indifferent sends the young cat or dog into transports of excitement; the dog seems to live as much in a world of smells as we do in a world of sights. The dog's "system of logic," if he had one, says Bradley, "would be simple, for it would begin, I am sure, and end with this axiom, 'What *is*, smells, and what does not smell, is nothing.' "[8] So exclusive is this preference among animals for some sensations rather than others that a major difficulty in training them is to get them to notice any but the familiar cues. Now such instinctive favoritism appears from the beginning in man also. The nipple of a bottle at an infant's lips is to him the most interesting thing in the world. From the very beginning a loud sound will arouse his fear. As his growth goes on and his instincts ripen, things that were before indifferent—toys, mechanical devices, games, members of the other sex—take on a special interest, not because he has learned from experience that it pays to attend to them, but because his nature dictates that at this stage he should find them appealing.

The proposal has been made by Professor Drever that this original and instinctive interest should be taken as the first form of meaning.[9] Now "meaning" usually refers to something in the way of thought. "Strictly," says Professor Broad, "a thing has meaning when acquaintance with, or knowledge about, it either enables one to infer

[6] Romanes, *Mental Evolution in Animals*, p. 161.
[7] *Ibid.*, p. 164. If the kittens would have behaved in this way, even without the puppy smell, as I suspect they would, the force of the example is still not wholly destroyed.
[8] *Logic*, I., 31.
[9] *Instinct in Man*, Chap. VI and App. I.

or causes one by association to think of something else." [10] Now when a sensation comes to us clothed in a special interest, is our thought being carried to something else? Clearly this is not necessary. Meaning as feeling is a different thing from meaning as thought, wherever it appears in the scale. How far apart they are may be seen from the fact that the very simplest thought-meaning that can enter into perception may in principle be mistaken, while the most developed of feeling-meanings could not possibly be mistaken. In sensation invested with such feeling-meanings we are not taking anything *for* anything; and hence we are strictly below the level of perceiving, thinking, or knowing. But Professor Drever's suggestion stresses a fact of the greatest importance in understanding the rise of perception, namely, that there is no democracy among the sensations with which we start, that some from the very beginning are weighted with "affective meaning." It is these that get the preference when explicit noticing arises.

But *why* this favoritism among sensations? Why should we find some interesting from the outset and others not? No answer need be expected in these pages; indeed it is more than possible that no answer will ever be found. Certain suggestions have been made that have often been taken for answers, but they will hardly bear examining. It has been suggested, for example, that we may look for the origin of the species of sensation where scientists commonly look for the origin of animal species, in natural selection. The animal or human child that was loftily indifferent to the sensations connected with eating, but found insistently attractive the sensations of falling or getting burned, would soon join the great majority who tell no tales. We find those sensations interesting which are useful to us in getting food, in avoiding danger, in preparing us, through playful experiment, for the exigencies of later life. This, at first, sounds plausible. But natural selection in the mind has precisely the defect of natural selection in biology. That theory, as has been pointedly said, explains the survival, but not the arrival, of the fittest. Given certain powers of dealing with nature, certain animals will survive, while those lacking them will not. True enough. But where is there anything in this to show how those that have them got them, and why those that lack them did not get them? This is the essential point, and natural selection does not touch it. There is a very simple fallacy in supposing that because possession of these powers explains survival, you can turn the argument around and say that survival explains their possession. To say this is like saying that a hole in a target accounts for a gun being fired.

When it is seen that natural selection will not serve, many inquirers turn to physiology. The explanation, they say, for our preferring some sensations to others, as indeed for our having sensations at all, is to be found in our brains and nervous systems. Some forms of stimulus, e.g., heat or friction, our nerves will respond to; to others, e.g., magnetism, they will not. When we do respond nervously we have the corresponding kind of sensation, and if some sensations are more interesting than others, that is because of the preformed nervous connections in our brains. Now that there is some causal connection between nervous change and sensation seems indubitable. But before anyone accepts this as an explanation of our sensing and feeling as we do, he may well reflect on the following points. (a) There is no connection in

10 *Perception, Physics and Reality,* p. 97.

the range of our knowledge that has proved more utterly opaque than the connection of body and mind. We have not the faintest notion how a change in a nerve could give rise to a pain. It is a complete mistake to suppose that such brilliant recent work as that of Adrian on the nervous impulse improves our understanding of how this impulse could generate experience. And if it is said that this is mere passing ignorance, that though we do not know as yet how one thing could produce another so very different, we may be sure of a point-for-point correspondence between changes . . . brain and mind, the answer is (b) that even so much is unwarranted. We shall see in that, in a course of reflection, the fact that A is seen to necessitate B may play a vital part in causing the thought of B to arise—that logical connection helps to determine psychological succession. But in the movements of physical particles, it is generally supposed that logical necessity plays no part. And when the laws of succession in the two series are thus so widely different, it is hard to believe that point-for-point correspondence is more than a provisional working assumption. It is true that in reflective thought we find the divergence at its widest, and that there is not *prima facie* an equal divergence if we choose, from the psychic series, a train of sensations. But even here we must be sceptical. For the content of sensation enters as an integral fact into the same mind that does the reasoning, and may figure in the reasoning itself. So far as it subjects itself to the laws that govern such reasoning it shares the divergence of that reasoning from the type of law that governs physical process. And thus even that modest form of explanation which consists in exhibiting detailed correspondence must, we suspect, be denied in the end to the physiological psychologist.

.   .   .

(3) Two factors have been mentioned that tend to break up the initial continuum and bring qualities into relief, the *intensity* of certain sensations and their *interest*. One other factor must be named. When a sensed quality appears in company with another, then, upon the reappearance of the first, the second also tends to recur. Now suppose that quality A appears successively with a number of other qualities B, C, D; that a shade of red presents itself first in a ball, then in a toy, and then in a dress. If the rule just laid down is correct, the red, on its second appearance, will tend to recall the *shape* that first came along with it. But this tendency is checked by the fact that there is now given a very different shape. The outcome is that the re-peated quality gets an emphasis that makes it stand out, while its conflicting as-sociates cancel each other. Similes are dangerous, but the process is rather like that of compound photographs in which, after many exposures to different faces, a film registers prominently the common features and shows only a blur for the differences. Since retention and association work from the beginning, this process also may be presumed at work. And it is an extremely important aid in making distinctions. For as a rule we can distinguish more completely sensations that come one after the other than sensations which we can hold before us both at once. If we are in doubt which of two tones is the higher, we shall not, if we are well advised, strike both at once; we shall sound first one and then the other. And so in most cases of touches, tastes, and odors.

We have now seen the general character of the experience in which we start and the chief factors which bring some elements rather than others into prominence. We do not suggest that these are the only factors. There are others of great importance; but since their effect is to bring into prominence things rather than sensations, they are more conveniently dealt with later. Nor is it suggested that sensed qualities are discriminated before things; the two kinds of discrimination grow up together. It is clear on the one hand that a thing can be discriminated before all its qualities are; but it is clear on the other hand that when we perceive a thing we seldom sense it as a whole; we take it to be there on the warrant of certain of its qualities that are sensed while others are not. The discrimination of qualities and the perception of things advance together and support each other.

· · ·

That there really is in the perception of things something that goes beyond sensation it is easy to show. Suppose that, glancing up at the sky, I see a tiny cross-shaped object and hear a certain pervasive hum. I at once recognize an airplane, and if questioned, I should say I "perceived" it. But how much have I actually seen or heard? I have seen little more than a speck, and have heard nothing but a peculiar hum. Now to say that a speck plus a hum *is* an airplane would of course be absurd, as absurd as to say that the tip of a cat's tail which I see vanishing through a door *is* the cat complete. Yet if the speck and hum are the only elements in the experience, how could I say I perceive an *airplane*? It is obvious that in perception something besides what is given in sensation is involved, and that in many cases this something else includes nearly everything of importance. In the actual work of perceiving, the relative parts of sensation and of this supplementary process vary greatly. When we perceive a slip of paper a few feet from our eyes, a large part of the perceived object is sensed, and the supplementary process has comparatively little to do; when we perceive a dot in the sky as an airplane, the role of sensation is relatively small and of the supplementary process large. Sir William Hamilton even laid it down as a precise law that "these elements are always found to exist in an inverse proportion," [11] and, as one might expect from Sir William, called in aid Joannes Secundus, "his learned commentator Bosscha," Cicero, and Shakespeare. We cannot follow him in his quantitative precision, but we can say at least that in all perception of things both processes are present. This may be proved by the ideal experiment of removing either one. Remove sensation and what is left? Some sort of reference or acceptance, no doubt, but nothing that anyone would call perception. Remove the supplementary process and what is left? Either pure sensation or, if it is doubted whether there is such a process, something which approaches it as a limit, and in any case falls short of the perception of things. In all such perception both processes are essential.

To one who has never reflected on the matter, the realization that perceiving involves this leap beyond the given comes as a surprise. But that it should come thus as a surprise is not itself a matter to be wondered at. In the business of making distinctions, the mind is capable of vast inertia; it is not accustomed to dissecting things except in the service of some practical end. And there is seldom any practical point in distinguishing the sensible from the non-sensible in perception, since the assumption that we see things whole and without any guesswork generally carries us through. But occasionally it does not, and nothing shows more clearly how we normally and without knowing it go beyond what is given than the way in which perception at times plays us false. A man "perceives a hundred-pound weight," braces himself to lift it, and finds that it is only paper. Certainly his perceiving the weight here is no process of sensation. A man "sees a ghost" in a moonlit hallway, takes his courage in

[11] *Lectures on Metaphysics*, II., 99.

his hands, runs to seize it, and finds himself in the embrace of the window curtain. Did he *see* the ghost at all? These cases may be unimportant and out-of-the-way, but it often happens, and particularly in studying perception, that the abnormal cases are the most enlightening ones. When we reflect on these instances it is plain that if we do not literally see and hear physical things when we perceive wrongly, neither do we see or hear them when we perceive rightly; all perception, true or false, involves a leap in the dark. . . .

·   ·   ·

THE PRIMACY OF PERCEPTION

maurice merleau-ponty

A Prospectus

We never cease living in the world of perception, but we bypass it in critical thought —almost to the point of forgetting the contribution of perception to our idea of truth. For critical thought encounters only *bare propositions* which it discusses, accepts, or rejects. Critical thought has broken with the naïve evidence of *things,* and when it affirms, it is because it no longer finds any means of denial. However necessary this activity of verification may be, specifying criteria and demanding from our experience its credentials of validity, it is not aware of our contact with the perceived world which is simply there before us, beneath the level of the verified true and the false. Nor does critical thought even define the positive steps of thinking or its most valid accomplishments.

. . .

The perceiving mind is an incarnated mind. I have tried, first of all, to reestablish the roots of the mind in its body and in its world, going against doctrines which treat perception as a simple result of the action of external things on our body as well as against those which insist on the autonomy of consciousness. These philosophies commonly forget—in favor of a pure exteriority or of a pure interiority—the insertion of the mind in corporeality, the ambiguous relation which we entertain with our body and, correlatively, with perceived things. When one attempts, as I have in *The Structure of Behavior,* to trace out, on the basis of modern psychology and physiology, the relationships which obtain between the perceiving organism and its milieu, one clearly finds that they are not those of an automatic machine which needs an outside agent to set off its pre-established mechanisms. And it is equally clear that one does not account for the facts by superimposing a pure, contemplative consciousness on a thinglike body. In the conditions of life—if not in the laboratory—the organism is

From "An Unpublished Text by Maurice Merleau-Ponty: A Prospectus of His Work," Arleen B. Dallery, trans., and "The Primacy of Perception and Its Philosophical Consequences," James M. Edie, trans., in Maurice Merleau-Ponty, *The Primacy of Perception,* James M. Edie, ed. (Evanston, Ill.: Northwestern University Press, 1964), pp. 3–6, 12–21, 24–25. Reprinted by permission of the publisher.
"The Primacy of Perception and Its Philosophical Consequences" was originally an address delivered to the Société française de philosophie on November 23, 1946.

less sensitive to certain isolated physical and chemical agents than to the constellation which they form and to the whole situation which they define. Behaviors reveal a sort of prospective activity in the organism, as if it were oriented toward the meaning of certain elementary situations, as if it entertained familiar relations with them, as if there were an "*a priori* of the organism," privileged conducts and laws of internal equilibrium which predisposed the organism to certain relations with its mileu. At this level there is no question yet of a real self-awareness or of intentional activity. Moreover, the organism's prospective capability is exercised only within defined limits and depends on precise, local conditions.

The functioning of the central nervous system presents us with similar paradoxes. In its modern forms, the theory of cerebral localizations has profoundly changed the relation of function to substrate. It no longer assigns, for instance, a pre-established mechanism to each perceptual behavior. "Coordinating centers" are no longer considered as storehouses of "cerebral traces," and their functioning is qualitatively different from one case to another, depending on the chromatic nuance to be evoked and the perceptual structure to be realized. Finally, this functioning reflects all the subtlety and all the variety of perceptual relationships.

The perceiving organism seems to show us a Cartesian mixture of the soul with the body. Higher-order behaviors give a new meaning to the life of the organism, but the mind here disposes of only a limited freedom; it needs simpler activities in order to stabilize itself in durable institutions and to realize itself truly as mind. Perceptual behavior emerges from these relations to a situation and to an environment which are not the workings of a pure, knowing subject.

In my work on the *Phenomenology of Perception* we are no longer present at the emergence of perceptual behaviors; rather we install ourselves in them in order to pursue the analysis of this exceptional relation between the subject and its body and its world. For contemporary psychology and psychopathology the body is no longer merely *an object in the world,* under the purview of a separated spirit. It is on the side of the subject; it is our *point of view on the world,* the place where the spirit takes on a certain physical and historical situation. As Descartes once said profoundly, the soul is not merely in the body like a pilot in his ship; it is wholly intermingled with the body. The body, in turn, is wholly animated, and all its functions contribute to the perception of objects—an activity long considered by philosophy to be pure knowledge.

We grasp external space through our bodily situation. A "corporeal or postural schema" gives us at every moment a global, practical, and implicit notion of the relation between our body and things, of our hold on them. A system of possible movements, or "motor projects," radiates from us to our environment. Our body is not in space like things; it inhabits or haunts space. It applies itself to space like a hand to an instrument, and when we wish to move about we do not move the body as we move an object. We transport it without instruments as if by magic, since it is ours and because through it we have direct access to space. For us the body is much more than an instrument or a means; it is our expression in the world, the visible form of our intentions. Even our most secret affective movements, those most deeply tied to the humoral infrastructure, help to shape our perception of things.

Now if perception is thus the common act of all our motor and affective functions, no less than the sensory, we must rediscover the structure of the perceived world through a process similar to that of an archaeologist. For the structure of the perceived world is buried under the sedimentations of later knowledge. Digging down to the perceived world, we see that sensory qualities are not opaque, indivisible "givens," which are simply exhibited to a remote consciousness—a favorite idea of classical philosophy. We see too that colors (each surrounded by an affective atmosphere which psychologists have been able to study and define) are themselves different modalities of our co-existence with the world. We also find that spatial forms or distances are not so much relations between different points in objective space as they are relations between these points and a central perspective—our body. In short, these relations are different ways for external stimuli to test, to solicit, and to vary our grasp on the world, our horizontal and vertical anchorage in a place and in a here-and-now. We find that perceived things, unlike geometrical objects, are not bounded entities whose laws of construction we possess a priori, but that they are open, inexhaustible systems which we recognize through a certain style of development, although we are never able, in principle, to explore them entirely, and even though they never give us more than profiles and perspectival views of themselves. Finally, we find that the perceived world, in its turn, is not a pure object of thought without fissures or lacunae; it is, rather, like a universal style shared in by all perceptual beings. While the world no doubt co-ordinates these perceptual beings, we can never presume that its work is finished. Our world, as Malebranche said, is an "unfinished task."

If we now wish to characterize a subject capable of this perceptual experience, it obviously will not be a self-transparent thought, absolutely present to itself without the interference of its body and its history. The perceiving subject is not this absolute thinker; rather, it functions according to a natal pact between our body and the world, between ourselves and our body. Given a perpetually new natural and historical situation to control, the perceiving subject undergoes a continued birth; at each instant it is something new. Every incarnate subject is like an open notebook in which we do not yet know what will be written. Or it is like a new language; we do not know what works it will accomplish but only that, once it has appeared, it cannot fail to say little or much, to have a history and a meaning. The very productivity or freedom of human life, far from denying our situation, utilizes it and turns it into a means of expression.

·   ·   ·

The Primacy of Perception and Its Philosophical Consequences

Preliminary summary of the argument

1   PERCEPTION AS AN ORIGINAL
    MODALITY OF CONSCIOUSNESS

The unprejudiced study of perception by psychologists has finally revealed that the perceived world is not a sum of objects (in the sense in which the sciences use this word), that our relation to the world is not that of a thinker to an object of thought, and finally that the unity of the perceived thing, as perceived by several consciousnesses, is not comparable to the unity of a proposition [*théorème*], as understood by several thinkers, any more than perceived existence is comparable to ideal existence.

As a result we cannot apply the classical distinction of form and matter to perception, nor can we conceive the perceiving subject as a consciousness which "interprets," "deciphers," or "orders" a sensible matter according to an ideal law which it possesses. Matter is "pregnant" with its form, which is to say that in the final analysis every perception takes place within a certain horizon and ultimately in the "world." We experience a perception and its horizon "in action" [*pratiquement*] rather than by "posing" them or explicitly "knowing" them. Finally the quasi-organic relation of the perceiving subject and the world involves, in principle, the contradiction of immanence and transcendence.

2   THE GENERALIZATION OF THESE RESULTS

Do these results have any value beyond that of psychological description? They would not if we could superimpose on the perceived world a world of ideas. But in reality the ideas to which we recur are valid only for a period of our lives or for a period in the history of our culture. Evidence is never apodictic, nor is thought timeless, though there is some progress in objectification and thought is always valid for more than an instant. The certainty of ideas is not the foundation of the certainty of perception but is, rather, based on it—in that it is perceptual experience which gives us the passage from one moment to the next and thus realizes the unity of time. In this sense all consciousness is perceptual, even the consciousness of ourselves.

3   CONCLUSIONS

The perceived world is the always presupposed foundation of all rationality, all value, and all existence. This thesis does not destroy either rationality or the absolute. It only tries to bring them down to earth.

Report of the session

M. Merleau-Ponty. The point of departure for these remarks is that the perceived world comprises relations and, in a general way, a type of organization which has not been recognized by classical psychology and philosophy.

If we consider an object which we perceive but one of whose sides we do not see, or if we consider objects which are not within our visual field at this moment— e.g., what is happening behind our back or what is happening in America or at the South Pole—how should we describe the existence of these absent objects or the nonvisible parts of present objects?

Should we say, as psychologists have often done, that I *represent* to myself the sides of this lamp which are not seen? If I say these sides are representations, I imply that they are not grasped as actually existing, because what is represented is not here before us, I do not actually perceive it. It is only a possible. But since the unseen sides of this lamp are not imaginary, but only hidden from view (to see them it suffices to move the lamp a little bit), I cannot say that they are representations.

Should I say that the unseen sides are somehow anticipated by me, as perceptions which would be produced necessarily if I moved, given the structure of the object? If, for example, I look at a cube, knowing the structure of the cube as it is defined in geometry, I can anticipate the perceptions which this cube will give me while I move around it. Under this hypothesis I would know the unseen side as the necessary consequence of a certain law of the development of my perception. But if I turn to perception itself, I cannot interpret it in this way because this analysis can be formulated as follows: It is *true* that the lamp has a back, that the cube has another side. But this formula, "It is true," does not correspond to what is given to me in perception. Perception does not give me truths like geometry but presences.

I grasp the unseen side as present, and I do not affirm that the back of the lamp exists in the same sense that I say the solution of a problem exists. The hidden side is present in its own way. It is in my vicinity.

Thus I should not say that the unseen sides of objects are simply possible perceptions, nor that they are the necessary conclusions of a kind of analysis or geometrical reasoning. It is not through an intellectual synthesis which would freely posit the total object that I am led from what is given to what is not actually given—that I am given, together with the visible sides of the object, the nonvisible sides as well. It is, rather, a kind of practical synthesis: I can touch the lamp, and not only the side turned toward me but also the other side; I have only to extend my hand to hold it.

The classical analysis of perception reduces all our experience to the single level of what, for good reasons, is judged to be true. But when, on the contrary, I consider the whole setting [*l'entourage*] of my perception, it reveals another modality which is neither the ideal and necessary being of geometry nor the simple sensory event, the *"percipi,"* and this is precisely what remains to be studied now.

But these remarks on the setting [*entourage*] of what is perceived enable us better to see the perceived itself. I perceive before me a road or a house, and I perceive them as having a certain dimension: the road may be a country road or a national highway; the house may be a shanty or a manor. These identifications presuppose that I recognize the true size of the object, quite different from that which appears to me from the point at which I am standing. It is frequently said that I restore the true size on the basis of the apparent size by analysis and conjecture. This is inexact for the very convincing reason that the apparent size of which we are speaking is not perceived by me. It is a remarkable fact that the uninstructed have no awareness of perspective and that it took a long time and much reflection for men to become aware of a perspectival deformation of objects. Thus there is no deciphering, no mediate inference from the sign to what is signified, because the alleged signs are not given to me separately from what they signify.

In the same way it is not true that I deduce the true color of an object on the basis of the color of the setting or of the lighting, which most of the time is not perceived. At this hour, since daylight is still coming through the windows, we perceive the yellowness of the artificial light, and it alters the color of objects. But when daylight disappears this yellowish color will no longer be perceived, and we will see the objects more or less in their true colors. The true color thus is not deduced, taking account of the lighting, because it appears precisely when daylight disappears.

If these remarks are true, what is the result? And how should we understand this "I perceive" which we are attempting to grasp?

We observe at once that it is impossible, as has often been said, to decompose a perception, to make it into a collection of sensations, because in it the whole is prior to the parts—and this whole is not an ideal whole. The meaning which I ultimately discover is not of the conceptual order. If it were a concept, the question would be how I can recognize it in the sense data, and it would be necessary for me to interpose between the concept and the sense data certain intermediaries, and then other intermediaries between these intermediaries, and so on. It is necessary that meaning and signs, the form and matter of perception, be related from the beginning and that, as we say, the matter of perception be "pregnant with its form."

In other words, the synthesis which constitutes the unity of the perceived objects and which gives meaning to the perceptual data is not an intellectual synthesis. Let us say with Husserl that it is a "synthesis of transition" [synthèse de transition] [1]— I anticipate the unseen side of the lamp because I can touch it—or a "horizontal synthesis" [synthèse d'horizon]—the unseen side is given to me as "visible from another standpoint," at once given but only immanently. What prohibits me from treating my perception as an intellectual act is that an intellectual act would grasp the object either as possible or as necessary. But in perception it is "real"; it is given as the infinite sum of an indefinite series of perspectival views in each of which the object is given but in none of which is it given exhaustively. It is not accidental for the object to be given to me in a "deformed" way, from the point of view [place] which I occupy. That is the price of its being "real." The perceptual synthesis thus must be accomplished by the subject, which can both delimit certain perspectival aspects in the object, the only ones actually given, and at the same time go beyond them. This subject, which takes a point of view, is my body as the field of perception and action [pratique]—in so far as my gestures have a certain reach and circumscribe as my domain the whole group of objects familiar to me. Perception is here understood as a reference to a whole which can be grasped, in principle, only through certain of its parts or aspects. The perceived thing is not an ideal unity in the possession of the intellect, like a geometrical notion, for example; it is rather a totality open to a horizon of an indefinite number of perspectival views which blend with one another according to a given style, which defines the object in question.

Perception is thus paradoxical. The perceived thing itself is paradoxical; it exists only in so far as someone can perceive it. I cannot even for an instant imagine an object in itself. As Berkeley said, if I attempt to imagine some place in the world which has never been seen, the very fact that I imagine it makes me present at that place. I thus cannot conceive a perceptible place in which I am not myself present. But even the places in which I find myself are never completely given to me; the things which I see are things for me only under the condition that they always recede beyond their immediately given aspects. Thus there is a paradox of immanence and transcendence in perception. Immanence, because the perceived object cannot be foreign to him who perceives; transcendence, because it always contains something more than what is actually given. And these two elements of perception are not, properly speaking, contradictory. For if we reflect on this notion of perspective, if we reproduce the perceptual experience in our thought, we see that the kind of evidence proper to the perceived, the appearance of "something," requires both this presence and this absence.

Finally, the world itself, which (to give a first, rough definition) is the totality of

---

[1] The more usual term in Husserl is "passive synthesis," which designates the "syntheses" of perceptual consciousness as opposed to the "active syntheses" of imagination and categorial thought. [Translator's note.]

perceptible things and the thing of all things, must be understood not as an object in the sense the mathematician or the physicist give to this word—that is, a kind of unified law which would cover all the partial phenomena or as a fundamental relation verifiable in all—but as the universal style of all possible perceptions. We must make this notion of the world, which guides the whole transcendental deduction of Kant, though Kant does not tell us its provenance, more explicit. "If a world is to be possible," he says sometimes, as if he were thinking before the origin of the world, as if he were assisting at its genesis and could pose its *a priori* conditions. In fact, as Kant himself said profoundly, we can only think the world because we have already experienced it; it is through this experience that we have the idea of being, and it is through this experience that the words "rational" and "real" receive a meaning simultaneously.

If I now consider not the problem of knowing how it is that there are things for me or how it is that I have a unified, unique, and developing perceptual experience of them, but rather the problem of knowing how my experience is related to the experience which others have of the same objects, perception will again appear as the paradoxical phenomenon which renders being accessible to us.

If I consider my perceptions as simple sensations, they are private; they are mine alone. If I treat them as acts of the intellect, if perception is an inspection of the mind, and the perceived object an idea, then you and I are talking about the same world, and we have *the right* to communicate among ourselves because the world has become an ideal existence and is the same for all of us—just like the Pythagorean theorem. But neither of these two formulas accounts for our experience. If a friend and I are standing before a landscape, and if I attempt to show my friend something which I see and which he does not yet see, we cannot account for the situation by saying that I see something in my own world and that I attempt, by sending verbal messages, to give rise to an analogous perception in the world of my friend. There are not two numerically distinct worlds plus a mediating language which alone would bring us together. There is—and I know it very well if I become impatient with him—a kind of demand that what I see be seen by him also. And at the same time this communication is required by the very thing which I am looking at, by the reflections of sunlight upon it, by its color, by its sensible evidence. The thing imposes itself not as true for every intellect, but as real for every subject who is standing where I am.

I will never know how you see red, and you will never know how I see it, but this separation of consciousnesses is recognized only after a failure of communication, and our first movement is to believe in an undivided being between us. There is no reason to treat this primordial communication as an illusion, as the sensationalists do, because even then it would become inexplicable. And there is no reason to base it on our common participation in the same intellectual consciousness because this would suppress the undeniable plurality of consciousnesses. It is thus necessary that, in the perception of another, I find myself in relation with another "myself," who is, in principle, open to the same truths as I am, in relation to the same being that I am. And this perception is realized. From the depths of my subjectivity I see another subjectivity invested with equal rights appear, because the behavior of the other takes place within my perceptual field. I understand this behavior, the words of another; I espouse his thought because this other, born in the midst of my phenomena, appropriates them and treats them in accord with typical behaviors which I myself have experienced. Just as my body, as the system of all my holds on the world, founds the unity of the objects which I perceive, in the same way the body of the other—as the bearer of symbolic behaviors and of the behavior of true reality— tears itself away from being one of my phenomena, offers me the task of a true communication, and confers on my objects the new dimension of intersubjective being or, in other words, of objectivity. Such are, in a quick résumé, the elements of a description of the perceived world.

•   •   •

. . . This leads us, therefore, to the second point which I propose to examine: What is the relation between intellectual consciousness and perceptual consciousness?

Before taking this up, let us say a word about the . . . objection which was addressed to us: You go back to the unreflected [irréfléchi]; therefore you renounce reflection. It is true that we discover the unreflected. But the unreflected we go back to is not that which is prior to philosophy or prior to reflection. It is the unreflected which is understood and conquered by reflection. Left to itself, perception forgets itself and is ignorant of its own accomplishments. Far from thinking that philosophy is a useless repetition of life I think, on the contrary, that without reflection life would probably dissipate itself in ignorance of itself or in chaos. But this does not mean that reflection should be carried away with itself or pretend to be ignorant of its origins. By fleeing difficulties it would only fail in its task.

Should we now generalize and say that what is true of perception is also true in the order of the intellect and that in a general way all our experience, all our knowledge, has the same fundamental structures, the same synthesis of transition, the same kind of horizons which we have found in perceptual experience?

No doubt the absolute truth or evidence of scientific knowledge would be opposed to this idea. But it seems to me that the acquisitions of the philosophy of the sciences confirm the primacy of perception. Does not the work of the French school at the beginning of this century, and the work of Brunschvicg, show that scientific knowledge cannot be closed in on itself, that it is always an approximate knowledge, and that it consists in clarifying a pre-scientific world the analysis of which will never be finished? Physico-mathematical relations take on a physical sense only to the extent that we at the same time represent to ourselves the sensible things to which these relations ultimately apply. Brunschvicg reproached positivism for its dogmatic illusion that the law is truer than the fact. The law, he adds, is conceived exclusively to make the fact intelligible. The perceived happening can never be reabsorbed in the complex of transparent relations which the intellect constructs because of the happening. But if this is the case, philosophy is not only consciousness of these relations; it is also consciousness of the obscure element and of the "non-relational foundation" on which these relations are based. Otherwise it would shirk its task of universal clarification. When I think the Pythagorean theorem and recognize it as true, it is clear that this truth is not for this moment only. Nevertheless later progress in knowledge will show that it is not yet a final, unconditioned evidence and that, if the Pythagorean theorem and the Euclidean system once appeared as final, unconditioned evidences, that is itself the mark of a certain cultural epoch. Later developments would not annul the Pythagorean theorem but would put it back in its place as a partial, and also an abstract, truth. Thus here also we do not have a timeless truth but rather the recovery of one time by another time, just as, on the level of perception, our certainty about perceiving a given thing does not guarantee that our experience will not be contradicted, or dispense us from a fuller experience of that thing. Naturally it is necessary to establish here a difference between ideal truth and perceived truth. I do not propose to undertake this immense task just now. I am only trying to show the organic tie, so to speak, between perception and intellection. Now it is incontestable that I dominate the stream of my conscious states and even that I am unaware of their temporal succession. At the moment when I am thinking or considering an idea, I am not divided into the instants of my life. But it is also incontestable that this domination of time, which is the work of thought, is always somewhat deceiving. Can I seriously say that I will always hold the ideas I do at present—and mean it? Do I not know that in six months, in a year, even if I use more or less the same formulas to express my thoughts, they will have changed their meaning slightly? Do I not know that there is a life of ideas, as there is a meaning of everything I experience, and that every one of my most convincing thoughts will need additions and then will be, not destroyed, but at least integrated into a new unity? This is the only conception of knowledge that is scientific and not mythological.

Thus perception and thought have this much in common—that both of them have a future horizon and a past horizon and that they appear to themselves as temporal, even though they do not move at the same speed nor in the same time. We must say that at each moment our ideas express not only the truth but also our capacity to attain it at that given moment. Scepticism begins if we conclude from this that our ideas are always false. But this can only happen with reference to some idol of absolute knowledge. We must say, on the contrary, that our ideas, however limited they may be at a given moment—since they always express our contact with being and with culture—are capable of being true provided we keep them open to the field of nature and culture which they must express. And this possibility is always open to us, just because we are temporal. The idea of going straight to the essence of things is an inconsistent idea if one thinks about it. What is given is a route, an experience which gradually clarifies itself, which gradually rectifies itself and proceeds by dialogue with itself and with others. Thus what we tear away from the dispersion of instants is not an already-made reason; it is, as has always been said, a natural light, our openness to *something*. What saves us is the possibility of a new development, and our power of making even what is false, true—by thinking through our errors and replacing them within the domain of truth.

.   .   .

Coming back to the perceived world as we have described it above, and basing our conception of reality on the phenomena, we do not in any way sacrifice objectivity to the interior life, as Bergson has been accused of doing. As Gestalt psychology has shown, structure, *Gestalt*, meaning are no less visible in objectively observable behavior than in the experience of ourselves—provided, of course, that objectivity is not confused with what is measurable. Is one truly objective with respect to man when he thinks he can take him as an object which can be explained as an intersection of processes and causalities? Is it not more objective to attempt to constitute a true science of human life based on the description of typical behaviors? Is it objective to apply tests to man which deal only with abstract aptitudes, or to attempt to grasp the situation of man as he is present to the world and to others by means of still more tests?

Psychology as a science has nothing to fear from a return to the perceived world, nor from a philosophy which draws out the consequences of this return. Far from hurting psychology, this attitude, on the contrary, clarifies the philosophical meaning of its discoveries. For there are not two truths; there is not an inductive psychology and an intuitive philosophy. Psychological induction is never more than the methodological means of bringing to light a certain typical behavior, and if induction includes intuition, conversely intuition does not occur in empty space. It exercises itself on the facts, on the material, on the phenomena brought to light by scientific research. There are not two kinds of knowledge, but two different degrees of clarification of the same knowledge. Psychology and philosophy are nourished by the same phenomena; it is only that the problems become more formalized at the philosophical level.

But the philosophers might say here that we are giving psychology too big a place, that we are compromising rationality by founding it on the texture of experience, as it is manifested in perceptual experience. But either the demand for an absolute rationality is only a wish, a personal preference which should not be confused with philosophy, or this point of view, to the extent that it is well-founded, satisfies it as well as, or even better than, any other. When philosophers wish to place reason above the vicissitudes of history they cannot purely and simply forget what psychology, sociology, ethnography, history, and psychiatry have taught us about the conditioning of human behavior. It would be a very romantic way of showing one's love for reason to base its reign on the disavowal of acquired knowledge. What can be validly demanded is that man never be submitted to the fate of an external nature or history and stripped of his consciousness. Now my philosophy satisfies this demand. In speaking of the primacy of perception, I have never, of course, meant to say (this would be a return to the theses of empiricism) that science, reflection, and philosophy are only transformed sensations or that values are deferred and calculated pleasures. By these words, the "primacy of perception," we mean that the experience of perception is our presence at the moment when things, truths, values are constituted for us; that perception is a nascent *logos;* that it teaches us, outside all dogmatism, the true conditions of objectivity itself; that it summons us to the tasks of knowledge and action. It is not a question of reducing human knowledge to sensation, but of assisting at the birth of this knowledge, to make it as sensible as the sensible, to recover the consciousness of rationality. This experience of rationality is lost when we take it for granted as self-evident, but is, on the contrary, rediscovered when it is made to appear against the background of non-human nature.

•   •   •

SELECTED BIBLIOGRAPHY FOR PART I

Armstrong, D. M. *Perception and the Physical World.* London: Routledge, 1961.

Austin, J. L. *Sense and Sensibilia.* Oxford: Clarendon Press, 1962.

Ayer, A. J. *The Foundations of Empirical Knowledge.* London: Macmillan, 1940.

————. *The Problem of Knowledge.* London: Macmillan, 1956. Chap. 3.

Broad, C. D. *The Mind and Its Place in Nature*. London: Kegan Paul, 1925. Chap. 4.

———. *Scientific Thought*. London: Kegan Paul, 1927. Chaps. 7–9.

Chisholm, Roderick M. *Perceiving: A Philosophical Study*. Ithaca, N.Y.: Cornell University Press, 1957.

Garnett, A. C. *The Perceptual Process*. Madison: University of Wisconsin Press, 1965.

Hamlyn, D. W. *Sensation and Perception*. London: Routledge, 1961.

Hirst, R. J. *The Problems of Perception*. New York: Macmillan, 1959.

———, ed. *Perception and the External World*. New York: Macmillan, 1965.

Lean, Martin. *Sense-Perception and Matter*. London: Routledge, 1953.

Lewis, C. I. *Mind and the World Order*. New York: Scribner, 1929.

Locke, Don. *Perception and Our Knowledge of the External World*. New York: Humanities Press, 1967.

Mandelbaum, Maurice. *Philosophy, Science, and Sense-Perception*. Baltimore: Johns Hopkins Press, 1964.

Merleau-Ponty, Maurice. *The Phenomenology of Perception*, trans. Colin Smith. London: Routledge, 1962.

Price, H. H. *Hume's Theory of the External World*. Oxford: Clarendon Press, 1940.

———. *Perception*. London: Methuen, 1932.

Prichard, H. A. *Knowledge and Perception*. Oxford: Clarendon Press, 1950.

Ryle, Gilbert. *The Concept of Mind*. London: Hutchinson, 1949. Chap. 7.

———. *Dilemmas*. Cambridge: Cambridge University Press, 1954. Chap. 7.

Sellars, Wilfred. *Science, Perception, and Reality*. London: Routledge, 1963. Chap. 3.

Smythies, J. R. *Analysis of Perception*. London: Routledge, 1956.

Straus, Erwin. *The Primary World of Senses, A Vindication of Sensory Experience*, trans. Jacob Needleman. New York: Free Press of Glencoe, 1963.

Swartz, Robert J., ed. *Perceiving, Sensing, and Knowing*. Garden City, N.J.: Anchor Books, 1965.

Warnock, G. J. *Berkeley*. London: Penguin Books, 1953.

———, ed. *The Philosophy of Perception*. Oxford: University Press, 1967.

part II

metaphysical

inquiries

INTRODUCTION

Western philosophy was born in the sixth century B.C., when the Greeks tried to discover the basic stuff of the universe and the process whereby this stuff changes into those things that we perceive and eventually returns to its elemental form. Thales, the first recorded Western philosopher, asserted that water was the basic stuff. This seemingly naïve answer is easily explained in the light of common experience. Water, when frozen, is a solid; when heated, a·vapor. It seems to mix with all things and to change itself into air, fire, and earth, the other elements recognized by the Greeks. Nevertheless, some of Thales' contemporaries did not find his explanation altogether satisfactory. If water is the dominant element, why does it change into the other elements? Why is there not only water? Thales' younger contemporary, Anaximenes, who believed that air, not water, was the basic stuff, improved logically upon Thales' explanation by attributing the apparent change into other elements to a process of condensation and rarefaction. This allowed for a universal basic stuff, a single substance, which changed its appearance when more or less of it occupied a given space.

As philosophy developed and men found out more about the world and about themselves, certain studies which were originally in the domain of philosophy became separate sciences. The questions the early Greeks raised are similar to those posed in a more sophisticated manner today by some scientists. Scientists attempt to discover the fundamental characteristics of certain kinds of entities and to show how these properties, once discovered, are related to the characteristics of other types of entities in the universe. The physicist, for example, deals primarily with inorganic matter; the biologist, with living things. When a scientist concludes from his various studies of organic and inorganic substances that some form of matter is the basic stuff of the universe, then he is doing metaphysics. Yet upon reflection we may note that dreaming, thinking, remembering, and imagining do not seem to be physical. These processes seem to belong to the realm of the mental, and seem to have characteristics which are distinct from those of matter. Whether these two kinds of things, matter and mind, can both be the basic stuff of the universe is the subject of some metaphysical inquiries. In metaphysics, the basic stuff, or ultimate nature of things, is called "reality" or the "real."

Metaphysics is sometimes characterized as the most fundamental or comprehensive of inquiries. It can be understood as the quest for the reality that underlies all specialized studies. Consequently, metaphysics may also make explicit the assumptions of the sciences. Aristotle, who was the first philosopher to separate what was known about the world into divisions that have come to be recognized as disciplines, devoted a collection of essays to the clarification of these assumptions. In the absence of any accurate classification, these essays came to be called the *metaphysika,* literally, the "after physics." "After physics" does not give us much of a clue to the subject matter of these essays. Aristotle explains their content as the study of "being qua being." For him the subject matter of metaphysics is comprised of certain concepts or categories presupposed by all kinds of change. One of the most fundamental of these concepts is substance; and how substances change is of major concern to Aristotle.

In the explanation of change, Aristotle distinguishes four kinds of causes: the *material, formal, efficient,* and *final causes.* In the explanation of any change all four causes must be present. The growth of an acorn into an oak tree depends, in part, upon the material or matter of which the acorn is composed. This is the *material cause* of the acorn's being what it is. The substance, or essence, of the acorn, its *formal cause,* is that by virtue of which it is the seed of an oak tree and not the seed of a maple or willow. The *efficient cause* supplies the motion or energy that results in the maturation of the seed. Under the efficient cause are those environmental conditions, such as the planting of the seed and a certain amount of rainfall, that foster its growth. These external conditions support the acorn's inner striving to become an oak tree. When the acorn becomes an oak it has attained the end of its striving or its *final cause.* When the principle of the four causes is applied to natural, as opposed to manufactured, objects, the formal cause and the final cause are the same. The formal cause is the essence, or the concept or idea, of the thing, and the final cause is the realization of the idea in actuality. The efficient cause also becomes the formal and final cause because the entity strives to become its form or essence. This striving may be supported or hindered by the external environment. The idea of internal purpose pervades Aristotle's universe and even extends to the heavenly bodies. We can describe Aristotle's universe as basically teleological in nature, as a universe governed primarily by purposes or ends.

Because it is extremely difficult, if not impossible, to examine through scientific methods these supposed teleological characteristics of nature, scientists have tended to be unsympathetic to teleological metaphysical positions. Rather, they have sought to restrict their activities, when they are interested in causes, to investigating what seems to correspond to Aristotle's efficient cause.

In sharp contrast to a teleological view of the universe that explains change by internal ideal principles, a mechanistic view explains change by invoking the laws of mechanics. Concepts that predominate in such a view are usually *matter, motion, space,* and *time.* A mechanist is usually a *materialist.* Materialism is the view that matter is the basic stuff of the universe and that mind is a consequence of matter or that there is no mind at all. The universal cause of change in a mechanistic materialism is mechanical motion. It follows from his appeal to the laws of science that the materialist assumes that the order in the universe is regular and without variation. When it is held that *all* change may be explained and predicted by scientific law, then the view is deterministic. In the history of Western philosophy most materialistic views have been deterministic. The most notable exception is the view of Lucretius, that atoms, the entities from which all else in the universe is formed, occasionally swerve from their normal path of downward motion. With the advent of quantum mechanics and the uncertainty principle, some modern materialists have also rejected determinism. The uncertainty principle states that it is impossible to specify or determine simultaneously the position and the velocity of a physical particle with full accuracy. And those who apply this principle against the mechanistic view ask how a system whose specific behavior is not predictable, and therefore is not *necessary*, can be said to be determined.

Thomas Hobbes, a British exponent of materialism, was committed to mechanism, and to determinism. Hobbes holds that matter is the fundamental substance of the universe and that all change is to be explained as the effect of one body upon another. The basic kind of motion in Hobbes' view is local motion, or the movement of a body from one place to another. This motion, for Hobbes, is mechanical, and its mechanical nature is the universal cause of every sort of change. Hobbes was a rigid determinist who maintained that effects can only be conceived as following necessarily from their causes. If we are not always successful in discovering the causes of a particular event, the difficulty is not with the causal laws but with our ignorance of the relevant factors. Hobbes explained in this manner not only change in physical bodies but also sensation, which results from the motions of external bodies acting upon the sense organs.

If philosophizing begins with the act of perception and not with the assumption that bodies have an existence independent of thought, then what is asserted about the world may be quite different from the view expounded by Hobbes. George Berkeley, an Anglo-Irish bishop who wrote during the first half of the eighteenth century, bases his metaphysics on an analysis of the perceptual act. With regard to the objects of perception, Berkeley maintains that *"esse est percipi," or* "to be is to be perceived." Berkeley's view and the arguments in its support were intended to invalidate the philosophical conception of matter without being inconsistent with the ordinary man's conception of sensible things. He maintains that what we perceive are ideas that do not correspond to anything material. In Berkeley's universe all that exists are minds, or spiritual substances and ideas. The view which claims that the real is mental is called *idealism.* Idealism has several forms, but, in general, idealistic philosophies emphasize the incorporeal, the nonspatial, the normative, and the teleological. The idealist's emphasis upon mind tends to commit him to a universe where God is the supreme spirit. In Berkeley's view, God causes the sensations that constitute, for us, trees, houses, etc. God is also the constant perceiver who preserves the continuity of existence.

David Hume, a successor of Berkeley, applied Berkeley's own criticisms of materialism to the concept of spiritual substance or mind. Hume's criticisms are extremely effective because, like Berkeley, he bases knowledge of existing things upon sensations which he calls impressions. Since we have no impressions of spiritual substance, but only of specific psychic events, Hume concludes that we cannot know that spiritual substance exists. He believes that one can philosophize only after one has determined the limits of the senses and of reason. His view of the limitations of man's faculties led him to challenge what most philosophers of his time accepted as knowledge. For this reason, he is called a sceptic.

Some contemporary philosophers maintain that the only meaningful statements about existence are propositions that can be empirically verified. Since most metaphysical statements cannot be verified in this manner many philosophers deny that these propositions are meaningful. Ernest Nagel accepts the verification criterion, although he admits that empirical observation alone does not prove those underlying assumptions, about the overall nature of things, about human destiny and the scope of human reason, which color "evaluations of major ideals and proposed policies." In making these assumptions explicit Nagel espouses a metaphysical view which is called "naturalism." The naturalist claims that what exists lies within the scope of scientific explanation, and that, therefore, God and other supernatural entities do not exist. A central thesis of Nagel's naturalism is that matter has both an existential and a causal primacy. This is not to say that only the material exists; for experience reveals modes of action, relations of meaning, dreams, plans, etc., which are not material. What naturalism does claim is that the activities of dreaming, planning, etc., do not occur as disembodied forces. Nagel's naturalism further claims that the irreducible variety of things in the universe supports a metaphysical pluralism. Nagel believes that naturalism is *supported*—if not proved—by existing empirical evidence, and that the view is not a result of dogmatic preference.

Up to this point in our discussion, the criteria for determining reality have been derived from perception, reason, the employment of the scientific method, and intuition. William James accepts none of these as the absolute determinant of reality. Men, according to James, recognize a number of sub-universes. Among these are the world of sense, of science, of ideal relations, of illusion and prejudice, of the supernatural, of individual opinion, and of madness and vagary. An individual's dominant habits of attention "elect from among the various worlds some one to be for him the world of ultimate realities." In the relative sense, that is, when we speak of one world or thing as having more reality than another and as being more believed than another, "reality means simply relation to our emotional and active life." In this sense, the sense of the practical, reality is what stimulates or interests us. James is claiming that as thinkers "with emotional reaction, we give what seems to us a still higher degree of reality to whatever things we select and emphasize and turn to with a will." James' emphasis upon the will is a form of voluntarism. A metaphysical voluntarism maintains that the will ultimately determines or constitutes reality.

We have in the course of this introduction made frequent reference to the "real." One of the major concerns of some metaphysicians has been that of distinguishing the real from the seemingly real. What criteria do we use to distinguish the true nature of a thing from its appearance? Can perception, reason, the scientific method, intuition, the will, or pure consciousness establish the nature of reality? In analyzing the ways in which we use the word "real" J. L. Austin concludes that there are no *general* criteria for distinguishing the real from the not real, although there are hundreds of particular criteria. When the distinction between the real and the not real is made its meaning is determined by the context, and is subject to alteration as the context shifts. The word "real" is meaningful only in cases where there is a clear sense of a "non-real" alternative. In the context of the hunt, the hunter must be able to distinguish the live or "real" duck from the decoy. However, in the context of the toy store, it is the manufactured imitation of a live duck that is the "real" toy and not the live duck. In each case the meaning of "real" is different and we are only able to make the distinction between "a real X" and "not a real X" because "there is a way of telling what is a real X and what is not." From Austin's position it follows that the metaphysical studies of Aristotle, Hobbes, Berkeley, and others are illegitimate because they attempt to establish general criteria for determining reality. These attempts do not account for restrictions governing the way in which the word "real" is used.

Whatever philosophic position one takes, the question of what is real, or that of what can be meant by the word "real," seems to arise. The readings which follow introduce the reader to some of the major positions on these questions.

THE REAL IS SUBSTANCE

aristotle

from the Metaphysics

The subject of our inquiry is substance; for the principles and the causes we are seeking are those of substances. For if the universe is of the nature of a whole, substance is its first part; and if it coheres merely by virtue of serial succession, on this view also substance is first, and is succeeded by quality, and then by quantity. At the same time these latter are not even being in the full sense, but are qualities and movements of it—or else even the not-white and the not-straight would be being; at least we say even these *are,* e.g., "there is a not-white." Further, none of the categories other than substance can exist apart. And the early philosophers also in practice testify to the primacy of substance; for it was of substance that they sought the principles and elements and causes. The thinkers of the present [1] day tend to rank universals as substances (for genera are universals, and these they tend to describe as principles and substances, owing to the abstract nature of their inquiry); but the thinkers of old ranked particular things as substances, e.g., fire and earth, not what is common to both, body.

There are three kinds of substance—one that is sensible (of which one sub-division is eternal and another is perishable; the latter is recognized by all men, and includes, e.g., plants and animals), of which we must grasp the elements, whether one or many; and another that is immovable, and this certain thinkers assert to be capable of existing apart, some dividing it into two, others identifying the Forms and the objects of mathematics, and others positing, of these two, only the objects of mathematics.[2] The former two kinds of substance are the subject of physics (for they imply movement); but the third kind belongs to another science, if there is no principle common to it and to the other kinds.

From the *Metaphysics,* trans. W. D. Ross, Book XII, Chaps. 1–3, pp. 872–874, and the *Physics,* trans. R. P. Hardie and R. K. Gaye, Book II, Chaps. 1, 3, 8, pp. 236–237, 240–241, 249–251, in *The Basic Works of Aristotle,* Richard McKeon, ed. copyright 1941 by Random House, Inc. Reprinted by permission.

[1] The Platonists.

[2] The three views appear to have been held respectively by Plato, Xenocrates, and Speusippus. [McKeon's note.]

Sensible substance is changeable. Now if change proceeds from opposites or from intermediates, and not from all opposites (for the voice is not-white [but it does not therefore change to white]), but from the contrary, there must be something underlying which changes into the contrary state; for the *contraries* do not change. Further, something persists, but the contrary does not persist; there is, then, some third thing besides the contraries, viz. the matter. Now since changes are of four kinds—either in respect of the "what" or of the quality or of the quantity or of the place, and change in respect of "thisness" is simple generation and destruction, and change in quantity is increase and diminution, and change in respect of an affection is alteration, and change of place is motion, changes will be from given states into those contrary to them in these several respects. The matter, then, which changes must be capable of both states. And since that which "is" has two senses, we must say that everything changes from that which is potentially to that which is actually, e.g., from potentially white to actually white, and similarly in the case of increase and diminution. Therefore not only can a thing come to be, incidentally, out of that which is not, but also all things come to be out of that which is, but is potentially, and is not actually. And this is the "One" of Anaxagoras; for instead of "all things were together"—and the "Mixture" of Empedocles and Anaximander and the account given by Democritus—it is better to say "all things were together potentially but not actually." Therefore these thinkers seem to have had some notion of matter. Now all things that change have matter, but different matter; and of eternal things those which are not generable but are movable in space have matter—not matter for generation, however, but for motion from one place to another.

One might raise the question from what sort of nonbeing generation proceeds; for "nonbeing" has three senses. If, then, one form of nonbeing exists potentially, still it is not by virtue of a potentiality for any and every thing, but different things come from different things; nor is it satisfactory to say that "all things were together"; for they differ in their matter, since otherwise why did an infinity of things come to be, and not one thing? For "reason" is one, so that if matter also were one, that must have come to be in actuality which the matter was in potency. The causes and the principles, then, are three, two being the pair of contraries of which one is definition and form and the other is privation, and the third being the matter.

Note, next, that neither the matter nor the form comes to be—and I mean the last matter and form. For everything that changes is something and is changed by something and into something. That by which it is changed is the immediate mover; that which is changed, the matter; that into which it is changed, the form. The process, then, will go on to infinity, if not only the bronze comes to be round but also the round or the bronze comes to be; therefore there must be a stop.

Note, next, that each substance comes into being out of something that shares its name. (Natural objects and other things both rank as substances.) For things come into being either by art or by nature or by luck or by spontaneity. Now art is a principle of movement in something other than the thing moved, nature is a principle in the thing itself (for man begets man), and the other causes are privations of these two.

There are three kinds of substance—the matter, which is a "this" in appearance (for all things that are characterized by contact and not by organic unity are matter and substratum, e.g., fire, flesh, head; for these are all matter, and the last matter is the matter of that which is in the full sense substance); the nature, which is a "this" or positive state toward which movement takes place; and again, thirdly, the particular substance which is composed of these two, e.g., Socrates or Callias. Now in some cases the "this" does not exist apart from the composite substance, e.g., the form of house does not so exist, unless the art of building exists apart (nor is there generation and destruction of these forms, but it is in another way that the house apart from its matter, and health, and all ideals of art, exist and do not exist); but if the "this" exists apart from the concrete thing, it is only in the case of natural objects. And so Plato was not far wrong when he said that there are as many Forms as there are kinds of natural object (if there *are* Forms distinct from the things of this earth). The moving causes exist as things preceding the effects, but causes in the sense of definitions are simultaneous with their effects. For when a man is healthy, then health also exists; and the shape of a bronze sphere exists at the same time as the bronze sphere. (But we must examine whether any form also survives afterwards. For in some cases there is nothing to prevent this; e.g., the soul may be of this sort—not all soul but the reason; for presumably it is impossible that *all* soul should survive.) Evidently then there is no necessity, on this ground at least, for the existence of the Ideas. For man is begotten by man, a given man by an individual father; and similarly in the arts; for the medical art is the formal cause of health.

· · · ·

from the Physics

Of things that exist, some exist by nature, some from other causes.

"By nature" the animals and their parts exist, and the plants and the simple bodies (earth, fire, air, water)—for we say that these and the like exist "by nature."

All the things mentioned present a feature in which they differ from things which are *not* constituted by nature. Each of them has *within itself* a principle of motion and of stationariness (in respect of place, or of growth and decrease, or by way of alteration). On the other hand, a bed and a coat and anything else of that sort, qua receiving these designations—i.e., in so far as they are products of art—have no innate impulse to change. But in so far as they happen to be composed of stone or of earth or of a mixture of the two, they *do* have such an impulse, and just to that extent—which seems to indicate that *nature is a source or cause of being moved and of being at rest in that to which it belongs primarily,* in virtue of itself and not in virtue of a concomitant attribute.

I say "not in virtue of a concomitant attribute," because (for instance) a man who is a doctor might cure himself. Nevertheless it is not in so far as he is a patient that he possesses the art of medicine: it merely has happened that the same man is doctor and patient—and that is why these attributes are not always found together. So it is with all other artificial products. None of them has in itself the source of its own production. But while in some cases (for instance houses and the other products of manual labor) that principle is in something else external to the thing, in others —those which may cause a change in themselves in virtue of a concomitant attribute— it lies in the things themselves (but not in virtue of what they are).

"Nature" then is what has been stated. Things "have a nature" which have a principle of this kind. Each of them is a substance; for it is a subject, and nature always implies a subject in which it inheres.

The term "according to nature" is applied to all these things and also to the attributes which belong to them in virtue of what they are, for instance the property of fire to be carried upward—which is not a "nature" nor "has a nature" but is "by nature" or "according to nature."

What nature is, then, and the meaning of the terms "by nature" and "according to nature," has been stated. *That* nature exists, it would be absurd to try to prove; for it is obvious that there are many things of this kind, and to prove what is obvious by what is not is the mark of a man who is unable to distinguish what is self-evident from what is not. (This state of mind is clearly possible. A man blind from birth might reason about colors. Presumably therefore such persons must be talking about words without any thought to correspond.)

· · ·

Now that we have established these distinctions, we must proceed to consider causes, their character and number. Knowledge is the object of our inquiry, and men do not think they know a thing till they have grasped the "why" of it (which is to grasp its primary cause). So clearly we too must do this as regards both coming to be and passing away and every kind of physical change, in order that, knowing their principles, we may try to refer to these principles each of our problems.

In one sense, then, (1) that out of which a thing comes to be and which persists, is called "cause," e.g., the bronze of the statue, the silver of the bowl, and the genera of which the bronze and the silver are species.

In another sense (2) the form or the archetype, i.e., the statement of the essence, and its genera, are called "causes" (e.g., of the octave the relation of 2 : 1, and generally number), and the parts in the definition.

Again (3) the primary source of the change or coming to rest; e.g., the man who gave advice is a cause, the father is cause of the child, and generally what makes of what is made and what causes change of what is changed.

Again (4) in the sense of end or "that for the sake of which" a thing is done, e.g., health is the cause of walking about. ("Why is he walking about?" we say. "To be healthy," and, having said that, we think we have assigned the cause.) The same is true also of all the intermediate steps which are brought about through the action of something else as means toward the end, e.g., reduction of flesh, purging, drugs, or surgical instruments are means toward health. All these things are "for the sake of" the end, though they differ from one another in that some are activities, others instruments.

This then perhaps exhausts the number of ways in which the term "cause" is used.

As the word has several senses, it follows that there are several causes of the same thing (not merely in virtue of a concomitant attribute), e.g., both the art of the sculptor and the bronze are causes of the statue. These are causes of the statue qua statue, not in virtue of anything else that it may be—only not in the same way, the one being the material cause, the other the cause whence the motion comes. Some things cause each other reciprocally, e.g., hard work causes fitness and vice versa, but again not in the same way, but the one as end, the other as the origin of change. Further the same thing is the cause of contrary results. For that which by its presence brings about one result is sometimes blamed for bringing about the contrary by its absence. Thus we ascribe the wreck of a ship to the absence of the pilot whose presence was the cause of its safety.

All the causes now mentioned fall into four familiar divisions. The letters are the causes of syllables, the material of artificial products, fire, etc., of bodies, the parts of the whole, and the premises of the conclusion, in the sense of "that from which." Of these pairs the one set are causes in the sense of substratum, e.g., the parts, the other set in the sense of essence—the whole and the combination and the form. But the seed and the doctor and the adviser, and generally the maker, are all sources whence the change or stationariness originates, while the others are causes in the sense of the end or the good of the rest; for "that for the sake of which" means what is best and the end of the things that lead up to it. (Whether we say the "good itself" or the "apparent good" makes no difference.)

Such then is the number and nature of the kinds of cause.

. . .

We must explain then (1) that Nature belongs to the class of causes which act for the sake of something; (2) about the necessary and its place in physical problems, for all writers ascribe things to this cause, arguing that since the hot and the cold, etc., are of such and such a kind, therefore certain things *necessarily* are and come to be—and if they mention any other cause (one [3] his "friendship and strife," another [4] his "mind"), it is only to touch on it, and then good-bye to it.

A difficulty presents itself: Why should not nature work, not for the sake of something, nor because it is better so, but just as the sky rains, not in order to make the corn grow, but of necessity? What is drawn up must cool, and what has been cooled must become water and descend, the result of this being that the corn grows. Similarly if a man's crop is spoiled on the threshing-floor, the rain did not fall for the sake of this—in order that the crop might be spoiled—but that result just followed. Why then should it not be the same with the parts in nature, e.g., that our teeth should come up *of necessity*—the front teeth sharp, fitted for tearing, the molars broad and useful for grinding down the food—since they did not arise for this end, but it was merely a coincident result; and so with all other parts in which we suppose that there is purpose? Wherever, then, all the parts came about just what they would have been if they had come to be for an end, such things survived, being organized spontaneously in a fitting way; whereas those which grew otherwise perished and continue to perish, as Empedocles says his "man-faced ox-progeny" did.

Such are the arguments (and others of the kind) which may cause difficulty on this point. Yet it is impossible that this should be the true view. For teeth and all other natural things either invariably or normally come about in a given way; but of not one of the results of chance or spontaneity is this true. We do not ascribe to chance or mere coincidence the frequency of rain in winter, but frequent rain in summer we do; nor heat in the dog days, but only if we have it in winter. If then, it is agreed that things are either the result of coincidence or for an end, and these cannot be the result of coincidence or spontaneity, it follows that they must be for an end; and that such things are all due to nature even the champions of the theory which is before us would agree. Therefore action for an end is present in things which come to be and are by nature.

[3] Empedocles.
[4] Anaxagoras.

Further, where a series has a completion, all the preceding steps are for the sake of that. Now surely as in intelligent action, so in nature; and as in nature, so it is in each action, if nothing interferes. Now intelligent action is for the sake of an end; therefore the nature of things also is so. Thus if a house, e.g., had been a thing made by nature, it would have been made in the same way as it is now by art; and if things made by nature were made also by art, they would come to be in the same way as by nature. Each step then in the series is for the sake of the next; and generally art partly completes what nature cannot bring to a finish, and partly imitates her. If, therefore, artificial products are for the sake of an end, so clearly also are natural products. The relation of the later to the earlier terms of the series is the same in both.

This is most obvious in the animals other than man: they make things neither by art nor after inquiry or deliberation. Wherefore people discuss whether it is by intelligence or by some other faculty that these creatures work,—spiders, ants, and the like. By gradual advance in this direction we come to see clearly that in plants too that is produced which is conducive to the end—leaves, e.g., grow to provide shade for the fruit. If then it is both by nature and for an end that the swallow makes its nest and the spider its web, and plants grow leaves for the sake of the fruit and send their roots down (not up) for the sake of nourishment, it is plain that this kind of cause is operative in things which come to be and are by nature. And since "nature" means two things, the matter and the form, of which the latter is the end, and since all the rest is for the sake of the end, the form must be the cause in the sense of "that for the sake of which."

Now mistakes come to pass even in the operations of art: the grammarian makes a mistake in writing and the doctor pours out the wrong dose. Hence clearly mistakes are possible in the operations of nature also. If then in art there are cases in which what is rightly produced serves a purpose, and if where mistakes occur there was a purpose in what was attempted, only it was not attained, so must it be also in natural products, and monstrosities will be failures in the purposive effort. Thus in the original combinations the "ox-progeny," if they failed to reach a determinate end, must have arisen through the corruption of some principle corresponding to what is now the seed.

Further, seed must have come into being first, and not straightway the animals: the words "whole-natured first . . ." [5] must have meant seed.

Again, in plants too we find the relation of means to end, though the degree of organization is less. Were there then in plants also "olive-headed vine-progeny," like the "man-headed ox-progeny," or not? An absurd suggestion; yet there must have been, if there were such things among animals.

Moreover, among the seeds anything must have come to be at random. But the person who asserts this entirely does away with "nature" and what exists "by nature." For those things are natural which, by a continuous movement originated from an internal principle, arrive at some completion: the same completion is not reached from every principle, nor any chance completion, but always the tendency in each is toward the same end, if there is no impediment.

The end and the means toward it may come about by chance. We say, for instance, that a stranger has come by chance, paid the ransom, and gone away, when

[5] Empedocles, Fr. 62. 4.

he does so as if he had come for that purpose, though it was not for that that he came. This is incidental, for chance is an incidental cause, as I remarked before. But when an event takes place always or for the most part, it is not incidental or by chance. In natural products the sequence is invariable, if there is no impediment.

It is absurd to suppose that purpose is not present because we do not observe the agent deliberating. Art does not deliberate. If the shipbuilding art were in the wood, it would produce the same results *by nature*. If, therefore, purpose is present in art, it is present also in nature. The best illustration is a doctor doctoring himself: nature is like that.

It is plain then that nature is a cause, a cause that operates for a purpose.

THE REAL IS MATTER

thomas hobbes

Of body and accident

1. Having understood what imaginary space is, in which we supposed nothing remaining without us, but all those things to be destroyed, that, by existing heretofore,
left images of themselves in our minds; let us now suppose some one of those things
to be placed again in the world, or created anew. It is necessary, therefore, that this
new-created or replaced thing do not only fill some part of the space above mentioned,
or be coincident and coextended with it, but also that it have no dependance upon
our thought. And this is that which, for the extension of it, we commonly call *body;*
and because it depends not upon our thought, we say is *a thing subsisting of itself;*
as also *existing,* because without us; and, lastly, it is called the *subject,* because it is
so placed in and *subjected* to imaginary space, that it may be understood by reason,
as well as perceived by sense. The definition, therefore, of *body* may be this, a *body
is that, which having no dependance upon our thought, is coincident or coextended
with some part of space.*

2. But what an *accident* is cannot so easily be explained by any definition, as by
examples. Let us imagine, therefore, that a body fills any space, or is coextended with
it; that coextension is not the coextended body: and, in like manner, let us imagine
that the same body is removed out of its place; that removing is not the removed
body: or let us think the same not removed; that not removing or rest is not the
resting body. What, then, are these things? They are *accidents* of that body. But
the thing in question is, *what is an accident?* which is an enquiry after that which
we know already, and not that which we should enquire after. For who does not
always and in the same manner understand him that says any thing is extended, or
moved, or not moved? But most men will have it be said that *an accident is something,* namely, some part of a natural thing, when, indeed, it is no part of the same.
To satisfy these men, as well as may be, they answer best that define an *accident* to be
the manner by which any body is conceived; which is all one as if they should say,

From *The Elements of Philosophy,* Vol. I, Chaps. VIII–IX, in *The English Works of
Thomas Hobbes,* William Molesworth, ed. (Aalen, Germany: Scientia Antiquariat und
Verlag, Schilling & Co., 1966), I:101–127. Reprinted by permission of the publisher.

an accident is that faculty of any body, by which it works in us a conception of itself. Which definition, though it be not an answer to the question propounded, yet it is an answer to that question which should have been propounded, namely, *whence does it happen that one part of any body appears here, another there?* For this is well answered thus: *it happens from the extension of that body.* Or, *how comes it to pass that the whole body, by succession, is seen now here, now there?* and the answer will be, *by reason of its motion.* Or, lastly, *whence is it that any body possesseth the same space for some time?* and the answer will be, *because it is not moved.* For if concerning the name of a body, that is, concerning a concrete name, it be asked, *what is it?* the answer must be made by definition; for the question is concerning the signification of the name. But if it be asked concerning an abstract name, *what is it?* the cause is demanded why a thing appears so or so. As if it be asked, *what is hard?* The answer will be, hard is that, whereof no part gives place, but when the whole gives place. But if it be demanded, *what is hardness?* a cause must be shewn why a part does not give place, except the whole give place. Wherefore, I define an *accident* to be *the manner of our conception of body.*

3. When an *accident* is said *to be in a body,* it is not so to be understood, as if anything were contained in that body; as if, for example, redness were in blood, in the same manner, as blood is in a bloody cloth, that is, as a part in the whole; for so, an accident would be a body also. But, as magnitude, or rest, or motion, is in that which is great, or which resteth, or which is moved (which, how it is to be understood, every man understands) so also, it is to be understood, that every other accident *is in* its subject. And this, also, is explicated by *Aristotle* no otherwise than negatively, namely, that *an accident is in its subject, not as any part thereof, but so as that it may be away, the subject still remaining;* which is right, saving that there are certain accidents which can never perish except the body perish also; for no body can be conceived to be without extension, or without figure. All other accidents, which are not common to all bodies, but peculiar to some only, as *to be at rest, to be moved, colour, hardness,* and the like, do perish continually, and are succeeded by others; yet so, as that the body never perisheth. And as for the opinion that some may have, that all other accidents are not in their bodies in the same manner that extension, motion, rest, or figure, are in the same; for example, that colour, heat, odour, virtue, vice, and the like, are otherwise in them, and, as they say, *inherent;* I desire they would suspend their judgment for the present, and expect a little, till it be found out by ratiocination, whether these very accidents are not also certain motions either of the mind of the perceiver, or of the bodies themselves which are perceived; for in the search of this, a great part of natural philosophy consists.

4. The *extension* of a body, is the same thing with the *magnitude* of it, or that which some call *real space.* But this *magnitude* does not depend upon our cogitation, as imaginary space doth; for this is an effect of our imagination, but *magnitude* is the cause of it; this is an accident of the mind, that of a body existing out of the mind.

5. That space, by which word I here understand imaginary space, which is coincident with the magnitude of any body, is called the *place* of that body; and the body itself is that which we call the *thing placed.* Now *place,* and the *magnitude* of the thing placed, differ. First in this, that a body keeps always the same *magnitude,* both when it is at rest, and when it is moved; but when it is moved, it does not keep the same *place.* Secondly in this, that *place* is a phantasm of any body of such and

such quantity and figure; but *magnitude* is the peculiar accident of every body; for one body may at several times have several places, but has always one and the same magnitude. Thirdly in this, that *place* is nothing out of the mind, nor *magnitude* anything within it. And lastly, *place* is feigned extension, but *magnitude* true extension; and a placed body is not extension, but a thing extended. Besides, *place is immovable;* for, seeing that which is moved, is understood to be carried from place to place, if place were moved, it would also be carried from place to place, so that one place must have another place, and that place another place, and so on infinitely, which is ridiculous. And as for those, that, by making *place* to be of the same nature with *real space,* would from thence maintain it to be immovable, they also make place, though they do not perceive they make it so, to be a mere phantasm. For whilst one affirms that place is therefore said to be immovable, because space in general is considered there; if he had remembered that nothing is general or universal besides names or signs, he would easily have seen that that space, which he says is considered in general, is nothing but a phantasm, in the mind or the memory, of a body of such magnitude and such figure. And whilst another says: real space is made immovable by the understanding; as when, under the superficies of running water, we imagine other and other water to come by continual succession, that superficies fixed there by the understanding, is the *immovable place* of the river: what else does he make it to be but a phantasm, though he do it obscurely and in perplexed words? Lastly, the nature of *place* does not consist in the *superficies of the ambient,* but in *solid space;* for the whole placed body is coextended with its whole place, and every part of it with every answering part of the same place; but seeing every placed body is a solid thing, it cannot be understood to be coextended with superficies. Besides, how can any whole body be moved, unless all its parts be moved together with it? Or how can the internal parts of it be moved, but by leaving their place? But the internal parts of a body cannot leave the superficies of an external part contiguous to it; and, therefore, it follows, that if place be the superficies of the ambient, then the parts of a body moved, that is, bodies moved, are not moved.

6. Space, or place, that is possessed by a body, is called *full,* and that which is not so possessed, is called *empty.*

. . .

10. Motion *is a continual relinquishing of one place, and acquiring of another;* and that place which is relinquished is commonly called the *terminus a quo,* as that which is acquired is called the *terminus ad quem;* I say a continual relinquishing, because no body, how little soever, can totally and at once go out of its former place into another, so, but that some part of it will be in a part of a place which is common to both, namely, to the relinquished and the acquired places. For example, let any

body be in the place A C B D; the same body cannot come into the place B D E F, but it must first be in G H I K, whose part G H B D is common to both the places A C B D, and G H I K, and whose part B D I K, is common to both the places G H I K, and B D E F. Now it cannot be conceived that anything can be moved without time; for time is, by the definition of it, a phantasm, that is, a conception of motion; and, therefore, to conceive that any thing may be moved without time, were to conceive motion without motion, which is impossible.

11. *That is said to be at rest, which, during any time, is in one place; and that to be moved, or to have been moved, which, whether it be now at rest or moved, was formerly in another place than that which it is now in.* From which definitions it may be inferred, first, that *whatsoever is moved, has been moved;* for if it be still in the same place in which it was formerly, it is at rest, that is, it is not moved, by the definition of *rest;* but if it be in another place, it has been moved, by the definition of *moved.* Secondly, that *what is moved, will yet be moved;* for that which is moved, leaveth the place where it is, and therefore will be in another place, and consequently will be moved still. Thirdly, that *whatsoever is moved, is not in one place during any time, how little soever that time be;* for by the definition of rest, that which is in one place during any time, is at rest.

There is a certain sophism against motion, which seems to spring from the not understanding of this last proposition. For they say, that, *if any body be moved, it is moved either in the place where it is, or in the place where it is not; both which are false; and therefore nothing is moved.* But the falsity lies in the major proposition; for that which is moved, is neither moved in the place where it is, nor in the place where it is not; but from the place where it is, to the place where it is not. Indeed it cannot be denied but that whatsoever is moved, is moved somewhere, that is, within some space; but then the place of that body is not that whole space, but a part of it . . . . From what is above demonstrated, namely, that whatsoever is moved, has also been moved, and will be moved, this also may be collected, that there can be no conception of motion, without conceiving past and future time.

· · ·

19. *Whatsoever is at rest, will always be at rest, unless there be some other body besides it, which, by endeavouring to get into its place by motion, suffers it no longer to remain at rest.* For suppose that some finite body exist and be at rest, and that all space besides be empty; if now this body begin to be moved, it will certainly be moved some way; seeing therefore there was nothing in that body which did not dispose it to rest, the reason why it is moved this way is in something out of it; and in like manner, if it had been moved any other way, the reason of motion that way had also been in something out of it; but seeing it was supposed that nothing is out of it, the reason of its motion one way would be the same with the reason of its motion every other way, wherefore it would be moved alike all ways at once; which is impossible.

In like manner, *whatsoever is moved, will always be moved, except there be some other body besides it, which causeth it to rest.* For if we suppose nothing to be without it, there will be no reason why it should rest now, rather than at another time; wherefore its motion would cease in every particle of time alike; which is not intelligible.

20. When we say a living creature, a tree, or any other specified body is *generated* or *destroyed,* it is not to be so understood as if there were made a body of that which is not-body, or not a body of a body, but of a living creature not a living creature, of a tree not a tree, &c. that is, that those accidents for which we call one thing a living creature, another thing a tree, and another by some other name, are generated and destroyed; and that therefore the same names are not to be given to them now, which were given them before. But that magnitude for which we give to any thing the name

of body is neither generated nor destroyed. For though we may feign in our mind that a point may swell to a huge bulk, and that this may again contract itself to a point; that is, though we may imagine something to arise where before was nothing, and nothing to be there where before was something, yet we cannot comprehend in our mind how this may possibly be done in nature. And therefore philosophers, who tie themselves to natural reason, suppose that a body can neither be generated nor destroyed, but only that it may appear otherwise than it did to us, that is, under different *species,* and consequently be called by other and other names; so that that which is now called man, may at another time have the name of not-man; but that which is once called body, can never be called not-body. But it is manifest, that all other accidents besides magnitude or extension may be generated and destroyed; as when a white thing is made black, the whiteness that was in it perisheth, and the blackness that was not in it is now generated; and therefore bodies, and the accidents under which they appear diversely, have this difference, that bodies are things, and not generated; accidents are generated, and not things.

21. And therefore, when any thing appears otherwise than it did by reason of other and other accidents, it is not to be thought that an accident goes out of one subject into another (for they are not, as I said above, in their subjects as a part in the whole, or as a contained thing in that which contains it, or as a master of a family in his house) but that one accident perisheth, and another is generated. For example, when the hand, being moved, moves the pen, motion does not go out of the hand into the pen; for so the writing might be continued though the hand stood still; but a new motion is generated in the pen, and is the pen's motion.

22. And therefore also it is improper to say, an accident is moved; as when, instead of saying, *figure is an accident of a body carried away,* we say, *a body carries away its figure.*

23. Now that accident for which we give a certain name to any body, or the accident which denominates its subject, is commonly called the ESSENCE thereof; as rationality is the essence of a man; whiteness, of any white thing, and extension the essence of a body. And the same essence, in as much as it is generated, is called the FORM. Again, a body, in respect of any accident, is called the SUBJECT, and in respect of the form it is called the MATTER.

Also, the production or perishing of any accident makes its subject be said *to be changed;* only the production or perishing of form makes it be said it is *generated* or *destroyed;* but in all generation and mutation, the name of *matter* still remains. For a table made of wood is not only wooden, but wood; and a statue of brass is brass as well as brazen; though Aristotle, in his *Metaphysics,* says, that whatsoever is made of any thing ought not to be called ἐκεινὸ, but ἐκείνινον; as that which is made of wood, but ξύλον, but ξύλινον, that is, not wood, but wooden.

24. And as for that matter which is common to all things, and which philosophers, following Aristotle, usually call *materia prima,* that is, *first matter,* it is not any body distinct from all other bodies, nor is it one of them. What then is it? A mere name; yet a name which is not of vain use; for it signifies a conception of body without the consideration of any form or other accident except only magnitude or extension, and aptness to receive form and other accident. So that whensoever we have use of the name *body in general,* if we use that of *materia prima,* we do well. For as when a man not knowing which was first, water or ice, would find out which of the two were the matter of both, he would be fain to suppose some third matter which were

neither of these two; so he that would find out what is the matter of all things, ought to suppose such as is not the matter of anything that exists. Wherefore *materia prima* is nothing; and therefore, they do not attribute to it either form or any other accident besides quantity; whereas all singular things have their forms and accidents certain.

Materia prima, therefore, is body in general, that is, body considered universally, not as having neither form nor any accident, but in which no form nor any other accident but quantity are at all considered, that is, they are not drawn into argumentation.

.   .   .

Of cause and effect

1. A BODY is said to work upon or *act,* that is to say, *do* something to another body, when it either generates or destroys some accident in it: and the body in which an accident is generated or destroyed is said to *suffer,* that is, to have something *done* to it by another body; as when one body by putting forwards another body generates motion in it, it is called the AGENT; and the body in which motion is so generated, is called the PATIENT; so fire that warms the hand is the *agent,* and the hand, which is warmed, is the *patient.* That accident, which is generated in the patient, is called the EFFECT.

2. When an agent and patient are contiguous to one another, their action and passion are then said to be *immediate,* otherwise, *mediate;* and when another body, lying betwixt the agent and patient, is contiguous to them both, it is then itself both an agent and a patient; an agent in respect of the body next after it, upon which it works, and a patient in respect of the body next before it, from which it suffers. Also, if many bodies be so ordered that every two which are next to one another be contiguous, then all those that are betwixt the first and the last are both agents and patients, and the first is an agent only, and the last a patient only.

3. An agent is understood to *produce* its determined or certain effect in the patient, according to some certain accident or accidents, with which both it and the patient are affected; that is to say, the agent hath its effect precisely such, not because it is a body, but because such a body, or so moved. For otherwise all agents, seeing they are all bodies alike, would produce like effects in all patients. And therefore the fire, for example, does not warm, because it is a body, but because it is hot; nor does one body put forward another body because it is a body, but because it is moved into the place of that other body. The cause, therefore, of all effects consists in certain accidents both in the agents and in the patients; which when they are all present, the effect is produced; but if any one of them be wanting, it is not produced; and that accident either of the agent or patient, without which the effect cannot be produced, is called *causa sine qua non,* or *cause necessary by supposition,* as also the *cause requisite for the production of the effect.* But a CAUSE simply, or *an entire cause, is the aggregate of all the accidents both of the agents how many soever they be, and of the patient, put together; which when they are all supposed to be present, it cannot be understood but that the effect is produced at the same instant; and if any one of them be wanting, it cannot be understood but that the effect is not produced.*

4. The aggregate of accidents in the agent or agents, requisite for the production of the effect, the effect being produced, is called the *efficient cause* thereof; and the aggregate of accidents in the patient, the effect being produced, is usually called the *material cause;* I say the effect being produced; for where there is no effect, there can be no cause; for nothing can be called a cause, where there is nothing that can be called an effect. But the efficient and material causes are both but partial causes, or parts of that cause, which in the next precedent article I called an entire cause. And from hence it is manifest, that the effect we expect, though the agents be not defective on their part, may nevertheless be frustrated by a defect in the patient; and when the patient is sufficient, by a defect in the agents.

5. An entire cause is always sufficient for the production of its effect, if the effect be at all possible. For let any effect whatsoever be propounded to be produced; if the same be produced, it is manifest that the cause which produced it was a sufficient cause; but if it be not produced, and yet be possible, it is evident that something was wanting either in some agent, or in the patient, without which it could not be produced; that is, that some accident was wanting which was requisite for its production; and therefore, that cause was not *entire,* which is contrary to what was supposed.

It follows also from hence, that in whatsoever instant the cause is entire, in the same instant the effect is produced. For if it be not produced, something is still wanting, which is requisite for the production of it; and therefore the cause was not entire, as was supposed.

And seeing a necessary cause is defined to be that, which being supposed, the effect cannot but follow; this also may be collected, that whatsoever effect is produced at any time, the same is produced by a necessary cause. For whatsoever is produced, in as much as it is produced, had an entire cause, that is, had all those things, which being supposed, it cannot be understood but that the effect follows; that is, it had a necessary cause. And in the same manner it may be shewn, that whatsoever effects are hereafter to be produced, shall have a necessary cause; so that all the effects that have been, or shall be produced, have their necessity in things antecedent.

6. And from this, that whensoever the cause is entire, the effect is produced in the same instant, it is manifest that causation and the production of effects consist in a certain continual progress; so that as there is a continual mutation in the agent or agents, by the working of other agents upon them, so also the patient, upon which they work, is continually altered and changed. For example: as the heat of the fire increases more and more, so also the effects thereof, namely, the heat of such bodies as are next to it, and again, of such other bodies as are next to them, increase more and more accordingly; which is already no little argument that all mutation consists in motion only; the truth whereof shall be further demonstrated in the ninth article. But in this progress of causation, that is, of action and passion, if any man comprehend in his imagination a part thereof, and divide the same into parts, the first part or beginning of it cannot be considered otherwise than as action or cause; for, if it should be considered as effect or passion, then it would be necessary to consider something before it, for its cause or action; which cannot be, for nothing can be before the beginning. And in like manner, the last part is considered only as effect; for it cannot be called cause, if nothing follow it; but after the last, nothing follows. And from hence it is, that in all action the beginning and cause are taken for the same thing. But every one of the intermediate parts are both action and passion,

and cause and effect, according as they are compared with the antecedent or subsequent part.

7. There can be no cause of motion, except in a body contiguous and moved. For let there be any two bodies which are not contiguous, and betwixt which the intermediate space is empty, or, if filled, filled with another body which is at rest; and let one of the propounded bodies be supposed to be at rest; I say it shall always be at rest. For if it shall be moved, the cause of that motion, by the 8th chapter, article 19, will be some external body; and, therefore, if between it and that external body there be nothing but empty space, then whatsoever the disposition be of that external body or of the patient itself, yet if it be supposed to be now at rest, we may conceive it will continue so till it be touched by some other body. But seeing cause, by the definition, is the aggregate of all such accidents, which being supposed to be present, it cannot be conceived but that the effect will follow, those accidents, which are either in external bodies, or in the patient itself, cannot be the cause of future motion. And in like manner, seeing we may conceive that whatsoever is at rest will still be at rest, though it be touched by some other body, except that other body be moved; therefore in a contiguous body, which is at rest, there can be no cause of motion. Wherefore there is no cause of motion in any body, except it be contiguous and moved.

The same reason may serve to prove that whatsoever is moved, will always be moved on in the same way and with the same velocity, except it be hindered by some other contiguous and moved body; and consequently that no bodies, either when they are at rest, or when there is an interposition of vacuum, can generate or extinguish or lessen motion in other bodies. There is one that has written that things moved are more resisted by things at rest, than by things contrarily moved; for this reason, that he conceived motion not to be so contrary to motion as rest. That which deceived him was, that the words *rest* and *motion* are but contradictory names; whereas motion, indeed, is not resisted by rest, but by contrary motion.

8. But if a body work upon another body at one time, and afterwards the same body work upon the same body at another time, so that both the agent and patient, and all their parts, be in all things as they were; and there be no difference, except only in time, that is, that one action be former, the other later in time; it is manifest of itself, that the effects will be equal and like, as not differing in anything besides time. And as effects themselves proceed from their causes, so the diversity of them depends upon the diversity of their causes also.

9. This being true, it is necessary that mutation can be nothing else but motion of the parts of that body which is changed. For first, we do not say anything is changed, but that which appears to our senses otherwise than it appeared formerly. Secondly, both those appearances are effects produced in the sentient; and, therefore, if they be different, it is necessary, by the preceding article, that either some part of the agent, which was formerly at rest, is now moved, and so the mutation consists in this motion; or some part, which was formerly moved, is now otherwise moved, and so also the mutation consists in this new motion; or which, being formerly moved, is now at rest, which, as I have shewn above, cannot come to pass without motion; and so again, mutation is motion; or lastly, it happens in some of these manners to the patient, or some of its parts; so that mutation, howsoever it be made, will consist in the motion of the parts, either of the body which is perceived, or of the sentient body, or of both. Mutation therefore is motion, namely, of the parts either

of the agent or of the patient; which was to be demonstrated. And to this it is consequent, that rest cannot be the cause of anything, nor can any action proceed from it; seeing neither motion nor mutation can be caused by it.

10. Accidents, in respect of other accidents which precede them, or are before them in time, and upon which they do not depend as upon their causes, are called *contingent* accidents; I say, in respect of those accidents by which they are not generated; for, in respect of their causes, all things come to pass with equal necessity; for otherwise they would have no causes at all; which, of things generated, is not intelligible.

THE REAL IS MIND

george berkeley

1. It is evident to anyone who takes a survey of the objects of human knowledge, that they are either ideas actually imprinted on the senses, or else such as are perceived by attending to the passions and operations of the mind, or lastly ideas formed by help of memory and imagination, either compounding, dividing, or barely representing those originally perceived in the aforesaid ways. By sight I have the ideas of light and colours with their several degrees and variations. By touch I perceive, for example, hard and soft, heat and cold, motion and resistance, and of all these more and less either as to quantity or degree. Smelling furnishes me with odours; the palate with tastes, and hearing conveys sounds to the mind in all their variety of tone and composition. And as several of these are observed to accompany each other, they come to be marked by one name, and so to be reputed as one thing. Thus, for example, a certain colour, taste, smell, figure, and consistence having been observed to go together, are accounted one distinct thing, signified by the name *apple*. Other collections of ideas constitute a stone, a tree, a book, and the like sensible things; which, as they are pleasing or disagreeable, excite the passions of love, hatred, joy, grief, and so forth.

2. But besides all that endless variety of ideas or objects of knowledge, there is likewise something which knows or perceives them, and exercises divers operations, as willing, imagining, remembering about them. This perceiving, active being is what I call *mind, spirit, soul,* or *my self*. By which words I do not denote any one of my ideas, but a thing entirely distinct from them, wherein they exist, or, which is the same thing, whereby they are perceived; for the existence of an idea consists in being perceived.

3. That neither our thoughts, nor passions, nor ideas formed by the imagination, exist without the mind, is what everybody will allow. And it seems no less evident that the various sensations or ideas imprinted on the sense, however blended or combined together (that is, whatever objects they compose) cannot exist otherwise than in a mind perceiving them. I think an intuitive knowledge may be obtained of this, by anyone that shall attend to what is meant by the term *exist* when applied to

From "The Principles of Human Knowledge," Part I, in *The Works of George Berkeley*, T. E. Jessop, ed. (London: Thomas Nelson and Sons Ltd., 1949), II:41–55. Reprinted by permission of the publisher.

sensible things. The table I write on, I say, exists, that is, I see and feel it; and if I were out of my study I should say it existed, meaning thereby that if I was in my study I might perceive it, or that some other spirit actually does perceive it. There was an odour, that is, it was smelled; there was a sound, that is to say, it was heard; a colour or figure, and it was perceived by sight or touch. This is all that I can understand by these and the like expressions. For as to what is said of the absolute existence of unthinking things without any relation to their being perceived, that seems perfectly unintelligible. Their *esse* is *percipi*, nor is it possible they should have any existence, out of the minds or thinking things which perceive them.

4. It is indeed an opinion strangely prevailing amongst men, that houses, mountains, rivers, and in a word all sensible objects have an existence natural or real, distinct from their being perceived by the understanding. But with how great an assurance and acquiescence soever this principle may be entertained in the world; yet whoever shall find in his heart to call it in question, may, if I mistake not, perceive it to involve a manifest contradiction. For what are the forementioned objects but the things we perceive by sense, and what do we perceive besides our own ideas or sensations; and is it not plainly repugnant that any one of these or any combination of them should exist unperceived?

5. If we throughly examine this tenet, it will, perhaps, be found at bottom to depend on the doctrine of *abstract ideas*. For can there be a nicer strain of abstraction than to distinguish the existence of sensible objects from their being perceived, so as to conceive them existing unperceived? Light and colours, heat and cold, extension and figures, in a word the things we see and feel, what are they but so many sensations, notions, ideas or impressions on the sense; and is it possible to separate, even in thought, any of these from perception? For my part I might as easily divide a thing from itself. I may indeed divide in my thoughts or conceive apart from each other those things which, perhaps, I never perceived by sense so divided. Thus I imagine the trunk of a human body without the limbs, or conceive the smell of a rose without thinking on the rose itself. So far I will not deny I can abstract, if that may properly be called *abstraction*, which extends only to the conceiving separately such objects, as it is possible may really exist or be actually perceived asunder. But my conceiving or imagining power does not extend beyond the possibility of real existence or perception. Hence as it is impossible for me to see or feel anything without an actual sensation of that thing, so is it impossible for me to conceive in my thoughts any sensible thing or object distinct from the sensation or perception of it.

6. Some truths there are so near and obvious to the mind, that a man need only open his eyes to see them. Such I take this important one to be, to wit, that all the choir of heaven and furniture of the earth, in a word all those bodies which compose the mighty frame of the world, have not any subsistence without a mind, that their being is to be perceived or known; that consequently so long as they are not actually perceived by me, or do not exist in my mind or that of any other created spirit, they must either have no existence at all, or else subsist in the mind of some eternal spirit: it being perfectly unintelligible and involving all the absurdity of abstraction, to attribute to any single part of them an existence independent of a spirit. To be convinced of which, the reader need only reflect and try to separate in his own thoughts the being of a sensible thing from its being perceived.

7. From what has been said it follows there is not any other substance than *spirit*, or that which perceives. But for the fuller proof of this point, let it be con-

sidered, the sensible qualities are colour, figure, motion, smell, taste, and such like, that is, the ideas perceived by sense. Now for an idea to exist in an unperceiving thing, is a manifest contradiction; for to have an idea is all one as to perceive: that therefore wherein colour, figure, and the like qualities exist, must perceive them; hence it is clear there can be no unthinking substance or *substratum* of those ideas.

8. But say you, though the ideas themselves do not exist without the mind, yet there may be things like them whereof they are copies or resemblances, which things exist without the mind, in an unthinking substance. I answer, an idea can be like nothing but an idea; a colour or figure can be like nothing but another colour or figure. If we look but ever so little into our thoughts, we shall find it impossible for us to conceive a likeness except only between our ideas. Again, I ask whether those supposed originals or external things, of which our ideas are the pictures or representations, be themselves perceivable or no? If they are, then they are ideas, and we have gained our point; but if you say they are not, I appeal to anyone whether it be sense, to assert a colour is like something which is invisible; hard or soft, like something which is intangible; and so of the rest.

9. Some there are who make a distinction betwixt *primary* and *secondary* qualities: by the former, they mean extension, figure, motion, rest, solidity or impenetrability, and number: by the latter they denote all other sensible qualities, as colours, sounds, tastes, and so forth. The ideas we have of these they acknowledge not to be the resemblances of anything existing without the mind or unperceived; but they will have our ideas of the primary qualities to be patterns or images of things which exist without the mind, in an unthinking substance which they call *matter*. By matter therefore we are to understand an inert, senseless substance, in which extension, figure, and motion, do actually subsist. But it is evident from what we have already shewn, that extension, figure and motion are only ideas existing in the mind, and that an idea can be like nothing but another idea, and that consequently neither they nor their archetypes can exist in an unperceiving substance. Hence it is plain, that the very notion of what is called *matter* or *corporeal substance,* involves a contradiction in it.

10. They who assert that figure, motion, and the rest of the primary or original qualities do exist without the mind, in unthinking substances, do at the same time acknowledge that colours, sounds, heat, cold, and such like secondary qualities, do not, which they tell us are sensations existing in the mind alone, that depend on and are occasioned by the different size, texture and motion of the minute particles of matter. This they take for an undoubted truth, which they can demonstrate beyond all exception. Now if it be certain, that those original qualities are inseparably united with the other sensible qualities, and not, even in thought, capable of being abstracted from them, it plainly follows that they exist only in the mind. But I desire anyone to reflect and try, whether he can by any abstraction of thought, conceive the extension and motion of a body, without all other sensible qualities. For my own part, I see evidently that it is not in my power to frame an idea of a body extended and moved, but I must withal give it some colour or other sensible quality which is acknowledged to exist only in the mind. In short, extension, figure, and motion, abstracted from all other qualities, are inconceivable. Where therefore the other sensible qualities are, there must these be also, to wit, in the mind and no where else.

11. Again, *great* and *small, swift* and *slow,* are allowed to exist nowhere with-

out the mind, being entirely relative, and changing as the frame or position of the organs of sense varies. The extension therefore which exists without the mind, is neither great nor small, the motion neither swift nor slow, that is, they are nothing at all. But say you, they are extension in general, and motion in general: thus we see how much the tenet of extended, moveable substances existing without the mind, depends on that strange doctrine of *abstract ideas*. And here I cannot but remark, how nearly the vague and indeterminate description of matter or corporeal substance, which the modern philosophers are run into by their own principles, resembles that antiquated and so much ridiculed notion of *materia prima*, to be met with in Aristotle and his followers. Without extension solidity cannot be conceived; since therefore it has been shewn that extension exists not in an unthinking substance, the same must also be true of solidity.

12. That number is entirely the creature of the mind, even though the other qualities be allowed to exist without, will be evident to whoever considers, that the same thing bears a different denomination of number, as the mind views it with different respects. Thus, the same extension is one or three or thirty six, according as the mind considers it with reference to a yard, a foot, or an inch. Number is so visibly relative, and dependent on men's understanding, that it is strange to think how anyone should give it an absolute existence without the mind. We say one book, one page, one line; all these are equally units, though some contain several of the others. And in each instance it is plain, the unit relates to some particular combination of ideas arbitrarily put together by the mind.

13. Unity I know some will have to be a simple or uncompounded idea, accompanying all other ideas into the mind. That I have any such idea answering the word *unity*, I do not find; and if I had, methinks I could not miss finding it; on the contrary it should be the most familiar to my understanding, since it is said to accompany all other ideas, and to be perceived by all the ways of sensation and reflexion. To say no more, it is an *abstract idea*.

14. I shall farther add, that after the same manner, as modern philosophers prove certain sensible qualities to have no existence in matter, or without the mind, the same thing may be likewise proved of all other sensible qualities whatsoever. Thus, for instance, it is said that heat and cold are affections only of the mind, and not at all patterns of real beings, existing in the corporeal substances which excite them, for that the same body which appears cold to one hand, seems warm to another. Now why may we not as well argue that figure and extension are not patterns or resemblances of qualities existing in matter, because to the same eye at different stations, or eyes of a different texture at the same station, they appear various, and cannot therefore be the images of anything settled and determinate without the mind? Again, it is proved that sweetness is not really in the sapid thing, because, the thing remaining unaltered, the sweetness is changed into bitter, as in case of a fever or otherwise vitiated palate. Is it not as reasonable to say that motion is not without the mind, since if the succession of ideas in the mind become swifter, the motion, it is acknowledged, shall appear slower without any alteration in any external object.

15. In short, let anyone consider those arguments which are thought manifestly to prove that colours and tastes exist only in the mind, and he shall find they may, with equal force, be brought to prove the same thing of extension, figure, and motion. Though it must be confessed this method of arguing doth not so much prove that there is no extension or colour in an outward object, as that we do not know by

sense which is the true extension or colour of the object. But the arguments foregoing plainly shew it to be impossible that any colour or extension at all, or other sensible quality whatsoever, should exist in an unthinking subject without the mind, or in truth, that there should be any such thing as an outward object.

16. But let us examine a little the received opinion. It is said extension is a mode or accident of matter, and that matter is the *substratum* that supports it. Now I desire that you would explain what is meant by matter's *supporting* extension: say you, I have no idea of matter, and therefore cannot explain it. I answer, though you have no positive, yet if you have any meaning at all, you must at least have a relative idea of matter; though you know not what it is, yet you must be supposed to know what relation it bears to accidents, and what is meant by its supporting them. It is evident *support* cannot here be taken in its usual or literal sense, as when we say that pillars support a building: in what sense therefore must it be taken?

17. If we inquire into what the most accurate philosophers declare themselves to mean by *material substance;* we shall find them acknowledge, they have no other meaning annexed to those sounds, but the idea of being in general, together with the relative notion of its supporting accidents. The general idea of being appeareth to me the most abstract and incomprehensible of all other; and as for its supporting accidents, this, as we have just now observed, cannot be understood in the common sense of those words; it must therefore be taken in some other sense, but what that is they do not explain. So that when I consider the two parts or branches which make the signification of the words *material substance,* I am convinced there is no distinct meaning annexed to them. But why should we trouble ourselves any farther, in discussing this material *substratum* or support of figure and motion, and other sensible qualities? Does it not suppose they have an existence without the mind? And is not this a direct repugnancy, and altogether inconceivable?

18. But though it were possible that solid, figured, moveable substances may exist without the mind, corresponding to the ideas we have of bodies, yet how is it possible for us to know this? Either we must know it by sense, or by reason. As for our senses, by them we have the knowledge only of our sensations, ideas, or those things that are immediately perceived by sense, call them what you will: but they do not inform us that things exist without the mind, or unperceived, like to those which are per-ceived. This the materialists themselves acknowledge. It remains therefore that if we have any knowledge at all of external things, it must be by reason, inferring their existence from what is immediately perceived by sense. But what reason can induce us to believe the existence of bodies without the mind, from what we perceive, since the very patrons of matter themselves do not pretend, there is any necessary con-nexion betwixt them and our ideas? I say it is granted on all hands (and what hap-pens in dreams, phrensies, and the like, puts it beyond dispute) that it is possible we might be affected with all the ideas we have now, though no bodies existed without, resembling them. Hence it is evident the supposition of external bodies is not neces-sary for the producing our ideas: since it is granted they are produced sometimes, and might possibly be produced always in the same order we see them in at present, without their concurrence.

19. But though we might possibly have all our sensations without them, yet perhaps it may be thought easier to conceive and explain the manner of their produc-tion, by supposing external bodies in their likeness rather than otherwise; and so it might be at least probable there are such things as bodies that excite their ideas in

our minds. But neither can this be said; for though we give the materialists their external bodies, they by their own confession are never the nearer knowing how our ideas are produced: since they own themselves unable to comprehend in what manner body can act upon spirit, or how it is possible it should imprint any idea in the mind. Hence it is evident the production of ideas or sensations in our minds, can be no reason why we should suppose matter or corporeal substances, since that is acknowledged to remain equally inexplicable with, or without this supposition. If therefore it were possible for bodies to exist without the mind, yet to hold they do so, must needs be a very precarious opinion; since it is to suppose, without any reason at all, that God has created innumerable beings that are entirely useless, and serve to no manner of purpose.

20. In short, if there were external bodies, it is impossible we should ever come to know it; and if there were not, we might have the very same reasons to think there were that we have now. Suppose, what no one can deny possible, an intelligence, without the help of external bodies, to be affected with the same train of sensations or ideas that you are, imprinted in the same order and with like vividness in his mind. I ask whether that intelligence hath not all the reason to believe the existence of corporeal substances, represented by his ideas, and exciting them in his mind, that you can possibly have for believing the same thing? Of this there can be no question; which one consideration is enough to make any reasonable person suspect the strength of whatever arguments he may think himself to have, for the existence of bodies without the mind.

21. Were it necessary to add any further proof against the existence of matter, after what has been said, I could instance several of those errors and difficulties (not to mention impieties) which have sprung from that tenet. It has occasioned numberless controversies and disputes in philosophy, and not a few of far greater moment in religion. But I shall not enter into the detail of them in this place, as well because I think, arguments à *posteriori* are unnecessary for confirming what has been, if I mistake not, sufficiently demonstrated à *priori,* as because I shall hereafter find occasion to say somewhat of them.

22. I am afraid I have given cause to think me needlessly prolix in handling this subject. For to what purpose is it to dilate on that which may be demonstrated with the utmost evidence in a line or two, to anyone that is capable of the least reflexion? It is but looking into your own thoughts, and so trying whether you can conceive it possible for a sound, or figure, or motion, or colour, to exist without the mind, or unperceived. This easy trial may make you see, that what you contend for, is a downright contradiction. Insomuch that I am content to put the whole upon this issue; if you can but conceive it possible for one extended moveable substance, or in general, for any one idea or anything like an idea, to exist otherwise than in a mind perceiving it, I shall readily give up the cause: And as for all that *compages* of external bodies which you contend for, I shall grant you its existence, though you cannot either give me any reason why you believe it exists, or assign any use to it when it is supposed to exist. I say, the bare possibility of your opinion's being true, shall pass for an argument that it is so.

23. But say you, surely there is nothing easier than to imagine trees, for instance, in a park, or books existing in a closet, and nobody by to perceive them. I answer, you may so, there is no difficulty in it: but what is all this, I beseech you, more than framing in your mind certain ideas which you call *books* and *trees,* and at the same

time omitting to frame the idea of anyone that may perceive them? But do not you yourself perceive or think of them all the while? This therefore is nothing to the purpose: it only shows you have the power of imagining or forming ideas in your mind; but it doth not shew that you can conceive it possible the objects of your thought may exist without the mind: to make out this, it is necessary that you conceive them existing unconceived or unthought of, which is a manifest repugnancy. When we do our utmost to conceive the existence of external bodies, we are all the while only contemplating our own ideas. But the mind taking no notice of itself, is deluded to think it can and doth conceive bodies existing unthought of or without the mind; though at the same time they are apprehended by or exist in itself. A little attention will discover to any one the truth and evidence of what is here said, and make it unnecessary to insist on any other proofs against the existence of material substance.

24. It is very obvious, upon the least inquiry into our own thoughts, to know whether it be possible for us to understand what is meant, by the *absolute existence of sensible objects in themselves, or without the mind.* To me it is evident those words mark out either a direct contradiction, or else nothing at all. And to convince others of this, I know no readier or fairer way, than to entreat they would calmly attend to their own thoughts: and if by this attention, the emptiness or repugnancy of those expressions does appear, surely nothing more is requisite for their conviction. It is on this therefore that I insist, to wit, that the absolute existence of unthinking things are words without a meaning, or which include a contradiction. This is what I repeat and inculcate, and earnestly recommend to the attentive thoughts of the reader.

25. All our ideas, sensations, or the things which we perceive, by whatsoever names they may be distinguished, are visibly inactive; there is nothing of power or agency included in them. So that one idea or object of thought cannot produce, or make any alteration in another. To be satisfied of the truth of this, there is nothing else requisite but a bare observation of our ideas. For since they and every part of them exist only in the mind, it follows that there is nothing in them but what is perceived. But whoever shall attend to his ideas, whether of sense or reflexion, will not perceive in them any power or activity; there is therefore no such thing contained in them. A little attention will discover to us that the very being of an idea implies passiveness and inertness in it, insomuch that it is impossible for an idea to do anything, or, strictly speaking, to be the cause of anything: neither can it be the resemblance or pattern of any active being, as is evident from *Sect.* 8. Whence it plainly follows that extension, figure and motion, cannot be the cause of our sensations. To say therefore, that these are the effects of powers resulting from the configuration, number, motion, and size of corpuscles, must certainly be false.

26. We perceive a continual succession of ideas, some are anew excited, others are changed or totally disappear. There is therefore some cause of these ideas whereon they depend, and which produces and changes them. That this cause cannot be any quality or idea or combination of ideas, is clear from the preceding section. It must therefore be a substance; but it has been shewn that there is no corporeal or material substance: it remains therefore that the cause of ideas is an incorporeal active substance or spirit.

27. A spirit is one simple, undivided, active being: as it perceives ideas, it is called the *understanding,* and as it produces or otherwise operates about them, it is

called the *will*. Hence there can be no idea formed of a soul or spirit: for all ideas whatever, being passive and inert, *vide Sect.* 25, they cannot represent unto us, by way of image or likeness, that which acts. A little attention will make it plain to anyone, that to have an idea which shall be like that active principle of motion and change of ideas, is absolutely impossible. Such is the nature of *spirit* or that which acts, that it cannot be of itself perceived, but only by the effects which it produceth. If any man shall doubt of the truth of what is here delivered, let him but reflect and try if he can frame the idea of any power or active being; and whether he hath ideas of two principal powers, marked by the names *will* and *understanding*, distinct from each other as well as from a third idea of substance or being in general, with a relative notion of its supporting or being the subject of the aforesaid powers, which is signified by the name *soul* or *spirit*. This is what some hold; but so far as I can see, the words *will, soul, spirit*, do not stand for different ideas, or in truth, for any idea at all, but for something which is very different from ideas, and which being an agent cannot be like unto, or represented by, any idea whatsoever. Though it must be owned at the same time, that we have some notion of soul, spirit, and the operations of the mind, such as willing, loving, hating, in as much as we know or understand the meaning of those words.

28. I find I can excite ideas in my mind at pleasure, and vary and shift the scene as oft as I think fit. It is no more than willing, and straightway this or that idea arises in my fancy: and by the same power it is obliterated, and makes way for another. This making and unmaking of ideas doth very properly denominate the mind active. Thus much is certain, and grounded on experience: but when we talk of unthinking agents, or of exciting ideas exclusive of volition, we only amuse ourselves with words.

29. But whatever power I may have over my own thoughts, I find the ideas actually perceived by sense have not a like dependence on my will. When in broad daylight I open my eyes, it is not in my power to choose whether I shall see or no, or to determine what particular objects shall present themselves to my view; and so likewise as to the hearing and other senses, the ideas imprinted on them are not creatures of my will. There is therefore some other will or spirit that produces them.

30. The ideas of sense are more strong, lively, and distinct than those of the imagination; they have likewise a steadiness, order, and coherence, and are not excited at random, as those which are the effects of human wills often are, but in a regular train or series, the admirable connexion whereof sufficiently testifies the wisdom and benevolence of its Author. Now the set rules or established methods, wherein the mind we depend on excites in us the ideas of sense, are called the *Laws of Nature:* and these we learn by experience, which teaches us that such and such ideas are attended with such and such other ideas, in the ordinary course of things.

31. This gives us a sort of foresight, which enables us to regulate our actions for the benefit of life. And without this we should be eternally at a loss: we could not know how to act anything that might procure us the least pleasure, or remove the least pain of sense. That food nourishes, sleep refreshes, and fire warms us; that to sow in the seed-time is the way to reap in the harvest, and, in general, that to obtain such or such ends, such or such means are conducive, all this we know, not by discovering any necessary connexion between our ideas, but only by the observation of the settled laws of Nature, without which we should be all in uncertainty and confusion, and a grown man no more know how to manage himself in the affairs of life, than an infant just born.

32. And yet this consistent uniform working, which so evidently displays the goodness and wisdom of that governing spirit whose will constitutes the Laws of Nature, is so far from leading our thoughts to him, that it rather sends them a wandering after second causes. For when we perceive certain ideas of sense constantly followed by other ideas, and we know this is not of our doing, we forthwith attribute power and agency to the ideas themselves, and make one the cause of another, than which nothing can be more absurd and unintelligible. Thus, for example, having observed that when we perceive by sight a certain round luminous figure, we at the same time perceive by touch the idea or sensation called *heat*, we do from thence conclude the sun to be the cause of heat. And in like manner perceiving the motion and collision of bodies to be attended with sound, we are inclined to think the latter an effect of the former.

33. The ideas imprinted on the senses by the Author of Nature are called *real things:* and those excited in the imagination being less regular, vivid and constant, are more properly termed *ideas,* or *images of things,* which they copy and represent. But then our sensations, be they never so vivid and distinct, are nevertheless *ideas,* that is, they exist in the mind, or are perceived by it, as truly as the ideas of its own framing. The ideas of sense are allowed to have more reality in them, that is, to be more strong, orderly, and coherent than the creatures of the mind; but this is no argument that they exist without the mind. They are also less dependent on the spirit, or thinking substance which perceives them, in that they are excited by the will of another and more powerful spirit: yet still they are *ideas,* and certainly no *idea,* whether faint or strong, can exist otherwise than in a mind perceiving it.

·   ·   ·

4

SCEPTICISM

david hume

Of the antient philosophy

.　.　.

'Tis confest by the most judicious philosophers, that our ideas of bodies are nothing but collections form'd by the mind of the ideas of the several distinct sensible qualities, of which objects are compos'd, and which we find to have a constant union with each other. But however these qualities may in themselves be entirely distinct, 'tis certain we commonly regard the compound, which they form, as ONE thing, and as continuing the SAME under very considerable alterations. The acknowledg'd composition is evidently contrary to this suppos'd *simplicity,* and the variation to the *identity.* It may, therefore, be worth while to consider the *causes,* which make us almost universally fall into such evident contradictions, as well as the *means* by which we endeavour to conceal them.

'Tis evident, that as the ideas of the several distinct *successive* qualities of objects are united together by a very close relation, the mind, in looking along the succession, must be carry'd from one part of it to another by an easy transition, and will no more perceive the change, than if it contemplated the same unchangeable object. This easy transition is the effect, or rather essence, of relation; and as the imagination readily takes one idea for another, where their influence on the mind is similar; hence it proceeds, that any such succession of related qualities is readily consider'd as one continu'd object, existing without any variation. The smooth and uninterrupted progress of the thought, being alike in both cases, readily deceives the mind, and makes us ascribe an identity to the changeable succession of connected qualities.

But when we alter our method of considering the succession, and instead of tracing it gradually thro' the successive points of time, survey at once any two distinct periods of its duration, and compare the different conditions of the successive qualities; in that case the variations, which were insensible when they arose gradually, do now appear of consequence, and seem entirely to destroy the identity. By this means there arises a kind of contrariety in our method of thinking, from the different points

4

From David Hume, *A Treatise of Human Nature,* L. A. Selby-Bigge, ed. (Oxford: The Clarendon Press, 1949), Book I, Part IV, Secs. III–IV, pp. 219–231. Reprinted by permission of the Clarendon Press.

of view, in which we survey the object, and from the nearness or remoteness of those instants of time, which we compare together. When we gradually follow an object in its successive changes, the smooth progress of the thought makes us ascribe an identity to the succession; because 'tis by a similar act of the mind we consider an unchangeable object. When we compare its situation after a considerable change the progress of the thought is broke; and consequently we are presented with the idea of diversity: In order to reconcile which contradictions the imagination is apt to feign something unknown and invisible, which it supposes to continue the same under all these variations; and this unintelligible something it calls a *substance, or original and first matter.*

We entertain a like notion with regard to the *simplicity* of substances, and from like causes. Suppose an object perfectly simple and indivisible to be presented, along with another object, whose *co-existent* parts are connected together by a strong relation, 'tis evident the actions of the mind, in considering these two objects, are not very different. The imagination conceives the simple object at once, with facility, by a single effort of thought, without change or variation. The connexion of parts in the compound object has almost the same effect, and so unites the object within itself, that the fancy feels not the transition in passing from one part to another. Hence the colour, taste, figure, solidity, and other qualities, combin'd in a peach or melon, are conceiv'd to form *one thing;* and that on account of their close relation, which makes them affect the thought in the same manner, as if perfectly uncompounded. But the mind rests not here. Whenever it views the object in another light, it finds that all these qualities are different, and distinguishable, and separable from each other; which view of things being destructive of its primary and more natural notions, obliges the imagination to feign an unknown something, or *original* substance and matter, as a principle of union or cohesion among these qualities, and as what may give the compound object a title to be call'd one thing, notwithstanding its diversity and composition.

The peripatetic philosophy asserts the *original* matter to be perfectly homogeneous in all bodies, and considers fire, water, earth, and air, as of the very same substance; on account of their gradual revolutions and changes into each other. At the same time it assigns to each of these species of objects a distinct *substantial form,* which it supposes to be the source of all those different qualities they possess, and to be a new foundation of simplicity and identity to each particular species. All depends on our manner of viewing the objects. When we look along the insensible changes of bodies, we suppose all of them to be of the same substance or essence. When we consider their sensible differences, we attribute to each of them a substantial and essential difference. And in order to indulge ourselves in both these ways of considering our objects, we suppose all bodies to have at once a substance and a substantial form.

The notion of *accidents* is an unavoidable consequence of this method of thinking with regard to substances and substantial forms; nor can we forbear looking upon colours, sounds, tastes, figures, and other properties of bodies, as existences, which cannot subsist apart, but require a subject of inhesion to sustain and support them. For having never discover'd any of these sensible qualities, where, for the reasons above-mention'd, we did not likewise fancy a substance to exist; the same habit, which makes us infer a connexion betwixt cause and effect, makes us here infer a dependance of every quality on the unknown substance. The custom of imagining a dependance has the same effect as the custom of observing it wou'd have. This conceit, however, is no more reasonable than any of the foregoing. Every quality being a distinct thing from another, may be conceiv'd to exist apart, and may exist apart, not only from every other quality, but from that unintelligible chimera of a substance.

But these philosophers carry their fictions still farther in their sentiments concerning *occult qualities,* and both suppose a substance supporting, which they do not understand, and an accident supported, of which they have as imperfect an idea. The whole system, therefore, is entirely incomprehensible, and yet is deriv'd from principles as natural as any of these above-explain'd.

In considering this subject we may observe a gradation of three opinions, that rise above each other, according as the persons, who form them, acquire new degrees of reason and knowledge. These opinions are that of the vulgar, that of a false philosophy, and that of the true; where we shall find upon enquiry, that the true philosophy approaches nearer to the sentiments of the vulgar, than to those of a mistaken knowledge. 'Tis natural for men, in their common and careless way of thinking, to imagine they perceive a connexion betwixt such objects as they have constantly found united together; and because custom has render'd it difficult to separate the ideas, they are apt to fancy such a separation to be in itself impossible and absurd. But philosophers, who abstract from the effects of custom, and compare the ideas of objects, immediately perceive the falsehood of these vulgar sentiments, and discover that there is no known connexion among objects. Every different object appears to them entirely distinct and separate; and they perceive, that 'tis not from a view of the nature and qualities of objects we infer one from another, but only when in several instances we observe them to have been constantly conjoin'd. But these philosophers, instead of drawing a just inference from this observation, and concluding, that we have no idea of power or agency, separate from the mind, and belonging to causes; I say, instead of drawing this conclusion, they frequently search for the qualities, in which this agency consists, and are displeased with every system, which their reason suggests to them, in order to explain it. They have sufficient force of genius to free them from the vulgar error, that there is a natural and perceivable connexion betwixt the several sensible qualities and actions of matter; but not sufficient to keep them from ever seeking for this connexion in matter, or causes. Had they fallen upon the just conclusion, they wou'd have return'd back to the situation of the vulgar, and wou'd have regarded all these disquisitions with indolence and indifference. At present they seem to be in a very lamentable condition, and such as the poets have given us but a faint notion of in their descriptions of the punishment of *Sisyphus* and *Tantalus.* For what can be imagin'd more tormenting, than to seek with eagerness, what for ever flies us; and seek for it in a place, where 'tis impossible it can ever exist?

But as nature seems to have observ'd a kind of justice and compensation in every thing, she has not neglected philosophers more than the rest of the creation; but has reserv'd them a consolation amid all their disappointments and afflictions. This consolation principally consists in their invention of the words *faculty* and *occult quality.* For it being usual, after the frequent use of terms, which are really significant and intelligible, to omit the idea, which we wou'd express by them, and to preserve only the custom, by which we recal the idea at pleasure; so it naturally happens, that after the frequent use of terms, which are wholly insignificant and unintelligible, we fancy them to be on the same footing with the precedent, and to have a secret meaning, which we might discover by reflection. The resemblance of their appearance deceives the mind, as is usual, and makes us imagine a thorough resemblance and conformity. By this means these philosophers set themselves at ease, and arrive at last, by an illusion, at the same indifference, which the people attain by their stupidity, and true philosophers by their moderate scepticism. They need only say, that any phænomenon, which puzzles them, arises from a faculty or an occult quality, and there is an end of all dispute and enquiry upon the matter.

But among all the instances, wherein the Peripatetics have shewn they were guided by every trivial propensity of the imagination, no one is more remarkable than their *sympathies, antipathies, and horrors of a vacuum.* There is a very remarkable inclination in human nature, to bestow on external objects the same emotions, which it observes in itself; and to find everywhere those ideas, which are most present to it. This inclination, 'tis true, is suppress'd by a little reflection, and only takes place in children, poets, and the antient philosophers. It appears in children, by their desire of beating the stones, which hurt them: In poets, by their readiness to personify every thing: And in the antient philosophers, by these fictions of sympathy and antipathy. We must pardon children, because of their age; poets, because they profess to follow implicitly the suggestions of their fancy: But what excuse shall we find to justify our philosophers in so signal a weakness?

Of the modern philosophy

.   .   .

The opinions of the antient philosophers, their fictions of substance and accident, and their reasonings concerning substantial forms and occult qualities, are like the spectres in the dark, and are deriv'd from principles, which, however common, are neither universal nor unavoidable in human nature. The *modern philosophy* pretends to be entirely free from this defect, and to arise only from the solid, permanent, and consistent principles of the imagination. Upon what grounds this pretension is founded must now be the subject of our enquiry.

The fundamental principle of that philosophy is the opinion concerning colours, sounds, tastes, smells, heat, and cold; which it asserts to be nothing but impressions in the mind, deriv'd from the operation of external objects, and without any resemblance to the qualities of the objects. Upon examination, I find only one of the reasons commonly produc'd for this opinion to be satisfactory, *viz.* that deriv'd from the variations of those impressions, even while the external object, to all appearance, continues the same. These variations depend upon several circumstances. Upon the different situations of our health: A man in a malady feels a disagreeable taste in meats, which before pleas'd him the most. Upon the different complexions and constitutions of men: That seems bitter to one, which is sweet to another. Upon the difference of their external situation and position: Colours reflected from the clouds change according to the distance of the clouds, and according to the angle they make with the eye and luminous body. Fire also communicates the sensation of pleasure at one distance, and that of pain at another. Instances of this kind are very numerous and frequent.

The conclusion drawn from them, is likewise as satisfactory as can possibly be imagin'd. 'Tis certain, that when different impressions of the same sense arise from any object, every one of these impressions has not a resembling quality existent in the object. For as the same object cannot, at the same time, be endow'd with different qualities of the same sense, and as the same quality cannot resemble impressions entirely different; it evidently follows, that many of our impressions have no external model or archetype. Now from like effects we presume like causes. Many of the impressions of colour, sound, &c., are confest to be nothing but internal existences, and to arise from causes, which no ways resemble them. These impressions are in appearance nothing different from the other impressions of colour, sound, &c. We conclude, therefore, that they are, all of them, deriv'd from a like origin.

This principle being once admitted, all the other doctrines of that philosophy seem to follow by an easy consequence. For upon the removal of sounds, colours, heat, cold, and other sensible qualities, from the rank of continu'd independent existences, we are reduc'd merely to what are called primary qualities, as the only *real* ones, of which we have any adequate notion. These primary qualities are extension and solidity, with their different mixtures and modifications; figure, motion, gravity, and cohesion. The generation, encrease, decay, and corruption of animals and vegetables, are nothing but changes of figure and motion; as also the operations of all bodies on each other; of fire, of light, water, air, earth, and of all the elements and powers of nature. One figure and motion produces another figure and motion; nor does there remain in the material universe any other principle, either active or passive, of which we can form the most distant idea.

I believe many objections might be made to this system: But at present I shall confine myself to one, which is in my opinion very decisive. I assert, that instead of explaining the operations of external objects by its means, we utterly annihilate all these objects, and reduce ourselves to the opinions of the most extravagant scepticism concerning them. If colours, sounds, tastes, and smells be merely perceptions, nothing we can conceive is possest of a real, continu'd, and independent existence; not even motion, extension and solidity, which are the primary qualities chiefly insisted on.

To begin with the examination of motion; 'tis evident this is a quality altogether inconceivable alone, and without a reference to some other object. The idea of motion necessarily supposes that of a body moving. Now what is our idea of the moving body, without which motion is incomprehensible? It must resolve itself into the idea of extension or of solidity; and consequently the reality of motion depends upon that of these other qualities.

This opinion, which is universally acknowledg'd concerning motion, I have prov'd to be true with regard to extension; and have shewn that 'tis impossible to conceive extension, but as compos'd of parts, endow'd with colour or solidity. The idea of extension is a compound idea; but as it is not compounded of an infinite number of parts or inferior ideas, it must at last resolve itself into such as are perfectly simple and indivisible. These simple and indivisible parts, not being ideas of extension, must be non-entities, unless conceiv'd as colour'd or solid. Colour is excluded from any real existence. The reality, therefore, of our idea of extension depends upon the reality of that of solidity, nor can the former be just while the latter is chimerical. Let us, then, lend our attention to the examination of the idea of solidity.

The idea of solidity is that of two objects, which being impell'd by the utmost force, cannot penetrate each other; but still maintain a separate and distinct existence. Solidity, therefore, is perfectly incomprehensible alone, and without the conception of some bodies, which are solid, and maintain this separate and distinct existence.

Now what idea have we of these bodies? The ideas of colours, sounds, and other secondary qualities are excluded. The idea of motion depends on that of extension, and the idea of extension on that of solidity. 'Tis impossible, therefore, that the idea of solidity can depend on either of them. For that wou'd be to run in a circle, and make one idea depend on another, while at the same time the latter depends on the former. Our modern philosophy, therefore, leaves us no just nor satisfactory idea of solidity; nor consequently of matter.

This argument will appear entirely conclusive to everyone that comprehends it; but because it may seem abstruse and intricate to the generality of readers, I hope to be excus'd, if I endeavour to render it more obvious by some variation of the expression. In order to form an idea of solidity, we must conceive two bodies pressing on each other without any penetration; and 'tis impossible to arrive at this idea, when we confine ourselves to one object, much more without conceiving any. Two non-entities cannot exclude each other from their places; because they never possess any place, nor can be endow'd with any quality. Now I ask, what idea do we form of these bodies or objects, to which we suppose solidity to belong? To say, that we conceive them merely as solid, is to run on *in infinitum*. To affirm, that we paint them out to ourselves as extended, either resolves all into a false idea, or returns in a circle. Extension must necessarily be consider'd either as colour'd, which is a false idea; or as solid, which brings us back to the first question. We may make the same observation concerning mobility and figure; and upon the whole must conclude, that after the exclusion of colours, sounds, heat and cold from the rank of external existences, there remains nothing, which can afford us a just and consistent idea of body.

Add to this, that, properly speaking, solidity or impenetrability is nothing, but an impossibility of annihilation, as has been already observ'd: For which reason 'tis the more necessary for us to form some distinct idea of that object, whose annihilation we suppose impossible. An impossibility of being annihilated cannot exist, and can never be conceived to exist, by itself; but necessarily requires some object or real existence, to which it may belong. Now the difficulty still remains, how to form an idea of this object or existence, without having recourse to the secondary and sensible qualities.

Nor must we omit on this occasion our accustom'd method of examining ideas by considering those impressions, from which they are deriv'd. The impressions, which enter by the sight and hearing, the smell and taste, are affirm'd by modern philosophy to be without any resembling objects; and consequently the idea of solidity, which is suppos'd to be real, can never be deriv'd from any of these senses. There remains, therefore, the feeling as the only sense, that can convey the impression, which is original to the idea of solidity; and indeed we naturally imagine, that we feel the solidity of bodies, and need but touch any object in order to perceive this quality. But this method of thinking is more popular than philosophical; as will appear from the following reflections.

First, 'Tis easy to observe, that tho' bodies are felt by means of their solidity, yet the feeling is a quite different thing from the solidity; and that they have not the least resemblance to each other. A man, who has the palsey in one hand, has as perfect an idea of impenetrability, when he observes that hand to be supported by the table, as when he feels the same table with the other hand. An object, that presses upon any of our members, meets with resistance; and that resistance, by the motion it gives to the nerves and animal spirits, conveys a certain sensation to the mind; but it does not follow, that the sensation, motion, and resistance are any ways resembling.

Secondly, The impressions of touch are simple impressions, except when consider'd with regard to their extension; which makes nothing to the present purpose: And from this simplicity I infer, that they neither represent solidity, nor any real object. For let us put two cases, *viz.* that of a man, who presses a stone, or any solid body, with his hand, and that of two stones, which press each other; 'twill readily be allow'd, that these two cases are not in every respect alike, but that in the former there is conjoin'd with the solidity, a feeling or sensation, of which there is no appearance in the latter. In order, therefore, to make these two cases alike, 'tis necessary to remove some part of the impression, which the man feels by his hand, or organ of sensation; and that being impossible in a simple impression, obliges us to remove the whole, and proves that this whole impression has no archetype or model in external objects. To which we may add, that solidity necessarily supposes two bodies, along with contiguity and impulse; which being a compound object, can never be represented by a simple impression. Not to mention, that tho' solidity continues always invariably the same, the impressions of touch change every moment upon us; which is a clear proof that the latter are not representations of the former.

Thus there is a direct and total opposition betwixt our reason and our senses; or more properly speaking, betwixt those conclusions we form from cause and effect, and those that persuade us of the continu'd and independent existence of body. When we reason from cause and effect, we conclude, that neither colour, sound, taste, nor smell have a continu'd and independent existence. When we exclude these sensible qualities there remains nothing in the universe, which has such an existence.

5

NATURALISM RECONSIDERED

ernest nagel

It is surely not the highest reach for a philosopher to be a combatant in the perennial wars between standaridized "isms" which fill conventional handbooks of philosophy. Philosophy at its best is a critical commentary upon existence and upon our claims to have knowledge of it; and its mission is to help illuminate what is obscure in experience and its objects, rather than to profess creeds or to repeat the battle cries of philosophical schools aiming at intellectual hegemony. The conception of philosophy as a struggle between competing systems is especially sterile when the "ism" defended or attacked covers as miscellaneous an assortment of not always congruous views as fly the banner of naturalism. The number of distinguishable doctrines for which the word "naturalism" has been a counter in the history of thought, is notorious. Even among contemporaries who proclaim themselves to be naturalists in philosophy, there are not only important differences in stress and perspective, but also in specific doctrines professed and in intellectual methods used to support commitments made. I am aware, therefore, that in taking naturalism as my subject this evening, I run the risk of becoming involved in futile polemics—a risk made graver by the fact that although the stated title of my address may have aroused different expectations, it is not my intention to recant and to confess past errors. I must explain why, notwithstanding the hazards of my theme, I have elected to discuss it.

The past quarter century has been for philosophy in many parts of the world a period of acute self-questioning, engendered in no small measure by developments in scientific and logical thought, and in part no doubt by fundamental changes in the social order. In any event, there has come about a general loss of confidence in the competence of philosophy to provide, by way of a distinctive intellectual method, a basic ground plan of the cosmos, or for that matter to contribute to knowledge of any primary subject matter except by becoming a specialized positive science and subjecting itself to the discipline of empirical inquiry. Although the abysses of human ignorance are undeniably profound, it has also become apparent that ignorance, like actual knowledge, is of many special and heterogeneous things; and we have come to

Reprinted from Ernest Nagel, *Logic Without Metaphysics*, pp. 3–16, by permission of the Macmillan Company. © by The Free Press, a corporation, 1956.
"Naturalism Reconsidered" was originally presented as the presidential address at the annual meeting of the Eastern Division of the American Philosophical Association at Goucher College, Baltimore, Maryland, December 1954.

think, like the fox and unlike the hedgehog of whom Mr. Isaiah Berlin has recently reminded us,[1] that there are a great many things which are already known or remain
to be discovered, but that there is no one "big thing" which, if known, would make
everything else coherent and unlock the mystery of creation. In consequence, many
of us have ceased to emulate the great system-builders in the history of philosophy. In
partial imitation of the strategy of modern science, and in the hope of achieving
responsibly held conclusions about matters concerning which we could acquire
genuine competence, we have tended to become specialists in our professional activities.
We have come to direct our best energies to the resolution of limited problems and
puzzles that emerge in the analysis of scientific and ordinary discourse, in the evaluation of claims to knowledge, in the interpretation and validation of ethical and
esthetic judgments, and in the assessment of types of human experience. I hope I
shall not be regarded as offensive in stating my impression that the majority of the
best minds among us have turned away from the conception of the philosopher as
the spectator of all time and existence, and have concentrated on restricted but
manageable questions, with almost deliberate unconcern for the bearing of their
often minute investigations upon an inclusive view of nature and man.

Some of us, I know, are distressed by the widespread scepticism of the traditional
claims for a *philosophia perennis*, and have dismissed as utterly trivial most, if not
all, the products of various current forms of analytical philosophy. I do not share
this distress, nor do I think the dismissal is uniformly perspicacious and warranted.
For in my judgment, the scepticism which many deplore is well founded. Even though
a fair-sized portion of recent analytical literature seems inconsequential also to me,
analytical philosophy in our own day is the continuation of a major philosophic tradition and can count substantial feats of clarification among its assets. Concentration on
limited and determinate problems has yielded valuable fruits, not least in the form of
an increased and refreshing sensitivity to the demands of responsible discourse.

On the other hand, philosophers, like other men, conduct their lives within the
framework of certain comprehensive, if not always explicit, assumptions about the
world they inhabit. These assumptions color evaluations of major ideals and proposed
policies. I also suspect that the directions taken by analyses of specific intellectual
problems are frequently if subtly controlled by the expressed or tacit beliefs philosophers hold concerning the overall nature of things, by their views on human
destiny, and by their conceptions of the scope of human reason. But, conversely,
resolutions of special problems made plausible by recent philosophical analysis, as
well as by the findings of various positive sciences, seem to me to support certain
broad generalizations about the cosmos and to disconfirm others. It is clearly desirable
that such basic intellectual commitments, which are at once the matrix and the outcome of inquiries into specific problems, be made as explicit as possible. A philosopher,
who is a reflective man by profession, certainly owes it to himself to articulate, if
only occasionally, what sort of world he thinks he inhabits, and to make clear to
himself where approximately lies the center of his convictions.

The discharge of the important obligation which is mine this evening, seems to
me an appropriate occasion for stating as simply and as succinctly as I can the sub-

[1] In *The Hedgehog and the Fox: An Essay on Tolstoy's View of History* (New York: New
American Library, a Mentor Book, 1957) Berlin makes reference to the following line from the
fragments of Archilochus: "The fox knows many things, but the hedgehog knows one big
thing." [Eds.]

stance of those intellectual commitments I like to call "naturalism." The label itself is of no importance, but I use it partly because of its historical associations, and partly because it is a reminder that the doctrines for which it is a name are neither new nor untried. With Santayana, I prefer not to accept in philosophic debate what I do not believe when I am not arguing; and naturalism as I construe it merely formulates what centuries of human experience have repeatedly confirmed. At any rate, naturalism seems to me a sound generalized account of the world encountered in practice and in critical reflection, and a just perspective upon the human scene. I wish to state briefly, and hence with little supporting argument, what I take to be its major tenets, and to defend it against some recent criticisms.

Claims to knowledge cannot ultimately be divorced from an evaluation of the intellectual methods used to support those claims. It is nevertheless unfortunate that in recent years naturalists in philosophy have so frequently permitted their allegiance to a dependable method of inquiry to obscure their substantive views on things in general. For it is the inclusive intellectual image of nature and man which naturalism supplies that sets it off from other comprehensive philosophies. In my conception of it, at any rate, naturalism embraces a generalized account of the cosmic scheme and of man's place in it, as well as a logic of inquiry.

I hasten to add, however, that naturalism does not offer a theory of nature in the sense that Newtonian mechanics, for example, provides a theory of motion. Naturalism does not, like the latter, specify a set of substantive principles with the help of which the detailed course of concrete happenings can be explained or understood. Moreover, the principles affirmed by naturalism are not proposed as competitors or underpinnings for any of the special theories which the positive sciences assert. Nor, finally, does naturalism offer its general view of nature and man as the product of some special philosophical mode of knowing. The account of things proposed by naturalism is a distillation from knowledge acquired in the usual way in daily encounters with the world or in specialized scientific inquiry. Naturalism articulates features of the world which, because they have become so obvious, are rarely mentioned in discussions of special subject matter, but which distinguish our actual world from other conceivable worlds. The major affirmations of naturalism are accordingly meager in content; but the principles affirmed are nevertheless effective guides in responsible criticism and evaluation.

Two theses seem to me central to naturalism as I conceive it. The first is the existential and causal primacy of organized matter in the executive order of nature. This is the assumption that the occurrence of events, qualities, and processes, and the characteristic behaviors of various individuals, are contingent on the organization of spatio-temporally located bodies, whose internal structures and external relations determine and limit the appearance and disappearance of everything that happens. That this is so, is one of the best-tested conclusions of experience. We are frequently ignorant of the special conditions under which things come into being or pass away; but we have also found repeatedly that when we look closely, we eventually ascertain at least the approximate and gross conditions under which events occur, and we discover that those conditions invariably consist of some more or less complex organization of material substances. Naturalism does not maintain that only what is material exists, since many things noted in experience—modes of action, relations of meaning, dreams, joys, plans, aspirations—are not, as such, material bodies or organizations of material bodies. What naturalism does assert as a truth about nature is that though *forms* of behavior or *functions* of material systems are indefeasibly parts of nature, forms and functions are not themselves agents in their own realization or in the realization of anything else. In the conception of nature's processes which naturalism affirms, there is no place for the operation of disembodied forces, no place for an immaterial spirit directing the course of events, no place for the survival of personality after the corruption of the body which exhibits it.

The second major contention of naturalism is that the manifest plurality and variety of things, of their qualities and their functions, are an irreducible feature of the cosmos, not a deceptive appearance cloaking some more homogeneous "ultimate reality" or transempirical substance, and that the sequential orders in which events occur or the manifold relations of dependence in which things exist are *contingent* connections, not the embodiments of a fixed and unified pattern of logically necessary links. The existential primacy of organized matter does not make illusory either the relatively permanent or the comparatively transient characters and forms which special configurations of bodies may possess. In particular, although the continued existence of the human scene is precarious and is dependent on a balance of forces that doubtless will not endure indefinitely, and even though its distinctive traits are not pervasive throughout space, it is nonetheless as much a part of the "ultimate" furniture of the world, and is as genuine a sample of what "really" exists, as are atoms and stars. There undoubtedly occur integrated systems of bodies, such as biological organisms, which have the capacity because of their material organization to maintain themselves and the direction of their characteristic activities. But there is no positive evidence, and much negative evidence, for the supposition that all existential structures are teleological systems in this sense, or for the view that whatever occurs is a phase in a unitary, teleologically organized, and all-inclusive, process or system. Modern physical cosmology does indeed supply some evidence for definite patterns of evolutionary development of stars, galactic systems, and even of the entire physical universe; and it is quite possible that the stage of cosmic evolution reached at any given time causally limits the types of things which can occur during that period. On the other hand, the patterns of change investigated in physical cosmogony are not patterns that are exhaustive of everything that happens; and nothing in these current physical speculations requires the conclusion that changes in one star or galaxy are related by inherent necessity to every action of biological organisms in some remote planet. Even admittedly teleological systems contain parts and processes which are causally irrelevant to some of the activities maintained by those systems; and the causal dependencies known to hold between the parts of any system, teleological or not, have never been successfully established as forms of logically necessary relations. In brief, if naturalism is true, irreducible variety and logical contingency are fundamental traits of the world we actually inhabit. The orders and connections of things are all accessible to rational inquiry; but these orders and connections are not all derivable by deductive methods from any set of premises that deductive reason can certify.

It is in this framework of general ideas that naturalism envisages the career and destiny of man. Naturalism views the emergence and the continuance of human society as dependent on physical and physiological conditions that have not always obtained and that will not permanently endure. But it does not, in consequence, regard man and his works as intrusions into nature, any more than it construes as intrusions the presence of heavenly bodies or of terrestrial protozoa. The stars are no more foreign to the cosmos than are men, even if the conditions for the existence of both stars and men are realized only occasionally or only in a few regions. Indeed, the conception of human life as a war with nature, as a struggle with an implacable foe that has doomed man to extinction, is but an inverted theology, with a malicious Devil in the seat of Omnipotence. It is a conception that is immodest, as well as anthropomorphic, in the importance it imputes to man in the scheme of things.

On the other hand, the affirmation that nature is man's "home" as much as it is the "home" of anything else, and the denial that cosmic forces are *intent* on destroying the human scene, do not warrant the interpretation that every sector of nature is explicable in terms of traits known to characterize only human individuals and human actions. Man undoubtedly possesses characteristics which are shared by everything that exists; but he also manifests traits and capacities that appear to be distinctive of him. Is anything gained but confusion when all forms of dependence between things, whether animate or inanimate, and all types of behaviors they display, are subsumed under distinctions that have an identifiable content only in reference to the human psyche? Measured by the illumination they bring, there is nothing to differentiate the thesis that human traits are nothing but the properties of bodies which can be formulated exclusively in the language of current physical theory, from the view that every change and every mode of operation, in whatever sector of the cosmos it may be encountered, is simply an illustration of some category pertinent to the description of human behavior.

Indeed, even some professed naturalists sometimes appear to promote the confusion when they make a fetish of continuity. Naturalists usually stress the emergence of novel forms in physical and biological evolution, thereby emphasizing the fact that human traits are not identical with the traits from which they emerge. Nevertheless, some distinguished contemporary naturalists also insist, occasionally with overtones of anxiety, that there is a "continuity" between the typically human on the one hand, and the physical and biological on the other. But is man's foothold in the scheme of things really made more secure by showing that his distinctive traits are in some sense "continuous" with features pervasive in nature, and would man's place in nature be less secure if such continuity did not obtain? The actual evidence for a continuity of development is conclusive in some instances of human traits, however it may be in others. But I sometimes suspect that the cardinal importance philosophers assign to the alleged universality of such continuity is a lingering survival of that ancient conception according to which things are intelligible only when seen as teleological systems producing definite ends, so that nature itself is properly understood only when construed as the habitat of human society. In any event, a naturalism that is not provincial in its outlook will not accept the intellectual incorporation of man into nature at the price of reading into all the processes of the cosmos the passions, the strivings, the defeats, and the glories of human life, and then exhibiting man as the most adequate, because most representative, expression of nature's inherent constitution. No, a mature naturalism seeks to understand what man is, not in terms of a discovered or postulated continuity between what is distinctive of him and what is pervasive in all things. Without denying that even the most distinctive human traits are dependent on things which are nonhuman, a mature naturalism attempts to assess man's nature in the light of *his* actions and achievements, *his* aspirations and capacities, *his* limitations and tragic failures, and *his* splendid works of ingenuity and imagination.

Human nature and history, in short, are *human* nature and history, not the history and nature of anything else, however much knowledge of other things contributes to a just appraisal of what man is. In particular, the adequacy of proposed ideals for human life must be judged, not in terms of their causes and origins, but in reference to how the pursuit and possible realization of ideals contribute to the organization and release of *human* energies. Men are animated by many springs of action, no one of which is intrinsically good or evil; and a moral ideal is the imagined satisfaction of some complex of impulses, desires, and needs. When ideals are handled responsibly, they therefore function as hypotheses for achieving a balanced exercise of human powers. Moral ideals are not self-certifying, any more than are the theories of the physical sciences; and evidence drawn from experienced satisfactions is required to validate them, however difficult may be the process of sifting and weighing the available data. Moral problems arise from a conflict of specific impulses and interests. They cannot, however, be effectively resolved by invoking standards derived from the study of nonhuman nature, or of what is allegedly beyond nature. If moral problems can be resolved at all, they can be resolved only in the light of specific human capacities, historical circumstance and acquired skills, and the opportunities (revealed by an imagination disciplined by knowledge) for altering the physical and social environment and for redirecting habitual behaviors. Moreover, since human virtues are in part the products of the society in which human powers are matured, a naturalistic moral theory is at the same time a critique of civilization—a critique of the institutions that channel human energies—so as to exhibit the possibilities and limitations of various forms and arrangements of society for bringing enduring satisfactions to individual human careers.

These are the central tenets of what I take to be philosophical naturalism. They are tenets which are supported by compelling empirical evidence, rather than dicta based on dogmatic preference. In my view of it, naturalism does not dismiss every other differing conception of the scheme of things as logically impossible; and it does not rule out all alternatives to itself on a priori grounds. It is possible, I think, to conceive without logical inconsistency a world in which disembodied forces are dynamic agents, or in which whatever happens is a manifestation of an unfolding logical pattern. In such possible worlds it would be an error to be a naturalist. But philosophy is not identical with pure mathematics, and its ultimate concern is with the actual world, even though philosophy must take cognizance of the fact that the actual world contains creatures who can envisage possible worlds and who employ different logical procedures for deciding which hypothetical world is the actual one. It is partly for this reason that contemporary naturalists devote so much attention to methods of evaluating evidence. When naturalists give their allegiance to the method of intelligence commonly designated as the method of modern empirical science, they do so because that method appears to be the most assured way of achieving reliable knowledge.

As judged by that method, the evidence in my opinion is at present conclusive for the truth of naturalism, and it is tempting to suppose that no one familiar with the evidence can fail to acknowledge that philosophy. Indeed, some commentators there are who assert that all philosophies are at bottom only expressions in different idioms of the same conceptions about the nature of things, so that the strife of philosophic systems is mainly a conflict over essentially linguistic matters. But too many thinkers for whom I have a profound respect explicitly reject naturalism, and their espousal of contrary views seems to me incompatible with the irenic claim that we really are in agreement on fundamentals.

Although I do not have the time this evening to consider systematically the criticisms currently made of naturalism, I do wish to examine briefly two repeatedly voiced objections which, if valid, would in my opinion seriously jeopardize the integrity and adequacy of naturalism as a philosophy. Stated summarily, the first objection is that in relying exclusively on the logico-empirical method of modern science for establishing cognitive claims, naturalists are in effect stacking the cards in their own favor, since thereby all alternative philosophies are antecedently disqualified. It is maintained, for example, that naturalism rejects any hypothesis about transempirical causes or time-transcending spiritual substances as factors in the order of things, not because such hypotheses are actually shown to be false, but simply because the logic of proof adopted dismisses as irrelevant any evidence which might establish them.

This criticism does not seem to me to have merit: the logico-empirical method of evaluating cognitive claims to which naturalists subscribe does not eliminate by fiat any hypothesis about existence for which evidence can be procured—evidence that in the last resort can be obtained through sensory or introspective observation. Thus, anyone who asserts a hypothesis postulating a transempirical ground for all existence, presumably seeks to understand in terms of that ground the actual occurrences in nature, and to account thereby for what actually happens as distinct from what is merely imagined to happen. There must therefore be some connection between the postulated character of the hypothetical transempirical ground and the empirically observable traits in the world around us; for otherwise the hypothesis is otiose, and not relevant to the spatio-temporal processes of nature. This does not mean, as some critics of naturalism suppose the latter to maintain, that the hypothetical transempirical ground must be characterized exclusively in terms of the observable properties of the world—any more than that the submicroscopic particles and processes which current physical theory postulates must be logical constructions out of the observable traits of macroscopic objects. But it does mean that unless the hypothesis implies, even if only by a circuitous route, some statements about empirical data, it is not adequate to the task for which it is proposed. If naturalists reject hypotheses about transempirical substances, they do not do so arbitrarily. They reject such hypotheses either because their relevance to the going concerns of nature is not established, or because, though their relevance is not in question, the actual evidence does not support them.

Nor does naturalism dismiss as unimportant and without consideration experiences such as of the holy, of divine illumination, or of mystical ecstasy—experiences which are of the greatest moment in the lives of many men, and which are often taken to signify the presence and operation of some purely spiritual reality. Such experiences have dimensions of meaning, for those who have undergone them, that are admittedly not on a par with the import of more common experiences like those of physical hunger, general well-being, or feelings of remorse and guilt. But such experiences are nonetheless events among other events; and though they may be evidence for something, their sheer occurrence does not certify *what* they are evidence for— any more than the sheer occurrence of dreams, hopes, and delusions authenticates the actual existence of their ostensible objects. In particular, whether the experience labelled as an experience of divine illumination is evidence for the existence of a divinity, is a question to be settled by inquiry, not by dogmatic affirmations or denials.

When naturalists refuse to acknowledge, merely on the strength of such experiences, the operation or presence of a divine power, they do so not because their commitment to a logical method prevents them from treating it seriously, but because independent inquiry fails to confirm it. Knowledge is knowledge, and cannot without confusion be identified with intuitive insight or with the vivid immediacy of profoundly moving experiences. Claims to knowledge must be capable of being tested; and the testing must be conducted by eventual reference to such evidence as counts in the responsible conduct of everyday affairs as well as of systematic inquiry in the sciences. Naturalists are therefore not engaged in question-begging when, through the use of the logic of scientific intelligence, they judge nonnaturalistic accounts of the order of things to be unfounded.

There is, however, a further objection to naturalism, to the effect that in committing itself to the logic of scientific proof, it is quite analogous to religious belief in resting on unsupported and indemonstrable faith. For that logic allegedly involves assumptions like the uniformity of nature or similar principles which transcend experience, cannot be justified empirically, and yet provide the premises that constitute the ultimate warrant for the conclusions of empirical inquiry. But if naturalism is thus based on unprovable articles of faith, on what cogent grounds can it reject a different conception of the true order of governance of events which rests on a different faith?

I cannot here deal adequately with the complex issues raised by this objection. Its point is not satisfactorily turned by claiming, as some have done, that instead of being articles of faith, the alleged indemonstrable postulates of scientific method are simply rules of the scientific game which *define* what in that game is to be understood by the words "knowledge" and "evidence." As I see it, however, the objection has force only for those whose ideal of reason is demonstration, and who therefore refuse to dignify anything as genuine knowledge unless it is demonstrable from self-luminous and self-evident premises. But if, as I also think, that ideal is not universally appropriate, and if, furthermore, a *wholesale* justification for knowledge and its method is an unreasonable demand and a misplaced effort, the objection appears as quite pointless. The warrant for a proposition about some specific interrelations of events does not derive from a faith in the uniformity of nature or in other principles with a cosmic scope. The warrant derives exclusively from the specific evidence available for that proposition, and from the contingent historical fact that the special ways employed in obtaining and appraising the evidence have been generally effective in yielding reliable knowledge. Subsequent inquiry may show that we were mistaken in accepting a proposition on the evidence available earlier; and further inquiry may also reveal that a given inductive policy, despite a record of successful past performance, requires correction if not total rejection. Fortunately, however, we are not always mistaken in accepting various propositions or in employing certain inductive policies, even though we are unable to demonstrate that we shall never fall into error. Accordingly, though many of our hopes for the stability of beliefs in the face of fresh experience may turn out to be baseless, and though no guarantees can be given that our most assured claims to knowledge may not eventually need revision, in adopting scientific method as the instrument for evaluating claims to knowledge, naturalists are not subscribing to an indemonstrable faith.

The bitter years of cataclysmic wars and social upheavals through which our generation has been passing, have also witnessed a general decline of earlier hopes in the possibilities of modern science for achieving a liberal and humane civilization. Indeed, as is well known, many men have become convinced that the progress and spread of science, and the consequent secularization of society, are the prime sources of our present ills; and a not inconsiderable number of thinkers have made widely popular various revised forms of older religious and irrationalistic philosophies as guides to human salvation. Moreover, since naturalists have not abandoned their firm adherence to the method of scientific intelligence, naturalism has been repeatedly charged with insensitivity toward spiritual values, with a shallow optimism toward science as an instrument for ennobling the human estate, and with a philistine blindness toward the ineradicable miseries of human existence. I want to conclude with a few brief comments on these allegations.

It is almost painful to have to make a point of the elementary fact that whatever may happen to be the range of special interests and sensibilities of individual naturalists, there is no incompatibility, whether logical or psychological, between maintaining that warranted knowledge is secured only through the use of a definite logical method, and recognizing that the world can be experienced in many other ways than by knowing it. It is a matter of record that outstanding exponents of naturalism, in our own time as well as in the past, have exhibited an unequaled and tender sensitivity to the esthetic and moral dimensions of human experience; and they have been not only movingly eloquent celebrants of the role of moral idealism and of intellectual and esthetic contemplation in human life, but also vigorous defenders of the distinctive character of these values against facile attempts to reduce them to something else.

It seems to me singularly inept, moveover, to indict naturalism as a philosophy without a sense for the tragic aspects of life. For unlike many world-views, naturalism offers no cosmic consolation for the unmerited defeats and undeserved sufferings which all men experience in one form or another. It has never sought to conceal its view of human destiny as an episode between two oblivions. To be sure, naturalism is not a philosophy of despair. For one facet in its radical pluralism is the truth that a human good is nonetheless a good, despite its transitory existence. There doubtless are foolish optimists among those professing naturalism, though naturalism has no monopoly in this respect, and it is from other quarters that one usually receives glad tidings of a universal nostrum. But in any event, neither the pluralism so central to naturalism, nor its cultivation of scientific reason, is compatible with any dogmatic assumption to the effect that men can be liberated from *all* the sorrows and evils to which they are now heirs, through the eventual advances of science and the institution of appropriate physical and social innovations. Indeed, why suppose that a philosophy which is wedded to the use of the sober logic of scientific intelligence should thereby be committed to the dogma that there are no irremediable evils? On the contrary, human reason is potent only against evils that are *remediable*. At the same time, since it is impossible to decide responsibly, *antecedent* to inquiry, *which* of the many human ills can be mitigated, if not eradicated, by extending the operations of scientific reason into human affairs, naturalism is not a philosophy of *general* renunciation—even though it recognizes that it is the better part of wisdom to be equably resigned to what, in the light of available evidence, cannot be avoided. Human reason is not an omnipotent instrument for the achievement of human goods; but it is the only instrument we do possess, and it is not a contemptible one. Although naturalism is acutely sensitive to the actual limitations of rational effort, those limitations do not warrant a romantic philosophy of general despair and they do not blind naturalism to the possibilities implicit in the exercise of disciplined reason for realizing human excellence.

6

THE PERCEPTION OF REALITY

william james

The various orders of reality

Suppose a newborn mind, entirely blank and waiting for experience to begin. Suppose that it begins in the form of a visual impression (whether faint or vivid is immaterial) of a lighted candle against a dark background, and nothing else, so that whilst this image lasts it constitutes the entire universe known to the mind in question. Suppose, moreover (to simplify the hypothesis), that the candle is only imaginary, and that no "original" of it is recognized by us psychologists outside. Will this hallucinatory candle be believed in, will it have a real existence for the mind?

What possible sense (for that mind) would a suspicion have that the candle was not real? What would doubt or disbelief of it imply? When *we,* the onlooking psychologists, say the candle is unreal, we mean something quite definite, viz., that there is a world known to *us* which *is* real, and to which we perceive that the candle does not belong; it belongs exclusively to that individual mind, has no *status* anywhere else, etc. It exists, to be sure, in a fashion, for it forms the content of that mind's hallucination; but the hallucination itself, though unquestionably it is a sort of existing fact, has no knowledge of *other* facts; and since those *other* facts are the realities *par excellence* for us, and the only things we believe in, the candle is simply outside of our reality and belief altogether.

By the hypothesis, however, the *mind which sees the candle* can spin no such considerations as these about it, for of other facts, actual or possible, it has no inkling whatever. That candle is its all, its absolute. Its entire faculty of attention is absorbed by it. It *is,* it is *that;* it is *there;* no other possible candle, or quality of this candle, no other possible place, or possible object in the place, no alternative, in short, suggests itself as even conceivable; so how can the mind help believing the candle real? The supposition that it might possibly not do so is, under the supposed conditions, unintelligible.

This is what Spinoza long ago announced:

> Let us conceive a boy [he said] imagining to himself a horse, and taking note of nothing else. As this imagination involves the existence of the horse,

From William James, *The Principles of Psychology* (New York: Henry Holt and Company, 1890), II:287–301.

and the boy has no perception which annuls its existence, he will necessarily contemplate the horse as present, nor will he be able to doubt of its existence, however little certain of it he may be. I deny that a man in so far as he imagines [*percipit*] affirms nothing. For what is it to imagine a winged horse but to affirm that the horse [that horse, namely] has wings? For if the mind had nothing before it but the winged horse it would contemplate the same as present, would have no cause to doubt of its existence, nor any power of dissenting from its existence, unless the imagination of the winged horse were joined to an idea which contradicted [*tollit*] its existence.[1]

The sense that anything we think of is unreal can only come, then, when that thing is contradicted by some other thing of which we think. *Any object which remains uncontradicted is* ipso facto *believed and posited as absolute reality.*

Now, how comes it that one thing thought of can be contradicted by another? It cannot unless it begins the quarrel by saying something inadmissible about that other. Take the mind with the candle, or the boy with the horse. If either of them say, "That candle or that horse, even when I don't see it, exists in *the outer world,*" he pushes into "the outer world" an object which may be incompatible with everything which he otherwise knows of that world. If so, he must take his choice of which to hold by, the present perceptions or the other knowledge of the world. If he holds to the other knowledge, the present perceptions are contradicted, *so far as their relation to that world goes.* Candle and horse, whatever they may be, are not existents in outward space. They are existents, of course; they are mental objects; mental objects have existence as mental objects. But they are situated in their own spaces, the space in which they severally appear, and neither of those spaces is the space in which the realities called "the outer world" exist.

Take again the horse with wings. If I merely dream of a horse with wings, my horse interferes with nothing else and has not to be contradicted. That horse, its wings, and its place, are all equally real. That horse exists no otherwise than as winged, and is moreover really there, for that place exists no otherwise than as the place of that horse, and claims as yet no connection with the other places of the world. But if with this horse I make an inroad into the *world otherwise known,* and say, for example, "That is my old mare Maggie, having grown a pair of wings where she stands in her stall," the whole case is altered; for now the horse and place are identified with a horse and place otherwise known, and *what* is known of the latter objects is incompatible with what is perceived with the former. "Maggie in her stall with wings! Never!" The wings are unreal, then, visionary. I have dreamed a lie about Maggie in her stall.

The reader will recognize in these two cases the two sorts of judgment called in the logic books existential and attributive, respectively. "The candle exists as an outer reality" is an existential, "My Maggie has got a pair of wings" is an attributive, proposition; and it follows from what was first said that *all propositions, whether attributive or existential, are believed through the very fact of being conceived, unless they clash with other propositions, believed at the same time, by affirming that their terms are the same with the terms of these other propositions.* A dream-candle has existence, true enough; but not the same existence (existence for itself, namely, or *extra mentem meam*) which the candles of waking perception have. A dream-horse has

[1] *Ethics,* II., 49, Scholium.

wings; but then neither horse nor wings are the same with any horses or wings known to memory. That we can at any moment think of the same thing which at any former moment we thought of is the ultimate law of our intellectual constitution. But when we now think of it incompatibly with our other ways of thinking it, then we must choose which way to stand by, for we cannot continue to think in two contradictory ways at once. *The whole distinction of real and unreal, the whole psychology of belief, disbelief, and doubt, is thus grounded on two mental facts—first, that we are liable to think differently of the same; and second, that when we have done so, we can choose which way of thinking to adhere to and which to disregard.*

The subjects adhered to become real subjects, the attributes adhered to, real attributes, the existence adhered to, real existence; whilst the subjects disregarded become imaginary subjects, the attributes disregarded, erroneous attributes, and the existence disregarded, an existence in no man's land, in the limbo "where footless fancies dwell." The real things are, in M. [Hippolyte] Taine's terminology, the *reductives* of the things judged unreal.

The many worlds

Habitually and practically we do not *count* these disregarded things as existents at all. For them *Vœ victis* is the law in the popular philosophy; they are not even treated as appearances; they are treated as if they were mere waste, equivalent to nothing at all. To the genuinely philosophic mind, however, they still have existence, though not the same existence, as the real things. *As* objects of fancy, *as* errors, *as* occupants of dreamland, etc., they are in their way as indefeasible parts of life, as undeniable features of the Universe, as the realities are in their way. The total world of which the philosophers must take account is thus composed of the realities *plus* the fancies and illusions.

Two sub-universes, at least, connected by relations which philosophy tries to ascertain! Really there are more then two sub-universes of which we take account, some of us of this one, and others of that. For there are various categories both of illusion and of reality, and alongside of the world of absolute error (i.e., error confined to single individuals) but still within the world of absolute reality (i.e., reality believed by the complete philosopher) there is the world of collective error, there are the worlds of abstract reality, of relative or practical reality, of ideal relations, and there is the supernatural world. The popular mind conceives of all these sub-worlds more or less disconnectedly; and when dealing with one of them, forgets for the time being its relations to the rest. The complete philosopher is he who seeks not only to assign to every given object of his thought its right place in one or other of these sub-worlds, but he also seeks to determine the relation of each sub-world to the others in the total world which *is*.

The most important sub-universes commonly discriminated from each other and recognized by most of us as existing, each with its own special and separate style of existence, are the following:

(1) The world of sense, or of physical "things" as we instinctively apprehend them, with such qualities as heat, color, and sound, and such "forces" as life, chemical affinity, gravity, electricity, all existing as such within or on the surface of the things.

(2) The world of science, or of physical things as the learned conceive them, with

secondary qualities and "forces" (in the popular sense) excluded, and nothing real but solids and fluids and their "laws" (i.e., customs) of motion.

(3) The world of ideal relations, or abstract truths believed or believable by all, and expressed in logical, mathematical, metaphysical, ethical, or aesthetic propositions.

(4) The world of "idols of the tribe," illusions or prejudices common to the race. All educated people recognize these as forming one sub-universe. The motion of the sky round the earth, for example, belongs to this world. That motion is not a recognized item of any of the other worlds; but as an "idol of the tribe" it really exists. For certain philosophers "matter" exists only as an idol of the tribe. For science, the "secondary qualities" of matter are but "idols of the tribe."

(5) The various supernatural worlds, the Christian heaven and hell, the world of the Hindoo mythology, the world of Swedenborg's *visa et audita,* etc. Each of these is a consistent system, with definite relations among its own parts. Neptune's trident, e.g., has no status of reality whatever in the Christian heaven; but within the classic Olympus certain definite things are true of it, whether one believe in the reality of the classic mythology as a whole or not. The various worlds of deliberate fable may be ranked with these worlds of faith—the world of the *Iliad,* that of *King Lear,* of the *Pickwick Papers,* etc.

(6) The various worlds of individual opinion, as numerous as men are.

(7) The worlds of sheer madness and vagary, also indefinitely numerous.

Every object we think of gets at last referred to one world or another of this or of some similar list. It settles into our belief as a common-sense object, a scientific object, an abstract object, a mythological object, an object of some one's mistaken conception, or a madman's object; and it reaches this state sometimes immediately, but often only after being hustled and bandied about amongst other objects until it finds some which will tolerate its presence and stand in relations to it which nothing contradicts. The molecules and ether-waves of the scientific world, for example, simply kick the object's warmth and color out, they refuse to have any relations with them. But the world of "idols of the tribe" stands ready to take them in. Just so the world of classic myth takes up the winged horse; the world of individual hallucination, the vision of the candle; the world of abstract truth, the proposition that justice is kingly, though no actual king be just. The various worlds themselves, however, appear (as aforesaid) to most men's minds in no very definitely conceived relation to each other, and our attention, when it turns to one, is apt to drop the others for the time being out of its account. Propositions concerning the different worlds are made from "different points of view"; and in this more or less chaotic state the consciousness of most thinkers remains to the end. Each world *whilst it is attended to* is real after its own fashion; only the reality lapses with the attention.

The world of "practical realities"

Each thinker, however, has dominant habits of attention; and these *practically elect from among the various worlds some one to be for him the world of ultimate realities.* From this world's objects he does not appeal. Whatever positively contradicts them must get into another world or die. The horse, e.g., may have wings to its heart's content, so long as it does not pretend to be the real world's horse—*that* horse is absolutely wingless. For most men, as we shall immediately see, the "things of sense" hold this prerogative position, and are the absolutely real world's nucleus. Other things, to be sure, may be real for this man or for that—things of science, abstract moral relations, things of the Christian theology, or what not. But even for the special man, these things are usually real with a less real reality than that of the things of sense. They are taken less seriously; and the very utmost that can be said for anyone's belief in them is that it is as strong as his "belief in his own senses."

In all this the everlasting partiality of our nature shows itself, our inveterate propensity to choice. For, in the strict and ultimate sense of the word existence, everything which can be thought of at all exists as *some* sort of object, whether mythical object, individual thinker's object, or object in outer space and for intelligence at large. Errors, fictions, tribal beliefs, are parts of the whole great Universe which God has made, and He must have meant all these things to be in it, each in its respective place. But for us finite creatures, " 'tis to consider too curiously to consider so." The mere fact of appearing as an object at all is not enough to constitute reality. That may be metaphysical reality, reality for God; but what we need is practical reality, reality for ourselves; and, to have that, an object must not only appear, but it must appear both *interesting* and *important*. The worlds whose objects are neither interesting nor important we treat simply negatively, we brand them as *un*real.

In the relative sense, then, the sense in which we contrast reality with simple *un*reality, and in which one thing is said to have *more* reality than another, and to be more believed, *reality means simply relation to our emotional and active life*. This is the only sense which the word ever has in the mouths of practical men. *In this sense, whatever excites and stimulates our interest is real;* whenever an object so appeals to us that we turn to it, accept it, fill our mind with it, or practically take account of it, so far it is real for us, and we believe it. Whenever, on the contrary, we ignore it, fail to consider it or act upon it, despise it, reject it, forget it, so far it is unreal for us and disbelieved. Hume's account of the matter was then essentially correct, when he said that belief in anything was simply the having the idea of it in a lively and active manner:

> I say, then, that belief is nothing but a more vivid, lively, forcible, firm, steady conception of an object than the imagination alone is ever able to attain. . . . It consists not in the peculiar nature or order of the ideas, but in the *manner* of their conception and in their *feeling* to the mind. I confess that it is impossible perfectly to explain this feeling or manner of conception. . . . Its true and proper name . . . is *belief,* which is a term that everyone sufficiently understands in common life. And in philosophy we can go no farther than assert that belief is something felt by the mind, which distinguishes the idea of the judgment from the fictions of the imagination. It gives them more weight and influence; makes them appear of greater importance; enforces them in the mind; gives them a superior influence on the passions, and renders them the governing principle in our actions.[2]

Or as Prof. Bain puts it: "In its essential character, belief is a phase of our active nature—otherwise called the Will." [3]

[2] *Inquiry Concerning Human Understanding*, sec. v., pt. 2 (slightly transposed in my quotation).
[3] Note to Jas. Mill's *Analysis*, I., 394.

The object of belief, then, reality or real existence, is something quite different from all the other predicates which a subject may possess. Those are properties intellectually or sensibly intuited. When we add any one of them to the subject, we increase the intrinsic content of the latter, we enrich its picture in our mind. But adding reality does not enrich the picture in any such inward way; it leaves it inwardly as it finds it, and only fixes it and stamps it in to *us*.

> The real [as Kant says] contains no more than the possible. A hundred real dollars do not contain a penny more than a hundred possible dollars. . . . By whatever, and by however many, predicates I may think a thing, nothing is added to it if I add that the thing exists. . . . Whatever, therefore, our concept of an object may contain, we must always step outside of it in order to attribute to it existence.[4]

The "stepping outside" of it is the establishment either of immediate practical relations between it and ourselves, or of relations between it and other objects with which we have immediate practical relations. Relations of this sort, which are as yet not transcended or superseded by others, are *ipso facto* real relations, and confer reality upon their objective term. *The* fons et origo *of all reality, whether from the absolute or the practical point of view, is thus subjective, is ourselves.* As bare logical thinkers, without emotional reaction, we give reality to whatever objects we think of, for they are really phenomena, or objects of our passing thought, if nothing more. But, *as thinkers with emotional reaction, we give what seems to us a still higher degree of reality to whatever things we select and emphasize and turn to* WITH A WILL. These are our *living* realities; and not only these, but all the other things which are intimately connected with these. Reality, starting from our Ego, thus sheds itself from point to point—first, upon all objects which have an immediate sting of interest for our Ego in them, and next, upon the objects most continuously related with these. It only fails when the connecting thread is lost. A whole system may be real, if it only hang to our Ego by one immediately *stinging* term. But what contradicts any such stinging term, even though it be another stinging term itself, is either not believed, or only believed after settlement of the dispute.

·   ·   ·

The paramount reality of sensations

But now we are met by questions of detail. What does this stirring, this exciting power, this interest, consist in, which some objects have? Which *are* those "intimate relations" with our life which give reality? And what things stand in these relations immediately, and what others are so closely connected with the former that (in Hume's language) we "carry our disposition" also on to them?

In a simple and direct way these questions cannot be answered at all. The whole history of human thought is but an unfinished attempt to answer them. For what have men been trying to find out, since men were men, but just those things: "Where do our true interests lie—which relations shall we call the intimate and real ones—which

4 *Critique of Pure Reason,* trans. Müller, II., 515–517.

things shall we call living realities and which not?" A few psychological points can, however, be made clear.

Any relation to our mind at all, in the absence of a stronger relation, suffices to make an object real. The barest appeal to our attention is enough for that. Revert to the beginning of the chapter, and take the candle entering the vacant mind. The mind was waiting for just some such object to make its spring upon. It makes its spring and the candle is believed. But when the candle appears at the same time with other objects, it must run the gauntlet of their rivalry, and then it becomes a question which of the various candidates for attention shall compel belief. As a rule we believe as much as we can. We would believe everything if we only could. When objects are represented by us quite unsystematically they conflict but little with each other, and the number of them which, in this chaotic manner, we can believe, is limitless. The primitive savage's mind is a jungle in which hallucinations, dreams, superstitions, conceptions, and sensible objects all flourish alongside of each other, unregulated except by the attention turning in this way or in that. The child's mind is the same. It is only as objects become permanent and their relations fixed that discrepancies and contradictions are felt and must be settled in some stable way. As a rule, the success with which a contradicted object maintains itself in our belief is proportional to several qualities which it must possess. Of these the one which would be put first by most people, because it characterizes objects of sensation, is its

(1) Coerciveness over attention, or the mere power to possess consciousness. Then follow:

(2) Liveliness, or sensible pungency, especially in the way of exciting pleasure or pain;

(3) Stimulating effect upon the will, i.e., capacity to arouse active impulses, the more instinctive the better;

(4) Emotional interest, as object of love, dread, admiration, desire, etc.;

(5) Congruity with certain favorite forms of contemplation—unity, simplicity, permanence, and the like;

(6) Independence of other causes, and its own causal importance.

These characters run into each other. Coerciveness is the result of liveliness or emotional interest. What is lively and interesting stimulates *eo ipso* the will; congruity holds of active impulses as well as of contemplative forms; causal independence and importance suit a certain contemplative demand, etc. I will therefore abandon all attempt at a formal treatment, and simply proceed to make remarks in the most convenient order of exposition.

As a whole, sensations are more lively and are judged more real than conceptions; things met with every hour more real than things seen once; attributes perceived when awake, more real than attributes perceived in a dream. But, owing to the *diverse relations contracted by the various objects with each other,* the simple rule that the lively and permanent is the real is often enough disguised. A conceived thing may be deemed more real than a certain sensible thing, if it only be intimately related to other sensible things more vivid, permanent, or interesting than the first one. Conceived molecular vibrations, e.g., are by the physicist judged more real than felt warmth, because so intimately related to all those other facts of motion in the world which he has made his special study. Similarly, a rare thing may be deemed more real than a permanent thing if it be more widely related to other permanent things. All the occasional crucial observations of science are examples of this. A rare experience, too, is likely to be judged more real than a permanent one, if it be more interesting and exciting. Such is the sight of Saturn through a telescope; such are the occasional insights and illuminations which upset our habitual ways of thought.

But no mere floating conception, no mere disconnected rarity, ever displaces vivid things or permanent things from our belief. A conception, to prevail, must *terminate* in the world of orderly sensible experience. A rare phenomenon, to displace frequent ones, must belong with others more frequent still. The history of science is strewn with wrecks and ruins of theory—essences and principles, fluids and forces— once fondly clung to, but found to hang together with no facts of sense. And exceptional phenomena solicit our belief in vain until such time as we chance to conceive them as of kinds already admitted to exist. What science means by "verification" is no more than this, that no object of conception shall be believed which sooner or later has not some permanent and vivid object of sensation for its *term. . . .*

Sensible objects are thus either our realities or the tests of our realities. Conceived objects must show sensible effects or else be disbelieved. And the effects, even though reduced to relative unreality when their causes come to view (as heat, which molecular vibrations make unreal), are yet the things on which our knowledge of the causes rests. Strange mutual dependence this, in which the appearance needs the reality in order to exist, but the reality needs the appearance in order to be known!

Sensible vividness or pungency is then the vital factor in reality when once the conflict between objects, and the connecting of them together in the mind, has begun. No object which neither possesses this vividness in its own right nor is able to borrow it from anything else has a chance of making headway against vivid rivals, or of rousing in us that reaction in which belief consists. On the vivid objects we *pin,* as the saying is, our faith in all the rest; and our belief returns instinctively even to those of them from which reflection has led it away. Witness the obduracy with which the popular world of colors, sounds, and smells holds its own against that of molecules and vibrations. Let the physicist himself but nod, like Homer, and the world of sense becomes his absolute reality again.

· · ·

7

THE WORD "REAL"

j. l. austin

But now, provoked largely by the frequent and unexamined occurrences of "real," "really," "real shape," etc., in the arguments we have just been considering, I want to take a closer look at this little word "real." I propose, if you like, to discuss the Nature of Reality—a genuinely important topic, though in general I don't much like making this claim.

There are two things, first of all, which it is immensely important to understand here.

1. "Real" is an absolutely *normal* word, with nothing newfangled or technical or highly specialized about it. It is, that is to say, already firmly established in, and very frequently used in, the ordinary language we all use every day. Thus *in this sense* it is a word which has a fixed meaning, and so can't, any more than can any other word which is firmly established, be fooled around with *ad lib*. Philosophers often seem to think that they can just "assign" any meaning whatever to any word; and so no doubt, in an absolutely trivial sense, they can (like Humpty-Dumpty). There are some expressions, of course, "material thing" for example, which only philosophers use, and in such cases they can, within reason, please themselves; but most words are *in fact* used in a particular way already, and this fact can't be just disregarded. (For example, some meanings that have been assigned to "know" and "certain" have made it seem outrageous that we should use these terms as we actually do; but what this shows is that the meanings assigned by some philosophers are *wrong*.) Certainly, when we have discovered how a word is in fact used, that may not be the end of the matter; there is certainly no reason why, in general, things should be left exactly as we find them; we may wish to tidy the situation up a bit, revise the map here and there, draw the boundaries and distinctions rather differently. But still, it is advisable always to bear in mind (*a*) that the distinctions embodied in our vast and, for the most part, relatively ancient stock of ordinary words are neither few nor always very obvious, and almost never just arbitrary; (*b*) that in any case, before indulging in any tampering on our own account, we need to find out what it is that we have to deal with; and

From J. L. Austin, *Sense and Sensibilia*, G. J. Warnock, ed. (Oxford: The Clarendon Press, 1962), Chap. VII, pp. 62–77. Reprinted by permission of the Clarendon Press.

(c) that tampering with words in what we take to be one little corner of the field is always *liable* to have unforeseen repercussions in the adjoining territory. Tampering, in fact, is not so easy as is often supposed, is not justified or needed so often as is often supposed, and is often thought to be necessary just because what we've got already has been misrepresented. And we must always be particularly wary of the philosophical habit of dismissing some of (if not all) the ordinary uses of a word as "unimportant," a habit which makes distortion practically unavoidable. For instance, if we are going to talk about "real," we must not dismiss as beneath contempt such humble but familiar expressions as "not real cream"; this may save us from saying, for example, or seeming to say that what is not real cream must be a fleeting product of our cerebral processes.

2. The other immensely important point to grasp is that "real" is *not* a normal word at all, but highly exceptional; exceptional in this respect that, unlike "yellow" or "horse" or "walk," it does not have one single, specifiable, always-the-same *meaning*. (Even Aristotle saw through this idea.) *Nor* does it have a large number of different meanings—it is not *ambiguous*, even "systematically." Now words of this sort have been responsible for a great deal of perplexity. Consider the expressions "cricket ball," "cricket bat," "cricket pavilion," "cricket weather." If someone did not know about cricket and were obsessed with the use of such "normal" words as "yellow," he might gaze at the ball, the bat, the building, the weather, trying to detect the "common quality" which (he assumes) is attributed to these things by the prefix "cricket." But no such quality meets his eye; and so perhaps he concludes that "cricket" must designate a *nonnatural* quality, a quality to be detected not in any ordinary way, but by *intuition*. If this story strikes you as too absurd, remember what philosophers have said about the word "good"; and reflect that many philosophers, failing to detect any ordinary quality common to real ducks, real cream, and real progress, have decided that Reality must be an *a priori* concept apprehended by reason alone.

Let us begin, then, with a preliminary, no doubt rather haphazard, survey of the complexities in the use of "real." Consider, for instance, a case which at first sight one might think was pretty straightforward—the case of "real color." What is meant by the "real" color of a thing? Well, one may say with some confidence, that's easy enough: the *real* color of the thing is the color that it looks to a normal observer in conditions of normal or standard illumination; and to find out what a thing's real color is, we just need to be normal and to observe it in those conditions.

But suppose (a) that I remark to you of a third party, "That isn't the real color of her hair." Do I mean by this that, if you were to observe her in conditions of standard illumination, you would find that her hair did not look that color? Plainly not—the conditions of illumination may be standard already. I mean, of course, that her hair has been *dyed,* and normal illumination just doesn't come into it at all. Or suppose that you are looking at a ball of wool in a shop, and I say, "That's not its real color." Here I *may* mean that it won't look that color in ordinary daylight; but I *may* mean that wool isn't that color before it's dyed. As so often, you can't tell what I mean just from the words that I use; it makes a difference, for instance, whether the thing under discussion is or is not of a type which is *customarily* dyed.

Suppose (b) that there is a species of fish which looks vividly multicolored, slightly glowing perhaps, at a depth of a thousand feet. I ask you what its real color is. So you catch a specimen and lay it out on deck, making sure the condition of the light is just about normal, and you find that it looks a muddy sort of grayish white.

Well, is *that* its real color? It's clear enough at any rate that we don't have to say so. In fact, is there any right answer in such a case?

Compare: "What is the real taste of saccharine?" We dissolve a tablet in a cup of tea and we find that it makes the tea taste sweet; we then take a tablet neat, and we find that it tastes bitter. Is it *really* bitter, or *really* sweet?

(*c*) What is the real color of the sky? Of the sun? Of the moon? Of a chameleon? We say that the sun in the evening sometimes looks red—well, what color is it *really*? (What are the "conditions of standard illumination" for the sun?)

(*d*) Consider a *pointilliste* painting of a meadow, say; if the general effect is of green, the painting may be composed of predominantly blue and yellow dots. What is the real color of the painting?

(*e*) What is the real color of an afterimage? The trouble with this one is that we have no idea what an alternative to its "real color" might be. Its apparent color, the color that it looks, the color that it appears to be?—but these phrases have no application here. (You might ask me, "What color is it really?" if you suspected that I had lied in telling you its color. But "What color is it really?" is not quite the same as "What is its real color?")

Or consider "real shape" for a moment. This notion cropped up, you may remember, seeming quite unproblematic, when we were considering the coin which was said to "look elliptical" from some points of view; it had a real shape, we insisted, which remained unchanged. But coins in fact are rather special cases. For one thing their outlines are well defined and very highly stable, and for another they have a *known* and a *nameable* shape. But there are plenty of things of which this is not true. What is the real shape of a cloud? And if it be objected, as I dare say it could be, that a cloud is not a "material thing" and so not the kind of thing which has to have a real shape, consider this case: what is the real shape of a cat? Does its real shape change whenever it moves? If not, in what posture *is* its real shape on display? Furthermore, is its real shape such as to be fairly smooth-outlined, or must it be finely enough serrated to take account of each hair? It is pretty obvious that there is *no* answer to these questions—no rules according to which, no procedure by which, answers are to be determined. Of course, there are plenty of shapes which the cat definitely is not—cylindrical, for instance. But only a desperate man would toy with the idea of ascertaining the cat's real shape "by elimination."

Contrast this with cases in which we *do* know how to proceed: "Are those real diamonds?," "Is that a real duck?" Items of jewelry that more or less closely resemble diamonds may not be real diamonds because they are paste or glass; that may not be a real duck because it is a decoy, or a toy duck, or a species of goose closely resembling a duck, or because I am having a hallucination. These are all of course quite different cases. And notice in particular (*a*) that, in most of them, "observation by a normal observer in standard conditions" is completely irrelevant; (*b*) that something which is not a real duck is not a *nonexistent* duck, or indeed a nonexistent anything; and (*c*) that something existent, e.g., a toy, may perfectly well not be real, e.g., not a real duck.

Perhaps by now we have said enough to establish that there is more in the use of "real" than meets the cursory eye; it has many and diverse uses in many diverse contexts. We must next, then, try to tidy things up a little; and I shall now mention under four headings what might be called the salient features of the use of "real"— though not *all* these features are equally conspicuous in all its uses.

1. First, "real" is a word that we may call *substantive-hungry*. Consider:

"These diamonds are real";
"These are real diamonds."

This pair of sentences looks like, in an obvious grammatical respect, this other pair:

"These diamonds are pink";
"These are pink diamonds."

But whereas we can *just* say of something "This is pink," we can't *just* say of something "This is real." And it is not very difficult to see why. We can perfectly well say of something that it is pink without knowing, without any reference to, what it *is*. But not so with "real." For one and the same object may be both a real *x* and not a real *y*; an object looking rather like a duck may be a real decoy duck (not just a toy) but not a real duck. When it isn't a real duck but a hallucination, it may still be a real hallucination—as opposed, for instance, to a passing quirk of a vivid imagination. That is, we must have an answer to the question "A real *what*?" if the question "Real or not?" is to have a definite sense, to get any foothold. And perhaps we should also mention here another point—that the question "Real or not?" does not always come up, can't always be raised. We *do* raise this question only when, to speak rather roughly, suspicion assails us—in some way or other things may be not what they seem; and we *can* raise this question only if there *is* a way, or ways, in which things may be not what they seem. What alternative is there to being a "real" afterimage?

"Real" is not, of course, the only word we have that is substantive-hungry. Other examples, perhaps better known ones, are "the same" and "one." The same *team* may not be the same *collection of players;* a body of troops may be one *company* and also three *platoons.* Then what about "good?" We have here a variety of gaps crying out for substantives: "A good *what?*," "Good *at* what?"; a good book, perhaps, but not a good novel; good at pruning roses, but not good at mending cars.

2. Next, "real" is what we may call a *trouser-word*. It is usually thought, and I dare say usually rightly thought, that what one might call the affirmative use of a term is basic—that, to understand "*x*," we need to know what it is to be *x,* or to be an *x,* and that knowing this apprises us of what it is *not* to be *x*, not to be an *x*. But with "real" (as we briefly noted earlier) it is the *negative* use that wears the trousers. That is, a definite sense attaches to the assertion that something is real, a real such-and-such, only in the light of a specific way in which it might be, or might have been, *not* real. "A real duck" differs from the simple "a duck" only in that it is used to exclude various ways of being not a real duck—but a dummy, a toy, a picture, a decoy, etc.; and moreover I don't know *just* how to take the assertion that it's a real duck unless I know *just* what, on that particular occasion, the speaker has it in mind to exclude. This, of course, is why the attempt to find a characteristic common to all things that are or could be called "real" is doomed to failure; the function of "real" is not to contribute positively to the characterization of anything, but to exclude possible ways of being *not* real—and these ways are both numerous for particular kinds of things, and liable to be quite different for things of different kinds. It is this identity of general function combined with immense diversity in specific applications which gives to the word "real" the, at first sight, baffling feature of having neither one single "meaning," nor yet ambiguity, a number of different meanings.

3. Thirdly, "real" is (like "good") a *dimension-word*. I mean by this that it is the most general and comprehensive term in a whole group of terms of the same kind, terms that fulfil the same function. Other members of this group, on the affirmative side, are, for example, "proper," "genuine," "live," "true," "authentic," "natural"; and on the negative side, "artificial," "fake," "false," "bogus," "makeshift," "dummy," "synthetic," "toy"—and such nouns as "dream," "illusion," "mirage," "hallucination," belong here as well. It is worth noticing here that, naturally enough, the *less* general terms on the affirmative side have the merit, in many cases, of suggesting more or less definitely what it is that is being excluded; they tend to pair off, that is, with particular terms on the negative side and thus, so to speak, to narrow the range of possibilities. If I say that I wish the university had a proper theatre, this suggests that it has at present a *makeshift* theatre; pictures are genuine as opposed to *fake,* silk is natural as opposed to *artificial,* ammunition is live as opposed to *dummy,* and so on. In practice, of course, we often get a clue to what it is that is in question from the substantive in the case, since we frequently have a well-founded antecedent idea in what respects the kind of thing mentioned could (and could not) be "not real." For instance, if you ask me "Is this real silk?" I shall tend to supply "as opposed to artificial," since I already know that silk is the kind of thing which can be very closely simulated by an artificial product. The notion of its being *toy* silk, for instance, will not occur to me.[1]

A large number of questions arise here—which I shall not go into—concerning both the composition of these families of "reality"-words and "unreality"-words, and also the distinctions to be drawn between their individual members. Why, for instance, is being a *proper* carving knife one way of being a real carving knife, whereas being *pure* cream seems not to be one way of being *real* cream? Or to put it differently: how does the distinction between real cream and synthetic cream differ from the distinction between pure cream and adulterated cream? Is it just that adulterated cream still is, after all, *cream*? And why are false teeth called "false" rather than, say, "artificial"? Why are artificial limbs so called, in *preference* to "false"? Is it that false teeth, besides doing much the same job as real teeth, look, and are meant to look, *deceptively* like real teeth? Whereas an artificial limb, perhaps, is meant to do the same job, but is neither intended, nor likely, to be *passed off* as a real limb.

Another philosophically notorious dimension-word, which has already been mentioned in another connection as closely comparable with "real," is "good." "Good" is the most general of a very large and diverse list of more specific words, which share with it the general function of expressing commendation, but differ among themselves in their aptness to, and implications in, particular contexts. It is a curious point, of which Idealist philosophers used to make much at one time, that "real" itself, in certain uses, may belong to this family. "Now this is a *real* carving knife!" may be one way of saying that this is a good carving knife. And it is sometimes said of a bad poem, for instance, that it isn't really a poem at all; a certain standard must be reached, as it were, even to *qualify*.

4. Lastly, "real" also belongs to a large and important family of words that we may call *adjuster-words*—words, that is, by the use of which other words are adjusted to meet the innumerable and unforeseeable demands of the world upon language. The

---

1 Why not? Because silk can't be "toy." Yes, but why not? Is it that a toy is, strictly speaking, something quite small, and specially made or designed to be manipulated in play? The water in toy beer-bottles is not toy beer, but *pretend* beer. Could a toy watch actually have clockwork inside and show the time correctly? Or would that be just a *miniature* watch?

position, considerably oversimplified no doubt, is that at a given time our language contains words that enable us (more or less) to say what we want to say in most situations that (we think) are liable to turn up. But vocabularies are finite; and the variety of possible situations that may confront us is neither finite nor precisely foreseeable. So situations are practically bound to crop up sometimes with which our vocabulary is not already fitted to cope in any tidy, straightforward style. We have the word "pig," for instance, and a pretty clear idea which animals, among those that we fairly commonly encounter, are and are not to be so called. But one day we come across a new kind of animal, which looks and behaves very much as pigs do, but not *quite* as pigs do; it is somehow different. Well, we might just keep silent, not knowing what to say; we don't want to say positively that it *is* a pig, or that it is *not*. Or we might, if for instance we expected to want to refer to these new creatures pretty often, invent a quite new word for them. But what we could do, and probably would do first of all, is to say, "It's *like* a pig." ("Like" is *the* great adjuster-word, or alternatively put, the main flexibility-device by whose aid, in spite of the limited scope of our vocabulary, we can always avoid being left completely speechless.) And then, having said of this animal that it's *like* a pig, we may proceed with the remark, "But it isn't a *real* pig"—or more specifically, and using a term that naturalists favor, "not a *true* pig." If we think of words as being shot like arrows at the world, the function of these adjuster-words is to free us from the disability of being able to shoot only straight ahead; by their use on occasion, such words as "pig" can be, so to speak, brought into connection with targets lying slightly off the simple, straightforward line on which they are ordinarily aimed. And in this way we gain, besides flexibility, precision; for if I can say, "Not a real pig, but like a pig," I don't have to tamper with the meaning of "pig" itself.

But, one might ask, do we *have* to have "like" to serve this purpose? We have, after all, other flexibility-devices. For instance, I might say that animals of this new species are "piggish"; I might perhaps call them "quasi-pigs," or describe them (in the style of vendors of peculiar wines) as "pig-type" creatures. But these devices, excellent no doubt in their way, can't be regarded as substitutes for "like," for this reason: they equip us simply with new expressions on the same level as, functioning in the same way as, the word "pig" itself; and thus, though they may perhaps help us out of our immediate difficulty, they themselves may land us in exactly the same *kind* of difficulty at any time. We have this kind of wine, not real port, but a tolerably close approximation to port, and we call it "port type." But then someone produces a new kind of wine, not port exactly, but also not quite the same as what we now call "port type." So what are we to say? Is it port-type type? It would be tedious to have to say so, and besides there would clearly be no future in it. But as it is we can say that it is *like* port-type wine (and for that matter rather like port, too); and in saying this we don't saddle ourselves with a *new word,* whose application may itself prove problematic if the vintners spring yet another surprise on us. The word "like" equips us *generally* to handle the unforeseen, in a way in which new words invented *ad hoc* don't, and can't.

(Why then do we need "real" as an adjuster-word as well as "like"? Why exactly do we want to say, sometimes "It is like a pig," sometimes "It is not a real pig"? To answer these questions properly would be to go a long way towards making really clear the use, the "meaning," of "real.")

It should be quite clear, then, that there are no criteria to be laid down *in general* for distinguishing the real from the not real. How this is to be done must depend on *what* it is with respect to which the problem arises in particular cases. Furthermore, even for particular kinds of things, there may be many different ways in which the distinction may be made (there is not just *one* way of being "not a real pig")—this depends on the number and variety of the surprises and dilemmas nature and our fellow men may spring on us, and on the surprises and dilemmas we have been faced with hitherto. And of course, if there is *never* any dilemma or surprise, the question simply doesn't come up; if we had simply never had occasion to distinguish anything as being in any way like a pig but not a *real* pig, then the words "real pig" themselves would have no application—as perhaps the words "real afterimage" have no application.

Again, the criteria we employ at a given time can't be taken as *final,* not liable to change. Suppose that one day a creature of the kind we now call a cat takes to talking. Well, we say to begin with, I suppose, "This cat can talk." But then other cats, not all, take to talking as well; we now have to say that some cats talk, we distinguish between talking and non-talking cats. But again we may, if talking becomes prevalent and the distinction between talking and not talking seems to us to be really important, come to insist that a *real* cat be a creature that can talk. And this will give us a new case of being "not a real cat," i.e., being a creature just like a cat except for not talking.

Of course—this may seem perhaps hardly worth saying, but in philosophy it seems it does need to be said—we make a distinction between "a real *x*" and "not a real *x*" only if there is a way of telling the difference between what is a real *x* and what is not. A distinction which we are not in fact able to draw is—to put it politely —not worth making.

SELECTED BIBLIOGRAPHY FOR PART II

Ayer, A. J. "Demonstration of the Impossibility of Metaphysics," *Mind,* XLIII (1934).

Baylis, C. A. *Metaphysics.* New York: Collier-Macmillan, 1965.

Bradley, F. H. *Appearance and Reality: A Metaphysical Essay.* London: Allen and Unwin, 1897.

Brightman, Edgar S. *Person and Reality: An Introduction to Metaphysics.* New York: Ronald Press, 1958.

Browning, Douglas, ed. *Philosophers of Process.* New York: Random House, 1965.

Carnap, Rudolf. "The Elimination of Metaphysics Through Logical Analysis of Language," in A. J. Ayer, ed. *Logical Positivism.* Glencoe, Ill.: Free Press, 1959.

Collingwood, R. G. *An Essay on Metaphysics.* Oxford: Clarendon Press, 1940.

DeGeorge, Richard. *Classical and Contemporary Metaphysics: A Source Book.* New York: Holt, Rinehart and Winston, 1962.

Dewey, John. "The Subject Matter of Metaphysics," *Journal of Philosophy,* XII (1915).

Drennen, D. A., ed. *A Modern Introduction to Metaphysics: Readings from Classical and Contemporary Sources.* New York: Free Press of Glencoe, 1962.

Emmet, Dorothy M. *The Nature of Metaphysical Thinking.* London: Macmillan, 1945.

Gilson, Etienne. *Being and Some Philosophers.* Toronto: Pontifical Institute of Medieval Studies, 1949.

Gotshalk, D. W. *Metaphysics in Modern Times: A Present-Day Perspective.* Chicago: University of Chicago Press, 1940.

Harris, Errol E. *The Foundations of Metaphysics in Science.* New York: Humanities Press, 1965.

Heidegger, Martin. *An Introduction to Metaphysics,* trans. Ralph Manheim. New Haven: Yale University Press, 1959.

Henle, R. J. *Method in Metaphysics.* Milwaukee: Marquette University Press, 1951.

Hocking, W. E. *Types of Philosophy.* New York: Scribner, 1939.

Kant, Immanuel. *Prolegomena to Any Future Metaphysics.* New York: Liberal Arts Press, 1951.

Lazerowitz, Morris. *The Structure of Metaphysics.* New York: Humanities Press, 1955.

Marcel, Gabriel. *Being and Having,* trans. Katharine Farrer. London: Collins, Fontana Library, 1965.

Maritain, Jacques. *A Preface to Metaphysics: Seven Lectures on Being.* New York: Sheed and Ward, 1939.

Pears, D. F., ed. *The Nature of Metaphysics.* London: Macmillan, 1957.

Pepper, S. C. *World Hypotheses: A Study in Evidence.* Berkeley and Los Angeles: University of California Press, 1961.

Ramsey, I. T., ed. *Prospect for Metaphysics: Essays of Metaphysical Exploration.* New York: Philosophical Library, 1961.

Santayana, George. *Realms of Being.* New York: Scribner, 1942.

Sartre, Jean-Paul. *Being and Nothingness: An Essay on Phenomenological Ontology.* New York: Philosophical Library, 1956.

Stace, W. T. *The Nature of the World: An Essay in Phenomenalist Metaphysics.* Princeton: Princeton University Press, 1940.

Strawson, P. F. *Individuals: An Essay in Descriptive Metaphysics.* London: Methuen, 1959.

Taylor, A. E. *Elements of Metaphysics.* London: Methuen, 1946.

Taylor, Richard. *Metaphysics.* Englewood Cliffs, N.J.: Prentice-Hall, 1963.

Tomlin, E. W. F. *The Approach to Metaphysics.* London: Routledge, 1947.

Walsh, W. H. *Metaphysics.* London: Hutchinson, 1963.

Wisdom, John. "Metaphysics and Verification," *Mind,* XLVII (1938).

part III

minds,

bodies,

and

selves

INTRODUCTION

The increasing complexity of society and the seeming loss of individuality give renewed importance to the ancient questions concerning man's nature. Since the seventeenth century the nature of man has been considered largely in terms of mind and body. Is man mind, body, or a complex of both? Our ordinary experience supports the view that man is both mind and body. We have bodies whose needs are satisfied by eating, sleeping, drinking, and other physical activities. In most cases these activities can be observed and measured by psychologists, physiologists, physicians, or other scientists. Yet we seem to be more than body. We feel, we dream, we think, and we have sense experiences which seem essentially private. Furthermore our observations seem to substantiate a causal connection between bodily processes and mental activities. A broken bone causes pain, sound waves bombarding the ear cause aural sensations, LSD causes hallucinations, and so forth. Mental states also seem to affect the body. Psychological depression causes loss of weight, shame causes blushing, anger or fear causes trembling, and so on.

For ancient and medieval thinkers the functions we generally attribute to the mind were performed by the soul. Thus man's nature was described in terms of a soul-body rather than a mind-body dichotomy. Some contemporary thinkers, such as Maurice Merleau-Ponty, still employ the soul-body dichotomy, but at the present time most philosophers express the duality in terms of mind and body.

A famous dualistic theory, consistent with common experience, was formulated by René Descartes, a seventeenth-century French philosopher and mathematician. Descartes, in his desire to establish philosophy on principles whose truth is absolute, finds that, at the outset, his own existence as a thinking being is the only piece of knowledge he cannot doubt. He establishes his philosophy on this principle, and after deducing the existence of God from it, he develops the view that man consists of both spiritual and material substances. Immaterial, spiritual substance is described as substance that thinks, feels, wills, and remembers; and material substance, as that which is extended. Man's extension, or body, is, like other physical entities in the universe, subject to the laws of nature; spiritual substance is not. Material and spiritual substances, as defined by Descartes, have no common attributes, and for most thinkers, their mutual exclusiveness seems to make their interaction impossible. But Descartes asserts that the intermediary between spiritual and material substance is the pineal gland. This resolution of the problem is, of course, questionable, but it is Descartes' way of accounting for those experiences where interaction seems to occur.

A materialistic interpretation of man, in denying the mind-body dichotomy, avoids the difficulties that the dualist faces when he attempts to explain the interaction between body and mind. In a materialistic view, man is body, and mind usually is either identified with bodily processes or described as an epiphenomenon, or appearance, which has no effect upon physical processes. Today the studies of psychologists and physiologists, which have made inroads into the explanation of the structure and the function of the brain and neurological processes, tend to support materialism. A result of these studies is the view that men, as well as animals, are physicochemical mechanisms. According to this view, man is distinguished from other animals by the complexity of his nervous system, and not by his mental states.

J. J. C. Smart, a contemporary philosopher, is committed to a materialistic view of man even though scientists have not, thus far, demonstrated that mind is brain and nothing more. Smart believes that identifying the mind with the brain results in a simpler and more elegant theory than the one which holds that there are psychic states over and above brain processes.

In contrast to the materialist, the metaphysical idealist identifies man with mind or spiritual substance and explains matter in terms of consciousness or ideas. For the idealist, the mind and its activities, rather than the complex human nervous system, are man's unique features. Josiah Royce, an American idealist, defines every real fact in the universe as "a meaning embodied in a conscious life." This definition, pertaining to both the human and physical domains, will be dealt with again later in this introduction.

Attempting to reconcile the opposition between idealism and materialism, Maurice Merleau-Ponty, a French phenomenologist, views the relationship of soul and body as a dialectic between a phenomenal object (the body) and consciousness (the soul). In his discussion of the soul-body problem Merleau-Ponty employs the categories of matter, life, and mind. None of these categories is reducible to the others, but the order of consciousness, or mind, is the foundation for the other two. When any of these planes of signification (matter, life, or mind) is related to the others, it is spoken of as being integrated with higher or lower levels. If the relationship is significant then the behavior is organized; if the relationship fails then the behavior is disorganized. When the relationship between body and soul (consciousness) is significant the body is always a body *for* consciousness, and consciousness experiences itself as inhering in an organism. Although there is a dualism when disorganization exists, there is no absolute distinction between body and soul. Nevertheless, insofar as he sees the objects of perception as phenomenal and consciousness itself as primary, Merleau-Ponty may be categorized as an idealist.

Another celebrated contemporary solution to the mind-body problem is presented in Gilbert Ryle's *The Concept of Mind*. Ryle speaks of the mind-body dualism as the "official theory," or the myth of "the ghost in the machine," promulgated by Descartes and others. This radical bifurcation of bodily and mental states and processes is, according to Ryle, a result of the misuse of expressions dealing with mental states. Such a misuse of expressions leads to the conclusion that there are physical and mental states and processes which are logically analogous but which are also logically independent. Ryle's criticism of the "official theory" is a prelude to his presentation of a view which conceives of mental activities as events which can be witnessed through the senses. *The Concept of Mind* is his endeavor to annihilate the mind-body dualism by presenting the proper use of mental expressions.

A comprehensive theory of man must cope not only with the mind-body problem but also with the problem of personal identity. This problem is related to the fact that change is a feature of both mental and physical processes. Some physical changes are immediately observable, others are more gradual. We can see the results of a crippling injury at once, but we cannot observe the growth a child undergoes in an hour or a day. Thoughts, feelings, and desires also change, sometimes perceptibly, and sometimes imperceptibly. A critical examination of long-accepted beliefs may strikingly alter one's thoughts and attitudes, as, for example, when a man's careful study of the platforms of the Republican and Democratic parties results in his switching his party allegiance. Other attitudes may change gradually through the course of a lifetime. The question that interests us here is not how change occurs but how a personal identity can persist amid change. We seek a basis for holding that we are now the same persons we were ten minutes ago or will be ten years from now.

The question of personal identity has not only philosophical but also legal and religious import. Legal judgments are often made upon the assumption that the person being tried for a crime is the person who committed the crime. The problem of identity becomes especially acute in legal cases when the defendant's personality has drastically changed since he committed the crime. The courts must then decide if this is the same person who committed the crime, and if he is to be held responsible for the crime. In a religious context, the nature of man's self has implications for the question of immortality. It would seem that immortality is meaningful only if a man's identity is maintained after death. However, if his identity resides in his body, it is difficult to see how he can survive death.

The problem of personal identity has been dealt with in various ways. The Scholastics and Descartes held the substantive theory in which the unity of person is maintained by substance. Substance, which may be either physical or mental, is sometimes referred to as the subject of our experiences. It remains unaltered by physical and mental processes and guarantees the integrity of personal identity from moment to moment. However, if one holds that the existence of mental and physical substances cannot be known, then one must explain identity in some other manner.

David Hume's scepticism in regard to the existence of spiritual and physical substances led him to adopt a serial, or bundle, conception of man. His consideration of the idea of self, a name for the identity or unity of person, led him to conclude that there are no impressions (sensations) of a unity which remains invariably the same throughout the whole course of our lives. When we try to discover this unity, what we stumble upon are "some perceptions or other, of heat or cold, light or shade, love or hatred, pain or pleasure." These separate impressions, according to this serial, or bundle, conception, compose the empirical ego. In asserting that the self consists of separate impressions, Hume denies the concept of a transcendental ego which, others claim, underlies impressions. The problem generated by identifying self with the empirical ego is that of determining the bond which unites separate impressions. Hume does not try to resolve this difficulty, but instead concludes that our conception of self is a fiction. The fiction arises because of memory, which "alone acquaints us with the continuance and extent of the succession of perceptions."

In directing his vision inward to discover the unity of person, Henri Bergson comes upon a solidified crust of perceptions and memories; but, for him, the unity of person is to be found not in these bundles of perceptions but in the continuous flux of the enduring self which is the center of one's inner life. The enduring self is not given by empirical or rational methods, but can be known only through intuition. The self that is so known endures in time.

In contrast to both Hume and Bergson, George Herbert Mead, an American pragmatist, believes that a man's self is not present at birth but develops through the individual's relations to others and to the social process as a whole. The self can have itself (in self-consciousness) as an object, but the object-self is experienced indirectly, as the individual takes "the attitudes of other individuals toward himself within a social environment or context of experience and behavior in which both he and they are involved." Thus the internal structure of the self mirrors the relationship between society and the individual.

Now let us return to the discussion of Royce, who not only presents an idealistic view of man but also considers those human characteristics which enable man to proclaim his unity or identity. Like Mead, Royce identifies the self with the meaning of the conscious life as developed within a community of selves. However, Royce bases the self primarily upon an ethical rather than a socio-behavioristic principle. This ethical aspect depends upon the self's internal nature, which is essentially purposive and which, in its development, comes to realize that the present moment is an expression of one's life "as friend, as worker, as loyal citizen, or in general as man, i.e., as one of God's expressions in human form." In other words, that which gives a man his continuing identity is the purpose around which his life is organized.

The various positions outlined above indicate that there are many conceptions of the self and of personal identity. Since the enunciation of Descartes' dualistic theory, philosophers have attempted to avoid such a radical bifurcation of mind and body. Some have sought the identity of self in materialism, others in idealism, and still others in positions which precisely fit neither of these metaphysical views. The readings which follow introduce the reader to difficult, yet exciting and significant, approaches to the questions concerning the nature of man.

THE SELF AS MIND AND BODY

rené descartes

Second meditation

OF THE NATURE OF THE HUMAN MIND; AND THAT
IT IS MORE EASILY KNOWN THAN THE BODY.

The Meditation of yesterday filled my mind with so many doubts that it is no longer in my power to forget them. And yet I do not see in what manner I can resolve them; and, just as if I had all of a sudden fallen into very deep water, I am so disconcerted that I can neither make certain of setting my feet on the bottom, nor can I swim and so support myself on the surface. I shall nevertheless make an effort and follow anew the same path as that on which I yesterday entered, i.e., I shall proceed by setting aside all that in which the least doubt could be supposed to exist, just as if I had discovered that it was absolutely false; and I shall ever follow in this road until I have met with something which is certain, or at least, if I can do nothing else, until I have learned for certain that there is nothing in the world that is certain. Archimedes, in order that he might draw the terrestrial globe out of its place, and transport it elsewhere, demanded only that one point should be fixed and immovable; in the same way I shall have the right to conceive high hopes if I am happy enough to discover one thing only which is certain and indubitable.

I suppose, then, that all the things that I see are false; I persuade myself that nothing has ever existed of all that my fallacious memory represents to me. I consider that I possess no senses; I imagine that body, figure, extension, movement, and place are but the fictions of my mind. What, then, can be esteemed as true? Perhaps nothing at all, unless that there is nothing in the world that is certain.

But how can I know there is not something different from those things that I have just considered, of which one cannot have the slightest doubt? Is there not some God, or some other being by whatever name we call it, who puts these reflections into my mind? That is not necessary, for is it not possible that I am capable of producing them myself? I myself, am I not at least something? But I have already denied that I

From the *Meditations on First Philosophy in the Philosophical Works of Descartes*, trans. Elizabeth S. Haldane and G. R. T. Ross (New York: Cambridge University Press, 1931), I:149–157, 189–192. Reprinted by permission of the publisher.

had senses and body. Yet I hesitate, for what follows from that? Am I so dependent on body and senses that I cannot exist without these? But I was persuaded that there was nothing in all the world, that there was no heaven, no earth, that there were no minds, nor any bodies: was I not then likewise persuaded that I did not exist? Not at all; of a surety I myself did exist since I persuaded myself of something [or merely because I thought of something].[1] But there is some deceiver or other, very powerful and very cunning, who ever employs his ingenuity in deceiving me. Then without doubt I exist also if he deceives me, and let him deceive me as much as he will, he can never cause me to be nothing so long as I think that I am something. So that after having reflected well and carefully examined all things, we must come to the definite conclusion that this proposition: I am, I exist, is necessarily true each time that I pronounce it, or that I mentally conceive it.

But I do not yet know clearly enough what I am, I who am certain that I am; and hence I must be careful to see that I do not imprudently take some other object in place of myself, and thus that I do not go astray in respect of this knowledge that I hold to be the most certain and most evident of all that I have formerly learned. That is why I shall now consider anew what I believed myself to be before I embarked upon these last reflections; and of my former opinions I shall withdraw all that might even in a small degree be invalidated by the reasons which I have just brought forward, in order that there may be nothing at all left beyond what is absolutely certain and indubitable.

What then did I formerly believe myself to be? Undoubtedly I believed myself to be a man. But what is a man? Shall I say a reasonable animal? Certainly not; for then I should have to inquire what an animal is, and what is reasonable; and thus from a single question I should insensibly fall into an infinitude of others more difficult; and I should not wish to waste the little time and leisure remaining to me in trying to unravel subtleties like these. But I shall rather stop here to consider the thoughts which of themselves spring up in my mind, and which were not inspired by anything beyond my own nature alone when I applied myself to the consideration of my being. In the first place, then, I considered myself as having a face, hands, arms, and all that system of members composed of bones and flesh as seen in a corpse which I designated by the name of body. In addition to this I considered that I was nourished, that I walked, that I felt, and that I thought, and I referred all these actions to the soul: but I did not stop to consider what the soul was, or if I did stop, I imagined that it was something extremely rare and subtle like a wind, a flame, or an ether, which was spread throughout my grosser parts. As to body, I had no manner of doubt about its nature, but thought I had a very clear knowledge of it; and if I had desired to explain it according to the notions that I had then formed of it, I should have described it thus: By the body I understand all that which can be defined by a certain figure: something which can be confined in a certain place, and which can fill a given space in such a way that every other body will be excluded from it; which can be perceived either by touch, or by sight, or by hearing, or by taste, or by smell: which can be moved in many ways not, in truth, by itself, but by something which is foreign to it, by which it is touched [and from which it receives impressions]: for to have the power of self-movement, as also of feeling or of thinking, I did not consider to

---

[1] Where it seems desirable an alternative reading from the French is given in square brackets. [Explanation from translators' preface.]

appertain to the nature of body: on the contrary, I was rather astonished to find that faculties similar to them existed in some bodies.

But what am I, now that I suppose that there is a certain genius which is extremely powerful, and, if I may say so, malicious, who employs all his powers in deceiving me? Can I affirm that I possess the least of all those things which I have just said pertain to the nature of body? I pause to consider, I revolve all these things in my mind, and I find none of which I can say that it pertains to me. It would be tedious to stop to enumerate them. Let us pass to the attributes of soul and see if there is any one which is in me? What of nutrition or walking [the first mentioned]? But if it is so that I have no body it is also true that I can neither walk nor take nourishment. Another attribute is sensation. But one cannot feel without body, and besides I have thought I perceived many things during sleep that I recognized in my waking moments as not having been experienced at all. What of thinking? I find here that thought is an attribute that belongs to me; it alone cannot be separated from me. I am, I exist, that is certain. But how often? Just when I think; for it might possibly be the case if I ceased entirely to think, that I should likewise cease altogether to exist. I do not now admit anything which is not necessarily true: to speak accurately I am not more than a thing which thinks, that is to say a mind or a soul, or an understanding, or a reason, which are terms whose significance was formerly unknown to me. I am, however, a real thing and really exist; but what thing? I have answered: a thing which thinks.

And what more? I shall exercise my imagination [in order to see if I am not something more]. I am not a collection of members which we call the human body: I am not a subtle air distributed through these members, I am not a wind, a fire, a vapor, a breath, nor anything at all which I can imagine or conceive; because I have assumed that all these were nothing. Without changing that supposition I find that I only leave myself certain of the fact that I am somewhat. But perhaps it is true that these same things which I supposed were nonexistent because they are unknown to me, are really not different from the self which I know. I am not sure about this, I shall not dispute about it now; I can only give judgment on things that are known to me. I know that I exist, and I inquire what I am, I whom I know to exist. But it is very certain that the knowledge of my existence taken in its precise significance does not depend on things whose existence is not yet known to me; consequently it does not depend on those which I can feign in imagination. And indeed the very term *feign* in imagination [2] proves to me my error, for I really do this if I image myself a something, since to imagine is nothing else than to contemplate the figure or image of a corporeal thing. But I already know for certain that I am, and that it may be that all these images, and, speaking generally, all things that relate to the nature of body are nothing but dreams [and chimeras]. For this reason I see clearly that I have as little reason to say, "I shall stimulate my imagination in order to know more distinctly what I am," than if I were to say, "I am now awake, and I perceive somewhat that is real and true: but because I do not yet perceive it distinctly enough, I shall go to sleep of express purpose, so that my dreams may represent the perception with greatest truth and evidence." And, thus, I know for certain that nothing of all that I can understand by means of my imagination belongs to this knowledge which I have of myself, and that it is necessary to recall the mind from this mode of thought with the

2 Or "form an image" (*effingo*). [Translators' note.]

utmost diligence in order that it may be able to know its own nature with perfect distinctness.

But what then am I? A thing which thinks. What is a thing which thinks? It is a thing which doubts, understands, [conceives], affirms, denies, wills, refuses, which also imagines and feels.

Certainly it is no small matter if all these things pertain to my nature. But why should they not so pertain? Am I not that being who now doubts nearly everything, who nevertheless understands certain things, who affirms that one only is true, who denies all the others, who desires to know more, is averse from being deceived, who imagines many things, sometimes indeed despite his will, and who perceives many likewise, as by the intervention of the bodily organs? Is there nothing in all this which is as true as it is certain that I exist, even though I should always sleep and though he who has given me being employed all his ingenuity in deceiving me? Is there likewise any one of these attributes which can be distinguished from my thought, or which might be said to be separated from myself? For it is so evident of itself that it is I who doubts, who understands, and who desires, that there is no reason here to add anything to explain it. And I have certainly the power of imagining likewise; for although it may happen (as I formerly supposed) that none of the things which I imagine are true, nevertheless this power of imagining does not cease to be really in use, and it forms part of my thought. Finally, I am the same who feels, that is to say, who perceives certain things, as by the organs of sense, since in truth I see light, I hear noise, I feel heat. But it will be said that these phenomena are false and that I am dreaming. Let it be so; still it is at least quite certain that it seems to me that I see light, that I hear noise, and that I feel heat. That cannot be false; properly speaking it is what is in me called feeling (sentire); and used in this precise sense that is no other thing than thinking.

From this time I begin to know what I am with a little more clearness and distinction than before; but nevertheless it still seems to me, and I cannot prevent myself from thinking, that corporeal things, whose images are framed by thought, which are tested by the senses, are much more distinctly known than that obscure part of me which does not come under the imagination. Although really it is very strange to say that I know and understand more distinctly these things whose existence seems to me dubious, which are unknown to me, and which do not belong to me, than others of the truth of which I am convinced, which are known to me and which pertain to my real nature, in a word, than myself. But I see clearly how the case stands: my mind loves to wander, and cannot yet suffer itself to be retained within the just limits of truth. Very good, let us once more give it the freest rein, so that, when afterwards we seize the proper occasion for pulling up, it may the more easily be regulated and controlled.

Let us begin by considering the commonest matters, those which we believe to be the most distinctly comprehended, to wit, the bodies which we touch and see; not indeed bodies in general, for these general ideas are usually a little more confused, but let us consider one body in particular. Let us take, for example, this piece of wax: it has been taken quite freshly from the hive, and it has not yet lost the sweetness of the honey which it contains; it still retains somewhat of the odor of the flowers from which it has been culled; its color, its figure, its size are apparent; it is hard, cold, easily handled, and if you strike it with the finger, it will emit a sound. Finally all the things which are requisite to cause us distinctly to recognize a body, are met with in it.

But notice that while I speak and approach the fire what remained of the taste is exhaled, the smell evaporates, the color alters, the figure is destroyed, the size increases, it becomes liquid, it heats, scarcely can one handle it, and when one strikes it, no sound is emitted. Does the same wax remain after this change? We must confess that it remains; none would judge otherwise. What then did I know so distinctly in this piece of wax? It could certainly be nothing of all that the senses brought to my notice, since all these things which fall under taste, smell, sight, touch, and hearing, are found to be changed, and yet the same wax remains.

Perhaps it was what I now think, viz., that this wax was not that sweetness of honey, nor that agreeable scent of flowers, nor that particular whiteness, nor that figure, nor that sound, but simply a body which a little while before appeared to me as perceptible under these forms, and which is now perceptible under others. But what, precisely, is it that I imagine when I form such conceptions? Let us attentively consider this, and, abstracting from all that does not belong to the wax, let us see what remains. Certainly nothing remains excepting a certain extended thing which is flexible and movable. But what is the meaning of flexible and movable? Is it not that I imagine that this piece of wax being round is capable of becoming square and of passing from a square to a triangular figure? No, certainly it is not that, since I imagine it admits of an infinitude of similar changes, and I nevertheless do not know how to compass the infinitude by my imagination, and consequently this conception which I have of the wax is not brought about by the faculty of imagination. What now is this extension? Is it not also unknown? For it becomes greater when the wax is melted, greater when it is boiled, and greater still when the heat increases; and I should not conceive [clearly] according to truth what wax is, if I did not think that even this piece that we are considering is capable of receiving more variations in extension than I have ever imagined. We must then grant that I could not even understand through the imagination what this piece of wax is, and that it is my mind (*entendement* F., *mens* L.) alone which perceives it. I say this piece of wax in particular, for as to wax in general it is yet clearer. But what is this piece of wax which cannot be understood excepting by the [understanding or] mind? It is certainly the same that I see, touch, imagine, and finally it is the same which I have always believed it to be from the beginning. But what must particularly be observed is that its perception is neither an act of vision, nor of touch, nor of imagination, and has never been such although it may have appeared formerly to be so, but only an intuition (*inspectio*) of the mind, which may be imperfect and confused as it was formerly, or clear and distinct as it is at present, according as my attention is more or less directed to the elements which are found in it, and of which it is composed.

Yet in the meantime I am greatly astonished when I consider [the great feebleness of mind] and its proneness to fall [insensibly] into error; for although without giving expression to my thoughts I consider all this in my own mind, words often impede me and I am almost deceived by the terms of ordinary language. For we say that we see the same wax, if it is present, and not that we simply judge that it is the same from its having the same color and figure. From this I should conclude that I knew the wax by means of vision and not simply by the intuition of the mind; unless by chance I remember that, when looking from a window and saying I see men who pass in the street, I really do not see them, but infer that what I see is men, just as I say that I see wax. And yet what do I see from the window but hats and coats which may cover automatic machines? Yet I judge these to be men. And similarly solely by the faculty of judgment which rests in my mind, I comprehend that which I believed I saw with my eyes.

A man who makes it his aim to raise his knowledge above the common should be ashamed to derive the occasion for doubting from the forms of speech invented by the vulgar; I prefer to pass on and consider whether I had a more evident and perfect conception of what the wax was when I first perceived it, and when I believed I knew it by means of the external senses or at least by the common sense (*sensus communis*) as it is called, that is to say by the imaginative faculty, or whether my present conception is clearer now that I have most carefully examined what it is, and in what way it can be known. It would certainly be absurd to doubt as to this. For what was there in this first perception which was distinct? What was there which might not as well have been perceived by any of the animals? But when I distinguish the wax from its external forms, and when, just as if I had taken from it its vestments, I consider it quite naked, it is certain that although some error may still be found in my judgment, I can nevertheless not perceive it thus without a human mind.

But finally what shall I say of this mind, that is, of myself, for up to this point I do not admit in myself anything but mind? What then, I who seem to perceive this piece of wax so distinctly, do I not know myself, not only with much more truth and certainty, but also with much more distinctness and clearness? For if I judge that the wax is or exists from the fact that I see it, it certainly follows much more clearly that I am or that I exist myself from the fact that I see it. For it may be that what I see is not really wax, it may also be that I do not possess eyes with which to see anything; but it cannot be that when I see, or (for I no longer take account of the distinction) when I think I see, that I myself who think am nought. So if I judge that the wax exists from the fact that I touch it, the same thing will follow, to wit, that I am; and if I judge that my imagination, or some other cause, whatever it is, persuades me that the wax exists, I shall still conclude the same. And what I have here remarked of wax may be applied to all other things which are external to me [and which are met with outside of me]. And further, if the [notion or] perception of wax has seemed to me clearer and more distinct, not only after the sight or the touch, but also after many other causes have rendered it quite manifest to me, with how much more [evidence] and distinctness must it be said that I now know myself, since all the reasons which contribute to the knowledge of wax, or any other body whatever, are yet better proofs of the nature of my mind! And there are so many other things in the mind itself which may contribute to the elucidation of its nature, that those which depend on body such as these just mentioned, hardly merit being taken into account.

But finally here I am, having insensibly reverted to the point I desired, for, since it is now manifest to me that even bodies are not properly speaking known by the senses or by the faculty of imagination, but by the understanding only, and since they are not known from the fact that they are seen or touched, but only because they are understood, I see clearly that there is nothing which is easier for me to know than my mind. But because it is difficult to rid oneself so promptly of an opinion to which one was accustomed for so long, it will be well that I should halt a little at this point, so that by the length of my meditation I may more deeply imprint on my memory this new knowledge.

Sixth meditation

OF THE EXISTENCE OF MATERIAL THINGS,
AND OF THE REAL DISTINCTION BETWEEN
THE SOUL AND BODY OF MAN

•   •   •

But now that I begin to know myself better, and to discover more clearly the author
of my being, I do not in truth think that I should rashly admit all the matters which
the senses seem to teach us, but, on the other hand, I do not think that I should
doubt them all universally.

And first of all, because I know that all things which I apprehend clearly and
distinctly can be created by God as I apprehend them, it suffices that I am able to
apprehend one thing apart from another clearly and distinctly in order to be certain
that the one is different from the other, since they may be made to exist in separation
at least by the omnipotence of God; and it does not signify by what power this separation is made in order to compel me to judge them to be different: and, therefore,
just because I know certainly that I exist, and that meanwhile I do not remark that
any other thing necessarily pertains to my nature or essence, excepting that I am a
thinking thing, I rightly conclude that my essence consists solely in the fact that I
am a thinking thing [or a substance whose whole essence or nature is to think]. And
although possibly (or rather certainly, as I shall say in a moment) I possess a body with
which I am very intimately conjoined, yet because, on the one side, I have a clear and
distinct idea of myself inasmuch as I am only a thinking and unextended thing, and as,
on the other, I possess a distinct idea of body, inasmuch as it is only an extended and
unthinking thing, it is certain that this I [that is to say, my soul by which I am what
I am], is entirely and absolutely distinct from my body, and can exist without it.

I further find in myself faculties employing modes of thinking peculiar to themselves, to wit, the faculties of imagination and feeling, without which I can easily
conceive myself clearly and distinctly as a complete being; while, on the other hand,
they cannot be so conceived apart from me, that is without an intelligent substance
in which they reside, for [in the notion we have of these faculties, or, to use the
language of the Schools] in their formal concept, some kind of intellection is comprised, from which I infer that they are distinct from me as its modes are from a
thing. I observe also in me some other faculties such as that of change of position,
the assumption of different figures and such like, which cannot be conceived, any
more than can the preceding, apart from some substance to which they are attached,
and consequently cannot exist without it; but it is very clear that these faculties, if it
be true that they exist, must be attached to some corporeal or extended substance, and
not to an intelligent substance, since in the clear and distinct conception of these there
is some sort of extension found to be present, but no intellection at all. There is
certainly further in me a certain passive faculty of perception, that is, of receiving
and recognizing the ideas of sensible things, but this would be useless to me [and
I could in no way avail myself of it], if there were not either in me or in some other
thing another active faculty capable of forming and producing these ideas. But this
active faculty cannot exist in me [inasmuch as I am a thing that thinks] seeing that

it does not presuppose thought, and also that those ideas are often produced in me without my contributing in any way to the same, and often even against my will; it is thus necessarily the case that the faculty resides in some substance different from me in which all the reality which is objectively in the ideas that are produced by this faculty is formally or eminently contained, as I remarked before. And this substance is either a body, that is, a corporeal nature in which there is contained formally [and really] all that which is objectively [and by representation] in those ideas, or it is God Himself, or some other creature more noble than body in which that same is contained eminently. But, since God is no deceiver, it is very manifest that He does not communicate to me these ideas immediately and by Himself, nor yet by the intervention of some creature in which their reality is not formally, but only eminently, contained. For since He has given me no faculty to recognize that this is the case, but, on the other hand, a very great inclination to believe [that they are sent to me or] that they are conveyed to me by corporeal objects, I do not see how He could be defended from the accusation of deceit if these ideas were produced by causes other than corporeal objects. Hence we must allow that corporeal things exist. However, they are perhaps not exactly what we perceive by the senses, since this comprehension by the senses is in many instances very obscure and confused; but we must at least admit that all things which I conceive in them clearly and distinctly, that is to say, all things which, speaking generally, are comprehended in the object of pure mathematics, are truly to be recognized as external objects.

As to other things, however, which are either particular only, as, for example, that the sun is of such and such a figure, etc., or which are less clearly and distinctly conceived, such as light, sound, pain and the like, it is certain that although they are very dubious and uncertain, yet on the sole ground that God is not a deceiver, and that consequently He has not permitted any falsity to exist in my opinion which He has not likewise given me the faculty of correcting, I may assuredly hope to conclude that I have within me the means of arriving at the truth even here. And first of all there is no doubt that in all things which nature teaches me there is some truth contained; for by nature, considered in general, I now understand no other thing than either God Himself or else the order and disposition which God has established in created things; and by my nature in particular I understand no other thing than the complexus of all the things which God has given me.

But there is nothing which this nature teaches me more expressly [nor more sensibly] than that I have a body which is adversely affected when I feel pain, which has need of food or drink when I experience the feelings of hunger and thirst, and so on; nor can I doubt there being some truth in all this.

Nature also teaches me by these sensations of pain, hunger, thirst, etc., that I am not only lodged in my body as a pilot in a vessel, but that I am very closely united to it, and so to speak so intermingled with it that I seem to compose with it one whole. For if that were not the case, when my body is hurt, I, who am merely a thinking thing, should not feel pain, for I should perceive this wound by the understanding only, just as the sailor perceives by sight when something is damaged in his vessel; and when my body has need of drink or food, I should clearly understand the fact without being warned of it by confused feelings of hunger and thirst. For all these sensations of hunger, thirst, pain, etc. are in truth none other than certain confused modes of thought which are produced by the union and apparent intermingling of mind and body.

.   .   .

SENSATIONS AND BRAIN PROCESSES

j. j. c. smart

This paper takes its departure from arguments to be found in U. T. Place's "Is Consciousness a Brain Process?" [1] I have had the benefit of discussing Place's thesis in a good many universities in the United States and Australia, and I hope that the present paper answers objections to his thesis which Place has not considered and that it presents his thesis in a more nearly unobjectionable form. This paper is meant also to supplement the paper "The 'Mental' and the 'Physical,'" by H. Feigl,[2] which in part argues for a similar thesis to Place's.

Suppose that I report that I have at this moment a roundish, blurry-edged afterimage which is yellowish toward its edge and is orange toward its center. What is it that I am reporting? One answer to this question might be that I am not reporting anything, that when I say that it looks to me as though there is a roundish yellowy-orange patch of light on the wall I am expressing some sort of *temptation,* the temptation to say that there *is* a roundish yellowy-orange patch on the wall (though I may know that there is not such a patch on the wall). This is perhaps Wittgenstein's view in the *Philosophical Investigations* (see §§ 367, 370). Similarly, when I "report" a pain, I am not really reporting anything (or, if you like, I am reporting in a queer sense of "reporting"), but am doing a sophisticated sort of wince. (See § 244: "The verbal expression of pain replaces crying and does not describe it." Nor does it describe anything else?) [3] I prefer most of the time to discuss an afterimage rather than a pain, because the word "pain" brings in something which is irrelevant to my purpose: the notion of "distress." I think that "He is in pain" entails "He is in distress," that is, that he is in a certain agitation-condition.[4] Similarly, to say "I am in pain"

J. J. C. Smart, "Sensations and Brain Processes" in *The Philosophy of Mind*, V. C. Chappell, ed., © 1962, pp. 60–72. Reprinted by permission of Prentice-Hall, Inc., Englewood Cliffs, New Jersey, and the author.

1 *British Journal of Psychology*, XLVII (1956), 44–50.

2 *Minnesota Studies in the Philosophy of Science*, Vol. II (Minneapolis: University of Minnesota Press, 1958), 370–497.

3 Some philosophers of my acquaintance, who have the advantage over me in having known Wittgenstein, would say that this interpretation of him is too behavioristic. However, it seems to me a very natural interpretation of his printed words, and whether or not it is Wittgenstein's real view it is certainly an interesting and important one. I wish to consider it here as a possible rival both to the "brain-process" thesis and to straight-out old-fashioned dualism.

4 Feigl, *op. cit.*, p. 428. Feigl uses the expression "nomological danglers" for the laws whereby the entities dangle: I have used the expression to refer to the dangling entities themselves.

may be to do more than "replace pain behavior": it may be partly to report something, though this something is quite nonmysterious, being an agitation-condition, and so susceptible of behavioristic analysis. The suggestion I wish if possible to avoid is a different one, namely that "I am in pain" is a genuine report, and that what it reports is an irreducibly psychical something. And similarly the suggestion I wish to resist is also that to say "I have a yellowish-orange afterimage" is to report something irreducibly psychical.

Why do I wish to resist this suggestion? Mainly because of Occam's razor. It seems to me that science is increasingly giving us a viewpoint whereby organisms are able to be seen as physicochemical mechanisms: it seems that even the behavior of man himself will one day be explicable in mechanistic terms. There does seem to be, so far as science is concerned, nothing in the world but increasingly complex arrangements of physical constituents. All except for one place: in consciousness. That is, for a full description of what is going on in a man you would have to mention not only the physical processes in his tissues, glands, nervous system, and so forth, but also his states of consciousness: his visual, auditory, and tactual sensations, his aches and pains. That these should be *correlated* with brain processes does not help, for to say that they are *correlated* is to say that they are something "over and above." You cannot correlate something with itself. You correlate footprints with burglars, but not Bill Sikes the burglar with Bill Sikes the burglar. So sensations, states of consciousness, do seem to be the one sort of thing left outside the physicalist picture, and for various reasons I just cannot believe that this can be so. That everything should be explicable in terms of physics (together of course with descriptions of the ways in which the parts are put together—roughly, biology is to physics as radio engineering is to electromagnetism) except the occurrence of sensations seems to me to be frankly unbelievable. Such sensations would be "nomological danglers," to use Feigl's expression.[4] It is not often realized how odd would be the laws whereby these nomological danglers would dangle. It is sometimes asked, "Why can't there be psychophysical laws which are of a novel sort, just as the laws of electricity and magnetism were novelties from the standpoint of Newtonian mechanics?" Certainly we are pretty sure in the future to come across new ultimate laws of a novel type, but I expect them to relate simple constituents: for example, whatever ultimate particles are then in vogue. I cannot believe that ultimate laws of nature could relate simple constituents to configurations consisting of perhaps billions of neurons (and goodness knows how many billion billions of ultimate particles) all put together for all the world as though their main purpose in life was to be a negative feedback mechanism of a complicated sort. Such ultimate laws would be like nothing so far known in science. They have a queer "smell" to them. I am just unable to believe in the nomological danglers themselves, or in the laws whereby they would dangle. If any philosophical arguments seemed to compel us to believe in such things, I would suspect a catch in the argument. In any case it is the object of this paper to show that there are no philosophical arguments which compel us to be dualists.

The above is largely a confession of faith, but it explains why I find Wittgenstein's position (as I construe it) so congenial. For on this view there are, in a sense, no sensations. A man is a vast arrangement of physical particles, but there are not, over and above this, sensations or states of consciousness. There are just behavioral facts about this vast mechanism, such as that it expresses a temptation (behavior disposition) to say "there is a yellowish-red patch on the wall" or that it goes through a sophisticated sort of wince, that is, says "I am in pain." Admittedly Wittgenstein says that though the sensation "is not a something," it is nevertheless "not a nothing either" (§ 304), but this need only mean that the word "ache" has a use. An ache is a thing, but only in the innocuous sense in which the plain man, in the first paragraph of Frege's *Foundations of Arithmetic,* answers the question "What is the number one?" by "a thing." It should be noted that when I assert that to say "I have a yellowish-orange afterimage" is to express a temptation to assert the physical-object statement "There is a yellowish-orange patch on the wall," I mean that saying "I have a yellowish-orange afterimage" is (partly) the exercise of the disposition [5] which is the temptation. It is not to *report* that I have the temptation, any more than is "I love you" normally a report that I love someone. Saying "I love you" is just part of the behavior which is the exercise of the disposition of loving someone.

Though for the reasons given above, I am very receptive to the above "expressive" account of sensation statements, I do not feel that it will quite do the trick. Maybe this is because I have not thought it out sufficiently, but it does seem to me as though, when a person says "I have an afterimage," he *is* making a genuine report, and that when he says "I have a pain," he *is* doing more than "replace pain-behavior," and that "this more" is not just to say that he is in distress. I am not so sure, however, that to admit this is to admit that there are nonphysical correlates of brain processes. Why should not sensations just be brain processes of a certain sort? There are, of course, well-known (as well as lesser-known) philosophical objections to the view that reports of sensations are reports of brain processes, but I shall try to argue that these arguments are by no means as cogent as is commonly thought to be the case.

Let me first try to state more accurately the thesis that sensations are brain processes. It is not the thesis that, for example, "afterimage" or "ache" means the same as "brain process of sort X" (where "X" is replaced by a description of a certain sort of brain process). It is that, in so far as "afterimage" or "ache" is a report of a process, it is a report of a process that *happens to be* a brain process. It follows that the thesis does not claim that sensation statements can be *translated* into statements about brain processes.[6] Nor does it claim that the logic of a sensation statement is the same as that of a brain-process statement. All it claims is that in so far as a sensation statement is a report of something, that something is in fact a brain process. Sensations are nothing over and above brain processes. Nations are nothing "over and above" citizens, but this does not prevent the logic of nation statements being very different from the logic of citizen statements, nor does it insure the translatability of nation statements into citizen statements. (I do not, however, wish to assert that the relation of sensation statements to brain-process statements is very like that of nation statements to citizen statements. Nations do not just *happen to be* nothing over and above citizens, for example. I bring in the "nations" example merely to make a negative point: that the fact that the logic of A-statements is different from that of B-statements does not insure that A's are anything over and above B's.)

---

[5] Wittgenstein did not like the word "disposition." I am using it to put in a nutshell (and perhaps inaccurately) the view which I am attributing to Wittgenstein. I should like to repeat that I do not wish to claim that my interpretation of Wittgenstein is correct. Some of those who knew him do not interpret him in this way. It is merely a view which I find myself extracting from his printed words and which I think is important and worth discussing for its own sake.

[6] See Place, *op. cit.,* p. 102, and Feigl, *op. cit.,* p. 390, near top.

Remarks on identity

When I say that a sensation is a brain process or that lightning is an electric discharge, I am using "is" in the sense of strict identity. (Just as in the—in this case necessary—proposition "7 is identical with the smallest prime number greater than 5.") When I say that a sensation is a brain process or that lightning is an electric discharge I do not mean just that the sensation is somehow spatially or temporally continuous with the brain process or that the lightning is just spatially or temporally continuous with the discharge. When on the other hand I say that the successful general is the same person as the small boy who stole the apples I mean only that the successful general I see before me is a time slice of the same four-dimensional object of which the small boy stealing apples is an earlier time slice. However, the four-dimensional object which has the general-I-see-before-me for its late time slice is identical in the strict sense with the four-dimensional object which has the small-boy-stealing-apples for an early time slice. I distinguish these two senses of "is identical with" because I wish to make it clear that the brain-process doctrine asserts identity in the *strict* sense.

I shall now discuss various possible objections to the view that the processes reported in sensation statements are in fact processes in the brain. Most of us have met some of these objections in our first year as philosophy students. All the more reason to take a good look at them. Others of the objections will be more recondite and subtle.

Objection 1. Any illiterate peasant can talk perfectly well about his afterimages, or how things look or feel to him, or about his aches and pains, and yet he may know nothing whatever about neurophysiology. A man may, like Aristotle, believe that the brain is an organ for cooling the body without any impairment of his ability to make true statements about his sensations. Hence the things we are talking about when we describe our sensations cannot be processes in the brain.

Reply. You might as well say that a nation of slugabeds, who never saw the Morning Star or knew of its existence, or who had never thought of the expression "the Morning Star," but who used the expression "the Evening Star" perfectly well, could not use this expression to refer to the same entity as we refer to (and describe as) "the Morning Star." [7]

You may object that the Morning Star is in a sense not the very same thing as the Evening Star, but only something spatiotemporally continuous with it. That is, you may say that the Morning Star is not the Evening Star in the strict sense of "identity" that I distinguished earlier.

There is, however, a more plausible example. Consider lightning. [8] Modern physical science tells us that lightning is a certain kind of electrical discharge due to ionization of clouds of water vapor in the atmosphere. This, it is now believed, is what

---

[7] Cf. Feigl, *op. cit.*, p. 439.
[8] See Place, *op. cit.*, p. 106; also Feigl, *op. cit.*, p. 438.

the true nature of lightning is. Note that there are not two things: a flash of lightning and an electrical discharge. There is one thing, a flash of lightning, which is described scientifically as an electrical discharge to the earth from a cloud of ionized water molecules. The case is not at all like that of explaining a footprint by reference to a burglar. We say that what lightning really is, what its true nature as revealed by science is, is an electrical discharge. (It is not the true nature of a footprint to be a burglar.)

To forestall irrelevant objections, I should like to make it clear that by "lightning" I mean the publicly observable physical object, lightning, not a visual sense-datum of lightning. I say that the publicly observable physical object lightning is in fact the electrical discharge, not just a correlate of it. The sense-datum, or rather the having of the sense-datum, the "look" of lightning, may well in my view be a correlate of the electrical discharge. For in my view it is a brain state *caused* by the lightning. But we should no more confuse sensations of lightning with lightning than we confuse sensations of a table with the table.

In short, the reply to Objection 1 is that there can be contingent statements of the form "A is identical with B," and a person may well know that something is an A without knowing that it is a B. An illiterate peasant might well be able to talk about his sensations without knowing about his brain processes, just as he can talk about lightning though he knows nothing of electricity.

Objection 2. It is only a contingent fact (if it is a fact) that when we have a certain kind of sensation there is a certain kind of process in our brain. Indeed it is possible, though perhaps in the highest degree unlikely, that our present physiological theories will be as out of date as the ancient theory connecting mental processes with goings on in the heart. It follows that when we report a sensation we are not reporting a brain process.

Reply. The objection certainly proves that when we say "I have an afterimage" we cannot *mean* something of the form "I have such and such a brain process." But this does not show that what we report (having an afterimage) is not *in fact* a brain process. "I see lightning" does not *mean* "I see an electrical discharge." Indeed, it is logically possible (though highly unlikely) that the electrical discharge account of lightning might one day be given up. Again, "I see the Evening Star" does not *mean* the same as "I see the Morning Star," and yet "The Evening Star and the Morning Star are one and the same thing" is a contingent proposition. Possibly Objection 2 derives some of its apparent strength from a "Fido"—Fido theory of meaning. If the meaning of an expression were what the expression named, then of course it *would* follow from the fact that "sensation" and "brain process" have different meanings that they cannot name one and the same thing.

Objection 3.[9] Even if Objections 1 and 2 do not prove that sensations are something over and above brain processes, they do prove that the qualities of sensations are something over and above the qualities of brain processes. That is, it may be

---

[9] I think this objection was first put to me by Professor Max Black. I think it is the most subtle of any of those I have considered, and the one which I am least confident of having satisfactorily met.

possible to get out of asserting the existence of irreducibly psychic processes, but not out of asserting the existence of irreducibly psychic *properties*. For suppose we identify the Morning Star with the Evening Star. Then there must be some properties which logically imply that of being the Morning Star, and quite distinct properties which entail that of being the Evening Star. Again, there must be some properties (for example, that of being a yellow flash) which are logically distinct from those in the physicalist story.

Indeed, it might be thought that the objection succeeds at one jump. For consider the property of "being a yellow flash." It might seem that this property lies inevitably outside the physicalist framework within which I am trying to work (either by "yellow" being an objective emergent property of physical objects, or else by being a power to produce yellow sense-data, where "yellow," in this second instantiation of the word, refers to a purely phenomenal or introspectible quality). I must therefore digress for a moment and indicate how I deal with secondary qualities. I shall concentrate on color.

First of all, let me introduce the concept of a normal percipient. One person is more a normal percipient than another if he can make color discriminations that the other cannot. For example, if A can pick a lettuce leaf out of a heap of cabbage leaves, whereas B cannot though he can pick a lettuce leaf out of a heap of beetroot leaves, then A is more normal than B. (I am assuming that A and B are not given time to distinguish the leaves by their slight difference in shape, and so forth.) From the concept of "more normal than" it is easy to see how we can introduce the concept of "normal." Of course, Eskimos may make the finest discriminations at the blue end of the spectrum, Hottentots at the red end. In this case the concept of a normal percipient is a slightly idealized one, rather like that of "the mean sun" in astronomical chronology. There is no need to go into such subtleties now. I say that "This is red" means something roughly like "A normal percipient would not easily pick this out of a clump of geranium petals though he would pick it out of a clump of lettuce leaves." Of course it does not exactly mean this: a person might know the meaning of "red" without knowing anything about geraniums, or even about normal percipients. But the point is that a person can be *trained* to say "This is red" of objects which would not easily be picked out of geranium petals by a normal percipient, and so on. (Note that even a color-blind person can reasonably assert that something is red, though of course he needs to use another human being, not just himself, as his "color meter.") This account of secondary qualities explains their unimportance in physics. For obviously the discriminations and lack of discriminations made by a very complex neurophysiological mechanism are hardly likely to correspond to simple and non-arbitrary distinctions in nature.

I therefore elucidate colors as powers, in Locke's sense, to evoke certain sorts of discriminatory responses in human beings. They are also, of course, powers to cause sensations in human beings (an account still nearer Locke's). But these sensations, I am arguing, are identifiable with brain processes.

Now how do I get over the objection that a sensation can be identified with a brain process only if it has some phenomenal property, not possessed by brain processes, whereby one-half of the identification may be, so to speak, pinned down?

Reply. My suggestion is as follows. When a person says, "I see a yellowish-orange afterimage," he is saying something like this: *"There is something going on which is like what is going on when* I have my eyes open, am awake, and there is an orange illuminated in good light in front of me, that is, when I really see an orange." (And there is no reason why a person should not say the same thing when he is having a veridical sense-datum, so long as we construe "like" in the last sentence in such a sense that something can be like itself.) Notice that the italicized words, namely "there is something going on which is like what is going on when," are all quasilogical or topic-neutral words. This explains why the ancient Greek peasant's reports about his sensations can be neutral between dualistic metaphysics or my materialistic metaphysics. It explains how sensations can be brain processes and yet how a man who reports them need know nothing about brain processes. For he reports them only very abstractly as "something going on which is like what is going on when. . . ." Similarly, a person may say "someone is in the room," thus reporting truly that the doctor is in the room, even though he has never heard of doctors. (There are not two people in the room: "someone" *and* the doctor.) This account of sensation statements also explains the singular elusiveness of "raw feels"—why no one seems to be able to pin any properties on them. Raw feels, in my view, are colorless for the very same reason that *something* is colorless. This does not mean that sensations do not have plenty of properties, for if they are brain processes they certainly have lots of neurological properties. It only means that in speaking of them as being like or unlike one another we need not know or mention these properties.

This, then, is how I would reply to Objection 3. The strength of my reply depends on the possibility of our being able to report that one thing is like another without being able to state the respect in which it is like. I do not see why this should not be so. If we think cybernetically about the nervous system we can envisage it as able to respond to certain likenesses of its internal processes without being able to do more. It would be easier to build a machine which would tell us, say on a punched tape, whether or not two objects were similar, than it would be to build a machine which would report wherein the similarities consisted.

Objection 4. The afterimage is not in physical space. The brain process is. So the afterimage is not a brain process.

Reply. This is an *ignoratio elenchi.* I am not arguing that the afterimage is a brain process, but that the experience of having an afterimage is a brain process. It is the *experience* which is reported in the introspective report. Similarly, if it is objected that the afterimage is yellowy-orange, my reply is that it is the experience of seeing yellowy-orange that is being described, and this experience is not a yellowy-orange something. So to say that a brain process cannot be yellowy-orange is not to say that a brain process cannot in fact be the experience of having a yellowy-orange afterimage. There is, in a sense, no such thing as an afterimage or a sense-datum, though there is such a thing as the experience of having an image, and this experience is described indirectly in material object language, not in phenomenal language, for there is no such thing. We describe the experience by saying, in effect, that it is like the experience we have when, for example, we really see a yellowy-orange patch on the wall. Trees and wallpaper can be green, but not the experience of seeing or imagining a tree or wallpaper. (Or if they are described as green or yellow this can only be in a derived sense.)

Objection 5. It would make sense to say of a molecular movement in the brain that it is swift or slow, straight or circular, but it makes no sense to say this of the experience of seeing something yellow.

Reply. So far we have not given sense to talk of experiences as swift or slow, straight or circular. But I am not claiming that "experience" and "brain process" mean the same or even that they have the same logic. "Somebody" and "the doctor" do not have the same logic, but this does not lead us to suppose that talking about somebody telephoning is talking about someone over and above, say, the doctor. The ordinary man, when he reports an experience, is reporting that something is going on, but he leaves it open as to what sort of thing is going on, whether in a material solid medium or perhaps in some sort of gaseous medium, or even perhaps in some sort of nonspatial medium (if this makes sense). All that I am saying is that "experience" and "brain process" may in fact refer to the same thing, and if so we may easily adopt a convention (which is not a change in our present rules for the use of experience words but an addition to them) whereby it would make sense to talk of an experience in terms appropriate to physical processes.

Objection 6. Sensations are private, brain processes are *public*. If I sincerely say, "I see a yellowish-orange afterimage," and I am not making a verbal mistake, then I cannot be wrong. But I can be wrong about a brain process. The scientist looking into my brain might be having an illusion. Moreover, it makes sense to say that two or more people are observing the same brain process but not that two or more people are reporting the same inner experience.

Reply. This shows that the language of introspective reports has a different logic from the language of material processes. It is obvious that until the brain-process theory is much improved and widely accepted there will be no *criteria* for saying "Smith has an experience of such-and-such a sort" *except* Smith's introspective reports. So we have adopted a rule of language that (normally) what Smith says goes.

Objection 7. I can imagine myself turned to stone and yet having images, aches, pains, and so on.

Reply. I can imagine that the electrical theory of lightning is false, that lightning is some sort of purely optical phenomenon. I can imagine that lightning is not an electrical discharge. I can imagine that the Evening Star is not the Morning Star. But it is. All the objection shows is that "experience" and "brain process" do not have the same meaning. It does not show that an experience is not in fact a brain process.

This objection is perhaps much the same as one which can be summed up by the slogan: "What can be composed of nothing cannot be composed of anything." [10] The argument goes as follows: On the brain-process thesis the identity between the brain process and the experience is a contingent one. So it is logically possible that there should be no brain process, and no process of any other sort either (no heart process, no kidney process, no liver process). There would be the experience but no

---

[10] I owe this objection to Dr. C. B. Martin. I gather that he no longer wishes to maintain this objection, at any rate in its present form.

"corresponding" physiological process with which we might be able to identify it empirically.

I suspect that the objector is thinking of the experience as a ghostly entity. So it is composed of something, not of nothing, after all. On his view it is composed of ghost stuff, and on mine it is composed of brain stuff. Perhaps the counter-reply will be [11] that the experience is simple and uncompounded, and so it is not composed of anything after all. This seems to be a quibble, for, if it were taken seriously, the remark "What can be composed of nothing cannot be composed of anything" could be recast as an a priori argument against Democritus and atomism and for Descartes and infinite divisibility. And it seems odd that a question of this sort could be settled a priori. We must therefore construe the word "composed" in a very weak sense, which would allow us to say that even an indivisible atom is composed of something (namely, itself). The dualist cannot really say that an experience can be composed of nothing. For he holds that experiences are something over and above material processes, that is, that they are a sort of ghost stuff. (Or perhaps ripples in an underlying ghost stuff.) I say that the dualist's hypothesis is a perfectly intelligible one. But I say that experiences are not to be identified with ghost stuff but with brain stuff. This is another hypothesis, and in my view a very plausible one. The present argument cannot knock it down a priori.

Objection 8. The "beetle in the box" objection (see Wittgenstein, *Philosophical Investigations*, § 293). How could descriptions of experiences, if these are genuine reports, get a foothold in language? For any rule of language must have public criteria for its correct application.

Reply. The change from describing how things are to describing how we feel is just a change from uninhibitedly saying "this is so" to saying "this looks so." That is, when the naïve person might be tempted to say, "There is a patch of light on the wall which moves whenever I move my eyes" or "A pin is being stuck into me," we have learned how to resist this temptation and say "It *looks as though* there is a patch of light on the wallpaper" or "It *feels as though* someone were sticking a pin into me." The introspective account tells us about the individual's state of consciousness in the same way as does "I see a patch of light" or "I feel a pin being stuck into me": it differs from the corresponding perception statement in so far as it withdraws any claim about what is actually going on in the external world. From the point of view of the psychologist, the change from talking about the environment to talking about one's perceptual sensations is simply a matter of disinhibiting certain reactions. These are reactions which one normally suppresses because one has learned that in the prevailing circumstances they are unlikely to provide a good indication of the state of the environment.[12] To say that something looks green to me is simply to say that my experience is like the experience I get when I see something that really is green. In my reply to Objection 3, I pointed out the extreme openness or generality of statements which report experiences. This explains why there is no language of private qualities. (Just as "someone," unlike "the doctor," is a colorless word.) [13]

11 Martin did not make this reply, but one of his students did.
12 I owe this point to Place, in correspondence.
13 The "beetle in the box" objection is, *if it is sound*, an objection to *any* view, and in particular the Cartesian one, that introspective reports are genuine reports. So it is no objection to a weaker thesis that I would be concerned to uphold, namely, that if introspective reports of "experiences" are genuinely reports, then the things they are reports of are in fact brain processes.

If it is asked what is the difference between those brain processes which, in my view, are experiences and those brain processes which are not, I can only reply that it is at present unknown. I have been tempted to conjecture that the difference may in part be that between perception and reception (in D. M. MacKay's terminology) and that the type of brain process which is an experience might be identifiable with MacKay's active "matching response." [14] This, however, cannot be the whole story, because sometimes I can perceive something unconsciously, as when I take a handkerchief out of a drawer without being aware that I am doing so. But at the very least, we can classify the brain processes which are experiences as those brain processes which are, or might have been, causal conditions of those pieces of verbal behavior which we call reports of immediate experience.

I have now considered a number of objections to the brain-process thesis. I wish now to conclude with some remarks on the logical status of the thesis itself. U. T. Place seems to hold that it is a straight-out scientific hypothesis. If so, he is partly right and partly wrong. If the issue is between (say) a brain-process thesis and a heart thesis, or a liver thesis, or a kidney thesis, then the issue is a purely empirical one, and the verdict is overwhelmingly in favor of the brain. The right sorts of things don't go on in the heart, liver, or kidney, nor do these organs possess the right sort of complexity of structure. On the other hand, if the issue is between a brain-or-liver-or-kidney thesis (that is, some form of materialism) on the one hand and epiphenomenalism on the other hand, then the issue is not an empirical one. For there is no conceivable experiment which could decide between materialism and epiphenomenalism. This latter issue is not like the average straight-out empirical issue in science, but like the issue between the nineteenth-century English naturalist Philip Gosse and the orthodox geologists and paleontologists of his day. According to Gosse, the earth was created about 4000 B.C. exactly as described in *Genesis,* with twisted rock strata, "evidence" of erosion, and so forth, and all sorts of fossils, all in their appropriate strata, just as if the usual evolutionist story had been true. Clearly this theory is in a sense irrefutable: no evidence can possibly tell against it. Let us ignore the theological setting in which Philip Gosse's hypothesis had been placed, thus ruling out objections of a theological kind, such as "what a queer God who would go to such elaborate lengths to deceive us." Let us suppose that it is held that the universe just *began* in 4004 B.C. with the initial conditions just everywhere as they were in 4004 B.C., and in particular that our own planet began with sediment in the rivers, eroded cliffs, fossils in the rocks, and so on. No scientist would ever entertain this as a serious hypothesis, consistent though it is with all possible evidence. The hypothesis offends against the principles of parsimony and simplicity. There would be far too many brute and inexplicable facts. Why are pterodactyl bones just as they are? No explanation in terms of the evolution of pterodactyls from earlier forms of life would any longer be possible. We would have millions of facts about the world as it was in 4004 B.C. that just have to be *accepted.*

The issue between the brain-process theory and epiphenomenalism seems to be of the above sort. (Assuming that a behavioristic reduction of introspective reports is not possible.) If it be agreed that there are no cogent philosophical arguments which force us into accepting dualism, and if the brain process theory and dualism are equally consistent with the facts, then the principles of parsimony and simplicity

[14] See his article "Towards an Information-Flow Model of Human Behaviour," *British Journal of Psychology,* XLVII (1956), 30–43.

seem to me to decide overwhelmingly in favor of the brain-process theory. As I pointed out earlier, dualism involves a large number of irreducible psychophysical laws (whereby the "nomological danglers" dangle) of a queer sort, that just have to be taken on trust, and are just as difficult to swallow as the irreducible facts about the paleontology of the earth with which we are faced on Philip Gosse's theory.

THE SELF AS AN ETHICAL CATEGORY

josiah royce

. . .

. . . The concept of the human Self, like the concept of Nature, comes to us, first, as an empirical concept, founded upon a certain class of experiences. But like the concept of Nature, the concept of the human Self tends far to outrun any directly observable present facts of human experience, and to assume forms which define the Self as having a nature and destiny which nò man directly observes or as yet can himself verify. If we consider first the empirical basis of the conception of the Self, and then the motives which lead us beyond our direct experience in our efforts to interpret the Self, we find, as a result of a general survey, three different kinds of conceptions of what it is that one means or ought to mean by the term Self as applied to the individual man. Each of these sorts of conception of the human Self is once more capable of a wide range of variation. Each can be used as a basis of different and, on occasion, of conflicting notions of what the Self is. But the three have their strong contrasts with one another, and each lays stress upon its own aspect of the facts.

First then, there is the more directly empirical way of conceiving the Self. In this sense, by a man's Self, you mean a certain totality of facts, viewed as more or less immediately given, and as distinguished from the rest of the world of Being. These facts may be predominantly corporeal facts, such as not only the man himself but also his neighbors may observe and comment upon. In this sense my countenance and my physical deeds, my body and my clothing—all these may be regarded as more or less a part of myself. My neighbor so views them. I may and very generally do so view them myself. If you changed or wholly removed such facts, my view of what I am would unquestionably alter. For to my neighbor as to myself, I am this man with these acts, this body, this presence. I cannot see these facts as my neighbor does, nor can he take my view of them. But we all regard such facts, not only as belonging to the Self, but as constituting, in a measure, what we regard as the Self of the present life. In addition to the external or corporeal Self of the phenomenal world, there is the equally empirical and phenomenal Self of the inner life, the series of states of consciousness, the feelings, thoughts, desires, memories, emotions, moods.

From "The Human Self" in Josiah Royce, *The World and the Individual* (New York: The Macmillan Company, 1913), Vol. II (*Nature, Man, and the Moral Order*), pp. 256–260, 265–277.

These, again, both my neighbor and myself regard as belonging to me, and as going to make up what I am. To be sure, within this inner empirical Self, we all make distinctions, now so freely illustrated, between what does and what does not essentially belong to the Self. When a man tells me a piece of interesting news, or expounds to me his opinions, I naturally regard the ideas which then arise in my mind as his and not as mine. I have to reflect in order to observe the somewhat recondite fact that the ideas which he seems to convey to me are in one sense ideas of my own, aroused in me according to laws of association. On the other hand, when I think alone by myself, the ideas which occur to me seem to be primarily mine. I have to reflect in order to remember how largely they have been derived from books, from nature, or from conversation, and how little I can call originally my own. And everywhere in the inner life, as it flits by, I observe a constantly shifting play of what I distinguish as more truly myself, from what I regard as relatively foreign. This feeling or purpose, this mood or this choice, is my own. That other emotion or idea is alien to me. It belongs to another. I do not recognize it as mine. The distinctions, thus empirically made, have no one rational principle. They are often founded upon the most arbitrary and unstable motives. The vacillation of common sense regarding the Self is endlessly repeated in my own inner life. I am constantly sure that there exists a Self, and that there I am, present to my own consciousness as the one whose experiences all these are, and who set myself over against the foreign non-Ego at every moment. But in distinguishing my empirical non-Ego from the Ego, I follow no stateable rule in my inner life from moment to moment. I even voluntarily play with the distinctions of Self and not-Self—dramatically address myself as if I were another, criticize and condemn myself, and upon occasion observe myself in a relatively impersonal fashion, as if I were a wholly alien personality. On the other hand, there are countless automatic processes that alter or that diminish the immediately given distinctions between Ego and non-Ego. The lover in Locksley Hall somewhat unobservantly tells us how

> Love took up the harp of life, and smote on all the chords with might;
> Smote the chord of Self that trembling, passed in music out of sight.

The lover admits that in the state which he thus describes, the Self, if invisible in the inner experience, was still able, most decidedly, to make itself heard. And, as a fact, one may well question whether, in view of what the lover in Locksley Hall tells us, the Self of this lover ever passed beyond his own range of vision at all, or was in the least out of sight. But the happy emotional confusion of self-consciousness here in question is familiar indeed to all who know joyous emotion. And in the sadder emotions one also has endless varieties in the intensity, clearness, and outlines which in our empirical consciousness characterize, from moment to moment, the relations of Self and not-Self.

But one may now ask, still dwelling upon the empirical Self, what manner of unity is left, in the midst of all these variations, as the unity that the concept of the Self can still be said to possess in our ordinary experience? And by what marks is the Self to be distinguished from the rest of the world? I reply, by pointing out a fact of central importance for the whole understanding of the empirical Ego. The variations of our experience and of our opinion concerning the empirical Self are countless in number. And no purely rational principle guides us in defining the Self from moment to moment in the world of common sense, or in distinguishing it from the not-Self. But there still does remain *one psychological principle* running through all these countless facts, and explaining, in general, both why they vary, and why yet we always suppose, despite the chaos of experiences, that the Self of our inner and outer life preserves a genuine, although to us hidden unity. This psychological principle is the simple one that, in us men, the distinction between Self and not-Self has a predominantly *Social origin,* and implies a more or less obviously present contrast between what we at any moment view as the life of another person, a fellow-being, or, as you may for short in general call him, an Alter, and the life, which by contrast with that of the Alter, is just then viewed as the life of the present Ego. To state the case more briefly, I affirm that our empirical self-consciousness, from moment to moment, depends upon a series of contrast-effects, whose psychological origin lies in our literal social life, and whose continuance in our present conscious life, whenever we are alone, is due to habit, to our memory of literal social relations, and to an imaginative idealization of these relations. Herein lies a large part of the explanation of those ambiguities of common sense upon which I have so far insisted.

·   ·   ·

The empirical Ego has now been, in outline, characterized. The source of its endless varieties has been sketched. Its unity has been found to be not, in our present form of existence, a fact that gets anywhere fully presented, as a rationally determined whole of life or of meaning. The empirical unity of the Ego depends merely upon a certain continuity of our social and of our inner life of experience and memory. The most stable feature about the empirical Ego, is that *sort of contrast in which it stands to the social world, literal and ideal, in which we live.* But precisely as here upon earth we have no abiding city, just so, in our present human form of consciousness, the Self is never presented except as a more or less imperfectly organized series of experiences, whose contrast with those of all other men fascinates us intensely, but whose final meaning can simply never be expressed in the type of experience which we men now have at our disposal. Were our life not hid in an infinitely richer and more significant life behind the veil, we who have once observed the essential fragmentariness of the empirical Ego would indeed have parted with our hope of a true Selfhood.

But the two other types of conception of the Self remain to be characterized. The one of these types, the second in our list of three, need detain us at this stage but little. The third type we shall at once so sketch as to define the momentous task that yet lies before us in our later lectures.

The second type of the conceptions of the Ego consists of all those views which regard the Self as in some metaphysical sense a real being, without defining the true Being of this Self in strictly idealistic terms. Such conceptions of the human Self as an entity are numerous in the history of philosophy. Their classification and further characterization will receive attention in the next lecture. For the moment I may exemplify them by mentioning as their most familiar examples, those views which conceive the human Self as, in some realistic sense, a distinct and independent entity. For such views the true Self is often essentially a Substance. Its individuality means that in essence it is separable, not only from the body, but from other souls. It preserves its unity despite the chaos of our experiences, just because in itself, and apart from all experience, it *is* One. It lies at the basis of our psychical life; and it must be sharply distinguished from the series of the states of consciousness, and even from their empirical organization. It is the source of all the order of our mental life; and all our self-consciousness is a more or less imperfect indication of its nature.

Such realistic views are well known to you. And you also know now why, without showing the least disrespect to their historical dignity, I can and must simply decline to follow them into their details in these lectures. They are all founded upon the realistic conception of Being. They must therefore all fall with that conception. Their true spirit indeed is often of far deeper moment than their mere letter. What doctrines of Soul-Substance have often meant to express, namely, a respect for human individuality, and an appreciation of its eternal worth in the life of the Universe, our own theory of the human individual will erelong develop in its own fashion. But taken literally, the doctrine that beneath or behind our conscious life there is a permanent substance, itself never either presented or presentable in consciousness, but real, and real in such wise that its Being is independent of any knowledge that from without refers to it—this whole doctrine, I say, simply perishes, for the purposes of our argument, together with Realism, and only its revised and purified inner meaning can reappear, in quite another guise, in the world of Idealism. Whatever the Self is, it is not a Thing. It is not, in Aristotle's or in Descartes' sense, a Substance. It is not a realistic entity of any type. Whether we men ever rightly come to know it or not, it exists only as somewhere known, and as a part of the fulfilment of meaning in the divine life. We are spared the trouble of proving this thesis here in detail, simply because our general proof of Idealism [1] has discounted the entire issue. We are not condemning Realism unheard; but only after the most careful analysis of its claims. But with Realism passes away every view which regards the real Self as anything but what every real fact in the universe is: A Meaning embodied in a conscious life, present as a relative whole within the unity of the Absolute life.

Well, there remains the third type of conception of the Self, namely, the strictly idealistic type. And precisely this type it was that I exemplified before, when I spoke of the way in which the Self has been distinguished, even by common sense, into a higher and a lower, a nobler and a baser Self. As stated in ordinary fashion, such concepts, as we saw, remain crude, and lead to frequent inconsistency. Revised with reference to the demands of our Idealism, the concept of the Self will assume a form which will reduce to unity these apparent inconsistencies of ethical common sense, and will also escape from bondage to those empirical complexities forced upon us by the Ego of the passing moment. We shall then see that the concept of the individual Self is, in its higher forms, in large measure an essentially Ethical Conception. And the third type of conceptions of the Ego consists of definitions which have always laid stress upon just this aspect. From this point of view, the Self is not a Thing, but a Meaning embodied in a conscious life. Its individuality, in case of any human being, implies the essential uniqueness of this life. Its unity, transcending as it does what we ever find presented in our present type of consciousness, implies that the true individual Self of any man gets its final expression in some form of consciousness different from that which we men now possess. The empirical variety, complexity, ambiguity, and inconsistency of our present consciousness of the Self, is to be explained as due to the fact that, in the moral order of the universe, no individual Self is or can be isolated, or in any sense sundered from other Selves, or

---

[1] This general proof is presented in the first series of Gifford lectures, comprising the first volume of *The World and the Individual*. [Eds.]

from the whole realm of the inner life of Nature itself. Consequently, even what is most individual about the Self never appears except in the closest connection with what transcends both the meaning and the life of the finite individual. Now, in our present form of conscious existence, we catch mere glimpses of the true meaning of the individual Self, as this meaning gets expressed in our deeds and in our ideals, and we also obtain equally fragmentary glimpses of the way in which this Self is linked to the lives of its fellows, or is dependent for its expression upon its relations to Nature, or is subject to the general moral order of the universe. These various transient flashes of insight constitute our present type of human experience. And it is their variety, their manifoldness, and their fragmentariness, which together are responsible for all those inconsistencies in our accounts of the Self—inconsistencies which our present discussion has been illustrating. But if you want to free yourself from hopeless bondage to such inconsistencies, you must look, not to some realistic conception of a Soul-Substance, but to some deeper account of the ethical meaning of our present life than we have yet formulated. And from this point of view we get a notion of Selfhood and of individuality which may be summarized at the present stage much as follows.

Our general idealistic theory asserts that the universe in its wholeness is the expression of a meaning in a life. What this view implies about every fragment and aspect of life that your attention may chance to select, or that your human experience may bring before you as the topic of inquiry, we have in former lectures repeatedly pointed out. Any instant of finite consciousness partially embodies a purpose, and so possesses its own Internal Meaning. Any such instant of finite consciousness also seeks, however, for other expression, for other objects, than are now present to just that instant, and so possesses what we have called its External Meaning. Our Idealism has depended, from the first, upon the thesis that the Internal and the External meaning of any finite process of experience are dependent each upon the other, so that if the whole meaning and intent of any finite instant of life is fully developed, and perfectly embodied, this Whole Meaning of the instant becomes identical with the Universe, with the Absolute, with the life of God. Even now, whatever you are or seek, the implied whole meaning of even your blindest striving is identical with the entire expression of the divine Will. And it is in this aspect of the world that we have found the unity of Being. On the other hand, as we have also seen, this unity of the world-life is no simple unity, such as the mystic sought. It is an infinitely complex unity. And of this complexity, of this wealth of life that the complete expression of even your most transient and finite glimpses of meaning implies, the foregoing facts about the Self are merely instances. If you are in company with a friend, the whole meaning of your thoughts and of your interests while you speak with him, not only requires for its complete expression his inner life as well as yours, and not only requires the genuine and conscious unity of his life and of yours by virtue of the ties of your friendship; but this same meaning also demands that, despite this unity of your life as friends—yes, even because of this unity—your friend and yourself shall remain also contrasted lives, whose unity includes and presupposes your variety as these two friends. For a friendship is not a simple unity of conscious life, but the unity of two conscious lives each of which contrasts itself with the other, and feels in the other's relative independence the fulfilment of its own purpose. And just so, when your meaning is not friendly but hostile, and when you stand in presence of your opponent, your rival, your enemy, your finite conscious meaning still implies, even in the midst of all its confused illusions, the demand that the very life of your enemy shall exist as the expression of your hostile intent to hold him as your real enemy, while nevertheless this life of his, other than your present conscious experience, and linked with your experience through the ties of meaning, is contrasted with your own life as the life that yours opposes and insofar seeks either to win over to your purposes, or to annul. Finite love and finite hate, and human experience of life in any form, always imply, therefore, that the will now present, but imperfectly expressed, in this passing instant, is genuinely expressed through other conscious life that, from the Absolute point of view, is at once in conscious unity with this instant's purpose, and also in conscious contrast with this instant's purpose.

Primarily then, the contrast of Self and not-Self comes to us as the contrast between the Internal and the External meaning of this present moment's purpose. In the narrowest sense, the Self is just your own present imperfectly expressed pulsation of meaning and purpose—this striving, this love, this hate, this hope, this fear, this inquiry, this inner speech of the instant's will, this thought, this deed, this desire—in brief, this idea taken as an Internal Meaning. In the widest sense, the not-Self is all the rest of the divine whole of conscious life—the Other, the outer World of expressed meaning taken as in contrast with what, just at this instant of our human form of consciousness, is observed, and, relatively speaking, possessed. Any finite idea is so far a Self; and I can, if you please, contrast my present Self with my past or my future Self, with yesterday's hopes or with tomorrow's deeds, quite as genuinely as with your inner life or with the whole society of which I am a member, or with the whole life of which our experience of Nature is a hint, or, finally, with the life of God in its entirety. In every such case, I take account of a true contrast between Self and not-Self. All such contrasts have a common character, namely, that in them an imperfectly expressed will is set over against its own richer expression, while stress is laid upon the fact—a perfectly genuine fact of Being—the fact that the whole expression always retains, and does not merely absorb or transmute, the very contrast between the finite Self and its desired or presupposed Other—its world of External Meanings. But if you ask how many such contrasts can be made, I reply, An infinite number. In countless ways can the Self of this instant's glimpse of conscious meaning be set into contrast with the not-Self, whose content may be the life of past and future, of friends and of enemies, of the social order and of Nature, of finite life in general, and of God's life in its wholeness.

But if the contrast of Self and not-Self can thus be defined with an infinite variety of emphasis, the unity of each of the two, Self and not-Self, can be emphasized in an equally infinite number of ways, whose depth and whose extent of meaning will vary with the range of life of which one takes account, and with the sort of contrast between Self and not-Self which one leaves still prominent over against the unity. Thus, in the familiar case of our ordinary social self-consciousness, I first view a certain realm of past and future experience as so bound up with the internal meaning of this instant's conscious experience, that I call this temporal whole of life the life of my own human Self, while I contrast this private existence of mine with that of my friends, my opponents, or of my other fellows, or with that of human society in general. The motives that lead to such an identification of the Self of the instant with a certain portion of that which is the instant's not-Self, namely, with a certain portion of past and future experience, are, as we have seen, extremely various, and in our empirical existence, both fickle and transitory. Whoever believes that he has any one rational principle for his usual identification of his past and future with the Self of this instant, has only to consider the psychological variations of self-consciousness before enumerated to discover his error. What will remain, after such an examination of the Self of common sense, will be the really deep and important persuasion that he *ought to possess* or to create for himself, despite this chaos, some one principle, some finally significant contrast, whereby he should be able, with an united and permanent meaning, to identify that portion of the world's life which is to be, in the larger sense, his own, and whereby he should become able to contrast with this, his larger Self, all the rest of the world of life.

And now this very consideration, this fact that one *ought to be able* to select from all the universe a certain portion of remembered and expected, of conceived and of intended life as that of his own true and individual Self, and that one ought to contrast with this whole of life, with this one's larger or truer individuality, the life of all other individual Selves, and the life of the Absolute in its wholeness—this consideration, I say, shows us at once the sense in which the Self is an Ethical Category. At this instant, as I have said, you can indeed identify the Self, if you please, with just the instant's passing glimpse of Internal Meaning; and in that case you can call all else the not-Self. To do this is to leave the Self a mere thrill of transient life—a fragment whose deeper meaning is wholly external to itself. But you can, and in general you do, first identify a remembered past, and an intended future, with the Self whose individuality is just now hinted to you; and this enlarged Self of memory and purpose you then oppose to a not-Self whose content is first the world of your fellowmen, and then the world of Nature and of the Absolute in its wholeness. Now what justification have you for this view of your larger Self? Apart from the capricious and shifting views of common sense, you can have, I reply, but one justification, namely this: You regard this present moment's life and striving as a glimpse of a certain task now assigned to you, the task of your life as friend, as worker, as loyal citizen, or in general as man, i.e., as one of God's expressions in human form. You conceive that, however far you might proceed towards the fulfilment of this task, however rich this individual life of yours might become, it would always remain, despite its unity with the world-life, in some true sense contrasted with the lives of your fellows, and with the life of God, just as now you stand in contrast to both. While your whole meaning is now, and will always remain one with the entire life of God, you conceive that this whole meaning expresses itself in the form of an articulate system of contrasting and cooperating lives, of which one, namely your own individual life, is more closely linked, in purpose, in task, in meaning, with the life of this instant, than is the life of any other individual. Or as you can say: "At this instant I am indeed one with God, in the sense that in Him my own absolute Selfhood is expressed. But God's will is expressed in a manifold life. And this life is a system of contrasted lives that are various even by virtue of their significant union. For true unity of meaning is best manifested in variety, just as the most intimate and wealthy friendship is that of strongly contrasting friends. And in the manifold lives that the world in its unity embodies, there is one, and only one, whose task is here hinted to me as my task, my life-plan—an ideal whose expression needs indeed the cooperation of countless other Selves, of a social order, of Nature, and of the whole universe, but whose individual significance remains contrasted with all other individual significance. If this is my task, if this is what my past life has meant, if this is what my future is to fulfil, if it is in this way that I do God's work, if my true relation to the Absolute is only to be won through the realization of this life-plan, and through the accomplishment of this unique task, then indeed I am a Self, and a Self who is nobody else, just precisely in so far as my life has this purpose and no other. *By this meaning of my life-plan, by this possession of an ideal, by this Intent always to remain another than my fellows despite my divinely planned unity with them—by this, and not by the possession of any Soul-Substance, I am defined and created a Self."*

Such, I say, will be your confession, if once you come to define the Self in the only genuine terms—namely, in ethical terms. If once you choose this definition, then the endless empirical varieties of self-consciousness, and the caprices of common sense, will not confuse you. You will know that since now we see through a glass darkly, you cannot expect at present to experience your human selfhood in any one consistent and final expression. But, too, you will know that you are a Self precisely insofar as you intend to accomplish God's will by becoming one; and that you are an individual precisely insofar as you purpose to do your Father's business in unique fashion, so that in this instant shall begin a work that can be finished only in eternity —a work that, however closely bound up it may be with all the rest of the divine life, still remains in its expression distinguishable from all this other life. You will indeed recognize that at every moment you receive from without, and from other Selves, the very experiences that give your Selfhood a chance to possess its meaning. You will know that of yourself alone you would be nothing. You will also know that as co-worker with your fellows, and as servant of God, you have a destiny of which our present life gives us but the dimmest hint.

·   ·   ·

4

IS THERE NOT A TRUTH
OF NATURALISM?

maurice merleau-ponty

Are we compelled in this direction by the preceding analyses? At least they lead to
the transcendental attitude, that is, to a philosophy which treats all conceivable
reality as an object of consciousness. It has seemed to us that matter, life, and mind
could not be defined as three orders of reality or three sorts of beings, but as three
planes of signification or three forms of unity. In particular, life would not be a force
which is added to physicochemical processes; its originality would be that of modes
of connection without equivalent in the physical domain, that of phenomena gifted
with a proper structure and which bind each other together according to a special
dialectic. In a living being, bodily movements and moments of behavior can be described and understood only in a specially tailored language and in accordance with
the categories of an original experience. And it is in this same sense that we have
recognized a psychological order and a mental order. But these distinctions then are
those of different regions of experience. We have been moved from the idea of a
nature as *omnitudo realitatis* to the idea of objects which could not be conceived in-
themselves (*en soi*), *partes extra partes,* and which are defined only by an idea in
which they participate, by a signification which is realized in them. Since the relations of the physical system and the forces which act upon it and those of the living
being and its milieu are not the external and blind relations of juxtaposed realities,
but dialectical relations in which the effect of each partial action is determined by
its signification for the whole, the human order of consciousness does not appear
as a third order superimposed on the two others, but as their condition of possibility
and their foundation.

The problem of the relations of the soul and the body seems to disappear from
the point of view of this absolute consciousness, milieu of the universe, as it did from
the critical point of view. There can be no question of a causal operation between
three planes of signification. One says that the soul "acts" on the body when it
happens that our conduct has a rational signification, that is, when it cannot be
understood by any play of physical forces or by any of the attitudes which are

characteristic of the vital dialectic. In reality the expression is improper: we have seen that the body is not a self-enclosed mechanism on which the soul could act from the outside. It is defined only by its functioning, which can present all degrees of integration. To say that the soul acts on the body is wrongly to suppose a univocal notion of the body and to add to it a second force which accounts for the rational signification of certain conducts. In this case it would be better to say that bodily functioning is integrated with a level which is higher than that of life and that the body has truly become a human body. Inversely one will say that the body has acted on the soul if the behavior can be understood without residue in terms of the vital dialectic or by known psychological mechanisms.

Here again one does not, properly speaking, have the right to imagine a transitive action from substance to substance, as if the soul were a constantly present force whose activity would be held in check by a more powerful force. It would be more exact to say that the behavior had become disorganized, leaving room for less integrated structures. In brief, the alleged reciprocal action is reducible to an alternation or a substitution of dialectics. Since the physical, the vital, and the mental individual are distinguished only as different degrees of integration, to the extent that man is completely identified with the third dialectic, that is, to the extent that he no longer allows systems of isolated conduct to function in him, his soul and his body are no longer distinguished.

If one supposes an anomaly of vision in El Greco, as has sometimes been done, it does not follow that the form of the body in his paintings, and consequently the style of the attitudes, admit of a "physiological explanation." When irremedial bodily peculiarities are integrated with the whole of our experience, they cease to have the dignity of a cause in us. A visual anomaly can receive a universal signification by the mediation of the artist and become for him the occasion of perceiving one of the "profiles" of human existence. The accidents of our bodily constitution can always play this revealing role on the condition that they become a means of extending our knowledge by the consciousness which we have of them, instead of being submitted to as pure facts which dominate us. Ultimately, El Greco's supposed visual disorder was conquered by him and so profoundly integrated into his manner of thinking and being that it appears finally as the necessary expression of his being much more than as a peculiarity imposed from the outside. It is no longer a paradox to say that "El Greco was astigmatic because he produced elongated bodies." [1] Everything which was accidental in the individual, that is, everything which revealed partial and independent dialectics without relationship to the total signification of his life, has been assimilated and centered in his deeper life. Bodily events have ceased to constitute autonomous cycles, to follow the abstract patterns of biology and psychology, and have received a new meaning. It is nevertheless the body, it will be said, which in the final analysis explains El Greco's vision; his liberty consisted only in justifying this accident of nature by infusing it with a metaphysical meaning. Unity does not furnish an adequate criterion of the liberty which has been won, since a man dominated by a complex, for example, and subject to the same psychological mechanism in all his undertakings, realizes unity in slavery. But here it is only a question of an apparent unity, of a stereotyped unity, which will not withstand an unexpected experience. It can be maintained only in a chosen milieu which the sick person has

---

[1] J. Cassou, Paris, Rieder, 1931, p. 35.

constructed for himself precisely by avoiding all situations in which the apparent coherence of his conduct would be disorganized. True unity on the contrary is recognized from the fact that it is not obtained by a restriction of the milieu. The same sensory or constitutional infirmity can be a cause of slavery if it imposes on man a type of vision and monotonous action from which he can no longer escape, or the occasion of a greater liberty if he makes use of it as an instrument. This supposes that he knows it instead of obeys it. For a being who lives at the simply biological level, it is a fatality.

For a being who has acquired the consciousness of self and his body, who has reached the dialectic of subject and object, the body is no longer the cause of the structure of consciousness; it has become the object of consciousness. Then one can no longer speak of a psychophysiological parallelism: only a disintegrated consciousness can be paralleled with physiological processes, that is, with a partial functioning of the organism. By acceding to true knowledge, by going beyond the dialectic of the living or the social being and its circumscribed milieu, by becoming the pure subject who knows the world objectively, man ultimately realizes that absolute consciousness with respect to which the body and individual existence are no longer anything but objects; death is deprived of meaning. Reduced to the status of object of consciousness, the body could not be conceived as an intermediary between "things" and the consciousness which knows them; and and since consciousness, having left the obscurity of instinct, no longer expresses the vital properties of objects but their *true* properties, the parallelism here is between consciousness and the true world which it knows directly. All the problems seem to be eliminated: the relations of the soul and the body—obscure as long as the body is treated in abstraction as a fragment of matter—are clarified when one sees in the body the bearer of a dialectic. Since the physical world and the organism can be conceptualized only as objects of consciousness or as significations, the problem of the relations of consciousness and its physical or organic "conditions" would exist only at the level of a confused thought which adheres to abstractions; it would disappear in the domain of truth in which the relation of the epistemological subject and its object alone subsists as original. This would constitute the only legitimate theme of philosophical reflection.

Let us consider a subject who turns his eyes toward a sensible object placed in front of him. Our preceding remarks permit us to say that the consecutive modification of his perceptual field is not an "effect" of the physical phenomenon of excitation or of the corresponding physiological phenomenon. We have shown that the most remarkable characteristics of the perceived object—its distance, its size, its apparent color—cannot be deduced from the physiological antecedents of perception. The modern theory of nerve functioning relates them to "transverse phenomena" of which there is neither a physical nor a physiological definition and which are conceived precisely by borrowing from the perceived world and the image of its descriptive properties. It becomes impossible to assign a *somatic* substrate of perception. The elaboration of stimuli and the distribution of motor influxes are accomplished according to articulations proper to the phenomenal field; what is introduced under the name of "transverse phenomena" is in reality the perceived field itself. For us this signifies that the living body and the nervous system, instead of being like annexes of the physical world in which the occasional causes of perception would be prepared, are "phenomena" emerging from among those which consciousness knows. Perceptual behavior, as science studies it, is not defined in terms of nerve cells and synapses;

it is not in the brain or even in the body; science has not been able to construct the "central sectors" of behavior from the outside like something which is enclosed within a cranial box; it can understand it only as a dialectic, the moments of which are not stimuli and movements but phenomenal objects and actions. The illusion of a transitive operation of stimuli on the sensory apparatus and of the latter "against" consciousness comes from the fact that we actualize separately the physical body, the body of the anatomists or even the organism of the physiologists, all of which are abstractions, snapshots taken from the functional body.

When its existence is accepted, the hallucinatory image is no longer treated in recent works as an isolated phenomenon which could be explained by some irritation of centers: it is connected with the whole of organic-vegetative functioning; which is to say that, rather than a perception without object, hallucination is a global conduct related to a global alteration of nerve functioning. It supposes a complete structure the description of which, like that of normal functioning, cannot be given in somatic terms. The somatic events do not act directly. Section of the optic nerve can be called the cause of blindness only in the sense in which Beethoven's deafness "explains" his last works. It provokes a change of the phenomenal field only by rendering impossible the functioning of the whole of the cortex under the action of luminous excitants. Is it this functioning itself which can be considered as a cause? No, if it is understood as the sum of the nerve events which are produced in each point of the cortex. This whole can be only the *condition of existence* of such and such a sensible scene; it accounts for the *fact that* I perceive but not for *that which* I perceive, not for the scene as such since this latter is presupposed in a complete definition of the nerve process. Everything takes place as if my perception opened out on a network of original significations. The passage of nerve influx in such and such conductors does not produce the visible scene; it does not even determine its structure in a univocal manner since it is organized according to laws of equilibrium which are neither those of a physical system nor those of the body considered as such. The somatic substrate is the passage point, the base of a dialectic. In the same way, nobody thinks of explaining the content of a delirium by its physiological conditions even though this form of consciousness presupposes *in existendo* some alteration of the brain.

Speaking generally, it seems that we are rejoining the critical idea. Whatever the external conditions may be—bodily, psychological, social—upon which the development of consciousness depends and even if it is only gradually constituted in history, the history itself out of which it comes is only a view which consciousness gives itself with regard to the acquired consciousness of self. A reversal of perspective is produced vis-à-vis adult consciousness: the historical becoming which prepared it was not *before* it, it is only *for* it; the time during which it progressed is no longer the time *of* its constitution, but a time which it constitutes; and the series of events is subordinated to its eternity. Such is the perpetual reply of critical thought to psychologism, sociologism, and historicism.

This discussion of causal thinking has seemed valid to us and we have pursued it at all levels of behavior. It leads, as we have just said, to the transcendental attitude. This is the first conclusion which we have to draw from the preceding chapters. It is not the only one, and it would even be necessary to say that this first conclusion stands in a relation of simple homonymy with a philosophy in the critical tradition. What is profound in the notion of "Gestalt" from which we started is not the idea of signification but that of *structure,* the joining of an idea and an existence which are indiscernible, the contingent arrangement by which materials begin to have meaning in our presence, intelligibility in the nascent state. The study of the reflex has shown us that the nervous system is the place in which an order without anatomical guarantee is realized by means of a continuing organization. It already permitted us to establish a rigorously reciprocal relation between function and substrate; there was not an area which was not linked in its functioning to the global activity of the nervous system, but also not a function which was not profoundly altered by the subtraction of a single one of these areas; and function was nothing outside the process which is delineated at each instant and which, based on the nerve mass, organizes itself.

The study of the "central sector" of behavior confirmed this ambiguity of bodily nature. On the one hand it appeared that absolutely no function could be localized, since each region plays a role only in the context of a global activity and since the diverse movements which it governs correspond to several modes of qualitatively distinct functioning rather than to several locally differentiated devices. On the other hand, it was equally clear that certain parts of the nerve substance are indispensable for the reception of certain stimuli, that the execution of certain movements are assigned to certain receptive regions or to some muscular ensemble, and that, even when nerve substance is not the depository of any special power of this kind, there can be no substitution for the nerve substance in each place. Thus, we were dealing less with two types of localization than with an inextricable intersecting of "horizontal" and "vertical" localizations—without the body being anywhere pure thing, *but also without it being anywhere pure idea.* It is not possible to designate separate contributions of the visual and auditive regions of the brain; both function only with the center; and integral thinking transfigures the hypothetical "visual contents" and "auditive contents" to the point of rendering them unrecognizable; but also the alteration of one of these regions is manifested in thought by a determinate deficit: it is the intuition of simultaneous wholes or that of successive wholes which becomes impossible. Thus the integration of the optic or auditive regions in a functional whole, although it infuses the corresponding "contents" with a new signification, does not annul their specificity; it uses and sublimates it.

For life, as for the mind, there is no past which is absolutely past; "the moments which the mind seems to have behind it are also borne in its present depths." [2] Higher behavior retains the subordinated dialectics in the present depths of its existence, from that of the physical system and its topographical conditions to that of the organism and its "milieu." They are not recognizable in the whole when it functions correctly, but the disintegration in case of partial lesion attests to their imminence. There is no essence of thinking which would receive the particular forms of "visual thought" and "auditive thought" by a contingency of our nerve organization and as a condition of existence. The alleged conditions of existence are indiscernible in the whole with which they collaborate *and reciprocally the essence of the whole cannot be concretely conceptualized without them and without its constitutive history.* Consequently, the relations of matter and form in the object-organism and the relations of the soul and body were found to be conceived differently than in critical thought.

<hr/>

2 Hegel, *Vorlesungen über die Philosophie der Geschichte,* in G. Lasson (ed.), *Hegels Sammtliche Werke kritische Ausgabe,* Leipzig, Meiner, 1905.

While critical philosophy, having step by step repressed quality and existence— residues of its ideal analysis—to place them finally in a matter about which nothing can be thought and which is for us therefore as if it were not, deploys a homogeneous activity of the understanding from one end of knowledge to the other; each "formation" (*mise en forme*) appears to us on the contrary to be an event in the world of ideas, the institution of a new dialectic, the opening of a new region of phenomena, and the establishment of a new constitutive layer which eliminates the preceding one as isolated moment, but conserves and integrates it. While critical thought pushed the problem of the relations of the soul and body back step by step by showing that we never deal with a body in-itself (*en soi*) but with a body for-a-consciousness and that thus we never have to put consciousness in contact with an opaque and foreign reality, for us consciousness experiences its inherence in an organism at each moment; for it is not a question of an inherence in material apparatuses, which as a matter of fact can be only *objects* for consciousness, but of a presence to consciousness of its proper history and of the dialectical stages which it has traversed.

Therefore, we could not accept any of the materialistic models to represent the relations of the soul and body—but neither could we accept the mentalistic models, for example, the Cartesian metaphor of the artisan and his tool. An organ cannot be compared to an instrument, as if it existed and could be conceived apart from integral functioning, nor the mind to an artisan who uses it: this would be to return to a wholly external relation like that of the pilot and his ship which was rightly rejected by Descartes. The mind does not use the body, but realizes itself through it while at the same time transferring the body outside of physical space. When we were describing the structures of behavior it was indeed to show that they are irreducible to the dialectic of physical stimulus and muscular contraction and that in this sense behavior, far from being a thing which exists in-itself (*en soi*), is a whole significative for a consciousness which considers it; but it was at the same time and reciprocally to make manifest in "expressive conduct" the *view of a consciousness* under our eyes, to show a mind which *comes into the world.*

Doubtless it is understood why we cannot even accept without reservations a relation of expression between the soul and the body comparable to that of the concept and the word, nor define the soul as the "meaning of the body," the body as the "manifestation of the soul." These formulae have the inconvenience of evoking two terms, solidary perhaps, but external to each other and the relation of which would be invariable. But sometimes our body manifests externally an intention arising from a dialectic which is higher than biology; sometimes, by a play of mechanisms which its past life has built up, it limits itself to mimicking intentions which it *does not have* any longer, as do the movements of a dying person for example; from one case to the other the relation of the soul and the body and even the terms themselves are modified depending on whether the "formation" succeeds or fails and whether the inertia of the subordinated dialectics allows itself to be surmounted or not. Our body does not always have meaning, and our thoughts, on the other hand—in timidity for example—do not always find in it the plenitude of their vital expression. In these cases of disintegration, the soul and the body are apparently distinct; and this is the truth of dualism. But the soul, if it possesses no means of expression—one should say rather, no means of actualizing itself—soon ceases to be *anything whatsoever* and in particular ceases to be the soul, as the thought of the aphasic weakens and becomes dissolved; the body which loses its meaning soon ceases to be a living body and falls back into the state of a physicochemical mass; it arrives at non-meaning only by dying. The two terms can never be distinguished absolutely without ceasing to be; thus their empirical connection is based on the original operation which establishes a meaning in a fragment of matter and makes it live, appear and be in it. In returning to this *structure* as the fundamental reality, we are rendering comprehensible both the distinction and the union of the soul and the body.

There is always a duality which reappears at one level or another: hunger or thirst prevents thought or feelings; the properly sexual dialectic ordinarily reveals itself through a passion; integration is never absolute and it always fails—at a higher level in the writer, at a lower level in the aphasic. There always comes a moment when we divest ourselves of a passion because of fatigue or self-respect. This duality is not a simple fact; it is founded in principle—all integration presupposing the normal functioning of subordinated formations, which always demand their own due.

But it is not a duality of substances; or, in other words, the notions of soul and body must be relativized: there is the body as mass of chemical components in interaction, the body as dialectic of living being and its biological milieu, and the body as dialectic of social subject and his group; even all our habits are an impalpable body for the ego of each moment. Each of these degrees is soul with respect to the preceding one, body with respect to the following one. The body in general is an ensemble of paths already traced, of powers already constituted; the body is the acquired dialectical soil upon which a higher "formation" is accomplished, and the soul is the meaning which is then established. The relations of the soul and the body can indeed be compared to those of concept and word, but on the condition of perceiving, beneath the separated products, the constituting operation which joins them and of rediscovering, beneath the empirical languages—the external accompaniment or contingent clothing of thought—the living *word* which is its unique actualization, in which the meaning is formulated for the first time and thus establishes itself as meaning and becomes available for later operations.

In this way our analyses have indeed led us to the ideality of the body, but it was a question of an idea which proffers itself and even constitutes itself in the contingency of existence. By a natural development the notion of "Gestalt" led us back to its Hegelian meaning, that is, to the concept before it has become consciousness of self. Nature, we said, is the exterior of a concept. But precisely the concept as concept has no exterior and the Gestalt still had to be conceptualized as unity of the interior and exterior, of nature and idea. Correlatively the consciousness *for* which the Gestalt exists was not intellectual consciousness but perceptual experience. Thus, it is perceptual consciousness which must be interrogated in order to find in it a definitive clarification. Let us limit ourselves here to indicating how the status of the object, the relations of form and matter, those of soul and body, and the individuality and plurality of consciousnesses are founded in it.

I cannot simply identify what I perceive and the thing itself. The real color of the object which I look at is and will always remain known to myself alone. I have no means whatsoever of knowing if the colored impression which it gives to others is identical to my own. Our intersubjective confrontations bear only upon the intelligible structure of the perceived world: I can assure myself that another viewer employs the same word as I to designate the color of this object and the same word, on the other hand, to qualify a series of other objects which I also call red objects. But, the relationships being conserved, it could happen that the scale of colors which he sees is completely different from mine. However, it is when objects give me the unique impression of the "sensed," when they have that direct manner of taking hold of me, that I say they are existing. It follows from this that perception, as knowledge of existing things, is an individual consciousness and not the consciousness in general of which we were speaking above. This sensible mass in which I live when I stare at a sector of the field without trying to recognize it, the "this" which my consciousness wordlessly intends, is not a signification or an idea, although subsequently it can serve as base for acts of logical explicitation and verbal expression. Already when I name the perceived or when I recognize it *as* a chair or tree, I substitute the subsumption under a concept for the experience of a fleeting reality; even when I pronounce the word "this," I already relate a singular and lived existence to the essence of lived existence. But these acts of expression or reflection intend an original text which cannot be deprived of meaning.

The signification which I find in a sensible whole was already adherent in it. When I "see" a triangle, my experience would be very poorly described by saying that I conceive or comprehend the triangle with respect to certain sensible givens. The signification is embodied. It is here and now that I perceive this triangle as such, while conception gives it to me as an eternal being whose meaning and properties, as Descartes said, owe nothing to the fact that I perceive it. It is not only the matter of perception which comes off the thing as it were and becomes a content of my individual consciousness. In a certain manner, the form also makes up a part of the psychological individual, or rather is related to it; and *this reference is included in its very meaning,* since it is the form *of* this or that thing which presents itself to me here and now and since this encounter, which is revealed to me by perception, does not in the least concern the proper nature of the thing and is, on the contrary, an episode of my life. If two subjects placed near each other look at a wooden cube, the total structure of the cube is the same for both; it has the value of intersubjective truth and this is what they both express in saying that there is a cube there. But it is not the same sides of the cube which, in each of them, are strictly seen and sensed.

We have said that this "perspectivism" of perception is not an indifferent fact, since without it the two subjects would not be aware of perceiving an existent cube subsisting beyond the sensible contents. If all the sides of the cube could be known at once, I would no longer be dealing with a thing which offers itself for inspection little by little, but with an idea which my mind would truly possess. This is what happens when I think of objects which I hold to be existent without actually perceiving them. In affirming that they continue to exist, I mean that a properly placed psychophysical subject would see this or that sensible sight, articulated in this or that way and connected with the view which I perceive here and now by such and such objective transitions.

But this *knowing about* the world must not be confused with my *perception of* this or that segment of the world and its immediate horizon. The objects which do not belong to the circle of the perceived exist in the sense in which truths do not cease to be true when I am not thinking about them: their mode of being is one of logical necessity and not of "reality." For I certainly suppose a "perspectivism" in them also, and it is essential to them to present themselves to a viewer through a multiplicity of "profiles." But since I do not perceive them, it is a question of a perspectivism in idea and of an essence of the viewer; the relation of the one to the other is itself a relation of significations. These objects belong therefore to the order of significations and not to that of existences.[3] A perception which would be coextensive with sensible things is inconceivable; and it is not physically but logically that it is impossible. For there to be perception, that is, apprehension of an existence, it is absolutely necessary that the object not be completely given to the look which rests on it, that aspects intended but not possessed in the present perception be kept in reserve. A seeing which would not take place from a certain point of view and which would give us, for example, all the sides of a cube at once is a pure contradiction in terms; for, in order to be visible all together, the sides of a wooden cube would have to be transparent, that is, would cease to be the sides of a wooden cube. And if each of the six sides of a transparent cube were visible as square, it is not a cube which we would be seeing. Thus the Bergsonian idea of a "pure perception," that is, adequate to the object or identical with it, is inconsistent. It is the cube as signification or geometrical idea which is made of six equal sides. The relation—unique and characteristic of existing things—of the "aspects" to the total object is not a logical relation like that of sign to signification: the sides of the chair are not its "signs," but precisely the sides.

In the same way the phenomena of my body should be distinguished from purely logical significations. What differentiates it from external things even as they are presented in lived perception is the fact that it is not, like them, accessible to an unlimited inspection. When it is a question of an external thing, I know that by changing place I could see the sides which are hidden from me; by occupying the position which was that of my neighbor a moment ago, I could obtain a new perspectival view and give a verbal account which would concur with the description of the object which my neighbor gave a moment ago. I do not have the same liberty with my body. I know very well that I will never see my eyes directly and that, even in a mirror, I cannot grasp their movement and their living expression. For me, my retinas are an absolute unknowable. This is, after all, only a particular case of the perspectival character of perception.

To say that I have a body is simply another way of saying that my knowledge is an individual dialectic in which intersubjective objects appear, that these objects, when they are given to knowledge in the mode of actual existence, present themselves to it by successive aspects which cannot coexist; finally, it is a way of saying that one of them offers itself obstinately "from the same side" without my being able to go around it. Reservation made for its image which mirrors give me (but *this image moves* as soon as I try to see it from different points of view, by leaning the head to the right and left; it is not a true "thing"), my body as given to me by sight is broken at the height of the shoulders and terminates in a tactile-muscular object. I am told that an object is visible for others in this lacuna in which my head is located; science teaches that organs, a brain and—each time that I perceive an external thing—"nerve influxes" in this visible object would be found by means of analyses. I will never see anything of all that. I could never make an actually present experience of my body adequately correspond to the signification, "human body," as it is given to me

[3] We reserve the question of whether there is not, as Heidegger suggests, a perception of the *world*, that is, a manner of acceding to an indefinite field of objects which gives them in their reality. What is certain is that the perceived is not limited to that which strikes my eyes. When I am sitting at my desk, the space is closed behind me not only in idea but also in reality. Even if the horizon of the perceived can be expanded to the limits of the world, the perceptual consciousness of the world as existing remains distinct from the intellectual consciousness of the world as object of an infinity of true judgments.

by science and witnesses. There are entities which will always remain pure significations for me under some of their aspects and which will never be offered to other
than lacunary perception. In itself, this structure is not much more mysterious than
that of external objects with which, moreover, it is one: how could I receive an
object "in a certain direction" if I, the perceiving subject, were not in some way hidden
in one of my phenomena, one which envelops me since I cannot go around it? Two
points are necessary for determining a direction.

We have not completely described the structure of the body proper, which also
includes an affective perspective, the importance of which is evident. But the preceding is sufficient to show that there is no enigma of "my body," nothing inexpressible
in its relation to myself. It is true that, by describing it, we are transforming into
signification the lived perspective which by definition is not one. But this alogical
essence of perceived beings can be clearly designated: one will say, for example, that
to offer themselves through profiles which I do not possess as I possess an idea is included in the idea of perceived being and of the body.

                                             •   •   •

5

DESCARTES' MYTH

gilbert ryle

1   The official doctrine

There is a doctrine about the nature and place of minds which is so prevalent among theorists and even among laymen that it deserves to be described as the official theory. Most philosophers, psychologists, and religious teachers subscribe, with minor reservations, to its main articles and, although they admit certain theoretical difficulties in it, they tend to assume that these can be overcome without serious modifications being made to the architecture of the theory. It will be argued here that the central principles of the doctrine are unsound and conflict with the whole body of what we know about minds when we are not speculating about them.

The official doctrine, which hails chiefly from Descartes, is something like this. With the doubtful exceptions of idiots and infants in arms every human being has both a body and a mind. Some would prefer to say that every human being is both a body and a mind. His body and his mind are ordinarily harnessed together, but after the death of the body his mind may continue to exist and function.

Human bodies are in space and are subject to the mechanical laws which govern all other bodies in space. Bodily processes and states can be inspected by external observers. So a man's bodily life is as much a public affair as are the lives of animals and reptiles and even as the careers of trees, crystals, and planets.

But minds are not in space, nor are their operations subject to mechanical laws. The workings of one mind are not witnessable by other observers; its career is private. Only I can take direct cognizance of the states and processes of my own mind. A person therefore lives through two collateral histories, one consisting of what happens in and to his body, the other consisting of what happens in and to his mind. The first is public, the second private. The events in the first history are events in the physical world, those in the second are events in the mental world.

It has been disputed whether a person does or can directly monitor all or only some of the episodes of his own private history; but, according to the official doctrine, of at least some of these episodes he has direct and unchallengeable cognizance. In

From Gilbert Ryle, *The Concept of Mind* (New York: Barnes & Noble, Inc., 1949), Chap. I, pp. 11–23. Reprinted by permission of the publisher and Hutchinson & Co. Ltd.

consciousness, self-consciousness, and introspection he is directly and authentically apprised of the present states and operations of his mind. He may have great or small uncertainties about concurrent and adjacent episodes in the physical world, but he can have none about at least part of what is momentarily occupying his mind.

It is customary to express this bifurcation of his two lives and of his two worlds by saying that the things and events which belong to the physical world, including his own body, are external, while the workings of his own mind are internal. This antithesis of outer and inner is of course meant to be construed as a metaphor, since minds, not being in space, could not be described as being spatially inside anything else, or as having things going on spatially inside themselves. But relapses from this good intention are common and theorists are found speculating how stimuli, the physical sources of which are yards or miles outside a person's skin, can generate mental responses inside his skull, or how decisions framed inside his cranium can set going movements of his extremities.

Even when "inner" and "outer" are construed as metaphors, the problem how a person's mind and body influence one another is notoriously charged with theoretical difficulties. What the mind wills, the legs, arms, and the tongue execute; what affects the ear and the eye has something to do with what the mind perceives; grimaces and smiles betray the mind's moods and bodily castigations lead, it is hoped, to moral improvement. But the actual transactions between the episodes of the private history and those of the public history remain mysterious, since by definition they can belong to neither series. They could not be reported among the happenings described in a person's autobiography of his inner life, but nor could they be reported among those described in some one else's biography of that person's overt career. They can be inspected neither by introspection nor by laboratory experiment. They are theoretical shuttlecocks which are forever being bandied from the physiologist back to the psychologist and from the psychologist back to the physiologist.

Underlying this partly metaphorical representation of the bifurcation of a person's two lives there is a seemingly more profound and philosophical assumption. It is assumed that there are two different kinds of existence or status. What exists or happens may have the status of physical existence, or it may have the status of mental existence. Somewhat as the faces of coins are either heads or tails, or somewhat as living creatures are either male or female, so, it is supposed, some existing is physical existing, other existing is mental existing. It is a necessary feature of what has physical existence that it is in space and time; it is a necessary feature of what has mental existence that it is in time but not in space. What has physical existence is composed of matter, or else is a function of matter; what has mental existence consists of consciousness, or else is a function of consciousness.

There is thus a polar opposition between mind and matter, an opposition which is often brought out as follows. Material objects are situated in a common field, known as "space," and what happens to one body in one part of space is mechanically connected with what happens to other bodies in other parts of space. But mental happenings occur in insulated fields, known as "minds," and there is, apart maybe from telepathy, no direct causal connection between what happens in one mind and what happens in another. Only through the medium of the public physical world can the mind of one person make a difference to the mind of another. The mind is its own place and in his inner life each of us lives the life of a ghostly Robinson Crusoe. People can see, hear, and jolt one another's bodies, but they are irremediably blind and deaf to the workings of one another's minds and inoperative upon them.

What sort of knowledge can be secured of the workings of a mind? On the one side, according to the official theory, a person has direct knowledge of the best imaginable kind of the workings of his own mind. Mental states and processes are (or are normally) conscious states and processes, and the consciousness which irradiates them can engender no illusions and leaves the door open for no doubts. A person's present thinkings, feelings, and willings, his perceivings, rememberings, and imaginings are intrinsically "phosphorescent"; their existence and their nature are inevitably betrayed to their owner. The inner life is a stream of consciousness of such a sort that it would be absurd to suggest that the mind whose life is that stream might be unaware of what is passing down it.

True, the evidence adduced recently by Freud seems to show that there exist channels tributary to this stream, which run hidden from their owner. People are actuated by impulses the existence of which they vigorously disavow; some of their thoughts differ from the thoughts which they acknowledge; and some of the actions which they think they will to perform they do not really will. They are thoroughly gulled by some of their own hypocrisies and they successfully ignore facts about their mental lives which on the official theory ought to be patent to them. Holders of the official theory tend, however, to maintain that anyhow in normal circumstances a person must be directly and authentically seized of the present state and workings of his own mind.

Besides being currently supplied with these alleged immediate data of consciousness, a person is also generally supposed to be able to exercise from time to time a special kind of perception, namely inner perception, or introspection. He can take a (non-optical) "look" at what is passing in his mind. Not only can he view and scrutinize a flower through his sense of sight and listen to and discriminate the notes of a bell through his sense of hearing; he can also reflectively or introspectively watch, without any bodily organ of sense, the current episodes of his inner life. This self-observation is also commonly supposed to be immune from illusion, confusion, or doubt. A mind's reports of its own affairs have a certainty superior to the best that is possessed by its reports of matters in the physical world. Sense perceptions can, but consciousness and introspection cannot, be mistaken or confused.

On the other side, one person has no direct access of any sort to the events of the inner life of another. He cannot do better than make problematic inferences from the observed behavior of the other person's body to the states of mind which, by analogy from his own conduct, he supposes to be signalized by that behavior. Direct access to the workings of a mind is the privilege of that mind itself; in default of such privileged access, the workings of one mind are inevitably occult to everyone else. For the supposed arguments from bodily movements similar to their own to mental workings similar to their own would lack any possibility of observational corroboration. Not unnaturally, therefore, an adherent of the official theory finds it difficult to resist this consequence of his premises, that he has no good reason to believe that there do exist minds other than his own. Even if he prefers to believe that to other human bodies there are harnessed minds not unlike his own, he cannot claim to be able to discover their individual characteristics, or the particular things that they undergo and do. Absolute solitude is on this showing the ineluctable destiny of the soul. Only our bodies can meet.

As a necessary corollary of this general scheme there is implicitly prescribed a special way of construing our ordinary concepts of mental powers and operations. The verbs, nouns, and adjectives, with which in ordinary life we describe the wits, characters, and higher-grade performances of the people with whom we have to do, are required to be construed as signifying special episodes in their secret histories, or else as signifying tendencies for such episodes to occur. When someone is described as knowing, believing, or guessing something, as hoping, dreading, intending, or shirking something, as designing this or being amused at that, these verbs are supposed to denote the occurrence of specific modifications in his (to us) occult stream of consciousness. Only his own privileged access to this stream in direct awareness and introspection could provide authentic testimony that these mental-conduct verbs were correctly or incorrectly applied. The onlooker, be he teacher, critic, biographer, or friend, can never assure himself that his comments have any vestige of truth. Yet it was just because we do in fact all know how to make such comments, make them with general correctness and correct them when they turn out to be confused or mistaken, that philosophers found it necessary to construct their theories of the nature and place of minds. Finding mental-conduct concepts being regularly and effectively used, they properly sought to fix their logical geography. But the logical geography officially recommended would entail that there could be no regular or effective use of these mental-conduct concepts in our descriptions of, and prescriptions for, other people's minds.

2   The absurdity of the official doctrine

Such in outline is the official theory. I shall often speak of it, with deliberate abusiveness, as "the dogma of the Ghost in the Machine." I hope to prove that it is entirely false, and false not in detail but in principle. It is not merely an assemblage of particular mistakes. It is one big mistake and a mistake of a special kind. It is, namely, a category-mistake. It represents the facts of mental life as if they belonged to one logical type or category (or range of types or categories), when they actually belong to another. The dogma is therefore a philosopher's myth. In attempting to explode the myth I shall probably be taken to be denying well-known facts about the mental life of human beings, and my plea that I aim at doing nothing more than rectify the logic of mental-conduct concepts will probably be disallowed as mere subterfuge.

I must first indicate what is meant by the phrase "Category-mistake." This I do in a series of illustrations.

A foreigner visiting Oxford or Cambridge for the first time is shown a number of colleges, libraries, playing fields, museums, scientific departments, and administrative offices. He then asks "But where is the University? I have seen where the members of the Colleges live, where the Registrar works, where the scientists experiment, and the rest. But I have not yet seen the University in which reside and work the members of your University." It has then to be explained to him that the University is not another collateral institution, some ulterior counterpart to the colleges, laboratories, and offices which he has seen. The University is just the way in which all that he has already seen is organized. When they are seen and when their coordination is understood, the University has been seen. His mistake lay in his innocent assumption that it was correct to speak of Christ Church, the Bodleian Library, the Ashmolean Museum, *and* the University, to speak, that is, as if "the University" stood for an extra member of the class of which these other units are members. He was mistakenly allocating the University to the same category as that to which the other institutions belong.

The same mistake would be made by a child witnessing the march-past of a division, who, having had pointed out to him such and such battalions, batteries, squadrons, etc., asked when the division was going to appear. He would be supposing that a division was a counterpart to the units already seen, partly similar to them and partly unlike them. He would be shown his mistake by being told that in watching the battalions, batteries, and squadrons marching past he had been watching the division marching past. The march-past was not a parade of battalions, batteries, squadrons, *and* a division; it was a parade of the battalions, batteries, and squadrons *of* a division.

One more illustration. A foreigner watching his first game of cricket learns what are the functions of the bowlers, the batsmen, the fielders, the umpires, and the scorers. He then says "But there is no one left on the field to contribute the famous element of team spirit. I see who does the bowling, the batting, and the wicketkeeping; but I do not see whose role it is to exercise *esprit de corps*." Once more, it would have to be explained that he was looking for the wrong type of thing. Team spirit is not another cricketing-operation supplementary to all of the other special tasks. It is, roughly, the keenness with which each of the special tasks is performed, and performing a task keenly is not performing two tasks. Certainly exhibiting team spirit is not the same thing as bowling or catching, but nor is it a third thing such that we can say that the bowler first bowls *and* then exhibits team spirit or that a fielder is at a given moment *either* catching *or* displaying *esprit de corps*.

These illustrations of category-mistakes have a common feature which must be noticed. The mistakes were made by people who did not know how to wield the concepts *University, division,* and *team spirit.* Their puzzles arose from inability to use certain items in the English vocabulary.

The theoretically interesting category-mistakes are those made by people who are perfectly competent to apply concepts, at least in the situations with which they are familiar, but are still liable in their abstract thinking to allocate those concepts to logical types to which they do not belong. An instance of a mistake of this sort would be the following story. A student of politics has learned the main differences between the British, the French, and the American Constitutions, and has learned also the differences and connections between the Cabinet, Parliament, the various Ministries, the Judicature, and the Church of England. But he still becomes embarrassed when asked questions about the connections between the Church of England, the Home Office, and the British Constitution. For while the Church and the Home Office are institutions, the British Constitution is not another institution in the same sense of that noun. So inter-institutional relations which can be asserted or denied to hold between the Church and the Home Office cannot be asserted or denied to hold between either of them and the British Constitution. "The British Constitution" is not a term of the same logical type as "the Home Office" and "the Church of England." In a partially similar way, John Doe may be a relative, a friend, an enemy, or a stranger to Richard Roe; but he cannot be any of these things to the Average Taxpayer. He knows how to talk sense in certain sorts of discussions about the Average Taxpayer, but he is baffled to say why he could not come across him in the street as he can come across Richard Roe.

It is pertinent to our main subject to notice that, so long as the student of politics continues to think of the British Constitution as a counterpart to the other institutions, he will tend to describe it as a mysteriously occult institution; and so long as John Doe continues to think of the Average Taxpayer as a fellow citizen, he will tend to think of him as an elusive insubstantial man, a ghost who is every-where yet nowhere.

My destructive purpose is to show that a family of radical category-mistakes is the source of the double-life theory. The representation of a person as a ghost mysteriously ensconced in a machine derives from this argument. Because, as is true, a person's thinking, feeling, and purposive doing cannot be described solely in the idioms of physics, chemistry, and physiology, therefore they must be described in counterpart idioms. As the human body is a complex organized unit, so the human mind must be another complex organized unit, though one made of a different sort of stuff and with a different sort of structure. Or, again, as the human body, like any other parcel of matter, is a field of causes and effects, so the mind must be another field of causes and effects, though not (Heaven be praised) mechanical causes and effects.

3   The origin of the category-mistake

One of the chief intellectual origins of what I have yet to prove to be the Cartesian category-mistake seems to be this. When Galileo showed that his methods of scientific discovery were competent to provide a mechanical theory which should cover every occupant of space, Descartes found in himself two conflicting motives. As a man of scientific genius he could not but endorse the claims of mechanics, yet as a religious and moral man he could not accept, as Hobbes accepted, the discouraging rider to those claims, namely that human nature differs only in degree of complexity from clockwork. The mental could not be just a variety of the mechanical.

He and subsequent philosophers naturally but erroneously availed themselves of the following escape route. Since mental-conduct words are not to be construed as signifying the occurrence of mechanical processes, they must be construed as signifying the occurrence of nonmechanical processes; since mechanical laws explain movements in space as the effects of other movements in space, other laws must ex-plain some of the nonspatial workings of minds as the effects of other nonspatial work-ings of minds. The difference between the human behaviors which we describe as intelligent and those which we describe as unintelligent must be a difference in their causation; so, while some movements of human tongues and limbs are the effects of mechanical causes, others must be the effects of nonmechanical causes, i.e., some issue from movements of particles of matter, others from workings of the mind.

The differences between the physical and the mental were thus represented as differences inside the common framework of the categories of "thing," "stuff," "attribute," "state," "process," "change," "cause," and "effect." Minds are things, but different sorts of things from bodies; mental processes are causes and effects, but different sorts of causes and effects from bodily movements. And so on. Somewhat as the foreigner expected the University to be an extra edifice, rather like a college but also considerably different, so the repudiators of mechanism represented minds as extra centers of causal processes, rather like machines but also considerably different from them. Their theory was a para-mechanical hypothesis.

That this assumption was at the heart of the doctrine is shown by the fact that there was from the beginning felt to be a major theoretical difficulty in explaining how minds can influence and be influenced by bodies. How can a mental process, such as willing, cause spatial movements like the movements of the tongue? How can a physical change in the optic nerve have among its effects a mind's perception of a flash of light? This notorious crux by itself shows the logical mold into which Descartes pressed his theory of the mind. It was the selfsame mold into which he and Galileo set their mechanics. Still unwittingly adhering to the grammar of mechanics, he tried to avert disaster by describing minds in what was merely an obverse vocabulary. The workings of minds had to be described by the mere negatives of the specific descriptions given to bodies; they are not in space, they are not motions, they are not modifications of matter, they are not accessible to public observation. Minds are not bits of clockwork, they are just bits of not-clockwork.

As thus represented, minds are not merely ghosts harnessed to machines, they are themselves just spectral machines. Though the human body is an engine, it is not quite an ordinary engine, since some of its workings are governed by another engine inside it—this interior governor-engine being one of a very special sort. It is invisible, inaudible, and it has no size or weight. It cannot be taken to bits and the laws it obeys are not those known to ordinary engineers. Nothing is known of how it governs the bodily engine.

A second major crux points the same moral. Since, according to the doctrine, minds belong to the same category as bodies and since bodies are rigidly governed by mechanical laws, it seemed to many theorists to follow that minds must be similarly governed by rigid nonmechanical laws. The physical world is a deterministic system, so the mental world must be a deterministic system. Bodies cannot help the modifications that they undergo, so minds cannot help pursuing the careers fixed for them. *Responsibility, choice, merit,* and *demerit* are therefore inapplicable concepts—unless the compromise solution is adopted of saying that the laws governing mental processes, unlike those governing physical processes, have the congenial attribute of being only rather rigid. The problem of the Freedom of the Will was the problem how to reconcile the hypothesis that minds are to be described in terms drawn from the categories of mechanics with the knowledge that higher-grade human conduct is not of a piece with the behavior of machines.

It is an historical curiosity that it was not noticed that the entire argument was broken-backed. Theorists correctly assumed that any sane man could already recognize the differences between, say, rational and nonrational utterances or between purposive and automatic behavior. Else there would have been nothing requiring to be salved from mechanism. Yet the explanation given presupposed that one person could in principle never recognize the difference between the rational and the irrational utterances issuing from other human bodies, since he could never get access to the postulated immaterial causes of some of their utterances. Save for the doubtful exception of himself, he could never tell the difference between a man and a Robot. It would have to be conceded, for example, that, for all that we can tell, the inner lives of persons who are classed as idiots or lunatics are as rational as those of anyone else. Perhaps only their overt behavior is disappointing; that is to say, perhaps "idiots" are not really idiotic, or "lunatics" lunatic. Perhaps, too, some of those who are classed as sane are really idiots. According to the theory, external observers could never know how the overt behavior of others is correlated with their mental powers and processes and so they could never know or even plausibly conjecture whether their applications of mental-conduct concepts to these other people were correct or incorrect. It would then be hazardous or impossible for a man to claim sanity or logical consistency even for himself, since he would be debarred from comparing his own performances with those of others. In short, our characterizations of persons and their performances as intelligent, prudent, and virtuous or as stupid, hypocritical, and cowardly could never have been made, so the problem of providing a special causal hypothesis to serve as the basis of such diagnoses would never have arisen. The question, "How do persons differ from machines?" arose just because everyone already knew how to apply mental-conduct concepts before the new causal hypothesis was introduced. This causal hypothesis could not therefore be the source of the criteria used in those applications. Nor, of course, has the causal hypothesis in any degree improved our handling of those criteria. We still distinguish good from bad arithmetic, politic from impolitic conduct, and fertile from infertile imaginations in the ways in which Descartes himself distinguished them before and after he speculated how the applicability of these criteria was compatible with the principle of mechanical causation.

He had mistaken the logic of his problem. Instead of asking by what criteria intelligent behavior is actually distinguished from non-intelligent behavior, he asked "Given that the principle of mechanical causation does not tell us the difference, what other causal principle will tell it us?" He realized that the problem was not one of mechanics and assumed that it must therefore be one of some counterpart to mechanics. Not unnaturally psychology is often cast for just this role.

When two terms belong to the same category, it is proper to construct conjunctive propositions embodying them. Thus a purchaser may say that he bought a left-hand glove and a right-hand glove, but not that he bought a left-hand glove, a right-hand glove, and a pair of gloves. "She came home in a flood of tears and a sedan chair" is a well-known joke based on the absurdity of conjoining terms of different types. It would have been equally ridiculous to construct the disjunction "She came home either in a flood of tears or else in a sedan chair." Now the dogma of the Ghost in the Machine does just this. It maintains that there exist both bodies and minds; that there occur physical processes and mental processes; that there are mechanical causes of corporeal movements and mental causes of corporeal movements. I shall argue that these and other analogous conjunctions are absurd; but, it must be noticed, the argument will not show that either of the illegitimately conjoined propositions is absurd in itself. I am not, for example, denying that there occur mental processes. Doing long division is a mental process and so is making a joke. But I am saying that the phrase "There occur mental processes" does not mean the same sort of thing as "There occur physical processes," and, therefore, that it makes no sense to conjoin or disjoin the two.

If my argument is successful, there will follow some interesting consequences. First, the hallowed contrast between Mind and Matter will be dissipated, but dissipated not by either of the equally hallowed absorptions of Mind by Matter or of Matter by Mind, but in quite a different way. For the seeming contrast of the two will be shown to be as illegitimate as would be the contrast of "She came home in a flood of tears" and "she came home in a sedan chair." The belief that there is a polar opposition between Mind and Matter is the belief that they are terms of the same logical type.

It will also follow that both Idealism and Materialism are answers to an improper question. The "reduction" of the material world to mental states and processes, as well as the "reduction" of mental states and processes to physical states and processes, presuppose the legitimacy of the disjunction "Either there exist minds or there exist bodies (but not both)." It would be like saying, "Either she bought a left-hand and a right-hand glove or she bought a pair of gloves (but not both)."

It is perfectly proper to say, in one logical tone of voice, that there exist minds and to say, in another logical tone of voice, that there exist bodies. But these expressions do not indicate two different species of existence, for "existence" is not a generic word like "colored" or "sexed." They indicate two different senses of "exist," somewhat as "rising" has different senses in "the tide is rising," "hopes are rising," and "the average age of death is rising." A man would be thought to be making a poor joke who said that three things are now rising, namely the tide, hopes, and the average age of death. It would be just as good or bad a joke to say that there exist prime numbers and Wednesdays and public opinions and navies; or that there exist both minds and bodies. In the succeeding chapters I try to prove that the official theory does rest on a batch of category-mistakes by showing that logically absurd corollaries follow from it. The exhibition of these absurdities will have the constructive effect of bringing out part of the correct logic of mental-conduct concepts.

•　　•　　•

6

OF PERSONAL IDENTITY

david hume

There are some philosophers, who imagine we are every moment intimately conscious of what we call our SELF; that we feel its existence and its continuance in existence; and are certain, beyond the evidence of a demonstration, both of its perfect identity and simplicity. The strongest sensation, the most violent passion, say they, instead of distracting us from this view, only fix it the more intensely, and make us consider their influence on *self* either by their pain or pleasure. To attempt a farther proof of this were to weaken its evidence; since no proof can be deriv'd from any fact, of which we are so intimately conscious; nor is there any thing, of which we can be certain, if we doubt of this.

Unluckily all these positive assertions are contrary to that very experience, which is pleaded for them, nor have we any idea of *self,* after the manner it is here explain'd. For from what impression cou'd this idea be deriv'd? This question 'tis impossible to answer without a manifest contradiction and absurdity; and yet 'tis a question, which must necessarily be answer'd, if we wou'd have the idea of self pass for clear and intelligible. It must be some one impression, that gives rise to every real idea. But self or person is not any one impression, but that to which our several impressions and ideas are suppos'd to have a reference. If any impression gives rise to the idea of self, that impression must continue invariably the same, thro' the whole course of our lives; since self is suppos'd to exist after that manner. But there is no impression constant and invariable. Pain and pleasure, grief and joy, passions and sensations succeed each other, and never all exist at the same time. It cannot, therefore, be from any of these impressions, or from any other, that the idea of self is deriv'd; and consequently there is no such idea.

But farther, what must become of all our particular perceptions upon this hypothesis? All these are different, and distinguishable, and separable from each other, and may be separately consider'd, and may exist separately, and have no need of any thing to support their existence. After what manner, therefore, do they belong to self; and how are they connected with it? For my part, when I enter most intimately into what I call *myself,* I always stumble on some particular perception or other, of heat or

From David Hume, *A Treatise of Human Nature,* L. A. Selby-Bigge, ed. (Oxford: The Clarendon Press, 1949), Book I, Part IV, Sec. VI, pp. 251–262. Reprinted by permission of the Clarendon Press.

cold, light or shade, love or hatred, pain or pleasure. I never can catch *myself* at any time without a perception, and never can observe any thing but the perception. When my perceptions are remov'd for any time, as by sound sleep; so long am I insensible of *myself*, and may truly be said not to exist. And were all my perceptions remov'd by death, and cou'd I neither think, nor feel, nor see, nor love, nor hate after the dissolution of my body, I shou'd be entirely annihilated, nor do I conceive what is farther requisite to make me a perfect non-entity. If any one upon serious and un-prejudic'd reflexion, thinks he has a different notion of *himself*, I must confess I can reason no longer with him. All I can allow him is, that he may be in the right as well as I, and that we are essentially different in this particular. He may, perhaps, perceive something simple and continu'd, which he calls *himself*; tho' I am certain there is no such principle in me.

But setting aside some metaphysicians of this kind, I may venture to affirm of the rest of mankind, that they are nothing but a bundle or collection of different percep-tions, which succeed each other with an inconceivable rapidity, and are in a perpetual flux and movement. Our eyes cannot turn in their sockets without varying our percep-tions. Our thought is still more variable than our sight; and all our other senses and faculties contribute to this change; nor is there any single power of the soul, which remains unalterably the same, perhaps for one moment. The mind is a kind of theatre, where several perceptions successively make their appearance; pass, re-pass, glide away, and mingle in an infinite variety of postures and situations. There is properly no *simplicity* in it at one time, nor *identity* in different; whatever natural propension we may have to imagine that simplicity and identity. The comparison of the theatre must not mislead us. They are the successive perceptions only, that constitute the mind; nor have we the most distant notion of the place, where these scenes are represented, or of the materials, of which it is compos'd.

What then gives us so great a propension to ascribe an identity to these successive perceptions, and to suppose ourselves possest of an invariable and uninterrupted existence thro' the whole course of our lives? In order to answer this question, we must distinguish betwixt personal identity, as it regards our thought or imagination, and as it regards our passions or the concern we take in ourselves. The first is our present subject; and to explain it perfectly we must take the matter pretty deep, and account for 'that identity, which we attribute to plants and animals; there being a great analogy betwixt it, and the identity of a self or person.

We have a distinct idea of an object, that remains invariable and uninterrupted thro' a suppos'd variation of time; and this idea we call that of *identity* or *sameness*. We have also a distinct idea of several different objects existing in succession, and connected together by a close relation; and this to an accurate view affords as perfect a notion of *diversity*, as if there was no manner of relation among the objects. But tho' these two ideas of identity, and a succession of related objects be in themselves perfectly distinct, and even contrary, yet 'tis certain, that in our common way of thinking they are generally confounded with each other. That action of the imagina-tion, by which we consider the uninterrupted and invariable object, and that by which we reflect on the succession of related objects, are almost the same to the feel-ing, nor is there much more effort of thought requir'd in the latter case than in the former. The relation facilitates the transition of the mind from one object to another, and renders its passage as smooth as if it contemplated one continu'd object. This resemblance is the cause of the confusion and mistake, and makes us substitute the notion of identity, instead of that of related objects. However at one instant we may consider the related succession as variable or interrupted, we are sure the next to ascribe to it a perfect identity, and regard it as invariable and uninterrupted. Our propensity to this mistake is so great from the resemblance above-mention'd, that we fall into it before we are aware; and tho' we incessantly correct ourselves by reflexion, and return to a more accurate method of thinking, yet we cannot long sustain our philosophy, or take off this biass from the imagination. Our last resource is to yield to it, and boldly assert that these different related objects are in effect the same, however interrupted and variable. In order to justify to ourselves this absurdity, we often feign some new and unintelligible principle, that connects the objects together, and prevents their interruption or variation. Thus we feign the continu'd existence of the perceptions of our senses, to remove the interruption; and run into the notion of a *soul,* and *self,* and *substance,* to disguise the variation. But we may farther observe, that where we do not give rise to such a fiction, our propension to confound identity with relation is so great, that we are apt to imagine something unknown and mysterious, connecting the parts, beside their relation; and this I take to be the case with regard to the identity we ascribe to plants and vegetables. And even when this does not take place, we still feel a propensity to confound these ideas, tho' we are not able fully to satisfy ourselves in that particular, nor find any thing invariable and uninterrupted to justify our notion of identity.

Thus the controversy concerning identity is not merely a dispute of words. For when we attribute identity, in an improper sense, to variable or interrupted objects, our mistake is not confin'd to the expression, but is commonly attended with a fiction, either of something invariable and uninterrupted, or of something mysterious and inexplicable, or at least with a propensity to such fictions. What will suffice to prove this hypothesis to the satisfaction of every fair enquirer, is to shew from daily experience and observation, that the objects, which are variable or interrupted, and yet are suppos'd to continue the same, are such only as consist of a succession of parts, connected together by resemblance, contiguity, or causation. For as such a succession answers evidently to our notion of diversity, it can only be by mistake we ascribe to it an identity; and as the relation of parts, which leads us into this mistake, is really nothing but a quality, which produces an association of ideas, and an easy transition of the imagination from one to another, it can only be from the resemblance, which this act of the mind bears to that, by which we contemplate one continu'd object, that the error arises. Our chief business, then, must be to prove, that all objects, to which we ascribe identity, without observing their invariableness and uninterruptedness, are such as consist of a succession of related objects.

In order to [do] this, suppose any mass of matter, of which the parts are contiguous and connected, to be plac'd before us; 'tis plain we must attribute a perfect identity to this mass, provided all the parts continue uninterruptedly and invariably the same, whatever motion or change of place we may observe either in the whole or in any of the parts. But supposing some very *small* or *inconsiderable* part to be added to the mass, or substracted from it; tho' this absolutely destroys the identity of the whole, strictly speaking; yet as we seldom think so accurately, we scruple not to pronounce a mass of matter the same, where we find so trivial an alteration. The passage of the thought from the object before the change to the object after it, is so smooth and easy, that we scarce perceive the transition, and are apt to imagine, that 'tis nothing but a continu'd survey of the same object.

There is a very remarkable circumstance, that attends this experiment; which is, that tho' the change of any considerable part in a mass of matter destroys the identity of the whole, yet we must measure the greatness of the part, not absolutely, but by its *proportion* to the whole. The addition or diminution of a mountain wou'd not be sufficient to produce a diversity in a planet; tho' the change of a very few inches wou'd be able to destroy the identity of some bodies. 'Twill be impossible to account for this, but by reflecting that objects operate upon the mind, and break or interrupt the continuity of its actions not according to their real greatness, but according to their proportion to each other: And therefore, since this interruption makes an object cease to appear the same, it must be the uninterrupted progress of the thought, which constitutes the imperfect identity.

This may be confirm'd by another phænomenon. A change in any considerable part of a body destroys its identity; but 'tis remarkable, that where the change is produc'd *gradually* and *insensibly* we are less apt to ascribe to it the same effect. The reason can plainly be no other, than that the mind, in following the successive changes of the body, feels an easy passage from the surveying its condition in one moment to the viewing of it in another, and at no particular time perceives any interruption in its actions. From which continu'd perception, it ascribes a continu'd existence and identity to the object.

But whatever precaution we may use in introducing the changes gradually, and making them proportionable to the whole, 'tis certain, that where the changes are at last observ'd to become considerable, we make a scruple of ascribing identity to such different objects. There is, however, another artifice, by which we may induce the imagination to advance a step farther; and that is, by producing a reference of the parts to each other, and a combination to some *common end* or purpose. A ship, of which a considerable part has been chang'd by frequent reparations, is still consider'd as the same; nor does the difference of the materials hinder us from ascribing an identity to it. The common end, in which the parts conspire, is the same under all their variations, and affords an easy transition of the imagination from one situation of the body to another.

But this is still more remarkable, when we add a *sympathy* of parts to their *common end*, and suppose that they bear to each other, the reciprocal relation of cause and effect in all their actions and operations. This is the case with all animals and vegetables; where not only the several parts have a reference to some general purpose, but also a mutual dependance on, and connexion with each other. The effect of so strong a relation is, that tho' every one must allow, that in a very few years both vegetables and animals endure a *total* change, yet we still attribute identity to them, while their form, size, and substance are entirely alter'd. An oak, that grows from a small plant to a large tree, is still the same oak; tho' there be not one particle of matter, or figure of its parts the same. An infant becomes a man, and is sometimes fat, sometimes lean, without any change in his identity.

We may also consider the two following phænomena, which are remarkable in their kind. The first is, that tho' we commonly be able to distinguish pretty exactly betwixt numerical and specific identity, yet it sometimes happens, that we confound them, and in our thinking and reasoning employ the one for the other. Thus a man, who hears a noise, that is frequently interrupted and renew'd, says, it is still the same noise; tho' 'tis evident the sounds have only a specific identity or resemblance, and there is nothing numerically the same, but the cause, which produc'd them. In like manner it may be said without breach of the propriety of language, that such a church, which was formerly of brick, fell to ruin, and that the parish rebuilt the same church of free-stone, and according to modern architecture. Here neither the form nor materials are the same, nor is there any thing common to the two objects, but their relation to the inhabitants of the parish; and yet this alone is sufficient to make us denominate them the same. But we must observe, that in these cases the first object is in a manner annihilated before the second comes into existence; by which means, we are never presented in any one point of time with the idea of difference and multiplicity; and for that reason are less scrupulous in calling them the same.

Secondly, We may remark, that tho' in a succession of related objects, it be in a manner requisite, that the change of parts be not sudden nor entire, in order to preserve the identity, yet where the objects are in their nature changeable and inconstant, we admit of a more sudden transition, than wou'd otherwise be consistent with that relation. Thus as the nature of a river consists in the motion and change of parts; tho' in less than four and twenty hours these be totally alter'd; this hinders not the river from continuing the same during several ages. What is natural and essential to any thing is, in a manner, expected; and what is expected makes less impression, and appears of less moment, than what is unusual and extraordinary. A considerable change of the former kind seems really less to the imagination, than the most trivial alteration of the latter; and by breaking less the continuity of the thought, has less influence in destroying the identity.

We now proceed to explain the nature of *personal identity,* which has become so great a question in philosophy, especially of late years in *England,* where all the abstruser sciences are study'd with a peculiar ardour and application. And here 'tis evident, the same method of reasoning must be continu'd, which has so successfully explain'd the identity of plants, and animals, and ships, and houses, and of all the compounded and changeable productions either of art or nature. The identity, which we ascribe to the mind of man, is only a fictitious one, and of a like kind with that which we ascribe to vegetables and animal bodies. It cannot, therefore, have a different origin, but must proceed from a like operation of the imagination upon like objects.

But lest this argument shou'd not convince the reader; tho' in my opinion perfectly decisive; let him weigh the following reasoning, which is still closer and more immediate. 'Tis evident, that the identity, which we attribute to the human mind, however perfect we may imagine it to be, is not able to run the several different perceptions into one, and make them lose their characters of distinction and difference, which are essential to them. 'Tis still true, that every distinct perception, which enters into the composition of the mind, is a distinct existence, and is different, and distinguishable, and separable from every other perception, either contemporary or successive. But, as, notwithstanding this distinction and separability, we suppose the whole train of perceptions to be united by identity, a question naturally arises concerning this relation of identity; whether it be something that really binds our several perceptions together, or only associates their ideas in the imagination. That is, in other words, whether in pronouncing concerning the identity of a person, we observe some real bond among his perceptions, or only feel one among the ideas we form of them. This question we might easily decide, if we wou'd recollect what has been already prov'd at large, that the understanding never observes any real connexion among objects, and that even the union of cause and effect, when strictly examin'd, resolves itself into a customary association of ideas. For from thence it evidently follows, that identity is nothing really belonging to these different perceptions, and uniting them together; but is merely a quality, which we attribute to them, because of the union of their ideas in the imagination, when we reflect upon them. Now the only qualities, which can give ideas an union in the imagination, are these three relations above-mention'd. These are the uniting principles in the ideal world, and without them every distinct object is separable by the mind, and may be separately consider'd, and appears not to have any more connexion with any other object, than if disjoin'd by the greatest difference and remoteness. 'Tis, therefore, on some of these three relations of resemblance, contiguity, and causation, that identity depends; and as the very essence of these relations consists in their producing an easy transition of ideas; it follows, that our notions of personal identity, proceed entirely from the smooth and uninterrupted progress of the thought along a train of connected ideas, according to the principles above-explain'd.

The only question, therefore, which remains, is, by what relations this uninterrupted progress of our thought is produc'd, when we consider the successive existence of a mind or thinking person. And here 'tis evident we must confine ourselves to resemblance and causation, and must drop contiguity, which has little or no influence in the present case.

To begin with *resemblance;* suppose we cou'd see clearly into the breast of another, and observe that succession of perceptions, which constitutes his mind or thinking principle, and suppose that he always preserves the memory of a considerable part of past perceptions; 'tis evident that nothing cou'd more contribute to the bestowing a relation on this succession amidst all its variations. For what is the memory but a faculty, by which we raise up the images of past perceptions? And as an image necessarily resembles its object, must not the frequent placing of these resembling perceptions in the chain of thought, convey the imagination more easily from one link to another, and make the whole seem like the continuance of one object? In this particular, then, the memory not only discovers the identity, but also contributes to its production, by producing the relation of resemblance among the perceptions. The case is the same whether we consider ourselves or others.

As to *causation;* we may observe, that the true idea of the human mind, is to consider it as a system of different perceptions or different existences, which are link'd together by the relation of cause and effect, and mutually produce, destroy, influence, and modify each other. Our impressions give rise to their correspondent ideas; and these ideas in their turn produce other impressions. One thought chases another, and draws after it a third, by which it is expell'd in its turn. In this respect, I cannot compare the soul more properly to any thing than to a republic or commonwealth, in which the several members are united by the reciprocal ties of government and subordination, and give rise to other persons, who propagate the same republic in the incessant changes of its parts. And as the same individual republic may not only change its members, but also its laws and constitutions; in like manner the same person may vary his character and disposition, as well as his impressions and ideas, without losing his identity. Whatever changes he endures, his several parts are still connected by the relation of causation. And in this view our identity with regard to the passions serves to corroborate that with regard to the imagination, by the making our distant perceptions influence each other, and by giving us a present concern for our past or future pains or pleasures.

As memory alone acquaints us with the continuance and extent of this succession of perceptions, 'tis to be consider'd, upon that account chiefly, as the source of personal identity. Had we no memory, we never shou'd have any notion of causation, nor consequently of that chain of causes and effects, which constitute our self or person. But having once acquir'd this notion of causation from the memory, we can extend the same chain of causes, and consequently the identity of our persons beyond our memory, and can comprehend times, and circumstances, and actions, which we have entirely forgot, but suppose in general to have existed. For how few of our past actions are there, of which we have any memory? Who can tell me, for instance, what were his thoughts and actions on the first of *January* 1715, the 11th of *March* 1719, and the 3d of *August* 1733? Or will he affirm, because he has entirely forgot the incidents of these days, that the present self is not the same person with the self of that time; and by that means overturn all the most establish'd notions of personal identity? In this view, therefore, memory does not so much *produce* as *discover* personal identity, by shewing us the relation of cause and effect among our different perceptions. 'Twill be incumbent on those who affirm that memory produces entirely our personal identity, to give a reason why we can thus extend our identity beyond our memory.

The whole of this doctrine leads us to a conclusion, which is of great importance in the present affair, *viz.* that all the nice and subtile questions concerning personal identity can never possibly be decided, and are to be regarded rather as grammatical than as philosophical difficulties. Identity depends on the relations of ideas; and these relations produce identity, by means of that easy transition they occasion. But as the relations, and the easiness of the transition may diminish by insensible degrees, we have no just standard, by which we can decide any dispute concerning the time, when they acquire or lose a title to the name of identity. All the disputes concerning the identity of connected objects are merely verbal, except so far as the relation of parts gives rise to some fiction or imaginary principle of union, as we have already observ'd.

·   ·   ·

7

THE SELF AS DURATION

henri bergson

There is one reality, at least, which we all seize from within, by intuition and not by simple analysis. It is our own personality in its flowing through time—our self which endures. We may sympathize intellectually with nothing else, but we certainly sympathize with our own selves.

When I direct my attention inward to contemplate my own self (supposed for the moment to be inactive), I perceive at first, as a crust solidified on the surface, all the perceptions which come to it from the material world. These perceptions are clear, distinct, juxtaposed or juxtaposable one with another; they tend to group themselves into objects. Next, I notice the memories which more or less adhere to these perceptions and which serve to interpret them. These memories have been detached, as it were, from the depth of my personality, drawn to the surface by the perceptions which resemble them; they rest on the surface of my mind without being absolutely myself. Lastly, I feel the stir of tendencies and motor habits—a crowd of virtual actions, more or less firmly bound to these perceptions and memories. All these clearly defined elements appear more distinct from me, the more distinct they are from each other. Radiating, as they do, from within outwards, they form, collectively, the surface of a sphere which tends to grow larger and lose itself in the exterior world. But if I draw myself in from the periphery toward the center, if I search in the depth of my being that which is most uniformly, most constantly, and most enduringly myself, I find an altogether different thing.

There is, beneath these sharply cut crystals and this frozen surface, a continuous flux which is not comparable to any flux I have ever seen. There is a succession of states, each of which announces that which follows and contains that which precedes it. They can, properly speaking, only be said to form multiple states when I have already passed them and turn back to observe their track. Whilst I was experiencing them they were so solidly organized, so profoundly animated with a common life, that I could not have said where any one of them finished or where another commenced. In reality no one of them begins or ends, but all extend into each other.

This inner life may be compared to the unrolling of a coil, for there is no living

From Henri Bergson, *An Introduction to Metaphysics*, pp. 24–38, T. E. Hulme, trans. Copyright © 1949, 1955, by The Liberal Arts Press, Inc. Reprinted by permission of the Liberal Arts Press Division of The Bobbs-Merrill Company, Inc., and Curtis Brown Ltd.

being who does not feel himself coming gradually to the end of his role; and to live is to grow old. But it may just as well be compared to a continual rolling up, like that of a thread on a ball, for our past follows us, it swells incessantly with the present that it picks up on its way; and consciousness means memory.

But actually it is neither an unrolling nor a rolling up, for these two similes evoke the idea of lines and surfaces whose parts are homogeneous and superposable on one another. Now, there are no two identical moments in the life of the same conscious being. Take the simplest sensation, suppose it constant, absorb in it the entire personality: the consciousness which will accompany this sensation cannot remain identical with itself for two consecutive moments, because the second moment always contains, over and above the first, the memory that the first has bequeathed to it. A consciousness which could experience two identical moments would be a consciousness without memory. It would die and be born again continually. In what other way could one represent unconsciousness?

It would be better, then, to use as a comparison the myriad-tinted spectrum, with its insensible gradations leading from one shade to another. A current of feeling which passed along the spectrum, assuming in turn the tint of each of its shades, would experience a series of gradual changes, each of which would announce the one to follow and would sum up those which preceded it. Yet even here the successive shades of the spectrum always remain external one to another. They are juxtaposed; they occupy space. But pure duration, on the contrary, excludes all idea of juxtaposition, reciprocal externality, and extension.

Let us, then, rather, imagine an infinitely small elastic body, contracted, if it were possible, to a mathematical point. Let this be drawn out gradually in such a manner that from the point comes a constantly lengthening line. Let us fix our attention not on the line as a line, but on the action by which it is traced. Let us bear in mind that this action, in spite of its duration, is indivisible if accomplished without stopping, that if a stopping-point is inserted, we have two actions instead of one, that each of these separate actions is then the indivisible operation of which we speak, and that it is not the moving action itself which is divisible, but, rather, the stationary line it leaves behind it as its track in space. Finally, let us free ourselves from the space which underlies the movement in order to consider only the movement itself, the act of tension or extension; in short, pure mobility. We shall have this time a more faithful image of the development of our self in duration.

However, even this image is incomplete, and, indeed, every comparison will be insufficient, because the unrolling of our duration resembles in some of its aspects the unity of an advancing movement and in others the multiplicity of expanding states; and, clearly, no metaphor can express one of these two aspects without sacrificing the other. If I use the comparison of the spectrum with its thousand shades, I have before me a thing already made, while duration is continually in the making. If I think of an elastic which is being stretched, or of a spring which is extended or relaxed, I forget the richness of color, characteristic of duration that is lived, to see only the simple movement by which consciousness passes from one shade to another. The inner life is all this at once: variety of qualities, continuity of progress, and unity of direction. It cannot be represented by images.

But it is even less possible to represent it by *concepts*, that is by abstract, general, or simple ideas. It is true that no image can reproduce exactly the original feeling I have of the flow of my own conscious life. But it is not even necessary that I should attempt to render it. If a man is incapable of getting for himself the intuition of the constitutive duration of his own being, nothing will ever give it to him, concepts no more than images. Here the single aim of the philosopher should be to promote a certain effort, which in most men is usually fettered by habits of mind more useful to life. Now the image has at least this advantage, that it keeps us in the concrete. No image can replace the intuition of duration, but many diverse images, borrowed from very different orders of things, may, by the convergence of their action, direct consciousness to the precise point where there is a certain intuition to be seized. By choosing images as dissimilar as possible, we shall prevent any one of them from usurping the place of the intuition it is intended to call up, since it would then be driven away at once by its rivals. By providing that, in spite of their differences of aspect, they all require from the mind the same kind of attention, and in some sort the same degree of tension, we shall gradually accustom consciousness to a particular and clearly defined disposition—that precisely which it must adopt in order to appear to itself as it really is, without any veil. But, then, consciousness must at least consent to make the effort. For it will have been shown nothing: it will simply have been placed in the attitude it must take up in order to make the desired effort, and so come by itself to the intuition. Concepts, on the contrary—especially if they are simple— have the disadvantage of being in reality symbols substituted for the object they symbolize, and demand no effort on our part. Examined closely, each of them, it would be seen, retains only that part of the object which is common to it and to others, and expresses, still more than the image does, a *comparison* between the object and others which resemble it. But as the comparison has made manifest a resemblance, as the resemblance is a property of the object, and as a property has every appearance of being a *part* of the object which possesses it, we easily persuade ourselves that by setting concept beside concept we are reconstructing the whole of the object with its parts, thus obtaining, so to speak, its intellectual equivalent. In this way we believe that we can form a faithful representation of duration by setting in line the concepts of unity, multiplicity, continuity, finite or infinite divisibility, etc. There precisely is the illusion. There also is the danger. Just in so far as abstract ideas can render service to analysis, that is, to the scientific study of the object in its relations to other objects, so far are they incapable of replacing intuition, that is, the metaphysical investigation of what is essential and unique in the object. For, on the one hand, these concepts, laid side by side, never actually give us more than an artificial reconstruction of the object, of which they can only symbolize certain general and, in a way, impersonal aspects; it is therefore useless to believe that with them we can seize a reality of which they present to us the shadow alone. And, on the other hand, besides the illusion there is also a very serious danger. For the concept generalizes at the same time as it abstracts. The concept can only symbolize a particular property by making it common to an infinity of things. It therefore always more or less deforms the property by the extension it gives to it. Replaced in the metaphysical object to which it belongs, a property coincides with the object, or at least molds itself on it, and adopts the same outline. Extracted from the metaphysical object, and presented in a concept, it grows indefinitely larger, and goes beyond the object itself, since henceforth it has to contain it, along with a number of other objects. Thus the different concepts that we form of the properties of a thing inscribe round it so many circles, each much too large and none of them fitting it exactly. And yet, in the thing itself the properties coincided with the thing, and coincided consequently with one another. So that if we are bent on reconstructing the object with concepts, some artifice must be sought whereby this coincidence of the object and its properties can be brought about. For example, we may choose one of the concepts and try, starting from it, to get round to the others. But we shall then soon discover that according as we start from one concept or another, the meeting and combination of the concepts will take place in an altogether different way. According as we start, for example, from unity or from multiplicity, we shall have to conceive differently the multiple unity of duration. Everything will depend on the weight we attribute to this or that concept, and this weight will always be arbitrary, since the concept extracted from the object has no weight, being only the shadow of a body. In this way, as many different *systems* will spring up as there are external points of view from which the reality can be examined, or larger circles in which it can be enclosed. Simple concepts have, then, not only the inconvenience of dividing the concrete unity of the object into so many symbolical expressions; they also divide philosophy into distinct schools, each of which takes its seat, chooses its counters, and carries on with the others a game that will never end. Either metaphysics is only this play of ideas, or else, if it is a serious occupation of the mind, if it is a science and not simply an exercise, it must transcend concepts in order to reach intuition. Certainly, concepts are necessary to it, for all the other sciences work as a rule with concepts, and metaphysics cannot dispense with the other sciences. But it is only truly itself when it goes beyond the concept, or at least when it frees itself from rigid and ready-made concepts in order to create a kind very different from those which we habitually use; I mean supple, mobile, and almost fluid representations, always ready to mold themselves on the fleeting forms of intuition. We shall return later to this important point. Let it suffice us for the moment to have shown that our duration can be presented to us directly in an intuition, that it can be suggested to us indirectly by images, but that it can never—if we confine the word concept to its proper meaning —be enclosed in a conceptual representation.

Let us try for an instant to consider our duration as a multiplicity. It will then be necessary to add that the terms of this multiplicity, instead of being distinct, as they are in any other multiplicity, encroach on one another; and that while we can no doubt, by an effort of imagination, solidify duration once it has elapsed, divide it into juxtaposed portions and count all these portions, yet this operation is accomplished on the frozen memory of the duration, on the stationary trace which the mobility of duration leaves behind it, and not on the duration itself. We must admit, therefore, that if there is a multiplicity here, it bears no resemblance to any other multiplicity we know. Shall we say, then, that duration has unity? Doubtless, a continuity of elements which prolong themselves into one another participates in unity as much as in multiplicity; but this moving, changing, colored, living unity has hardly anything in common with the abstract, motionless, and empty unity which the concept of pure unity circumscribes. Shall we conclude from this that duration must be defined as unity and multiplicity at the same time? But singularly enough, however much I manipulate the two concepts, portion them out, combine them differently, practice on them the most subtle operations of mental chemistry, I never obtain anything which resembles the simple intuition that I have of duration; while, on the contrary, when I replace myself in duration by an effort of intuition, I immediately perceive how it is unity, multiplicity, and many other things besides. These different concepts, then, were only so many standpoints from which we could consider duration. Neither separated nor reunited have they made us penetrate into it.

We do penetrate into it, however, and that can only be by an effort of intuition. In this sense, an inner, absolute knowledge of the duration of the self by the self is possible. But if metaphysics here demands and can obtain an intuition, science has none the less need of an analysis. Now it is a confusion between the function of analysis and that of intuition which gives birth to the discussions between the schools and the conflicts between systems.

Psychology, in fact, proceeds like all the other sciences by analysis. It resolves the self, which has been given to it at first in a simple intuition, into sensations, feelings, ideas, etc., which it studies separately. It substitutes, then, for the self a series of elements which form the facts of psychology. But are these *elements* really *parts?* That is the whole question, and it is because it has been evaded that the problem of human personality has so often been stated in insoluble terms.

It is incontestable that every psychical state, simply because it belongs to a person, reflects the whole of a personality. Every feeling, however simple it may be, contains virtually within it the whole past and present of the being experiencing it, and, consequently, can only be separated and constituted into a "state" by an effort of abstraction or of analysis. But it is no less incontestable that without this effort of abstraction or analysis there would be no possible development of the science of psychology. What, then, exactly, is the operation by which a psychologist detaches a mental state in order to erect it into a more or less independent entity? He begins by neglecting that special coloring of the personality which cannot be expressed in known and common terms. Then he endeavors to isolate, in the person already thus simplified, some aspect which lends itself to an interesting inquiry. If he is considering inclination, for example, he will neglect the inexpressible shade which colors it, and which makes the inclination mine and not yours; he will fix his attention on the movement by which our personality *leans toward* a certain object: he will isolate this attitude, and it is this special aspect of the personality, this snapshot of the mobility of the inner life, this "diagram" of concrete inclination, that he will erect into an independent fact. There is in this something very like what an artist passing through Paris does when he makes, for example, a sketch of a tower of Notre Dame. The tower is inseparably united to the building, which is itself no less inseparably united to the ground, to its surroundings, to the whole of Paris, and so on. It is first necessary to detach it from all these; only one aspect of the whole is noted, that formed by the tower of Notre Dame. Moreover, the special form of this tower is due to the grouping of the stones of which it is composed; but the artist does not concern himself with these stones, he notes only the silhouette of the tower. For the real and internal organization of the thing he substitutes, then, an external and schematic representation. So that, on the whole, his sketch corresponds to an observation of the object from a certain point of view and to the choice of a certain means of representation. But exactly the same thing holds true of the operation by which the psychologist extracts a single mental state from the whole personality. This isolated psychical state is hardly anything but a sketch, the commencement of an artificial reconstruction; it is the whole considered under a certain elementary aspect in which we are specially interested and which we have carefully noted. It is not a part, but an element. It has not been obtained by a natural dismemberment, but by analysis.

Now beneath all the sketches he has made at Paris the visitor will probably, by way of memento, write the word "Paris." And as he has really seen Paris, he will be able, with the help of the original intuition he had of the whole, to place his sketches therein, and so join them up together. But there is no way of performing the inverse operation; it is impossible, even with an infinite number of accurate sketches, and even with the word "Paris" which indicates that they must be combined together, to get back to an intuition that one has never had, and to give oneself an impression of what Paris is like if one has never seen it. This is because we are not dealing here with real *parts,* but with mere *notes* of the total impression. To take a still more striking example, where the notation is more completely symbolic, suppose that I am shown, mixed together at random, the letters which make up a poem I am ignorant of. If the letters were *parts* of the poem, I could attempt to reconstitute the poem with them by trying the different possible arrangements, as a child does with the pieces of a Chinese puzzle. But I should never for a moment think of attempting such a thing in this case, because the letters are not *component parts,* but only *partial expressions,* which is quite a different thing. That is why, if I know the poem, I at once put each of the letters in its proper place and join them up without difficulty by a continuous connection, while the inverse operation is impossible. Even when I believe I am actually attempting this inverse operation, even when I put the letters end to end, I begin by thinking of some plausible meaning. I thereby give myself an intuition, and from this intuition I attempt to redescend to the elementary symbols which would reconstitute its expression. The very idea of reconstituting a thing by operations practiced on symbolic elements alone implies such an absurdity that it would never occur to anyone if they recollected that they were not dealing with fragments of the thing, but only, as it were, with fragments of its symbol.

Such is, however, the undertaking of the philosophers who try to reconstruct personality with psychical states, whether they confine themselves to those states alone, or whether they add a kind of thread for the purpose of joining the states together. Both empiricists and rationalists are victims of the same fallacy. Both of them mistake *partial notations* for *real parts,* thus confusing the point of view of analysis and of intuition, of science and of metaphysics.

The empiricists say quite rightly that psychological analysis discovers nothing more in personality than psychical states. Such is, in fact, the function, and the very definition of analysis. The psychologist has nothing else to do but analyze personality, that is, to note certain states; at the most he may put the label "ego" on these states in saying they are "states of the ego," just as the artist writes the word "Paris" on each of his sketches. On the level at which the psychologist places himself, and on which he must place himself, the "ego" is only a sign by which the primitive, and moreover very confused, intuition which has furnished the psychologist with his subject matter is recalled; it is only a word, and the great error here lies in believing that while remaining on the same level we can find behind the word a thing. Such has been the error of those philosophers who have not been able to resign themselves to being only psychologists in psychology, Taine and Stuart Mill, for example. Psychologists in the method they apply, they have remained metaphysicians in the object they set before themselves. They desire an intuition, and by a strange inconsistency they seek this intuition in analysis which is the very negation of it. They look for the ego, and they claim to find it in psychical states, though this diversity of states has itself only been obtained, and could only be obtained, by transporting oneself outside the ego altogether, so as to make a series of sketches, notes, and more or less symbolic and schematic diagrams. Thus, however much they place the states side by side, multiplying points of contact and exploring the intervals, the ego always escapes them, so that they finish by seeing in it nothing but a vain phantom. We might as well deny that the *Iliad* had a meaning, on the ground that we had looked in vain for that meaning in the intervals between the letters of which it is composed.

Philosophical empiricism is born here, then, of a confusion between the point of view of intuition and that of analysis. Seeking for the original in the translation, where naturally it cannot be, it denies the existence of the original on the ground that it is not found in the translation. It leads of necessity to negations; but on examining the matter closely, we perceive that these negations simply mean that analysis is not intuition, which is self-evident. From the original, and, one must add, very indistinct intuition which gives positive science its material, science passes immediately to analysis, which multiplies to infinity its observations of this material from outside points of view. It soon comes to believe that by putting together all these diagrams it can reconstitute the object itself. No wonder, then, that it sees this object fly before it, like a child that would like to make a solid plaything out of the shadows outlined along the wall!

But rationalism is the dupe of the same illusion. It starts out from the same confusion as empiricism, and remains equally powerless to reach the inner self. Like empiricism, it considers psychical states as so many fragments detached from an ego that binds them together. Like empiricism, it tries to join these fragments together in order to re-create the unity of the self. Like empiricism, finally, it sees this unity of the self, in the continually renewed effort it makes to clasp it, steal away indefinitely like a phantom. But while empiricism, weary of the struggle, ends by declaring that there is nothing else but the multiplicity of psychical states, rationalism persists in affirming the unity of the person. It is true that, seeking this unity on the level of the psychical states themselves, and obliged, besides, to put down to the account of these states all the qualities and determinations that it finds by analysis (since analysis by its very definition leads always to *states*), nothing is left to it, for the unity of personality, but something purely negative, the absence of all determination. The psychical states having necessarily in this analysis taken and kept for themselves everything that can serve as matter, the "unity of the ego" can never be more than a form without content. It will be absolutely indeterminate and absolutely void. To these detached psychical states, to these shadows of the ego, the sum of which was for the empiricists the equivalent of the self, rationalism, in order to reconstitute personality, adds something still more unreal, the void in which these shadows move—a place for shadows, one might say. How could this "form," which is in truth formless, serve to characterize a living, active, concrete personality, or to distinguish Peter from Paul? Is it astonishing that the philosophers who have isolated this "form" of personality should, then, find it insufficient to characterize a definite person, and that they should be gradually led to make their empty ego a kind of bottomless receptacle, which belongs no more to Peter than to Paul, and in which there is room, according to our preference, for entire humanity, for God, or for existence in general? I see in this matter only one difference between empiricism and rationalism. The former, seeking the unity of the ego in the gaps, as it were, between the psychical states, is led to fill the gaps with other states, and so on indefinitely, so that the ego, compressed in a constantly narrowing interval, tends towards zero, as analysis is pushed farther and farther; while rationalism, making the ego the place where mental states are lodged, is confronted with an empty space which we have no reason to limit here rather than there, which goes beyond each of the successive boundaries that we try to assign to it, which constantly grows larger, and which tends to lose itself no longer in zero, but in the infinite.

The distance, then, between a so-called "empiricism" like that of Taine and the most transcendental speculations of certain German pantheists is very much less than is generally supposed. The method is analogous in both cases; it consists in reasoning about the *elements* of a translation as if they were *parts* of the original. But a true empiricism is that which proposes to get as near to the original itself as possible, to search deeply into its life, and so, by a kind of *intellectual auscultation,* to feel the throbbings of its soul; and this true empiricism is the true metaphysics. It is true that the task is an extremely difficult one, for none of the ready-made conceptions which thought employs in its daily operations can be of any use. Nothing is more easy than to say that the ego is multiplicity, or that it is unity, or that it is the synthesis of both. Unity and multiplicity are here representations that we have no need to cut out on the model of the object; they are found ready-made, and have only to be chosen from a heap. They are stock-size clothes which do just as well for Peter as for Paul, for they set off the form of neither. But an empiricism worthy of the name, an empiricism which works only to measure, is obliged for each new object that it studies to make an absolutely fresh effort. It cuts out for the object a concept which is appropriate to that object alone, a concept which can as yet hardly be called a concept, since it applies to this one thing. It does not proceed by combining current ideas like unity and multiplicity; but it leads us, on the contrary, to a simple, unique representation, which, however once formed, enables us to understand easily how it is that we can place it in the frames unity, multiplicity, etc., all much larger than itself. In short, philosophy thus defined does not consist in the choice of certain concepts, and in taking sides with a school, but in the search for a unique intuition from which we can descend with equal ease to different concepts, because we are placed above the divisions of the schools.

That personality has unity cannot be denied; but such an affirmation teaches one nothing about the extraordinary nature of the particular unity presented by personality. That our self is multiple I also agree, but then it must be understood that it is a multiplicity which has nothing in common with any other multiplicity. What is really important for philosophy is to know exactly what unity, what multiplicity, and what reality superior both to abstract unity and multiplicity the multiple unity of the self actually is. Now philosophy will know this only when it recovers possession of the simple intuition of the self by the self. Then, according to the direction it chooses for its descent from this summit, it will arrive at unity or multiplicity, or at any one of the concepts by which we try to define the moving life of the self. But no mingling of these concepts would give anything which at all resembles the self that endures.

If we are shown a solid cone, we see without any difficulty how it narrows towards the summit and tends to be lost in a mathematical point, and also how it enlarges in the direction of the base into an indefinitely increasing circle. But neither the point nor the circle, nor the juxtaposition of the two on a plane, would give us the least idea of a cone. The same thing holds true of the unity and multiplicity of mental life, and of the zero and the infinite towards which empiricism and rationalism conduct personality.

.   .   .

8

THE SELF AND THE ORGANISM

george h. mead

In our statement of the development of intelligence we have already suggested that the language process is essential for the development of the self. The self has a character which is different from that of the physiological organism proper. The self is something which has a development; it is not initially there, at birth, but arises in the process of social experience and activity, that is, develops in the given individual as a result of his relations to that process as a whole and to other individuals within that process. The intelligence of the lower forms of animal life, like a great deal of human intelligence, does not involve a self. In our habitual actions, for example, in our moving about in a world that is simply there and to which we are so adjusted that no thinking is involved, there is a certain amount of sensuous experience such as persons have when they are just waking up, a bare thereness of the world. Such characters about us may exist in experience without taking their place in relationship to the self. One must, of course, under those conditions, distinguish between the experience that immediately takes place and our own organization of it into the experience of the self. One says upon analysis that a certain item had its place in his experience, in the experience of his self. We do inevitably tend at a certain level of sophistication to organize all experience into that of a self. We do so intimately identify our experiences, especially our affective experiences, with the self that it takes a moment's abstraction to realize that pain and pleasure can be there without being the experience of the self. Similarly, we normally organize our memories upon the string of our self. If we date things we always date them from the point of view of our past experiences. We frequently have memories that we cannot date, that we cannot place. A picture comes before us suddenly and we are at a loss to explain when that experience originally took place. We remember perfectly distinctly the picture, but we do not have it definitely paced, and until we can place it in terms of our past experience we are not satisfied. Nevertheless, I think it is obvious when one comes to consider it that the self is not necessarily involved in the life of the organism, nor involved in what we term our sensuous experience, that is, experience in a world about us for which we have habitual reactions.

From George H. Mead, *Mind, Self and Society* (Chicago: University of Chicago Press, 1947), Part III, Sec. 18, pp. 135–144. Reprinted by permission of the publisher.

We can distinguish very definitely between the self and the body. The body can be there and can operate in a very intelligent fashion without there being a self involved in the experience. The self has the characteristic that it is an object to itself, and that characteristic distinguishes it from other objects and from the body. It is perfectly true that the eye can see the foot, but it does not see the body as a whole. We cannot see our backs; we can feel certain portions of them, if we are agile, but we cannot get an experience of our whole body. There are, of course, experiences which are somewhat vague and difficult of location, but the bodily experiences are for us organized about a self. The foot and hand belong to the self. We can see our feet, especially if we look at them from the wrong end of an opera glass, as strange things which we have difficulty in recognizing as our own. The parts of the body are quite distinguishable from the self. We can lose parts of the body without any serious invasion of the self. The mere ability to experience different parts of the body is not different from the experience of a table. The table presents a different feel from what the hand does when one hand feels another, but it is an experience of something with which we come definitely into contact. The body does not experience itself as a whole, in the sense in which the self in some way enters into the experience of the self.

It is the characteristic of the self as an object to itself that I want to bring out. This characteristic is represented in the word "self," which is a reflexive, and indicates that which can be both subject and object. This type of object is essentially different from other objects, and in the past it has been distinguished as conscious, a term which indicates an experience with, an experience of, one's self. It was assumed that consciousness in some way carried this capacity of being an object to itself. In giving a behavioristic statement of consciousness we have to look for some sort of experience in which the physical organism can become an object to itself.

When one is runnning to get away from someone who is chasing him, he is entirely occupied in this action, and his experience may be swallowed up in the objects about him, so that he has, at the time being, no consciousness of self at all. We must be, of course, very completely occupied to have that take place, but we can, I think, recognize that sort of a possible experience in which the self does not enter. We can, perhaps, get some light on that situation through those experiences in which in very intense action there appear in the experience of the individual, back of this intense action, memories and anticipations. Tolstoi as an officer in the war gives an account of having pictures of his past experience in the midst of his most intense action. There are also the pictures that flash into a person's mind when he is drowning. In such instances there is a contrast between an experience that is absolutely wound up in outside activity in which the self as an object does not enter, and an activity of memory and imagination in which the self is the principal object. The self is then entirely distinguishable from an organism that is surrounded by things and acts with reference to things, including parts of its own body. These latter may be objects like other objects, but they are just objects out there in the field, and they do not involve a self that is an object to the organism. This is, I think, frequently overlooked. It is that fact which makes our anthropomorphic reconstructions of animal life so fallacious. How can an individual get outside himself (experientially) in such a way as to become an object to himself? This is the essential psychological problem of selfhood or of self-consciousness; and its solution is to be found by referring to the process of social conduct or activity in which the given person or individual is implicated. The apparatus of reason would not be complete unless it swept itself into its own analysis of the field of experience; or unless the individual brought himself into the same experiential field as that of the other individual selves in relation to whom he acts in any given social situation. Reason cannot become impersonal unless it takes an objective, non-affective attitude toward itself; otherwise we have just consciousness, not *self*-consciousness. And it is necessary to rational conduct that the individual should thus take an objective, impersonal attitude toward himself, that he should become an object to himself. For the individual organism is obviously an essential and important fact or constituent element of the empirical situation in which it acts; and without taking objective account of itself as such, it cannot act intelligently, or rationally.

The individual experiences himself as such, not directly, but only indirectly, from the particular standpoints of other individual members of the same social group, or from the generalized standpoint of the social group as a whole to which he belongs. For he enters his own experience as a self or individual not directly or immediately, not by becoming a subject to himself, but only in so far as he first becomes an object to himself just as other individuals are objects to him or in his experience; and he becomes an object to himself only by taking the attitudes of other individuals toward himself within a social environment or context of experience and behavior in which both he and they are involved.

The importance of what we term "communication" lies in the fact that it provides a form of behavior in which the organism or the individual may become an object to himself. It is that sort of communication which we have been discussing—not communication in the sense of the cluck of the hen to the chickens, or the bark of a wolf to the pack, or the lowing of a cow, but communication in the sense of significant symbols, communication which is directed not only to others but also to the individual himself. So far as that type of communication is a part of behavior it at least introduces a self. Of course, one may hear without listening; one may see things that he does not realize; do things that he is not really aware of. But it is where one does respond to that which he addresses to another and where that response of his own becomes a part of his conduct, where he not only hears himself but responds to himself, talks and replies to himself as truly as the other person replies to him, that we have behavior in which the individuals become objects to themselves.

Such a self is not, I would say, primarily the physiological organism. The physiological organism is essential to it, but we are at least able to think of a self without it. Persons who believe in immortality, or believe in ghosts, or in the possibility of the self leaving the body, assume a self which is quite distinguishable from the body. How successfully they can hold these conceptions is an open question, but we do, as a fact, separate the self and the organism. It is fair to say that the beginning of the self as an object, so far as we can see, is to be found in the experiences of people that lead to the conception of a "double." Primitive people assume that there is a double, located presumably in the diaphragm, that leaves the body temporarily in sleep and completely in death. It can be enticed out of the body of one's enemy and perhaps killed. It is represented in infancy by the imaginary playmates which children set up, and through which they come to control their experiences in their play.

The self, as that which can be an object to itself, is essentially a social structure, and it arises in social experience. After a self has arisen, it in a certain sense provides for itself its social experiences, and so we can conceive of an absolutely solitary self. But it is impossible to conceive of a self arising outside of social experience. When it has arisen we can think of a person in solitary confinement for the rest of his life, but who still has himself as a companion, and is able to think and to converse with himself as he had communicated with others. That process to which I have just referred, of responding to one's self as another responds to it, taking part in one's own conversation with others, being aware of what one is saying and using that awareness of what one is saying to determine what one is going to say thereafter—that is a process with which we are all familiar. We are continually following up our own address to other persons by an understanding of what we are saying, and using that understanding in the direction of our continued speech. We are finding out what we are going to say, what we are going to do, by saying and doing, and in the process we are continually controlling the process itself. In the conversation of gestures what we say calls out a certain response in another and that in turn changes our own action, so that we shift from what we started to do because of the reply the other makes. The conversation of gestures is the beginning of communication. The individual comes to carry on a conversation of gestures with himself. He says something, and that calls out a certain reply in himself which makes him change what he was going to say. One starts to say something, we will presume an unpleasant something, but when he starts to say it he realizes it is cruel. The effect on himself of what he is saying checks him; there is here a conversation of gestures between the individual and himself. We mean by significant speech that the action is one that affects the individual himself, and that the effect upon the individual himself is part of the intelligent carrying-out of the conversation with others. Now we, so to speak, amputate that social phase and dispense with it for the time being, so that one is talking to one's self as one would talk to another person.

This process of abstraction cannot be carried on indefinitely. One inevitably seeks an audience, has to pour himself out to somebody. In reflective intelligence one thinks to act, and to act solely so that this action remains a part of a social process. Thinking becomes preparatory to social action. The very process of thinking is, of course, simply an inner conversation that goes on, but it is a conversation of gestures which in its completion implies the expression of that which one thinks to an audience. One separates the significance of what he is saying to others from the actual speech and gets it ready before saying it. He thinks it out, and perhaps writes it in the form of a book; but it is still a part of social intercourse in which one is addressing other persons and at the same time addressing one's self, and in which one controls the address to other persons by the response made to one's own gesture. That the person should be responding to himself is necessary to the self, and it is this sort of social conduct which provides behavior within which that self appears. I know of no other form of behavior than the linguistic in which the individual is an object to himself, and, so far as I can see, the individual is not a self in the reflexive sense unless he is an object to himself. It is this fact that gives a critical importance to communication, since this is a type of behavior in which the individual does so respond to himself.

We realize in everyday conduct and experience that an individual does not mean a great deal of what he is doing and saying. We frequently say that such an individual is not himself. We come away from an interview with a realization that we have left out important things, that there are parts of the self that did not get into what was said. What determines the amount of the self that gets into communication is the social experience itself. Of course, a good deal of the self does not need to get expression. We carry on a whole series of different relationships to different people. We are one thing to one man and another thing to another. There are parts of the self which exist only for the self in relationship to itself. We divide ourselves up in all sorts of different selves with reference to our acquaintances. We discuss politics with one and religion with another. There are all sorts of different selves answering to all sorts of different social reactions. It is the social process itself that is responsible for the appearance of the self; it is not there as a self apart from this type of experience.

A multiple personality is in a certain sense normal, as I have just pointed out. There is usually an organization of the whole self with reference to the community to which we belong, and the situation in which we find ourselves. What the society is, whether we are living with people of the present, people of our own imaginations, people of the past, varies, of course, with different individuals. Normally, within the sort of community as a whole to which we belong, there is a unified self, but that may be broken up. To a person who is somewhat unstable nervously and in whom there is a line of cleavage, certain activities become impossible, and that set of activities may separate and evolve another self. Two separate "me's" and "I's," two different selves, result, and that is the condition under which there is a tendency to break up the personality. There is an account of a professor of education who disappeared, was lost to the community, and later turned up in a logging camp in the West. He freed himself of his occupation and turned to the woods where he felt, if you like, more at home. The pathological side of it was the forgetting, the leaving out of the rest of the self. This result involved getting rid of certain bodily memories which would identify the individual to himself. We often recognize the lines of cleavage that run through us. We would be glad to forget certain things, get rid of things the self is bound up with in past experiences. What we have here is a situation in which there can be different selves, and it is dependent upon the set of social reactions that is involved as to which self we are going to be. If we can forget everything involved in one set of activities, obviously we relinquish that part of the self. Take a person who is unstable, get him occupied by speech, and at the same time get his eye on something you are writing so that he is carrying on two separate lines of communication, and if you go about it in the right way you can get those two currents going so that they do not run into each other. You can get two entirely different sets of activities going on. You can bring about in that way the dissociation of a person's self. It is a process of setting up two sorts of communication which separate the behavior of the individual. For one individual it is this thing said and heard, and for the other individual there exists only that which he sees written. You must, of course, keep one experience out of the field of the other. Dissociations are apt to take place when an event leads to emotional upheavals. That which is separated goes on in its own way.

The unity and structure of the complete self reflects the unity and structure of the social process as a whole; and each of the elementary selves of which it is composed reflects the unity and structure of one of the various aspects of that process in which the individual is implicated. In other words, the various elementary selves which constitute, or are organized into, a complete self are the various aspects of the structure of that complete self answering to the various aspects of the structure of the social process as a whole; the structure of the complete self is thus a reflection of the complete social process. The organization and unification of a social group is identical with the organization and unification of any one of the selves arising within the social process in which that group is engaged, or which it is carrying on.

The phenomenon of dissociation of personality is caused by a breaking up of the complete, unitary self into the component selves of which it is composed, and which respectively correspond to different aspects of the social process in which the person is involved, and within which his complete or unitary self has arisen; these aspects being the different social groups to which he belongs within that process.

SELECTED BIBLIOGRAPHY FOR PART III

Anderson, Alan, ed. *Minds and Machines*. Englewood Cliffs, N.J.: Prentice-Hall, 1964.

Aune, Bruce. *Knowledge, Mind, and Nature*. New York: Random House, 1967.

Ayer, A. J. *The Concept of Person and Other Essays*. London: Macmillan, 1963.

Broad, C. D. *The Mind and Its Place in Nature*. New York: Harcourt, Brace, 1925.

Castell, Alburey. *The Self in Philosophy*. New York: Macmillan, 1965.

Chappell, Vere, ed. *Philosophy of Mind*. Englewood Cliffs, N.J.: Prentice-Hall, 1962.

Ducasse, C. J. *Nature, Mind and Death*. La Salle, Ill.: Open Court, 1951.

Feigl, Herbert. *The "Mental" and "Physical."* Minneapolis: University of Minnesota Press, 1967.

———. "Other Minds and the Egocentric Predicament," *Journal of Philosophy*, LV (1958).

Flew, Antony. *Body, Mind, and Death*. New York: Macmillan, 1964.

Grice, H. P. "Personal Identity," *Mind*, L (1941).

Grossmann, Reinhardt. *The Structure of Mind*. Madison, Wisconsin: University of Wisconsin Press, 1965.

Gustafson, Donald. *Essays in Philosophical Psychology*. Garden City: Doubleday, 1964.

Hampshire, Stuart, ed. *Philosophy of Mind*. New York: Harper and Row, 1966.

Hook, Sidney, ed. *Dimensions of Mind*. New York: New York University Press, 1960.

Laird, John. *Our Minds and Their Bodies*. London: Oxford University Press, 1925.

———. *The Problem of the Self*. London: Macmillan, 1917.

Lovejoy, Arthur. *The Revolt Against Dualism*. La Salle, Ill.: Open Court, 1930.

Morick, Harold, ed. *Wittgenstein and the Problem of Other Minds*. New York: McGraw-Hill, 1967.

Penelhum, Terence. "Hume on Personal Identity," *Philosophical Review*, LXIV (1955).

Place, U. T. "Materialism as a Scientific Hypothesis," *Philosophical Review*, LXIX (1960).

Plato. *Phaedo,* trans. R. Hackforth. Indianapolis, Ind.: Liberal Arts Press, 1955.

Scriven, Michael. "The Mechanical Concept of Mind," *Mind*, LXII (1953).

Shaffer, Jerome. "Could Mental States be Brain Processes?" *Journal of Philosophy,* LVIII (1961).

Shoemaker, Sydney S. "Personal Identity and Memory," *Journal of Philosophy,* LVI (1959).

————. *Self-Knowledge and Self-Identity.* (Ithaca, N.Y.: Cornell University Press, 1963.

Sibley, Frank. "A Theory of Mind," *Review of Metaphysics,* IV (1950–51).

Skinner, B. F. *Science and Human Behavior.* New York: Macmillan, 1953.

Smart, J. J. C. "Materialism," *Journal of Philosophy,* LX (1963).

————. *Philosophy and Scientific Realism.* New York: Humanities Press, 1963.

Smythies, J. R., ed. *Brain and Mind.* New York: Humanities Press, 1965.

Strawson, P. F. *Individuals: An Essay in Descriptive Metaphysics.* London: Methuen, 1959.

Stout, G. F. *Mind and Matter.* Cambridge: Cambridge University Press, 1931.

Vesey, G. N. A., ed. *Body and Mind.* London: Allen and Unwin, 1964.

White, Alan R. *The Philosophy of Mind.* New York: Random House, 1967.

Williams, B. A. O. "Personal Identity and Individuation," *Proceedings of the Aristotelian Society,* LVII (1956–57).

Wisdom, John. *Problems of Mind and Matter.* Cambridge: Cambridge University Press, 1934.

Wittgenstein, Ludwig. *Philosophical Investigations,* trans. G. E. M. Anscombe. New York: Macmillan, 1953.

part IV

GOD

∴...does he exist?

INTRODUCTION

Metaphysical inquiry into the nature of man and of the universe is incomplete without consideration of the question of God's existence. Supernaturalism, a religious view held by millions today, is the belief that there is, above man and outside of nature, a superior being (or beings). It is a belief which finds social expression in the doctrines and practices of some orthodox Eastern and Western religions. Orthodox religions usually prescribe for their members rituals of worship and codes of morality. For example, some Christian sects prescribe a morality based upon the ten commandments, and hold that the universe was created by God and that through the grace of God man's immortal soul may be saved. On the other hand, some theologically unorthodox views, generally naturalistic or materialistic ones, claim that there is only nature or matter, and present man as a creature whose meaning, purpose, and morality are found exclusively in this world, rather than in a supernatural realm. The tenability of either a religious or nonreligious position depends ultimately upon the justification which can be given for belief in the existence or nonexistence of God.

The problem of God's existence has received both philosophic and non-philosophic treatment. Most people are familiar with the approach taken in revealed religion, where God's existence is verified in a non-philosophic manner. The theologian who appeals to revelation to prove God's existence cites the authority of sacred literature. Sacred literature, in turn, derives its authority from God himself. It is His revelations which are recorded in the Bible, Koran, and other sacred writings. In the authentication of ancient scriptures, scholars have performed extensive analyses and employed scientific techniques, but the word of God as recorded in a validated manuscript is not subject, according to the theology of revelation, to critical examination and must be accepted without question. Unlike the fact that Caesar crossed the Rubicon or that George Washington was the first President of the United States, the word of God cannot be tested and verified. Hence revelation, according to its defenders, cannot be disputed philosophically. In contrast to those theologians who depend upon revelation, the philosopher bases his consideration of God's existence upon arguments open to criticism. A philosophic approach to the question of God's existence or nonexistence—the sort of approach to be found in Part IV—is based upon human reason or experience.

Theism, under its most general definition, is the belief that there is a God. It is a view that has several forms. Orthodox theists usually hold that God created the universe, answers prayers, and upon occasion intervenes in human affairs. In contrast, deism, in the sense most often used today, maintains that God created the universe but does not interfere with its natural laws or with human affairs. Accordingly, the prayers and supplications of man go unheeded. According to pantheism, a special form of theism,[1] God is not a separate, external being, but *is* the universe, with all its forces and laws. In these disparate positions there is disagreement about the nature of God and his relation to the universe, but in none of them is there dispute about the existence of God.

One of the most famous arguments in support of theism was formulated in the eleventh century by St. Anselm of Canterbury. His famous ontological argument attempts to demonstrate the existence of God from man's conception of God as "a being than which nothing greater can be thought." Because of God's perfection, Anselm concludes that God must exist. (If God, the supreme being, did not exist, then He would not be the greatest being one could conceive. Thus existence is seen as an attribute necessary for God's perfection.) Anselm infers the necessity of God's existence from his conception of God. For him, the ontological argument is a rational attempt to understand his faith in God. Because Anselm bases his argument for God's existence solely upon the activity of reason (the mind's conception of God), rather than upon his observation of the world, the argument is called an *a priori,* or rational, proof of God's existence.

The ontological argument was criticized, shortly after its enunciation, by Gaunilo, a contemporary of Anselm. Gaunilo maintains that the existence of God cannot be inferred from Anselm's definition. He supports his argument by the famous example of the perfect island that can be conceived but whose existence cannot be inferred from its conception.

Because the essence of God is not self-evident, Thomas Aquinas, a thirteenth-century Dominican, also discounts Anselm's *a priori* evidence as proof of God's existence. Aquinas holds that God's existence and attributes are inferred from the observed facts of experience. In this kind of argument the existence of God is derived from statements that describe His effects. Aquinas formulates five such proofs of God's existence.

Ernest Nagel criticizes both the ontological argument and Aquinas' empirical arguments for the existence of God. Because he finds these arguments untenable, Nagel opts for atheism. The atheist claims that there is no God. Nagel maintains that this position has a positive as well as a negative role. Atheism's negative aspect is its criticism of the prevailing arguments for the existence of God, while its positive role is that of formulating a world view to replace that of theism.

Upon careful examination of the arguments for and against the existence of God some thinkers contend that there is no conclusive evidence for either view. Thomas Huxley, a nineteenth-century English scientist, finds himself in this position, which he calls "agnosticism." He elects to suspend judgment on the matter of God's existence until adequate evidence for either theism or atheism is available. Huxley does not believe that the suspension of judgment is a danger to social bonds or morality since

[1] Under a more restrictive definition of theism than that used above, pantheism may be considered to be distinct from theism, rather than a form of it. See, for example, Nagel, p. 216.

orderly society and moral behavior are older than Christianity, and are based on human needs rather than on religious precepts.

Can we really suspend judgment on the question of God's existence? William James believes that we cannot. Sometimes we are confronted with a situation where a choice between alternative beliefs is forced upon us, but where conclusive evidence for one alternative or the other is lacking. In such a situation, James argues, we have the right to choose one of the alternatives in the interest of effective living. For him, belief in God is such a genuine choice. Hence, in the absence of sufficient evidence, we have the right to will to believe that God exists. James' famous doctrine of "the will to believe" involves faith that is not substantiated by fact or reason.

The traditional use of the vague and ambiguous word "faith" to describe religious beliefs has resulted in confusion, distortion, and intellectual resistance. In the attempt to eliminate these difficulties, Paul Tillich, an existential theologian of the twentieth century, redefines "faith." In sharp contrast to James, Tillich holds that faith is not an act of the will but a commitment of the total self to an "ultimate concern." Since man cannot avoid his involvement with an "ultimate concern," the problem vital to religion is not whether God exists, but which of the various symbols of faith is the most appropriate expression of this concern.

Like Tillich, A. J. Ayer doubts the legitimacy of the problem of God's existence. However, his rejection of the problem is not based upon an existential "faith" but upon the principle of verification, which supplies a criterion for determining whether or not a sentence is literally meaningful. To be meaningful, an assertion about existence must be empirically verifiable. A statement about God's existence is not verifiable because there are no direct or indirect observations which give meaning to the term "God." Ayer concludes, then, that theism is nonsense. Agnosticism and atheism are also illegitimate positions because they presuppose the meaningfulness of the term "God."

Need the radical character of Ayer's position follow from his assumptions? John Wisdom accepts Ayer's assumption that the question of God's existence is not an experimental matter, but he asserts that the reasonableness of such beliefs involves a logic of attitude as well as a logic of fact. Two persons who know the same facts may disagree in their attitudes toward these facts. Disputes involving such disagreement may be resolved by one disputant's pointing out features ignored by his opponent. The logic of attitude is similar to that employed by a judge in connecting the facts of a case to previous cases and to other facts which together substantiate his ruling. Or the logic is like that employed by two people who disagree about the aesthetic value of a scene or work of art. One tries to persuade the other by pointing out different features of the work so that it is seen from a different perspective, a perspective which suits the divergent attitude. When facts themselves are inconclusive, then conclusions are reached by decisions as to which facts ought to be emphasized. Such a logic, Wisdom maintains, is applicable to arguments for the existence of God, and, he implies, might be the basis for a fruitful reëxamination of the issue.

The following selections examine in detail the views discussed above. They provide alternative answers to the question of God's existence, answers which may assist in the development of a consistent philosophy of man and of the universe.

THE ONTOLOGICAL ARGUMENT

st. anselm

from the Proslogium

Chapter two

And so, Lord, do thou, who dost give understanding to faith, give me, so far as thou knowest it to be profitable, to understand that thou art as we believe; and that thou art that which we believe. And, indeed, we believe that thou art a being than which nothing greater can be conceived. Or is there no such nature, since the fool hath said in his heart, there is no God? (Psalms xiv. 1.) But, at any rate, this very fool, when he hears of this being of which I speak—a being than which nothing greater can be conceived—understands what he hears, and what he understands is in his understanding; although he does not understand it to exist.

For, it is one thing for an object to be in the understanding, and another to understand that the object exists. When a painter first conceives of what he will afterwards perform, he has it in his understanding, but he does not yet understand it to be, because he has not yet performed it. But after he has made the painting, he both has it in his understanding, and he understands that it exists, because he has made it.

Hence, even the fool is convinced that something exists in the understanding, at least, than which nothing greater can be conceived. For, when he hears of this, he understands it. And whatever is understood, exists in the understanding. And assuredly that, than which nothing greater can be conceived, cannot exist in the understanding alone. For, suppose it exists in the understanding alone: then it can be conceived to exist in reality, which is greater.

Therefore, if that, than which nothing greater can be conceived, exists in the understanding alone, the very being, than which nothing greater can be conceived, is one, than which a greater can be conceived. But obviously this is impossible. Hence, there is no doubt that there exists a being, than which nothing greater can be conceived, and it exists both in the understanding and in reality.

From *St. Anselm: Basic Writings*, S. N. Deane, trans. (La Salle, Ill.: Open Court Publishing Company, 1961), pp. 7–10, 145–152. Reprinted by permission of the publisher.

Chapter three

And it assuredly exists so truly, that it cannot be conceived not to exist. For, it is possible to conceive of a being which cannot be conceived not to exist; and this is greater than one which can be conceived not to exist. Hence, if that, than which nothing greater can be conceived, can be conceived not to exist, it is not that, than which nothing greater can be conceived. But this is an irreconcilable contradiction. There is, then, so truly a being than which nothing greater can be conceived to exist, that it cannot even be conceived not to exist; and this being thou art, O Lord, our God.

So truly, therefore, dost thou exist, O Lord, my God, that thou canst not be conceived not to exist; and rightly. For, if a mind could conceive of a being better than thee, the creature would rise above the Creator; and this is most absurd. And, indeed, whatever else there is, except thee alone, can be conceived not to exist. To thee alone, therefore, it belongs to exist more truly than all other beings, and hence in a higher degree than all others. For, whatever else exists does not exist so truly, and hence in a less degree it belongs to it to exist. Why, then, has the fool said in his heart, there is no God (Psalms xiv. 1), since it is so evident, to a rational mind, that thou dost exist in the highest degree of all? Why, except that he is dull and a fool?

Chapter four

But how has the fool said in his heart what he could not conceive; or how is it that he could not conceive what he said in his heart? since it is the same to say in the heart, and to conceive.

But, if really, nay, since really, he both conceived, because he said in his heart; and did not say in his heart, because he could not conceive; there is more than one way in which a thing is said in the heart or conceived. For, in one sense, an object is conceived, when the word signifying it is conceived; and in another, when the very entity, which the object is, is understood.

In the former sense, then, God can be conceived not to exist; but in the latter, not at all. For no one who understands what fire and water are can conceive fire to be water, in accordance with the nature of the facts themselves, although this is possible according to the words. So, then, no one who understands what God is can conceive that God does not exist; although he says these words in his heart, either without any, or with some foreign, signification. For, God is that than which a greater cannot be conceived. And he who thoroughly understands this, assuredly understands that this being so truly exists, that not even in concept can it be nonexistent. Therefore, he who understands that God so exists, cannot conceive that he does not exist.

·   ·   ·

In Behalf of the Fool

An answer to the argument of Anselm in the
Proslogium *by Gaunilo, a monk of Marmoutier*

1. If one doubts or denies the existence of a being of such a nature that nothing greater than it can be conceived, he receives this answer:

The existence of this being is proved, in the first place, by the fact that he himself, in his doubt or denial regarding this being, already has it in his understanding; for in hearing it spoken of he understands what is spoken of. It is proved, therefore, by the fact that what he understands must exist not only in his understanding, but in reality also.

And the proof of this is as follows. It is a greater thing to exist both in the understanding and in reality than to be in the understanding alone. And if this being is in the understanding alone, whatever has, even in the past, existed in reality will be greater than this being. And so that which was greater than all beings will be less than some being, and will not be greater than all—which is a manifest contradiction.

And hence, that which is greater than all, already proved to be in the understanding, must exist not only in the understanding, but also in reality: for otherwise it will not be greater than all other beings.

2. The fool might make this reply:

This being is said to be in my understanding already, only because I understand what is said. Now could it not with equal justice be said that I have in my understanding all manner of unreal objects, having absolutely no existence in themselves, because I understand these things if one speaks of them, whatever they may be?

Unless indeed it is shown that this being is of such a character that it cannot be held in concept like all unreal objects, or objects whose existence is uncertain: and hence I am not able to conceive of it when I hear of it, or to hold it in concept; but I must understand it and have it in my understanding; because, it seems, I cannot conceive of it in any other way than by understanding it, that is, by comprehending in my knowledge its existence in reality.

But if this is the case, in the first place there will be no distinction between what has precedence in time—namely, the having of an object in the understanding—and what is subsequent in time—namely, the understanding that an object exists; as in the example of the picture, which exists first in the mind of the painter, and afterwards in his work.

Moreover, the following assertion can hardly be accepted: that this being, when it is spoken of and heard of, cannot be conceived not to exist in the way in which even God can be conceived not to exist. For if this is impossible, what was the object of this argument against one who doubts or denies the existence of such a being?

Finally, that this being so exists that it cannot be perceived by an understanding convinced of its own indubitable existence, unless this being is afterwards conceived of—this should be proved to me by an indisputable argument, but not by that which you have advanced: namely, that what I understand, when I hear it, already is in my understanding. For thus in my understanding, as I still think, could be all sorts of things whose existence is uncertain, or which do not exist at all, if some one whose words I should understand mentioned them. And so much the more if I should be deceived, as often happens, and believe in them, though I do not yet believe in the being whose existence you would prove.

3. Hence, your example of the painter who already has in his understanding what he is to paint cannot agree with this argument. For the picture, before it is made, is contained in the artificer's art itself; and any such thing, existing in the art of an artificer, is nothing but a part of his understanding itself. A joiner, St. Augustine says, when he is about to make a box in fact, first has it in his art. The box which is made in fact is not life; but the box which exists in his art is life. For the artificer's soul lives, in which all these things are, before they are produced. Why, then, are these things life in the living soul of the artificer, unless because they are nothing else than the knowledge or understanding of the soul itself?

With the exception, however, of those facts which are known to pertain to the mental nature, whatever, on being heard and thought out by the understanding, is perceived to be real, undoubtedly that real object is one thing, and the understanding itself, by which the object is grasped, is another. Hence, even if it were true that there is a being than which a greater is inconceivable, yet to this being, when heard of and understood, the not yet created picture in the mind of the painter is not analogous.

4. Let us notice also the point touched on above, with regard to this being which is greater than all which can be conceived, and which, it is said, can be none other than God himself. I, so far as actual knowledge of the object, either from its specific or general character, is concerned, am as little able to conceive of this being when I hear of it, or to have it in my understanding, as I am to conceive of or understand God himself, whom, indeed, for this very reason I can conceive not to exist. For I do not know that reality itself which God is, nor can I form a conjecture of that reality from some other like reality. For you yourself assert that that reality is such that there can be nothing else like it.

For, suppose that I should hear something said of a man absolutely unknown to me, of whose very existence I was unaware. Through that special or general knowledge by which I know what man is, or what men are, I could conceive of him also, according to the reality itself, which man is. And yet it would be possible, if the person who told me of him deceived me, that the man himself, of whom I conceived, did not exist; since that reality according to which I conceived of him, though a no less indisputable fact, was not that man, but any man.

Hence, I am not able, in the way in which I should have this unreal being in concept or in understanding, to have that being of which you speak in concept or in understanding, when I hear the word *God* or the words, *a being greater than all other beings*. For I can conceive of the man according to a fact that is real and familiar to me: but of God, or a being greater than all others, I could not conceive at all, except merely according to the word. And an object can hardly or never be conceived according to the word alone.

For when it is so conceived, it is not so much the word itself (which is, indeed, a real thing—that is, the sound of the letters and syllables) as the signification of the word, when heard, that is conceived. But it is not conceived as by one who knows what is generally signified by the word, by whom, that is, it is conceived according to a reality and in true conception alone. It is conceived as by a man who does not know the object, and conceives of it only in accordance with the movement of his mind produced by hearing the word, the mind attempting to image for itself the signification of the word that is heard. And it would be surprising if in the reality of fact it could ever attain to this.

Thus, it appears, and in no other way, this being is also in my understanding, when I hear and understand a person who says that there is a being greater than all conceivable beings. So much for the assertion that this supreme nature already is in my understanding.

5. But that this being must exist, not only in the understanding but also in reality, is thus proved to me:

If it did not so exist, whatever exists in reality would be greater than it. And so the being which has been already proved to exist in my understanding, will not be greater than all other beings.

I still answer: if it should be said that a being which cannot be even conceived in terms of any fact, is in the understanding, I do not deny that this being is, accordingly, in my understanding. But since through this fact it can in no wise attain to real existence also, I do not yet concede to it that existence at all, until some certain proof of it shall be given.

For he who says that this being exists, because otherwise the being which is greater than all will not be greater than all, does not attend strictly enough to what he is saying. For I do not yet say, no, I even deny or doubt that this being is greater than any real object. Nor do I concede to it any other existence than this (if it should be called existence) which it has when the mind, according to a word merely heard, tries to form the image of an object absolutely unknown to it.

How, then, is the veritable existence of that being proved to me from the assumption, by hypothesis, that it is greater than all other beings? For I should still deny this, or doubt your demonstration of it, to this extent, that I should not admit that this being is in my understanding and concept even in the way in which many objects whose real existence is uncertain and doubtful, are in my understanding and concept. For it should be proved first that this being itself really exists somewhere, and then, from the fact that it is greater than all, we shall not hesitate to infer that it also subsists in itself.

6. For example: it is said that somewhere in the ocean is an island, which, because of the difficulty, or rather the impossibility, of discovering what does not exist, is called the lost island. And they say that this island has an inestimable wealth of all manner of riches and delicacies in greater abundance than is told of the Islands of the Blest, and that having no owner or inhabitant, it is more excellent than all other countries, which are inhabited by mankind, in the abundance with which it is stored.

Now if some one should tell me that there is such an island, I should easily understand his words, in which there is no difficulty. But suppose that he went on to say, as if by a logical inference: "You can no longer doubt that this island which is more excellent than all lands exists somewhere, since you have no doubt that it is in your understanding. And since it is more excellent not to be in the understanding alone, but to exist both in the understanding and in reality, for this reason it must exist. For if it does not exist, any land which really exists will be more excellent than it; and so the island already understood by you to be more excellent will not be more excellent."

If a man should try to prove to me by such reasoning that this island truly exists, and that its existence should no longer be doubted, either I should believe that he was jesting, or I know not which I ought to regard as the greater fool: myself, supposing that I should allow this proof; or him, if he should suppose that he had established with any certainty the existence of this island. For he ought to show first that the hypothetical excellence of this island exists as a real and indubitable fact, and in no wise as any unreal object, or one whose existence is uncertain, in my understanding.

7. This, in the mean time, is the answer the fool could make to the arguments urged against him. When he is assured in the first place that this being is so great that its nonexistence is not even conceivable, and that this in turn is proved on no other ground than the fact that otherwise it will not be greater than all things, the fool may make the same answer, and say:

When did I say that any such being exists in reality, that is, a being greater than all others?—that on this ground it should be proved to me that it also exists in reality to such a degree that it cannot even be conceived not to exist? Whereas in the first place it should be in some way proved that a nature which is higher, that is, greater and better, than all other natures, exists; in order that from this we may then be able to prove all attributes which necessarily the being that is greater and better than all possesses.

Moreover, it is said that the nonexistence of this being is inconceivable. It might better be said, perhaps, that its nonexistence, or the possibility of its nonexistence, is unintelligible. For according to the true meaning of the word, unreal objects are unintelligible. Yet their existence is conceivable in the way in which the fool conceived of the nonexistence of God. I am most certainly aware of my own existence; but I know, nevertheless, that my nonexistence is possible. As to that supreme being, moreover, which God is, I understand without any doubt both his existence, and the impossibility of his nonexistence. Whether, however, so long as I am most positively aware of my existence, I can conceive of my nonexistence, I am not sure. But if I can, why can I not conceive of the nonexistence of whatever else I know with the same certainty? If, however, I cannot, God will not be the only being of which it can be said, it is impossible to conceive of his nonexistence.

·   ·   ·

THE EXISTENCE OF GOD

st. thomas aquinas

. . .

First Article: Whether the existence of God is self-evident?

We proceed thus to the First Article:

Objection 1. It seems that the existence of God is self-evident. For those things are said to be self-evident to us the knowledge of which exists naturally in us, as we can see in regard to first principles. But as Damascene says, *the knowledge of God is naturally implanted in all.* Therefore the existence of God is self-evident.

Obj. 2. Further, those things are said to be self-evident which are known as soon as the terms are known, which the Philosopher [i.e., Aristotle] says is true of the first principles of demonstration. Thus, when the nature of a whole and of a part is known, it is at once recognized that every whole is greater than its part. But as soon as the signification of the name *God* is understood, it is at once seen that God exists. For by this name is signified that thing than which nothing greater can be conceived. But that which exists actually and mentally is greater than that which exists only mentally. Therefore, since as soon as the name *God* is understood it exists mentally, it also follows that it exists actually. Therefore the proposition *God exists* is self-evident.

Obj. 3. Further, the existence of truth is self-evident. For whoever denies the existence of truth grants that truth does not exist: and, if truth does not exist, then the proposition *Truth does not exist* is true: and if there is anything true, there must be truth. But God is truth itself: *I am the way, the truth, and the life* (Jo. xiv. 6). Therefore *God exists* is self-evident.

On the contrary, No one can mentally admit the opposite of what is self-evident, as the Philosopher states concerning the first principles of demonstration. But the opposite of the proposition *God is* can be mentally admitted: *The fool said in his heart, There is no God* (Ps. lii. 1). Therefore, that God exists is not self-evident.

I answer that, A thing can be self-evident in either of two ways: on the one hand, self-evident in itself, though not to us; on the other, self-evident in itself, and to us. A proposition is self-evident because the predicate is included in the essence of the subject: *e.g., Man is an animal,* for animal is contained in the essence of man. If, therefore, the essence of the predicate and subject be known to all, the proposition will be self-evident to all; as is clear with regard to the first principles of demonstration, the terms of which are certain common notions that no one is ignorant of, such as being and nonbeing, whole and part, and the like. If, however, there are some to whom the essence of the predicate and subject is unknown, the proposition will be self-evident in itself, but not to those who do not know the meaning of the predicate and subject of the proposition. Therefore, it happens, as Boethius says, that there are some notions of the mind which are common and self-evident only to the learned, as that incorporeal substances are not in space. Therefore I say that this proposition, *God exists,* of itself is self-evident, for the predicate is the same as the subject, because God is His own existence as will be hereafter shown. Now because we do not know the essence of God, the proposition is not self-evident to us, but needs to be demonstrated by things that are more known to us, though less known in their nature —namely, by His effects.

Reply Obj. 1. To know that God exists in a general and confused way is implanted in us by nature, inasmuch as God is man's beatitude. For man naturally desires happiness, and what is naturally desired by man is naturally known by him. This, however, is not to know absolutely that God exists, just as to know that someone is approaching is not the same as to know that Peter is approaching, even though it is Peter who is approaching; for there are many who imagine that man's perfect good, which is happiness, consists in riches, and others in pleasures, and others in something else.

Reply Obj. 2. Perhaps not everyone who hears this name *God* understands it to signify something than which nothing greater can be thought, seeing that some have believed God to be a body. Yet, granted that everyone understands that by this name *God* is signified something than which nothing greater can be thought, nevertheless, it does not therefore follow that he understands that what the name signifies exists actually, but only that it exists mentally. Nor can it be argued that it actually exists, unless it be admitted that there actually exists something than which nothing greater can be thought; and this precisely is not admitted by those who hold that God does not exist.

Reply Obj. 3. The existence of truth in general is self-evident, but the existence of a Primal Truth is not self-evident to us.

Second Article: Whether it can be demonstrated that God exists?

We proceed thus to the Second Article:

Objection 1. It seems that the existence of God cannot be demonstrated. For it is an article of faith that God exists. But what is of faith cannot be demonstrated, because a demonstration produces scientific knowledge, whereas faith is of the unseen, as is clear from the Apostle (Heb. xi. 1). Therefore it cannot be demonstrated that God exists.

Obj. 2. Further, essence is the middle term of demonstration. But we cannot know in what God's essence consists, but solely in what it does not consist, as Damascene says. Therefore we cannot demonstrate that God exists.

Obj. 3. Further, if the existence of God were demonstrated, this could only be from His effects. But His effects are not proportioned to Him, since He is infinite and His effects are finite, and between the finite and infinite there is no proportion. Therefore, since a cause cannot be demonstrated by an effect not proportioned to it, it seems that the existence of God cannot be demonstrated.

On the contrary, The Apostle says: *The invisible things of Him are clearly seen, being understood by the things that are made* (Rom. i. 20). But this would not be unless the existence of God could be demonstrated through the things that are made; for the first thing we must know of anything is, whether it exists.

I answer that, Demonstration can be made in two ways: One is through the cause, and is called *propter quid,* and this is to argue from what is prior absolutely. The other is through the effect, and is called a demonstration *quia;* this is to argue from what is prior relatively only to us. When an effect is better known to us than its cause, from the effect we proceed to the knowledge of the cause. And from every effect the existence of its proper cause can be demonstrated, so long as its effects are better known to us, because, since every effect depends upon its cause, if the effect exists, the cause must pre-exist. Hence the existence of God, in so far as it is not self-evident to us, can be demonstrated from those of His effects which are known to us.

Reply Obj. 1. The existence of God and other like truths about God, which can be known by natural reason, are not articles of faith, but are preambles to the articles; for faith presupposes natural knowledge, even as grace presupposes nature and perfection the perfectible. Nevertheless, there is nothing to prevent a man, who cannot grasp a proof, from accepting, as a matter of faith, something which in itself is capable of being scientifically known and demonstrated.

Reply Obj. 2. When the existence of a cause is demonstrated from an effect, this effect takes the place of the definition of the cause in proving the cause's existence. This is especially the case in regard to God, because, in order to prove the existence of anything, it is necessary to accept as a middle term the meaning of the name, and not its essence, for the question of its essence follows on the question of its existence. Now the names given to God are derived from His effects, as will be later shown. Consequently, in demonstrating the existence of God from His effects, we may take for the middle term the meaning of the name *God.*

Reply Obj. 3. From effects not proportioned to the cause no perfect knowledge of that cause can be obtained. Yet from every effect the existence of the cause can be clearly demonstrated, and so we can demonstrate the existence of God from His effects, though from them we cannot know God perfectly as He is in His essence.

Third Article: Whether God Exists?

We proceed thus to the Third Article:
Objection 1. It seems that God does not exist, because if one of two contraries be infinite, the other would be altogether destroyed. But the name *God* means that He

is infinite goodness. If, therefore, God existed, there would be no evil discoverable; but there is evil in the world. Therefore God does not exist.

Obj. 2. Further, it is superfluous to suppose that what can be accounted for by a few principles has been produced by many. But it seems that everything we see in the world can be accounted for by other principles, supposing God did not exist. For all natural things can be reduced to one principle, which is nature; and all voluntary things can be reduced to one principle, which is human reason, or will. Therefore there is no need to suppose God's existence.

On the contrary, It is said in the person of God: *I am Who am* (Exod. iii. 14).

I answer that, The existence of God can be proved in five ways.

The first and more manifest way is the argument from motion. It is certain, and evident to our senses, that in the world some things are in motion. Now whatever is moved is moved by another, for nothing can be moved except it is in potentiality to that towards which it is moved, whereas a thing moves inasmuch as it is in act. For motion is nothing else than the reduction of something from potentiality to actuality. But nothing can be reduced from potentiality to actuality, except by something in a state of actuality. Thus that which is actually hot, as fire, makes wood, which is potentially hot, to be actually hot, and thereby moves and changes it. Now it is not possible that the same thing should be at once in actuality and potentiality in the same respect, but only in different respects. For what is actually hot cannot simultaneously be potentially hot; but it is simultaneously potentially cold. It is therefore impossible that in the same respect and in the same way a thing should be both mover and moved, i.e., that it should move itself. Therefore, whatever is moved must be moved by another. If that by which it is moved be itself moved, then this also must needs be moved by another, and that by another again. But this cannot go on to infinity, because then there would be no first mover, and, consequently, no other mover, seeing that subsequent movers move only inasmuch as they are moved by the first mover; as the staff moves only because it is moved by the hand. Therefore it is necessary to arrive at a first mover, moved by no other; and this everyone understands to be God.

The second way is from the nature of efficient cause. In the world of sensible things we find there is an order of efficient causes. There is no case known (neither is it, indeed, possible) in which a thing is found to be the efficient cause of itself; for so it would be prior to itself, which is impossible. Now in efficient causes it is not possible to go on to infinity, because in all efficient causes following in order, the first is the cause of the intermediate cause, and the intermediate is the cause of the ultimate cause, whether the intermediate cause be several, or one only. Now to take away the cause is to take away the effect. Therefore, if there be no first cause among efficient causes, there will be no ultimate, nor any intermediate, cause. But if in efficient causes it is possible to go on to infinity, there will be no first efficient cause, neither will there be an ultimate effect, nor any intermediate efficient causes; all of which is plainly false. Therefore it is necessary to admit a first efficient cause, to which everyone gives the name of God.

The third way is taken from possibility and necessity, and runs thus. We find in nature things that are possible to be and not to be, since they are found to be generated, and to be corrupted, and consequently, it is possible for them to be and not to be. But it is impossible for these always to exist, for that which can not-be at some time is not. Therefore, if everything can not-be, then at one time there was nothing in existence. Now if this were true, even now there would be nothing in existence, because that which does not exist begins to exist only through something already existing. Therefore, if at one time nothing was in existence, it would have been impossible for anything to have begun to exist; and thus even now nothing would be in existence—which is absurd. Therefore, not all beings are merely possible, but there must exist something the existence of which is necessary. But every necessary thing either has its necessity caused by another, or not. Now it is impossible to go on to infinity in necessary things which have their necessity caused by another, as has been already proved in regard to efficient causes. Therefore we cannot but admit the existence of some being having of itself its own necessity, and not receiving it from another, but rather causing in others their necessity. This all men speak of as God.

The fourth way is taken from the gradation to be found in things. Among beings there are some more and some less good, true, noble, and the like. But *more* and *less* are predicated of different things according as they resemble in their different ways something which is the maximum, as a thing is said to be hotter according as it more nearly resembles that which is hottest; so that there is something which is truest, something best, something noblest, and, consequently, something which is most being, for those things that are greatest in truth are greatest in being, as it is written in [Aristotle's] *Metaph*. ii. Now the maximum in any genus is the cause of all in that genus, as fire, which is the maximum of heat, is the cause of all hot things, as is said in the same book. Therefore there must also be something which is to all beings the cause of their being, goodness, and every other perfection; and this we call God.

The fifth way is taken from the governance of the world. We see that things which lack knowledge, such as natural bodies, act for an end, and this is evident from their acting always, or nearly always, in the same way, so as to obtain the best result. Hence it is plain that they achieve their end, not fortuitously, but designedly. Now whatever lacks knowledge cannot move towards an end, unless it be directed by some being endowed with knowledge and intelligence; as the arrow is directed by the archer. Therefore some intelligent being exists by whom all natural things are directed to their end; and this being we call God.

Reply Obj. 1. As Augustine says: *Since God is the highest good, He would not allow any evil to exist in His works, unless His omnipotence and goodness were such as to bring good even out of evil.* This is part of the infinite goodness of God, that He should allow evil to exist, and out of it produce good.

Reply Obj. 2. Since nature works for a determinate end under the direction of a higher agent, whatever is done by nature must be traced back to God as to its first cause. So likewise whatever is done voluntarily must be traced back to some higher cause other than human reason and will, since these can change and fail; for all things that are changeable and capable of defect must be traced back to an immovable and self-necessary first principle, as has been shown.

PHILOSOPHICAL CONCEPTS OF ATHEISM

ernest nagel

. . .

1

I must begin by stating what sense I am attaching to the word "atheism," and how I am construing the theme of this paper. I shall understand by "atheism" a critique and a denial of the major claims of all varieties of theism. And by theism I shall mean the view which holds, as one writer has expressed it, "that the heavens and the earth and all that they contain owe their existence and continuance in existence to the wisdom and will of a supreme, self-consistent, omnipotent, omniscient, righteous, and benevolent being, who is distinct from, and independent of, what he has created." Several things immediately follow from these definitions.

In the first place, atheism is not necessarily an irreligious concept, for theism is just one among many views concerning the nature and origin of the world. The denial of theism is logically compatible with a religious outlook upon life, and is in fact characteristic of some of the great historical religions. For as readers of this volume will know, early Buddhism is a religion which does not subscribe to any doctrine about a god; and there are pantheistic religions and philosophies which, because they deny that God is a being separate from and independent of the world, are not theistic in the sense of the word explained above.

The second point to note is that atheism is not to be identified with sheer unbelief, or with disbelief in some particular creed of a religious group. Thus, a child who has received no religious instruction and has never heard about God, is not an atheist—for he is not denying any theistic claims. Similarly in the case of an adult who, if he has withdrawn from the faith of his fathers without reflection or because of frank indifference to any theological issue, is also not an atheist—for such an adult is not challenging theism and is not professing any views on the subject. Moreover, though the term "atheist" has been used historically as an abusive label for those who do not happen to subscribe to some regnant orthodoxy (for example, the ancient

Reprinted with a slight omission, from *Basic Beliefs: The Religious Philosophies of Mankind*, J. E. Fairchild, ed. (New York: Sheridan House, Inc., 1959), pp. 167–186, by permission of the publisher.

Romans called the early Christians atheists, because the latter denied the Roman divinities), or for those who engage in conduct regarded as immoral, it is not in this sense that I am discussing atheism.

One final word of preliminary explanation. I propose to examine some *philosophic* concepts of atheism, and I am not interested in the slightest in the many considerations atheists have advanced against the evidences for some particular religious and theological doctrine—for example, against the truth of the Christian story. What I mean by "philosophical" in the present context is that the views I shall consider are directed against any form of theism, and have their origin and basis in a logical analysis of the theistic position, and in a comprehensive account of the world believed to be wholly intelligible without the adoption of a theistic hypothesis.

Theism as I conceive it is a theological proposition, not a statement of a position that belongs primarily to religion. On my view, religion as a historical and social phenomenon is primarily an institutionalized *cultus* or practice, which possesses identifiable social functions and which expresses certain attitudes men take toward their world. Although it is doubtful whether men ever engage in religious practices or assume religious attitudes without some more or less explicit interpretation of their ritual or some rationale for their attitude, it is still the case that it is possible to distinguish religion as a social and personal phenomenon from the theological doctrines which may be developed as justifications for religious practices. Indeed, in some of the great religions of the world the profession of a creed plays a relatively minor role. In short, religion is a form of social communion, a participation in certain kinds of ritual (whether it be a dance, worship, prayer, or the like), and a form of experience (sometimes, though not invariably, directed to a personal confrontation with divine and holy things). Theology is an articulated and, at its best, a rational attempt at understanding these feelings and practices, in the light of their relation to other parts of human experience, and in terms of some hypothesis concerning the nature of things entire.

2

As I see it, atheistic philosophies fall into two major groups: 1) those which hold that the theistic doctrine is meaningful, but reject it either on the ground that, (a) the positive evidence for it is insufficient, or (b) the negative evidence is quite overwhelming; and 2) those who hold that the theistic thesis is not even meaningful, and reject it (a) as just nonsense or (b) as literally meaningless, but interpreting it as a symbolic rendering of human ideals, thus reading the theistic thesis in a sense that most believers in theism would disavow. It will not be possible in the limited space at my disposal to discuss the second category of atheistic critiques; and in any event, most of the traditional atheistic critiques of theism belong to the first group.

But before turning to the philosophical examination of the major classical arguments for theism, it is well to note that such philosophical critiques do not quite convey the passion with which atheists have often carried on their analyses of theistic views. For historically, atheism has been, and indeed continues to be, a form of social and political protest, directed as much against institutionalized religion as against theistic doctrine. Atheism has been, in effect, a moral revulsion against the undoubted abuses of the secular power exercised by religious leaders and religious institutions.

Religious authorities have opposed the correction of glaring injustices, and encouraged politically and socially reactionary policies. Religious institutions have been havens of obscurantist thought and centers for the dissemination of intolerance. Religious creeds have been used to set limits to free inquiry, to perpetuate inhumane treatment of the ill and the underprivileged, and to support moral doctrines insensitive to human suffering.

These indictments may not tell the whole story about the historical significance of religion; but they are at least an important part of the story. The refutation of theism has thus seemed to many as an indispensable step not only towards liberating men's minds from superstition, but also towards achieving a more equitable reordering of society. And no account of even the more philosophical aspects of atheistic thought is adequate, which does not give proper recognition to the powerful social motives that actuate many atheistic arguments.

But however this may be, I want now to discuss three classical arguments for the existence of God, arguments which have constituted at least a partial basis for theistic commitments. As long as theism is defended simply as a dogma, asserted as a matter of direct revelation or as the deliverance of authority, belief in the dogma is impregnable to rational argument. In fact, however, reasons are frequently advanced in support of the theistic creed, and these reasons have been the subject of acute philosophical critiques.

One of the oldest intellectual defenses of theism is the cosmological argument, also known as the argument from a first cause. Briefly put, the argument runs as follows. Every event must have a cause. Hence an event A must have as cause some event B, which in turn must have a cause C, and so on. But if there is no end to this backward progression of causes, the progression will be infinite; and in the opinion of those who use this argument, an infinite series of actual events is unintelligible and absurd. Hence there must be a first cause, and this first cause is God, the initiator of all change in the universe.

The argument is an ancient one, and is especially effective when stated within the framework of assumptions of Aristotelian physics; and it has impressed many generations of exceptionally keen minds. The argument is nonetheless a weak reed on which to rest the theistic thesis. Let us waive any question concerning the validity of the principle that every event has a cause, for though the question is important its discussion would lead us far afield. However, if the principle is assumed, it is surely incongruous to postulate a first cause as a way of escaping from the coils of an infinite series. For if everything must have a cause, why does not God require one for His own existence? The standard answer is that He does not need any, because He is self-caused. But if God can be self-caused, why cannot the world itself be self-caused? Why do we require a God transcending the world to bring the world into existence and to initiate changes in it? On the other hand, the supposed inconceivability and absurdity of an infinite series of regressive causes will be admitted by no one who has competent familiarity with the modern mathematical analysis of infinity. The cosmological argument does not stand up under scrutiny.

The second "proof" of God's existence is usually called the ontological argument. It too has a long history going back to early Christian days, though it acquired great prominence only in medieval times. The argument can be stated in several ways, one of which is the following. Since God is conceived to be omnipotent, he is a perfect being. A perfect being is defined as one whose essence or nature lacks no attributes (or properties) whatsoever, one whose nature is complete in every respect. But it is evident that we have an idea of a perfect being, for we have just defined the idea; and since this is so, the argument continues, God, who is the perfect being, must exist. Why must he? Because his existence follows from his defined nature. For if God lacked the attribute of existence, he would be lacking at least one attribute, and would therefore not be perfect. To sum up, since we have an idea of God as a perfect being, God must exist.

There are several ways of approaching this argument, but I shall consider only one. The argument was exploded by the eighteenth-century philosopher Immanuel Kant. The substance of Kant's criticism is that it is just a confusion to say that existence is an attribute, and that though the *word* "existence" may occur as the grammatical predicate in a sentence no attribute is being predicated of a thing when we say that the thing exists or has existence. Thus, to use Kant's example, when we think of $100 we are thinking of the nature of this sum of money; but the nature of $100 remains the same whether we have $100 in our pockets or not. Accordingly, we are confounding grammar with logic if we suppose that some characteristic is being attributed to the nature of $100 when we say that a hundred dollar bill exists in someone's pocket.

To make the point clearer, consider another example. When we say that a lion has a tawny color, we are predicating a certain attribute of the animal, and similarly when we say that the lion is fierce or is hungry. But when we say the lion exists, all that we are saying is that something is (or has the nature of) a lion; we are not specifying an attribute which belongs to the nature of anything that is a lion. In short, the word "existence" does not signify any attribute, and in consequence no attribute that belongs to the nature of anything. Accordingly, it does not follow from the assumption that we have an idea of a perfect being that such a being exists. For the idea of a perfect being does not involve the attribute of existence as a constituent of that idea, since there is no such attribute. The ontological argument thus has a serious leak, and it can hold no water.

3

The two arguments discussed thus far are purely dialectical, and attempt to establish God's existence without any appeal to empirical data. The next argument, called the argument from design, is different in character, for it is based on what purports to be empirical evidence. I wish to examine two forms of this argument.

One variant of it calls attention to the remarkable way in which different things and processes in the world are integrated with each other, and concludes that this mutual "fitness" of things can be explained only by the assumption of a divine architect who planned the world and everything in it. For example, living organisms can maintain themselves in a variety of environments, and do so in virtue of their delicate mechanisms which adapt the organisms to all sorts of environmental changes. There is thus an intricate pattern of means and ends throughout the animate world. But the existence of this pattern is unintelligible, so the argument runs, except on the hypothesis that the pattern has been deliberately instituted by a Supreme Designer. If we find a watch in some deserted spot, we do not think it came into existence by chance, and we do not hesitate to conclude that an intelligent creature designed and made it. But the world and all its contents exhibit mechanisms and mutual adjustments that are far more complicated and subtle than are those of a watch. Must we not therefore conclude that these things too have a Creator?

The conclusion of this argument is based on an inference from analogy: the watch and the world are alike in possessing a congruence of parts and an adjustment of means to ends; the watch has a watch-maker; hence the world has a world-maker. But is the analogy a good one? Let us once more waive some important issues, in particular the issue whether the universe is the unified system such as the watch admittedly is. And let us concentrate on the question what is the ground for our assurance that watches do not come into existence except through the operations of intelligent manufacturers. The answer is plain. We have never run across a watch which has not been deliberately made by someone. But the situation is nothing like this in the case of the innumerable animate and inanimate systems with which we are familiar. Even in the case of living organisms, though they are generated by their parent organisms, the parents do not "make" their progeny in the same sense in which watch-makers make watches. And once this point is clear, the inference from the existence of living organisms to the existence of a supreme designer no longer appears credible.

Moreover, the argument loses all its force if the facts which the hypothesis of a divine designer is supposed to explain can be understood on the basis of a better-supported assumption. And indeed, such an alternative explanation is one of the achievements of Darwinian biology. For Darwin showed that one can account for the variety of biological species, as well as for their adaptations to their environments, without invoking a divine creator and acts of special creation. The Darwinian theory explains the diversity of biological species in terms of chance variations in the structure of organisms, and of a mechanism of selection which retains those variant forms that possess some advantages for survival. The evidence for these assumptions is considerable; and developments subsequent to Darwin have only strengthened the case for a thoroughly naturalistic explanation of the facts of biological adaptation. In any event, this version of the argument from design has nothing to recommend it.

A second form of this argument has been recently revived in the speculations of some modern physicists. No one who is familiar with the facts, can fail to be impressed by the success with which the use of mathematical methods has enabled us to obtain intellectual mastery of many parts of nature. But some thinkers have therefore concluded that since the book of nature is ostensibly written in mathematical language, nature must be the creation of a divine mathematician. However, the argument is most dubious. For it rests, among other things, on the assumption that mathematical tools can be successfully used only if the events of nature exhibit some *special* kind of order, and on the further assumption that if the structure of things were different from what they are mathematical language would be inadequate for describing such structure. But it can be shown that no matter what the world were like—even if it impressed us as being utterly chaotic—it would still possess some order, and would in principle be amenable to a mathematical description. In point of fact, it makes no sense to say that there is absolutely *no* pattern in any conceivable subject matter. To be sure, there are differences in complexities of structure, and if the patterns of events were sufficiently complex we might not be able to unravel them. But however that may be, the success of mathematical physics in giving us some understanding of the world around us does not yield the conclusion that only a mathematician could have devised the patterns of order we have discovered in nature.

4

The inconclusiveness of the three classical arguments for the existence of God was already made evident by Kant, in a manner substantially not different from the above discussion. There are, however, other types of arguments for theism that have been influential in the history of thought, two of which I wish to consider, even if only briefly.

Indeed, though Kant destroyed the classical intellectual foundations for theism, he himself invented a fresh argument for it. Kant's attempted proof is not intended to be a purely theoretical demonstration, and is based on the supposed facts of our moral nature. It has exerted an enormous influence on subsequent theological speculation. In barest outline, the argument is as follows. According to Kant, we are subject not only to physical laws like the rest of nature, but also to moral ones. These moral laws are categorical imperatives, which we must heed not because of their utilitarian consequences, but simply because as autonomous moral agents it is our duty to accept them as binding. However, Kant was keenly aware that though virtue may be its reward, the virtuous man (that is, the man who acts out of a sense of duty and in conformity with the moral law) does not always receive his just desserts in this world; nor did he shut his eyes to the fact that evil men frequently enjoy the best things this world has to offer. In short, virtue does not always reap happiness. Nevertheless, the highest human good is the realization of happiness commensurate with one's virtue; and Kant believed that it is a practical postulate of the moral life to promote this good. But what can guarantee that the highest good is realizable? Such a guarantee can be found only in God, who must therefore exist if the highest good is not to be a fatuous ideal. The existence of an omnipotent, omniscient, and omnibenevolent God is thus postulated as a necessary condition for the possibility of a moral life.

Despite the prestige this argument has acquired, it is difficult to grant it any force. It is easy enough to postulate God's existence. But as Bertrand Russell observed in another connection, postulation has all the advantages of theft over honest toil. No postulation carries with it any assurance that what is postulated is actually the case. And though we may postulate God's existence as a means to guaranteeing the possibility of realizing happiness together with virtue, the postulation establishes neither the actual realizability of this ideal nor the fact of his existence. Moreover, the argument is not made more cogent when we recognize that it is based squarely on the highly dubious conception that considerations of utility and human happiness must not enter into the determination of what is morally obligatory. Having built his moral theory on a radical separation of means from ends, Kant was driven to the desperate postulation of God's existence in order to relate them again. The argument is thus at best a *tour de force,* contrived to remedy a fatal flaw in Kant's initial moral assumptions. It carries no conviction to anyone who does not commit Kant's initial blunder.

One further type of argument, pervasive in much Protestant theological literature, deserves brief mention. Arguments of this type take their point of departure from the psychology of religious and mystical experience. Those who have undergone such experiences, often report that during the experience they feel themselves to be in the presence of the divine and holy, that they lose their sense of self-identity and become merged with some fundamental reality, or that they enjoy a feeling of total dependence upon some ultimate power. The overwhelming sense of transcending one's finitude which characterizes such vivid periods of life, and of coalescing with some ultimate source of all existence, is then taken to be compelling evidence for the existence of a supreme being. In a variant form of this argument, other theologians have identified God as the object which satisfies the commonly experienced need for integrating one's scattered and conflicting impulses into a coherent unity, or as the subject which is of ultimate concern to us. In short, a proof of God's existence is found in the occurrence of certain distinctive experiences.

It would be flying in the face of well-attested facts were one to deny that such experiences frequently occur. But do these facts constitute evidence for the conclusion based on them? Does the fact, for example, that an individual experiences a profound sense of direct contact with an alleged transcendent ground of all reality, constitute competent evidence for the claim that there is such a ground and that it is the immediate cause of the experience? If well-established canons for evaluating evidence are accepted, the answer is surely negative. No one will dispute that many men do have vivid experiences in which such things as ghosts or pink elephants appear before them; but only the hopelessly credulous will without further ado count such experiences as establishing the existence of ghosts and pink elephants. To establish the existence of such things, evidence is required that is obtained under controlled conditions and that can be confirmed by independent inquirers. Again, though a man's report that he is suffering pain may be taken at face value, one cannot take at face value the claim, were he to make it, that it is the food he ate which is the cause (or a contributory cause) of his felt pain—not even if the man were to report a vivid feeling of abdominal disturbance. And similarly, an overwhelming feeling of being in the presence of the Divine is evidence enough for admitting the genuineness of such feeling; it is no evidence for the claim that a supreme being with a substantial existence independent of the experience is the cause of the experience.

5

Thus far the discussion has been concerned with noting inadequacies in various arguments widely used to support theism. However, much atheistic criticism is also directed toward exposing incoherencies in the very thesis of theism. I want therefore to consider this aspect of the atheistic critique, though I will restrict myself to the central difficulty in the theistic position which arises from the simultaneous attribution of omnipotence, omniscience, and omnibenevolence to the Deity. The difficulty is that of reconciling these attributes with the occurrence of evil in the world. Accordingly, the question to which I now turn is whether, despite the existence of evil, it is possible to construct a theodicy which will justify the ways of an infinitely powerful and just God to man.

Two main types of solutions have been proposed for this problem. One way that is frequently used is to maintain that what is commonly called evil is only an illusion, or at worst only the "privation" or absence of good. Accordingly, evil is not "really real," it is only the "negative" side of God's beneficence, it is only the product of our limited intelligence which fails to plumb the true character of God's creative bounty. A sufficient comment on this proposed solution is that facts are not altered or abolished by rebaptizing them. Evil may indeed be only an appearance and not genuine. But this does not eliminate from the realm of appearance the tragedies, the sufferings, and the iniquities which men so frequently endure. And it raises once more, though on another level, the problem of reconciling the fact that there is evil in the realm of appearance with God's alleged omnibenevolence. In any event, it is small comfort to anyone suffering a cruel misfortune for which he is in no way responsible, to be told that what he is undergoing is only the absence of good. It is a gratuitous insult to mankind, a symptom of insensitivity and indifference to human suffering, to be assured that all the miseries and agonies men experience are only illusory.

Another gambit often played in attempting to justify the ways of God to man is to argue that the things called evil are evil only because they are viewed in isolation; they are not evil when viewed in proper perspective and in relation to the rest of creation. Thus, if one attends to but a single instrument in an orchestra, the sounds issuing from it may indeed be harsh and discordant. But if one is placed at a proper distance from the whole orchestra, the sounds of that single instrument will mingle with the sounds issuing from the other players to produce a marvellous bit of symphonic music. Analogously, experiences we call painful undoubtedly occur and are real enough. But the pain is judged to be an evil only because it is experienced in a limited perspective—the pain is there for the sake of a more inclusive good, whose reality eludes us because our intelligences are too weak to apprehend things in their entirety.

It is an appropriate retort to this argument that of course we judge things to be evil in a human perspective, but that since we are not God this is the only proper perspective in which to judge them. It may indeed be the case that what is evil for us is not evil for some other part of creation. However, we are not this other part of creation, and it is irrelevant to argue that were we something other than what we are, our evaluations of what is good and bad would be different. Moreover, the worthlessness of the argument becomes even more evident if we remind ourselves that it is unsupported speculation to suppose that whatever is evil in a finite perspective is good from the purported perspective of the totality of things. For the argument can be turned around: What we judge to be a good is a good only because it is viewed in isolation; when it is viewed in proper perspective, and in relation to the entire scheme of things, it is an evil. This is in fact a standard form of the argument for a universal pessimism. Is it any worse than the similar argument for a universal optimism? The very raising of this question is a *reductio ad absurdum* of the proposed solution to the ancient problem of evil.

I do not believe it is possible to reconcile the alleged omnipotence and omnibenevolence of God with the unvarnished facts of human existence. In point of fact, many theologians have concurred in this conclusion; for in order to escape from the difficulty which the traditional attributes of God present, they have assumed that God is not all-powerful, and that there are limits as to what He can do in his efforts to establish a righteous order in the universe. But whether such a modified theology is better off, is doubtful; and in any event, the question still remains whether the facts of human life support the claim that an omnibenevolent Deity, though limited in power, is revealed in the ordering of human history. It is pertinent to note in this connection that though there have been many historians who have made the effort, no historian has yet succeeded in showing to the satisfaction of his professional colleagues that the hypothesis of a Divine Providence is capable of explaining anything which cannot be explained just as well without this hypothesis.

6

This last remark naturally leads to the question whether, apart from their polemics against theism, philosophical atheists have not shared a common set of positive views, a common set of philosophical convictions which set them off from other groups of thinkers. In one very clear sense of this query the answer is indubitably negative. For there never has been what one might call a "school of atheism," in the way in which there has been a Platonic school or even a Kantian school. In point of fact, atheistic critics of theism can be found among many of the conventional groupings of philosophical thinkers—even, I venture to add, among professional theologians in recent years who in effect preach atheism in the guise of language taken bodily from the Christian tradition.

Nevertheless, despite the variety of philosophic positions to which at one time or another in the history of thought atheists have subscribed, it seems to me that atheism is not simply a negative standpoint. At any rate, there is a certain quality of intellectual temper that has characterized, and continues to characterize, many philosophical atheists. (I am excluding from consideration the so-called "village atheist," whose primary concern is to twit and ridicule those who accept some form of theism, or for that matter those who have any religious convictions.) Moreover, their rejection of theism is based not only on the inadequacies they have found in the arguments for theism, but often also on the positive ground that atheism is a corollary to a better-supported general outlook upon the nature of things. I want therefore to conclude this discussion with a brief enumeration of some points of positive doctrine to which, by and large, philosophical atheists seem to me to subscribe. These points fall into three major groups.

In the first place, philosophical atheists reject the assumption that there are disembodied spirits, or that incorporeal entities of any sort can exercise a causal agency. On the contrary, atheists are generally agreed that if we wish to achieve any understanding of what takes place in the universe, we must look to the operations of organized bodies. Accordingly, the various processes taking place in nature, whether animate or inanimate, are to be explained in terms of the properties and structures of identifiable and spatiotemporally located objects. Moreover, the present variety of systems and activities found in the universe is to be accounted for on the basis of the transformations things undergo when they enter into different relations with one another—transformations which often result in the emergence of novel kinds of objects. On the other hand, though things are in flux and undergo alteration, there is no all-encompassing unitary pattern of change. Nature is ineradicably plural, both in respect to the individuals occurring in it as well as in respect to the processes in which things become involved. Accordingly, the human scene and the human perspective are not illusory; and man and his works are no less and no more "real" than are other parts or phases of the cosmos. At the risk of using a possibly misleading characterization, all of this can be summarized by saying that an atheistic view of things is a form of materialism.

In the second place, atheists generally manifest a marked empirical temper, and often take as their ideal the intellectual methods employed in the contemporaneous empirical sciences. Philosophical atheists differ considerably on important points of detail in their account of how responsible claims to knowledge are to be established. But there is substantial agreement among them that controlled sensory observation is the court of final appeal in issues concerning matters of fact. It is indeed this commitment to the use of an empirical method which is the final basis of the atheistic critique of theism. For at bottom this critique seeks to show that we can understand whatever a theistic assumption is alleged to explain, through the use of the proved methods of the positive sciences and without the introduction of empirically unsupported *ad hoc* hypotheses about a Deity. It is pertinent in this connection to recall a familiar legend about the French mathematical physicist Laplace. According to the story, Laplace made a personal presentation of a copy of his now famous book on celestial mechanics to Napoleon. Napoleon glanced through the volume, and finding no reference to the Deity asked Laplace whether God's existence played any role in the analysis. "Sire, I have no need for that hypothesis," Laplace is reported to have replied. The dismissal of sterile hypotheses characterizes not only the work of Laplace; it is the uniform rule in scientific inquiry. The sterility of the theistic assumption is one of the main burdens of the literature of atheism both ancient and modern.

And finally, atheistic thinkers have generally accepted a utilitarian basis for judging moral issues, and they have exhibited a libertarian attitude toward human needs and impulses. The conceptions of the human good they have advocated are conceptions which are commensurate with the actual capacities of mortal men, so that it is the satisfaction of the complex needs of the human creature which is the final standard for evaluating the validity of a moral ideal or moral prescription.

In consequence, the emphasis of atheistic moral reflection has been this-worldly rather than other-worldly, individualistic rather than authoritarian. The stress upon a good life that must be consummated in this world, has made atheists vigorous opponents of moral codes which seek to repress human impulses in the name of some unrealizable other-worldly ideal. The individualism that is so pronounced a strain in many philosophical atheists has made them tolerant of human limitations and sensitive to the plurality of legitimate moral goals. On the other hand, this individualism has certainly not prevented many of them from recognizing the crucial role which institutional arrangements can play in achieving desirable patterns of human living. In consequence, atheists have made important contributions to the development of a climate of opinion favorable to pursuing the values of a liberal civilization and they have played effective roles in attempts to rectify social injustices.

Atheists cannot build their moral outlook on foundations upon which so many men conduct their lives. In particular, atheism cannot offer the incentives to conduct and the consolations for misfortune which theistic religions supply to their adherents. It can offer no hope of personal immortality, no threats of Divine chastisement, no promise of eventual recompense for injustices suffered, no blueprints to sure salvation. For on its view of the place of man in nature, human excellence and human dignity must be achieved within a finite life-span, or not at all, so that the rewards of moral endeavor must come from the quality of civilized living, and not from some source of disbursement that dwells outside of time. Accordingly, atheistic moral reflection at its best does not culminate in a quiescent ideal of human perfection, but is a vigorous call to intelligent activity—activity for the sake of realizing human potentialities and for eliminating whatever stands in the way of such realization. Nevertheless, though slavish resignation to remediable ills is not characteristic of atheistic thought, responsible atheists have never pretended that human effort can invariably achieve the heart's every legitimate desire. A tragic view of life is thus an uneliminable ingredient in atheistic thought. This ingredient does not invite or generally produce lugubrious lamentation. But it does touch the atheist's view of man and his place in nature with an emotion that makes the philosophical atheist a kindred spirit to those who, within the frameworks of various religious traditions, have developed a serenely resigned attitude toward the inevitable tragedies of the human estate.

AGNOSTICISM

thomas huxley

. . .

The people who call themselves "Agnostics" have been charged with doing so because they have not the courage to declare themselves "Infidels." It has been insinuated that they have adopted a new name in order to escape the unpleasantness which attaches to their proper denomination. To this wholly erroneous imputation, I have replied by showing that the term "Agnostic" did, as a matter of fact, arise in a manner which negatives it; and my statement has not been, and cannot be, refuted. Moreover, speaking for myself, and without impugning the right of any other person to use the term in another sense, I further say that Agnosticism is not properly described as a "negative" creed, nor indeed as a creed of any kind, except in so far as it expresses absolute faith in the validity of a principle, which is as much ethical as intellectual. This principle may be stated in various ways, but they all amount to this: that it is wrong for a man to say that he is certain of the objective truth of any proposition unless he can produce evidence which logically justifies that certainty. This is what Agnosticism asserts; and, in my opinion, it is all that is essential to Agnosticism. That which Agnostics deny and repudiate, as immoral, is the contrary doctrine, that there are propositions which men ought to believe, without logically satisfactory evidence; and that reprobation ought to attach to the profession of disbelief in such inadequately supported propositions. The justification of the Agnostic principle lies in the success which follows upon its application, whether in the field of natural, or in that of civil, history; and in the fact that, so far as these topics are concerned, no sane man thinks of denying its validity.

Still speaking for myself, I add, that though Agnosticism is not, and cannot be, a creed, except in so far as its general principle is concerned; yet that the application of that principle results in the denial of, or the suspension of judgment concerning, a number of propositions respecting which our contemporary ecclesiastical "gnostics" profess entire certainty. And, in so far as these ecclesiastical persons can be justified in their old-established custom (which many nowadays think more honoured in the breach than the observance) of using opprobrious names to those who differ from them, I fully admit their right to call me and those who think with me "Infidels"; all

From "Agnosticism and Christianity," in Thomas Huxley, *Science and Christian Tradition* (New York: Appleton and Company, 1896), pp. 309–318.

I have ventured to urge is that they must not expect us to speak of ourselves by that title.

The extent of the region of the uncertain, the number of the problems the investigation of which ends in a verdict of not proven, will vary according to the knowledge and the intellectual habits of the individual Agnostic. I do not very much care to speak of anything as "unknowable." What I am sure about is that there are many topics about which I know nothing; and which, so far as I can see, are out of reach of my faculties. But whether these things are knowable by any one else is exactly one of those matters which is beyond my knowledge, though I may have a tolerably strong opinion as to the probabilities of the case. Relatively to myself, I am quite sure that the region of uncertainty—the nebulous country in which words play the part of realities—is far more extensive than I could wish. Materialism and Idealism, Theism and Atheism, the doctrine of the soul and its mortality or immortality—appear in the history of philosophy like the shades of Scandinavian heroes, eternally slaying one another and eternally coming to life again in a metaphysical "Nifelheim." It is getting on for twenty-five centuries, at least, since mankind began seriously to give their minds to these topics. Generation after generation, philosophy has been doomed to roll the stone uphill; and, just as all the world swore it was at the top, down it has rolled to the bottom again. All this is written in innumerable books; and he who will toil through them will discover that the stone is just where it was when the work began. Hume saw this; Kant saw it; since their time, more and more eyes have been cleansed of the films which prevented them from seeing it; until now the weight and number of those who refuse to be the prey of verbal mystifications has begun to tell in practical life.

It was inevitable that a conflict should arise between Agnosticism and Theology; or rather, I ought to say, between Agnosticism and Ecclesiasticism. For Theology, the science, is one thing; and Ecclesiasticism, the championship of a foregone conclusion as to the truth of a particular form of Theology, is another. With scientific Theology, Agnosticism has no quarrel. On the contrary, the Agnostic, knowing too well the influence of prejudice and idiosyncrasy, even on those who desire most earnestly to be impartial, can wish for nothing more urgently than that the scientific theologian should not only be at perfect liberty to thresh out the matter in his own fashion; but that he should, if he can, find flaws in the Agnostic position; and, even if demonstration is not to be had, that he should put, in their full force, the grounds of the conclusions he thinks probable. The scientific theologian admits the Agnostic principle, however widely his results may differ from those reached by the majority of Agnostics.

But, as between Agnosticism and Ecclesiasticism, or, as our neighbours across the Channel call it, Clericalism, there can be neither peace nor truce. The Cleric asserts that it is morally wrong not to believe certain propositions, whatever the results of a strict scientific investigation of the evidence of these propositions. He tells us "that religious error is, in itself, of an immoral nature." [1] He declares that he has prejudged certain conclusions, and looks upon those who show cause for arrest of judgment as emissaries of Satan. It necessarily follows that, for him, the attainment of faith, not the ascertainment of truth, is the highest aim of mental life. And, on careful analysis of the nature of this faith, it will too often be found to be, not the mystic process

---

[1] Dr. Newman, *Essay on Development*, p. 357.

of unity with the Divine, understood by the religious enthusiast; but that which the candid simplicity of a Sunday scholar once defined it to be. "Faith," said this unconscious plagiarist of Tertullian, "is the power of saying you believe things which are incredible."

Now I, and many other Agnostics, believe that faith, in this sense, is an abomination; and though we do not indulge in the luxury of self-righteousness so far as to call those who are not of our way of thinking hard names, we do not feel that the disagreement between ourselves and those who hold this doctrine is even more moral than intellectual. It is desirable there should be an end of any mistakes on this topic. If our clerical opponents were clearly aware of the real state of the case, there would be an end of the curious delusion, which often appears between the lines of their writings, that those whom they are so fond of calling "Infidels" are people who not only ought to be, but in their hearts are, ashamed of themselves. It would be discourteous to do more than hint the antipodal opposition of this pleasant dream of theirs to facts.

The clerics and their lay allies commonly tell us, that if we refuse to admit that there is good ground for expressing definite convictions about certain topics, the bonds of human society will dissolve and mankind lapse into savagery. There are several answers to this assertion. One is that the bonds of human society were formed without the aid of their theology; and, in the opinion of not a few competent judges, have been weakened rather than strengthened by a good deal of it. Greek science, Greek art, the ethics of old Israel, the social organisation of old Rome, contrived to come into being, without the help of any one who believed in a single distinctive article of the simplest of the Christian creeds. The science, the art, the jurisprudence, the chief political and social theories, of the modern world have grown out of those of Greece and Rome—not by favour of, but in the teeth of, the fundamental teachings of early Christianity, to which science, art, and any serious occupation with the things of this world, were alike despicable.

Again, all that is best in the ethics of the modern world, in so far as it has not grown out of Greek thought, or Barbarian manhood, is the direct development of the ethics of old Israel. There is no code of legislation, ancient or modern, at once so just and so merciful, so tender to the weak and poor, as the Jewish law; and, if the Gospels are to be trusted, Jesus of Nazareth himself declared that he taught nothing but that which lay implicitly, or explicitly, in the religious and ethical system of his people.

> And the scribe said unto him, Of a truth, Teacher, thou hast well said that he is one; and there is none other but he, and to love him with all the heart, and with all the understanding, and with all the strength, and to love his neighbour as himself, is much more than all whole burnt offerings and sacrifices. (Mark xii. 32, 33.)

Here is the briefest of summaries of the teaching of the prophets of Israel of the eighth century; does the Teacher, whose doctrine is thus set forth in his presence, repudiate the exposition? Nay; we are told, on the contrary, that Jesus saw that he "answered discreetly," and replied, "Thou art not far from the kingdom of God."

So that I think that even if the creeds, from the so-called "Apostles," to the so-called "Athanasian," were swept into oblivion; and even if the human race should arrive at the conclusion that whether a bishop washes a cup or leaves it unwashed is not a matter of the least consequence, it will get on very well. The causes which have led to the development of morality in mankind, which have guided or impelled us all the way from the savage to the civilised state, will not cease to operate because a number of ecclesiastical hypotheses turn out to be baseless. And, even if the absurd notion that morality is more the child of speculation than of practical necessity and inherited instinct, had any foundation; if all the world is going to thieve, murder, and otherwise misconduct itself as soon as it discovers that certain portions of ancient history are mythical, what is the relevance of such arguments to any one who holds by the Agnostic principle?

Surely, the attempt to cast out Beelzebub by the aid of Beelzebub is a hopeful procedure as compared to that of preserving morality by the aid of immorality. For I suppose it is admitted that an Agnostic may be perfectly sincere, may be competent, and may have studied the question at issue with as much care as his clerical opponents. But, if the Agnostic really believes what he says, the "dreadful-consequence" argufier (consistently, I admit, with his own principles) virtually asks him to abstain from telling the truth, or to say what he believes to be untrue, because of the supposed injurious consequences to morality. "Beloved brethren, that we may be spotlessly moral, before all things let us lie," is the sum total of many an exhortation addressed to the "Infidel." Now, as I have already pointed out, we cannot oblige our exhorters. We leave the practical application of the convenient doctrines of "Reserve" and "Non-natural interpretation" to those who invented them.

I trust that I have now made amends for any ambiguity, or want of fulness, in my previous exposition of that which I hold to be the essence of the Agnostic doctrine. Henceforward, I might hope to hear no more of the assertion that we are necessarily Materialists, Idealists, Atheists, Theists, or any other *ists,* if experience had led me to think that the proved falsity of a statement was any guarantee against its repetition. And those who appreciate the nature of our position will see, at once, that when Ecclesiasticism declares that we ought to believe this, that, and the other, and are very wicked if we don't, it is impossible for us to give any answer but this: We have not the slightest objection to believe anything you like, if you will give us good grounds for belief; but, if you cannot, we must respectfully refuse, even if that refusal should wreck mortality and insure our own damnation several times over. We are quite content to leave that to the decision of the future. The course of the past has impressed us with the firm conviction that no good ever comes of falsehood, and we feel warranted in refusing even to experiment in that direction.

·   ·   ·

THE WILL TO BELIEVE

william james

In the recently published Life by Leslie Stephen of his brother, Fitz-James, there is an account of a school to which the latter went when he was a boy. The teacher, a certain Mr. Guest, used to converse with his pupils in this wise: "Gurney, what is the difference between justification and sanctification?—Stephen, prove the omnipotence of God!" etc. In the midst of our Harvard freethinking and indifference we are prone to imagine that here at your good old orthodox College conversation continues to be somewhat upon this order; and to show you that we at Harvard have not lost all interest in these vital subjects, I have brought with me tonight something like a sermon on justification by faith to read to you—I mean an essay in justification *of* faith, a defence of our right to adopt a believing attitude in religious matters, in spite of the fact that our merely logical intellect may not have been coerced. "The Will to Believe," accordingly, is the title of my paper.

I have long defended to my own students the lawfulness of voluntarily adopted faith; but as soon as they have got well imbued with the logical spirit, they have, as a rule, refused to admit my contention to be lawful philosophically, even though, in point of fact, they were personally all the time chock-full of some faith or other themselves. I am all the while, however, so profoundly convinced that my own position is correct, that your invitation has seemed to me a good occasion to make my statements more clear. Perhaps your minds will be more open than those with which I have hitherto had to deal. I will be as little technical as I can, though I must begin by setting up some technical distinctions that will help us in the end.

1

Let us give the name of *hypothesis* to anything that may be proposed to our belief; and just as the electricians speak of live and dead wires, let us speak of any hypothesis as either *live* or *dead*. A live hypothesis is one which appeals as a real possibility to him to whom it is proposed. If I ask you to believe in the Mahdi, the notion makes

From "The Will to Believe," in William James, *The Will to Believe and Other Essays in Popular Philosophy* (New York: Longmans, Green & Co. Ltd., 1896), pp. 1–30. Reprinted by permission of David McKay and Company.

no electric connection with your nature—it refuses to scintillate with any credibility at all. As an hypothesis it is completely dead. To an Arab, however (even if he be not one of the Mahdi's followers), the hypothesis is among the mind's possibilities: it is alive. This shows that deadness and liveness in an hypothesis are not intrinsic properties, but relations to the individual thinker. They are measured by his willingness to act. The maximum of liveness in an hypothesis means willingness to act irrevocably. Practically, that means belief; but there is some believing tendency wherever there is willingness to act at all.

Next, let us call the decision between two hypotheses an *option*. Options may be of several kinds. They may be—1. *living* or *dead;* 2. *forced* or *avoidable;* 3. *momentous* or *trivial;* and for our purposes we may call an option a *genuine* option when it is of the forced, living, and momentous kind.

1. A living option is one in which both hypotheses are live ones. If I say to you: "Be a theosophist or be a Mohammedan," it is probably a dead option, because for you neither hypothesis is likely to be alive. But if I say: "Be an agnostic or be a Christian," it is otherwise: trained as you are, each hypothesis makes some appeal, however small, to your belief.

2. Next, if I say to you: "Choose between going out with your umbrella or without it," I do not offer you a genuine option, for it is not forced. You can easily avoid it by not going out at all. Similarly, if I say, "Either love me or hate me," "Either call my theory true or call it false," your option is avoidable. You may remain indifferent to me, neither loving nor hating, and you may decline to offer any judgment as to my theory. But if I say, "Either accept this truth or go without it," I put on you a forced option, for there is no standing place outside of the alternative. Every dilemma based on a complete logical disjunction, with no possibility of not choosing, is an option of this forced kind.

3. Finally, if I were Dr. Nansen and proposed to you to join my North Pole expedition, your option would be momentous; for this would probably be your only similar opportunity, and your choice now would either exclude you from the North Pole sort of immortality altogether or put at least the chance of it into your hands. He who refuses to embrace a unique opportunity loses the prize as surely as if he tried and failed. *Per contra,* the option is trivial when the opportunity is not unique, when the stake is insignificant, or when the decision is reversible if it later prove unwise. Such trivial options abound in the scientific life. A chemist finds an hypothesis live enough to spend a year in its verification: he believes in it to that extent. But if his experiments prove inconclusive either way, he is quit for his loss of time, no vital harm being done.

It will facilitate our discussion if we keep all these distinctions well in mind.

2

The next matter to consider is the actual psychology of human opinion. When we look at certain facts, it seems as if our passional and volitional nature lay at the root of all our convictions. When we look at others, it seems as if they could do nothing when the intellect had once said its say. Let us take the latter facts up first.

Does it not seem preposterous on the very face of it to talk of our opinions being modifiable at will? Can our will either help or hinder our intellect in its perceptions of truth? Can we, by just willing it, believe that Abraham Lincoln's existence is a myth, and that the portraits of him in McClure's Magazine are all of someone else? Can we, by any effort of our will, or by any strength of wish that it were true, believe ourselves well and about when we are roaring with rheumatism in bed, or feel certain that the sum of the two one-dollar bills in our pocket must be a hundred dollars? We can *say* any of these things, but we are absolutely impotent to believe them; and of just such things is the whole fabric of the truths that we do believe in made up, —matters of fact, immediate or remote, as Hume said, and relations between ideas, which are either there or not there for us if we see them so, and which if not there cannot be put there by any action of our own.

In Pascal's *Thoughts* there is a celebrated passage known in literature as Pascal's wager. In it he tries to force us into Christianity by reasoning as if our concern with truth resembled our concern with the stakes in a game of chance. Translated freely his words are these:

> You must either believe or not believe that God is—which will you do? Your human reason cannot say. A game is going on between you and the nature of things which at the day of judgment will bring out either heads or tails. Weigh what your gains and your losses would be if you should stake all you have on heads, or God's existence: if you win in such case, you gain eternal beatitude; if you lose, you lose nothing at all. If there were an infinity of chances, and only one for God in this wager, still you ought to stake your all on God; for though you surely risk a finite loss by this procedure, any finite loss is reasonable, even a certain one is reasonable, if there is but the possibility of infinite gain. Go, then, and take holy water, and have masses said; belief will come and stupefy your scruples—*Cela vous fera croire et vous abêtira.* Why should you not? At bottom, what have you to lose?

You probably feel that when religious faith expresses itself thus, in the language of the gaming-table, it is put to its last trumps. Surely Pascal's own personal belief in masses and holy water had far other springs; and this celebrated page of his is but an argument for others, a last desperate snatch at a weapon against the hardness of the unbelieving heart. We feel that a faith in masses and holy water adopted wilfully after such a mechanical calculation would lack the inner soul of faith's reality; and if we were ourselves in the place of the Deity, we should probably take particular pleasure in cutting off believers of this pattern from their infinite reward. It is evident that unless there be some pre-existing tendency to believe in masses and holy water, the option offered to the will by Pascal is not a living option. Certainly no Turk ever took to masses and holy water on its account; and even to us Protestants these means of salvation seem such foregone impossibilities that Pascal's logic, invoked for them specifically, leaves us unmoved. As well might the Mahdi write to us, saying, "I am the Expected One whom God has created in his effulgence. You shall be infinitely happy if you confess me; otherwise you shall be cut off from the light of the sun. Weigh, then, your infinite gain if I am genuine against your finite sacrifice if I am not!" His logic would be that of Pascal; but he would vainly use it on us, for the hypothesis he offers us is dead. No tendency to act on it exists in us to any degree.

The talk of believing by our volition seems, then, from one point of view, simply silly. From another point of view it is worse than silly, it is vile. When one turns to the magnificent edifice of the physical sciences, and sees how it was reared; what thousands of disinterested moral lives of men lie buried in its mere foundations; what patience and postponement, what choking down of preference, what submission to the icy laws of outer fact are wrought into its very stones and mortar; how absolutely impersonal it stands in its vast augustness—then how besotted and contemptible seems every little sentimentalist who comes blowing his voluntary smoke-wreaths, and pretending to decide things from out of his private dream! Can we wonder if those bred in the rugged and manly school of science should feel like spewing such subjectivism out of their mouths? The whole system of loyalties which grow up in the schools of science go dead against its toleration; so that it is only natural that those who have caught the scientific fever should pass over to the opposite extreme, and write sometimes as if the incorruptibly truthful intellect ought positively to prefer bitterness and unacceptableness to the heart in its cup.

> It fortifies my soul to know
> That, though I perish, Truth is so—

sings Clough, while Huxley exclaims:

> My only consolation lies in the reflection that, however bad our posterity may become, so far as they hold by the plain rule of not pretending to believe what they have no reason to believe, because it may be to their advantage so to pretend [the word "pretend" is surely here redundant], they will not have reached the lowest depth of immorality.

And that delicious *enfant terrible* Clifford writes:

> Belief is desecrated when given to unproved and unquestioned statements for the solace and private pleasure of the believer. . . . Whoso would deserve well of his fellows in this matter will guard the purity of his belief with a very fanaticism of jealous care, lest at any time it should rest on an unworthy object, and catch a stain which can never be wiped away. . . . If [a] belief has been accepted on insufficient evidence [even though the belief be true, as Clifford on the same page explains] the pleasure is a stolen one. . . . It is sinful because it is stolen in defiance of our duty to mankind. That duty is to guard ourselves from such beliefs as from a pestilence which may shortly master our own body and then spread to the rest of the town. . . . It is wrong always, everywhere, and for every one, to believe anything upon insufficient evidence.

3

All this strikes one as healthy, even when expressed, as by Clifford, with somewhat too much of robustious pathos in the voice. Free-will and simple wishing do seem, in the matter of our credences, to be only fifth wheels to the coach. Yet if any one should thereupon assume that intellectual insight is what remains after wish and will and sentimental preference have taken wing, or that pure reason is what then settles our opinions, he would fly quite as directly in the teeth of the facts.

It is only our already dead hypotheses that our willing nature is unable to bring to life again. But what has made them dead for us is for the most part a previous action of our willing nature of an antagonistic kind. When I say "willing nature," I do not mean only such deliberate volitions as may have set up habits of belief that we cannot now escape from—I mean all such factors of belief as fear and hope, prejudice and passion, imitation and partisanship, the circumpressure of our caste and set. As a matter of fact we find ourselves believing, we hardly know how or why. Mr. Balfour gives the name of "authority" to all those influences, born of the intellectual climate, that make hypotheses possible or impossible for us, alive or dead. Here in this room, we all of us believe in molecules and the conservation of energy, in democracy and necessary progress, in Protestant Christianity and the duty of fighting for "the doctrine of the immortal Monroe," all for no reasons worthy of the name. We see into these matters with no more inner clearness, and probably with much less, than any disbeliever in them might possess. His unconventionality would probably have some grounds to show for its conclusions; but for us, not insight, but the *prestige* of the opinions, is what makes the spark shoot from them and light up our sleeping magazines of faith. Our reason is quite satisfied, in nine hundred and ninety-nine cases out of every thousand of us, if it can find a few arguments that will do to recite in case our credulity is criticised by someone else. Our faith is faith in someone else's faith, and in the greatest matters this is most the case. Our belief in truth itself, for instance, that there is a truth, and that our minds and it are made for each other— what is it but a passionate affirmation of desire, in which our social system backs us up? We want to have a truth; we want to believe that our experiments and studies and discussions must put us in a continually better and better position towards it; and on this line we agree to fight out our thinking lives. But if a pyrrhonistic sceptic asks us *how we know* all this, can our logic find a reply? No! Certainly it cannot. It is just one volition against another—we willing to go in for life upon a trust or assumption which he, for his part, does not care to make.

As a rule we disbelieve all facts and theories for which we have no use. Clifford's cosmic emotions find no use for Christian feelings. Huxley belabors the bishops because there is no use for sacerdotalism in his scheme of life. Newman, on the contrary, goes over to Romanism, and finds all sorts of reasons good for staying there, because a priestly system is for him an organic need and delight. Why do so few "scientists" even look at the evidence for telepathy, so-called? Because they think, as a leading biologist, now dead, once said to me, that even if such a thing were true, scientists ought to band together to keep it suppressed and concealed. It would undo the uniformity of Nature and all sorts of other things without which scientists cannot carry on their pursuits. But if this very man had been shown something which, as a scientist, he might *do* with telepathy, he might not only have examined the evidence, but even have found it good enough. This very law which the logicians would impose upon us—if I may give the name of logicians to those who would rule out our willing nature here—is based on nothing but their own natural wish to exclude all elements for which they, in their professional quality of logicians, can find no use.

Evidently, then, our non-intellectual nature does influence our convictions. There are passional tendencies and volitions which run before and others which come after belief, and it is only the latter that are too late for the fair; and they are not too late when the previous passional work has been already in their own direction. Pascal's argument, instead of being powerless, then seems a regular clincher, and is the last stroke needed to make our faith in masses and holy water complete. The state of things is evidently far from simple; and pure insight and logic, whatever they might do ideally, are not the only things that really do produce our creeds.

4

Our next duty, having recognized this mixed-up state of affairs, is to ask whether it be simply reprehensible and pathological, or whether, on the contrary, we must treat it as a normal element in making up our minds. The thesis I defend is, briefly stated, this: *Our passional nature not only lawfully may, but must, decide an option between propositions, whenever it is a genuine option that cannot by its nature be decided on intellectual grounds; for to say, under such circumstances, "Do not decide, but leave the question open," is itself a passional decision—just like deciding yes or no—and is attended with the same risk of losing the truth. . . .*

· · ·

8

And now, after all this introduction, let us go straight at our question. I have said, and now repeat it, that not only as a matter of fact do we find our passional nature influencing us in our opinions, but that there are some options between opinions in which this influence must be regarded both as an inevitable and as a lawful determinant of our choice.

I fear here that some of you my hearers will begin to scent danger, and lend an inhospitable ear. Two first steps of passion you have indeed had to admit as necessary—we must think so as to avoid dupery, and we must think so as to gain truth; but the surest path to those ideal consummations, you will probably consider, is from now onwards to take no further passional step.

Well, of course, I agree as far as the facts will allow. Wherever the option between losing truth and gaining it is not momentous, we can throw the chance of *gaining truth* away, and at any rate save ourselves from any chance of *believing falsehood*, by not making up our minds at all till objective evidence has come. In scientific questions, this is almost always the case; and even in human affairs in general, the need of acting is seldom so urgent that a false belief to act on is better than no belief at all. Law courts, indeed, have to decide on the best evidence attainable for the moment, because a judge's duty is to make law as well as to ascertain it, and (as a learned judge once said to me) few cases are worth spending much time over: the great thing is to have them decided on *any* acceptable principle, and got out of the way. But in our dealings with objective nature we obviously are recorders, not makers, of the truth; and decisions for the mere sake of deciding promptly and getting on to the next business would be wholly out of place. Throughout the breadth of physical nature facts are what they are quite independently of us, and seldom is there any such hurry about them that the risks of being duped by believing a premature theory need be faced. The questions here are always trivial options, the hypotheses are hardly living (at any rate not living for us spectators), the choice between believing truth or falsehood is seldom forced. The attitude of sceptical balance is therefore the absolutely wise one if we would escape mistakes. What difference, indeed, does it make to most of us whether we have or have not a theory of the Röntgen rays, whether we believe or not in mind-stuff, or have a conviction about the causality of conscious states? It makes no difference. Such options are not forced on us. On every account it is better not to make them, but still keep weighing reasons *pro et contra* with an indifferent hand.

I speak, of course, here of the purely judging mind. For purposes of discovery such indifference is to be less highly recommended, and science would be far less advanced than she is if the passionate desires of individuals to get their own faiths confirmed had been kept out of the game. See for example the sagacity which Spencer and Weismann now display. On the other hand, if you want an absolute duffer in an investigation, you must, after all, take the man who has no interest whatever in its results: he is the warranted incapable, the positive fool. The most useful investigator, because the most sensitive observer, is always he whose eager interest in one side of the question is balanced by an equally keen nervousness lest he become deceived. Science has organized this nervousness into a regular *technique*, her so-called method of verification; and she has fallen so deeply in love with the method that one may even say she has ceased to care for truth by itself at all. It is only truth as technically verified that interests her. The truth of truths might come in merely affirmative form, and she would decline to touch it. Such truth as that, she might repeat with Clifford, would be stolen in defiance of her duty to mankind. Human passions, however, are stronger than technical rules. *"Le cœur a ses raisons,"* as Pascal says, *"que la raison ne connaît pas";* and however indifferent to all but the bare rules of the game the umpire, the abstract intellect, may be, the concrete players who furnish him the materials to judge of are usually, each one of them, in love with some pet "live hypothesis" of his own. Let us agree, however, that wherever there is no forced option, the dispassionately judicial intellect with no pet hypothesis, saving us, as it does, from dupery at any rate, ought to be our ideal.

The question next arises: Are there not somewhere forced options in our speculative questions, and can we (as men who may be interested at least as much in positively gaining truth as in merely escaping dupery) always wait with impunity till the coercive evidence shall have arrived? It seems *a priori* improbable that the truth should be so nicely adjusted to our needs and powers as that. In the great boarding-house of nature, the cakes and the butter and the syrup seldom come out so even and leave the plates so clean. Indeed, we should view them with scientific suspicion if they did.

9

Moral questions immediately present themselves as questions whose solution cannot wait for sensible proof. A moral question is a question not of what sensibly exists, but of what is good, or would be good if it did exist. Science can tell us what exists; but to compare the *worths*, both of what exists and of what does not exist, we must consult not science, but what Pascal calls our heart. Science herself consults her heart when she lays it down that the infinite ascertainment of fact and correction of false belief are the supreme goods for man. Challenge the statement, and science can only repeat it oracularly, or else prove it by showing that such ascertainment and correction bring man all sorts of other goods which man's heart in turn declares. The question of having moral beliefs at all or not having them is decided by our will. Are our moral preferences true or false, or are they only odd biological phenomena, making things good or bad for *us,* but in themselves indifferent? How can your pure intellect decide? If your heart does not *want* a world of moral reality, your head will assuredly never make you believe in one. Mephistophelian scepticism, indeed, will satisfy the head's play-instincts much better than any rigorous idealism can. Some men (even at the student age) are so naturally cool-hearted that the moralistic hypothesis never has for them any pungent life, and in their supercilious presence the hot young moralist always feels strangely ill at ease. The appearance of knowingness is on their side, of *naïveté* and gullibility on his. Yet, in the inarticulate heart of him, he clings to it that he is not a dupe, and that there is a realm in which (as Emerson says) all their wit and intellectual superiority is no better than the cunning of a fox. Moral scepticism can no more be refuted or proved by logic than intellectual scepticism can. When we stick to it that there *is* truth (be it of either kind), we do so with our whole nature, and resolve to stand or fall by the results. The sceptic with his whole nature adopts the doubting attitude; but which of us is the wiser, Omniscience only knows.

Turn now from these wide questions of good to a certain class of questions of fact, questions concerning personal relations, states of mind between one man and another. *Do you like me or not?*—for example. Whether you do or not depends, in countless instances, on whether I meet you half-way, am willing to assume that you must like me, and show you trust and expectation. The previous faith on my part in your liking's existence is in such cases what makes your liking come. But if I stand aloof, and refuse to budge an inch until I have objective evidence, until you shall have done something apt, as the absolutists say, *ad extorquendum assensum meum,* ten to one your liking never comes. How many women's hearts are vanquished by the mere sanguine insistence of some man that they *must* love him! He will not consent to the hypothesis that they cannot. The desire for a certain kind of truth here brings about that special truth's existence; and so it is in innumerable cases of other sorts. Who gains promotions, boons, appointments, but the man in whose life they are seen to play the part of live hypotheses, who discounts them, sacrifices other things for their sake before they have come, and takes risks for them in advance? His faith acts on the powers above him as a claim, and creates its own verification.

A social organism of any sort whatever, large or small, is what it is because each member proceeds to his own duty with a trust that the other members will simultaneously do theirs. Wherever a desired result is achieved by the co-operation of many independent persons, its existence as a fact is a pure consequence of the precursive faith in one another of those immediately concerned. A government, an army, a commercial system, a ship, a college, an athletic team, all exist on this condition, without which not only is nothing achieved, but nothing is even attempted. A whole train of passengers (individually brave enough) will be looted by a few highwaymen, simply because the latter can count on one another, while each passenger fears that if he makes a movement of resistance, he will be shot before any one else backs him up. If we believed that the whole car-full would rise at once with us, we should each severally rise, and train-robbing would never even be attempted. There are, then, cases where a fact cannot come at all unless a preliminary faith exists in its coming. *And where faith in a fact can help create the fact,* that would be an insane logic which should say that faith running ahead of scientific evidence is the "lowest kind of immorality" into which a thinking being can fall. Yet such is the logic by which our scientific absolutists pretend to regulate our lives!

10

In truths dependent on our personal action, then, faith based on desire is certainly a lawful and possibly an indispensable thing.

But now, it will be said, these are all childish human cases, and have nothing to do with great cosmical matters, like the question of religious faith. Let us then pass on to that. Religions differ so much in their accidents that in discussing the religious question we must make it very generic and broad. What then do we now mean by the religious hypothesis? Science says things are; morality says some things are better than other things; and religion says essentially two things.

First, she says that the best things are the more eternal things, the overlapping things, the things in the universe that throw the last stone, so to speak, and say the final word. "Perfection is eternal"—this phrase of Charles Secrétan seems a good way of putting this first affirmation of religion, an affirmation which obviously cannot yet be verified scientifically at all.

The second affirmation of religion is that we are better off even now if we believe her first affirmation to be true.

Now, let us consider what the logical elements of this situation are *in case the religious hypothesis in both its branches be really true.* (Of course, we must admit that possibility at the outset. If we are to discuss the question at all, it must involve a living option. If for any of you religion be a hypothesis that cannot, by any living possibility be true, then you need go no farther. I speak to the "saving remnant" alone.) So proceeding, we see, first, that religion offers itself as a *momentous* option. We are supposed to gain, even now, by our belief, and to lose by our nonbelief, a certain vital good. Secondly, religion is a *forced* option, so far as that good goes. We cannot escape the issue by remaining sceptical and waiting for more light, because, although we do avoid error in that way *if religion be untrue,* we lose the good, *if it be true,* just as certainly as if we positively chose to disbelieve. It is as if a man should hesitate indefinitely to ask a certain woman to marry him because he was not perfectly sure that she would prove an angel after he brought her home. Would he not cut himself off from that particular angel-possibility as decisively as if he went and married someone else? Scepticism, then, is not avoidance of option; it is option of a certain particular kind of risk. *Better risk loss of truth than chance of error*—that is your faith-vetoer's exact position. He is actively playing his stake as much as the believer is; he is backing the field against the religious hypothesis, just as the believer is backing the religious hypothesis against the field. To preach scepticism to us as a duty until "sufficient evidence" for religion be found, is tantamount therefore to telling us, when in presence of the religious hypothesis, that to yield to our fear of its being error is wiser and better than to yield to our hope that it may be true. It is not intellect against all passions, then; it is only intellect with one passion laying down its law. And by what, forsooth, is the supreme wisdom of this passion warranted? Dupery for dupery, what proof is there that dupery through hope is so much worse than dupery through fear? I, for one, can see no proof; and I simply refuse obedience to the scientist's command to imitate his kind of option, in a case where my own stake is important enough to give me the right to choose my own form of risk. If religion be true and the evidence for it be still insufficient, I do not wish, by putting your extinguisher upon my nature (which feels to me as if it had after all some business in this matter), to forfeit my sole chance in life of getting upon the winning side— that chance depending, of course, on my willingness to run the risk of acting as if my passional need of taking the world religiously might be prophetic and right.

All this is on the supposition that it really may be prophetic and right, and that, even to us who are discussing the matter, religion is a live hypothesis which may be true. Now, to most of us religion comes in a still further way that makes a veto on our active faith even more illogical. The more perfect and more eternal aspect of the universe is represented in our religions as having personal form. The universe is no longer a mere *It* to us, but a *Thou,* if we are religious; and any relation that may be possible from person to person might be possible here. For instance, although in one sense we are passive portions of the universe, in another we show a curious autonomy, as if we were small active centres on our own account. We feel, too, as if the appeal of religion to us were made to our own active good-will, as if evidence might be forever withheld from us unless we met the hypothesis half-way. To take a trivial illustration: just as a man who in a company of gentlemen made no advances, asked a warrant for every concession, and believed no one's word without proof, would cut himself off by such churlishness from all the social rewards that a more trusting spirit would earn—so here, one who should shut himself up in snarling logicality and try to make the gods extort his recognition willy-nilly, or not get it at all, might cut himself off forever from his only opportunity of making the gods' acquaintance. This feeling, forced on us we know not whence, that by obstinately believing that there are gods (although not to do so would be so easy both for our logic and our life) we are doing the universe the deepest service we can, seems part of the living essence of the religious hypothesis. If the hypothesis *were* true in all its parts, including this one, then pure intellectualism, with its veto on our making willing advances, would be an absurdity; and some participation of our sympathetic nature would be logically required. I, therefore, for one, cannot see my way to accepting the agnostic rules of truth-seeking, or wilfully agree to keep my willing nature out of the game. I cannot do so for this plain reason, that *a rule of thinking which would absolutely prevent me from acknowledging certain kinds of truth if those kinds of truth were really there, would be an irrational rule.* That for me is the long and short of the formal logic of the situation, no matter what the kinds of truth might materially be.

I confess I do not see how this logic can be escaped. But sad experience makes me fear that some of you may still shrink from radically saying with me, *in abstracto,* that we have the right to believe at our own risk any hypothesis that is live enough to tempt our will. I suspect, however, that if this is so, it is because you have got away from the abstract logical point of view altogether, and are thinking (perhaps without realizing it) of some particular religious hypothesis which for you is dead. The freedom to "believe what we will" you apply to the case of some patent superstition; and the faith you think of is the faith defined by the schoolboy when he said, "Faith is when you believe something that you know ain't true." I can only repeat that this is misapprehension. *In concreto,* the freedom to believe can only cover living options which the intellect of the individual cannot by itself resolve; and living options never seem absurdities to him who has them to consider. When I look at the religious question as it really puts itself to concrete men, and when I think of all the possibilities which both practically and theoretically it involves, then this command that we shall put a stopper on our heart, instincts, and courage, and *wait*—acting of course meanwhile more or less as if religion were *not* true—till doomsday, or till such time as our intellect and senses working together may have raked in evidence enough—this command, I say, seems to me the queerest idol ever manufactured in the philosophic cave. Were we scholastic absolutists, there might be more excuse. If we had an infallible intellect with its objective certitudes, we might feel ourselves disloyal to such a perfect organ of knowledge in not trusting to it exclusively, in not waiting for its releasing word. But if we are empiricists, if we believe that no bell in us tolls to let us know for certain when truth is in our grasp, then it seems a piece of idle fantasticality to preach so solemnly our duty of waiting for the bell. Indeed we *may* wait if we will—I hope you do not think that I am denying that—but if we do so, we do so at our peril as much as if we believed. In either case we *act,* taking our life in our hands. No one of us ought to issue vetoes to the other, nor should we bandy words of abuse. We ought, on the contrary, delicately and profoundly to respect one another's mental feedom: then only shall we bring about the intellectual republic; then only shall we have that spirit of inner tolerance without which all our outer tolerance is soulless, and which is empiricism's glory; then only shall we live and let live, in speculative as well as in practical things.

· · ·

6

THE SYMBOL OF ULTIMATE CONCERN

paul tillich

What Faith Is Not

1 The intellectualistic distortion of the meaning of faith

Our positive description of what faith is implies the rejection of interpretations that dangerously distort the meaning of faith. It is necessary to make these implicit rejections explicit, because the distortions exercise a tremendous power over popular thinking and have been largely responsible for alienating many from religion since the beginning of the scientific age. It is not only the popular mind which distorts the meaning of faith. Behind it lie philosophical and theological thoughts which in a more refined way also miss the meaning of faith.

The different distorted interpretations of the meaning of faith can be traced to one source. Faith as being ultimately concerned is a centered act of the whole personality. If one of the functions which constitute the totality of the personality is partly or completely identified with faith, the meaning of faith is distorted. Such interpretations are not altogether wrong because every function of the human mind participates in the act of faith. But the element of truth in them is embedded in a whole of error.

The most ordinary misinterpretation of faith is to consider it an act of knowledge that has a low degree of evidence. Something more or less probable or improbable is affirmed in spite of the insufficiency of its theoretical substantiation. This situation is very usual in daily life. If this is meant, one is speaking of *belief* rather than of faith. One believes that one's information is correct. One believes that records of past events are useful for the reconstruction of facts. One believes that a scientific theory is adequate for the understanding of a series of facts. One believes that a person will act in a specific way or that a political situation will change in a certain direction. In all these cases the belief is based on evidence sufficient to make the event probable. Sometimes, however, one believes something which has low probability or is strictly improbable, though not impossible. The causes for all these theoretical and practical beliefs are rather varied. Some things are believed because we have good though not complete evidence about them; many more things are believed because they are stated by good authorities. This is the case whenever we accept the evidence which others accepted as sufficient for belief, even if we cannot approach the evidence directly (for example, all events of the past). Here a new element comes into the picture, namely, the trust in the authority which makes a statement probable for us. Without such trust we could not believe anything except the objects of our immediate experience. The consequence would be that our world would be infinitely smaller than it actually is. It is rational to trust in authorities which enlarge our consciousness without forcing us into submission. If we use the word "faith" for this kind of trust we can say that most of our knowledge is based on faith. But it is not appropriate to do so. We believe the authorities, we trust their judgment, though never unconditionally, but we do not have faith in them. Faith is more than trust in authorities, although trust is an element of faith. This distinction is important in view of the fact that some earlier theologians tried to prove the unconditional authority of the Biblical writers by showing their trustworthiness as witnesses. The Christian may believe the Biblical writers, but not unconditionally. He does not have faith in them. He should not even have faith in the Bible. For faith is more than trust in even the most sacred authority. It is participation in the subject of one's ultimate concern with one's whole being. Therefore, the term "faith" should not be used in connection with theoretical knowledge, whether it is a knowledge on the basis of immediate, prescientific or scientific evidence, or whether it is on the basis of trust in authorities who themselves are dependent on direct or indirect evidence.

The terminological inquiry has led us into the material problem itself. Faith does not affirm or deny what belongs to the prescientific or scientific knowledge of our world, whether we know it by direct experience or through the experience of others. The knowledge of our world (including ourselves as a part of the world) is a matter of inquiry by ourselves or by those in whom we trust. It is not a matter of faith. The dimension of faith is not the dimension of science, history, or psychology. The acceptance of a probable hypothesis in these realms is not faith, but preliminary belief, to be tested by scholarly methods and to be changed by every new discovery. Almost all the struggles between faith and knowledge are rooted in the wrong understanding of faith as a type of knowledge which has a low degree of evidence but is supported by religious authority. It is, however, not only confusion of faith with knowledge that is responsible for the world historical conflicts between them; it is also the fact that matters of faith in the sense of ultimate concern lie hidden behind an assumedly scientific method. Whenever this happens, faith stands against faith and not against knowledge.

The difference between faith and knowledge is also visible in the kind of certitude each gives. There are two types of knowledge which are based on complete evidence and give complete certitude. The one is the immediate evidence of sense perception. He who sees a green color sees a green color and is certain about it. He cannot be certain whether the thing which seems to him green is really green. He may be under a deception. But he cannot doubt that he sees green. The other complete evidence is that of the logical and mathematical rules which are presupposed even if their formulation admits different and sometimes conflicting methods. One cannot discuss logic without presupposing those implicit rules which make the discussion meaningful. Here we have absolute certitude; but we have no reality, just as in the case of mere sense perception. Nevertheless, this certitude is not without value. No truth is possible without the material given by sense perception and without the form given by the logical and mathematical rules which express the structure in which all reality stands. One of the worst errors of theology and popular religion is to make statements which intentionally or unintentionally contradict the structure of reality. Such an attitude is an expression not of faith but of the confusion of faith with belief.

Knowledge of reality has never the certitude of complete evidence. The process of knowing is infinite. It never comes to an end except in a state of knowledge of the whole. But such knowledge transcends infinitely every finite mind and can be ascribed only to God. Every knowledge of reality by the human mind has the character of higher or lower probability. The certitude about a physical law, a historical fact, or a psychological structure can be so high that, for all practical purposes, it is certain. But theoretically the incomplete certitude of belief remains and can be undercut at any moment by criticism and new experience. The certitude of faith has not this character. Neither has it the character of formal evidence. The certitude of faith is "existential," meaning that the whole existence of man is involved. It has, as we indicated before, two elements: the one, which is not a risk but a certainty about one's own being, namely, on being related to something ultimate or unconditional; the other, which is a risk and involves doubt and courage, namely, the surrender to a concern which is not really ultimate and may be destructive if taken as ultimate. This is not a theoretical problem of the kind of higher or lower evidence, of probability or improbability, but it is an existential problem of "to be or not to be." It belongs to a dimension other than any theoretical judgment. Faith is not belief and it is not knowledge with a low degree of probability. Its certitude is not the uncertain certitude of a theoretical judgment.

2   The voluntaristic distortion of the meaning of faith

One can divide this form of the distorted interpretation of faith into a Catholic and a Protestant type. The Catholic type has a great tradition in the Roman Church. It goes back to Thomas Aquinas, who emphasized that the lack of evidence which faith has must be complemented by an act of will. This, first of all, presupposes that faith is understood as an act of knowledge with a limited evidence and that the lack of evidence is made up by an act of will. We have seen that this way of understanding faith does not do justice to the existential character of faith. Our criticism of the intellectualistic distortion of the meaning of faith hits basically also the voluntaristic distortion of the meaning of faith. The former is the basis of the latter. Without a theoretically formulated content the "will to believe" would be empty. But the content which is meant in the will to believe is given to the will by the intellect. For instance, someone has doubts about the so-called "immortality of the soul." He realizes that this assertion that the soul continues to live after the death of the body cannot be proved either by evidence or by trustworthy authority. It is a questionable proposition of theoretical character. But there are motives driving people to this assertion. They decide to believe, and make up in this way for the lack of evidence. If this belief is called "faith," it is a misnomer, even if much evidence were collected for the belief in a continuation of life after death. In classical Roman Catholic theology the "will to believe" is not an act which originates in man's striving, but it is given by grace to him whose will is moved by God to accept the truth of what the Church teaches. Even so, it is not the intellect which is determined by its content to believe, but it is the will which performs what the intellect alone cannot do. This kind of interpretation agrees with the authoritarian attitude of the Roman Church. For it is the authority of the Church which gives the contents, to be affirmed by the intellect under the impact of the will. If the idea of grace mediated by the Church and motivating the will is rejected, as in pragmatism, the will to believe becomes willfulness. It becomes an arbitrary decision which may be supported by some insufficient arguments but which could have gone in other directions with equal justification. Such belief as the basis of the will to believe is certainly not faith.

The Protestant form of the will to believe is connected with the moral interpretation of religion by Protestants. One demands "obedience of faith," following a Paulinian phrase. The term can mean two different things. It can mean the element of commitment which is implied in the state of ultimate concern. If this is meant, one simply says that in the state of ultimate concern all mental functions participate— which certainly is true. Or the term "obedience of faith" can mean subjection to the command to believe as it is given in prophetic and apostolic preaching. Certainly, if a prophetic word is accepted as prophetic, i.e., as coming from God, obedience of faith does not mean anything other than accepting a message as coming from God. But if there is doubt whether a "word" is prophetic, the term "obedience of faith" loses its meaning. It becomes an arbitrary "will to believe." Yet one may describe the situation in a more refined way and point to the fact that we are often grasped by something, e.g., Biblical passages, as expressions of the objectively ultimate concern, but we hesitate to accept them as our subjective ultimate concern for escapist reasons. In such cases, one says, the appeal to the will is justified and does not ask for a willful decision. This is true; but such an act of will does not produce faith—faith as ultimate concern is already given. The demand to be obedient is the demand to be what one already is, namely, committed to the ultimate concern from which one tries to escape. Only if this is the situation can obedience of faith be demanded; but then faith precedes the obedience and is not the product of it. No command to believe and no will to believe can create faith.

This is important for religious education, counseling, and preaching. One should never convey the impression to those whom one wants to impress, that faith is a demand made upon them, the rejection of which is lack of good will. Finite man cannot produce infinite concern. Our oscillating will cannot produce the certainty which belongs to faith. This is in strict analogy to what we said about the impossibility of reaching the truth of faith by arguments and authorities, which in the best case give finite knowledge of a more or less probable character. Neither arguments for belief nor the will to believe can create faith.

3 The emotionalistic distortion of the meaning of faith

The difficulty of understanding faith either as a matter of the intellect or as a matter of will, or of both in mutual support, has led to the interpretation of faith as emotion. This solution was, and partly is, supported from both the religious and the secular side. For the defenders of religion it was a retreat to a seemingly safe position after the battle about faith as a matter of knowledge or will had been lost. The father of all modern Protestant theology, Schleiermacher, has described religion as the feeling of unconditional dependence. Of course, feeling so defined does not mean in religion what it means in popular psychology. It is not vague and changing, but has a definite content: unconditional dependence, a phrase related to what we have called ultimate concern. Nevertheless, the word "feeling" has induced many people to believe that faith is a matter of merely subjective emotions, without a content to be known and a demand to be obeyed.

This interpretation of faith was readily accepted by representatives of science and ethics, because they took it as the best way to get rid of interference from the side of religion in the processes of scientific research and technical organization. If religion is mere feeling it is innocuous. The old conflicts between religion and culture are finished. Culture goes its way, directed by scientific knowledge, and religion is the private affair of every individual and a mere mirror of his emotional life. No claims for truth can be made by it. No competition with science, history, psychology, politics is possible. Religion, put safely into the corner of subjective feelings, has lost its danger for man's cultural activities.

Neither of the two sides, the religious and the cultural, could keep this well-defined covenant of peace. Faith as the state of ultimate concern claims the whole man and cannot be restricted to the subjectivity of mere feeling. It claims truth for its concern and commitment to it. It does not accept the situation "in the corner" of mere feeling. If the whole man is grasped, all his functions are grasped. If this claim of religion is denied, religion itself is denied. It was not only religion which could not accept the restriction of faith to feeling. It was also not accepted by those who were especially interested in pushing religion into the emotional corner. Scientists, artists, moralists showed clearly that they also were ultimately concerned. Their concern expressed itself even in those creations in which they wanted most radically to deny religion. A keen analysis of most philosophical, scientific, and ethical systems shows how much ultimate concern is present in them, even if they are leading in the fight against what they call religion.

This shows the limits of the emotionalist definition of faith. Certainly faith as an act of the whole personality has strong emotional elements within it. Emotion always expresses the involvement of the whole personality in an act of life or spirit. But emotion is not the source of faith. Faith is definite in its direction and concrete in its content. Therefore, it claims truth and commitment. It is directed toward the unconditional, and appears in a concrete reality that demands and justifies such commitment.

Symbols of Faith

1   The meaning of symbol

Man's ultimate concern must be expressed symbolically, because symbolic language alone is able to express the ultimate. This statement demands explanation in several respects. In spite of the manifold research about the meaning and function of symbols which is going on in contemporary philosophy, every writer who uses the term "symbol" must explain his understanding of it.

Symbols have one characteristic in common with signs; they point beyond themselves to something else. The red sign at the street corner points to the order to stop the movements of cars at certain intervals. A red light and the stopping of cars have essentially no relation to each other, but conventionally they are united as long as the convention lasts. The same is true of letters and numbers and partly even words. They point beyond themselves to sounds and meanings. They are given this special function by convention within a nation or by international conventions, as the mathematical signs. Sometimes such signs are called symbols; but this is unfortunate because it makes the distinction between signs and symbols more difficult. Decisive is the fact that signs do not participate in the reality of that to which they point, while symbols do. Therefore, signs can be replaced for reasons of expediency or convention, while symbols cannot.

This leads to the second characteristic of the symbol: It participates in that to which it points: the flag participates in the power and dignity of the nation for which it stands. Therefore, it cannot be replaced except after an historic catastrophe that changes the reality of the nation which it symbolizes. An attack on the flag is felt as an attack on the majesty of the group in which it is acknowledged. Such an attack is considered blasphemy.

The third characteristic of a symbol is that it opens up levels of reality which otherwise are closed for us. All arts create symbols for a level of reality which cannot be reached in any other way. A picture and a poem reveal elements of reality which cannot be approached scientifically. In the creative work of art we encounter reality in a dimension which is closed for us without such works. The symbol's fourth characteristic not only opens up dimensions and elements of reality which otherwise would remain unapproachable but also unlocks dimensions and elements of our soul which correspond to the dimensions and elements of reality. A great play gives us not only a new vision of the human scene, but it opens up hidden depths of our own being. Thus we are able to receive what the play reveals to us in reality. There are within us dimensions of which we cannot become aware except through symbols, as melodies and rhythms in music.

Symbols cannot be produced intentionally—this is the fifth characteristic. They grow out of the individual or collective unconscious and cannot function without being accepted by the unconscious dimension of our being. Symbols which have an especially social function, as political and religious symbols, are created or at least accepted by the collective unconscious of the group in which they appear.

The sixth and last characteristic of the symbol is a consequence of the fact that symbols cannot be invented. Like living beings, they grow and they die. They grow when the situation is ripe for them, and they die when the situation changes. The symbol of the "king" grew in a special period of history, and it died in most parts of the world in our period. Symbols do not grow because people are longing for them, and they do not die because of scientific or practical criticism. They die because they can no longer produce response in the group where they originally found expression.

These are the main characteristics of every symbol. Genuine symbols are created in several spheres of man's cultural creativity. We have mentioned already the political and the artistic realm. We could add history and, above all, religion, whose symbols will be our particular concern.

2 Religious symbols

We have discussed the meaning of symbols generally because, as we said, man's ultimate concern must be expressed symbolically! One may ask: Why can it not be expressed directly and properly? If money, success, or the nation is someone's ultimate concern, can this not be said in a direct way without symbolic language? Is it not only in those cases in which the content of the ultimate concern is called "God" that we are in the realm of symbols? The answer is that everything which is a matter of un-conditional concern is made into a god. If the nation is someone's ultimate concern, the name of the nation becomes a sacred name and the nation receives divine qualities which far surpass the reality of the being and functioning of the nation. The nation then stands for and symbolizes the true ultimate, but in an idolatrous way. Success as ultimate concern is not the natural desire of actualizing potentialities, but is readiness to sacrifice all other values of life for the sake of a position of power and social pre-dominance. The anxiety about not being a success is an idolatrous form of the anxiety about divine condemnation. Success is grace; lack of success, ultimate judg-ment. In this way concepts designating ordinary realities become idolatrous symbols of ultimate concern.

The reason for this transformation of concepts into symbols is the character of ultimacy and the nature of faith. That which is the true ultimate transcends the realm of finite reality infinitely. Therefore, no finite reality can express it directly and properly. Religiously speaking, God transcends his own name. This is why the use of his name easily becomes an abuse or a blasphemy. Whatever we say about that which concerns us ultimately, whether or not we call it God, has a symbolic meaning. It points beyond itself while participating in that to which it points. In no other way can faith express itself adequately. The language of faith is the language of symbols. If faith were what we have shown that it is not, such an assertion could not be made. But faith, understood as the state of being ultimately concerned, has no language other than symbols. When saying this I always expect the question: Only a symbol? He who asks this question shows that he has not understood the difference between signs and symbols nor the power of symbolic language, which surpasses in quality and strength the power of any nonsymbolic language. One should never say "only a symbol," but one should say "not less than a symbol." With this in mind we can now describe the different kinds of symbols of faith.

The fundamental symbol of our ultimate concern is God. It is always present in any act of faith, even if the act of faith includes the denial of God. Where there is ultimate concern, God can be denied only in the name of God. One God can deny the other one. Ultimate concern cannot deny its own character as ultimate. Therefore, it affirms what is meant by the word "God." Atheism, consequently, can only mean the attempt to remove any ultimate concern—to remain unconcerned about the meaning of one's existence. Indifference toward the ultimate question is the only imaginable form of atheism. Whether it is possible is a problem which must remain unsolved at this point. In any case, he who denies God as a matter of ultimate concern affirms

God, because he affirms ultimacy in his concern. God is the fundamental symbol for what concerns us ultimately. Again it would be completely wrong to ask: So God is nothing but a symbol? Because the next question has to be: A symbol for what? And then the answer would be: For God! God is symbol for God. This means that in the notion of God we must distinguish two elements: the element of ultimacy, which is a matter of immediate experience and not symbolic in itself, and the element of concreteness, which is taken from our ordinary experience and symbolically applied to God. The man whose ultimate concern is a sacred tree has both the ultimacy of concern and the concreteness of the tree which symbolizes his relation to the ultimate. The man who adores Apollo is ultimately concerned, but not in an abstract way. His ultimate concern is symbolized in the divine figure of Apollo. The man who glorifies Jahweh, the God of the Old Testament, has both an ultimate concern and a concrete image of what concerns him ultimately. This is the meaning of the seemingly cryptic statement that God is the symbol of God. In this qualified sense God is the fundamental and universal content of faith.

It is obvious that such an understanding of the meaning of God makes the discussions about the existence or nonexistence of God meaningless. It is meaningless to question the ultimacy of an ultimate concern. This element in the idea of God is in itself certain. The symbolic expression of this element varies endlessly through the whole history of mankind. Here again it would be meaningless to ask whether one or another of the figures in which an ultimate concern is symbolized does "exist." If "existence" refers to something which can be found within the whole of reality, no divine being exists. The question is not this, but: Which of the innumerable symbols of faith is most adequate to the meaning of faith? In other words, which symbol of ultimacy expresses the ultimate without idolatrous elements? This is the problem, and not the so-called "existence of God"—which is in itself an impossible combination of words. God as the ultimate in man's ultimate concern is more certain than any other certainty, even that of oneself. God as symbolized in a divine figure is a matter of daring faith, of courage and risk.

God is the basic symbol of faith, but not the only one. All the qualities we attribute to him, power, love, justice, are taken from finite experiences and applied symbolically to that which is beyond finitude and infinity. If faith calls God "almighty," it uses the human experience of power in order to symbolize the content of its infinite concern, but it does not describe a highest being who can do as he pleases. So it is with all the other qualities and with all the actions, past, present, and future, which men attribute to God. They are symbols taken from our daily experience, and not information about what God did once upon a time or will do sometime in the future. Faith is not the belief in such stories, but it is the acceptance of symbols that express our ultimate concern in terms of divine actions.

Another group of symbols of faith are manifestations of the divine in things and events, in persons and communities, in words and documents. This whole realm of sacred objects is a treasure of symbols. Holy things are not holy in themselves, but they point beyond themselves to the source of all holiness, that which is of ultimate concern.

·   ·   ·

7

CRITIQUE OF THEOLOGY

a. j. ayer

.   .   .

It is now generally admitted, at any rate by philosophers, that the existence of a being having the attributes which define the god of any non-animistic religion cannot be demonstratively proved. To see that this is so, we have only to ask ourselves what are the premises from which the existence of such a god could be deduced. If the conclusion that a god exists is to be demonstratively certain, then these premises must be certain; for, as the conclusion of a deductive argument is already contained in the premises, any uncertainty there may be about the truth of the premises is necessarily shared by it. But we know that no empirical proposition can ever be anything more than probable. It is only *a priori* propositions that are logically certain. But we cannot deduce the existence of a god from an *a priori* proposition. For we know that the reason why *a priori* propositions are certain is that they are tautologies. And from a set of tautologies nothing but a further tautology can be validly deduced. It follows that there is no possibility of demonstrating the existence of a god.

What is not so generally recognized is that there can be no way of proving that the existence of a god, such as the God of Christianity, is even probable. Yet this also is easily shown. For if the existence of such a god were probable, then the proposition that he existed would be an empirical hypothesis. And in that case it would be possible to deduce from it, and other empirical hypotheses, certain experiential propositions which were not deducible from those other hypotheses alone. But in fact this is not possible. It is sometimes claimed, indeed, that the existence of a certain sort of regularity in nature constitutes sufficient evidence for the existence of a god. But if the sentence "God exists" entails no more than that certain types of phenomena occur in certain sequences, then to assert the existence of a god will be simply equivalent to asserting that there is the requisite regularity in nature; and no religious man would admit that this was all he intended to assert in asserting the existence of a god. He would say that in talking about God, he was talking about a transcendent being who might be known through certain empirical manifestations, but certainly could not be defined in terms of those manifestations. But in that case the term "god"

From A. J. Ayer, *Language, Truth and Logic* (London: Victor Gollancz, 1948), pp. 114–120. Reprinted by permission of the publisher and Dover Publications, Inc.

is a metaphysical term. And if "god" is a metaphysical term, then it cannot be even probable that a god exists. For to say that "God exists" is to make a metaphysical utterance which cannot be either true or false. And by the same criterion, no sentence which purports to describe the nature of a transcendent god can possess any literal significance.

It is important not to confuse this view of religious assertions with the view that is adopted by atheists, or agnostics. For it is characteristic of an agnostic to hold that the existence of a god is a possibility in which there is no good reason either to believe or disbelieve; and it is characteristic of an atheist to hold that it is at least probable that no god exists. And our view that all utterances about the nature of God are nonsensical, so far from being identical with, or even lending any support to, either of these familiar contentions, is actually incompatible with them. For if the assertion that there is a god is nonsensical, then the atheist's assertion that there is no god is equally nonsensical, since it is only a significant proposition that can be significantly contradicted. As for the agnostic, although he refrains from saying either that there is or that there is not a god, he does not deny that the question whether a transcendent god exists is a genuine question. He does not deny that the two sentences "There is a transcendent god" and "There is no transcendent god" express propositions one of which is actually true and the other false. All he says is that we have no means of telling which of them is true, and therefore ought not to commit ourselves to either. But we have seen that the sentences in question do not express propositions at all. And this means that agnosticism also is ruled out.

Thus we offer the theist the same comfort as we gave to the moralist. His assertions cannot possibly be valid, but they cannot be invalid either. As he says nothing at all about the world, he cannot justly be accused of saying anything false, or anything for which he has insufficient grounds. It is only when the theist claims that in asserting the existence of a transcendent god he is expressing a genuine proposition that we are entitled to disagree with him.

It is to be remarked that in cases where deities are identified with natural objects, assertions concerning them may be allowed to be significant. If, for example, a man tells me that the occurrence of thunder is alone both necessary and sufficient to establish the truth of the proposition that Jehovah is angry, I may conclude that, in his usage of words, the sentence "Jehovah is angry" is equivalent to "It is thundering." But in sophisticated religions, though they may be to some extent based on men's awe of natural process which they cannot sufficiently understand, the "person" who is supposed to control the empirical world is not himself located in it; he is held to be superior to the empirical world, and so outside it; and he is endowed with superempirical attributes. But the notion of a person whose essential attributes are nonempirical is not an intelligible notion at all. We may have a word which is used as if it named this "person," but, unless the sentences in which it occurs express propositions which are empirically verifiable, it cannot be said to symbolize anything. And this is the case with regard to the word "god," in the usage in which it is intended to refer to a transcendent object. The mere existence of the noun is enough to foster the illusion that there is a real, or at any rate a possible entity corresponding to it. It is only when we inquire what God's attributes are that we discover that "God," in this usage, is not a genuine name.

It is common to find belief in a transcendent god conjoined with belief in an afterlife. But, in the form which it usually takes, the content of this belief is not a genuine hypothesis. To say that men do not ever die, or that the state of death is merely a state of prolonged insensibility, is indeed to express a significant proposition, though all the available evidence goes to show that it is false. But to say that there is something imperceptible inside a man, which is his soul or his real self, and that it goes on living after he is dead, is to make a metaphysical assertion which has no more factual content than the assertion that there is a transcendent god.

It is worth mentioning that, according to the account which we have given of religious assertions, there is no logical ground for antagonism between religion and natural science. As far as the question of truth or falsehood is concerned, there is no opposition between the natural scientist and the theist who believes in a transcendent god. For since the religious utterances of the theist are not genuine propositions at all, they cannot stand in any logical relation to the propositions of science. Such antagonism as there is between religion and science appears to consist in the fact that science takes away one of the motives which make men religious. For it is acknowledged that one of the ultimate sources of religious feeling lies in the inability of men to determine their own destiny; and science tends to destroy the feeling of awe with which men regard an alien world, by making them believe that they can understand and anticipate the course of natural phenomena, and even to some extent control it. The fact that it has recently become fashionable for physicists themselves to be sympathetic towards religion is a point in favor of this hypothesis. For this sympathy towards religion marks the physicists' own lack of confidence in the validity of their hypotheses, which is a reaction on their part from the anti-religious dogmatism of nineteenth-century scientists, and a natural outcome of the crisis through which physics has just passed.

It is not within the scope of this inquiry to enter more deeply into the causes of religious feeling, or to discuss the probability of the continuance of religious belief. We are concerned only to answer those questions which arise out of our discussion of the possibility of religious knowledge. The point which we wish to establish is that there cannot be any transcendent truths of religion. For the sentences which the theist uses to express such "truths" are not literally significant.

An interesting feature of this conclusion is that it accords with what many theists are accustomed to say themselves. For we are often told that the nature of God is a mystery which transcends the human understanding. But to say that something transcends the human understanding is to say that it is unintelligible. And what is unintelligible cannot significantly be described. Again, we are told that God is not an object of reason but an object of faith. This may be nothing more than an admission that the existence of God must be taken on trust, since it cannot be proved. But it may also be an assertion that God is the object of a purely mystical intuition, and cannot therefore be defined in terms which are intelligible to the reason. And I think there are many theists who would assert this. But if one allows that it is impossible to define God in intelligible terms, then one is allowing that it is impossible for a sentence both to be significant and to be about God. If a mystic admits that the object of his vision is something which cannot be described, then he must also admit that he is bound to talk nonsense when he describes it.

For his part, the mystic may protest that his intuition does reveal truths to him, even though he cannot explain to others what these truths are; and that we who do not possess this faculty of intuition can have no ground for denying that it is a cognitive faculty. For we can hardly maintain *a priori* that there are no ways of discovering true propositions except those which we ourselves employ. The answer is that we set no limit to the number of ways in which one may come to formulate a true proposition. We do not in any way deny that a synthetic truth may be discovered by purely intuitive methods as well as by the rational method of induction. But we do say that every synthetic proposition, however it may have been arrived at, must be subject to the test of actual experience. We do not deny *a priori* that the mystic is able to discover truths by his own special methods. We wait to hear what are the propositions which embody his discoveries, in order to see whether they are verified or confuted by our empirical observations. But the mystic, so far from producing propositions which are empirically verified, is unable to produce any intelligible propositions at all. And therefore we say that his intuition has not revealed to him any facts. It is no use his saying that he has apprehended facts but is unable to express them. For we know that if he really had acquired any information, he would be able to express it. He would be able to indicate in some way or other how the genuineness of his discovery might be empirically determined. The fact that he cannot reveal what he "knows," or even himself devise an empirical test to validate his "knowledge," shows that his state of mystical intuition is not a genuinely cognitive state. So that in describing his vision the mystic does not give us any information about the external world; he merely gives us indirect information about the condition of his own mind.

These considerations dispose of the argument from religious experience, which many philosophers still regard as a valid argument in favor of the existence of a god. They say that it is logically possible for men to be immediately acquainted with God, as they are immediately acquainted with a sense-content, and that there is no reason why one should be prepared to believe a man when he says that he is seeing a yellow patch, and refuse to believe him when he says that he is seeing God. The answer to this is that if the man who asserts that he is seeing God is merely asserting that he is experiencing a peculiar kind of sense-content, then we do not for a moment deny that his assertion may be true. But, ordinarily, the man who says that he is seeing God is saying not merely that he is experiencing a religious emotion, but also that there exists a transcendent being who is the object of this emotion; just as the man who says that he sees a yellow patch is ordinarily saying not merely that his visual sense-field contains a yellow sense-content, but also that there exists a yellow object to which the sense-content belongs. And it is not irrational to be prepared to believe a man when he asserts the existence of a yellow object, and to refuse to believe him when he asserts the existence of a transcendent god. Whereas the sentence "There exists here a yellow-colored material thing" expresses a genuine synthetic proposition which could be empirically verified, the sentence "There exists a transcendent god" has, as we have seen, no literal significance.

We conclude, therefore, that the argument from religious experience is altogether fallacious. The fact that people have religious experiences is interesting from the psychological point of view, but it does not in any way imply that there is such a thing as religious knowledge, any more than our having moral experiences implies that there is such a thing as moral knowledge. The theist, like the moralist, may believe that his experiences are cognitive experiences, but, unless he can formulate his "knowledge" in propositions that are empirically verifiable, we may be sure that he is deceiving himself. It follows that those philosophers who fill their books with assertions that they intuitively "know" this or that moral or religious "truth" are merely providing material for the psychoanalyst. For no act of intuition can be said to reveal a truth about any matter of fact unless it issues in verifiable propositions. And all such propositions are to be incorporated in the system of empirical propositions which constitutes science.

8

GODS

john wisdom

1. *The existence of God is not an experimental issue in the way it was.* An atheist or agnostic might say to a theist "You still think there are spirits in the trees, nymphs in the streams, a God of the world." He might say this because he noticed the theist in time of drought pray for rain and make a sacrifice and in the morning look for rain. But disagreement about whether there are gods is now less of this experimental or betting sort than it used to be. This is due in part, if not wholly, to our better knowledge of why things happen as they do.

It is true that even in these days it is seldom that one who believes in God has no hopes or fears which an atheist has not. Few believers now expect prayer to still the waves, but some think it makes a difference to people and not merely in ways the atheist would admit. Of course with people, as opposed to waves and machines, one never knows what they won't do next, so that expecting prayer to make a difference to them is not so definite a thing as believing in its mechanical efficacy. Still, just as primitive people pray in a businesslike way for rain so some people still pray for others with a real feeling of doing something to help. However, in spite of this persistence of an experimental element in some theistic belief, it remains true that Elijah's method on Mount Carmel of settling the matter of what god or gods exist would be far less appropriate today than it was then.

2. *Belief in gods is not merely a matter of expectation of a world to come.* Someone may say "The fact that a theist no more than an atheist expects prayer to bring down fire from heaven or cure the sick does not mean that there is no difference between them as to the facts, it does not mean that the theist has no expectations different from the atheist's. For very often those who believe in God believe in another world and believe that God is there and that we shall go to that world when we die."

This is true, but I do not want to consider here expectations as to what one will see and feel after death nor what sort of reasons these logically unique expectations could have. So I want to consider those theists who do not believe in a future life, or rather, I want to consider the differences between atheists and theists insofar as these differences are not a matter of belief in a future life.

Reprinted from *Logic and Language*, Anthony Flew, ed. (London: Basil Blackwell & Mott Ltd., 1960), pp. 187–206, by permission of the publisher and the Aristotelian Society, London.

3. What are these differences? And is it that theists are superstitious or that atheists are blind? A child may wish to sit a while with his father and he may, when he has done what his father dislikes, fear punishment and feel distress at causing vexation, and while his father is alive he may feel sure of help when danger threatens and feel that there is sympathy for him when disaster has come. When his father is dead he will no longer expect punishment or help. Maybe for a moment an old fear will come or a cry for help escape him but he will at once remember that this is no good now. He may feel that his father is no more until perhaps someone says to him that his father is still alive though he lives now in another world and one so far away that there is no hope of seeing him or hearing his voice again. The child may be told that nevertheless his father can see him and hear all he says. When he has been told this the child will still fear no punishment nor expect any sign of his father, but now, even more than he did when his father was alive, he will feel that his father sees him all the time and will dread distressing him and when he has done something wrong he will feel separated from his father until he has felt sorry for what he has done. Maybe when he himself comes to die he will be like a man who expects to find a friend in the strange country where he is going. But even when this is so, it is by no means all of what makes the difference between a child who believes that his father lives still in another world and one who does not.

Likewise one who believes in God may face death differently from one who does not, but there is other difference between them beside this. This other difference may still be described as belief in another world, only this belief is not a matter of expecting one thing rather than another here or hereafter, it is not a matter of a world to come but of a world that now is, though beyond our senses.

We are at once reminded of those other unseen worlds which some philosophers "believe in" and others "deny," while non-philosophers unconsciously "accept" them by using them as models with which to "get the hang of" the patterns in the flux of experience. We recall the timeless entities whose changeless connections we seek to represent in symbols, and the values which stand firm amidst our flickering satisfaction and remorse, and the physical things which, though not beyond the corruption of moth and rust, are yet more permanent than the shadows they throw upon the screen before our minds. We recall, too, our talk of souls and of what lies in their depths and is manifested to us partially and intermittently in our own feelings and the behavior of others. The hypothesis of mind, of other human minds and of animal minds, is reasonable because it explains for each of us why certain things behave so cunningly all by themselves unlike even the most ingenious machines. Is the hypothesis of minds in flowers and trees reasonable for like reasons? Is the hypothesis of a world mind reasonable for like reasons—someone who adjusts the blossom to the bees, someone whose presence may at times be felt—in a garden in high summer, in the hills when clouds are gathering, but not, perhaps, in a cholera epidemic?

4. The question "Is belief in gods reasonable?" has more than one source. It is clear now that in order to grasp fully the logic of belief in divine minds we need to examine the logic of belief in animal and human minds. But we cannot do that here and so for the purposes of this discussion about divine minds let us acknowledge the reasonableness of our belief in human minds without troubling ourselves about its logic. The question of the reasonableness of belief in divine minds then becomes a matter of whether there are facts in nature which support claims about divine minds in the way facts in nature support our claims about human minds.

In this way we resolve the force behind the problem of the existence of gods into two components, one metaphysical and the same which prompts the question "Is there *ever any* behavior which gives reason to believe in *any* sort of mind?" and one which finds expression in "Are there other mind-patterns in nature beside the human and animal patterns which we can all easily detect, and are these other mind-patterns superhuman?"

Such over-determination of a question syndrome is common. Thus, the puzzling questions "Do dogs think?" "Do animals feel?" are partly metaphysical puzzles and partly scientific questions. They are not purely metaphysical; for the reports of scientists about the poor performances of cats in cages and old ladies' stories about the remarkable performances of their pets are not irrelevant. But nor are these questions purely scientific; for the stories never settle them and therefore they have other sources. One other source is the metaphysical source we have already noticed, namely, the difficulty about getting behind an animal's behavior to its mind, whether it is a nonhuman animal or a human one.

But there's a third component in the force behind these questions; these disputes have a third source, and it is one which is important in the dispute which finds expression in the words "I believe in God," "I do not." This source comes out well if we consider the question "Do flowers feel?" Like the questions about dogs and animals this question about flowers comes partly from the difficulty we sometimes feel over inference from *any* behavior to thought or feeling and partly from ignorance as to what behavior is to be found. But these questions, as opposed to a like question about human beings, come also from hesitation as to whether the behavior in question is *enough* mind-like, that is, is it enough similar to or superior to human behavior to be called "mind-proving"? Likewise, even when we are satisfied that human behavior shows mind and even when we have learned whatever mind-suggesting things there are in nature which are not explained by human and animal minds, we may still ask "But are these things sufficiently striking to be called a mind-pattern? Can we fairly call them manifestations of a divine being?"

"The question," someone may say, "has then become merely a matter of the application of a name. And 'What's in a name?' "

5. *But the line between a question of fact and a question or decision as to the application of a name is not so simple as this way of putting things suggests.* The question "What's in a name?" is engaging because we are inclined to answer both "Nothing" and "Very much." And this "Very much" has more than one source. We might have tried to comfort Heloise by saying "It isn't that Abelard no longer loves you, for this man isn't Abelard"; we might have said to poor Mr. Tebrick in Mr. Garnett's *Lady into Fox* "But this is no longer Silvia." But if Mr. Tebrick replied "Ah, but it is!" this might come not at all from observing facts about the fox which we had not observed, but from noticing facts about the fox which we had missed, although we had in a sense observed all that Mr. Tebrick had observed. It is possible to have before one's eyes all the items of a pattern and still to miss the pattern. Consider the following conversation:

> "And I think Kay and I are pretty happy. We've always been happy."
> Bill lifted up his glass and put it down without drinking.
> "Would you mind saying that again?" he asked.
> "I don't see what's so queer about it. Taken all in all, Kay and I have really been happy."

"All right" Bill said gently, "Just tell me how you and Kay have been happy."

Bill had a way of being amused by things which I could not understand.

"It's a little hard to explain," I said. "It's like taking a lot of numbers that don't look alike and that don't mean anything until you add them all together."

I stopped, because I hadn't meant to talk to him about Kay and me.

"Go ahead," Bill said. "What about the numbers." And he began to smile.

"I don't know why you think it's so funny," I said. "All the things that two people do together, two people like Kay and me, add up to something. There are the kids and the house and the dog and all the people we have known and all the times we've been out to dinner. Of course, Kay and I do quarrel sometimes but when you add it all together, all of it isn't as bad as the parts of it seem. I mean, maybe that's all there is to anybody's life."

Bill poured himself another drink. He seemed about to say something and checked himself. He kept looking at me.[1]

Or again, suppose two people are speaking of two characters in a story which both have read or of two friends which both have known, and one says "Really she hated him," and the other says "She didn't, she loved him." Then the first may have noticed what the other has not although he knows no incident in the lives of the people they are talking about which the other doesn't know too and the second speaker may say "She didn't, she loved him" because he hasn't noticed what the first noticed, although he can remember every incident the first can remember. But then again he may say "She didn't, she loved him" not because he hasn't noticed the patterns in time which the first has noticed but because though he has noticed them he doesn't feel he still needs to emphasize them with "Really she hated him." The line between using a name because of how we feel and because of what we have noticed isn't sharp. "A difference as to the facts," "a discovery," "a revelation," these phrases cover many things. Discoveries have been made not only by Christopher Columbus and Pasteur, but also by Tolstoy and Dostoyevsky and Freud. Things are revealed to us not only by the scientists with microscopes but also by the poets, the prophets, and the painters. What is so isn't merely a matter of "the facts." For sometimes when there is agreement as to the facts there is still argument as to whether defendant did or did not "exercise reasonable care," was or was not "negligent."

And though we shall need to emphasize how much "There is a God" evinces an attitude to the familiar we shall find in the end that it also evinces some recognition of patterns in time easily missed and that, therefore, difference as to there being any gods is in part a difference as to what is so and therefore as to the facts, though not in the simple ways which first occurred to us.

6. *Let us now approach these same points by a different road.*

6.1. *How it is that an explanatory hypothesis, such as the existence of God, may start by being experimental and gradually become something quite different can be seen from the following story:*

Two people return to their long neglected garden and find among the weeds a few of the old plants surprisingly vigorous. One says to the other "It must be that a gardener has been coming and doing something about these plants." Upon inquiry

[1] *H. M. Pulham, Esq.,* p. 320, by John P. Marquand.

they find that no neighbor has ever seen anyone at work in their garden. The first man says to the other "He must have worked while people slept." The other says "No, someone would have heard him and besides, anybody who cared about the plants would have kept down these weeds." The first man says "Look at the way these are arranged. There is purpose and a feeling for beauty here. I believe that someone comes, someone invisible to mortal eyes. I believe that the more carefully we look the more we shall find confirmation of this." They examine the garden ever so carefully and sometimes they come on new things suggesting that a gardener comes and sometimes they come on new things suggesting the contrary and even that a malicious person has been at work. Besides examining the garden carefully they also study what happens to gardens left without attention. Each learns all the other learns about this and about the garden. Consequently, when after all this, one says "I still believe a gardener comes" while the other says "I don't" their different words now reflect no difference as to what they have found in the garden, no difference as to what they would find in the garden if they looked further, and no difference about how fast untended gardens fall into disorder. At this stage, in this context, the gardener hypothesis has ceased to be experimental; the difference between one who accepts and one who rejects it is now not a matter of the one expecting something the other does not expect. What is the difference between them? The one says: "A gardener comes unseen and unheard. He is manifested only in his works with which we are all familiar." The other says "There is no gardener." And with this difference in what they say about the gardener goes a difference in how they feel toward the garden, in spite of the fact that neither expects anything of it which the other does not expect.

But is this the whole difference between them—that the one calls the garden by one name and feels one way toward it, while the other calls it by another name and feels in another way toward it? And if this is what the difference has become, then is it any longer appropriate to ask "Which is right?" or "Which is reasonable?"

And yet surely such questions *are* appropriate when one person says to another "You still think the world's a garden and not a wilderness, and that the gardener has not forsaken it" or "You still think there are nymphs of the streams, a presence in the hills, a spirit of the world." Perhaps when a man sings "God's in his heaven" we need not take this as more than an expression of how he feels. But when Bishop Gore or Dr. Joad write about belief in God and young men read them in order to settle their religious doubts, the impression is not simply that of persons choosing exclamations with which to face nature and the "changes and chances of this mortal life." The disputants speak as if they are concerned with a matter of scientific fact, or of trans-sensual, trans-scientific, and metaphysical fact, but still of fact and still a matter about which reasons for and against may be offered, although no scientific reasons in the sense of field surveys for fossils or experiments on delinquents are to the point.

6.2. *Now can an interjection have a logic?* Can the manifestation of an attitude in the utterance of a word, in the application of a name, have a logic? When all the facts are known how can there still be a question of fact? How can there still be a question? Surely as Hume says ". . . after every circumstance, every relation is known, the understanding has no further room to operate." [2]

---

2 *An Enquiry concerning the Principles of Morals.* Appendix I.

6.3. When the madness of these questions leaves us for a moment *we can all easily recollect disputes which, though they cannot be settled by experiment, are yet disputes in which one party may be right and the other wrong* and in which both parties may offer reasons and the one better reasons than the other. *This may happen in pure and applied mathematics and logic.* Two accountants or two engineers provided with the same data may reach different results and this difference is resolved not by collecting further data but by going over the calculations again. Such differences indeed share with differences as to what will win a race the honor of being among the most "settlable" disputes in the language.

6.4. *But it won't do to describe the theistic issue as one settlable by such calculation,* or as one about what can be deduced in this *vertical* fashion from the facts we know. No doubt, dispute about God has sometimes, perhaps especially in medieval times, been carried on in this fashion. But nowadays it is not, and we must look for some other analogy, some other case in which a dispute is settled but not by experiment.

6.5. *In courts of law* it sometimes happens that opposing counsel are agreed as to the facts and are not trying to settle a question of further fact, are not trying to settle whether the man who admittedly had quarrelled with the deceased did or did not murder him, but are concerned with whether Mr. A who admittedly handed his long-trusted clerk signed blank checks did or did not exercise reasonable care, whether a ledger is or is not a document, whether a certain body was or was not a public authority.

In such cases we notice that the process of argument is not a *chain* of demonstrative reasoning. It is a presenting and re-presenting of those features of the case which *severally cooperate* in favor of the conclusion, in favor of saying what the reasoner wishes said, in favor of calling the situation by the name by which he wishes to call it. The reasons are like the legs of a chair, not the links of a chain. Consequently although the discussion is *a priori* and the steps are not a matter of experience, the procedure resembles scientific argument in that the reasoning is not *vertically* extensive but *horizontally* extensive—it is a matter of the cumulative effect of several independent premises, not of the repeated transformation of one or two. And because the premises are severally inconclusive the process of deciding the issue becomes a matter of weighing the cumulative effect of one group of severally inconclusive items against the cumulative effect of another group of severally inconclusive items, and thus lends itself to description in terms of conflicting "probabilities." This encourages the feeling that the issue is one of fact—that it is a matter of guessing from the premises at a further fact, at what is to come. But this is a muddle. *The dispute does not cease to be* a priori *because it is a matter of the cumulative effect of severally inconclusive premises.* The logic of the dispute is not that of a chain of deductive reasoning as in a mathematic calculation. But nor is it a matter of collecting from several inconclusive items of information an expectation as to something further, as when a doctor from a patient's symptoms guesses at what is wrong, or a detective from many clues guesses the criminal. It has its own sort of logic and its own sort of end—the solution of the question at issue is a decision, a ruling by the judge. But it is not an arbitrary decision though the rational connections are neither quite like those in vertical deductions nor like those in inductions in which from many signs we guess at what is to come; and though the decision manifests itself in the application of a name it is no more merely the application of a name than is the pinning on of a medal merely the pinning on of a bit of metal. Whether a lion with stripes is a tiger or a lion is, if you like, merely a matter of the application of a name. Whether Mr. So and So, of whose conduct we have so complete a record, did or did not exercise reasonable care is not merely a matter of the application of a name or, if we choose to say it is, then we must remember that with this name a game is lost and won, and a game with very heavy stakes. With the judges choice of a name for the facts goes an attitude, and the declaration, the ruling, is an exclamation evincing that attitude. But *it is an exclamation which not only has a purpose but also has a logic,* a logic surprisingly like that of "futile," "deplorable," "graceful," "grand," "divine."

6.6. *Suppose two people are looking at a picture or natural scene.* One says "Excellent" or "Beautiful" or "Divine"; the other says "I don't see it." He means he doesn't see the beauty. And this reminds us of how we felt the theist accuse the atheist of blindness and the atheist accuse the theist of seeing what isn't there. And yet surely each sees what the other sees. It isn't that one can see part of the picture which the other can't see. So the difference is in a sense not one as to the facts. And so it cannot be removed by the one disputant discovering to the other what so far he hasn't seen. It isn't that the one sees the picture in a different light and so, as we might say, sees a different picture. Consequently the difference between them cannot be resolved by putting the picture in a different light. And yet surely this is just what can be done in such a case—not by moving the picture, but by talk perhaps. To settle a dispute as to whether a piece of music is good or better than another we listen again, with a picture we look again. Someone perhaps points to emphasize certain features and we see it in a different light. Shall we call this "field work" and "the last of observation" or shall we call it "reviewing the premises" and "the beginning of deduction (horizontal)"?

If, in spite of all this, we choose to say that a difference as to whether a thing is beautiful is not a factual difference, we must be careful to remember that there is a procedure for settling these differences, and that this consists not only in reasoning and redescription as in the legal case, but also in a more literal re-setting-before with re-looking or re-listening.

6.7. *And if we say, as we did at the beginning, that when a difference as to the existence of a God is not one as to future happenings, then it is not experimental and therefore not as to the facts, we must not forthwith assume that there is no right and wrong about it,* no rationality or irrationality, no appropriateness or inappropriateness, no procedure which tends to settle it, *nor even that this procedure is in no sense a discovery of new facts.* After all, even in science this is not so. Our two gardeners even when they had reached the stage when neither expected any experimental result which the other did not, might yet have continued the dispute, each presenting and re-presenting the features of the garden favoring his hypothesis, that is, fitting his model for describing the accepted fact; each emphasizing the pattern he wishes to emphasize. True, in science, there is seldom or never a pure instance of this sort of dispute, for nearly always with difference of hypothesis goes some difference of expectation as to the facts. But scientists argue about rival hypotheses with a vigor which is not exactly proportioned to difference in expectations of experimental results.

The difference as to whether a God exists involves our feelings more than most scientific disputes, and, in this respect, is more like a difference as to whether there is beauty in a thing.

7. *The Connecting Technique*. Let us consider again the technique used in revealing or proving beauty, in removing a blindness, in inducing an attitude which is lacking, in reducing a reaction that is inappropriate. Besides running over in a special way the features of the picture, tracing the rhythms, making sure that this and that are not only seen but noticed, and their relation to each other—besides all this— there are other things we can do to justify our attitude and alter that of the man who cannot see. For features of the picture may be brought out by setting beside it other pictures; just as the merits of an argument may be brought out, proved, by setting beside it other arguments, in which striking but irrelevant features of the original are changed and relevant features emphasized; just as the merits and demerits of a line of action may be brought out by setting beside it other actions. To use Susan Stebbing's example: Nathan brought out for David certain features of what David had done in the matter of Uriah the Hittite by telling him a story about two sheep owners. This is the kind of thing we very often do when someone is "inconsistent" or unreasonable. This is what we do in referring to other cases in law. The paths we need to trace from other cases to the case in question are often numerous and difficult to detect and the person with whom we are discussing the matter may well draw attention to connections which, while not incompatible with those we have tried to emphasize, are of an opposite inclination. A may have noticed in B subtle and hidden likenesses to an angel and reveal these to C, while C has noticed in B subtle and hidden likenesses to a devil which he reveals to A.

Imagine that a man picks up some flowers that lie half withered on a table and gently puts them in water. Another man says to him "You believe flowers feel." He says this although he knows that the man who helps the flowers doesn't expect anything of them which he himself doesn't expect; for he himself expects the flowers to be "refreshed" and to be easily hurt, injured, I mean, by rough handling, while the man who puts them in water does not expect them to whisper "Thank you." The Sceptic says "You believe flowers feel" because something about the way the other man lifts the flowers and puts them in water suggests an attitude to the flowers which he feels inappropriate, although perhaps he would not feel it inappropriate to butterflies. He feels that this attitude to flowers is somewhat crazy *just as it is sometimes felt that a lover's attitude is somewhat crazy even when this is not a matter of his having false hopes about how the person he is in love with will act.* It is often said in such cases that reasoning is useless. But the very person who says this feels that the lover's attitude is crazy, is inappropriate, like some dreads and hatreds, such as some horrors of enclosed places. And often one who says "It is useless to reason" proceeds at once to reason with the lover, nor is this reasoning always quite without effect. We may draw the lover's attention to certain things done by her he is in love with and trace for him a path to these from things done by others at other times [3] which have disgusted and infuriated him. And by this means we may weaken his admiration and confidence, make him feel it unjustified and arouse his suspicion and contempt and make him feel our suspicion and contempt reasonable. It is possible, of course, that he has already noticed the analogies, the connections, we point out and that he has accepted them—that is, he has not denied them nor passed them off. He has recognized them, and they have altered his attitude, altered his love; but he

---

[3] Thus, like the scientist, the critic is concerned to show up the irrelevance of time and space.

still loves. We then feel that perhaps it is we who are blind and cannot see what he can see.

8. *Connecting and Disconnecting.* But before we confess ourselves thus inadequate there are other fires his admiration must pass through. For when a man has an attitude which it seems to us he should not have, or lacks one which it seems to us he should have, then, not only do we suspect that he is not influenced by connections which we feel should influence him, and draw his attention to these, but also we suspect he is influenced by connections which should not influence him, and draw his attention to these. It may, for a moment, seem strange that we should draw his attention to connections which we feel should not influence him, and which, since they do influence him, he has in a sense already noticed. But we do—such is our confidence in "the light of reason."

Sometimes the power of these connections comes mainly from a man's mismanagement of the language he is using. This is what happens in the Monte Carlo fallacy, where, by mismanaging the laws of chance, a man passes from noticing that a certain color or number has not turned up for a long while to an improper confidence that now it soon will turn up. In such cases our showing up of the false connections is a process we call "explaining a fallacy in reasoning." To remove fallacies in reasoning we urge a man to call a spade a spade, ask him what he means by "the State," and, having pointed out ambiguities and vaguenesses, ask him to reconsider the steps in his argument.

10. *Unspoken Connections. Usually, however, wrongheadedness or wronghearted-ness in a situation, blindness to what is there or seeing what is not, does not arise merely from mismanagement of language, but is more due to connections which are not mishandled in language, for the reason that they are not put into language at all.* And often these misconnections too, weaken in the light of reason, if only we can guess where they lie and turn it on them. In so far as these connections are not presented in language, the process of removing their power is not a process of correcting the mismanagement of language. But it is still akin to such a process; for though it is not a process of setting out fairly what has been set out unfairly, it is a process of setting out fairly what has not been set out at all. And we must remember that the line between connections ill-presented or half-presented in language and connections operative but not presented in language, or only hinted at, is not a sharp one.

Whether or not we call the process of showing up these connections "reasoning to remove bad unconscious reasoning," it is certain that in order to settle in ourselves what weight we shall attach to someone's confidence or attitude we not only ask him for his reasons but also look for unconscious reasons both good and bad; that is, for reasons which he can't put into words, isn't explicitly aware of, is hardly aware of, isn't aware of at all—perhaps it's long experience, which he *doesn't* recall, which lets him know a squall is coming; perhaps it's old experience, which he *can't* recall, which makes the cake in the tea mean so much and makes Odette so fascinating.[4]

I am well aware of the distinction between the question "What reasons are there for the belief that S is P?" and the question "What are the sources of beliefs that S

[4] Proust. *Swann's Way*, Vol. 1, p. 58, Vol. 2. Phoenix Edition.

is P?" There are cases where investigation of the rationality of a claim which certain persons make is done with very little inquiry into why they say what they do, into the causes of their beliefs. This is so when we have very definite ideas about what is really logically relevant to their claim and what is not. Offered a mathematical theorem, we ask for the proof; offered the generalization that parental discord causes crime, we ask for the correlation coefficients. But even in this last case, if we fancy that only the figures are reasons, we underestimate the complexity of the logic of our conclusion; and yet it is difficult to describe the other features of the evidence which have weight, and there is apt to be disagreement about the weight they should have. In criticizing other conclusions and especially conclusions which are largely the expression of an attitude, we have not only to ascertain what reasons there are for them but also to decide what things are reasons and how much. This latter process of sifting reasons from causes is part of the critical process for every belief, but in some spheres it has been done pretty fully already. In these spheres we don't need to examine the actual processes to belief and distill from them a logic. But in other spheres this remains to be done. Even in science or on the stock exchange or in ordinary life we sometimes hesitate to condemn a belief or a hunch merely because those who believe it cannot offer the sort of reasons we had hoped for. And now suppose Miss Gertrude Stein finds excellent the work of a new artist while we see nothing in it. We nervously recall, perhaps, how pictures by Picasso which Miss Stein admired and others rejected, later came to be admired by many who gave attention to them, and we wonder whether the case is not a new instance of her perspicacity and our blindness. But if, upon giving all our attention to the work in question, we still do not respond to it, and we notice that the subject matter of the new pictures is, perhaps, birds in wild places and learn that Miss Stein is a bird-watcher, then we begin to trouble ourselves less about her admiration.

It must not be forgotten that our attempt to show up misconnections in Miss Stein may have an opposite result and reveal to us connections we had missed. Thinking to remove the spell exercised upon his patient by the old stories of the Greeks the psychoanalyst may himself fall under that spell and find in them what his patient has found, and, incidentally, what made the Greeks tell those tales.

11. *Now what happens, what should happen, when we inquire in this way into the reasonableness, the propriety of belief in gods?* The answer is: A double and opposite-phased change. Wordsworth writes:

> . . . And I have felt
> A presence that disturbs me with the joy
> Of elevated thoughts, a sense sublime
> Of something far more deeply interfused,
> Whose dwelling is the light of setting suns,
> And the round ocean and the living air,
> And the blue sky, and in the mind of man
> A motion and a spirit, that impels
> All thinking things, all objects of all thoughts,
> And rolls through all things . . .[5]

We most of us know this feeling. But is it well placed like the feeling that here is first-rate work, which we sometimes rightly have even before we have fully grasped the

[5] Tintern Abbey.

picture we are looking at or the book we are reading? Or is it misplaced like the
feeling in a house that has long been empty that someone secretly lives there still.
Wordsworth's feeling *is* the feeling that the world is haunted, that something watches
in the hills and manages the stars. The child feels that the stone tripped him when he
stumbled, that the bough struck him when it flew back in his face. He has to learn
that the wind isn't buffeting him, that there is not a devil in it, that he was wrong,
that his attitude was inappropriate. And as he learns that the wind wasn't hindering
him so he also learns it wasn't helping him. But we know how, though he learns, his
attitude lingers. It is plain that Wordsworth's feeling is of this family.

Belief in gods, it is true, is often very different from belief that stones are
spiteful, the sun kindly. For the gods appear in human form and from the waves
and control these things and by so doing reward and punish us. But varied as are
the stories of the gods they have a family likeness and we have only to recall them
to feel sure of the other main sources which cooperate with animism to produce them.

What are the stories of the gods? What are our feelings when we believe in
God? They are feelings of awe before power, dread of the thunderbolts of Zeus,
confidence in the everlasting arms, unease beneath the all-seeing eye. They are feelings of guilt and inescapable vengeance, of smothered hate and of a security we
can hardly do without. We have only to remind ourselves of these feelings and the
stories of the gods and goddesses and heroes in which these feelings find expression, to be reminded of how we felt as children to our parents and the big people
of our childhood. Writing of a first telephone call from his grandmother Proust says:

> . . . it was rather that this isolation of the voice was like a symbol, a presenta-
> tion, a direct consequence of another isolation, that of my grandmother,
> separated for the first time in my life, from myself. The orders or prohibitions
> which she addressed to me at every moment in the ordinary cause of my life,
> the tedium of obedience, or the fire of rebellion which neutralized the affection
> that I felt for her were at this moment eliminated. . . . "Granny!" I cried to
> her . . . but I had beside me only that voice, a phantom, as unpalpable as
> that which would come to revisit me when my grandmother was dead. "Speak
> to me!" but then it happened that, left more solitary still, I ceased to catch
> the sound of her voice. My grandmother could no longer hear me . . . I con-
> tinued to call her, sounding the empty night, in which I felt that her appeals
> also must be straying. I was shaken by the same anguish which, in the distant
> past, I had felt once before, one day when, a little child, in a crowd, I had lost
> her.

Giorgio de Chirico, writing of Courbet, says:

> The word "yesterday" envelopes us with its yearning echo, just as, on waking,
> when the sense of time and the logic of things remain a while confused, the
> memory of a happy hour we spent the day before may sometimes linger re-
> verberating within us. At times we think of Courbet and his work as we do
> of our own father's youth.

When a man's father fails him by death or weakness how much he needs another
father, one in the heavens with whom is "no variableness nor shadow of turning."

We understood Mr. Kenneth Graham when he wrote of the Golden Age we feel we have lived in under the Olympians. Freud says:

> The ordinary man cannot imagine this Providence in any other form but that of a greatly exalted father, for only such a one could understand the needs of the sons of men, or be softened by their prayers and be placated by the signs of their remorse. The whole thing is so patently infantile, so incongruous with reality . . . .

"So incongruous with reality"! It cannot be denied.

But here a new aspect of the matter may strike us. For the very facts which make us feel that now we can recognize systems of superhuman, subhuman, elusive, beings for what they are—the persistent projections of infantile phantasies—include facts which make these systems less fantastic. What are these facts? They are patterns in human reactions which are well described by saying that we are as if there were hidden within us powers, persons, not ourselves and stronger than ourselves. That this is so may perhaps be said to have been common knowledge yielded by ordinary observation of people, but we did not know the degree in which this is so until recent study of extraordinary cases in extraordinary conditions had revealed it. I refer, of course, to the study of multiple personalities and the wider studies of psychoanalysts. Even when the results of this work are reported to us that is not the same as tracing the patterns in the details of the cases on which the results are based; and even that is not the same as taking part in the studies oneself. One thing not sufficiently realized is that some of the things shut within us are not bad but good.

Now the gods, good and evil and mixed, have always been mysterious powers outside us rather than within. But they have also been within. It is not a modern theory but an old saying that in each of us a devil sleeps. Eve said: "The serpent beguiled me." Helen says to Menelaus:

> . . . And yet how strange it is!
> I ask not thee; I ask my own sad thought,
> What was there in my heart, that I forgot
> My home and land and all I loved, to fly
> With a strange man? Surely it was not I,
> But Cypris there!" [6]

Elijah found that God was not in the wind, nor in the thunder, but in a still small voice. The kingdom of Heaven is within us, Christ insisted, though usually about the size of a grain of mustard seed, and he prayed that we should become one with the Father in Heaven.

New knowledge made it necessary either to give up saying "The sun is sinking" or to give the words a new meaning. In many contexts we preferred to stick to the old words and give them a new meaning which was not entirely new but, on the contrary, *practically* the same as the old. The Greeks did not speak of the dangers of repressing instincts, but they did speak of the dangers of thwarting Dionysus, of neglecting Cypris for Diana, of forgetting Poseidon for Athena. We have eaten of the fruit of a garden we can't forget though we were never there, a garden we still look

---

[6] Euripides. *The Trojan Women*, Gilbert Murray's Translation.

for though we can never find it. Maybe we look for too simple a likeness to what we dreamed. Maybe we are not as free as we fancy from the old idea that Heaven is a happy hunting ground, or a city with streets of gold. Lately Mr. Aldous Huxley has recommended our seeking not somewhere beyond the sky or late in time but a timeless state not made of the stuff of this world, which he rejects, picking it into worthless pieces. But this sounds to me still too much a looking for another place, not indeed one filled with sweets, but instead so empty that some of us would rather remain in the Lamb or the Elephant, where, as we know, they stop whimpering with another bitter, and, so far from sneering at all things, hang pictures of winners at Kempton and stars of the 'nineties. Something good we have for each other is freed there, and, in some degree and for a while, the miasma of time is rolled back without obliging us to deny the present.

The artists who do most for us don't tell us only of fairylands. Proust, Manet, Breughel, even Botticelli and Vermeer show us reality. And yet they give us, for a moment, exhilaration without anxiety, peace without boredom. And those who, like Freud, work in a different way against that which too often comes over us and forces us into deadness or despair, also deserve critical, patient, and courageous attention. For they, too, work to release us from human bondage into human freedom.

Many have tried to find ways of salvation. The reports they bring back are always incomplete and apt to mislead even when they are not in words, but in music or paint. But they are by no means useless; and not the worst of them are those which speak of oneness with God. But insofar as we become one with Him He becomes one with us. St. John says He is in us as we love one another.

This love, I suppose, is not benevolence but something that comes of the one-ness with one another of which Christ spoke.[7] Sometimes it momentarily gains strength. Hate and the Devil do too. And what is oneness without otherness?

Selected Bibliography for part IV

Alston, W. P., ed. *Religious Belief and Philosophical Thought: Readings in Philosophy of Religion*. New York: Harcourt, Brace and World, 1963.

Bertocci, Peter. *An Introduction to the Philosophy of Religion*. New York: Prentice-Hall, 1951.

Blackstone, W. T. *The Problem of Religious Knowledge*. Englewood Cliffs, N.J.: Prentice-Hall, 1963.

Braithwaite, R. B. *An Empiricist's View of the Nature of Religious Belief*. Cambridge: Cambridge University Press, 1955.

Collins, James. *God in Modern Philosophy*. Chicago: H. Regnery, 1959.

Danielou, Jean. *God and the Ways of Knowing*, trans. Walter Roberts. New York: Meridian Books, 1957.

[7] St. John xvi, 21.

Darrow, Clarence. "Why I Am an Agnostic," reprinted in A. & L. Weinberg, eds. *Verdicts Out of Court*. Chicago: Quadrangle Books, 1963.

Dewey, John. *A Common Faith*. New Haven: Yale University Press, 1934.

Ferré, Frederick. *Basic Modern Philosophy of Religion*. New York: Scribner, 1967.

Fishler, Max. *What the Great Philosophers Thought About God*. Los Angeles: University Book Publishers, 1958.

Flew, Antony, and MacIntyre, Alasdair, eds. *New Essays in Philosophical Theology*. New York: Macmillan, 1955.

Hartshorne, Charles. *The Logic of Perfection*. La Salle, Ill.: Open Court, 1962.

———. *Man's Vision of God and the Logic of Theism*. New York: Willett, 1941.

———, and Reese, W. L., eds. *Philosophers Speak of God*. Chicago: University of Chicago Press, 1953.

Hick, John, ed. *The Existence of God*. New York: Macmillan, 1964.

———. *Faith and Knowledge: A Modern Introduction to the Problem of Religious Knowledge*. Ithaca, N. Y.: Cornell University Press, 1957.

———. *Philosophy of Religion*. Englewood Cliffs, N.J.: Prentice-Hall, 1963.

Hicks, G. Dawes. *The Philosophical Bases of Theism*. New York: Macmillan, 1937.

Hook, Sidney, ed. *Religious Experience and Truth*. New York: New York University Press, 1961.

Hume, David. *Dialogues Concerning Natural Religion*. London: T. Nelson, 1947.

James, William. *The Varieties of Religious Experience: A Study in Human Nature*. New Hyde Park, N.Y.: University Books, 1963.

Kierkegaard, Søren. *Concluding Unscientific Postscript*, trans. D. F. Swenson. Princeton: Princeton University Press, 1941.

———. *Philosophical Fragments*. trans. D. F. Swenson. Princeton: Princeton University Press, 1936.

Lewis, H. D. *Our Experience of God*. New York: Macmillan, 1959.

McTaggart, J. M. E. *Some Dogmas of Religion*. London: E. Arnold, 1906.

Marcel, Gabriel. *Creative Fidelity*, trans. Robert Rosthal. New York: Farrar, Straus, 1964.

Maritain, Jacques. *Approaches to God*, trans. Peter O'Reilly. New York: Harper, 1954.

Mavrodes, George I., and Hackett, Stuart C., eds. *Problems and Perspectives in the Philosophy of Religion*. Boston: Allyn and Bacon, 1967.

Mill, John Stuart. *Three Essays on Religion*. New York: Henry Holt, 1884.

Mourant, John, ed. *Readings in the Philosophy of Religion*. New York: Crowell, 1954.

Ogletree, Thomas W. *The Death of God Controversy*. Nashville: Abingdon Press, 1966.

Paley, William. *Natural Theology: Or Evidences of the Existence and Attributes of the Deity*, ed. F. Ferré. Indianapolis: Bobbs-Merrill, 1963.

Plantinga, Alvin. *The Ontological Argument, from St. Anselm to Contemporary Philosophers*. Garden City, N.Y.: Anchor Books, 1965.

Rashdall, Hastings. *Philosophy and Religion*. London: Duckworth, 1909.

Royce, Josiah. *The Religious Aspect of Philosophy: A Critique of the Bases of Conduct and of Faith.* New York: Harper, 1958.

———. *The Sources of Religious Insight.* New York: Scribner, 1940.

Russell, Bertrand. *Religion and Science.* London: T. Butterworth, 1935.

Smith, Huston. *The Religions of Man.* New York: Harper and Row, 1958.

Smith, John E., ed. *Philosophy of Religion.* New York: Macmillan, 1965.

———, ed. *Religion and Empiricism.* Milwaukee: Marquette University Press, 1967.

Stace, W. T. *Mysticism and Philosophy.* Philadelphia: Lippincott, 1960.

Taylor, A. E. *Does God Exist?* New York: Macmillan, 1947.

Tenant, F. R. *Philosophical Theology,* Vol. II. Cambridge: Cambridge University Press, 1930.

ethical theories

part V

INTRODUCTION

"The unexamined life is not worth living." With this provocative declaration Socrates, the first great moral philosopher of the western world, sought to prompt men to examine their most basic moral beliefs. Since Socrates' time it has been the goal of moral philosophy to discover and justify by rational means the principles that men should utilize in making moral judgments. We all make moral judgments; they are a part of our daily lives. Should I serve in the armed forces? Should I tell my friend the truth? Should I falsify my income tax return? Should I oppose capital punishment? In order to answer these and similar questions, the individual must make moral judgments.

When we consider moral judgments, we usually ask either what acts are right or what is a moral man. As these questions suggest, moral philosophy is more interested in man's obligations and values, than in a description of his behavior. For example, the moral philosopher is more interested in the principle "killing is wrong" than in statistics on homicides or investigations of their probable causes. At the same time, however, he does not deny that men should consider facts in making moral decisions, or that the social sciences, with their descriptive orientation, frequently provide information that is relevant to ethical deliberations.

Throughout history philosophers have been concerned with *normative ethics*, i.e., with ethical theories that provide standards for making moral judgments. Although normative ethics continues to challenge some philosophers, many others are directing their attention to *meta-ethics*. Those working in the area of meta-ethics usually consider the following basic problems: (1) What do ethical terms such as "good" and "wrong" *mean*? (2) Can ethical theories and moral judgments be justified or proved, and if so, how? In other words, those who do meta-ethics are concerned with clarifying ethical concepts and examining the possibility of justifying ethical judgments, rather than with attempts to prove that men should act in a certain way or have a certain kind of character. While meta-ethics is commonly contrasted with normative ethics, the two are related in that meta-ethics clarifies the concepts used in normative theories, and in that those who set forth normative theories are interested in their justification.

The standards of moral judgments

Within the field of normative ethics two types of moral judgments are most often considered: those that answer the question "What ought I to do?" and those that answer the question "What kind of person should I be?" Judgments about right and wrong acts are usually called *judgments of moral obligation.* In contrast, judgments concerning persons, their intentions, their motives, and their virtues are called *judgments of moral value.* For example, the judgment that "We ought to tell the truth" is a judgment of moral obligation, while the judgment that "Those who tell the truth are good" is a judgment of moral value. Care should be taken not to confuse judgments of moral value with other value judgments that fall outside the realm of ethics. Consider these judgments:

> He has a good car.
> This work of art is really beautiful.
> I had a good time last Saturday night.

Each of these judgments is about a thing or an experience; none is about man's actions or his character, and hence none of them is a judgment of moral value.

As we have seen, theories of moral obligation are concerned with our actions. *Teleological theories* of moral obligation affirm that our actions should be evaluated in terms of their consequences. According to the teleologist an action is right if and only if it leads to good consequences. However a problem immediately confronts the teleologist: how can he decide if a given result is good or bad? Moral philosophers have proposed a variety of criteria. The *hedonist,* for example, claims that those acts that yield pleasure are right and that those that result in pain are wrong.

Another problem must be considered by the teleologist: whose good should he seek? *Ethical egoists* maintain that the individual should seek his own good. Epicurus was both an ethical egoist and a hedonist: he held that a man should seek his own pleasure. In contrast to ethical egoism, *utilitarianism* claims that the individual should seek the general good. Most utilitarians are also hedonists and hence recommend that one should do that which brings the greatest pleasure to men in general. J. S. Mill held this view. Some utilitarians, however, are not hedonists. These philosophers do not identify the good with pleasure, but claim that there are other goods, such as friendship, that men should seek. This view, so that it may be distinguished from the common hedonistic utilitarianism, is usually called *ideal utilitarianism.* G. E. Moore is an exponent of this position.

Deontological theories, in contrast to teleological ones, assert that there are considerations other than the value of the consequences that make an act right or wrong. Some deontologists list the consequences as one of several considerations to be weighed in evaluating an action; others deny the relevance of results altogether. Deontologists may be divided into act-deontologists and rule-deontologists. *Act-deontologists* contend that our judgments of obligation are particular, i.e., that a judgment about what is right in a given case is based upon the unique circumstances of the situation, and not upon some general rule. While we may, on the basis of similar experiences, generalize and formulate some rules, it should be noted that these guidelines are derived by induction from particular acts. Søren Kierkegaard presents an act-deontological theory when he claims that in a particular situation he has a specific duty to God and this specific duty is not determined by reference to an established set of rules. Thus, according to Kierkegaard, an act is right if it conforms to the specific will of God; the consequences of it for the agent or others are irrelevant. *Rule-deontologists,* by contrast, argue that there are one or more rules that are the criteria of right and wrong. These rules are fundamental and are not induced from particular acts. Immanuel Kant, a rule-deontologist, argues that there is one basic rule, the "categorical imperative."

To be complete, a moral theory should include both a theory of obligation and a theory of moral value. In dealing with judgments of moral obligation, we have been concerned with the question "What ought I to do?" Judgments of moral value occur when we answer the question "What kind of person should I be?" Aristotle and Hume are two philosophers who consider seriously the problem of moral values. Aristotle describes at length his concept of the good man—the man who possesses the intellectual and moral virtues. Similarly David Hume argues that "personal merit" consists exclusively of the possession of certain mental qualities that are "useful or agreeable to the person himself or to others." He particularly stresses benevolence, which he feels is naturally implanted in every man.

We have described a variety of normative ethical positions. Confronted by such a multiplicity, we may well wonder if there is one true standard by which we ought to make our moral judgments. Ethical *absolutists* assert that there is. *Relativists,* on the other hand, argue that there is no one standard for all men. Rather, they hold, that what is morally right for some men is morally wrong for others. W. T. Stace describes this view. Such an ethical relativism should not be confused with the descriptive realtivism of the anthropologist, who merely observes how the basic ethical standards of various cultures differ. Similarly, the relativism characterized by Stace should not be confused with the meta-ethical view that there is no rational way to justify one moral judgment as opposed to another. The relativist, as described by Stace, holds the normative principle that what is right for some may be wrong for others.

The meaning of moral judgments and the problem of moral responsibility

We have already noted that meta-ethics is concerned with two basic problems: the meaning of ethical terms, and the justification of ethical judgments. Since the majority of moral philosophers seem to be more interested in the second problem, and since considerations of this problem usually involve the first, we shall consider only the question of justification. Some philosophers argue that normative judgments can be established by rational arguments based upon empirical facts. However, most recent attempts to justify ethical judgments can be classified as either intuitive or noncognitive. Intuitionism asserts that our basic moral principles and values are self-evident, i.e., intuited. Hence a rational justification of them is neither necessary nor possible. Noncognitivism, by contrast, argues that moral principles and value judgments cannot be justified by either reason or intuition. The noncognitivist maintains that ethical statements are not descriptive of actions or persons, but are simply expressions of the speaker's emotions, attitudes, or recommendations. W. D. Ross (like Moore) argues for the intuitive justification of ethical judgments. And among the many philosophers who hold the noncognitivist position, Hare presents a recent and moderate view.

One of the most important problems in philosophy is that of man's freedom and responsibility. Metaphysics considers the question "Are man's choices free or determined?"; ethics considers, among others, the question "When is it right to hold a person responsible for his actions?" To this basic question moral philosophers have given several opposing answers. The so-called "hard determinists" argue that all events including our choices are totally caused by other events, and that, as a result, man is neither free nor responsible. The majority of philosophers, however, have defended "soft determinism." The soft determinist agrees that all events, including our choices, are caused. Nevertheless, he rejects the conclusion that man is therefore neither free nor responsible. He argues that there is no contradiction between determinism and the assertion that human beings are free agents. "Free," he maintains, does not mean uncaused: one is free simply if one has the ability to act according to his choices and desires. Indeed, one's choice or desire may be one of the causes of a free action. On the basis of this definition of "free," the soft determinist argues that, although men's actions are determined, men are at least sometimes free and responsible.

Opposing the arguments of the determinists, some philosophers argue for indeterminism. The indeterminist maintains that some of man's decisions are independent of antecedent psychological and physiological causes. That is to say, man's will sometimes has complete freedom to determine a course of action, and man is in such cases morally responsible.

Among the many philosophers who ask when it is right to hold a person morally responsible are John Hospers, Jean-Paul Sartre, and P. H. Nowell-Smith. Hospers cannot accurately be classified as either a hard or a soft determinist. On the level of actions he denies a hard determinism and asserts that men are at least sometimes free to act differently than they do act, and hence that in these cases they can be said to be responsible. However, on the more basic level of the "springs of action," words like "could have," "free," and "responsible" are without meaning. On this level "we must admit that we are ultimately the kind of persons we are because of conditions occurring outside us, over which we had no control." In sharp contrast to Hospers, Sartre presents a view that may be characterized as indeterministic and libertarian. He asserts that a man is what he wills himself to be. The individual is free—totally free—and hence totally responsible. Nowell-Smith, on the other hand, approaches the question analytically. He carefully analyzes the meanings of "could have" and critically examines the criteria used by the courts to determine when persons are to be held responsible for their actions.

The selections that follow, then, present possible solutions to the ethical problems outlined above—the standards of moral judgments; the meaning and justification of moral judgments; and the question of moral responsibility.

The standards
of moral judgments

EGOISTIC HEDONISM

epicurus

No one should postpone the study of philosophy when he is young, nor should he weary of it when he becomes mature, because the search for mental health is never untimely or out of season. To say that the time to study philosophy has not yet arrived or that it is past is like saying that the time for happiness is not yet at hand or is no longer present. Thus both the young and the mature should pursue philosophy, the latter in order to be rejuvenated as they age by the blessings that accrue from pleasurable past experience, and the youthful in order to become mature immediately through having no fear of the future. Hence we should make a practice of the things that make for happiness, for assuredly when we have this we have everything, and we do everything we can to get it when we don't have it.

This selection consists of Epicurus' *Letter to Menoeceus*, reprinted from *The Philosophy of Epicurus*, George K. Strodach, ed. (Evanston, Ill.: Northwestern University Press, 1963), pp. 178–185, by permission of the publisher.

The Preconditions of Happiness

You should do and practice all the things I constantly recommended to you, with the knowledge that they are the fundamentals of the good life. (1) First of all, you should think of deity as imperishable and blessed being (as delineated in the universal conception of it common to all men), and you should not attribute to it anything foreign to its immortality or inconsistent with its blessedness. On the contrary, you should hold every doctrine that is capable of safeguarding its blessedness in common with its imperishability. The gods do indeed exist, since our knowledge of them is a matter of clear and distinct perception; but they are not like what the masses suppose them to be, because most people do not maintain the pure conception of the gods. The irreligious man is not the person who destroys the gods of the masses but the person who imposes the ideas of the masses on the gods. The opinions held by most people about the gods are not true conceptions of them but fallacious notions, according to which awful penalties are meted out to the evil and the greatest of blessings to the good. The masses, by assimilating the gods in every respect to their own moral qualities, accept deities similar to themselves and regard anything not of this sort as alien.

(2) Second, you should accustom yourself to believing that death means nothing to us, since every good and every evil lies in sensation; but death in the privation of sensation. Hence a correct comprehension of the fact that death means nothing to us makes the mortal aspect of life pleasurable, not by conferring on us a boundless period of time but by removing the yearning for deathlessness. There is nothing fearful in living for the person who has really laid hold of the fact that there is nothing fearful in not living. So it is silly for a person to say that he dreads death—not because it will be painful when it arrives but because it pains him now as a future certainty; for that which makes no trouble for us when it arrives is a meaningless pain when we await it. This, the most horrifying of evils, means nothing to us, then, because so long as we are existent death is not present and whenever it is present we are nonexistent. Thus it is of no concern either to the living or to those who have completed their lives. For the former it is nonexistent, and the latter are themselves nonexistent.

Most people, however, recoil from death as though it were the greatest of evils; at other times they welcome it as the end-all of life's ills. The sophisticated person, on the other hand, neither begs off from living nor dreads not living. Life is not a stumbling block to him, nor does he regard not being alive as any sort of evil. As in the case of food he prefers the most savory dish to merely the larger portion, so in the case of time he garners to himself the most agreeable moments rather than the longest span.

Anyone who urges the youth to lead a good life but counsels the older man to end his life in good style is silly, not merely because of the welcome character of life but because of the fact that living well and dying well are one and the same discipline. Much worse off, however, is the person who says it were well not to have been born "but once born to pass Hades' portals as swiftly as may be." Now if he says such a thing from inner persuasion why does he not withdraw from life? Everything is in readiness for him once he has firmly resolved on this course. But if he speaks facetiously he is a trifler standing in the midst of men who do not welcome him.

It should be borne in mind, then, that the time to come is neither ours nor altogether not ours. In this way we shall neither expect the future outright as something destined to be nor despair of it as something absolutely not destined to be.

The good life

It should be recognized that within the category of desire certain desires are natural, certain others unnecessary and trivial; that in the case of the natural desires certain ones are necessary, certain others merely natural; and that in the case of necessary desires certain ones are necessary for happiness, others to promote freedom from bodily discomfort, others for the maintenance of life itself. A steady view of these matters shows us how to refer all moral choice and aversion to bodily health and imperturbability of mind, these being the twin goals of happy living. It is on this account that we do everything we do—to achieve freedom from pain and freedom from fear. When once we come by this, the tumult in the soul is calmed and the human being does not have to go about looking for something that is lacking or to search for something additional with which to supplement the welfare of soul and body. Accordingly we have need of pleasure only when we feel pain because of the absence of pleasure, but whenever we do not feel pain we no longer stand in need of pleasure. And so we speak of pleasure as the starting point and the goal of the happy life because we realize that it is our primary native good, because every act of choice and aversion originates with it, and because we come back to it when we judge every good by using the pleasure feeling as our criterion.

Because of the very fact that pleasure is our primary and congenital good we do not select every pleasure; there are times when we forgo certain pleasures, particularly when they are followed by too much unpleasantness. Furthermore, we regard certain states of pain as preferable to pleasures, particularly when greater satisfaction results from our having submitted to discomforts for a long period of time. Thus every pleasure is a good by reason of its having a nature akin to our own, but not every pleasure is desirable. In like manner, every state of pain is an evil, but not all pains are uniformly to be rejected. At any rate, it is our duty to judge all such cases by measuring pleasures against pains, with a view to their respective assets and liabilities, inasmuch as we do experience the good as being bad at times and, contrariwise, the bad as being good.

In addition, we consider limitation of the appetites a major good, and we recommend this practice not for the purpose of enjoying just a few things and no more, but rather for the purpose of enjoying those few in case we do not have much. We are firmly convinced that those who need expensive fare least are the ones who relish it most keenly and that a natural way of life is easily procured, while trivialities are hard to come by. Plain foods afford pleasure equivalent to that of a sumptuous diet, provided that the pains of penury are wholly eliminated. Barley bread and water yield the peak of pleasure whenever a person who needs them sets them in front of himself. Hence becoming habituated to a simple rather than a lavish way of life provides us with the full complement of health; it makes a person ready for the necessary business of life; it puts us in a position of advantage when we happen upon sumptuous fare at intervals and prepares us to be fearless in facing fortune.

Thus when I say that pleasure is the goal of living I do not mean the pleasures of libertines or the pleasures inherent in positive enjoyment, as is supposed by certain persons who are ignorant of our doctrine or who are not in agreement with it or who interpret it preversely. I mean, on the contrary, the pleasure that consists in freedom from bodily pain and mental agitation. The pleasant life is not the product of one drinking party after another or of sexual intercourse with women and boys or of the seafood and other delicacies afforded by a luxurious table. On the contrary, it is the result of sober thinking—namely, investigation of the reasons for every act of choice and aversion, and elimination of those false ideas about the gods and death which are the chief source of mental disturbances.

The starting point of this whole scheme and the most important of its values is good judgment, which consequently is more highly esteemed even than philosophy. All the other virtues stem from sound judgment, which shows us that it is impossible to live the pleasant Epicurean life without also living sensibly, nobly, and justly and, vice versa, that it is impossible to live sensibly, nobly, and justly without living pleasantly. The traditional virtues grow up together with the pleasant life; they are indivisible. Can you think of anyone more moral than the person who has devout beliefs about the gods, who is consistently without fears about death, and who has pondered man's natural end? Or who realizes that the goal of the good life is easily gained and achieved and that the term of evil is brief, both in extent of time and duration of pain. Or the man who laughs at the "decrees of Fate," a deity whom some people have set up as sovereign of all?

The good Epicurean believes that certain events occur deterministically, that others are chance events, and that still others are in our own hands. He sees also that necessity cannot be held morally responsible and that chance is an unpredictable thing, but that what is in our own hands, since it has no master, is naturally associated with blameworthiness and the opposite. (Actually it would be better to subscribe to the popular mythology than to become a slave by accepting the determinism of the natural philosophers, because popular religion underwrites the hope of supplicating the gods by offerings but determinism contains an element of necessity, which is inexorable.) As for chance, the Epicurean does not assume that it is a deity (as in popular belief) because a god does nothing irregular; nor does he regard it as an unpredictable cause of all events. It is his belief that good and evil are not the chance contributions of a deity, donated to mankind for the happy life, but rather that the initial circumstances for great good and evil are sometimes provided by chance. He thinks it preferable to have bad luck rationally than good luck irrationally. In other words, in human action it is better for a rational choice to be unsuccessful than for an irrational choice to succeed through the agency of chance.

Think about these and related matters day and night, by yourself and in company with someone like yourself. If you do, you will never experience anxiety, waking or sleeping, but you will live like a god among men. For a human being who lives in the midst of immortal blessings is in no way like mortal man!

UTILITARIANISM

john stuart mill

What utilitarianism is

A passing remark is all that needs be given to the ignorant blunder of supposing that those who stand up for utility as the test of right and wrong, use the term in that restricted and merely colloquial sense in which utility is opposed to pleasure. An apology is due to the philosophical opponents of utilitarianism, for even the momentary appearance of confounding them with anyone capable of so absurd a misconception; which is the more extraordinary, inasmuch as the contrary accusation, of referring everything to pleasure, and that too in its grossest form, is another of the common charges against utilitarianism: and, as has been pointedly remarked by an able writer, the same sort of persons, and often the very same persons, denounce the theory "as impracticably dry when the word utility precedes the word pleasure, and as too practicably voluptuous when the word pleasure precedes the word utility." Those who know anything about the matter are aware that every writer, from Epicurus to Bentham, who maintained the theory of utility, meant by it, not something to be contradistinguished from pleasure, but pleasure itself, together with exemption from pain; and instead of opposing the useful to the agreeable or the ornamental, have always declared that the useful means these, among other things. Yet the common herd, including the herd of writers, not only in newspapers and periodicals, but in books of weight and pretension, are perpetually falling into this shallow mistake. Having caught up the word utilitarian, while knowing nothing whatever about it but its sound, they habitually express by it the rejection, or the neglect, of pleasure in some of its forms; of beauty, of ornament, or of amusement. Nor is the term thus ignorantly misapplied solely in disparagement, but occasionally in compliment; as though it implied superiority to frivolity and the mere pleasures of the moment. And this perverted use is the only one in which the word is popularly known, and the one from which the new generation are acquiring their sole notion of its meaning. Those who introduced the word, but who had for many years discontinued it as a distinctive appellation, may well feel themselves called upon to resume it, if by

From John Stuart Mill, *Utilitarianism*, 13th ed. (London: Longmans, Green & Co. Ltd., 1897), Chaps. II, III, IV, pp. 8–17, 39–43, 52–56. Reprinted by permission of David McKay and Company.

doing so they can hope to contribute anything towards rescuing it from this utter degradation.

The creed which accepts as the foundation of morals, Utility, or the Greatest Happiness Principle, holds that actions are right in proportion as they tend to promote happiness, wrong as they tend to produce the reverse of happiness. By happiness is intended pleasure, and the absence of pain; by unhappiness, pain, and the privation of pleasure. To give a clear view of the moral standard set up by the theory, much more requires to be said; in particular, what things it includes in the ideas of pain and pleasure; and to what extent this is left an open question. But these supplementary explanations do not affect the theory of life on which this theory of morality is grounded—namely, that pleasure, and freedom from pain, are the only things desirable as ends; and that all desirable things (which are as numerous in the utilitarian as in any other scheme) are desirable either for the pleasure inherent in themselves, or as means to the promotion of pleasure and the prevention of pain.

Now, such a theory of life excites in many minds, and among them in some of the most estimable in feeling and purpose, inveterate dislike. To suppose that life has (as they express it) no higher end than pleasure—no better and nobler object of desire and pursuit—they designate as utterly mean and grovelling; as a doctrine worthy only of swine, to whom the followers of Epicurus were, at a very early period, contemptuously likened; and modern holders of the doctrine are occasionally made the subject of equally polite comparisons by its German, French, and English assailants.

When thus attacked, the Epicureans have always answered, that it is not they, but their accusers, who represent human nature in a degrading light; since the accusation supposes human beings to be capable of no pleasures except those of which swine are capable. If this supposition were true, the charge could not be gainsaid, but would then be no longer an imputation: for if the sources of pleasure were precisely the same to human beings and to swine, the rule of life which is good enough for the one would be good enough for the other. The comparison of the Epicurean life to that of beasts is felt as degrading, precisely because a beast's pleasures do not satisfy a human being's conceptions of happiness. Human beings have faculties more elevated than the animal appetites, and when once made conscious of them, do not regard anything as happiness which does not include their gratification. I do not, indeed, consider the Epicureans to have been by any means faultless in drawing out their scheme of consequences from the utilitarian principle. To do this in any sufficient manner, many Stoic, as well as Christian elements require to be included. But there is no known Epicurean theory of life which does not assign to the pleasures of the intellect, of the feelings and imagination, and of the moral sentiments, a much higher value as pleasures than to those of mere sensation. It must be admitted, however, that utilitarian writers in general have placed the superiority of mental over bodily pleasures chiefly in the greater permanency, safety, uncostliness, &c., of the former—that is, in their circumstantial advantages rather than in their intrinsic nature. And on all these points utilitarians have fully proved their case; but they might have taken the other, and, as it may be called, higher ground, with entire consistency. It is quite compatible with the principle of utility to recognize the fact, that some *kinds* of pleasure are more desirable and more valuable than others. It would be absurd that while, in estimating all other things, quality is considered as well as quantity, the estimation of pleasures should be supposed to depend on quantity alone.

If I am asked, what I mean by difference of quality in pleasures, or what makes one pleasure more valuable than another, merely as a pleasure, except its being greater in amount, there is but one possible answer. Of two pleasures, if there be one to which all or almost all who have experience of both give a decided preference, irrespective of any feeling of moral obligation to prefer it, that is the more desirable pleasure. If one of the two is, by those who are competently acquainted with both, placed so far above the other that they prefer it, even though knowing it to be attended with a greater amount of discontent, and would not resign it for any quantity of the other pleasure which their nature is capable of, we are justified in ascribing to the preferred enjoyment a superiority in quality, so far outweighing quantity as to render it, in comparison, of small account.

Now it is an unquestionable fact that those who are equally acquainted with, and equally capable of appreciating and enjoying, both, do give a most marked preference to the manner of existence which employs their higher faculties. Few human creatures would consent to be changed into any of the lower animals, for a promise of the fullest allowance of a beast's pleasures; no intelligent human being would consent to be a fool, no instructed person would be an ignoramus, no person of feeling and conscience would be selfish and base, even though they should be persuaded that the fool, the dunce, or the rascal is better satisfied with his lot than they are with theirs. They would not resign what they possess more than he, for the most complete satisfaction of all the desires which they have in common with him. If they ever fancy they would, it is only in cases of unhappiness so extreme, that to escape from it they would exchange their lot for almost any other, however undesirable in their own eyes. A being of higher faculties requires more to make him happy, is capable probably of more acute suffering, and is certainly accessible to it at more points, than one of an inferior type; but in spite of these liabilities, he can never really wish to sink into what he feels to be a lower grade of existence. We may give what explanation we please of this unwillingness; we may attribute it to pride, a name which is given indiscriminately to some of the most and to some of the least estimable feelings of which mankind are capable; we may refer it to the love of liberty and personal independence, an appeal to which was with the Stoics one of the most effective means for the inculcation of it; to the love of power, or to the love of excitement, both of which do really enter into and contribute to it: but its most appropriate appellation is a sense of dignity, which all human beings possess in one form or other, and in some, though by no means in exact, proportion to their higher faculties, and which is so essential a part of the happiness of those in whom it is strong, that nothing which conflicts with it could be, otherwise than momentarily, an object of desire to them. Whoever supposes that this preference takes place at a sacrifice of happiness—that the superior being, in anything like equal circumstances, is not happier than the inferior—confounds the two very different ideas, of happiness, and content. It is indisputable that the being whose capacities of enjoyment are low, has the greatest chance of having them fully satisfied; and a highly-endowed being will always feel that any happiness which he can look for, as the world is constituted, is imperfect. But he can learn to bear its imperfections, if they are at all bearable; and they will not make him envy the being who is indeed unconscious of the imperfections, but only because he feels not at all the good which those imperfections qualify. It is better to be a human being dissatisfied than a pig satisfied; better to be Socrates dissatisfied than a fool satisfied. And if the fool, or the pig, is of a different opinion, it is because they only know their own side of the question. The other party to the comparison knows both sides.

It may be objected, that many who are capable of the higher pleasures, occasionally, under the influence of temptation, postpone them to the lower. But this is quite compatible with a full appreciation of the intrinsic superiority of the higher. Men often, from infirmity of character, make their election for the nearer good, though they know it to be the less valuable; and this no less when the choice is between two bodily pleasures, than when it is between bodily and mental. They pursue sensual indulgences to the injury of health, though perfectly aware that health is the greater good. It may be further objected, that many who begin with youthful enthusiasm for everything noble, as they advance in years sink into indolence and selfishness. But I do not believe that those who undergo this very common change, voluntarily choose the lower description of pleasures in preference to the higher. I believe that before they devote themselves exclusively to the one, they have already become incapable of the other. Capacity for the nobler feelings is in most natures a very tender plant, easily killed, not only by hostile influences, but by mere want of sustenance; and in the majority of young persons it speedily dies away if the occupations to which their position in life has devoted them, and the society into which it has thrown them, are not favourable to keeping that higher capacity in exercise. Men lose their high aspirations as they lose their intellectual tastes, because they have not time or opportunity for indulging them; and they addict themselves to inferior pleasures, not because they deliberately prefer them, but because they are either the only ones to which they have access, or the only ones which they are any longer capable of enjoying. It may be questioned whether any one who has remained equally susceptible to both classes of pleasures, ever knowingly and calmly preferred the lower; though many, in all ages, have broken down in an ineffectual attempt to combine both.

From this verdict of the only competent judges, I apprehend there can be no appeal. On a question which is the best worth having of two pleasures, or which of two modes of existence is the most grateful to the feelings, apart from its moral attributes and from its consequences, the judgment of those who are qualified by knowledge of both, or, if they differ, that of the majority among them, must be admitted as final. And there needs be the less hesitation to accept this judgment respecting the quality of pleasures, since there is no other tribunal to be referred to even on the question of quantity. What means are there of determining which is the acutest of two pains, or the intensest of two pleasurable sensations, except the general suffrage of those who are familiar with both? Neither pains nor pleasures are homogeneous, and pain is always heterogeneous with pleasure. What is there to decide whether a particular pleasure is worth purchasing at the cost of a particular pain, except the feelings and judgment of the experienced? When, therefore, those feelings and judgment declare the pleasures derived from the higher faculties to be preferable *in kind,* apart from the question of intensity, to those of which the animal nature, disjoined from the higher faculties, is susceptible, they are entitled on this subject to the same regard.

I have dwelt on this point, as being a necessary part of a perfectly just conception of Utility or Happiness, considered as the directive rule of human conduct. But it is by no means an indispensable condition to the acceptance of the utilitarian standard; for that standard is not the agent's own greatest happiness, but the greatest amount of happiness altogether; and if it may possibly be doubted whether a noble character is always the happier for its nobleness, there can be no doubt that it makes other people happier, and that the world in general is immensely a gainer by it. Utilitarianism, therefore, could only attain its end by the general cultivation of nobleness of character, even if each individual were only benefited by the nobleness of others, and his own, so far as happiness is concerned, were a sheer deduction from the benefit. But the bare enunciation of such an absurdity as this last, renders refutation superfluous.

According to the Greatest Happiness Principle, as above explained, the ultimate end, with reference to and for the sake of which all other things are desirable (whether we are considering our own good or that of other people), is an existence exempt as far as possible from pain, and as rich as possible in enjoyments, both in point of quantity and quality; the test of quality, and the rule for measuring it against quantity, being the preference felt by those who, in their opportunities of experience, to which must be added their habits of self-consciousness and self-observation, are best furnished with the means of comparison. This, being, according to the utilitarian opinion, the end of human action, is necessarily also the standard of morality; which may accordingly be defined, the rules and precepts for human conduct, by the observance of which an existence such as has been described might be, to the greatest extent possible, secured to all mankind; and not to them only, but, so far as the nature of things admits, to the whole sentient creation.

·   ·   ·

Of the ultimate sanction of the principle of utility

The question is often asked, and properly so, in regard to any supposed moral standard—What is its sanction? What are the motives to obey? Or more specifically, what is the source of its obligation? Whence does it derive its binding force? It is a necessary part of moral philosophy to provide the answer to this question; which, though frequently assuming the shape of an objection to the utilitarian morality, as if it had some special applicability to that above others, really arises in regard to all standards. It arises, in fact, whenever a person is called on to *adopt* a standard or refer morality to any basis on which he has not been accustomed to rest it. For the customary morality, that which education and opinion have consecrated, is the only one which presents itself to the mind with the feeling of being *in itself* obligatory; and when a person is asked to believe that this morality *derives* its obligation from some general principle round which custom has not thrown the same halo, the assertion is to him a paradox; the supposed corollaries seem to have a more binding force than the original theorem; the superstructure seems to stand better without, than with, what is represented as its foundation. He says to himself, I feel that I am bound not to rob or murder, betray or deceive; but why am I bound to promote the general happiness? If my own happiness lies in something else, why may I not give that the preference?

If the view adopted by the utilitarian philosophy of the nature of the moral sense be correct, this difficulty will always present itself, until the influences which form moral character have taken the same hold of the principle which they have taken of some of the consequences—until, by the improvement of education, the feeling of unity with our fellow creatures shall be (what it cannot be doubted that Christ intended it to be) as deeply rooted in our character, and to our own consciousness as completely a part of our nature, as the horror of crime is in an ordinarily well-brought-up young person. In the meantime, however, the difficulty has no peculiar application to the doctrine of utility, but is inherent in every attempt to analyse morality and reduce it to principles; which, unless the principle is already in men's minds invested with as much sacredness as any of its applications, always seems to divest them of a part of their sanctity.

The principle of utility either has, or there is no reason why it might not have, all the sanctions which belong to any other system of morals. Those sanctions are either external or internal. Of the external sanctions it is not necessary to speak at any length. They are, the hope of favour and the fear of displeasure from our fellow creatures or from the Ruler of the Universe, along with whatever we may have of sympathy or affection for them or of love and awe of Him, inclining us to do His will independently of selfish consequences. There is evidently no reason why all these motives for observance should not attach themselves to the utilitarian morality, as completely and as powerfully as to any other. Indeed, those of them which refer to our fellow creatures are sure to do so, in proportion to the amount of general intelligence; for whether there be any other ground of moral obligation than the general happiness or not, men do desire happiness; and however imperfect may be their own practice, they desire and commend all conduct in others towards themselves, by which they think their happiness is promoted. With regard to the religious motive, if men believe, as most profess to do, in the goodness of God, those who think that conduciveness to the general happiness is the essence, or even only the criterion, of good, must necessarily believe that it is also that which God approves. The whole force therefore of external reward and punishment, whether physical or moral, and whether proceeding from God or from our fellow men, together with all that the capacities of human nature admit, of disinterested devotion to either, become available to enforce the utilitarian morality, in proportion as that morality is recognised; and the more powerfully, the more the appliances of education and general cultivation are bent to the purpose.

So far as to external sanctions. The internal sanction of duty, whatever our standard of duty may be, is one and the same—a feeling in our own mind; a pain, more or less intense, attendant on violation of duty, which in properly cultivated moral natures rises, in the more serious cases, into shrinking from it as an impossibility. This feeling, when disinterested, and connecting itself with the pure idea of duty, and not with some particular form of it, or with any of the merely accessory circumstances, is the essence of Conscience; though in that complex phenomenon as it actually exists, the simple fact is in general all encrusted over with collateral associations, derived from sympathy, from love, and still more from fear; from all the forms of religious feeling; from the recollections of childhood and of all our past life; from self-esteem, desire of the esteem of others, and occasionally even self-abasement. This extreme complication is, I apprehend, the origin of the sort of mystical character which, by a tendency of the human mind of which there are many other examples, is apt to be attributed to the idea of moral obligation, and which leads people to believe that the idea cannot possibly attach itself to any other objects than those which, by a supposed mysterious law, are found in our present experience to excite it. Its binding force, however, consists in the existence of a mass of feeling which must be broken through in order to do what violates our standard of right, and which, if we do nevertheless violate that standard, will probably have to be encountered afterwards in the form of remorse. Whatever theory we have of the nature or origin of conscience, this is what essentially constitutes it.

The ultimate sanction, therefore, of all morality (external motives apart) being a subjective feeling in our own minds, I see nothing embarrassing to those whose standard is utility, in the question, What is the sanction of that particular standard? We may answer, The same as of all other moral standards—the conscientious feelings of mankind. Undoubtedly this sanction has no binding efficacy on those who do not possess the feelings it appeals to; but neither will these persons be more obedient to any other moral principle than to the utilitarian one. On them morality of any kind has no hold but through the external sanctions. Meanwhile the feelings exist, a fact in human nature, the reality of which, and the great power with which they are capable of acting on those in whom they have been duly cultivated, are proved by experience. No reason has ever been shown why they may not be cultivated to as great intensity in connection with the utilitarian, as with any other rule of morals.

· · ·

Of what sort of proof the principle of utility is susceptible

It has already been remarked, that questions of ultimate ends do not admit of proof, in the ordinary acceptation of the term. To be incapable of proof by reasoning is common to all first principles; to the first premises of our knowledge, as well as to those of our conduct. But the former, being matters of fact, may be the subject of a direct appeal to the faculties which judge of fact—namely, our senses, and our internal consciousness. Can an appeal be made to the same faculties on questions of practical ends? Or by what other faculty is cognizance taken of them?

Questions about ends are, in other words, questions what things are desirable. The utilitarian doctrine is, that happiness is desirable, and the only thing desirable, as an end; all other things being only desirable as means to that end. What ought to be required of this doctrine—what conditions is it requisite that the doctrine should fulfil—to make good its claim to be believed?

The only proof capable of being given that an object is visible, is that people actually see it. The only proof that a sound is audible, is that people hear it; and so of the other sources of our experience. In like manner, I apprehend, the sole evidence it is possible to produce that anything is desirable, is that people do actually desire it. If the end which the utilitarian doctrine proposes to itself were not, in theory and in practice, acknowledged to be an end, nothing could ever convince any person that it was so. No reason can be given why the general happiness is desirable, except that each person, so far as he believes it to be attainable, desires his own happiness. This, however, being a fact, we have not only all the proof which the case admits of, but all which it is possible to require, that happiness is a good: that each person's happiness is a good to that person, and the general happiness, therefore, a good to the aggregate of all persons. Happiness has made out its title as *one* of the ends of conduct, and consequently one of the criteria of morality.

But it has not, by this alone, proved itself to be the sole criterion. To do that, it would seem, by the same rule, necessary to show, not only that people desire happiness, but that they never desire anything else. Now it is palpable that they do desire things which, in common language, are decidedly distinguished from happiness. They desire, for example, virtue, and the absence of vice, no less really than pleasure and the absence of pain. The desire of virtue is not as universal, but it is as authentic a fact, as the desire of happiness. And hence the opponents of the utilitarian standard deem that they have a right to infer that there are other ends of human action besides happiness, and that happiness is not the standard of approbation and disapprobation.

But does the utilitarian doctrine deny that people desire virtue, or maintain that virtue is not a thing to be desired? The very reverse. It maintains not only that virtue is to be desired, but that it is to be desired disinterestedly, for itself. Whatever may be the opinion of utilitarian moralists as to the original conditions by which virtue is made virtue; however they may believe (as they do) that actions and dispositions are only virtuous because they promote another end than virtue; yet this being granted, and it having been decided, from considerations of this description, which *is* virtuous, they not only place virtue at the very head of the things which are good as means to the ultimate end, but they also recognise as a psychological fact the possibility of its being, to the individual, a good in itself, without looking to any end beyond it; and hold, that the mind is not in a right state, not in a state conformable to Utility, not in the state most conducive to the general happiness, unless it does love virtue in this manner—as a thing desirable in itself, even although, in the individual instance, it should not produce those other desirable consequences which it tends to produce, and on account of which it is held to be virtue. This opinion is not, in the smallest degree, a departure from the Happiness principle. The ingredients of happiness are very various, and each of them is desirable in itself, and not merely when considered as swelling an aggregate. The principle of utility does not mean that any given pleasure, as music, for instance, or any given exemption from pain, as for example, health, are to be looked upon as means to a collective something termed happiness, and to be desired on that account. They are desired and desirable in and for themselves; besides being means, they are a part of the end. Virtue, according to the utilitarian doctrine, is not naturally and originally part of the end, but it is capable of becoming so; and in those who love it disinterestedly it has become so, and is desired and cherished, not as a means to happiness, but as a part of their happiness.

To illustrate this farther, we may remember that virtue is not the only thing, originally a means, and which if it were not a means to anything else, would be and remain indifferent, but which by association with what it is a means to, comes to be desired for itself, and that too with the utmost intensity. What, for example, shall we say of the love of money? There is nothing originally more desirable about money than about any heap of glittering pebbles. Its worth is solely that of the things which it will buy; the desires for other things than itself, which it is a means of gratifying. Yet the love of money is not only one of the strongest moving forces of human life, but money is, in many cases, desired in and for itself; the desire to possess it is often stronger than the desire to use it, and goes on increasing when all the desires which point to ends beyond it, to be compassed by it, are falling off. It may then be said truly, that money is desired not for the sake of an end, but as part of the end. From being a means to happiness, it has come to be itself a principal ingredient of the individual's conception of happiness. The same may be said of the majority of the great objects of human life—power, for example, or fame; except that to each of these there is a certain amount of immediate pleasure annexed, which has at least the semblance of being naturally inherent in them; a thing which cannot be said of money. Still, however, the strongest natural attraction, both of power and of fame, is the immense aid they give to the attainment of our other wishes; and it is the strong association thus generated between them and all our objects of desire, which gives to the direct desire of them the intensity it often assumes, so as in some characters to surpass in strength all other desires. In these cases the means have become a part of the end, and a more important part of it than any of the things which they are means to. What was once desired as an instrument for the attainment of happiness, has come to be desired for its own sake. In being desired for its own sake it is, however, desired as *part* of happiness. The person is made, or thinks he would be made, happy by its mere possession; and is made unhappy by failure to obtain it. The desire of it is not a different thing from the desire of happiness, any more than the love of music, or the desire of health. They are included in happiness. They are some of the elements of which the desire of happiness is made up. Happiness is not an abstract idea, but a concrete whole; and these are some of its parts. And the utilitarian standard sanctions and approves their being so. Life would be a poor thing, very ill provided with sources of happiness, if there were not this provision of nature, by which things originally indifferent, but conducive to, or otherwise associated with, the satisfaction of our primitive desires, become in themselves sources of pleasure more valuable than the primitive pleasures, both in permanency, in the space of human existence that they are capable of covering, and even in intensity.

•   •   •

WHAT IS GOOD?
THE SUBJECT MATTER OF ETHICS

g. e. moore

1. It is very easy to point out some among our everyday judgments, with the truth of which Ethics is undoubtedly concerned. Whenever we say, "So and so is a good man," or "That fellow is a villain"; whenever we ask, "What ought I to do?" or "Is it wrong for me to do like this?"; whenever we hazard such remarks as "Temperance is a virtue and drunkenness a vice"—it is undoubtedly the business of Ethics to discuss such questions and such statements; to argue what is the true answer when we ask what it is right to do, and to give reasons for thinking that our statements about the character of persons or the morality of actions are true or false. In the vast majority of cases, where we make statements involving any of the terms "virtue," "vice," "duty," "right," "ought," "good," "bad," we are making ethical judgments; and if we wish to discuss their truth, we shall be discussing a point of Ethics.

So much as this is not disputed; but it falls very far short of defining the province of Ethics. That province may indeed be defined as the whole truth about that which is at the same time common to all such judgments and peculiar to them. But we have still to ask the question: What is it that is thus common and peculiar? And this is a question to which very different answers have been given by ethical philosophers of acknowledged reputation, and none of them, perhaps, completely satisfactory.

2. If we take such examples as those given above, we shall not be far wrong in saying that they are all of them concerned with the question of "conduct"—with the question, what, in the conduct of us, human beings, is good, and what is bad, what is right, and what is wrong. For when we say that a man is good, we commonly mean that he acts rightly; when we say that drunkenness is a vice, we commonly mean that to get drunk is a wrong or wicked action. And this discussion of human conduct is, in fact, that with which the name "Ethics" is most intimately associated. It is so associated by derivation; and conduct is undoubtedly by far the commonest and most generally interesting object of ethical judgments.

Accordingly, we find that many ethical philosophers are disposed to accept as an adequate definition of "Ethics" the statement that it deals with the question what is

From G. E. Moore, *Principia Ethica* (Cambridge: Cambridge University Press, 1948), Chap. I, pp. 1–15. Reprinted by permission of the publisher.

good or bad in human conduct. They hold that its enquiries are properly confined to "conduct" or to "practice"; they hold that the name "practical philosophy" covers all the matter with which it has to do. Now, without discussing the proper meaning of the word (for verbal questions are properly left to the writers of dictionaries and other persons interested in literature; philosophy, as we shall see, has no concern with them), I may say that I intend to use "Ethics" to cover more than this—a usage, for which there is, I think, quite sufficient authority. I am using it to cover an inquiry for which, at all events, there is no other word: the general enquiry into what is good.

Ethics is undoubtedly concerned with the question what good conduct is; but, being concerned with this, it obviously does not start at the beginning, unless it is prepared to tell us what is good as well as what is conduct. For "good conduct" is a complex notion: all conduct is not good; for some is certainly bad and some may be indifferent. And on the other hand, other things, beside conduct, may be good; and if they are so, then, "good" denotes some property, that is common to them and conduct; and if we examine good conduct alone of all good things, then we shall be in danger of mistaking for this property, some property which is not shared by those other things: and thus we shall have made a mistake about Ethics even in this limited sense; for we shall not know what good conduct really is. This is a mistake which many writers have actually made, from limiting their inquiry to conduct. And hence I shall try to avoid it by considering first what is good in general; hoping, that if we can arrive at any certainty about this, it will be much easier to settle the question of good conduct: for we all know pretty well what "conduct" is. This, then, is our first question: What is good? and What is bad? and to the discussion of this question (or these questions) I give the name of Ethics, since that science must, at all events, include it.

3. But this is a question which may have many meanings. If, for example, each of us were to say "I am doing good now" or "I had a good dinner yesterday," these statements would each of them be some sort of answer to our question, although perhaps a false one. So, too, when A asks B what school he ought to send his son to, B's answer will certainly be an ethical judgment. And similarly all distribution of praise or blame to any personage or thing that has existed, now exists, or will exist, does give some answer to the question "What is good?" In all such cases some particular thing is judged to be good or bad: the question "What?" is answered by "This." But this is not the sense in which a scientific Ethics asks the question. Not one, of all the many million answers of this kind, which must be true, can form a part of an ethical system; although that science must contain reasons and principles sufficient for deciding on the truth of all of them. There are far too many persons, things, and events in the world, past, present, or to come, for a discussion of their individual merits to be embraced in any science. Ethics, therefore, does not deal at all with facts of this nature, facts that are unique, individual, absolutely particular; facts with which such studies as history, geography, astronomy, are compelled, in part at least, to deal. And, for this reason, it is not the business of the ethical philosopher to give personal advice or exhortation.

4. But there is another meaning which may be given to the question "What is good?" "Books are good" would be an answer to it, though an answer obviously false; for some books are very bad indeed. And ethical judgments of this kind do indeed belong to Ethics; though I shall not deal with many of them. Such is the judgment "Pleasure is good"—a judgment, of which Ethics should discuss the truth,

although it is not nearly as important as that other judgment, with which we shall be much occupied presently—"Pleasure *alone* is good." It is judgments of this sort, which are made in such books on Ethics as contain a list of "virtues"—in Aristotle's *Ethics* for example. But it is judgments of precisely the same kind, which form the substance of what is commonly supposed to be a study different from Ethics, and one much less respectable—the study of Casuistry. We may be told that Casuistry differs from Ethics, in that it is much more detailed and particular, Ethics much more general. But it is most important to notice that Casuistry does not deal with anything that is absolutely particular—particular in the only sense in which a perfectly precise line can be drawn between it and what is general. It is not particular in the sense just noticed, the sense in which this book is a particular book, and A's friend's advice particular advice. Casuistry may indeed be *more* particular and Ethics *more* general; but that means that they differ only in degree and not in kind. And this is universally true of "particular" and "general," when used in this common, but inaccurate, sense. So far as Ethics allows itself to give lists of virtues or even to name constituents of the Ideal, it is indistinguishable from Casuistry. Both alike deal with what is general, in the sense in which physics and chemistry deal with what is general. Just as chemistry aims at discovering what are the properties of oxygen, *wherever it occurs,* and not only of this or that particular specimen of oxygen; so Casuistry aims at discovering what actions are good, *whenever they occur.* In this respect Ethics and Casuistry alike are to be classed with such sciences as physics, chemistry, and physiology, in their absolute distinction from those of which history and geography are instances. And it is to be noted that, owing to their detailed nature, casuistical investigations are actually nearer to physics and to chemistry than are the investigations usually assigned to Ethics. For just as physics cannot rest content with the discovery that light is propagated by waves of ether, but must go on to discover the particular nature of the ether waves corresponding to each several color; so Casuistry, not content with the general law that charity is a virtue must attempt to discover the relative merits of every different form of charity. Casuistry forms, therefore, part of the ideal of ethical science: Ethics cannot be complete without it. The defects of Casuistry are not defects of principle; no objection can be taken to its aim and object. It has failed only because it is far too difficult a subject to be treated adequately in our present state of knowledge. The casuist has been unable to distinguish, in the cases which he treats, those elements upon which their value depends. Hence he often thinks two cases to be alike in respect of value, when in reality they are alike only in some other respect. It is to mistakes of this kind that the pernicious influence of such investigations has been due. For Casuistry is the goal of ethical investigation. It cannot be safely attempted at the beginning of our studies, but only at the end.

5. But our question "What is good?" may have still another meaning. We may, in the third place, mean to ask, not what thing or things are good, but how "good" is to be defined. This is an inquiry which belongs only to Ethics, not to Casuistry; and this is the inquiry which will occupy us first.

It is an inquiry to which most special attention should be directed; since this question, how "good" is to be defined, is the most fundamental question in all Ethics. That which is meant by "good" is, in fact, except its converse "bad," the *only* simple object of thought which is peculiar to Ethics. Its definition is, therefore, the most essential point in the definition of Ethics; and moreover, a mistake with regard to it entails a far larger number of erroneous ethical judgments than any other. Unless this first question be fully understood, and its true answer clearly recognized, the rest of Ethics is as good as useless from the point of view of systematic knowledge. True ethical judgments, of the two kinds last dealt with, may indeed be made by those who do not know the answer to this question as well as by those who do; and it goes without saying that the two classes of people may lead equally good lives. But it is extremely unlikely that the *most general* ethical judgments will be equally valid, in the absence of a true answer to this question: I shall presently try to show that the gravest errors have been largely due to beliefs in a false answer. And, in any case, it is impossible that, till the answer to this question be known, any one should know *what is the evidence* for any ethical judgment whatsoever. But the main object of Ethics, as a systematic science, is to give correct *reasons* for thinking that this or that is good; and, unless this question be answered, such reasons cannot be given. Even, therefore, apart from the fact that a false answer leads to false conclusions, the present inquiry is a most necessary and important part of the science of Ethics.

6. What, then, is good? How is good to be defined? Now, it may be thought that this is a verbal question. A definition does indeed often mean the expressing of one word's meaning in other words. But this is not the sort of definition I am asking for. Such a definition can never be of ultimate importance in any study except lexicography. If I wanted that kind of definition I should have to consider in the first place how people generally used the word "good"; but my business is not with its proper usage, as established by custom. I should, indeed, be foolish, if I tried to use it for something which it did not usually denote: if, for instance, I were to announce that, whenever I used the word "good," I must be understood to be thinking of that object which is usually denoted by the word "table." I shall, therefore, use the word in the sense in which I think it is ordinarily used; but at the same time I am not anxious to discuss whether I am right in thinking that it is so used. My business is solely with that object or idea, which I hold, rightly or wrongly, that the word is generally used to stand for. What I want to discover is the nature of that object or idea, and about this I am extremely anxious to arrive at an agreement.

But, if we understand the question in this sense, my answer to it may seem a very disappointing one. If I am asked "What is good?" my answer is that good is good, and that is the end of the matter. Or if I am asked "How is good to be defined?" my answer is that it cannot be defined, and that is all I have to say about it. But disappointing as these answers may appear, they are of the very last importance. To readers who are familiar with philosophic terminology, I can express their importance by saying that they amount to this: That propositions about the good are all of them synthetic and never analytic; and that is plainly no trivial matter. And the same thing may be expressed more popularly, by saying that, if I am right, then nobody can foist upon us such an axiom as that "Pleasure is the only good" or that "The good is the desire" on the pretence that this is "the very meaning of the word."

7. Let us, then, consider this position. My point is that "good" is a simple notion, just as "yellow" is a simple notion; that, just as you cannot, by any manner of means, explain to any one who does not already know it, what yellow is, so you cannot explain what good is. Definitions of the kind that I was asking for, definitions which describe the real nature of the object or notion denoted by a word, and which do not merely tell us what the word is used to mean, are only possible when the object or notion in question is something complex. You can give a definition of a horse, because a horse has many different properties and qualities, all of which you can

enumerate. But when you have enumerated them all, when you have reduced a horse to his simplest terms, then you can no longer define those terms. They are simply something which you think of or perceive, and to any one who cannot think of or perceive them, you can never, by any definition, make their nature known. It may perhaps be objected to this that we are able to describe to others, objects which they have never seen or thought of. We can, for instance, make a man understand what a chimera is, although he has never heard of one or seen one. You can tell him that it is an animal with a lioness' head and body, with a goat's head growing from the middle of its back, and with a snake in place of a tail. But here the object which you are describing is a complex object; it is entirely composed of parts, with which we are all perfectly familiar—a snake, a goat, a lioness; and we know, too, the manner in which those parts are to be put together, because we know what is meant by the middle of a lioness's back, and where her tail is wont to grow. And so it is with all objects, not previously known, which we are able to define: they are all complex; all composed of parts, which may themselves, in the first instance, be capable of similar definition, but which must in the end be reducible to simplest parts, which can no longer be defined. But yellow and good, we say, are not complex: they are notions of that simple kind, out of which definitions are composed and with which the power of further defining ceases.

8. When we say, as Webster says, "The definition of horse is 'A hoofed quadruped of the genus Equus,'" we may, in fact, mean three different things. (1) We may mean merely: "When I say 'horse,' you are to understand that I am talking about a hoofed quadruped of the genus Equus." This might be called the arbitrary verbal definition: and I do not mean that good is indefinable in that sense. (2) We may mean, as Webster ought to mean: "When most English people say 'horse,' they mean a hoofed quadruped of the genus Equus." This may be called the verbal definition proper, and I do not say that good is indefinable in this sense either; for it is certainly possible to discover how people use a word: otherwise, we could never have known that "good" may be translated by *"gut"* in German and by *"bon"* in French. But (3) we may, when we define horse, mean something much more important. We may mean that a certain object, which we all of us know, is composed in a certain manner: that it has four legs, a head, a heart, a liver, etc., etc., all of them arranged in definite relations to one another. It is in this sense that I deny good to be definable. I say that it is not composed of any parts, which we can substitute for it in our minds when we are thinking of it. We might think just as clearly and correctly about a horse, if we thought of all its parts and their arrangement instead of thinking of the whole: we could, I say, think how a horse differed from a donkey just as well, just as truly, in this way, as now we do, only not so easily; but there is nothing whatsoever which we could so substitute for good; and that is what I mean, when I say that good is indefinable.

9. But I am afraid I have still not removed the chief difficulty which may prevent acceptance of the proposition that good is indefinable. I do not mean to say that *the* good, that which is good, is thus indefinable; if I did think so, I should not be writing on Ethics, for my main object is to help toward discovering that definition. It is just because I think there will be less risk of error in our search for a definition of "the good," that I am now insisting that *good* is indefinable. I must try to explain the difference between these two. I suppose it may be granted that "good" is an adjective. Well "the good," "that which is good," must therefore be the substantive to which the adjective "good" will apply: it must be the whole of that to which the adjective

will apply, and the adjective must *always* truly apply to it. But if it is that to which the adjective will apply, it must be something different from that adjective itself; and the whole of that something different, whatever it is, will be our definition of *the* good. Now it may be that this something will have other adjectives, beside "good," that will apply to it. It may be full of pleasure, for example; it may be intelligent: and if these two adjectives are really part of its definition, then it will certainly be true, that pleasure and intelligence are good. And many people appear to think that, if we say "Pleasure and intelligence are good," or if we say "Only pleasure and intelligence are good," we are defining "good." Well, I cannot deny that propositions of this nature may sometimes be called definitions; I do not know well enough how the word is generally used to decide upon this point. I only wish it to be understood that that is not what I mean when I say there is no possible definition of good, and that I shall not mean this if I use the word again. I do most fully believe that some true proposition of the form "Intelligence is good and intelligence alone is good" can be found; if none could be found, our definition of *the* good would be impossible. As it is, I believe *the* good to be definable; and yet I still say that good itself is indefinable.

10. "Good," then, if we mean by it that quality which we assert to belong to a thing, when we say that the thing is good, is incapable of any definition, in the most important sense of that word. The most important sense of "definition" is that in which a definition states what are the parts which invariably compose a certain whole; and in this sense "good" has no definition because it is simple and has no parts. It is one of those innumerable objects of thought which are themselves incapable of definition, because they are the ultimate terms by reference to which whatever *is* capable of definition must be defined. That there must be an indefinite number of such terms is obvious, on reflection; since we cannot define anything except by an analysis, which, when carried as far as it will go, refers us to something, which is simply different from anything else, and which by that ultimate difference explains the peculiarity of the whole which we are defining: for every whole contains some parts which are common to other wholes also. There is, therefore, no intrinsic difficulty in the contention that "good" denotes a simple and indefinable quality. There are many other instances of such qualities.

Consider yellow, for example. We may try to define it, by describing its physical equivalent; we may state what kind of light-vibrations must stimulate the normal eye, in order that we may perceive it. But a moment's reflection is sufficient to show that those light-vibrations are not themselves what we mean by yellow. *They* are not what we perceive. Indeed we should never have been able to discover their existence, unless we had first been struck by the patent difference of quality between the different colors. The most we can be entitled to say of those vibrations is that they are what corresponds in space to the yellow which we actually perceive.

Yet a mistake of this simple kind has commonly been made about "good." It may be true that all things which are good are *also* something else, just as it is true that all things which are yellow produce a certain kind of vibration in the light. And it is a fact, that Ethics aims at discovering what are those other properties belonging to all things which are good. But far too many philosophers have thought that when they named those other properties they were actually defining good; that these properties, in fact, were simply not "other," but absolutely and entirely the same with goodness. This view I propose to call the "naturalistic fallacy" and of it I shall now endeavor to dispose.

11. Let us consider what it is such philosophers say. And first it is to be noticed that they do not agree among themselves. They not only say that they are right as to what good is, but they endeavor to prove that other people who say that it is something else, are wrong. One, for instance, will affirm that good is pleasure, another, perhaps, that good is that which is desired; and each of these will argue eagerly to prove that the other is wrong. But how is that possible? One of them says that good is nothing but the object of desire, and at the same time tries to prove that it is not pleasure. But from his first assertion, that good just means the object of desire, one of two things must follow as regards his proof:

(1) He may be trying to prove that the object of desire is not pleasure. But, if this be all, where is his Ethics? The position he is maintaining is merely a psychological one. Desire is something which occurs in our minds, and pleasure is something else which so occurs; and our would-be ethical philosopher is merely holding that the latter is not the object of the former. But what has that to do with the question in dispute? His opponent held the ethical proposition that pleasure was the good, and although he should prove a million times over the psychological proposition that pleasure is not the object of desire, he is no nearer proving his opponent to be wrong. The position is like this. One man says a triangle is a circle: another replies "A triangle is a straight line, and I will prove to you that I am right: *for*" (this is the only argument) "a straight line is not a circle." "That is quite true," the other may reply; "but nevertheless a triangle is a circle, and you have said nothing whatever to prove the contrary. What is proved is that one of us is wrong, for we agree that a triangle cannot be both a straight line and a circle: but which is wrong, there can be no earthly means of proving, since you define triangle as straight line and I define it as circle."—Well, that is one alternative which any naturalistic Ethics has to face; if good is *defined* as something else, it is then impossible either to prove that any other definition is wrong or even to deny such definition.

(2) The other alternative will scarcely be more welcome. It is that the discussion is after all a verbal one. When A says "Good means pleasant" and B says "Good means desire," they may merely wish to assert that most people have used the word for what is pleasant and for what is desired respectively. And this is quite an interesting subject for discussion: only it is not a whit more an ethical discussion than the last was. Nor do I think that any exponent of naturalistic Ethics would be willing to allow that this was all he meant. They are all so anxious to persuade us that what they call the good is what we really ought to do. "Do, pray, act so, because the word 'good' is generally used to denote actions of this nature": such, on this view, would be the substance of their teaching. And in so far as they tell us how we ought to act, their teaching is truly ethical, as they mean it to be. But how perfectly absurd is the reason they would give for it! "You are to do this, because most people use a certain word to denote conduct such as this." "You are to say the thing which is not, because most people call it lying." That is an argument just as good!—My dear sirs, what we want to know from you as ethical teachers, is not how people use a word; it is not even, what kind of actions they approve, which the use of this word "good" may certainly imply: what we want to know is simply what *is* good. We may indeed agree that what most people do think good, is actually so; we shall at all events be

glad to know their opinions: but when we say their opinions about what *is* good, we do mean what we say; we do not care whether they call that thing which they mean "horse" or "table" or "chair," "*gut*" or "*bon*" or "ἀγαθός"; we want to know what it is that they so call. When they say "Pleasure is good," we cannot believe that they merely mean "Pleasure is pleasure" and nothing more than that.

12. Suppose a man says "I am pleased"; and suppose that is not a lie or a mistake but the truth. Well, if it is true, what does that mean? It means that his mind, a certain definite mind, distinguished by certain definite marks from all others, has at this moment a certain definite feeling called pleasure. "Pleased *means* nothing but having pleasure, and though we may be more pleased or less pleased, and even, we may admit for the present, have one or another kind of pleasure; yet in so far as it is pleasure we have, whether there be more or less of it, and whether it be of one kind or another, what we have is one definite thing, absolutely indefinable, some one thing that is the same in all the various degrees and in all the various kinds of it that there may be. We may be able to say how it is related to other things: that, for example, it is in the mind, that it causes desire, that we are conscious of it, etc., etc. We can, I say, describe its relations to other things, but define it we can *not*. And if anybody tried to define pleasure for us as being any other natural object; if anybody were to say, for instance, that pleasure *means* the sensation of red, and were to proceed to deduce from that that pleasure is a color, we should be entitled to laugh at him and to distrust his future statements about pleasure. Well, that would be the same fallacy which I have called the naturalistic fallacy. That "pleased" does not mean "having the sensation of red," or anything else whatever, does not prevent us from understanding what it does mean. It is enough for us to know that "pleased" does mean "having the sensation of pleasure," and though pleasure is absolutely indefinable, though pleasure is pleasure and nothing else whatever, yet we feel no difficulty in saying that we are pleased. The reason is, of course, that when I say "I am pleased," I do *not* mean that "I" am the same thing as "having pleasure." And similarly no difficulty need be found in my saying that "pleasure is good" and yet not meaning that "pleasure" is the same thing as "good," that pleasure *means* good, and that good *means* pleasure. If I were to imagine that when I said "I am pleased," I meant that I was exactly the same thing as "pleased," I should not indeed call that a naturalistic fallacy, although it would be the same fallacy as I have called naturalistic with reference to Ethics. The reason of this is obvious enough. When a man confuses two natural objects with one another, defining the one by the other, if for instance, he confuses himself, who is one natural object, with "pleased" or with "pleasure" which are others, then there is no reason to call the fallacy naturalistic. But if he confuses "good," which is not in the same sense a natural object, with any natural object whatever, then there is a reason for calling that a naturalistic fallacy; its being made with regard to "good" marks it as something quite specific, and this specific mistake deserves a name because it is so common. As for the reasons why good is not to be considered a natural object, they may be reserved for discussion in another place. But, for the present, it is sufficient to notice this: Even if it were a natural object, that would not alter the nature of the fallacy nor diminish its imporance one whit. All that I have said about it would remain quite equally true: only the name which I have called it would not be so appropriate as I think it is. And I do not care about the name: what I do care about is the fallacy. It does not matter what we call it, provided we recognize it when we meet with it. It is to be met with in almost every

book on Ethics; and yet it is not recognized: and that is why it is necessary to multiply illustrations of it, and convenient to give it a name. It is a very simple fallacy indeed. When we say that an orange is yellow, we do not think our statement binds us to hold that "orange" means nothing else than "yellow," or that nothing can be yellow but an orange. Supposing the orange is also sweet! Does that bind us to say that "sweet" is exactly the same thing as "yellow," that "sweet" must be defined as "yellow"? And supposing it be recognized that "yellow" just means "yellow" and nothing else whatever, does that make it any more difficult to hold that oranges are yellow? Most certainly it does not: on the contrary, it would be absolutely meaningless to say that oranges were yellow, unless yellow did in the end mean just "yellow" and nothing else whatever—unless it was absolutely indefinable. We should not get any very clear notion about things, which are yellow—we should not get very far with our science, if we were bound to hold that everything which was yellow, *meant* exactly the same thing as yellow. We should find we had to hold that an orange was exactly the same thing as a stool, a piece of paper, a lemon, anything you like. We could prove any number of absurdities; but should we be the nearer to the truth? Why, then, should it be different with "good"? Why, if good is good and indefinable, should I be held to deny that pleasure is good? Is there any difficulty in holding both to be true at once? On the contrary, there is no meaning in saying that pleasure is good, unless good is something different from pleasure. It is absolutely useless, so far as Ethics is concerned, to prove as Mr. Spencer tries to do, that increase of pleasure coincides with increase of life, unless good *means* something different from either life or pleasure. He might just as well try to prove that an orange is yellow by showing that it always is wrapped up in paper.

13. In fact, if it is not the case that "good" denotes something simple and indefinable, only two alternatives are possible: either it is a complex, a given whole, about the correct analysis of which there may be disagreement; or else it means nothing at all, and there is no such subject as Ethics. In general, however, ethical philosophers have attempted to define good, without recognizing what such an attempt must mean. They actually use arguments which involve one or both of the absurdities considered in § 11. We are, therefore, justified in concluding that the attempt to define good is chiefly due to want of clearness as to the possible nature of definition. There are, in fact, only two serious alternatives to be considered, in order to establish the conclusion that "good" does denote a simple and indefinable notion. It might possibly denote a complex, as "horse" does; or it might have no meaning at all. Neither of these possibilities has, however, been clearly conceived and seriously maintained, as such, by those who presume to define good; and both may be dismissed by a simple appeal to facts.

·   ·   ·

ON ABSOLUTE DUTY

søren kierkegaard

Is there such a thing as a teleological suspension of the ethical?

The ethical as such is the universal: it applies to everyone; and the same thing is expressed from another point of view by saying that it applies every instant. It reposes immanently in itself, it has nothing without itself which is its *telos,* but is itself *telos* for everything outside it, and when this has been incorporated by the ethical it can go no further. Conceived immediately as physical and psychical, the particular individual is the particular which has its *telos* in the universal, and its task is to express itself constantly in it, to abolish its particularity in order to become the universal. As soon as the individual would assert himself in his particularity over against the universal he sins, and only by recognizing this can he again reconcile himself with the universal. Whenever the individual after he has entered the universal feels an impulse to assert himself as the particular, he is in temptation (*Anfechtung*), and he can labor himself out of this only by abandoning himself as the particular in the universal. If this be the highest thing that can be said of man and of his existence, then the ethical has the same character as man's eternal blessedness, which to all eternity and at every instant is his *telos,* since it would be a contradiction to say that this might be abandoned (i.e., teleologically suspended), inasmuch as this is no sooner suspended than it is forfeited, whereas in other cases what is suspended is not forfeited but is preserved precisely in that higher thing which is its *telos.*

If such be the case, then Hegel is right when in his chapter on "The Good and the Conscience," [1] he characterizes man merely as the particular and regards this character as "a moral form of the evil" which is to be annulled in the teleology of the moral, so that the individual who remains in this stage is either sinning or subjected to temptation (*Anfechtung*). On the other hand, he is wrong in talking of faith, wrong in not protesting loudly and clearly against the fact that Abraham

From Søren Kierkegaard, *Fear and Trembling,* Walter Lowrie, trans. (Copyright 1941, 1954 by Princeton University Press), Problems I, II, pp. 79–84, 87–89, 102–108. Reprinted by permission of Princeton University Press.

1 Cf. *Philosophie des Rechts,* 2nd ed. (1840) §§129–141 and Table of Contents p. xix. [Eds.]

enjoys honor and glory as the father of faith, whereas he ought to be prosecuted and convicted of murder.

For faith is this paradox, that the particular is higher than the universal—yet in such a way, be it observed, that the movement repeats itself, and that consequently the individual, after having been in the universal, now as the particular isolated himself as higher than the universal. If this be not faith, then Abraham is lost, then faith has never existed in the world . . . because it has always existed. For if the ethical (i.e., the moral) is the highest thing, and if nothing incommensurable remains in man in any other way but as the evil (i.e., the particular which has to be expressed in the universal), then one needs no other categories besides those which the Greeks possessed or which by consistent thinking can be derived from them. This fact Hegel ought not to have concealed, for after all he was acquainted with Greek thought.

One not infrequently hears it said by men who for lack of losing themselves in studies are absorbed in phrases that a light shines upon the Christian world whereas a darkness broods over paganism. This utterance has always seemed strange to me, inasmuch as every profound thinker and every serious artist is even in our day rejuvenated by the eternal youth of the Greek race. Such an utterance may be explained by the consideration that people do not know what they ought to say but only that they must say something. It is quite right for one to say that paganism did not possess faith, but if with this one is to have said something, one must be a little clearer about what one understands by faith, since otherwise one falls back into such phrases. To explain the whole of existence and faith along with it is easy, and that man does not make the poorest calculation in life who reckons upon admiration when he possesses such an explanation; for, as Boileau says, *"un sot trouve toujours un plus sot qui l'admire."*

Faith is precisely this paradox, that the individual as the particular is higher than the universal, is justified over against it, is not subordinate but superior—yet in such a way, be it observed, that it is the particular individual who, after he has been subordinated as the particular to the universal, now through the universal becomes the individual who as the particular is superior to the universal, for the fact that the individual as the particular stands in an absolute relation to the absolute. This position cannot be mediated, for all mediation comes about precisely by virtue of the universal; it is and remains to all eternity a paradox, inaccessible to thought. And yet faith is this paradox—or else (these are the logical deductions which I would beg the reader to have *in mente* at every point, though it would be too prolix for me to reiterate them on every occasion)—or else there never has been faith . . . precisely because it always has been. In other words, Abraham is lost.

That for the particular individual this paradox may easily be mistaken for a temptation (*Anfechtung*) is indeed true, but one ought not for this reason to conceal it. That the whole constitution of many persons may be such that this paradox repels them is indeed true, but one ought not for this reason to make faith something different in order to be able to possess it, but ought rather to admit that one does not possess it, whereas those who possess faith should take care to set up certain criteria so that one might distinguish the paradox from a temptation (*Anfechtung*).

Now the story of Abraham contains such a teleological suspension of the ethical. There have not been lacking clever pates and profound investigators who have found analogies to it. Their wisdom is derived from the pretty proposition that at bottom everything is the same. If one will look a little more closely, I have not much doubt that in the whole world one will not find a single analogy (except a later instance which proves nothing), if it stands fast that Abraham is the representative of faith, and that faith is normally expressed in him whose life is not merely the most paradoxical that can be thought but so paradoxical that it cannot be thought at all. He acts by virtue of the absurd, for it is precisely absurd that he as the particular is higher than the universal. This paradox cannot be mediated; for as soon as he begins to do this he has to admit that he was in temptation (*Anfechtung*), and if such was the case, he never gets to the point of sacrificing Isaac, or, if he has sacrificed Isaac, he must turn back repentantly to the universal. By virtue of the absurd he gets Isaac again. Abraham is therefore at no instant a tragic hero but something quite different, either a murderer or a believer. The middle term which saves the tragic hero, Abraham has not. Hence it is that I can understand the tragic hero but cannot understand Abraham, though in a certain crazy sense I admire him more than all other men.

Abraham's relation to Isaac, ethically speaking, is quite simply expressed by saying that a father shall love his son more dearly than himself. Yet within its own compass the ethical has various gradations. Let us see whether in this story there is to be found any higher expression for the ethical such as would ethically explain his conduct, ethically justify him in suspending the ethical obligation toward his son, without in this search going beyond the teleology of the ethical.

. . . .

The difference between the tragic hero and Abraham is clearly evident. The tragic hero still remains within the ethical. He lets one expression of the ethical find its *telos* in a higher expression of the ethical; the ethical relation between father and son, or daughter and father, he reduces to a sentiment which has its dialectic in the the idea of morality. Here there can be no question of a teleological suspension of the ethical.

With Abraham the situation was different. By his act he overstepped the ethical entirely and possessed a higher *telos* outside of it, in relation to which he suspended the former. For I should very much like to know how one would bring Abraham's act into relation with the universal, and whether it is possible to discover any connection whatever between what Abraham did and the universal . . . except the fact that he transgressed it. It was not for the sake of saving a people, not to maintain the idea of the state, that Abraham did this, and not in order to reconcile angry deities. If there could be a question of the deity being angry, he was angry only with Abraham, and Abraham's whole action stands in no relation to the universal, is a purely personal undertaking. Therefore, whereas the tragic hero is great by reason of his moral virtue, Abraham is great by reason of a personal virtue. In Abraham's life there is no higher expression for the ethical than this, that the father shall love his son. Of the ethical in the sense of morality there can be no question in this instance. In so far as the universal was present, it was indeed cryptically present in Isaac, hidden as it were in Isaac's loins, and must therefore cry out with Isaac's mouth, "Do it not! Thou art bringing everything to naught."

Why then did Abraham do it? For God's sake, and (in complete identity with this) for his own sake. He did it for God's sake because God required this proof of his faith; for his own sake he did it in order that he might furnish the proof. The unity of these two points of view is perfectly expressed by the word which has always been used to characterize this situation: it is a trial, a temptation (*Fristelse*). A temptation—but what does that mean? What ordinarily tempts a man is that which would keep him from doing his duty, but in this case the temptation is itself the ethical . . . which would keep him from doing God's will.

• • •

Is there such a thing as an absolute duty toward God?

The ethical is the universal, and as such it is again the divine. One has therefore a right to say that fundamentally every duty is a duty toward God; but if one cannot say more, then one affirms at the same time that properly I have no duty toward God. Duty becomes duty by being referred to God, but in duty itself I do not come into relation with God. Thus it is a duty to love one's neighbor, but in performing this duty I do not come into relation with God but with the neighbor whom I love. If I say then in this connection that it is my duty to love God, I am really uttering only a tautology, inasmuch as "God" is in this instance used in an entirely abstract sense as the divine, i.e., the universal, i.e., duty. So the whole existence of the human race is rounded off completely like a sphere, and the ethical is at once its limit and its content. God becomes an invisible vanishing point, a powerless thought, His power being only in the ethical which is the content of existence. If in any way it might occur to any man to want to love God in any other sense than that here indicated, he is romantic, he loves a phantom which, if it had merely the power of being able to speak, would say to him, "I do not require your love. Stay where you belong." If in any way it might occur to a man to want to love God otherwise, this love would be open to suspicion, like that of which Rousseau speaks, referring to people who love the Kaffirs instead of their neighbors.

So in case what has been expounded here is correct, in case there is no incommensurability in a human life, and what there is of the incommensurable is only such by an accident from which no consequences can be drawn, in so far as existence is regarded in terms of the idea, Hegel is right; but he is not right in talking about faith or in allowing Abraham to be regarded as the father of it; for by the latter he has pronounced judgment both upon Abraham and upon faith. In the Hegelian philosophy *das Äussere (die Entäusserung)* is higher than *das Innere*. This is frequently illustrated by an example. The child is *das Innere,* the man *das Äussere.* Hence it is that the child is defined by the outward, and, conversely, the man, as *das Innere,* is defined precisely by *das Innere.* Faith, on the contrary, is the paradox that inwardness is higher than outwardness—or, to recall an expression used above, the uneven number is higher than the even. In the ethical way of regarding life it is therefore the task of the individual to divest himself of the inward determinants and express them in an outward way. Whenever he shrinks from this, whenever he is inclined to persist in or to slip back again into the inward determinants of feeling, mood, etc., he sins, he succumbs to a temptation *(Anfechtung).* The paradox of faith is this, that there is an inwardness which is incommensurable for the outward, an inwardness, be it observed, which is not identical with the first but is a new inwardness. This must not be overlooked. Modern philosophy has taken the liberty of substituting without more ado the word faith for the immediate. When one does that it is ridiculous to deny that faith has existed in all ages. In that way faith comes into rather simple company along with feeling, mood, idiosyncrasy, vapors, etc. To this extent philosophy may be right in saying that one ought not to stop there. But there is nothing to justify philosophy in using this phrase with regard to faith. Before faith there goes a movement of infinity, and only then, *necopinate,* by virtue of the absurd, faith enters upon the scene. This I can well understand without maintaining on that account that I have faith. If faith is nothing but what philosophy makes it out to be, then Socrates already went further, much further, whereas the contrary is true, that he never reached it. In an intellectual respect he made the movement of infinity. His ignorance is infinite resignation. This task in itself is a match for human powers, even though people in our time disdain it; but only after it is done, only when the individual has evacuated himself in the infinite, only then is the point attained where faith can break forth.

The paradox of faith is this, that the individual is higher than the universal, that the individual (to recall a dogmatic distinction now rather seldom heard) determines his relation to the universal by his relation to the absolute, not his relation to the absolute by his relation to the universal. The paradox can also be expressed by saying that there is an absolute duty toward God; for in this relationship of duty the individual as an individual stands related absolutely to the absolute. So when in this connection it is said that it is a duty to love God, something different is said from that in the foregoing; for if this duty is absolute, the ethical is reduced to a position of relativity. From this, however, it does not follow that the ethical is to be abolished, but it acquires an entirely different expression, the paradoxical expression—that, for example, love to God may cause the knight of faith to give his love to his neighbor the opposite expression to that which, ethically speaking, is required by duty.

If such is not the case, then faith has no proper place in existence, then faith is a temptation (*Anfechtung*), and Abraham is lost, since he gave in to it.

This paradox does not permit of mediation, for it is founded precisely upon the fact that the individual is only the individual. As soon as this individual desires to express his absolute duty in the universal, to become conscious of this duty in that, he is in temptation (*Anfechtung*) and, even supposing he puts up a resistance to this, he never gets to the point of fulfilling the so-called absolute duty, and if he does not resist, then he sins, even though *realiter* his act was that which it was his absolute duty to do. So what should Abraham do? If he would say to another person, "Isaac I love more dearly than everything in the world, and hence it is so hard for me to sacrifice him"; then surely the other would have shrugged his shoulders and said, "Why will you sacrifice him then?"—or if the other had been a sly fellow, he surely would have seen through Abraham and perceived that he was making a show of feelings which were in strident contradiction to his act.

In the story of Abraham we find such a paradox. His relation to Isaac, ethically expressed, is this, that the father should love the son. This ethical relation is reduced to a relative position in contrast with the absolute relation to God. To the question, "Why?" Abraham has no answer except that it is a trial, a temptation (*Fristelse*)— terms which, as was remarked above, express the unity of the two points of view: that it is for God's sake and for his own sake. In common usage these two ways of regarding the matter are mutually exclusive. Thus when we see a man do something which does not comport with the universal, we say that he scarcely can be doing it for God's sake, and by that we imply that he does it for his own sake. The paradox of faith has lost the intermediate term, i.e., the universal. On the one side it has the expression for the extremest egoism (doing the dreadful thing it does for one's own sake);

on the other side the expression for the most absolute self-sacrifice (doing it for God's sake). Faith is this paradox, and the individual absolutely cannot make himself intelligible to anybody. People imagine maybe that the individual can make himself intelligible to another individual in the same case. Such a notion would be unthinkable if in our time people did not in so many ways seek to creep slyly into greatness. The one knight of faith can render no aid to the other. Either the individual becomes a knight of faith by assuming the burden of the paradox, or he never becomes one. In these regions partnership is unthinkable. Every more precise explication of what is to be understood by Isaac the individual can give only to himself. And even if one were able, generally speaking, to define ever so precisely what should be intended by Isaac (which moreover would be the most ludicrous self-contradiction, i.e., that the particular individual who definitely stands outside the universal is subsumed under universal categories precisely when he has to act as the individual who stands outside the universal), the individual nevertheless will never be able to assure himself by the aid of others that this application is appropriate, but he can do so only by himself as the individual. Hence even if a man were cowardly and paltry enough to wish to become a knight of faith on the responsibility and at the peril of an outsider, he will never become one; for only the individual becomes a knight of faith as the particular individual, and this is the greatness of this knighthood, as I can well understand without entering the order; but this is also its terror, as I can comprehend even better.

5

THE CATEGORICAL IMPERATIVE

immanuel kant

First Section:

Transition from the common rational
knowledge of morals to the philosophical

Nothing in the world—indeed nothing even beyond the world—can possibly be conceived which could be called good without qualification except a *good will*. Intelligence, wit, judgment, and the other talents of the mind, however they may be named, or courage, resoluteness, and perseverance as qualities of temperament, are doubtless in many respects good and desirable. But they can become extremely bad and harmful if the will, which is to make use of these gifts of nature and which in its special constitution is called character, is not good. It is the same with the gifts of fortune. Power, riches, honor, even health, general well-being, and the contentment with one's condition which is called happiness, make for pride and even arrogance if there is not a good will to correct their influence on the mind and on its principles of action so as to make it universally conformable to its end. It need hardly be mentioned that the sight of a being adorned with no feature of a pure and good will, yet enjoying uninterrupted prosperity, can never give pleasure to a rational impartial observer. Thus the good will seems to constitute the indispensable condition even of worthiness to be happy.

Some qualities seem to be conducive to this good will and can facilitate its action, but, in spite of that, they have no intrinsic unconditional worth. They rather presuppose a good will, which limits the high esteem which one otherwise rightly has for them and prevents their being held to be absolutely good. Moderation in emotions and passions, self-control, and calm deliberation not only are good in many respects but even seem to constitute a part of the inner worth of the person. But however unconditionally they were esteemed by the ancients, they are far from being good without qualification. For without the principle of a good will they can become extremely

From Immanuel Kant, *Foundations of the Metaphysics of Morals (Grundlegung zur Metaphysik der Sitten)*, Lewis White Beck, trans., pp. 9–10, 13–17, 29–30, 38–42, 47–49. Copyright © 1959 by the Liberal Arts Press, Inc. Reprinted by permission of the Liberal Arts Press Division of the Bobbs-Merrill Company, Inc.

bad, and the coolness of a villain makes him not only far more dangerous but also more directly abominable in our eyes than he would have seemed without it.

The good will is not good because of what it effects or accomplishes or because of its adequacy to achieve some proposed end; it is good only because of its willing, i.e., it is good of itself. And, regarded for itself, it is to be esteemed incomparably higher than anything which could be brought about by it in favor of any inclination or even of the sum total of all inclinations. Even if it should happen that, by a particularly unfortunate fate or by the niggardly provision of a stepmotherly nature, this will should be wholly lacking in power to accomplish its purpose, and if even the greatest effort should not avail it to achieve anything of its end, and if there remained only the good will (not as a mere wish but as the summoning of all the means in our power), it would sparkle like a jewel in its own right, as something that had its full worth in itself. Usefulness or fruitlessness can neither diminish nor augment this worth. Its usefulness would be only its setting, as it were, so as to enable us to handle it more conveniently in commerce or to attract the attention of those who are not yet connoisseurs, but not to recommend it to those who are experts or to determine its worth.

.   .   .

We have, then, to develop the concept of a will which is to be esteemed as good of itself without regard to anything else. It dwells already in the natural sound understanding and does not need so much to be taught as only to be brought to light. In the estimation of the total worth of our actions it always takes first place and is the condition of everything else. In order to show this, we shall take the concept of duty. It contains that of a good will, though with certain subjective restrictions and hindrances; but these are far from concealing it and making it unrecognizable, for they rather bring it out by contrast and make it shine forth all the brighter.

I here omit all actions which are recognized as opposed to duty, even though they may be useful in one respect or another, for with these the question does not arise at all as to whether they may be carried out *from* duty, since they conflict with it. I also pass over the actions which are really in accordance with duty and to which one has no direct inclination, rather executing them because impelled to do so by another inclination. For it is easily decided whether an action in accord with duty is performed from duty or for some selfish purpose. It is far more difficult to note this difference when the action is in accordance with duty and, in addition, the subject has a direct inclination to do it. For example, it is in fact in accordance with duty that a dealer should not overcharge an inexperienced customer, and wherever there is much business the prudent merchant does not do so, having a fixed price for everyone, so that a child may buy of him as cheaply as any other. Thus the customer is honestly served. But this is far from sufficient to justify the belief that the merchant has behaved in this way from duty and principles of honesty. His own advantage required this behavior; but it cannot be assumed that over and above that he had a direct inclination to the purchaser and that, out of love, as it were, he gave none an advantage in price over another. Therefore the action was done neither from duty nor from direct inclination but only for a selfish purpose.

On the other hand, it is a duty to preserve one's life, and moreover everyone has a direct inclination to do so. But for that reason the often anxious care which most men take of it has no intrinsic worth, and the maxim of doing so has no moral import. They preserve their lives according to duty, but not from duty. But if adversities and hopeless sorrow completely take away the relish for life. if an unfortunate man, strong in soul, is indignant rather than despondent or dejected over his fate and wishes for death, and yet preserves his life without loving it and from neither inclination nor fear but from duty—then his maxim has a moral import.

To be kind where one can is duty, and there are, moreover, many persons so sympathetically constituted that without any motive of vanity or selfishness they find an inner satisfaction in spreading joy, and rejoice in the contentment of others which they have made possible. But I say that, however dutiful and amiable it may be, that kind of action has no true moral worth. It is on a level with [actions arising from] other inclinations, such as the inclination to honor, which, if fortunately directed to what in fact accords with duty and is generally useful and thus honorable, deserve praise and encouragement but no esteem. For the maxim lacks the moral import of an action done not from inclination but from duty. But assume that the mind of that friend to mankind was clouded by a sorrow of his own which extinguished all sympathy with the lot of others and that he still had the power to benefit others in distress, but that their need left him untouched because he was preoccupied with his own need. And now suppose him to tear himself, unsolicited by inclination, out of this dead insensibility and to perform this action only from duty and without any inclination—then for the first time his action has genuine moral worth. Furthermore, if nature has put little sympathy in the heart of a man, and if he, though an honest man, is by temperament cold and indifferent to the sufferings of others, perhaps because he is provided with special gifts of patience and fortitude and expects or even requires that others should have the same—and such a man would certainly not be the meanest product of nature—would not he find in himself a source from which to give himself a far higher worth than he could have got by having a good-natured temperament? This is unquestionably true even though nature did not make him philanthropic, for it is just here that the worth of the character is brought out, which is morally and incomparably the highest of all: he is beneficent not from inclination but from duty.

To secure one's own happiness is at least indirectly a duty, for discontent with one's condition under pressure from many cares and amid unsatisfied wants could easily become a great temptation to transgress duties. But without any view to duty all men have the strongest and deepest inclination to happiness, because in this idea all inclinations are summed up. But the percept of happiness is often so formulated that it definitely thwarts some inclinations, and men can make no definite and certain concept of the sum of satisfaction of all inclinations which goes under the name of happiness. It is not to be wondered at, therefore, that a single inclination, definite as to what it promises and as to the time at which it can be satisfied, can outweigh a fluctuating idea, and that, for example, a man with the gout can choose to enjoy what he likes and to suffer what he may, because according to his calculations at least on this occasion he has not sacrificed the enjoyment of the present moment to a perhaps groundless expectation of a happiness supposed to lie in health. But even in this case, if the universal inclination to happiness did not determine his will, and if health were not at least for him a necessary factor in these calculations, there yet would remain, as in all other cases, a law that he ought to promote his happiness, not from inclination but from duty. Only from this law would his conduct have true moral worth.

It is in this way, undoubtedly, that we should understand those passages of

Scripture which command us to love our neighbor and even our enemy, for love as an inclination cannot be commanded. But beneficence from duty, when no inclination impels it and even when it is opposed by a natural and unconquerable aversion, is practical love, not pathological love; it resides in the will and not in the propensities of feeling, in principles of action and not in tender sympathy; and it alone can be commanded.

[Thus the first proposition of morality is that to have moral worth an action must be done from duty.] The second proposition is: An action performed from duty does not have its moral worth in the purpose which is to be achieved through it but in the maxim by which it is determined. Its moral value, therefore, does not depend on the realization of the object of the action but merely on the principle of volition by which the action is done, without any regard to the objects of the faculty of desire. From the preceding discussion it is clear that the purposes we may have for our actions and their effects as ends and incentives of the will cannot give the actions any unconditional and moral worth. Wherein, then, can this worth lie, if it is not in the will in relation to its hoped-for effect? It can lie nowhere else than in the principle of the will, irrespective of the ends which can be realized by such action. For the will stands, as it were, at the crossroads halfway between its *a priori* principle which is formal and its *a posteriori* incentive which is material. Since it must be determined by something, if it is done from duty it must be determined by the formal principle of volition as such since every material principle has been withdrawn from it.

The third principle, as a consequence of the two preceding, I would express as follows: Duty is the necessity of an action executed from respect for law. I can certainly have an inclination to the object as an effect of the proposed action, but I can never have respect for it precisely because it is a mere effect and not an activity of a will. Similarly, I can have no respect for any inclination whatsoever, whether my own or that of another; in the former case I can at most approve of it and in the latter I can even love it, i.e., see it as favorable to my own advantage. But that which is connected with my will merely as ground and not as consequence, that which does not serve my inclination but overpowers it or at least excludes it from being considered in making a choice—in a word, law itself—can be an object of respect and thus a command. Now as an act from duty wholly excludes the influence of inclination and therewith every object of the will, nothing remains which can determine the will objectively except the law, and nothing subjectively except pure respect for this practical law. This subjective element is the maxim [1] that I ought to follow such a law even if it thwarts all my inclinations.

Thus the moral worth of an action does not lie in the effect which is expected from it or in any principle of action which has to borrow its motive from this expected effect. For all these effects (agreeableness of my own condition, indeed even the promotion of the happiness of others) could be brought about through other causes and would not require the will of a rational being, while the highest and unconditional good can be found only in such a will. Therefore, the preëminent good can consist only in the conception of the law in itself (which can be present only in a rational being) so far as this conception and not the hoped-for effect is the determining ground of the will. This preëminent good, which we call moral, is already present

[1] A maxim is the subjective principle of volition. The objective principle (i.e., that which would serve all rational beings also subjectively as a practical principle if reason had full power over the faculty of desire) is the practical law.

in the person who acts according to this conception, and we do not have to look for it first in the result.[2]

· · ·

Second Section:

Transition from the popular moral philosophy to the metaphysics of morals

· · ·

In this study we do not advance merely from the common moral judgment (which here is very worthy of respect) to the philosophical, as this has already been done, but we advance by natural stages from a popular philosophy (which goes no further than it can grope by means of examples) to metaphysics (which is not held back by anything empirical and which, as it must measure out the entire scope of rational knowledge of this kind, reaches even Ideas, where examples fail us). In order to make this advance, we must follow and clearly present the practical faculty of reason from its universal rules of determination to the point where the concept of duty arises from it.

Everything in nature works according to laws. Only a rational being has the capacity of acting according to the conception of laws, i.e., according to principles. This capacity is will. Since reason is required for the derivation of actions from laws, will is nothing else than practical reason. If reason infallibly determines the will, the actions which such a being recognizes as objectively necessary are also subjectively necessary. That is, the will is a faculty of choosing only that which reason, independently of inclination, recognizes as practically necessary, i.e., as good. But if reason of itself does not sufficiently determine the will, and if the will is subjugated to subjective conditions (certain incentives) which do not always agree with objective conditions; in a word, if the will is not of itself in complete accord with reason (the actual case of men), then the actions which are recognized as objectively necessary are subjectively contingent, and the determination of such a will according to objective laws is constraint. That is, the relation of objective laws to a will which is not completely good is conceived as the determination of the will of a rational being by principles of reason to which this will is not by nature necessarily obedient.

[2] It might be objected that I seek to take refuge in an obscure feeling behind the word "respect," instead of clearly resolving the question with a concept of reason. But though respect is a feeling, it is not one received through any [outer] influence but is self-wrought by a rational concept; thus it differs specifically from all feelings of the former kind which may be referred to inclination or fear. What I recognize directly as a law for myself I recognize with respect, which means merely the consciousness of the submission of my will to a law without the intervention of other influences on my mind. The direct determination of the will by the law and the consciousness of this determination is respect; thus respect can be regarded as the effect of the law on the subject and not as the cause of the law. Respect is properly the conception of a worth which thwarts my self-love. Thus it is regarded as an object neither of inclination nor of fear, though it has something analogous to both. The only object of respect is the law, and indeed only the law which we impose on ourselves and yet recognize as necessary in itself. As a law we are subject to it without consulting self-love; as imposed on us by ourselves, it is consequence of our will. In the former respect it is analogous to fear and in the latter to inclination. All respect for a person is only respect for the law (of righteousness, etc.) of which the person provides an example. Because we see the improvement of our talents as a duty, we think of a person of talents as the example of a law, as it were (the law that we should by practice become like him in his talents), and that constitutes our respect. All so-called moral interest consists solely in respect for the law.

The conception of an objective principle, so far as it constrains a will, is a command (of reason), and the formula of this command is called an *imperative*.

All imperatives are expressed by an "ought" and thereby indicate the relation of an objective law of reason to a will which is not in its subjective constitution necessarily determined by this law. This relation is that of constraint. Imperatives say that it would be good to do or to refrain from doing something, but they say it to a will which does not always do something simply because it is presented as a good thing to do. Practical good is what determines the will by means of the conception of reason and hence not by subjective causes but, rather, objectively, i.e., on grounds which are valid for every rational being as such. It is distinguished from the pleasant as that which has an influence on the will only by means of a sensation from merely subjective causes, which hold only for the senses of this or that person and not as a principle of reason which holds for everyone.

A perfectly good will, therefore, would be equally subject to objective laws (of the good), but it could not be conceived as constrained by them to act in accord with them, because, according to its own subjective constitution, it can be determined to act only through the conception of the good. Thus no imperatives hold for the divine will or, more generally, for a holy will. The "ought" is here out of place, for the volition of itself is necessarily in unison with the law. Therefore imperatives are only formulas expressing the relation of objective laws of volition in general to the subjective imperfection of the will of this or that rational being, e.g., the human will.

All imperatives command either hypothetically or categorically. The former present the practical necessity of a possible action as a means to achieving something else which one desires (or which one may possibly desire). The categorical imperative would be one which presented an action as of itself objectively necessary, without regard to any other end.

Since every practical law presents a possible action as good and thus as necessary for a subject practically determinable by reason, all imperatives are formulas of the determination of action which is necessary by the principle of a will which is in any way good. If the action is good only as a means to something else, the imperative is hypothetical; but if it is thought of as good in itself, and hence as necessary in a will which of itself conforms to reason as the principle of this will, the imperative is categorical.

· · ·

If I think of a hypothetical imperative as such, I do not know what it will contain until the condition is stated [under which it is an imperative]. But if I think of a categorical imperative, I know immediately what it contains. For since the imperative contains besides the law only the necessity that the maxim [3] should accord with this law, while the law contains no condition to which it is restricted, there is nothing remaining in it except the universality of law as such to which the maxim of the action should conform; and in effect this conformity alone is represented as necessary by the imperative.

There is, therefore, only one categorical imperative. It is: Act only according to

---

[3] A maxim is the subjective principle of acting and must be distinguished from the objective principle, i.e., the practical law. The former contains the practical rule which reason determines according to the conditions of the subject (often its ignorance or inclinations) and is thus the principle according to which the subject acts. The law, on the other hand, is the objective principle valid for every rational being, and the principle by which it ought to act, i.e., an imperative.

that maxim by which you can at the same time will that it should become a universal law.

Now if all imperatives of duty can be derived from this one imperative as a principle, we can at least show what we understand by the concept of duty and what it means, even though it remain undecided whether that which is called duty is an empty concept or not.

The universality of law according to which effects are produced constitutes what is properly called nature in the most general sense (as to form), i.e., the existence of things so far as it is determined by universal laws. [By analogy], then, the universal imperative of duty can be expressed as follows: Act as though the maxim of your action were by your will to become a universal law of nature.

We shall now enumerate some duties, adopting the usual division of them into duties to ourselves and to others and into perfect and imperfect duties.

1. A man who is reduced to despair by a series of evils feels a weariness with life but is still in possession of his reason sufficiently to ask whether it would not be contrary to his duty to himself to take his own life. Now he asks whether the maxim of his action could become a universal law of nature. His maxim, however, is: For love of myself, I make it my principle to shorten my life when by a longer duration it threatens more evil than satisfaction. But it is questionable whether this principle of self-love could become a universal law of nature. One immediately sees a contradiction in a system of nature whose law would be to destroy life by the feeling whose special office is to impel the improvement of life. In this case it would not exist as nature; hence that maxim cannot obtain as a law of nature, and thus it wholly contradicts the supreme principle of all duty.

2. Another man finds himself forced by need to borrow money. He well knows that he will not be able to repay it, but he also sees that nothing will be loaned him if he does not firmly promise to repay it at a certain time. He desires to make such a promise, but he has enough conscience to ask himself whether it is not improper and opposed to duty to relieve his distress in such a way. Now, assuming he does decide to do so, the maxim of his action would be as follows: When I belive myself to be in need of money, I will borrow money and promise to repay it, although I know I shall never do so. Now this principle of self-love or of his own benefit may very well be compatible with his whole future welfare, but the question is whether it is right. He changes the pretension of self-love into a universal law and then puts the question: How would it be if my maxim became a universal law? He immediately sees that it could never hold as a universal law of nature and be consistent with itself; rather it must necessarily contradict itself. For the universality of a law which says that anyone who believes himself to be in need could promise what he pleased with the intention of not fulfilling it would make the promise itself and the end to be accomplished by it impossible; no one would believe what was promised to him but would only laugh at any such assertion as vain pretense.

3. A third finds in himself a talent which could, by means of some cultivation, make him in many respects a useful man. But he finds himself in comfortable circumstances and prefers indulgence in pleasure to troubling himself with broadening and improving his fortunate natural gifts. Now, however, let him ask whether his maxim of neglecting his gifts, besides agreeing with his propensity to idle amusement, agrees also with what is called duty. He sees that a system of nature could indeed exist in accordance with such a law, even though man (like the inhabitants of the

South Sea Islands) should let his talents rust and resolve to devote his life merely to idleness, indulgence, and propagation—in a word, to pleasure. But he cannot possibly will that this should become a universal law of nature or that it should be implanted in us by a natural instinct. For, as a rational being, he necessarily wills that all his faculties should be developed, inasmuch as they are given to him for all sorts of possible purposes.

4. A fourth man, for whom things are going well, sees that others (whom he could help) have to struggle with great hardships, and he asks, "What concern of mine is it? Let each one be as happy as heaven wills, or as he can make himself; I will not take anything from him or even envy him; but to his welfare or to his assistance in time of need I have no desire to contribute." If such a way of thinking were a universal law of nature, certainly the human race could exist, and without doubt even better than in a state where everyone talks of sympathy and good will, or even exerts himself occasionally to practice them while, on the other hand, he cheats when he can and betrays or otherwise violates the rights of man. Now although it is possible that a universal law of nature according to that maxim could exist, it is nevertheless impossible to will that such a principle should hold everywhere as a law of nature. For a will which resolved this would conflict with itself, since instances can often arise in which he would need the love and sympathy of others, and in which he would have robbed himself, by such a law of nature springing from his own will, of all hope of the aid he desires.

The foregoing are a few of the many actual duties, or at least of duties we hold to be actual, whose derivation from the one stated principle is clear. We must be able to will that a maxim of our action become a universal law; this is the canon of the moral estimation of our action generally. Some actions are of such a nature that their maxim cannot even be *thought* as a universal law of nature without contradiction, far from it being possible that one could will that it should be such. In others this internal impossiblity is not found, though it is still impossible to *will* that their maxim should be raised to the universality of a law of nature, because such a will would contradict itself. We easily see that the former maxim conflicts with the stricter or narrower (imprescriptible) duty, the latter with broader (meritorious) duty. Thus all duties, so far as the kind of obligation (not the object of their action) is concerned, have been completely exhibited by these examples in their dependence on the one principle.

·   ·   ·

Thus if there is to be a supreme practical principle and a categorical imperative for the human will, it must be one that forms an objective principle of the will from the conception of that which is necessarily an end for everyone because it is an end in itself. Hence this objective principle can serve as a universal practical law. The ground of this principle is: rational nature exists as an end in itself. Man necessarily thinks of his own existence in this way; thus far it is a subjective principle of human actions. Also every other rational being thinks of his existence by means of the same rational ground which holds also for myself; thus it is at the same time an objective principle from which, as a supreme practical ground, it must be possible to derive all laws of the will. The practical imperative, therefore, is the following: Act so that you treat humanity, whether in your own person or in that of another, always as an end and never as a means only. Let us now see whether this can be achieved.

To return to our previous examples:

First, according to the concept of necessary duty to one's self, he who contemplates suicide will ask himself whether his action can be consistent with the idea of humanity as an end in itself. If, in order to escape from burdensome circumstances, he destroys himself, he uses a person merely as a means to maintain a tolerable condition up to the end of life. Man, however, is not a thing, and thus not something to be used merely as a means; he must always be regarded in all his actions as an end in himself. Therefore, I cannot dispose of man in my own person so as to mutilate, corrupt, or kill him. (It belongs to ethics proper to define more accurately this basic principle so as to avoid all misunderstanding, e.g., as to the amputation of limbs in order to preserve myself, or to exposing my life to danger in order to save it; I must, therefore, omit them here.)

Second, as concerns necessary or obligatory duties to others, he who intends a deceitful promise to others sees immediately that he intends to use another man merely as a means, without the latter containing the end in himself at the same time. For he whom I want to use for my own purposes by means of such a promise cannot possibly assent to my mode of acting against him and cannot contain the end of this action in himself. This conflict against the principle of other men is even clearer if we cite examples of attacks on their freedom and property. For then it is clear that he who transgresses the rights of men intends to make use of the persons of others merely as a means, without considering that, as rational beings, they must always be esteemed at the same time as ends, i.e., only as beings who must be able to contain in themselves the end of the very same action.[4]

Third, with regard to contingent (meritorious) duty to one's self, it is not sufficient that the action not conflict with humanity in our person as an end in itself; it must also harmonize with it. Now in humanity there are capacities for greater perfection which belong to the end of nature with respect to humanity in our own person; to neglect these might perhaps be consistent with the preservation of humanity as an end in itself but not with the furtherance of that end.

Fourth, with regard to meritorious duty to others, the natural end which all men have is their own happiness. Humanity might indeed exist if no one contributed to the happiness of others, provided he did not intentionally detract from it; but this harmony with humanity as an end in itself is only negative rather than positive if everyone does not also endeavor, so far as he can, to further the ends of others. For the ends of any person, who is an end in himself, must as far as possible also be my end, if that conception of an end in itself is to have its full effect on me.

This principle of humanity and of every rational creature as an end in itself is the supreme limiting condition on freedom of the actions of each man. It is not borrowed from experience, first, because of its universality, since it applies to all rational beings generally and experience does not suffice to determine anything about them; and, secondly, because in experience humanity is not thought of (subjectively) as the end of men, i.e., as an object which we of ourselves really make our end. Rather it is thought of as the objective end which should constitute the supreme limit-

---

4 Let it not be thought that the banal *"quod tibi non vis fieri, etc.,"* could here serve as guide or principle, for it is only derived from the principle and is restricted by various limitations. It cannot be a universal law, because it contains the ground neither of duties to one's self nor of the benevolent duties to others (for many a man would gladly consent that others should not benefit him, provided only that he might be excused from showing benevolence to them). Nor does it contain the ground of obligatory duties to another, for the criminal would argue on this ground against the judge who sentences him. And so on.

ing condition of all subjective ends, whatever they may be. Thus this principle must arise from pure reason. Objectively the ground of all practical legislation lies (according to the first principle) in the rule and in the form of universality, which makes it capable of being a law (at most a natural law); subjectively, it lies in the end. But the subject of all ends is every rational being as an end in itself (by the second principle); from this there follows the third practical principle of the will as the supreme condition of its harmony with universal practical reason, viz., the idea of the will of every rational being as making universal law.

·   ·   ·

6

VIRTUES

aristotle

1

Every art and every inquiry, and similarly every action and pursuit, is thought to aim at some good; and for this reason the good has rightly been declared to be that at which all things aim. But a certain difference is found among ends; some are activities, others are products apart from the activities that produce them. Where there are ends apart from the actions, it is the nature of the products to be better than the activities. Now, as there are many actions, arts, and sciences, their ends also are many; the end of the medical art is health, that of shipbuilding a vessel, that of strategy victory, that of economics wealth. But where such arts fall under a single capacity—as bridle-making and the other arts concerned with the equipment of horses fall under the art of riding, and this and every military action under strategy, in the same way other arts fall under yet others—in all of these the ends of the master arts are to be preferred to all the subordinate ends; for it is for the sake of the former that the latter are pursued. It makes no difference whether the activities themselves are the ends of the actions, or something else apart from the activities, as in the case of the sciences just mentioned.

If, then, there is some end of the things we do, which we desire for its own sake (everything else being desired for the sake of this), and if we do not choose everything for the sake of something else (for at that rate the process would go on to infinity, so that our desire would be empty and vain), clearly this must be the good and the chief good. Will not the knowledge of it, then, have a great influence on life? Shall we not, like archers who have a mark to aim at, be more likely to hit upon what is right? If so, we must try, in outline at least to determine what it is, and of which of the sciences or capacities it is the object. It would seem to belong to the most authoritative art and that which is most truly the master art. And politics appears to be of this nature; for it is this that ordains which of the sciences should be studied in a state, and which each class of citizens should learn and up to what point they should learn them; and we see even the most highly esteemed of capacities to fall under this, e.g., strategy, economics, rhetoric; now, since politics uses the rest of the sciences, and since, again, it legislates as to what we are to do and what we are to abstain from, the end of this science must include those of the others, so that this end must be the good for man. For even if the end is the same for a single man and for a state, that of the state seems at all events something greater and more complete whether to attain or to preserve; though it is worthwhile to attain the end merely for one man, it is finer and more godlike to attain it for a nation or for city-states. These, then, are the ends at which our inquiry aims, since it is political science, in one sense of that term.

Our discussion will be adequate if it has as much clearness as the subject matter admits of, for precision is not to be sought for alike in all discussions, any more than in all the products of the crafts. Now fine and just actions, which political science investigates, admit of much variety and fluctuation of opinion, so that they may be thought to exist only by convention, and not by nature. And goods also give rise to a similar fluctuation because they bring harm to many people; for before now men have been undone by reason of their wealth, and others by reason of their courage. We must be content, then, in speaking of such subjects and with such premises to indicate the truth roughly and in outline, and in speaking about things which are only for the most part true and with premises of the same kind to reach conclusions that are no better. In the same spirit, therefore, should each type of statement be *received;* for it is the mark of an educated man to look for precision in each class of things just so far as the nature of the subject admits; it is evidently equally foolish to accept probable reasoning from a mathematician and to demand from a rhetorician scientific proofs.

Now each man judges well the things he knows, and of these he is a good judge. And so the man who has been educated in a subject is a good judge of that subject, and the man who has received an all-round education is a good judge in general. Hence a young man is not a proper hearer of lectures on political science; for he is inexperienced in the actions that occur in life, but its discussions start from these and are about these; and, further, since he tends to follow his passions, his study will be vain and unprofitable, because the end aimed at is not knowledge but action. And it makes no difference whether he is young in years or youthful in character; the defect does not depend on time, but on his living, and pursuing each successive object, as passion directs. For to such persons, as to the incontinent, knowledge brings no profit; but to those who desire and act in accordance with a rational principle knowledge about such matters will be of great benefit.

These remarks about the student, the sort of treatment to be expected, and the purpose of the inquiry, may be taken as our preface.

Let us resume our inquiry and state, in view of the fact that all knowledge and every pursuit aims at some good, what it is that we say political science aims at and what is the highest of all goods achievable by action. Verbally there is very general agreement; for both the general run of men and people of superior refinement say that it is happiness, and identify living well and doing well with being happy; but with regard to what happiness is they differ, and the many do not give the same account as the wise. For the former think it is some plain and obvious thing, like pleasure, wealth, or honor; they differ, however, from one another—and often even the same man identifies it with different things, with health when he is ill, with wealth when he is poor; but, conscious of their ignorance, they admire those who proclaim some great ideal that is above their comprehension. Now some [1] thought that apart from these many goods there is another which is self-subsistent and causes the goodness of all these as well. To examine all the opinions that have been held were perhaps somewhat fruitless; enough to examine those that are most prevalent or that seem to be arguable.

•   •   •

. . . To judge from the lives that men lead, most men, and men of the most vulgar type, seem (not without some ground) to identify the good, or happiness, with pleasure; which is the reason why they love the life of enjoyment. For there are, we may say, three prominent types of life—that just mentioned, the political, and thirdly the contemplative life. Now the mass of mankind are evidently quite slavish in their tastes, preferring a life suitable to beasts, but they get some ground for their view from the fact that many of those in high places share the tastes of Sardanapalus. A consideration of the prominent types of life shows that people of superior refinement and of active disposition identify happiness with honor; for this is, roughly speaking, the end of the political life. But it seems too superficial to be what we are looking for, since it is thought to depend on those who bestow honor rather than on him who receives it, but the good we divine to be something proper to a man and not easily taken from him. Further, men seem to pursue honor in order that they may be assured of their goodness; at least it is by men of practical wisdom that they seek to be honored, and among those who know them, and on the ground of their virtue; clearly, then, according to them, at any rate, virtue is better. And perhaps one might even suppose this to be, rather than honor, the end of the political life. But even this appears somewhat incomplete; for possession of virtue seems actually compatible with being asleep, or with lifelong inactivity, and, further, with the greatest sufferings and misfortunes; but a man who was living so no one would call happy, unless he were maintaining a thesis at all costs. But enough of this; for the subject has been sufficiently treated even in the current discussions. Third comes the contemplative life, which we shall consider later.

The life of moneymaking is one undertaken under compulsion, and wealth is evidently not the good we are seeking; for it is merely useful and for the sake of something else. And so one might rather take the aforenamed objects to be ends; for they are loved for themselves. But it is evident that not even these are ends; yet many arguments have been thrown away in support of them. Let us leave this subject, then.

•   •   •

Let us again return to the good we are seeking, and ask what it can be. It seems different in different actions and arts; it is different in medicine, in strategy, and in the other arts likewise. What then is the good of each? Surely that for whose sake everything else is done. In medicine this is health, in strategy victory, in architecture a house, in any other sphere something else, and in every action and pursuit the end; for it is for the sake of this that all men do whatever else they do. Therefore, if there is an end for all that we do, this will be the good achievable by action, and if there are more than one, these will be the goods achievable by action.

So the argument has by a different course reached the same point; but we must try to state this even more clearly. Since there are evidently more than one end, and

[1] The Platonic School.

we choose some of these (e.g., wealth, flutes, and, in general, instruments) for the sake of something else, clearly not all ends are final ends; but the chief good is evidently something final. Therefore, if there is only one final end, this will be what we are seeking, and if there are more than one, the most final of these will be what we are seeking. Now we call that which is in itself worthy of pursuit more final than that which is worthy of pursuit for the sake of something else, and that which is never desirable for the sake of something else more final than the things that are desirable both in themselves and for the sake of that other thing, and therefore we call final without qualification that which is always desirable in itself and never for the sake of something else.

Now such a thing as happiness, above all else, is held to be; for this we choose always for itself and never for the sake of something else, but honor, pleasure, reason, and every virtue we choose indeed for themselves (for if nothing resulted from them we should still choose each of them), but we choose them also for the sake of happiness, judging that by means of them we shall be happy. Happiness, on the other hand, no one chooses for the sake of these, nor, in general, for anything other than itself.

From the point of view of self-sufficiency the same result seems to follow; for the final good is thought to be self-sufficient. Now by self-sufficient we do not mean that which is sufficient for a man by himself, for one who lives a solitary life, but also for parents, children, wife, and in general for his friends and fellow citizens, since man is born for citizenship. But some limit must be set to this; for if we extend our requirement to ancestors and descendants and friends' friends we are in for an infinite series. Let us examine this question, however, on another occasion; the self-sufficient we now define as that which when isolated makes life desirable and lacking in nothing; and such we think happiness to be; and further we think it most desirable of all things, without being counted as one good thing among others—if it were so counted it would clearly be made more desirable by the addition of even the least of goods; for that which is added becomes an excess of goods, and of goods the greater is always more desirable. Happiness, then, is something final and self-sufficient, and is the end of action.

Presumably, however, to say that happiness is the chief good seems a platitude, and a clearer account of what it is is still desired. This might perhaps be given, if we could first ascertain the function of man. For just as for a flute-player, a sculptor, or any artist, and, in general, for all things that have a function or activity, the good and the "well" is thought to reside in the function, so would it seem to be for man, if he has a function. Have the carpenter, then, and the tanner certain functions or activities, and has man none? Is he born without a function? Or as eye, hand, foot, and in general each of the parts evidently has a function, may one lay it down that man similarly has a function apart from all these? What then can this be? Life seems to be common even to plants, but we are seeking what is peculiar to man. Let us exclude, therefore, the life of nutrition and growth. Next there would be a life of perception, but *it* also seems to be common even to the horse, the ox, and every animal. There remains, then, an active life of the element that has a rational principle; of this, one part has such a principle in the sense of being obedient to one, the other in the sense of possessing one and exercising thought. And, as "life of the rational element" also has two meanings, we must state that life in the sense of activity is what we mean; for this seems to be the more proper sense of the term. Now if the function of man is an activity of soul which follows or implies a rational principle, and if we say "a-so-and-so" and "a good so-and-so" have a function which is the same in kind, e.g., a lyre player and a good lyre player, and so without qualification in all cases, eminence in respect of goodness being added to the name of the function (for the function of a lyre player is to play the lyre, and that of a good lyre player is to do so well): if this is the case, [and we state the function of man to be a certain kind of life, and this to be an activity or actions of the soul implying a rational principle, and the function of a good man to be the good and noble performance of these, and if any action is well performed when it is performed in accordance with the appropriate excellence: if this is the case,] human good turns out to be activity of soul in accordance with virtue, and if there are more than one virtue, in accordance with the best and most complete.

But we must add "in a complete life." For one swallow does not make a summer, nor does one day; and so too one day, or a short time, does not make a man blessed and happy.

.   .   .

Yet evidently, as we said, it [happiness] needs the external goods as well; for it is impossible, or not easy, to do noble acts without the proper equipment. In many actions we use friends and riches and political power as instruments; and there are some things the lack of which takes the luster from happiness, as good birth, goodly children, beauty; for the man who is very ugly in appearance or ill-born or solitary and childless is not very likely to be happy, and perhaps a man would be still less likely if he had thoroughly bad children or friends or had lost good children or friends by death. As we said, then, happiness seems to need this sort of prosperity in addition; for which reason some identify happiness with good fortune, though others identify it with virtue.

.   .   .

2

Virtue, then, being of two kinds, intellectual and moral, intellectual virtue in the main owes both its birth and its growth to teaching (for which reason it requires experience and time), while moral virtue comes about as a result of habit, whence also its name *ethike* is one that is formed by a slight variation from the word *ethos* (habit). From this it is also plain that none of the moral virtues arises in us by nature; for nothing that exists by nature can form a habit contrary to its nature. For instance the stone which by nature moves downwards cannot be habituated to move upwards, not even if one tries to train it by throwing it up ten thousand times; nor can fire be habituated to move downwards, nor can anything else that by nature behaves in one way be trained to behave in another. Neither by nature, then, nor contrary to nature do the virtues arise in us; rather we are adapted by nature to receive them, and are made perfect by habit.

Again, of all the things that come to us by nature we first acquire the potentiality and later exhibit the activity (this is plain in the case of the senses; for it was not by often seeing or often hearing that we got these senses, but on the contrary we had them before we used them, and did not come to have them by using them); but the virtues we get by first exercising them, as also happens in the case of the arts as well. For the things we have to learn before we can do them, we learn by doing them, e.g., men become builders by building and lyre players by playing the lyre; so too we become just by doing just acts, temperate by doing temperate acts, brave by doing brave acts.

This is confirmed by what happens in states; for legislators make the citizens good by forming habits in them, and this is the wish of every legislator, and those who do not effect it miss their mark, and it is in this that a good constitution differs from a bad one.

Again, it is from the same causes and by the same means that every virtue is both produced and destroyed, and similarly every art; for it is from playing the lyre that both good and bad lyre players are produced. And the corresponding statement is true of builders and of all the rest; men will be good or bad builders as a result of building well or badly. For if this were not so, there would have been no need of a teacher, but all men would have been born good or bad at their craft. This, then, is the case with the virtues also; by doing the acts that we do in our transactions with other men we become just or unjust, and by doing the acts that we do in the presence of danger, and being habituated to feel fear or confidence, we become brave or cowardly. The same is true of appetites and feelings of anger; some men become temperate and good-tempered, others self-indulgent and irascible, by behaving in one way or the other in the appropriate circumstances. Thus, in one word, states of character arise out of like activities. This is why the activities we exhibit must be of a certain kind; it is because the states of character correspond to the differences between these. It makes no small difference, then, whether we form habits of one kind or of another from our very youth; it makes a very great difference, or rather *all* the difference.

Since, then, the present inquiry does not aim at theoretical knowledge like the others (for we are inquiring not in order to know what virtue is, but in order to become good, since otherwise our inquiry would have been of no use), we must examine the nature of actions, namely how we ought to do them; for these determine also the nature of the states of character that are produced, as we have said. Now, that we must act according to the right rule is a common principle and must be assumed— it will be discussed later, i.e., both what the right rule is, and how it is related to the other virtues. But this must be agreed upon beforehand, that the whole account of matters of conduct must be given in outline and not precisely, as we said at the very beginning that the accounts we demand must be in accordance with the subject matter; matters concerned with conduct and questions of what is good for us have no fixity, any more than matters of health. The general account being of this nature, the account of particular cases is yet more lacking in exactness; for they do not fall under any art of precept but the agents themselves must in each case consider what is appropriate to the occasion, as happens also in the art of medicine or of navigation.

But though our present account is of this nature we must give what help we can. First, then, let us consider this, that it is the nature of such things to be destroyed by defect and excess, as we see in the case of strength and of health (for to gain light on things imperceptible we must use the evidence of sensible things); both excessive and defective exercise destroys the strength, and similarly drink or food which is above or below a certain amount destroys the health, while that which is proportionate both produces and increases and preserves it. So too is it, then, in the case of temperance and courage and the other virtues. For the man who flies from and fears everything and does not stand his ground against anything becomes a coward, and the man who fears nothing at all but goes to meet every danger becomes rash; and similarly the man who indulges in every pleasure and abstains from ·none becomes self-indulgent, while the man who shuns every pleasure, as boors do, becomes in a way insensible; temperance and courage, then, are destroyed by excess and defect, and preserved by the men.

But not only are the sources and causes of their origination and growth the same as those of their destruction, but also the sphere of their actualization will be the same; for this is also true of the things which are more evident to sense, e.g., of strength; it is produced by taking much food and undergoing much exertion, and it is the strong man that will be most able to do these things. So too is it with the virtues; by abstaining from pleasures we become temperate, and it is when we have become so that we are most able to abstain from them; and similarly too in the case of courage; for by being habituated to despise things that are terrible and to stand our ground against them we become brave, and it is when we have become so that we shall be most able to stand our ground against them.

We must take as a sign of states of character the pleasure or pain that ensues on acts; for the man who abstains from bodily pleasures and delights in this very fact is temperate, while the man who is annoyed at it is self-indulgent, and he who stands his ground against things that are terrible and delights in this or at least is not pained is brave, while the man who is pained is a coward. For moral excellence is concerned with pleasures and pains; it is on account of the pleasure that we do bad things, and on account of the pain that we abstain from noble ones. Hence we ought to have been brought up in a particular way from our very youth, as Plato says, so as both to delight in and to be pained by the things that we ought; for this is the right education.

.   .   .

Next we must consider what virtue is. Since things that are found in the soul are of three kinds—passions, faculties, states of character—virtue must be one of these. By passions I mean appetite, anger, fear, confidence, envy, joy, friendly feeling, hatred, longing, emulation, pity, and in general the feelings that are accompanied by pleasure or pain; by faculties the things in virtue of which we are said to be capable of feeling these, e.g., of becoming angry or being pained or feeling pity; by states of character the things in virtue of which we stand well or badly with reference to the passions, e.g., with reference to anger we stand badly if we feel it violently or too weakly, and well if we feel it moderately; and similarly with reference to the other passions.

Now neither the virtues nor the vices are *passions,* because we are not called good or bad on the ground of our passions, but are so called on the ground of our virtues and our vices, and because we are neither praised nor blamed for our passions (for the man who feels fear or anger is not praised, nor is the man who simply feels anger blamed, but the man who feels it in a certain way), but for our virtues and our vices we *are* praised or blamed.

Again, we feel anger and fear without choice, but the virtues are modes of choice or involve choice. Further, in respect of the passions we are said to be moved, but in respect of the virtues and the vices we are said not to be moved but to be disposed in a particular way.

For these reasons also they are not *faculties;* for we are neither called good nor bad, nor praised nor blamed, for the simple capacity of feeling the passions; again, we have the faculties by nature, but we are not made good or bad by nature; we have spoken of this before.

If, then, the virtues are neither passions nor faculties, all that remains is that they should be *states of character*.

Thus we have stated what virtue is in respect of its genus.

We must, however, not only describe virtue as a state of character, but also say what sort of state it is. We may remark, then, that every virtue or excellence both brings into good condition the thing of which it is the excellence and makes the work of that thing be done well; e.g., the excellence of the eye makes both the eye and its work good; for it is by the excellence of the eye that we see well. Similarly the excellence of the horse makes a horse both good in itself and good at running and at carrying its rider and at awaiting the attack of the enemy. Therefore, if this is true in every case, the virtue of man also will be the state of character which makes a man good and which makes him do his own work well.

How this is to happen we have stated already, but it will be made plain also by the following consideration of the specific nature of virtue. In everything that is continuous and divisible it is possible to take more, less, or an equal amount, and that either in terms of the thing itself or relatively to us; and the equal is an intermediate excess and defect. By the intermediate in the object I mean that which is equidistant from each of the extremes, which is one and the same for all men; by the intermediate relatively to us that which is neither too much nor too little—and this is not one, nor the same for all. For instance, if ten is many and two is few, six is the intermediate, taken in terms of the object; for it exceeds and is exceeded by an equal amount; this is intermediate according to arithmetical proportion. But the intermediate relatively to us is not to be taken so; if ten pounds are too much for a particular person to eat and two too little, it does not follow that the trainer will order six pounds; for this also is perhaps too much for the person who is to take it, or too little—too little for Milo,[2] too much for the beginner in athletic exercises. The same is true of running and wrestling. Thus a master of any art avoids excess and defect, but seeks the intermediate and chooses this—the intermediate not in the object but relatively to us.

It is is thus, then, that every art does its work well—by looking to the intermediate and judging its works by this standard (so that we often say of good works of art that it is not possible either to take away or to add anything, implying that excess and defect destroy the goodness of works of art, while the mean preserves it; and good artists, as we say, look to this in their work), and if, further, virtue is more exact and better than any art, as nature also is, then virtue must have the quality of aiming at the intermediate. I mean moral virtue; for it is this that is concerned with passions and actions, and in these there is excess, defect, and the intermediate. For instance, both fear and confidence and appetite and anger and pity and in general pleasure and pain may be felt both too much and too little, and in both cases not well; but to feel them at the right times, with reference to the right objects, towards the right people, with the right motive, and in the right way, is what is both intermediate and best, and this is characteristic of virtue. Similarly with regard to actions also there is excess, defect, and the intermediate. Now virtue is concerned with passions and actions, in which excess is a form of failure, and so is defect, while the intermediate

2 A famous wrestler. [Eds.]

is praised and is a form of success; and being praised and being successful are both characteristics of virtue. Therefore virtue is a kind of mean, since, as we have seen, it aims at what is intermediate.

Again, it is possible to fail in many ways (for evil belongs to the class of the unlimited, as the Pythagoreans conjectured, and good to that of the limited), while to succeed is possible only in one way (for which reason also one is easy and the other difficult—to miss the mark easy, to hit it difficult); for these reasons also, then, excess and defect are characteristic of vice, and the mean of virtue;

For men are good in but one way, but bad in many.

Virtue, then, is a state of character concerned with choice, lying in a mean, i.e., the mean relative to us, this being determined by a rational principle, and by that principle by which the man of practical wisdom would determine it. Now it is a mean between two vices, that which depends on excess and that which depends on defect; and again it is a mean because the vices respectively fall short of or exceed what is right in both passions and actions, while virtue both finds and chooses that which is intermediate. Hence in respect of its substance and the definition which states its essence virtue is a mean, with regard to what is best and right an extreme.

But not every action nor every passion admits of a mean; for some have names that already imply badness, e.g., spite, shamelessness, envy, and in the case of actions adultery, theft, murder; for all of these and suchlike things imply by their names that they are themselves bad, and not the excesses or deficiencies of them. It is not possible, then, ever to be right with regard to them; one must always be wrong. Nor does goodness or badness with regard to such things depend on committing adultery with the right woman, at the right time, and in the right way, but simply to do any of them is to go wrong. It would be equally absurd, then, to expect that in unjust, cowardly, and voluptuous action there should be a mean, an excess, and a deficiency; for at that rate there would be a mean of excess and of deficiency, an excess of excess, and a deficiency of deficiency. But as there is no excess and deficiency of temperance and courage because what is intermediate is in a sense an extreme, so too of the actions we have mentioned there is no mean nor any excess and deficiency, but however they are done they are wrong; for in general there is neither a mean of excess and deficiency, nor excess and deficiency of a mean.

•   •   •

7

CONCERNING MORAL SENTIMENT

david hume

Of the general principles of morals . . .

There has been a controversy started of late . . . concerning the general foundation
of Morals; whether they be derived from Reason, or from Sentiment; whether we
attain the knowledge of them by a chain of argument and induction, or by an immediate feeling and finer internal sense; whether, like all sound judgment of truth
and falsehood, they should be the same to every rational intelligent being; or whether,
like the perception of beauty and deformity, they be founded entirely on the particular fabric and constitution of the human species.

The ancient philosophers, though they often affirm, that virtue is nothing but conformity to reason, yet, in general, seem to consider morals as deriving their existence
from taste and sentiment. On the other hand, our modern enquirers, though they also
talk much of the beauty of virtue, and deformity of vice, yet have commonly en-
deavoured to account for these distinctions by metaphysical reasonings, and by deductions from the most abstract principles of the understanding. Such confusion reigned
in these subjects that an opposition of the greatest consequence could prevail between
one system and another, and even in the parts of almost each individual system; and
yet nobody, till very lately, was ever sensible of it. The elegant Lord Shaftesbury, who
first gave occasion to remark this distinction, and who, in general, adhered to the
principles of the ancients, is not, himself, entirely free from the same confusion.

It must be acknowledged, that both sides of the question are susceptible of
specious arguments. Moral distinctions, it may be said, are discernible by pure *reason*:
else, whence the many disputes that reign in common life, as well as in philosophy,
with regard to this subject: the long chain of proofs often produced on both sides;
the examples cited, the authorities appealed to, the analogies employed, the fallacies
detected, the inferences drawn, and the several conclusions adjusted to their proper
principles. Truth is disputable; not taste: what exists in the nature of things is the

From *An Enquiry Concerning the Principles of Morals*, Secs. I, IX, in David Hume, *Enquiries
Concerning the Human Understanding and Concerning the Principles of Morals*, 2nd. ed.,
L. A. Selby-Bigge, ed. (Oxford: The Clarendon Press, 1961), pp. 170–173, 268–271, 278–282.
Reprinted by permission of the Clarendon Press.

standard of our judgment; what each man feels within himself is the standard of sentiment. Propositions in geometry may be proved, systems in physics may be controverted; but the harmony of verse, the tenderness of passion, the brilliancy of wit, must give immediate pleasure. No man reasons concerning another's beauty; but frequently concerning the justice or injustice of his actions. In every criminal trial the first object of the prisoner is to disprove the facts alleged, and deny the actions imputed to him: the second to prove, that, even if these actions were real, they might be justified, as innocent and lawful. It is confessedly by deductions of the understanding, that the first point is ascertained: how can we suppose that a different faculty of the mind is employed in fixing the other?

On the other hand, those who would resolve all moral determinations into *sentiment,* may endeavour to show, that it is impossible for reason ever to draw conclusions of this nature. To virtue, say they, it belongs to be *amiable,* and vice *odious.* This forms their very nature or essence. But can reason or argumentation distribute these different epithets to any subjects, and pronounce beforehand, that this must produce love, and that hatred? Or what other reason can we ever assign for these affections, but the original fabric and formation of the human mind, which is naturally adapted to receive them?

The end of all moral speculations is to teach us our duty; and, by proper representations of the deformity of vice and beauty of virtue, beget correspondent habits, and engage us to avoid the one, and embrace the other. But is this ever to be expected from inferences and conclusions of the understanding, which of themselves have no hold of the affections or set in motion the active powers of men? They discover truths: but where the truths which they discover are indifferent, and beget no desire or aversion, they can have no influence on conduct and behavior. What is honorable, what is fair, what is becoming, what is noble, what is generous, takes possession of the heart, and animates us to embrace and maintain it. What is intelligible, what is evident, what is probable, what is true, procures only the cool assent of the understanding; and gratifying a speculative curiosity, puts an end to our researches.

Extinguish all the warm feelings and prepossessions in favor of virtue, and all disgust or aversion to vice: render men totally indifferent towards these distinctions; and morality is no longer a practical study, nor has any tendency to regulate our lives and actions.

These arguments on each side (and many more might be produced) are so plausible, that I am apt to suspect, they may, the one as well as the other, be solid and satisfactory, and that *reason* and *sentiment* concur in almost all moral determinations and conclusions. The final sentence, it is probable, which pronounces characters and actions amiable or odious, praise-worthy or blameable; that which stamps on them the mark of honour or infamy, approbation or censure; that which renders morality an active principle and constitutes virtue our happiness, and vice our misery: it is probable, I say, that this final sentence depends on some internal sense or feeling, which nature has made universal in the whole species. For what else can have an influence of this nature? But in order to pave the way for such a sentiment, and give a proper discernment of its object, it is often necessary, we find, that much reasoning should precede, that nice distinctions be made, just conclusions drawn, distant comparisons formed, complicated relations examined, and general facts fixed and ascertained. Some species of beauty, especially the natural kinds, on their first appearance, command our affection and approbation; and where they fail of this effect, it is impossible for any reasoning to redress their influence, or adapt them better to our taste and sentiment. But in many orders of beauty, particularly those of the finer arts, it is requisite to employ much reasoning, in order to feel the proper sentiment; and a false relish may frequently be corrected by argument and reflection. There are just grounds to conclude, that moral beauty partakes much of this latter species, and demands the assistance of our intellectual faculties, in order to give it a suitable influence on the human mind.

· · ·

Conclusion

It may justly appear surprising that any man in so late an age, should find it requisite to prove, by elaborate reasoning, that Personal Merit consists altogether in the possession of mental qualities, *useful* or *agreeable* to the *person himself* or to *others*. It might be expected that this principle would have occurred even to the first rude, unpractised enquirers concerning morals, and been received from its own evidence, without any argument or disputation. Whatever is valuable in any kind, so naturally classes itself under the division of *useful* or *agreeable,* the *utile* or the *dulce,* that it is not easy to imagine why we should ever seek further, or consider the question as a matter of nice research or inquiry. And as everything useful or agreeable must possess these qualities with regard either to the *person himself* or to *others,* the complete delineation or description of merit seems to be performed as naturally as a shadow is cast by the sun, or an image is reflected upon water. If the ground, on which the shadow is cast, be not broken and uneven; nor the surface from which the image is reflected, disturbed and confused; a just figure is immediately presented, without any art or attention. And it seems a reasonable presumption, that systems and hypotheses have perverted our natural understanding, when a theory, so simple and obvious, could so long have escaped the most elaborate examination.

But however the case may have fared with philosophy, in common life these principles are still implicitly maintained; nor is any other topic of praise or blame ever recurred to, when we employ any panegyric or satire, any applause or censure of human action and behaviour. If we observe men, in every intercourse of business or pleasure, in every discourse and conversation, we shall find them nowhere, except in the schools, at any loss upon this subject. What so natural, for instance, as the following dialogue? You are very happy, we shall suppose one to say, addressing himself to another, that you have given your daughter to Cleanthes. He is a man of honour and humanity. Everyone, who has any intercourse with him, is sure of *fair* and *kind* treatment.[1] I congratulate you too, says another, on the promising expectations of this son-in-law; whose assiduous application to the study of the laws, whose quick penetration and early knowledge both of men and business, prognosticate the greatest honours and advancements.[2] You surprise me, replies a third, when you talk of Cleanthes as a man of business and application. I met him lately in a circle of the gayest company, and he was the very life and soul of our conversation: so much wit with good manners; so much gallantry without affectation; so much ingenious knowl-

---

[1] Qualities useful to others.
[2] Qualities useful to the person himself.

edge so genteelly delivered, I have never before observed in any one.[3] You would admire him still more, says a fourth, if you knew him more familiarly. That cheerfulness, which you might remark in him, is not a sudden flash struck out by company: it runs through the whole tenor of his life, and preserves a perpetual serenity on his countenance, and tranquillity in his soul. He has met with severe trials, misfortunes as well as dangers; and by his greatness of mind, was still superior to all of them.[4] The image, gentlemen, which you have here delineated of Cleanthes, cried I, is that of accomplished merit. Each of you has given a stroke of the pencil to his figure; and you have unawares exceeded all the pictures drawn by Gratian or Castiglione. A philosopher might select this character as a model of perfect virtue.

And as every quality which is useful or agreeable to ourselves or others is, in common life, allowed to be a part of personal merit; so no other will ever be received, where men judge of things by their natural, unprejudiced reason, without the delusive glosses of superstition and false religion. Celibacy, fasting, penance, mortification, self-denial, humility, silence, solitude, and the whole train of monkish virtues; for what reason are they everywhere rejected by men of sense, but because they serve to no manner of purpose; neither advance a man's future in the world, nor render him a more valuable member of society; neither qualify him for the entertainment of company, nor increase his power of self-enjoyment? We observe, on the contrary, that they cross all these desirable ends; stupify the understanding and harden the heart, obscure the fancy and sour the temper. We justly, therefore, transfer them to the opposite column, and place them in the catalogue of vices; nor has any superstition force sufficient among men of the world, to pervert entirely these natural sentiments. A gloomy, hair-brained enthusiast, after his death, may have a place in the calendar; but will scarcely ever be admitted, when alive, into intimacy and society, except by those who are as delirious and dismal as himself.

It seems a happiness in the present theory, that it enters not into that vulgar dispute concerning the *degrees* of benevolence or self-love, which prevail in human nature; a dispute which is never likely to have any issue, both because men, who have taken part, are not easily convinced, and because the phenomena, which can be produced on either side, are so dispersed, so uncertain, and subject to so many interpretations, that it is scarcely possible accurately to compare them, or draw from them any determinate inference or conclusion. It is sufficient for our present purpose, if it be allowed, what surely, without the greatest absurdity cannot be disputed, that there is some benevolence, however small, infused into our bosom; some spark of friendship for human kind; some particle of the dove kneaded into our frame, along with the elements of the wolf and serpent. Let these generous sentiments be supposed ever so weak; let them be insufficient to move even a hand or finger of our body, they must still direct the determinations of our mind, and where everything else is equal, produce a cool preference of what is useful and serviceable to mankind, above what is pernicious and dangerous. A *moral distinction*, therefore, immediately arises; a general sentiment of blame and approbation; a tendency, however faint, to the objects of the one, and a proportionable aversion to those of the other. Nor will those reasoners, who so earnestly maintain the predominant selfishness of human kind, be any wise scandalized at hearing of the weak sentiments of virtue implanted in our nature. On

[3] Qualities immediately agreeable to others.
[4] Qualities immediately agreeable to the person himself.

the contrary, they are found as ready to maintain the one tenet as the other; and their spirit of satire (for such it appears, rather than of corruption) naturally gives rise to both opinions; which have, indeed, a great and almost an indissoluble connexion together.

. . .

I am sensible, that nothing can be more unphilosophical than to be positive or dogmatical on any subject; and that, even if *excessive* scepticism could be maintained, it would not be more destructive to all just reasoning and enquiry. I am convinced that, where men are the most sure and arrogant, they are commonly the most mistaken, and have there given reins to passion, without that proper deliberation and suspense, which can alone secure them from the grossest absurdities. Yet, I must confess, that this enumeration puts the matter in so strong a light, that I cannot, *at present,* be more assured of any truth, which I learn from reasoning and argument, than that personal merit consists entirely in the usefulness or agreeableness of qualities to the person himself possessed of them, or to others, who have any intercourse with him. But when I reflect that, though the bulk and figure of the earth have been measured and delineated, though the motions of the tides have been accounted for, the order and economy of the heavenly bodies subjected to their proper laws, and Infinite itself reduced to calculation; yet men still dispute concerning the foundation of their moral duties. When I reflect on this, I say, I fall back into diffidence and scepticism, and suspect that an hypothesis, so obvious, had it been a true one, would, long ere now, have been received by the unanimous suffrage and consent of mankind.

Having explained the moral *approbation* attending merit or virtue, there remains nothing but briefly to consider our interested *obligation* to it, and to enquire whether every man, who has any regard to his own happiness and welfare, will not best find his account in the practice of every moral duty. If this can be clearly ascertained from the foregoing theory, we shall have the satisfaction to reflect, that we have advanced principles, which not only, it is hoped, will stand the test of reasoning and enquiry, but may contribute to the amendment of men's lives, and their improvement in morality and social virtue. And though the philosophical truth of any proposition by no means depends on its tendency to promote the interests of society; yet a man has but a bad grace, who delivers a theory, however true, which, he must confess, leads to a practice dangerous and pernicious. Why rake into those corners of nature which spread a nuisance all around? Why dig up the pestilence from the pit in which it is buried? The ingenuity of your researches may be admired, but your systems will be detested; and mankind will agree, if they cannot refute them, to sink them, at least, in eternal silence and oblivion. Truths which are *pernicious* to society, if any such there be, will yield to errors which are salutary and *advantageous.*

But what philosophical truths can be more advantageous to society, than those here delivered, which represent virtue in all her genuine and most engaging charms, and makes us approach her with ease, familiarity, and affection? The dismal dress falls off, with which many divines, and some philosophers, have covered her; and nothing appears but gentleness, humanity, beneficence, affability; nay, even at proper intervals, play, frolic, and gaiety. She talks not of useless austerities and rigours, suffering and self-denial. She declares that her sole purpose is to make her votaries and all mankind, during every instant of their existence, if possible, cheerful and happy; nor does she ever willingly part with any pleasure but in hopes of ample compensation in some other period of their lives. The sole trouble which she demands, is that of just calculation, and a steady preference of the greater happiness. And if any austere pretenders approach her, enemies to joy and pleasure, she either rejects them as hypocrites and deceivers; or, if she admit them in her train, they are ranked, however, among the least favoured of her votaries.

And, indeed, to drop all figurative expression, what hopes can we ever have of engaging mankind to a practice which we confess full of austerity and rigour? Or what theory of morals can ever serve any useful purpose, unless it can show, by a particular detail, that all the duties which it recommends, are also the true interest of each individual? The peculiar advantage of the foregoing system seems to be, that it furnishes proper mediums for that purpose.

That the virtues which are immediately *useful* or *agreeable* to the person possessed of them, are desirable in a view to self-interest, it would surely be superfluous to prove. Moralists, indeed, may spare themselves all the pains which they often take in recommending these duties. To what purpose collect arguments to evince that temperance is advantageous, and the excesses of pleasure hurtful, when it appears that these excesses are only denominated such, because they are hurtful; and that, if the unlimited use of strong liquors, for instance, no more impaired health or the faculties of mind and body than the use of air or water, it would not be a whit more vicious or blameable?

It seems equally superfluous to prove, that the *companionable* virtues of good manners and wit, decency and genteelness, are more desirable than the contrary qualities. Vanity alone, without any other consideration, is a sufficient motive to make us wish for the possession of these accomplishments. No man was ever willingly deficient in this particular. All our failures here proceed from bad education, want of capacity, or a perverse and unpliable disposition. Would you have your company coveted, admired, followed; rather than hated, despised, avoided? Can any one seriously deliberate in the case? As no enjoyment is sincere, without some reference to company and society; so no society can be agreeable, or even tolerable, where a man feels his presence unwelcome, and discovers all around him symptoms of disgust and aversion.

But why, in the greater society or confederacy of mankind, should not the case be the same as in particular clubs and companies? Why is it more doubtful, that the enlarged virtues of humanity, generosity, beneficence, are desirable with a view of happiness and self-interest, than the limited endowments of ingenuity and politeness? Are we apprehensive lest those social affections interfere, in a greater and more immediate degree than any other pursuits, with private utility, and cannot be gratified, without some important sacrifice of honour and advantage? If so, we are but ill-instructed in the nature of the human passions, and are more influenced by verbal distinctions than by real differences.

Whatever contradiction may vulgarly be supposed between the *selfish* and *social* sentiments or dispositions, they are really no more opposite than selfish and ambitious, selfish and revengeful, selfish and vain. It is requisite that there be an original propensity of some kind, in order to be a basis to self-love, by giving a relish to the objects of its pursuit; and none more fit for this purpose than benevolence or humanity. The goods of fortune are spent in one gratification or another: the miser who accumulates his annual income, and lends it out at interest, has really spent it in the gratification of his avarice. And it would be difficult to show why a man is more a loser by a generous action, than by any other method of expense; since the utmost which he can attain by the most elaborate selfishness, is the indulgence of some affection.

Now if life, without passion, must be altogether insipid and tiresome; let a man suppose that he has full power of modelling his own disposition, and let him deliberate what appetite or desire he would choose for the foundation of his happiness and enjoyment. Every affection, he would observe, when gratified by success, gives a satisfaction proportioned to its force and violence; but besides this advantage, common to all, the immediate feeling of benevolence and friendship, humanity and kindness, is sweet, smooth, tender, and agreeable, independent of all fortune and accidents. These virtues are besides attended with a pleasing consciousness or remembrance, and keep us in humour with ourselves as well as others; while we retain the agreeable reflection of having done our part towards mankind and society. And though all men show a jealousy of our success in the pursuits of avarice and ambition; yet are we almost sure of their good-will and good wishes, so long as we persevere in the paths of virtue, and employ ourselves in the execution of generous plans and purposes. What other passion is there where we shall find so many advantages united; an agreeable sentiment, a pleasing consciousness, a good reputation? But of these truths, we may observe, men are, of themselves, pretty much convinced; nor are they deficient in their duty to society, because they would not wish to be generous, friendly, and humane; but because they do not feel themselves such.

•   •   •

8

ETHICAL RELATIVITY

w. t. stace

There is an opinion widely current nowadays in philosophical circles which passes under the name of "ethical relativity." Exactly what this phrase means or implies is certainly far from clear. But unquestionably it stands as a label for the opinions of a group of ethical philosophers whose position is roughly on the extreme left wing among the moral theorizers of the day. And perhaps one may best understand it by placing it in contrast with the opposite kind of extreme view against which, un-doubtedly, it has arisen as a protest. For among moral philosophers one may clearly distinguish a left and a right wing. Those of the left wing are the ethical relativists. They are the revolutionaries, the clever young men, the up-to-date. Those of the right wing we may call the ethical absolutists. They are the conservatives and the old-fashioned.

According to the absolutists there is but one eternally true and valid moral code. This moral code applies with rigid impartiality to all men. What is a duty for me must likewise be a duty for you. And this will be true whether you are an Englishman, a Chinaman, or a Hottentot. If cannibalism is an abomination in England or America, it is an abomination in central Africa, notwithstanding that the African may think other-wise. The fact that he sees nothing wrong in his cannibal practices does not make them for him morally right. They are as much contrary to morality for him as they are for us. The only difference is that he is an ignorant savage who does not know this. There is not one law for one man or race of men, another for another. There is not one moral standard for Europeans, another for Indians, another for Chinese. There is but one law, one standard, one morality, for all men. And this standard, this law, is absolute and unvarying.

Moreover, as the one moral law extends its dominion over all the corners of the earth, so too it is not limited in its application by any considerations of time or period. That which is right now was right in the centuries of Greece and Rome, nay, in the very ages of the cave man. That which is evil now was evil then. If slavery is morally wicked today, it was morally wicked among the ancient Athenians, notwithstanding that their greatest men accepted it as a necessary condition of human society. Their opinion did not make slavery a moral good for them. It only showed that they were,

From W. T. Stace, *The Concept of Morals,* Chap. I, pp. 1–12. Reprinted by permission of the Macmillan Company. Copyright, 1937, 1962 by The Macmillan Company.

in spite of their otherwise noble conceptions, ignorant of what is truly right and good in this matter.

The ethical absolutist recognizes as a fact that moral customs and moral ideas differ from country to country and from age to age. This indeed seems manifest and not to be disputed. We think slavery morally wrong, the Greeks though it morally unobjectionable. The inhabitants of New Guinea certainly have very different moral ideas from ours. But the fact that the Greeks or the inhabitants of New Guinea think something right does not make it right, even for them. Nor does the fact that we think the same things wrong make them wrong. They are *in themselves* either right or wrong. What we have to do is to discover which they are. What anyone thinks makes no difference. It is here just as it is in matters of physical science. We believe the earth to be a globe. Our ancestors may have thought it flat. This does not show that it was *flat,* and is *now* a globe. What it shows is that men, having in other ages been ignorant about the shape of the earth, have now learned the truth. So if the Greeks thought slavery morally legitimate, this does not indicate that it was for them and in that age morally legitimate, but rather that they were ignorant of the truth of the matter.

The ethical absolutist is not indeed committed to the opinion that his own, or our own, moral code is the true one. Theoretically at least he might hold that slavery is ethically justifiable, that the Greeks knew better than we do about this, that ignorance of the true morality lies with use and not with them. All that he is actually committed to is the opinion that, whatever the true moral code may be, it is always the same for all men in all ages. His view is not at all inconsistent with the belief that humanity has still much to learn in moral matters. If anyone were to assert that in five hundred years the moral conceptions of the present day will appear as barbarous to the people of that age as the moral conceptions of the middle ages appear to us now, he need not deny it. If anyone were to assert that the ethics of Christianity are by no means final, and will be superseded in future ages by vastly nobler moral ideals, he need not deny this either. For it is of the essence of his creed to believe that morality is in some sense objective, not man-made, not produced by human opinion; that its principles are real truths about which men have to learn—just as they have to learn about the shape of the world—about which they may have been ignorant in the past, and about which therefore they may well be ignorant now.

Thus although absolutism is conservative in the sense that it is regarded by the more daring spirits as an out of date opinion, it is not necessarily conservative in the sense of being committed to the blind support of existing moral ideas and institutions. If ethical absolutists are sometimes conservative in this sense too, that is their personal affair. Such conservativism is accidental, not essential to the absolutist's creed. There is no logical reason, in the nature of the case, why an absolutist should not be a communist, an anarchist, a surrealist, or an upholder of free love. The fact that he is usually none of these things may be accounted for in various ways. But it has nothing to do with the sheer logic of his ethical position. The sole opinion to which he is committed is that whatever is morally right (or wrong)—be it free love or monogamy or slavery or cannibalism or vegetarianism—is morally right (or wrong) for all men at all times.

Usually the absolutist goes further than this. He often maintains, not merely that the moral law is the same for all the men on this planet—which is, after all, a tiny speck in space—but that in some way or in some sense it has application everywhere in the universe. He may express himself by saying that it applies to all "rational beings"—which would apparently include angels and the men on Mars (if they are rational). He is apt to think that the moral law is a part of the fundamental structure of the universe. But with this aspect of absolutism we need not, at the moment, concern ourselves. At present we may think of it as being simply the opinion that there is a single moral standard for all human beings.

This brief and rough sketch of ethical absolutism is intended merely to form a background against which we may the more clearly indicate, by way of contrast, the theory of ethical relativity. Up to the present, therefore, I have not given any of the reasons which the absolutist can urge in favor of his case. It is sufficient for my purpose at the moment to state *what* he believes, without going into the question of *why* he believes it. But before proceeding to our next step—the explanation of ethical relativity—I think it will be helpful to indicate some of the historical causes (as distinguished from logical reasons) which have helped in the past to render absolutism a plausible interpretation of morality as understood by European peoples.

Our civilization is a Christian civilization. It has grown up, during nearly two thousand years, upon the soil of Christian monotheism. In this soil, our whole outlook upon life, and consequently all our moral ideas, have their roots. They have been molded by this influence. The wave of religious scepticism which, during the last half century, has swept over us, has altered this fact scarcely at all. The moral ideas even of those who most violently reject the dogmas of Christianity with their intellects are still Christian ideas. This will probably remain true for many centuries even if Christian theology, as a set of intellectual beliefs, comes to be wholly rejected by every educated person. It will probably remain true so long as our civilization lasts. A child cannot, by changing in later life his intellectual creed, strip himself of the early formative moral influences of his childhood, though he can no doubt modify their results in various minor ways. With the outlook on life which was instilled into him in his early days he, in large measure, lives and dies. So it is with a civilization. And our civilization, whatever religious or irreligious views it may come to hold or reject, can hardly escape within its lifetime the molding influences of its Christian origin. Now ethical absolutism was, in its central ideas, the product of Christian theology.

The connection is not difficult to detect. For morality has been conceived, during the Christian dispensation, as issuing from the will of God. That indeed was its single and all-sufficient source. There would be no point, for the naïve believer in the faith, in the philosopher's questions regarding the foundations of morality and the basis of moral obligation. Even to ask such questions is a mark of incipient religious scepticism. For the true believer the author of the moral law is God. What pleases God, what God commands—that is the definition of right. What displeases God, what he forbids—that is the definition of wrong. Now there is, for the Christian monotheist, only one God ruling over the entire universe. And this God is rational, self-consistent. He does not act upon whims. Consequently his will and his commands must be the same everywhere. They will be unvarying for all peoples and in all ages. If the heathen have other moral ideas than ours—inferior ideas—that can only be because they live in ignorance of the true God. If they knew God and his commands, their ethical precepts would be the same as ours.

Polytheistic creeds may well tolerate a number of diverse moral codes. For the God of the western hemisphere might have different views from those entertained by the God of the eastern hemisphere. And the God of the north might issue to his worshippers commands at variance with the commands issued to other peoples by the God of the south. But a monotheistic religion implies a single universal and absolute morality.

This explains why ethical absolutism, until very recently, was not only believed by philosophers but *taken for granted without any argument.* The ideas of philosophers, like the ideas of everyone else, are largely molded by the civilizations in which they live. Their philosophies are largely attempts to state in abstract terms and in self-consistent language the stock of ideas which they have breathed in from the atmosphere of their social environment. This accounts for the large number of so-called "unrecognized presuppositions" with which systems of philosophy always abound. These presuppositions are simply the ideas which the authors of the systems have breathed in with the intellectual atmospheres by which they happen to be surrounded —which they have taken over, therefore, as a matter of course, without argument, without criticism, without even a suspicion that they might be false.

It is not therefore at all surprising to find that Immanuel Kant, writing in the latter half of the eighteenth century, not only took the tenets of ethical absolutism for granted, but evidently considered that no instructed person would dispute them. It is a noticeable feature of his ethical philosophy that he gives no reasons whatever to support his belief in the existence of a universally valid moral law. He assumes as a matter of course that his readers will accept this view. And he proceeds at once to inquire what is the metaphysical foundation of the universal moral law. That alone is what interests him. *Assuming* that there does exist such a law, how, he asks, can this be the case, and what, in the way of transcendental truth, does it imply? It never occurs to him to reflect that any philosopher who should choose to question his fundamental assumption could outflank his whole ethical position; and that if this assumption should prove false his entire moral philosophy would fall to the ground like a pack of cards.

We can now turn to the consideration of ethical relativity which is the proper subject of this chapter. The revolt of the relativists against absolutism is, I believe, part and parcel of the general revolutionary tendency of our times. In particular it is a result of the decay of belief in the dogmas of orthodox religion. Belief in absolutism was supported, as we have seen, by belief in Christian monotheism. And now that, in an age of widespread religious scepticism, that support is withdrawn, absolutism tends to collapse. Revolutionary movements are as a rule, at any rate in their first onset, purely negative. They attack and destroy. And ethical relativity is, in its essence, a purely negative creed. It is simply a denial of ethical absolutism. That is why the best way of explaining it is to begin by explaining ethical absolutism. If we understand that what the latter asserts the former denies, then we understand ethical relativity.

Any ethical position which denies that there is a single moral standard which is equally applicable to all men at all times may fairly be called a species of ethical relativity. There is not, the relativist asserts, merely one moral law, one code, one standard. There are many moral laws, codes, standards. What morality ordains in one place or age may be quite different from what morality ordains in another place or age. The moral code of Chinamen is quite different from that of Europeans, that of African savages quite different from both. Any morality, therefore, is relative to the age, the place, and the circumstances in which it is found. It is in no sense absolute.

This does not mean merely—as one might at first sight be inclined to suppose—

that the very same kind of action which is *thought* right in one country and period may be *thought* wrong in another. This would be a mere platitude, the truth of which everyone would have to admit. Even the absolutist would admit this—would even wish to emphasize it—since he is well aware that different peoples have different sets of moral ideas, and his whole point is that some of these sets of ideas are false. What the relativist means to assert is, not this platitude, but that the very same kind of action which *is* right in one country and period may *be* wrong in another. And this, far from being a platitude, is a very startling assertion.

It is very important to grasp thoroughly the difference between the two ideas. For there is reason to think that many minds tend to find ethical relativity attractive because they fail to keep them clearly apart. It is so very obvious that moral ideas differ from country to country and from age to age. And it is so very easy, if you are mentally lazy, to suppose that to say this means the same as to say that no universal moral standard exists—or in other words that it implies ethical relativity. We fail to see that the word "standard" is used in two different senses. It is perfectly true that, in one sense, there are many variable moral standards. We speak of judging a man by the standard of his time. And this implies that different times have different standards. And this, of course, is quite true. But when the word "standard" is used in this sense it means simply the set of moral ideas current during the period in question. It means what people *think* right, whether as a matter of fact it *is* right or not. On the other hand when the absolutist asserts that there exists a single universal moral "standard," he is not using the word in this sense at all. He means by "standard" what *is* right as distinct from what people merely think right. His point is that although what people think right varies in different countries and periods, yet what actually is right is everywhere and always the same. And it follows that when the ethical relativist disputes the position of the absolutist and denies that any universal moral standard exists he too means by "standard" what actually is right. But it is exceedingly easy, if we are not careful, to slip loosely from using the word in the first sense to using it in the second sense, and to suppose that the variability of moral beliefs is the same thing as the variability of what really is moral. And unless we keep the two senses of the word "standard" distinct, we are likely to think the creed of ethical relativity much more plausible than it actually is.

The genuine relativist, then, does not merely mean that Chinamen may think right what Frenchmen think wrong. He means that what *is* wrong for the Frenchman may *be* right for the Chinaman. And if one inquires how, in those circumstances, one is to know what actually is right in China or in France, the answer comes quite glibly. What is right in China is the same as what people think right in China; and what is right in France is the same as what people think right in France. So that, if you want to know what is moral in any particular country or age all you have to do is to ascertain what are the moral ideas current in that age or country. Those ideas are, *for that age or country*, right. Thus what is morally right is identified with what is thought to be morally right, and the distinction which we made above between these two is simply denied. To put the same thing in another way, it is denied that there can be or ought to be any distinction between the two senses of the word "standard." There is only one kind of standard of right and wrong, namely, the moral ideas current in any particular age or country.

Moral right *means* what people think morally right. It has no other meaning. What Frenchmen think right is, therefore, right *for Frenchmen*. And evidently one must conclude—though I am not aware that relativists are anxious to draw one's attention to such unsavory but yet absolutely necessary conclusions from their creed— that cannibalism is right for people who believe in it, that human sacrifice is right for those races which practice it, and that burning widows alive was right for Hindus until the British stepped in and compelled the Hindus to behave immorally by allowing their widows to remain alive.

When it is said that, according to the ethical relativist, what is thought right in any social group is right for that group, one must be careful not to misinterpret this. The relativist does not, of course, mean that there actually is an objective moral standard in France and a different objective standard in England, and that French and British opinions respectively give us correct information about these different standards. His point is rather that there are no objectively true moral standards at all. There is no single universal objective standard. Nor are there a variety of local objective standards. All standards are subjective. People's subjective feelings about morality are the only standards which exist.

To sum up. The ethical relativist consistently denies, it would seem, whatever the ethical absolutist asserts. For the absolutist there is a single universal moral standard. For the relativist there is no such standard. There are only local, ephemeral, and variable standards. For the absolutist there are two senses of the word "standard." Standards in the sense of sets of current moral ideas are relative and changeable. But the standard in the sense of what is actually morally right is absolute and unchanging. For the relativist no such distinction can be made. There is only one meaning of the word standard, namely, that which refers to local and variable sets of moral ideas. Or if it is insisted that the word must be allowed two meanings, then the relativist will say that there is at any rate no actual example of a standard in the absolute sense, and that the word as thus used is an empty name to which nothing in reality corresponds; so that the distinction between the two meanings becomes empty and useless. Finally—though this is merely saying the same thing in another way—the absolutist makes a distinction between what actually is right and what is thought right. The relativist rejects this distinction and identifies what is moral with what is thought moral by certain human beings or groups of human beings.

It is true that the relativist may object to my statement of his case on the ground that it does not specify precisely *who* the human beings are whose thinking makes what is right right and what is wrong wrong; and that he himself would not think of defining right as "that which people think right"—using the vague word "people" as if morality were determined by what any chance persons, anyone or everyone, happen to think moral. We shall see later that there is a real and incurable ambiguity in the relativist's position here (and not merely in my statement of it), and that he himself has difficulty in saying who are the "people" whose ideas are to constitute moral standards. But he cannot deny, at any rate, that his creed does identify morality with the subjective thinking of human beings. And that is the only point which I am at present trying to make clear. To *what* human beings he means to refer will be a matter for our future discussion.

•   •   •

The meaning of moral judgments
and the problem of moral responsibility

9

WHAT MAKES RIGHT ACTS RIGHT?

w. d. ross

The real point at issue between hedonism and utilitarianism on the one hand and their opponents on the other is not whether "right" means "productive of so and so"; for it cannot with any plausibility be maintained that it does. The point at issue is that to which we now pass, viz., whether there is any general character which makes right acts right, and if so, what it is. Among the main historical attempts to state a single characteristic of all right actions which is the foundation of their rightness are those made by egoism and utilitarianism. But I do not propose to discuss these, not because the subject is unimportant, but because it has been dealt with so often and so well already, and because there has come to be so much agreement among moral philosophers that neither of these theories is satisfactory. A much more attractive theory has been put forward by Professor [G. E.] Moore: that what makes actions right is that they are productive of more *good* than could have been produced by any other action open to the agent.

This theory is in fact the culmination of all the attempts to base rightness on productivity of some sort of result. The first form this attempt takes is the attempt to

From W. D. Ross, *The Right and the Good* (Oxford: The Clarendon Press, 1930), Chap. II, pp. 16–34. Reprinted by permission of the Clarendon Press.

base rightness on conduciveness to the advantage or pleasure of the agent. This theory comes to grief over the fact, which stares us in the face, that a great part of duty consists in an observance of the rights and a furtherance of the interests of others, whatever the cost to ourselves may be. Plato and others may be right in holding that a regard for the rights of others never in the long run involves a loss of happiness for the agent, that "the just life profits a man." But this, even if true, is irrelevant to the rightness of the act. As soon as a man does an action *because* he thinks he will promote his own interests thereby, he is acting not from a sense of its rightness but from self-interest.

To the egoistic theory hedonistic utilitarianism supplies a much-needed amendment. It points out correctly that the fact that a certain pleasure will be enjoyed by the agent is no reason why he *ought* to bring it into being rather than an equal or greater pleasure to be enjoyed by another, though, human nature being what it is, it makes it not unlikely that he *will* try to bring it into being. But hedonistic utilitarianism in its turn needs a correction. On reflection it seems clear that pleasure is not the only thing in life that we think good in itself, that for instance we think the possession of a good character, or an intelligent understanding of the world, as good or better. A great advance is made by the substitution of "productive of the greatest good" for "productive of the greatest pleasure."

Not only is this theory more attractive than hedonistic utilitarianism, but its logical relation to that theory is such that the latter could not be true unless *it* were true, while it might be true though hedonistic utilitarianism were not. It is in fact one of the logical bases of hedonistic utilitarianism. For the view that what produces the maximum pleasure is right has for its bases the views (1) that what produces the maximum good is right, and (2) that pleasure is the only thing good in itself. If they were not assuming that what produces the maximum *good* is right, the utilitarians' attempt to show that pleasure is the only thing good in itself, which is in fact the point they take most pains to establish, would have been quite irrelevant to their attempt to prove that only what produces the maximum *pleasure* is right. If, therefore, it can be shown that productivity of the maximum good is not what makes all right actions right, we shall *a fortiori* have refuted hedonistic utilitarianism.

When a plain man fulfills a promise because he thinks he ought to do so, it seems clear that he does so with no thought of its total consequences, still less with any opinion that these are likely to be the best possible. He thinks in fact much more of the past than of the future. What makes him think it right to act in a certain way is the fact that he has promised to do so—that and, usually, nothing more. That his act will produce the best possible consequences is not his reason for calling it right. What lends color to the theory we are examining, then, is not the actions (which form probably a great majority of our actions) in which some such reflection as "I have promised" is the only reason we give ourselves for thinking a certain action right, but the exceptional cases in which the consequences of fulfilling a promise (for instance) would be so disastrous to others that we judge it right not to do so. It must of course be admitted that such cases exist. If I have promised to meet a friend at a particular time for some trivial purpose, I should certainly think myself justified in breaking my engagement if by doing so I could prevent a serious accident or bring relief to the victims of one. And the supporters of the view we are examining hold that my thinking so is due to my thinking that I shall bring more good into existence by the one action than by the other. A different account may, however, be given of the matter, an account which will, I believe, show itself to be the true one. It may be said that besides the duty of fulfilling promises I have and recognize a duty of relieving distress, and that when I think it right to do the latter at the cost of not doing the former, it is not because I think I shall produce more good thereby but because I think it the duty which is in the circumstances more of a duty. This account surely corresponds much more closely with what we really think in such a situation. If, so far as I can see, I could bring equal amounts of good into being by fulfilling my promise and by helping some one to whom I had made no promise, I should not hesitate to regard the former as my duty. Yet on the view that what is right is right because it is productive of the most good I should not so regard it.

There are two theories, each in its way simple, that offer a solution of such cases of conscience. One is the view of Kant, that there are certain duties of perfect obligation, such as those of fulfilling promises, of paying debts, of telling the truth, which admit of no exception whatever in favor of duties of imperfect obligation, such as that of relieving distress. The other is the view of, for instance, Professor Moore and Dr. Rashdall, that there is only the duty of producing good, and that all "conflicts of duties" should be resolved by asking "by which action will most good be produced?" But it is more important that our theory fit the facts than that it be simple, and the account we have given above corresponds (it seems to me) better than either of the simpler theories with what we really think, viz., that normally promise-keeping, for example, should come before benevolence, but that when and only when the good to be produced by the benevolent act is very great and the promise comparatively trivial, the act of benevolence becomes our duty.

In fact the theory of "ideal utilitarianism," if I may for brevity refer so to the theory of Professor Moore, seems to simplify unduly our relations to our fellows. It says, in effect, that the only morally significant relation in which my neighbors stand to me is that of being possible beneficiaries by my action. They do stand in this relation to me, and this relation is morally significant. But they may also stand to me in the relation of promisee to promiser, of creditor to debtor, of wife to husband, of child to parent, of friend to friend, of fellow countryman to fellow countryman, and the like; and each of these relations is the foundation of a *prima facie* duty, which is more or less incumbent on me according to the circumstances of the case. When I am in a situation, as perhaps I always am, in which more than one of the *prima facie* duties is incumbent on me, what I have to do is to study the situation as fully as I can until I form the considered opinion (it is never more) that in the circumstances one of them is more incumbent than any other; then I am bound to think that to do this *prima facie* duty is my duty *sans phrase* in the situation.

I suggest "*prima facie* duty" or "conditional duty" as a brief way of referring to the characteristic (quite distinct from that of being a duty proper) which an act has, in virtue of being of a certain kind (e.g., the keeping of a promise), of being an act which would be a duty proper if it were not at the same time of another kind which is morally significant. Whether an act is a duty proper or actual duty depends on *all* the morally significant kinds it is an instance of. The phrase "*prima facie* duty" must be apologized for, since (1) it suggests that what we are speaking of is a certain kind of duty, whereas it is in fact not a duty, but something related in a special way to duty. Strictly speaking, we want not a phrase in which duty is qualified by an adjective, but a separate noun. (2) "*Prima*" *facie* suggests that one is speaking only of an appearance which a moral situation presents at first sight, and which may turn out to be illusory; whereas what I am speaking of is an objective fact involved in the nature of the situation, or more strictly in an element of its nature, though not, as duty proper does, arising from its *whole* nature. I can, however, think of no term which fully meets the case. "Claim" has been suggested by Professor Prichard. The word "claim" has the advantage of being quite a familiar one in this connection, and it seems to cover much of the ground. It would be quite natural to say, "a person to whom I have made a promise has a claim on me," and also, "a person whose distress I could relieve (at the cost of breaking the promise) has a claim on me." But (1) while "claim" is appropriate from *their* point of view, we want a word to express the corresponding fact from the agent's point of view—the fact of his being subject to claims that can be made against him; and ordinary language provides us with no such correlative to "claim." And (2) (what is more important) "claim seems inevitably to suggest two persons, one of whom might make a claim on the other; and while this covers the ground of social duty, it is inappropriate in the case of that important part of duty which is the duty of cultivating a certain kind of character in oneself. It would be artificial, I think, and at any rate metaphorical, to say that one's character has a claim on oneself.

There is nothing arbitrary about these *prima facie* duties. Each rests on a definite circumstance which cannot seriously be held to be without moral significance. Of *prima facie* duties I suggest, without claiming completeness or finality for it, the following division.[1]

(1) Some duties rest on previous acts of my own. These duties seem to include two kinds, (*a*) those resting on a promise or what may fairly be called an implicit promise, such as the implicit undertaking not to tell lies which seems to be implied in the act of entering into conversation (at any rate by civilized men), or of writing books that purport to be history and not fiction. These may be called the duties of fidelity. (*b*) Those resting on a previous wrongful act. These may be called the duties of reparation. (2) Some rest on previous acts of other men, i.e., services done by them to me. These may be loosely described as the duties of gratitude. (3) Some rest on the fact or possibility of a distribution of pleasure or happiness (or of the means thereto) which is not in accordance with the merit of the persons concerned; in such cases there arises a duty to upset or prevent such a distribution. These are the duties of justice. (4) Some rest on the mere fact that there are other beings in the world whose condition we can make better in respect of virtue, or of intelligence, or of pleasure. These are the duties of beneficence. (5) Some rest on the fact that we can improve our own condition in respect of virtue or of intelligence. These are the duties of self-improvement. (6) I think that we should distinguish from (4) the duties that may be summed up under the title of "not injuring others." No doubt to injure others is incidentally to fail to do them good; but it seems to me clear that non-

---

[1] I should make it plain at this stage that I am *assuming* the correctness of some of our main convictions as to *prima facie* duties, or, more strictly, am claiming that we *know* them to be true. To me it seems as self-evident as anything could be, that to make a promise, for instance, is to create a moral claim on us in someone else. Many readers will perhaps say that they do *not* know this to be true. If so, I certainly cannot prove it to them; I can only ask them to reflect again, in the hope that they will ultimately agree that they also know it to be true. The main moral convictions of the plain man seem to me to be, not opinions which it is for philosophy to prove or disprove, but knowledge from the start; and in my own case I seem to find little difficulty in distinguishing these essential convictions from other moral convictions which I also have, which are merely fallible opinions based on an imperfect study of the working for good or evil of certain institutions or types of action.

maleficence is apprehended as a duty distinct from that of beneficence, and as a duty of a more stringent character. It will be noticed that this alone among the types of duty has been stated in a negative way. An attempt might no doubt be made to state this duty, like the others, in a positive way. It might be said that it is really the duty to prevent ourselves from acting either from an inclination to harm others or from an inclination to seek our own pleasure, in doing which we should incidentally harm them. But on reflection it seems clear that the primary duty here is the duty not to harm others, this being a duty whether or not we have an inclination that if followed would lead to our harming them; and that when we have such an inclination the primary duty not to harm others gives rise to a consequential duty to resist the inclination. The recognition of this duty of non-maleficence is the first step on the way to the recognition of the duty of beneficence; and that accounts for the prominence of the commands "thou shalt not kill," "thou shalt not commit adultery," "thou shalt not steal," "thou shalt not bear false witness," in so early a code as the Decalogue. But even when we have come to recognize the duty of beneficence, it appears to me that the duty of non-maleficence is recognized as a distinct one, and as *prima facie* more binding. We should not in general consider it justifiable to kill one person in order to keep another alive, or to steal from one in order to give alms to another.

The essential defect of the "ideal utilitarian" theory is that it ignores, or at least does not do full justice to, the highly personal character of duty. If the only duty is to produce the maximum of good, the question who is to have the good—whether it is myself, or my benefactor, or a person to whom I have made a promise to confer that good on him, or a mere fellow man to whom I stand in no such special relation—should make no difference to my having a duty to produce that good. But we are all in fact sure that it makes a vast difference.

One or two other comments must be made on this provisional list of the divisions of duty. (1) The nomenclature is not strictly correct. For by "fidelity" or "gratitude" we mean, strictly, certain states of motivation; and, as I have urged, it is not our duty to have certain motives, but to do certain acts. By "fidelity," for instance, is meant, strictly, the disposition to fulfill promises and implicit promises *because we have made them*. We have no general word to cover the actual fulfillment of promises and implicit promises *irrespective of motive;* and I use "fidelity," loosely but perhaps conveniently, to fill this gap. So too I use "gratitude" for the returning of services, irrespective of motive. The term "justice" is not so much confined, in ordinary usage, to a certain state of motivation, for we should often talk of a man as acting justly even when we did not think his motive was the wish to do what was just simply for the sake of doing so. Less apology is therefore needed for our use of "justice" in this sense. And I have used the word "beneficence" rather than "benevolence," in order to emphasize the fact that it is our duty to do certain things, and not to do them from certain motives.

(2) If the objection be made, that this catalogue of the main types of duty is an unsystematic one resting on no logical principle, it may be replied, first, that it makes no claim to being ultimate. It is a *prima facie* classification of the duties which reflection on our moral convictions seems actually to reveal. And if these convictions are, as I would claim that they are, of the nature of knowledge, and if I have not misstated them, the list will be a list of authentic conditional duties, correct as far as it goes though not necessarily complete. The list of *goods* put forward by the rival

theory is reached by exactly the same method—the only sound one in the circumstances —viz., that of direct reflection on what we really think. Loyalty to the facts is worth more than a symmetrical architectonic or a hastily reached simplicity. If further reflection discovers a perfect logical basis for this or for a better classification, so much the better.

(3)It may, again, be objected that our theory that there are these various and often conflicting types of *prima facie* duty leaves us with no principle upon which to discern what is our actual duty in particular circumstances. But this objection is not one which the rival theory is in a position to bring forward. For when we have to choose between the production of two heterogeneous goods, say knowledge and pleasure, the "ideal utilitarian" theory can only fall back on an opinion, for which no logical basis can be offered, that one of the goods is the greater; and this is no better than a similar opinion that one of two duties is the more urgent. And again, when we consider the infinite variety of the effects of our actions in the way of pleasure, it must surely be admitted that the claim which *hedonism* sometimes makes that it offers a readily applicable criterion of right conduct, is quite illusory.

I am unwilling, however, to content myself with an *argumentum ad hominem,* and I would contend that in principle there is no reason to anticipate that every act that is our duty is so for one and the same reason. Why should two sets of circumstances, or one set of circumstances, *not* possess different characteristics, any one of which makes a certain act our *prima facie* duty? When I ask what it is that makes me in certain cases sure that I have a *prima facie* duty to do so and so, I find that it lies in the fact that I have made a promise; when I ask the same question in another case, I find the answer lies in the fact that I have done a wrong. And if on reflection I find (as I think I do) that neither of these reasons is reducible to the other, I must not on any *a priori* ground assume that such a reduction is possible.

An attempt may be made to arrange in a more systematic way the main types of duty which we have indicated. In the first place it seems self-evident that if there are things that are intrinsically good, it is *prima facie* a duty to bring them into existence rather than not to do so, and to bring as much of them into existence as possible. It will be argued in our fifth chapter that there are three main things that are intrinsically good—virtue, knowledge, and, with certain limitations, pleasure. And since a given virtuous disposition, for instance, is equally good whether it is realized in myself or in another, it seems to be my duty to bring it into existence whether in myself or in another. So too with a given piece of knowledge.

The case of pleasure is difficult; for while we clearly recognize a duty to produce pleasure for others, it is by no means so clear that we recognize a duty to produce pleasure for ourselves. This appears to arise from the following facts. The thought of an act as our duty is one that presupposes a certain amount of reflection about the act; and for that reason does not normally arise in connection with acts towards which we are already impelled by another strong impulse. So far, the cause of our not thinking of the promotion of our own pleasure as a duty is analogous to the cause which usually prevents a highly sympathetic person from thinking of the promotion of the pleasure of others as a duty. He is impelled so strongly by direct interest in the well-being of others towards promoting their pleasure that he does not stop to ask whether it is his duty to promote it; and we are all impelled so strongly towards the promotion of our own pleasure that we do not stop to ask whether it is a duty or not. But there is a futrher reason why even when we stop to think about the matter it does not usually present itself as a duty: viz., that, since the performance of most of our duties involves the giving up of some pleasure that we desire, the doing of duty and the getting of pleasure for ourselves come by a natural association of ideas to be thought of as incompatible things. This association of ideas is in the main salutary in its operation, since it puts a check on what but for it would be much too strong, the tendency to pursue one's own pleasure without thought of other considerations. Yet if pleasure is good, it seems in the long run clear that it is right to get it for ourselves as well as to produce it for others, when this does not involve the failure to discharge some more stringent *prima facie* duty. The question is a very difficult one, but it seems that this conclusion can be denied only on one or other of three grounds: (1) that pleasure is not *prima facie* good (i.e., good when it is neither the actualization of a bad disposition nor undeserved), (2) that there is no *prima facie* duty to produce as much that is good as we can, or (3) that though there is a *prima facie* duty to produce other things that are good, there is no *prima facie* duty to produce pleasure which will be enjoyed by ourselves. I give reasons later for not accepting the first contention. The second hardly admits of argument but seems to me plainly false. The third seems plausible only if we hold that an act that is pleasant or brings pleasure to ourselves must for that reason not be a duty; and this would lead to paradoxical consequences, such as that if a man enjoys giving pleasure to others or working for their moral improvement, it cannot be his duty to do so. Yet it seems to be a very stubborn fact, that in our ordinary consciousness we are not aware of a duty to get pleasure for ourselves; and by way of partial explanation of this I may add that though, as I think, one's own pleasure is a good and there is a duty to produce it, it is only if we *think* of our own pleasure not as simply our own pleasure, but as an objective good, something that an impartial spectator would approve, that we can think of the getting it as a duty; and we do not habitually think of it in this way.

If these contentions are right, what we have called the duty of beneficence and the duty of self-improvement rest on the same ground. No different principles of duty are involved in the two cases. If we feel a special responsibility for improving our own character rather than that of others, it is not because a special principle is involved, but because we are aware that the one is more under our control than the other. It was on this ground that Kant expressed the practical law of duty in the form "seek to make yourself good and other people happy." He was so persuaded of the internality of virtue that he regarded any attempt by one person to produce virtue in another as bound to produce, at most, only a counterfeit of virtue, the doing of externally right acts not from the true principle of virtuous action but out of regard to another person. It must be admitted that one man cannot compel another to be virtuous; compulsory virtue would just not be virtue. But experience clearly shows that Kant overshoots the mark when he contends that one man cannot do anything to *promote* virtue in another, to bring such influences to bear upon him that his own response to them is more likely to be virtuous than his response to other influences would have been. And our duty to do this is not different in kind from our duty to improve our own characters.

It is equally clear, and clear at an earlier stage of moral development, that if there are things that are bad in themselves we ought, *prima facie,* not to bring them upon others; and on this fact rests the duty of non-maleficence.

The duty of justice is particularly complicated, and the word is used to cover things which are really very different—things such as the payment of debts, the reparation of injuries done by oneself to another, and the bringing about of a distribution of happiness between other people in proportion to merit. I use the word to denote only the last of these three. In the fifth chapter I shall try to show that besides the three (comparatively) simple goods, virtue, knowledge, and pleasure, there is a more complex good, not reducible to these, consisting in the proportionment of happiness to virtue. The bringing of this about is a duty which we owe to all men alike, though it may be reinforced by special responsibilities that we have undertaken to particular men. This, therefore, with beneficence and self-improvement, comes under the general principle that we should produce as much good as possible, though the good here involved is different in kind from any other.

But besides this general obligation, there are special obligations. These may arise, in the first place, incidentally, from acts which were not essentially meant to create such an obligation, but which nevertheless create it. From the nature of the case such acts may be of two kinds—the infliction of injuries on others, and the acceptance of benefits from them. It seems clear that these put us under a special obligation to other men, and that only these acts can do so incidentally. From these arise the twin duties of reparation and gratitude.

And finally there are special obligations arising from acts the very intention of which, when they were done, was to put us under such an obligation. The name for such acts is "promises"; the name is wide enough if we are willing to include under it implicit promises, i.e., modes of behavior in which without explicit verbal promise we intentionally create an expectation that we can be counted on to behave in a certain way in the interest of another person.

These seem to be, in principle, all the ways in which *prima facie* duties arise. In actual experience they are compounded together in highly complex ways. Thus, for example, the duty of obeying the laws of one's country arises partly (as Socrates contends in the *Crito*) from the duty of gratitude for the benefits one has received from it; partly from the implicit promise to obey which seems to be involved in permanent residence in a country whose laws we know we are *expected* to obey, and still more clearly involved when we ourselves invoke the protection of its laws (this is the truth underlying the doctrine of the social contract); and partly (if we are fortunate in our country) from the fact that its laws are potent instruments for the general good.

Or again, the sense of a general obligation to bring about (so far as we can) a just apportionment of happiness to merit is often greatly reinforced by the fact that many of the existing injustices are due to a social and economic system which we have, not indeed created, but taken part in and assented to; the duty of justice is then reinforced by the duty of reparation.

It is necessary to say something by way of clearing up the relation between *prima facie* duties and the actual or absolute duty to do one particular act in particular circumstances. If, as almost all moralists except Kant are agreed, and as most plain men think, it is sometimes right to tell a lie or to break a promise, it must be maintained that there is a difference between *prima facie* duty and actual or absolute duty. When we think ourselves justified in breaking, and indeed morally obliged to break, a promise in order to relieve someone's distress, we do not for a moment cease to recognize a *prima facie* duty to keep our promise, and this leads us to feel, not indeed shame or repentance, but certainly compunction, for behaving as we do;

we recognize, further, that it is our duty to make up somehow to the promisee for
the breaking of the promise. We have to distinguish from the characteristic of being
our duty that of tending to be our duty. Any act that we do contains various elements
in virtue of which it falls under various categories. In virtue of being the breaking of
a promise, for instance, it tends to be wrong; in virtue of being an instance of relieving distress it tends to be right. Tendency to be one's duty may be called a parti-
resultant attribute, i.e., one which belongs to an act in virtue of some one component
in its nature. *Being* one's duty is a toti-resultant attribute, one which belongs to an act
in virtue of its whole nature and of nothing less than this. . . .

Another instance of the same distinction may be found in the operation of
natural laws. *Qua* subject to the force of gravitation towards some other body, each
body tends to move in a particular direction with a particular velocity; but its actual
movement depends on *all* the forces to which it is subject. It is only by recognizing this
distinction that we can preserve the absoluteness of laws of nature, and only by
recognizing a corresponding distinction that we can preserve the absoluteness of the
general principles of morality. But an important difference between the two cases
must be pointed out. When we say that in virtue of gravitation a body tends to move
in a certain way, we are referring to a causal influence actually exercised on it by
another body or other bodies. When we say that in virtue of being deliberately untrue
a certain remark tends to be wrong, we are referring to no causal relation, to no
relation that involves succession in time, but to such a relation as connects the various
attributes of a mathematical figure. And if the word "tendency" is thought to suggest
too much a causal relation, it is better to talk of certain types of act as being *prima
facie* right or wrong (or of different persons as having different and possibly conflicting claims upon us), than of their tending to be right or wrong.

Something should be said of the relation between our apprehension of the
prima facie rightness of certain types of act and our mental attitude towards particular acts. It is proper to use the word "apprehension" in the former case and not
in the latter. That an act, *qua* fulfilling a promise, or *qua* effecting a just distribution
of good, or *qua* returning services rendered, or *qua* promoting the good of others, or
qua promoting the virtue or insight of the agent, is *prima facie* right, is self-evident;
not in the sense that it is evident from the beginning of our lives, or as soon as we
attend to the proposition for the first time, but in the sense that when we have
reached sufficient mental maturity and have given sufficient attention to the proposition
it is evident without any need of proof, or of evidence beyond itself. It is self-
evident just as a mathematical axiom, or the validity of a form of inference, is
evident. The moral order expressed in these propositions is just as much part of the
fundamental nature of the universe (and, we may add, of any possible universe in
which there were moral agents at all) as is the spatial or numerical structure expressed
in the axioms of geometry or arithmetic. In our confidence that these propositions are
true there is involved the same trust in our reason that is involved in our confidence
in mathematics; and we should have no justification for trusting it in the latter
sphere and distrusting it in the former. In both cases we are dealing with propositions
that cannot be proved, but that just as certainly need no proof.

Some of these general principles of *prima facie* duty may appear to be open to
criticism. It may be thought, for example, that the principle of returning good for
good is a falling off from the Christian principle, generally and rightly recognized

as expressing the highest morality, of returning good for evil. To this it may be replied that I do not suggest that there is a principle commanding us to return good for good and forbidding us to return good for evil, and that I do suggest that there is a positive duty to seek the good of all men. What I maintain is that an act in which good is returned for good is recognized as *specially* binding on us just because it is of that character, and that *ceteris paribus* any one would think it his duty to help his benefactors rather than his enemies, if he could not do both; just as it is generally recognized that *ceteris paribus* we should pay our debts rather than give our money in charity, when we cannot do both. A benefactor is not only a man, calling for our effort on his behalf on that ground, but also our benefactor, calling for our *special* effort on *that* ground.

Our judgments about our actual duty in concrete situations have none of the certainty that attaches to our recognition of the general principles of duty. A state-ment is certain, i.e., is an expression of knowledge, only in one or other of two cases: when it is either self-evident, or a valid conclusion from self-evident premises. And our judgments about our particular duties have neither of these characters. (1) They are not self-evident. Where a possible act is seen to have two characteristics, in virtue of one of which it is *prima facie* right, and in virtue of the other *prima facie* wrong, we are (I think) well aware that we are not certain whether we ought or ought not to do it; that whether we do it or not, we are taking a moral risk. We come in the long run, after consideration, to think one duty more pressing than the other, but we do not feel certain that it is so. And though we do not always recognize that a possible act has two such characteristics, and though there *may* be cases in which it has not, we are never certain that any particular possible act has not, and therefore never certain that it is right, nor certain that it is wrong. For, to go no further in the analysis, it is enough to point out that any particular act will in all probability in the course of time contribute to the bringing about of good or of evil for many human beings, and thus have a *prima facie* rightness or wrongness of which we know nothing. (2) Again, our judgments about our particular duties are not logical conclusions from self-evident premises. The only possible premises would be the general principles stating their *prima facie* rightness or wrongness *qua* having the different characteristics they do have; and even if we could (as we cannot) apprehend the extent to which an act will tend on the one hand, for example, to bring about advantages for our benefactors, and on the other hand to bring about disadvantages for fellow men who are not our benefactors, there is no principle by which we can draw the conclusion that it is on the whole right or on the whole wrong. In this respect the judgment as to the rightness of a particular act is just like the judgment as to the beauty of a particular natural object or work of art. A poem is, for instance, in respect of certain qualities beautiful and in respect of certain others not beautiful; and our judgment as to the degree of beauty it possesses on the whole is never reached by logical reasoning from the apprehension of its particular beauties or particular defects. Both in this and in the moral case we have more or less probable opinions which are not logically justified conclusions from the general principles that are recognized as self-evident.

There is therefore much truth in the description of the right act as a fortunate act. If we cannot be certain that it is right, it is our good fortune if the act we do is the right act. This consideration does not, however, make the doing of our duty a mere matter of chance. There is a parallel here between the doing of duty and the doing of what will be to our personal advantage. We never *know* what act will in the long run be to our advantage. Yet it is certain that we are more likely in general to secure our advantage if we estimate to the best of our ability the probable tendencies of our actions in this respect, than if we act on caprice. And similarly we are more likely to do our duty if we reflect to the best of our ability on the *prima facie* rightness or wrongness of various possible acts in virtue of the characteristics we perceive them to have, than if we act without reflection. With this greater likelihood we must be content.

Many people would be inclined to say that the right act for me is not that whose general nature I have been describing, viz., that which if I were omniscient I should see to be my duty, but that which on all the evidence available to me I should think to be my duty. But suppose that from the state of partial knowledge in which I think act A to be my duty, I could pass to a state of perfect knowledge in which I saw act B to be my duty, should I not say "act B was the right act for me to do"? I should no doubt add "though I am not to be blamed for doing act A." But in adding this, am I not passing from the question "what is right" to the question "what is morally good"? At the same time I am not making the *full* passage from the one notion to the other; for in order that the act should be morally good, or an act I am not to be blamed for doing, it must not merely be the act which it is reasonable for me to think my duty; it must also be done for that reason, or from some other morally good motive. Thus the conception of the right act as the act which it is reasonable for me to think my duty is an unsatisfactory compromise between the true notion of the right act and the notion of the morally good action.

The general principles of duty are obviously not self-evident from the beginning of our lives. How do they come to be so? The answer is, that they come to be self-evident to us just as mathematical axioms do. We find by experience that this couple of matches and that couple make four matches, that this couple of balls on a wire and that couple make four balls: and by reflection on these and similar discoveries we come to see that it is of the nature of two and two to make four. In a precisely similar way, we see the *prima facie* rightness of an act which would be the fulfillment of a particular promise, and of another which would be the fulfillment of another promise; and when we have reached sufficient maturity to think in general terms, we apprehend *prima facie* rightness to belong to the nature of any fulfillment of promise. What comes first in time is the apprehension of the self-evident *prima facie* rightness of an individual act of a particular type. From this we come by reflection to apprehend the self-evident general principle of *prima facie* duty. From this, too, perhaps along with the apprehension of the self-evident *prima facie* rightness of the same act in virtue of its having another characteristic as well, and perhaps in spite of the apprehension of it *prima facie* wrongness in virtue of its having some third characteristic, we come to believe something not self-evident at all, but an object of probable opinion, viz., that this particular act is (not *prima facie* but) actually right.

In this respect there is an important difference between rightness and mathematical properties. A triangle which is isosceles necessarily has two of its angles equal, whatever other characteristics the triangle may have—whatever, for instance, be its area, or the size of its third angle. The equality of the two angles is a parti-resultant attribute. And the same is true of all mathematical attributes. It is true, I may add, of *prima facie* rightness. But no act is ever, in virtue of falling under some general description, necessarily actually right; its rightness depends on its whole nature [2] and not on any element in it. The reason is that no mathematical object (no figure, for instance, or angle) ever has two characteristics that tend to give it opposite resultant characteristics, while moral acts often (as every one knows) and indeed always (as on reflection we must admit) have different characteristics that tend to make them at the same time *prima facie* right and *prima facie* wrong; there is probably no act, for instance, which does good to anyone without doing harm to some one else, and *vice versa*.

. . .

[2] To avoid complicating unduly the statement of the general view I am putting forward, I have here rather overstated it. Any act is the origination of a great variety of things many of which make no difference to its rightness or wrongness. But there are always many elements in its nature (i.e., in what it is the origination of) that make a difference to its rightness or wrongness, and no element in its nature can be dismissed without consideration as indifferent.

10

THE LANGUAGE OF MORALS:
DESCRIPTION AND EVALUATION

r. m. hare

1. Of all the problems raised by the preceding argument, the key problem is as follows: there are two sorts of things that we can say, for example, about strawberries; the first sort is usually called *descriptive,* the second sort *evaluative.* Examples of the first sort of remark are, "This strawberry is sweet" and "This strawberry is large, red, and juicy." Examples of the second sort of remark are "This is a good strawberry" and "This strawberry is just as strawberries ought to be." The first sort of remark is often given as a reason for making the second sort of remark; but the first sort does not by itself entail the second sort, nor vice versa. Yet there seems to be some close logical connection between them. Our problem is: "What is this connection?" For no light is shed by saying that there is a connection, unless we can say what it is.

The problem may also be put in this way: If we knew all the descriptive properties which a particular strawberry had (knew, of every descriptive sentence relating to the strawberry, whether it was true or false), and if we knew also the meaning of the word "good," then what else should we require to know, in order to be able to tell whether a strawberry was a good one? Once the question is put in this way, the answer should be apparent. We should require to know, what are the criteria in virtue of which a strawberry is to be called a good one, or what are the characteristics that make a strawberry a good one, or what is the standard of goodness in strawberries. We should require to be given the major premise. We have already seen that we can know the meaning of "good strawberry" without knowing any of these latter things—though there is also a sense of the sentence "what does it mean to call a strawberry a good one?" in which we should not know the answer to it, unless we also knew the answer to these other questions. It is now time to elucidate and distinguish these two ways in which we can be said to know what it means to call an object a good member of its class. This will help us to see more clearly both the differences and the similarities between "good" and words like "red" and "sweet."

Since we have been dwelling for some time on the differences, it will do no harm now to mention some of the similarities. For this purpose, let us consider the two sentences "M is a red motorcar" and "M is a good motorcar." It will be noticed that

From R. M. Hare, *The Language of Morals* (Oxford: The Clarendon Press, 1952), Chap. 7, pp. 111–126. Reprinted by permission of the Clarendon Press.

"motorcar," unlike "strawberry," is a functional word, as defined in the preceding chapter.[1] Reference to the *Shorter Oxford English Dictionary* shows that a motorcar is a carriage, and a carriage a means of conveyance. Thus, if a motorcar will not convey anything, we know from the definition of motorcar that it is not a good one. But when we know this, we know so little, compared with what is required in order to know the full criteria of a good motorcar, that I propose in what follows to ignore, for the sake of simplicity, this complicating factor. I shall treat "motorcar" as if it did not have to be defined functionally: that is to say, I shall assume that we could learn the meaning of "motorcar" (as in a sense we can) simply by being shown examples of motorcars. It is, of course, not always easy to say whether or not a word is a functional word; it depends, like all questions of meaning, on how the word is taken by a particular speaker.

The first similarity between "M is a red motorcar" and "M is a good motorcar" is that both can be, and often are, used for conveying information of a purely factual or descriptive character. If I say to someone "M is a good mortocar," and he himself has not seen, and knows nothing of M, but does on the other hand know what sorts of motorcar we are accustomed to call "good" (knows what is the accepted standard of goodness in motorcars), he undoubtedly receives information from my remark about what sort of motorcar it is. He will complain that I have misled him, if he subsequently discovers that M will not go over 30 m.p.h., or uses as much oil as petrol, or is covered with rust, or has large holes in the roof. His reason for complaining will be the same as it would have been if I had said that the car was red and he subsequently discovered that it was black. I should have led him to expect the motorcar to be of a certain description when in fact it was of a quite different description.

The second similarity between the two sentences is this. Sometimes we use them, not for actually conveying information, but for putting our hearer into a position subsequently to use the word "good" or "red" for giving or getting information. Suppose, for example, that he is utterly unfamiliar with motorcars in the same sort of way as most of us are unfamiliar with horses nowadays, and knows no more about motorcars than is necessary in order to distinguish a motorcar from a hansom cab. In that case, my saying to him "M is a good motorcar" will not give him any information about M, beyond the information that it is a motorcar. But if he is able then or subsequently to examine M, he will have learnt something. He will have learnt that some of the characteristics which M has, are characteristics which make people— or at any rate me—call it a good motorcar. This may not be to learn very much. But suppose that I make judgments of this sort about a great many motorcars, calling some good and some not good, and he is able to examine all or most of the motorcars about which I am speaking; he will in the end learn quite a lot, always presuming that I observe a consistent standard in calling them good or not good. He will eventually, if he pays careful attention, get into the position in which he knows, after I have said that a motorcar is a good one, what sort of a motorcar he may expect it to be—for example fast, stable on the road, and so on.

Now if we were dealing, not with "good," but with "red," we should call this processing "explaining the meaning of the word"—and we might indeed, in a sense, say that what I have been doing is explaining what one means by "a good motorcar."

[1] Hare's definition is as follows: "A word is a functional word if, in order to explain its meaning fully, we have to say what the object it refers to is *for*, or what it is supposed to do." [Eds.]

This is a sense of "mean" about which, as we have seen, we must be on our guard. The processes, however, are very similar. I might explain the meaning of "red" by continually saying of various mortorcars "M is a red motorcar," "N is not a red motorcar," and so on. If he were attentive enough, he would soon get into a position in which he was able to use the word "red" for giving or getting information, at any rate about motorcars. And so, both with "good" and with "red," there is this process, which in the case of "red" we may call "explaining the meaning," but in the case of "good" may only call it so loosely and in a secondary sense; to be clear we must call it something like "explaining or conveying or setting forth the standard of goodness in motorcars."

The standard of goodness, like the meaning of "red," is normally something which is public and commonly accepted. When I explain to someone the meaning of "red motorcar," he expects, unless I am known to be very eccentric, that he will find other people using it in the same way. And similarly, at any rate with objects like motorcars where there is a commonly accepted standard, he will expect, having learned from me what is the standard of goodness in motorcars, to be able, by using the expression "good motorcar," to give information to other people, and get it from them, without confusion.

A third respect in which "good motorcar" resembles "red motorcar" is the following: both "good" and "red" can vary as regards the exactitude or vagueness of the information which they do or can convey. We normally use the expression "red motorcar" very loosely. Any motorcar that lies somewhere between the unmistakably purple and the unmistakably orange could without abuse of language be called a red motorcar. And similarly, the standard for calling motorcars good is commonly very loose. There are certain characteristics, such as inability to exceed 30 m.p.h., which to anyone but an eccentric would be sufficient conditions for refusing to call it a good motorcar; but there is no precise set of accepted criteria such that we can say "If a motorcar satisfies these conditions, it is a good one; if not, not." And in both cases we could be precise if we wanted to. We could, for certain purposes, agree not to say that a motorcar was "really red" unless the redness of its paint reached a certain measurable degree of purity and saturation; and similarly, we might adopt a very exact standard of goodness in motorcars. We might refuse the name "good motorcar" to any car that would not go round a certain racetrack without mishap in a certain limited time, that did not conform to certain other rigid specifications as regards accommodation, etc. This sort of thing has not been done for the expression "good motorcar"; but, as Mr. Urmson has pointed out, it has been done by the Ministry of Agriculture for the expression "super apple." [2]

It is important to notice that the exactness or looseness of their criteria does absolutely nothing to distinguish words like "good" from words like "red." Words in both classes may be descriptively loose or exact, according to how rigidly the criteria have been laid down by custom or convention. It certainly is not true that value-words are distinguished from descriptive words in that the former are looser, descriptively, than the latter. There are loose and rigid examples of both sorts of word. Words like "red" can be extremely loose, without becoming to the least degree evaluative; and expressions like "good sewage effluent" can be the subject of very rigid criteria, without in the least ceasing to be evaluative.

[2] *Mind,* lix (1950), 152 (also in *Logic and Language,* ii, ed. Flew, 166).

It is important to notice also, how easy it is, in view of these resemblances be-tween "good" and "red," to think that there are no differences—to think that to set forth the standard of goodness in motorcars is to set forth the meaning, in all senses that there are of that word, of the expression "good motorcar"; to think that "M is a good motorcar" means neither more nor less than "M has certain characteristics of which 'good' is the name."

2. It is worth noticing here that the functions of the word "good" which are concerned with information could be performed equally well if "good" had no com-mendatory function at all. This can be made clear by substituting another word, made up for the purpose, which is to be supposed to lack the commendatory force of "good." Let us use "doog" as this new word. "Doog," like "good," can be used for conveying information only if the criteria for its application are known; but this makes it, unlike "good," altogether meaningless until these criteria are made known. I make the criteria known by pointing out various motorcars, and saying "M is a doog motorcar," "N is not a doog motorcar," and so on. We must imagine that, although "doog" has no commendatory force, the criteria for doogness in motorcars which I am employing are the same as those which, in the previous example, I employed for goodness in motorcars. And so, as in the previous example, the learner, if he is suf-ficiently attentive, becomes able to use the word "doog" for giving or getting informa-tion; when I say to him "Z is a doog motorcar," he knows what characteristics to expect it to have; and if he wants to convey to someone else that a motorcar Y has those same characteristics, he can do so by saying "Y is a doog motorcar."

Thus the word "doog" does (though only in connection with motorcars) half the jobs that the word "good" does—namely, all those jobs that are concerned with the giving, or learning to give or get, information. It does not do those jobs which are concerned with commendation. Thus we might say that "doog" functions just like a descriptive word. First my learner learns to use it by my giving him examples of its application, and then he uses it by applying it to fresh examples. It would be quite natural to say that what I was doing was teaching my learner the *meaning* of "doog"; and this shows us again how natural it is to say that, when we are learning a similar lesson for the expression "good motorcar" (i.e., learning the criteria of its application), we are learning its meaning. But with the word "good" it is misleading to say this; for the meaning of good motorcar" (in another sense of "meaning") is something that might be known by someone who did not know the criteria of its application; he would know, if someone said that a motorcar was a good one, that he was commending it; and to know that, would be to know the meaning of the expression. Further . . . someone might know about "good" all the things which my learner learned about the the word "doog" (namely, how to apply the word to the right objects, and use it for giving and getting information) and yet be said not to know its meaning; for he might not know that to call a motorcar good was to commend it.

3. It may be objected by some readers that to call the descriptive or informative job of "good" its *meaning* in any sense is illegitimate. Such objectors might hold that the meaning of "good" is adequately characterized by saying that it is used for com-mending, and that any information we get from its use is not a question of meaning at all. When I say "M is a good motorcar," my meaning, on this view, is to commend M; if a hearer gets from my remark, together with his knowledge of the standard habitually used by me in assessing the merits of motorcars, information about what description of motorcar it is, this is not part of my meaning; all my hearer has done

is to make an inductive inference from "Hare has usually in the past commended motor cars of a certain description" and "Hare has commended M" to "M is of the same description." I suspect that this objection is largely a verbal one, and I have no wish to take sides against it. On the one hand, we must insist that to know the criteria for applying the word "good" to motorcars is not to know—at any rate in the full or primary sense—the meaning of the expression "good motorcar"; to this extent the objection must be agreed with. On the other hand, the relation of the expression "good motorcar" to the criteria for its application is very like the relation of a descriptive expression to its defining characteristics, and this likeness finds an echo in our language when we ask "What do you mean, good?" and get the answer "I mean it'll do So and never breaks down." In view of this undoubted fact of usage, I deem it best to adopt the term "descriptive meaning." Moreover, it is natural to say that a sentence has descriptive meaning, if the speaker intends it primarily to convey information; and when a newspaper says that X opened the batting on a good wicket, its intention is not primarily to commend the wicket, but to inform its readers what description of wicket it was.

4. It is time now to justify my calling the descriptive meaning of "good" secondary to the evaluative meaning. My reasons for doing so are two. First, the evaluative meaning is constant for every class of object for which the word is used. When we call a motorcar or a chronometer or a cricket-bat or a picture good, we are commending all of them. But because we are commending all of them for different reasons, the descriptive meaning is different in all cases. We have knowledge of the evaluative meaning of "good" from our earliest years; but we are constantly learning to use it in new descriptive meanings, as the classes of objects whose virtues we learn to distinguish grow more numerous. Sometimes we learn to use "good" in a new descriptive meaning through being taught it by an expert in a particular field—for example, a horseman might teach me how to recognize a good hunter. Sometimes, on the other hand, we make up a new descriptive meaning for ourselves. This happens when we start having a standard for a class of objects, certain members of which we have started needing to place in order of merit, but for which there has hitherto been no standard. . . .

The second reason for calling the evaluative meaning primary is, that we can use the evaluative force of the word in order to *change* the descriptive meaning for any class of objects. This is what the moral reformer often does in morals; but the same process occurs outside morals. It may happen that motorcars will in the near future change considerably in design (e.g., by our seeking economy at the expense of size). It may be that then we shall cease giving the name "a good motorcar" to a car that now would rightly and with the concurrence of all be allowed that name. How, linguistically speaking, would this have happened? At present, we are roughly agreed (though only roughly) on the necessary and sufficient criteria for calling a motorcar a good one. If what I have described takes place, we may begin to say "No cars of the nineteen-fifties were really good; there weren't any good ones till 1960." Now here we cannot be using "good" with the same descriptive meaning as it is now generally used with; for some of the cars of 1950 do indubitably have those characteristics which entitle them to the name "good motorcar" in the 1950 descriptive sense of that word. What is happening is that the evaluative meaning of the word is being used in order to shift the descriptive meaning; we are doing what would be called, if "good" were a purely descriptive word, redefining it. But we cannot call it that, for the evaluative meaning remains constant; we are rather altering the standard. This is similar to the process called by Professor Stevenson "persuasive definition"; [3] the process is not necessarily, however, highly colored with emotion.

We may notice here that there are two chief ways in which a change in standard may be reflected in, and indeed partly effected by, a change in language. The first is the one which I have just illustrated; the evaluative meaning of "good" is retained, and is used in order to alter the descriptive meaning and so establish a new standard. The second does not often occur with the word "good"; for that word is so well-established as a value-word that the procedure would be practically impossible. This procedure is for the word to be gradually emptied of its evaluative meaning through being used more and more in what I shall call a conventional or "inverted-commas" [i.e., "quotation-marks"] way; when it has lost all its evaluative meaning it comes to be used as a purely descriptive word for designating certain characteristics of the object, and, when it is required to commend or condemn objects in this class, some quite different value-word is imported for the purpose. The two processes may be illustrated and contrasted by a somewhat over-schematized account of what has happened in the last two centuries to the expression "eligible bachelor." "Eligible" started off as a value-word, meaning "such as should be chosen (sc., as a husband for one's daughters)." Then, because the criteria of eligibility came to be fairly rigid, it acquired a descriptive meaning too; a person, if said to be eligible, might, in the eighteenth century, have been expected to have large landed estates and perhaps a title. By the nineteenth century, however, the criteria of eligibility have changed; what makes a bachelor eligible is no longer necessarily landed property or a title; it is substantial wealth of any kind provided that it is well-secured. We might imagine a nineteenth-century mother saying "I know he is not of noble birth; but he's eligible all the same, because he has £3,000 a year in the Funds, and much more besides when his father dies." This would be an example of the first method. On the other hand, in the twentieth century, partly as a reaction from the over-rigid standards of the nineteenth, which resulted in the word "eligible" lapsing into a conventional use, the second method has been adopted. If now someone said "He is an eligible bachelor," we could almost feel the inverted commas round the word, and even the irony; we should feel that if that was all that could be said for him, there must be something wrong with him. For commending bachelors, on the other hand, we now use quite different words; we say "He is likely to make a very *good* husband for Jane," or "She was very *sensible* to say 'yes.' "

The close connection of standards of values with language is illustrated by the plight of the truly bilingual. A writer equally at home in English and French relates that once, when walking in the park on a rainy day, he met a lady dressed in a way which the English would call sensible, but the French *ridicule;* his mental reaction to this had to be expressed bilingually, because the standards he was applying were of diverse origin; he found himself saying to himself (slipping from English into French) "Pretty adequate armor. How uncomfortable though. Why go for a walk if you feel like this? *Elle est parfaitement ridicule.*" This cleavage of standards is said sometimes to produce neuroses in bilinguals, as might be expected in view of the close bearing of standards of values upon action.

5. Although with "good" the evaluative meaning is primary, there are other

---

[3] *Ethics and Language,* ch. ix.

words in which the evaluative meaning is secondary to the descriptive. Such words are "tidy" and "industrious." Both are normally used to commend; but we·can say, without any hint of irony, "too tidy" or "too industrious." It is the descriptive meaning of these words that is most firmly attached to them; and therefore, although we must for certain purposes class them as value-words (for if we treat them as purely descriptive, logical errors result), they are so in a less full sense than "good." If the evaluative meaning of a word, which was primary, comes to be secondary, that is a sign that the standard to which the word appeals has become conventional. It is, of course, impossible to say *exactly* when this has happened; it is a process like the coming of winter.

Although the evaluative meaning of "good" is primary, the secondary descriptive meaning is never wholly absent. Even when we are using the word "good" evaluatively in order to set up a new standard, the word still has a descriptive meaning, not in the sense that it is used to *convey* information, but in the sense that its use in setting up the new standard is an essential preliminary—like definition in the case of a purely descriptive word—to its subsequent use with a new descriptive meaning. It is also to be noticed that the relative prominence of the descriptive and evaluative meanings of "good" varies according to the class of objects within which commendation is being given. We may illustrate this by taking two extreme examples. If I talk of "a good egg," it is at once known to what description of egg I am referring—namely, one that is not decomposed. Here the descriptive meaning predominates, because we have very fixed standards for assessing the goodness of eggs. On the other hand, if I say that a poem is a good one, very little information is given about what description of poem it is—for there is no accepted standard of goodness in poems. But it must not be thought that "good egg" is exclusively descriptive, or "good poem" exclusively evaluative. If, as the Chinese are alleged to do, we chose to eat eggs that are decomposed, we should call that kind of egg good, just as, because we choose to eat game that is slightly decomposed, we call it "well-hung" (compare also the expression "good Stilton cheese"). And if I said that a poem was good, and was not a very eccentric person, my hearer would be justified in assuming that the poem was not "Happy birthday to you!"

In general, the more fixed and accepted the standard, the more information is conveyed. But it must not be thought that the evaluative force of the word varies at all exactly in inverse proportion to the descriptive. The two vary independently: where a standard is firmly established and is as firmly believed in, a judgment containing "good" may be highly informative, without being any the less commendatory. Consider the following description of the Oxford Sewage Farm:

> The method employed is primitive but efficient. The farm is unsightly, obnoxious to people dwelling near it, and not very remunerative, but the effluent from it is, in the technical sense, good.

Now here, as may be seen by consulting handbooks on the subject, there are perfectly well-recognized tests for determining whether effluent is good or bad. One manual gives a simple field test, and another gives a series of more comprehensive tests which

---

4 P. H. J. Lagarde-Quost, "The Bilingual Citizen," *Britain Today*, Dec. 1947, p. 13; Jan. 1948, p. 13.

take up seventeen pages. This might tempt us to say that the word is used in a purely descriptive sense and has no evaluative force. But, although admittedly in calling effluent good in this technical sense we are commending it as effluent and not as perfume, we are nevertheless commending it; it is not a neutral chemical or biological fact about it that it is good; to say that it was bad would be to give a very good reason for sacking the sewage-farmer or taking other steps to see that it was good in future. The proper comment on such a lapse was made by a former Archbishop of York, speaking to the Congress of the Royal Sanitary Institute, 1912:

> There is now, I hope, no need of the trenchant eloquence of that noble-hearted pioneer of sanitary science, Charles Kingsley, to insist that it is not religion, but something more nearly approaching blasphemy, to say that an outbreak of disease is God's will being done, when patently it is man's duty which is being left undone.

It is true that, if the word "good" in a certain sentence has very little evaluative meaning, it is likely that it has a fair amount of descriptive meaning, and vice versa. That is because, if it had very little of either, it would have very little meaning at all, and would not be worth uttering. To this extent the meanings vary inversely. But this is only a tendency; we may do justice to the logical phenomena by saying that "good" normally has at least some of both sorts of meaning; that it normally has sufficient of both sorts taken together to make it worth uttering; and that, provided that the first two conditions are satisfied, the amounts of the two sorts of meaning vary independently.

There are, however, cases in which we use the word "good" with no commendatory meaning at all. We must distinguish several kinds of such non-commendatory uses. The first has been called the *inverted-commas* use. If I were not accustomed to commend any but the most modern styles of architecture, I might still say "The new chamber of the House of Commons is very good Gothic revival." I might mean this in several senses. The first is that in which it is equivalent to "a good example to choose, if one is seeking to illustrate the typical features of Gothic revival" or "a good specimen of Gothic revival." This is a specialized evaluative sense, with which we are not here concerned. I might mean, on the other hand, "genuinely preferable to most other examples of Gothic revival, and therefore to be commended *within* the class of Gothic revival buildings, though not within the class of buildings in general." With this sense, too, we are not now concerned; it is a commendatory use, with a limited class of comparison. The sense with which we are concerned is that in which it means, roughly, "the sort of Gothic revival building about which a certain sort of people—you know who—would say 'that is a good building.'" It is characteristic of this use of "good" that in expanding it we often want to put the word "good" inside inverted commas; hence the name. We are, in this use, not making a value-judgment ourselves, but alluding to the value-judgments of other people. This type of use is extremely important for the logic of moral judgments, in which it has caused some confusion.

It is to be noticed that it is easiest to use "good" in an inverted-commas sense when a certain class of people, who are sufficiently numerous and prominent for their value-judgments to be well known (e.g., the "best" people in any field), have a rigid standard of commendation for that class of object. In such cases, the inverted-commas use can verge into an *ironic* use, in which not only is no commendation being given, but rather the reverse. If I had a low opinion of Carlo Dolci, I might say "If you want to see a really 'good' Carlo Dolci, go and look at the one in. . . ."

There is another use in which the absence of evaluative content is not sufficiently obvious to the speaker for us to call it either an inverted-commas or an ironic use. This is the *conventional* use, in which the speaker is merely paying lip service to a convention, by commending, or saying commendatory things about, an object just because everyone else does. I might, if I myself had no preference at all about the design of furniture, still say "This piece of furniture is of good design," not because I wished to guide my own or anyone else's choice of furniture, but simply because I had been taught the characteristics which are generally held to be criteria of good design, and wished to show that I had "good taste" in furniture. It would be difficult in such a case to say whether I was evaluating the furniture or not. If I were not a logician, I should not ask myself the questions which would determine whether I was. Such a question would be "If someone (not connected in any way with the furniture trade), consistently and regardless of cost filled his house with furniture not conforming to the canons by which you judge the design of this furniture to be good, would you regard that as evidence that he did not agree with you?" If I replied "No, I would not; for what furniture is of good design is one question, and what furniture one chooses for oneself is another," then we might conclude that I had not been really commending the design by calling it good, but only paying lip service to a convention.

These are only some of the many ways in which we use the word "good." A logician cannot do justice to the infinite subtlety of language; all he can do is to point out some of the main features of our use of a word, and thereby put people on their guard against the main dangers. A full understanding of the logic of value-terms can only be achieved by continual and sensitive attention to the way we use them.

11

WHAT MEANS THIS FREEDOM?

john hospers

I am in agreement to a very large extent with the conclusions of Professor Edwards' paper, and am happy in these days of "soft determinism" to hear the other view so forcefully and fearlessly stated. As a preparation for developing my own views on the subject, I want to mention a factor that I think is of enormous importance and relavance: namely, unconscious motivation. There are many actions—not those of an insane person (however the term "insane" be defined), nor of a person ignorant of the effects of his action, nor ignorant of some relevant fact about the situation, nor in any obvious way mentally deranged—for which human beings in general and the courts in particular are inclined to hold the doer responsible, and for which, I would say, he should not be held responsible. The deed may be planned, it may be carried out in cold calculation, it may spring from the agent's character and be continuous with the rest of his behavior, and it may be perfectly true that he could have done differently *if* he had wanted to; nonetheless his behavior was brought about by unconscious conflicts developed in infancy, over which he had no control and of which (without training in psychiatry) he does not even have knowledge. He may even *think* he knows why he acted as he did, he may *think* he has conscious control over his actions, he may even *think* he is fully responsible for them; but he is not. Psychiatric casebooks provide hundreds of examples. The law and common sense, though puzzled sometimes by such cases, are gradually becoming aware that they exist; but at this early stage countless tragic blunders still occur because neither the law nor the public in general is aware of the genesis of criminal actions. The mother blames her daughter for choosing the wrong men as candidates for husbands; but though the daughter thinks she is choosing freely and spends a considerable amount of time "deciding" among them, the identification with her sick father, resulting from Oedipal fantasies in early childhood, prevents her from caring for any but sick men, twenty or thirty years older than herself. Blaming her is beside the point; she cannot help it, and she cannot change it. Countless criminal acts are thought out in great detail; yet the participants are (without their own knowledge) acting out fantasies, fears, and defenses from early childhood, over whose coming and going they have no conscious control.

Reprinted from *Determinism and Freedom in the Age of Modern Science,* Sidney Hook, ed. (New York: New York University Press, 1958), pp. 113–130, by permission of the publisher.

Now, I am not saying that none of these persons should be in jails or asylums. Often society must be protected against them. Nor am I saying that people should cease the practices of blaming and praising, punishing and rewarding; in general these devices are justified by the results—although very often they have practically no effect; the deeds are done from inner compulsion, which is not lessened when the threat of punishment is great. I am only saying that frequently persons we think responsible are not properly to be called so; we mistakenly think them responsible because we assume they are like those in whom no unconscious drive (toward this type of behavior) is present, and that their behavior can be changed by reasoning, exhorting, or threatening.

1

I have said that these persons are not responsible. But what is the criterion for responsibility? Under precisely what conditions is a person to be held morally responsible for an action? Disregarding here those conditions that have to do with a person's *ignorance* of the situation or the effects of his action, let us concentrate on those having to do with his "inner state." There are several criteria that might be suggested:

1. The first idea that comes to mind is that responsibility is determined by the presence or absence of *premeditation*—the opposite of "premeditated" being, presumably, "unthinking" or "impulsive." But this will not do—both because some acts are not premeditated but responsible, and because some are premeditated and not responsible.

Many acts we call responsible can be as unthinking or impulsive as you please. If you rush across the street to help the victim of an automobile collision, you are (at least so we would ordinarily say) acting responsibly, but you did not do so out of premeditation; you saw the accident, you didn't think, you rushed to the scene without hesitation. It was like a reflex action. But you acted responsibly: unlike the knee jerk, the act was the result of past training and past thought about situations of this kind; that is why you ran to help instead of ignoring the incident or running away. When something done originally from conviction or training becomes habitual, it becomes *like* a reflex action. As Aristotle said, virtue should become second nature through habit: a virtuous act should be performed *as if* by instinct; this, far from detracting from its moral worth, testifies to one's mastery of the desired type of behavior; one does not have to make a moral effort each time it is repeated.

There are also premeditated acts for which, I would say, the person is not responsible. Premeditation, especially when it is so exaggerated as to issue in no action at all, can be the result of neurotic disturbance or what we sometimes call an emotional "block," which the person inherits from long-past situations. In Hamlet's revenge on his uncle (I use this example because it is familiar to all of us), there was no lack, but rather a surfeit, of premeditation; his actions were so exquisitely premeditated as to make Freud and Dr. Ernest Jones look more closely to find out what lay behind them. The very premeditation camouflaged unconscious motives of which Hamlet himself was not aware. I think this is an important point, since it seems that the courts often assume that premeditation is a criterion of responsibility. If failure to kill his uncle had been considered a crime, every court in the land would have convicted Hamlet. Again: a woman's decision to stay with her husband in spite of endless "mental cruelty" is, if she is the victim of an unconscious masochistic "will to punishment," one for which she is not responsible; she is the victim and not the agent, no matter how profound her conviction that she is the agent; she is caught in a masochistic web (of complicated genesis) dating back to babyhood, perhaps a repetition of a comparable situation involving her own parents, a repetition-compulsion that, as Freud said, goes "beyond the pleasure principle." Again: a criminal whose crime was carefully planned step by step is usually considered responsible, but as we shall see in later examples, the overwhelming impulse toward it, stemming from an unusually humiliating ego defeat in early childhood, was as compulsive as any can be.

2. Shall we say, then, that a person is not responsible for his act unless he can *defend it with reasons?* I am afraid that this criterion is no better than the previous one. First, intellectuals are usually better at giving reasons than nonintellectuals, and according to this criterion would be more responsible than persons acting from moral conviction not implemented by reasoning; yet it is very doubtful whether we should want to say that the latter are the more responsible. Second, the giving of reasons itself may be suspect. The reasons may be rationalizations camouflaging unconscious motives of which the agent knows nothing. Hamlet gave many reasons for not doing what he felt it was his duty to do: the time was not right, his uncle's soul might go to heaven, etc. His various "reasons" contradicted one another, and if an overpowering compulsion had not been present, the highly intellectual Hamlet would not have been taken in for a moment by these rationalizations. The real reason, the Oedipal conflict that made his uncle's crime the accomplishment of his own deepest desire, binding their fates into one and paralyzing him into inaction, was unconscious and, of course, unknown to him. One's intelligence and reasoning power do not enable one to escape from unconsciously motivated behavior; it only gives one greater facility in rationalizing that behavior; one's intelligence is simply used in the interests of the neurosis—it is pressed into service to justify with reasons what one does quite independently of the reasons.

If these two criteria are inadequate, let us seek others.

3. Shall we say that a person is responsible for his action unless it is the *result of unconscious forces* of which he knows nothing? Many psychoanalysts would probably accept this criterion. If it is not largely reflected in the language of responsibility as ordinarily used, this may be due to ignorance of fact: most people do not know that there are such things as unconscious motives and unconscious conflicts causing human beings to act. But it may be that if they did, perhaps they would refrain from holding persons responsible for certain actions.

I do not wish here to quarrel with this criterion of responsibility. I only want to point out the fact that if this criterion is employed a far greater number of actions will be excluded from the domain of responsibility than we might at first suppose. Whether we are neat or untidy, whether we are selfish or unselfish, whether we provoke scenes or avoid them, even whether we can exert our powers of will to change our behavior—all these may, and often do, have their source in our unconscious life.

4. Shall we say that a person is responsible for his act unless it is *compelled?* Here we are reminded of Aristotle's assertion (*Nicomachean Ethics*, Book III) that a person is responsible for his act except for reasons of either ignorance or compulsion. Ignorance is not part of our problem here (unless it is unconsciously induced ignorance of facts previously remembered and selectively forgotten—in which case the forgetting is again compulsive), but compulsion is. How will compulsion do as a criterion? The difficulty is to state just what it means. When we say an act is com-

pelled in a psychological sense, our language is metaphorical—which is not to say that there is no point in it or that, properly interpreted, it is not true. Our actions are compelled in a literal sense if someone has us in chains or is controlling our bodily movements. When we say that the storm compelled us to jettison the cargo of the ship (Aristotle's example), we have a less literal sense of compulsion, for at least it is open to us to go down with the ship. When psychoanalysts say that a man was compelled by unconscious conflicts to wash his hands constantly, this is also not a literal use of "compel"; for nobody forced his hands under the tap. Still, it is a typical example of what psychologists call *compulsive* behavior: it has unconscious causes inaccessible to introspection, and moreover nothing can change it—it is as inevitable for him to do it as it would be if someone were forcing his hands under the tap. In this it is exactly like the action of a powerful external force; it is just as little within one's conscious control.

In its area of application this interpretation of responsibility comes to much the same as the previous one. And this area is very great indeed. For if we cannot be held responsible for the infantile situations (in which we were after all passive victims), then neither, it would seem, can we be held responsible for compulsive actions occurring in adulthood that are inevitable consequences of those infantile situations. And, psychiatrists and psychoanalysts tell us, actions fulfilling this description are characteristic of all people some of the time and some people most of the time. Their occurrence, once the infantile events have taken place, is inevitable, just as the explosion is inevitable once the fuse has been lighted; there is simply more "delayed action" in the psychological explosions than there is in the physical ones.

(I have not used the word "inevitable" here to mean "causally determined," for according to such a definition every event would be inevitable if one accepted the causal principle in some form or other; and probably nobody except certain philosophers uses "inevitable" in this sense. Rather, I use "inevitable" in its ordinary sense of "cannot be avoided." To the extent, therefore, that adult neurotic manifestations *can* be avoided, once the infantile patterns have become set, the assertion that they are inevitable is not true.)

5. There is still another criterion, which I prefer to the previous ones, by which a man's responsibility for an act can be measured: the degree to which that act can (or could have been) *changed by the use of reasons.* Suppose that the man who washes his hands constantly does so, he says, for hygienic reasons, believing that if he doesn't do so he will be poisoned by germs. We now convince him, on the best medical authority, that his belief is groundless. Now, the test of his responsibility is whether the changed belief will result in changed behavior. If it does not, as with the compulsive hand-washer, he is not acting responsibly, but if it does, he is. It is not the *use* of reasons, but their *efficacy in changing behavior,* that is being made the criterion of responsibility. And clearly in neurotic cases no such change occurs; in fact, this is often made the defining characteristic of neurotic behavior: it is unchangeable by any rational considerations.

2

I have suggested these criteria to distinguish actions for which we can call the agent responsible from those for which we cannot. Even persons with extensive knowledge of psychiatry do not, I think, use any one of these criteria to the exclusion of the others; a conjunction of two or more may be used at once. But however they may be combined or selected in actual application, I believe we can make the distinction along some such lines as we have suggested.

But is there not still another possible meaning of "responsibility" that we have not yet mentioned? Even after we have made all the above distinctions, there remains a question in our minds whether we are, in the final analysis, *responsible for any of our actions at all*. The issue may be put this way: How can anyone be responsible for his actions, since they grow out of his character, which is shaped and molded and made what it is by influences—some hereditary, but most of them stemming from early parental environment—that were not of his own making or choosing? This question, I believe, still troubles many people who would agree to all the distinctions we have just made but still have the feeling that "this isn't all." They have the uneasy suspicion that there is a more ultimate sense, a "deeper" sense, in which we are *not* responsible for our actions, since we are not responsible for the character out of which those actions spring. This, of course, is the sense Professor Edwards was describing.

Let us take as an example a criminal who, let us say, strangled several persons and is himself now condemned to die in the electric chair. Jury and public alike hold him fully responsible (at least they utter the words "he is responsible"), for the murders were planned down to the minutest detail, and the defendant tells the jury exactly how he planned them. But now we find out how it all came about; we learn of parents who rejected him from babyhood, of the childhood spent in one foster home after another, where it was always plain to him that he was not wanted; of the constantly frustrated early desire for affection, the hard shell of nonchalance and bitterness that he assumed to cover the painful and humiliating fact of being unwanted, and his subsequent attempts to heal these wounds to his shattered ego through defensive aggression.

> The criminal is the most passive person in this world, helpless as a baby in his motorically inexpressible fury. Not only does he try to wreak revenge on the mother of the earliest period of his babyhood; his criminality is based on the inner feeling of being incapable of making the mother even feel that the child seeks revenge on her. The situation is that of a dwarf trying to annoy a giant who superciliously refuses to see these attempts. . . . Because of his inner feeling of being a dwarf, the criminotic uses, so to speak, dynamite. Of that the giant must take cognizance. True, the "revenge" harms the avenger. He may be legally executed. However, the primary inner aim of forcing the giant to acknowledge the dwarf's fury is fulfilled.[1]

The poor victim is not conscious of the inner forces that exact from him this ghastly toll; he battles, he schemes, he revels in pseudo-aggression, he is miserable, but he does not know what works within him to produce these catastrophic acts of crime. His aggressive actions are the wriggling of a worm on a fisherman's hook. And if this is so, it seems difficult to say any longer, "He is responsible." Rather, we shall put him behind bars for the protection of society, but we shall no longer flatter our feeling of moral superiority by calling him personally responsible for what he did.

[1] Edmund Bergler, *The Basic Neurosis* (New York: Grune and Stratton, 1949), p. 305.

Let us suppose it were established that a man commits murder only if, sometime during the previous week, he has eaten a certain combination of foods—say, tuna fish salad at a meal also including peas, mushroom soup, and blueberry pie. What if we were to track down the factors common to all murders committed in this country during the last twenty years and found this factor present in all of them, and only in them? The example is of course empirically absurd; but may it not be that there is *some* combination of factors that regularly leads to homicide, factors such as are described in general terms in the above quotation? (Indeed the situation in the quotation is less fortunate than in our hypothetical example, for it is easy to avoid certain foods once we have been warned about them, but the situation of the infant is thrust on him; something has already happened to him once and for all, before he knows it has happened.) When such specific factors are discovered, won't they make it clear that it is foolish and pointless, as well as immoral, to hold human beings responsible for crimes? Or, if one prefers biological to psychological factors, suppose a neurologist is called in to testify at a murder trial and produces X-ray pictures of the brain of the criminal; anyone can see, he argues, that the *cella turcica* was already calcified at the age of nineteen; it should be a flexible bone, growing, enabling the gland to grow.[2] All the defendant's disorders might have resulted from this early calcification. Now, this particular explanation may be empirically false; but who can say that no such factors, far more complex, to be sure, exist?

When we know such things as these, we no longer feel so much tempted to say that the criminal is responsible for his crime; and we tend also (do we not?) to excuse him—not legally (we still confine him to prison) but morally; we no longer call him a monster or hold him personally responsible for what he did. Moreover, we do this in general, not merely in the case of crime: "You must excuse Grandmother for being irritable; she's really quite ill and is suffering some pain all the time." Or: "The dog always bites children after she's had a litter of pups; you can't blame her for it: she's not feeling well, and besides she naturally wants to defend them." Or: "She's nervous and jumpy, but do excuse her: she has a severe glandular disturbance."

Let us note that the more *thoroughly* and *in detail* we know the causal factors leading a person to behave as he does, the more we tend to exempt him from responsibility. When we know nothing of the man except what we see him do, we say he is an ungrateful cad who expects much of other people and does nothing in return, and we are usually indignant. When we learn that his parents were the same way and, having no guilt feelings about this mode of behavior themselves, brought him up to be greedy and avaricious, we see that we could hardly expect him to have developed moral feelings in this direction. When we learn, in addition, that he is not aware of being ungrateful or selfish, but unconsciously represses the memory of events unfavorable to himself, we feel that the situation is unfortunate but "not really his fault." When we know that this behavior of his, which makes others angry, occurs more constantly when he feels tense or insecure, and that he now feels tense and insecure, and that relief from pressure will diminish it, then we tend to "feel sorry for the poor guy" and say he's more to be pitied than censured. We no longer want to say that he is personally responsible; we might rather blame nature or his parents for having given him an unfortunate constitution or temperament.

[2] Meyer Levin, *Compulsion* (New York: Simon and Schuster, 1956), p. 403.

In recent years a new form of punishment has been imposed on middle-aged and elderly parents. Their children, now in their twenties, thirties or even forties, present them with a modern grievance: "My analysis proves that *you* are responsible for my neurosis." Overawed by these authoritative statements, the poor tired parents fall easy victims to the newest variations on the scapegoat theory.

In my opinion, this senseless cruelty—which disinters educational sins which had been buried for decades, and uses them as the basis for accusations which the victims cannot answer—is unjustified. Yes, "the truth loves to be centrally located" (Melville), and few parents—since they are human—have been perfect. But granting their mistakes, they acted as *their* neurotic difficulties forced them to act. To turn the tables and declare the children not guilty because of the *impersonal* nature of their own neuroses, while at the same time the parents are *personally* blamed, is worse than illogical; it is profoundly unjust.[3]

And so, it would now appear, neither of the parties is responsible: "they acted as their neurotic difficulties forced them to act." The patients are not responsible for their neurotic manifestations, but then neither are the parents responsible for theirs; and so, of course, for their parents in turn, and theirs before them. It is the twentieth-century version of the family curse, the curse on the House of Atreus.

"But," a critic complains, "it's immoral to exonerate people indiscriminately in this way. I might have thought it fit to excuse somebody because he was born on the other side of the tracks, if I didn't know so many bank presidents who were also born on the other side of the tracks." Now, I submit that the most immoral thing in this situation is the critic's caricature of the conditions of the excuse. Nobody is excused merely because he was born on the other side of the tracks. But if he was born on the other side of the tracks *and* was a highly narcissistic infant to begin with *and* was repudiated or neglected by his parents *and* . . . (here we list a finite number of conditions), and if this complex of factors is *regularly* followed by certain behavior traits in adulthood, and moreover *unavoidably* so—that is, they occur no matter what he or anyone else tries to do—then we excuse him morally and say he is not responsible for his deed. If he is not responsible for A, a series of events occurring in his babyhood, then neither is he responsible for B, a series of things he does in adulthood, provided that B inevitably—that is, unavoidably—follows upon the occurrence of A. And according to psychiatrists and psychoanalysts, this often happens.

But one may still object that so far we have talked only about neurotic behavior. Isn't nonneurotic or normal or not unconsciously motivated (or whatever you want to call it) behavior still within the area of responsibility? There are reasons for answering "No" even here; for the normal person no more than the neurotic one has caused his own character, which makes him what he is. Granted that neurotics are not responsible for their behavior (that part of it which we call neurotic) because it stems from undigested infantile conflicts that they had no part in bringing about, and that are external to them just as surely as if their behavior had been forced on them by a malevolent deity (which is indeed one theory on the subject); but the so-called normal person is equally the product of causes in which his volition took no part. And if,

[3] Edmund Bergler, *The Superego* (New York: Grune and Stratton, 1952), p. 320.

unlike the neurotic's, his behavior is changeable by rational considerations, and if he has the willpower to overcome the effects of an unfortunate early environment, this again is no credit to him; he is just lucky. If energy is available to him in a form in which it can be mobilized for constructive purposes, this is no credit to him, for this too is part of his psychic legacy. Those of us who can discipline ourselves and develop habits of concentration of purpose tend to blame those who cannot, and call them lazy and weak-willed; but what we fail to see is that they literally *cannot* do what we expect; if their psyches were structured like ours, they could, but as they are burdened with a tyrannical superego (to use psychoanalytic jargon for the moment), and a weak defenseless ego whose energies are constantly consumed in fighting endless charges of the superego, they simply cannot do it, and it is irrational to expect it of them. We cannot with justification blame them for their inability, any more than we can congratulate ourselves for our ability. This lesson is hard to learn, for we constantly and naïvely assume that other people are constructed as we ourselves are.

For example: A child raised under slum conditions, whose parents are socially ambitious and envy families with money, but who nevertheless squander the little they have on drink, may simply be unable in later life to mobilize a drive sufficient to overcome these early conditions. Common sense would expect that he would develop the virtue of thrift; he would make quite sure that he would never again endure the grinding poverty he had experienced as a child. But in fact it is not so: the exact conditions are too complex to be specified in detail here, but when certain conditions are fulfilled (concerning the subject's early life), he will always thereafter be a spendthrift, and no rational considerations will be able to change this. He will listen to the rational considerations and see the force of these, but they will not be able to change him, even if he tries; he cannot change his wasteful habits any more than he can lift the Empire State Building with his bare hands. We moralize and plead with him to be thrifty, but we do not see how strong, how utterly overpowering, and how constantly with him, is the opposite drive, which is so easily manageable with us. But he is possessed by the all-consuming, all-encompassing urge to make the world see that he belongs, that he has arrived, that he is just as well off as anyone else, that the awful humiliations were not real, that they never actually occurred, for isn't he now able to spend and spend? The humiliation must be blotted out; and conspicuous, flashy, expensive, and wasteful buying will do this; it shows the world what the world must know! True, it is only for the moment; true, it is in the end self-defeating, for wasteful consumption is the best way to bring poverty back again; but the person with an overpowering drive to mend a lesion to his narcissism cannot resist the avalanche of that drive with this puny rational consideration. A man with his back against the wall and a gun at his throat doesn't think of what may happen ten years hence. (Consciously, of course, he knows nothing of this drive; all that appears to consciousness is its shattering effects; he knows only that he must keep on spending —not why—and that he is unable to resist.) He hasn't in him the psychic capacity, the energy to stem the tide of a drive that at that moment is all-powerful. We, seated comfortably away from this flood, sit in judgment on him and blame him and exhort him and criticize him; but he, carried along by the flood, cannot do otherwise than he does. He may fight with all the strength of which he is capable, but it is not enough. And we, who are rational enough at least to exonerate a man in a situation of "overpowering impulse" when we recognize it to be one, do not even recognize this as an example of it; and so, in addition to being swept away in the flood that childhood conditions rendered inevitable, he must also endure our lectures, our criticisms, and our moral excoriation.

But, one will say, he could have overcome his spendthrift tendencies; some people do. Quite true: some people do. They are lucky. They have it in them to overcome early deficiencies by exerting great effort, and they are capable of exerting the effort. Some of us, luckier still, can overcome them with but little effort; and a few, the luckiest, haven't the deficiencies to overcome. It's all a matter of luck. The least lucky are those who can't overcome them, even with great effort, and those who haven't the ability to exert the effort.

But, one persists, it isn't a matter simply of luck; it *is* a matter of effort. Very well then, it's a matter of effort; without exerting the effort you may not overcome the deficiency. But whether or not you are the kind of person who has it in him to exert the effort is a matter of luck.

All this is well known to psychoanalysts. They can predict, from minimal cues that most of us don't notice, whether a person is going to turn out to be lucky or not. "The analyst," they say, "must be able to use the residue of the patient's unconscious guilt so as to remove the symptom or character trait that creates the guilt. The guilt must not only be present, but *available* for use, *mobilizable*. If it is used up (absorbed) in criminal activity, or in an excessive amount of self-damaging tendencies, then it cannot be used for therapeutic purposes, and the prognosis is negative." Not all philosophers will relish the analyst's way of putting the matter, but at least as a physician he can soon detect whether the patient is lucky or unlucky—and he knows that whichever it is, it *isn't the patient's fault*. The patient's conscious volition cannot remedy the deficiency. Even whether he will cooperate with the analyst is really out of the patient's hands: if he continually projects the denying-mother fantasy on the analyst and unconsciously identifies him always with the cruel, harsh forbidder of the nursery, thus frustrating any attempt at impersonal observation, the sessions are useless; yet if it happens that way, he can't help that either. That fatal projection is not under his control; whether it occurs or not depends on how his unconscious identifications have developed since his infancy. He can try, yes—but the ability to try enough for the therapy to have effect is also beyond his control; the capacity to try more than just so much is either there or it isn't—and either way "it's in the lap of the gods."

The position, then, is this: if we *can* overcome the effects of early environment, the ability to do so is itself a product of the early environment. We did not give ourselves this ability; and if we lack it we cannot be blamed for not having it. Sometimes, to be sure, moral exhortation brings out an ability that is there but not being used, and in this lies its *occasional* utility; but very often its use is pointless, because the ability is not there. The only thing that can overcome a desire, as Spinoza said, is a stronger contrary desire; and many times there simply is no wherewithal for producing a stronger contrary desire. Those of us who do have the wherewithal are lucky.

There is one possible practical advantage in remembering this. It may prevent us (unless we are compulsive blamers) from indulging in righteous indignation and committing the sin of spiritual pride, thanking God that we are not as this publican here. And it will protect from our useless moralizings those who are least equipped by nature for enduring them.

As with responsibility, so with deserts. Someone commits a crime and is punished by the state; "he deserved it," we say self-righteously—as if we were moral and he immoral, when in fact we are lucky and he is unlucky—forgetting that there, but for the grace of God and a fortunate early environment, go we. Or, as Clarence Darrow said in his speech for the defense in the Loeb-Leopold case:

> I do not believe that people are in jail because they deserve to be. . . . I know what causes the emotional life. . . . I know it is practically left out of some. Without it they cannot act with the rest. They cannot feel the moral shocks which safeguard others. Is [this man] to blame that his machine is imperfect? Who is to blame? I do not know. I have never in my life been interested so much in fixing blame as I have in relieving people from blame. I am not wise enough to fix it.[4]

3

I want to make it quite clear that I have not been arguing for determinism. Though I find it difficult to give any sense to the term "indeterminism," because I do not know what it would be like to come across an uncaused event, let us grant indeterminists everything they want, at least in words—influences that suggest but do not constrain, a measure of acausality in an otherwise rigidly causal order, and so on— whatever these phrases may mean. With all this granted, exactly the same situation faces the indeterminist and the determinist; all we have been saying would still hold true. "Are our powers innate or acquired?"

> Suppose the powers are declared innate; then the villain may sensibly ask whether he is responsible for what he was born with. A negative reply is inevitable. Are they then acquired? Then the ability to acquire them—was *that* innate? or acquired? It is innate? Very well then. . . .[5]

The same fact remains—that we did not cause our characters, that the influences that made us what we are are influences over which we had no control and of whose very existence we had no knowledge at the time. This fact remains for "determinism" and "indeterminism" alike. And it is this fact to which I would appeal, not the specific tenets of traditional forms of "determinism," which seem to me, when analyzed, empirically empty.

"But," it may be asked, "isn't it your view that nothing ultimately *could* be other than it is? And isn't this deterministic? And isn't it deterministic if you say that human beings could never act otherwise than they do, and that their desires and temperaments could not, when you consider their antecedent conditions, be other than they are?"

I reply that all these charges rest on confusions.

1. To say that nothing *could* be other than it is, is, taken literally, nonsense; and if taken as a way of saying something else, misleading and confusing. If you say, "I

---

[4] Levin, *op. cit.*, pp. 439–40, 469.

[5] W. I. Matson, "The Irrelevance of Free Will to Moral Responsibility," *Mind*, LXV (October 1956), p. 495.

can't do it," this invites the question, "No? Not even if you want to?" "Can" and "could" are power words, used in the context of human action; when applied to nature they are merely anthropomorphic. "Could" has no application to nature—unless, of course, it is uttered in a theological context: one might say that God *could* have made things different. But with regard to inanimate nature "could" has no meaning. Or perhaps it is intended to mean that the order of nature is in some sense *necessary*. But in that case the sense of "necessary" must be specified. I know what "necessary" means when we are talking about propositions, but not when we are talking about the sequence of events in nature.

2. What of the charge that we could never have acted otherwise than we did? This, I submit, is simply not true. Here the exponents of Hume-Mill-Schlick-Ayer "soft determinism" are quite right. I could have gone to the opera today instead of coming here; that is, if certain conditions had been different, I should have gone. I could have done many other things instead of what I did, if some condition or other had been different, specifically if my desire had been different. I repeat that "could" is a power word, and "I could have done this" means approximately "I *should* have done this *if* I had wanted to." In this sense, all of us could often have done otherwise than we did. I would not want to say that I should have done differently even if *all* the conditions leading up to my action had been the same (this is generally not what we mean by "could" anyway); but to assert that I could have is empty, for if I *did* act differently from the time before, we would automatically say that one or more of the conditions were different, whether we had independent evidence for this or not, thus rendering the assertion immune to empirical refutation. (Once again, the vacuousness of "determinism.")

3. Well, then, could we ever have, not acted, but desired otherwise than we did desire? This gets us once again to the heart of the matter we were discussing in the previous section. Russell said, "We can do as we please but we can't please as we please." But I am persuaded that even this statement conceals a fatal mistake. Let us follow the same analysis through. "I could have done X" means "I should have done X if I had wanted to." "I could have wanted X" by the same analysis would mean "I should have wanted X if I had wanted to"—which seems to make no sense at all. (What does Russell want? To please as he doesn't please?)

What does this show? It shows, I think, that the only meaningful context of "can" and "could have" is that of *action*. "Could have acted differently" makes sense; "could have desired differently," as we have just seen, does not. Because a word or phrase makes good sense in one context, let us not assume that it does so in another.

I conclude, then, with the following suggestion: that we operate on two levels of moral discourse, which we shouldn't confuse; one (let's call it the upper level) is that of actions; the other (the lower, or deeper, level) is that of the springs of action. Most moral talk occurs on the upper level. It is on this level that the Hume-Mill-Schlick-Ayer analysis of freedom fully applies. As we have just seen, "can" and "could" acquire their meaning on this level; so, I suspect, does "freedom." So does the distinction between compulsive and noncompulsive behavior, and among the senses of "responsibility," discussed in the first section of this paper, according to which we are responsible for some things and not for others. All these distinctions are perfectly valid on this level (or in this dimension) of moral discourse; and it is, after all, the usual one—we are practical beings interested in changing the course of human behavior, so it is natural enough that 99 per cent of our moral talk occurs here.

But when we descend to what I have called the lower level of moral discourse, as we occasionally do in thoughtful moments when there is no immediate need for action, then we must admit that we are ultimately the kind of persons we are because of conditions occurring outside us, over which we had no control. But while this is true, we should beware of extending the moral terminology we used on the other level to this one also. "Could" and "can," as we have seen, no longer have meaning here. "Right" and "wrong," which apply only to actions, have no meaning here either. I suspect that the same is true of "responsibility," for now that we have recalled often forgotten facts about our being the product of outside forces, we must ask in all seriousness what would be added by saying that we are not *responsible* for our own characters and temperaments. What would it mean even? Has it a significant opposite? What would it be like to be responsible for one's own character? What possible situation is describable by this phrase? Instead of saying that it is *false* that we are responsible for our own characters, I should prefer to say that the utterance is meaningless—meaningless in the sense that it describes no possible situation, though it *seems* to because the word "responsible" is the same one we used on the upper level, where it marks a real distinction. If this is so, the result is that *moral* terms—at least the terms "could have" and "responsible"—simply drop out on the lower level. What remains, shorn now of moral terminology, is the point we tried to bring out in Part II: whether or not we have personality disturbances, whether or not we have the ability to overcome deficiences of early environment, is like the answer to the question whether or not we shall be struck down by a dread disease: "it's all a matter of luck." It is important to keep this in mind, for people almost always forget it, with consequences in human intolerance and unnecessary suffering that are incalculable.

12

FREEDOM

jean-paul sartre

. . .

Atheistic existentialism, of which I am a representative, declares with greater consistency that if God does not exist there is at least one being whose existence comes before its essence, a being which exists before it can be defined by any conception of it. That being is man or, as Heidegger has it, the human reality. What do we mean by saying that existence precedes essence? We mean that man first of all exists, encounters himself, surges up in the world—and defines himself afterwards. If man as the existentialist sees him is not definable, it is because to begin with he is nothing. He will not be anything until later, and then he will be what he makes of himself. Thus, there is no human nature, because there is no God to have a conception of it. Man simply is. Not that he is simply what he conceives himself to be, but he is what he wills, and as he conceives himself after already existing—as he wills to be after that leap towards existence. Man is nothing else but that which he makes of himself. That is the first principle of existentialism. And this is what people call its "subjectivity," using the word as a reproach against us. But what do we mean to say by this, but that man is of a greater dignity than a stone or a table? For we mean to say that man primarily exists—that man is, before all else, something which propels itself towards a future and is aware that it is doing so. Man is, indeed, a project which possesses a subjective life, instead of being a kind of moss, or a fungus or a cauliflower. Before that projection of the self nothing exists; not even in the heaven of intelligence: man will only attain existence when he is what he purposes to be. Not, however, what he may wish to be. For what we usually understand by wishing or willing is a conscious decision taken—much more often than not—after we have made ourselves what we are. I may wish to join a party, to write a book, or to marry—but in such a case what is usually called my will is probably a manifestation of a prior and more spontaneous decision. If, however, it is true that existence is prior to essence, man is responsible for what he is. Thus, the first effect of existentialism is that it puts every man in possession of himself as he is, and places the entire responsibility

From Jean-Paul Sartre, *Existentialism and Humanism*, Philip Mairet, trans. (London: Methuen & Co., Ltd., 1949). Reprinted by permission of Methuen & Co., Ltd. and Philosophical Library.

for his existence squarely upon his own shoulders. And, when we say that man is responsible for himself, we do not mean that he is responsible only for his own individuality, but that he is responsible for all men. The word "subjectivism" is to be understood in two senses, and our adversaries play upon only one of them. Subjectivism means, on the one hand, the freedom of the individual subject and, on the other, that man cannot pass beyond human subjectivity. It is the latter which is the deeper meaning of existentialism. When we say that man chooses himself, we do mean that every one of us must choose himself; but by that we also mean that in choosing for himself he chooses for all men. For, in effect, of all the actions a man may take in order to create himself as he wills to be, there is not one which is not creative, at the same time, of an image of man such as he believes he ought to be. To choose between this or that is at the same time to affirm the value of that which is chosen; for we are unable ever to choose the worse. What we choose is always the better; and nothing can be better for us unless it is better for all. If, moreover, existence precedes essence and we will to exist at the same time as we fashion our image, that image is valid for all and for the entire epoch in which we find ourselves. Our responsibility is thus much greater than we had supposed, for it concerns mankind as a whole. If I am a worker, for instance, I may choose to join a Christian rather than a Communist trade union. And if, by that membership, I choose to signify that resignation is, after all, the attitude that best becomes a man, that man's kingdom is not upon this earth, I do not commit myself alone to that view. Resignation is my will for everyone, and my action is, in consequence, a commitment on behalf of all mankind. Or if, to take a more personal case, I decide to marry and to have children, even though this decision proceeds simply from my situation, from my passion or my desire, I am thereby committing not only myself, but humanity as a whole, to the practice of monogamy. I am thus responsible for myself and for all men, and I am creating a certain image of man as I would have him to be. In fashioning myself I fashion man.

This may enable us to understand what is meant by such terms—perhaps a little grandiloquent—as anguish, abandonment, and despair. As you will soon see, it is very simple. First, what do we mean by anguish? The existentialist frankly states that man is in anguish. His meaning is as follows: When a man commits himself to anything, fully realizing that he is not only choosing what he will be, but is thereby at the same time a legislator deciding for the whole of mankind—in such a moment a man cannot escape from the sense of complete and profound responsibility. There are many, indeed, who show no such anxiety. But we affirm that they are merely disguising their anguish or are in flight from it. Certainly, many people think that in what they are doing they commit no one but themselves to anything: and if you ask them, "What would happen if everyone did so?" they shrug their shoulders and reply, "Everyone does not do so." But in truth, one ought always to ask oneself what would happen if everyone did as one is doing; nor can one escape from that disturbing thought except by a kind of self-deception. The man who lies in self-excuse, by saying "Everyone will not do it" must be ill at ease in his conscience, for the act of lying implies the universal value which it denies. By its very disguise his anguish reveals itself. This is the anguish that Kierkegaard called "the anguish of Abraham." You know the story: An angel commanded Abraham to sacrifice his son: and obedience was obligatory, if it really was an angel who had appeared and said, "Thou, Abraham, shalt sacrifice thy son." But anyone in such a case would wonder, first, whether it was indeed an angel and secondly, whether I am really Abraham. Where are the proofs? A certain mad woman who suffered from hallucinations said that people were telephoning to her, and giving her orders. The doctor asked, "But who is it that speaks to you?" She replied: "He says it is God." And what, indeed, could prove to her that it was God? If an angel appears to me, what is the proof that it is an angel; or, if I hear voices, who can prove that they proceed from heaven and not from hell, or from my own subconsciousness or some pathological condition? Who can prove that they are really addressed to me?

Who, then, can prove that I am the proper person to impose, by my own choice, my conception of man upon mankind? I shall never find any proof whatever; there will be no sign to convince me of it. If a voice speaks to me, it is still I myself who must decide whether the voice is or is not that of an angel. If I regard a certain course of action as good, it is only I who choose to say that it is good and not bad. There is nothing to show that I am Abraham: nevertheless I also am obliged at every instant to perform actions which are examples. Everything happens to every man as though the whole human race had its eyes fixed upon what he is doing and regulated its conduct accordingly. So every man ought to say, "Am I really a man who has the right to act in such a manner that humanity regulates itself by what I do." If a man does not say that, he is dissembling his anguish. Clearly, the anguish with which we are concerned here is not one that could lead to quietism or inaction. It is anguish pure and simple, of the kind well known to all those who have borne responsibilities. When, for instance, a military leader takes upon himself the responsibility for an attack and sends a number of men to their death, he chooses to do it and at bottom he alone chooses. No doubt he acts under a higher command, but its orders, which are more general, require interpretation by him and upon that interpretation depends the life of ten, fourteen, or twenty men. In making the decision, he cannot but feel a certain anguish. All leaders know that anguish. It does not prevent their acting; on the contrary, it is the very condition of their action, for the action presupposes that there is a plurality of possibilities, and in choosing one of these, they realize that it has value only because it is chosen. Now it is anguish of that kind which existentialism describes, and moreover, as we shall see, makes explicit through direct responsibility toward other men who are concerned. Far from being a screen which could separate us from action, it is a condition of action itself.

And when we speak of "abandonment"—a favorite word of Heidegger—we only mean to say that God does not exist, and that it is necessary to draw the consequences of his absence right to the end. The existentialist is strongly opposed to a certain type of secular moralism which seeks to suppress God at the least possible expense. Towards 1880, when the French professors endeavored to formulate a secular morality, they said something like this: God is a useless and costly hypothesis, so we will do without it. However, if we are to have morality, a society, and a law-abiding world, it is essential that certain values should be taken seriously; they must have an *a priori* existence ascribed to them. It must be considered obligatory *a priori* to be honest, not to lie, not to beat one's wife, to bring up children, and so forth; so we are going to do a little work on this subject, which will enable us to show that these values exist all the same, inscribed in an intelligible heaven although, of course, there is no God. In other words—and this is, I believe, the purport of all that we in France call radicalism—nothing will be changed if God does not exist; we shall rediscover the same norms of honesty, progress, and humanity, and we shall have disposed of God as an out-of-date hypothesis which will die away quietly of itself. The existentialist, on the contrary, finds it extremely embarrassing that God does not exist, for there disappears with Him all possibility of finding values in an intelligible heaven. There can no longer be any good *a priori,* since there is no infinite and perfect consciousness to think it. It is nowhere written that "the good" exists, that one must be honest or must not lie, since we are now upon the plane where there are only men. Dostoyevsky once wrote "If God did not exist, everything would be permitted"; and that, for existentialism, is the starting point. Everything is indeed permitted if God does not exist, and man is in consequence forlorn, for he cannot find anything to depend upon either within or outside himself. He discovers forthwith, that he is without excuse. For if, indeed, existence precedes essence, one will never be able to explain one's action by reference to a given and specific human nature; in other words, there is no determinism—man is free, man *is* freedom. Nor, on the other hand, if God does not exist, are we provided with any values or commands that could legitimize our behavior. Thus we have neither behind us, nor before us in a luminous realm of values, any means of justification or excuse. We are left alone, without excuse. That is what I mean when I say that man is condemned to be free. Condemned, because he did not create himself, yet is nevertheless at liberty, and from the moment that he is thrown into this world he is responsible for everything he does. The existentialist does not believe in the power of passion. He will never regard a grand passion as a destructive torrent upon which a man is swept into certain actions as by fate, and which, therefore, is an excuse for them. He thinks that man is responsible for his passion. Neither will an existentialist think that a man can find help through some sign being vouchsafed upon earth for his orientation: for he thinks that the man himself interprets the sign as he chooses. He thinks that every man, without any support or help whatever, is condemned at every instant to invent man. As Ponge has written in a very fine article, "Man is the future of man." That is exactly true. Only, if one took this to mean that the future is laid up in Heaven, that God knows what it is, it would be false, for then it would no longer even be a future. If, however, it means that, whatever man may now appear to be, there is a future to be fashioned, a virgin future that awaits him—then it is a true saying. But in the present, one is forsaken.

As an example by which you may the better understand this state of abandonment, I will refer to the case of a pupil of mine, who sought me out in the following circumstances. His father was quarrelling with his mother and was also inclined to be a "collaborator"; his elder brother had been killed in the German offensive of 1940 and this young man, with a sentiment somewhat primitive but generous, burned to avenge him. His mother was living alone with him, deeply afflicted by the semi-treason of his father and by the death of her eldest son, and her one consolation was in this young man. But he, at this moment, had the choice between going to England to join the Free French Forces or of staying near his mother and helping her to live. He fully realized that this woman lived only for him and that his disappearance—or perhaps his death—would plunge her into despair. He also realized that, concretely and in fact, every action he performed on his mother's behalf would be sure of effect in the sense of aiding her to live, whereas anything he did in order to go and fight would be an ambiguous action which might vanish like water into sand and serve no purpose. For instance, to set out for England he would have to wait indefinitely in a Spanish camp on the way through Spain; or, on arriving in England or in Algiers, he might be put into an office to fill up forms. Consequently, he found himself confronted by two very different modes of action: the one concrete, immediate, but directed towards only one individual; and the other an action addressed to an end infinitely greater, a national collectivity, but for that very reason ambiguous—and it might be frustrated on the way. At the same time, he was hesitating between two kinds of morality; on the one side the morality of sympathy, of personal devotion, and, on the other side, a morality of wider scope but of more debatable validity. He had to choose between those two. What could help him to choose? Could the Christian doctrine? No. Christian doctrine says: Act with charity, love your neighbor, deny yourself for others, choose the way which is hardest, and so forth. But which is the harder road? To whom does one owe the more brotherly love, the patriot or the mother? Which is the more useful aim, the general one of fighting in and for the whole community, or the precise aim of helping one particular person to live? Who can give an answer to that *a priori?* No one. Nor is it given in any ethical scripture. The Kantian ethic says, Never regard another as a means, but always as an end. Very well; if I remain with my mother, I shall be regarding her as the end and not as a means: but by the same token I am in danger of treating as means those who are fighting on my behalf; and the converse is also true, that if I go to the aid of the combatants I shall be treating them as the end at the risk of treating my mother as a means.

If values are uncertain, if they are still too abstract to determine the particular, concrete case under consideration, nothing remains but to trust in our instincts. That is what this young man tried to do; and when I saw him he said, "In the end, it is feeling that counts; the direction in which it is really pushing me is the one I ought to choose. If I feel that I love my mother enough to sacrifice everything else for her —my will to be avenged, all my longings for action and adventure—then I stay with her. If, on the contrary, I feel that my love for her is not enough, I go." But how does one estimate the strength of a feeling? The value of his feeling for his mother was determined precisely by the fact that he was standing by her. I may say that I love a certain friend enough to sacrifice such or such a sum of money for him, but I cannot prove that unless I have done it. I may say, "I love my mother enough to remain with her," if actually I have remained with her. I can only estimate the strength of this affection if I have performed an action by which it is defined and ratified. But if I then appeal to this affection to justify my action, I find myself drawn into a vicious circle.

Moreover, as Gide has very well said, a sentiment which is play-acting and one which is vital are two things that are hardly distinguishable one from another. To decide that I love my mother by staying beside her, and to play a comedy the upshot of which is that I do so—these are nearly the same thing. In other words, feeling is formed by the deeds that one does; therefore I cannot consult it as a guide to action. And that is to say that I can neither seek within myself for an authentic impulse to action, nor can I expect, from some ethic, formulae that will enable me to act. You may say that the youth did, at least, go to a professor to ask for advice. But if you seek counsel—from a priest, for example—you have selected that priest; and at bottom you already knew, more or less, what he would advise. In other words, to choose an adviser is nevertheless to commit oneself by that choice. If you are a Christian, you will say, Consult a priest; but there are collaborationists, priests who are resisters, and priests who wait for the tide to turn: which will you choose? Had this young man chosen a priest of the resistance, or one of the collaboration, he would have decided beforehand the kind of advice he was to receive. Similarly, in coming to me, he knew what advice I should give him, and I had but one reply to make. You are free, therefore choose—that is to say, invent. No rule of general morality can show you what you ought to do: no signs are vouchsafed in this world. The Catholics will reply, "Oh, but they are!" Very well; still, it is I myself, in every case, who have to interpret the signs. While I was imprisoned, I made the acquaintance of a somewhat remarkable man, a Jesuit, who had become a member of that order in the following manner. In his life he had suffered a succession of rather severe setbacks. His father had died when he was a child, leaving him in poverty, and he had been awarded a free scholarship in a religious institution, where he had been made continually to feel that he was accepted for charity's sake, and, in consequence, he had been denied several of those distinctions and honors which gratify children. Later, about the age of eighteen, he came to grief in a sentimental affair; and finally, at twenty-two—this was a trifle in itself, but it was the last drop that overflowed his cup—he failed in his military examination. This young man, then, could regard himself as a total failure: it was a sign—but a sign of what? He might have taken refuge in bitterness or despair. But he took it—very cleverly for him—as a sign that he was not intended for secular successes, and that only the attainments of religion, those of sanctity and of faith, were accessible to him. He interpreted his record as a message from God, and became a member of the Order. Who can doubt but that this decision as to the meaning of the sign was his, and his alone? One could have drawn quite different conclusions from such a series of reverses—as, for example, that he had better become a carpenter or a revolutionary. For the decipherment of the sign, however, he bears the entire responsibility. That is what "abandonment" implies, that we ourselves decide our being. And with this abandonment goes anguish.

As for "despair," the meaning of this expression is extremely simple. It merely means that we limit ourselves to a reliance upon that which is within our wills, or within the sum of the probabilities which render our action feasible. Whenever one wills anything, there are always these elements of probability. If I am counting upon a visit from a friend, who may be coming by train or by tram, I presuppose that the train will arrive at the appointed time, or that the tram will not be derailed. I remain in the realm of possibilities; but one does not rely upon any possibilities beyond those that are strictly concerned in one's action. Beyond the point at which the possibilities under consideration cease to affect my action, I ought to disinterest myself. For there is no God and no prevenient design, which can adapt the world and all its possibilities to my will. When Descartes said, "Conquer yourself rather than the world," what he meant was, at bottom, the same—that we should act without hope.

Marxists, to whom I have said this, have answered: "Your action is limited, obviously, by your death; but you can rely upon the help of others. That is, you can count both upon what the others are doing to help you elsewhere, as in China and in Russia, and upon what they will do later, after your death, to take up your action and carry it forward to its final accomplishment which will be the revolution. Moreover you must rely upon this; not to do so is immoral." To this I rejoin, first, that I shall always count upon my comrades-in-arms in the struggle, in so far as they are committed, as I am, to a definite, common cause; and in the unity of a party or a group which I can more or less control—that is, in which I am enrolled as a militant and whose movements at every moment are known to me. In that respect, to rely upon the unity and the will of the party is exactly like my reckoning that the train will run to time or that the tram will not be derailed. But I cannot count upon men whom I do not know, I cannot base my confidence upon human goodness or upon man's interest in the good of society, seeing that man is free and that there is no human nature which I can take as foundational. I do not know where the Russian revolution will lead. I can admire it and take it as an example in so far as it is evident, today, that the proletariat plays a part in Russia which it has attained in no other nation. But I cannot affirm that this will necessarily lead to the triumph of the proletariat: I must confine myself to what I can see. Nor can I be sure that comrades-in-arms will take up my work after my death and carry it to the maximum perfection, seeing that those men are free agents and will freely decide, tomorrow, what man is then to be. Tomorrow, after my death, some men may decide to establish Fascism, and the others may be so cowardly or so slack as to let them do so. If so, Fascism will then be the truth of man, and so much the worse for us. In reality, things will be such as men have decided they shall be. Does that mean that I should abandon myself to quietism? No. First I ought to commit myself and then act my commitment, according to the time-honored formula that "one need not hope in order to undertake one's work." Nor does this mean that I should not belong to a party, but only that I should be without illusion and that I should do what I can. For instance, if I ask myself "Will the social ideal as such, ever become a reality?" I cannot tell, I only know that whatever may be in my power to make it so, I shall do; beyond that, I can count upon nothing.

Quietism is the attitude of people who say, "let others do what I cannot do." The doctrine I am presenting before you is precisely the opposite of this, since it declares that there is no reality except in action. It goes further, indeed, and adds, "Man is nothing else but what he purposes, he exists only in so far as he realizes himself, he is therefore nothing else but the sum of his actions, nothing else but what his life is." Hence we can well understand why some people are horrified by our teaching. For many have but one resource to sustain them in their misery, and that is to think, "Circumstances have been against me; I was worthy to be something much better than I have been. I admit I have never had a great love or a great friendship; but that is because I never met a man or a woman who were worthy of it; if I have not written any very good books, it is because I had not the leisure to do so; or, if I have had no children to whom I could devote myself it is because I did not find the man I could have lived with. So there remains within me a wide range of abilities, inclinations, and potentialities, unused but perfectly viable, which endow me with a worthiness that could never be inferred from the mere history of my actions." But in reality, and for the existentialist, there is no love apart from the deeds of love; no potentiality of love other than that which is manifested in loving; there is no genius other than that which is expressed in works of art. The genius of Proust is the totality of the works of Proust; the genius of Racine is the series of his tragedies, outside of which there is nothing. Why should we attribute to Racine the capacity to write yet another tragedy when that is precisely what he did not write? In life, a man commits himself, draws his own portrait and there is nothing but that portrait. No doubt this thought may seem comfortless to one who has not made a success of his life. On the other hand, it puts everyone in a position to understand that reality alone is reliable; that dreams, expectations, and hopes serve to define a man only as deceptive dreams, abortive hopes, expectations unfulfilled; that is to say, they define him negatively, not positively. Nevertheless, when one says, "You are nothing else but what you live," it does not imply that an artist is to be judged solely by his works of art, for a thousand other things contribute no less to his definition as a man. What we mean to say is that a man is no other than a series of undertakings, that he is the sum, the organization, the set of relations, that constitute these undertakings.

In the light of all this, what people reproach us with is not, after all, our pessimism, but the sternness of our optimism. If people condemn our works of fiction, in which we describe characters that are base, weak, cowardly, and sometimes even frankly evil, it is not only because those characters are base, weak, cowardly, or evil. For suppose that, like Zola, we showed that the behavior of these characters was caused by their heredity, or by the action of their environment upon them, or by determining factors, psychic or organic. People would be reassured; they would say, "You see, that is what we are like, no one can do anything about it." But the existentialist, when he portrays a coward, shows him as responsible for his cowardice. He is not like that on account of a cowardly heart or lungs or cerebrum; he has not become like that through his physiological organism; he is like that because he has made himself into a coward by his actions. There is no such thing as a cowardly temperament. There are nervous temperaments; there is what is called impoverished blood, and there are also rich temperaments. But the man whose blood is poor is not a coward for all that, for what produces cowardice is the act of giving up or giving way; and a temperament is not an action. A coward is defined by the deed that he has done. What people feel obscurely, and with horror, is that the coward as we present him is guilty of being a coward. What people would prefer would be to be born either a coward or a hero. One of the charges most often laid against the *Chemins de la Liberté* is something like this—"But, after all, these people being so base, how can you make them into heroes?" That objection is really rather comic, for it implies that people are born heroes: and that is, at bottom, what such people would like to think. If you are born cowards, you can be quite content: you can do nothing about it and you will be cowards all your lives whatever you do; and if you are born heroes you can again be quite content: you will be heroes all your lives, eating and drinking heroically. Whereas the existentialist says that the coward makes himself cowardly, the hero makes himself heroic; and that there is always a possibility for the coward to give up cowardice and for the hero to stop being a hero. What counts is the total commitment, and it is not by a particular case or particular action that you are committed altogether.

We have now, I think, dealt with a certain number of the reproaches against existentialism. You have seen that it cannot be regarded as a philosophy of quietism since it defines man by his action; nor as a pessimistic description of man, for no doctrine is more optimistic: the destiny of man is placed within himself. Nor is it an attempt to discourage man from action, since it tells him that there is no hope except in his action, and that the one thing which permits him to have life is the deed. Upon this level therefore, what we are considering is an ethic of action and self-commitment. However, we are still reproached, upon these few data, for confining man within his individual subjectivity. There again people badly misunderstand us.

Our point of departure is, indeed, the subjectivity of the individual, and that for strictly philosophic reasons. It is not because we are bourgeois, but because we seek to base our teaching upon the truth, and not upon a collection of fine theories, full of hope but lacking real foundations. And at the point of departure there cannot be any other truth than this: *I think, therefore I am,* which is the absolute truth of consciousness as it attains to itself. Every theory which begins with man, outside of this moment of self-attainment, is a theory which thereby suppresses the truth, for outside of the Cartesian *cogito,* all objects are no more than probable, and any doctrine of probabilities which is not attached to a truth will crumble into nothing. In order to define the probable one must possess the true. Before there can be any truth whatever, then, there must be an absolute truth, and there is such a truth which is simple, easily attained, and within the reach of everybody; it consists in one's immediate sense of one's self.

In the second place, this theory alone is compatible with the dignity of man: it is the only one which does not make man into an object. All kinds of materialism lead one to treat every man including oneself as an object—that is, as a set of pre-determined reactions, in no way different from the patterns of qualities and phenomena which constitute a table, or a chair, or a stone. Our aim is precisely to establish the human kingdom as a pattern of values in distinction from the material world. But the subjectivity which we thus postulate as the standard of truth is no narrowly individual subjectivism, for as we have demonstrated, it is not only one's own self that one discovers in the *cogito,* but those of others too. Contrary to the philosophy of Descartes, contrary to that of Kant, when we say "I think" we are attaining to ourselves in the presence of the other, and we are just as certain of the other as we are of ourselves. Thus the man who discovers himself directly in the *cogito* also discovers all the others, and discovers them as the condition of his own existence. He recognizes that he cannot be anything (in the sense in which one says one is spiritual, or that one is wicked or jealous) unless others recognize him as such. I cannot obtain any truth whatsoever about myself, except through the mediation of another. The other is indispensable to my existence, and equally so to any knowledge I can have of myself. Under these conditions, the intimate discovery of myself is at the same time the revelation of the other as a freedom which confronts mine, and which cannot think or will without doing so either for or against me. Thus, at once, we find ourselves in a world which is, let us say, that of "inter-subjectivity." It is in this world that man has to decide what he is and what others are.

Furthermore, although it is impossible to find in each and every man a universal essence that can be called human nature, there is nevertheless a human universality of *condition.* It is not by chance that the thinkers of today are so much more ready to speak of the condition than of the nature of man. By his condition they understand, with more or less clarity, all the *limitations* which *a priori* define man's fundamental situation in the universe. His historical situations are variable: man may be born a slave in a pagan society, or may be a feudal baron, or a proletarian. But what never vary are the necessities of being in the world, of having to labor and to die there. These limitations are neither subjective nor objective, or rather there is both a subjective and an objective aspect of them. Objective, because we meet with them everywhere and they are everywhere recognizable; and subjective because they are *lived* and are nothing if man does not live them—if, that is to say, he does not freely determine himself and his existence in relation to them. And, diverse though man's purposes may be, at least none of them is wholly foreign to me, since every human purpose presents itself as an attempt either to surpass these limitations, or to widen them, or else to deny or to accommodate oneself to them. Consequently every purpose, however individual it may be, is of universal value. Every purpose, even that of a Chinese, an Indian, or a Negro, can be understood by a European. To say it can be understood, means that the European of 1945 may be striving out of a certain situation towards the same limitations in the same way, and that he may reconceive in himself the purpose of the Chinese, of the Indian or the African. In every purpose there is universality, in this sense that every purpose is comprehensible to every man. Not that this or that purpose defines man for ever, but that it may be entertained again and again. There is always some way of understanding an idiot, a child, a primitive man or a foreigner if one has sufficient information. In this sense we may say that there is a human universality, but it is not something given; it is being perpetually made. I make this universality in choosing myself; I also make it by understanding the purpose of any other man, of whatever epoch. This absoluteness of the act of choice does not alter the relativity of each epoch.

What is at the very heart and center of existentialism, is the absolute character of the free commitment, by which every man realizes himself in realizing a type of humanity—a commitment always understandable, to no matter whom in no matter what epoch—and its bearing upon the relativity of the cultural pattern which may result from such absolute commitment. One must observe equally the relativity of Cartesianism and the absolute character of the Cartesian commitment. In this sense you may say, if you like, that every one of us makes the absolute by breathing, by eating, by sleeping or by behaving in any fashion whatsoever. There is no difference between free being—being as self-committal, as existence choosing its essence—and absolute being. And there is no difference whatever between being as an absolute, temporarily localized—that is, localized in history—and universally intelligible being.

This does not completely refute the charge of subjectivism. Indeed that objection appears in several other forms, of which the first is as follows. People say to us, "Then it does not matter what you do," and they say this in various ways. First they tax us with anarchy; then they say, "You cannot judge others, for there is no reason for preferring one purpose to another"; finally, they may say, "Everything being merely voluntary in this choice of yours, you give away with one hand what you pretend to gain with the other." These three are not very serious objections. As to the first, to say that it does not matter what you choose is not correct. In one sense choice is possible, but what is not possible is not to choose. I can always choose, but I must know that if I do not choose, that is still a choice. This, although it may appear merely formal, is of great importance as a limit to fantasy and caprice. For, when I confront a real situation—for example, that I am a sexual being, able to have relations with a being of the other sex and able to have children—I am obliged to choose my attitude to it, and in every respect I bear the responsibility of the choice which, in committing myself, also commits the whole of humanity. Even if my choice is determined by no *a priori* value whatever, it can have nothing to do with caprice: and if anyone thinks that this is only Gide's theory of the *acte gratuit* over again, he has failed to see the enormous difference between this theory and that of Gide. Gide does not know what a situation is; his "act" is one of pure caprice. In our view, on the contrary, man finds himself in an organized situation in which he is himself involved: his choice involves mankind in its entirety, and he cannot avoid choosing. Either he must remain single, or he must marry without having children, or he must marry and have children. In any case, and whichever he may choose, it is impossible for him, in respect of this situation, not to take complete responsibility. Doubtless he chooses without reference to any pre-established values, but it is unjust to tax him with caprice. Rather let us say that the moral choice is comparable to the construction of a work of art.

But here I must at once digress to make it quite clear that we are not propounding an aesthetic morality, for our adversaries are disingenuous enough to reproach us even with that. I mention the work of art only by way of comparison. That being understood, does anyone reproach an artist, when he paints a picture, for not following rules established *a priori?* Does one ever ask what is the picture that he ought to paint? As everyone knows, there is no pre-defined picture for him to make; the artist applies himself to the composition of a picture, and the picture that ought to be made is precisely that which he will have made. As everyone knows, there are no aesthetic values *a priori,* but there are values which will appear in due course in the coherence of the picture, in the relation between the will to create and the finished work. No one can tell what the painting of tomorrow will be like; one cannot judge a painting until it is done. What has that to do with morality? We are in the same creative situation. We never speak of a work of art as irresponsible; when we are discussing a canvas by Picasso, we understand very well that the composition became what it is at the time when he was painting it, and that his works are part and parcel of his entire life.

It is the same upon the plane of morality. There is this in common between art and morality, that in both we have to do with creation and invention. We cannot decide *a priori* what it is that should be done. I think it was made sufficiently clear to you in the case of that student who came to see me, that to whatever ethical system he might appeal, the Kantian or any other, he could find no sort of guidance whatever; he was obliged to invent the law for himself. Certainly we cannot say that this man, in choosing to remain with his mother—that is, in taking sentiment, personal devotion and concrete charity as his moral foundations—would be making an irresponsible choice, nor could we do so if he preferred the sacrifice of going away to England. Man makes himself; he is not found ready-made; he makes himself by the choice of his morality, and he cannot but choose a morality, such is the pressure of circumstances upon him. We define man only in relation to his commitments; it is therefore absurd to reproach us for irresponsibility in our choice.

In the second place, people say to us, "You are unable to judge others." This is true in one sense and false in another. It is true in this sense, that whenever a man chooses his purpose and his commitment in all clearness and in all sincerity, whatever that purpose may be, it is impossible for him to prefer another. It is true in the sense that we do not believe in progress. Progress implies amelioration; but man is always the same, facing a situation which is always changing, and choice remains always a choice in the situation. The moral problem has not changed since the time when it was a choice between slavery and anti-slavery—from the time of the war of Secession, for example, until the present moment when one chooses between the M.R.P. [*Mouvement Rèpublicain Populaire*] and the Communists.

We can judge, nevertheless, for, as I have said, one chooses in view of others, and in view of others one chooses himself. One can judge, first—and perhaps this is not a judgment of value, but it is a logical judgment—that in certain cases choice is founded upon an error, and in others upon the truth. One can judge a man by saying that he deceives himself. Since we have defined the situation of man as one of free choice, without excuse and without help, any man who takes refuge behind the excuse of his passions, or by inventing some deterministic doctrine, is a self-deceiver. One may object: "But why should he not choose to deceive himself?" I reply that it is not for me to judge him morally, but I define his self-deception as an error. Here one cannot avoid pronouncing a judgment of truth. The self-deception is evidently a falsehood, because it is a dissimulation of man's complete liberty of commitment. Upon this same level, I say that it is also a self-deception if I choose to declare that certain values are incumbent upon me; I am in contradiction with myself if I will these values and at the same time say that they impose themselves upon me. If anyone says to me, "And what if I wish to deceive myself?" I answer, "There is no reason why you should not, but I declare that you are doing so, and that the attitude of strict consistency alone is that of good faith." Furthermore, I can pronounce a moral judgment. For I declare that freedom, in respect of concrete circumstances, can have no other end and aim but itself; and when once a man has seen that values depend upon himself, in that state of forsakenness he can will only one thing, and that is freedom as the foundation of all values. That does not mean that he wills it in the abstract: it simply means that the actions of men of good faith have, as their ultimate significance, the quest of freedom itself as such. A man who belongs to some communist or revolutionary society wills certain concrete ends, which imply the will to freedom, but that freedom is willed in community. We will freedom for freedom's sake, in and through particular circumstances. And in thus willing freedom, we discover that it depends entirely upon the freedom of others and that the freedom of others depends upon our own. Obviously, freedom as the definition of a man does not depend upon others, but as soon as there is a commitment, I am obliged to will the liberty of others at the same time as my own. I cannot make liberty my aim unless I make that of others equally my aim. Consequently, when I recognize, as entirely authentic, that man is a being whose existence precedes his essence, and that he is a free being who cannot, in any circumstances, but will his freedom, at the same time I realize that I cannot not will the freedom of others. Thus, in the name of that will to freedom which is implied in freedom itself, I can form judgments upon those who seek to hide from themselves the wholly voluntary nature of their existence and its complete freedom. Those who hide from this total freedom, in a guise of solemnity or with deterministic excuses, I shall call cowards. Others, who try to show that their existence is necessary, when it is merely an accident of the appearance of the human race on earth—I shall call scum. But neither cowards nor scum can be identified except upon the plane of strict authenticity. Thus, although the content of morality is variable, a certain form of this morality is universal. Kant declared that freedom is a will both to itself and to the freedom of others. Agreed: but he thinks that the formal and the universal suffice for the constitution of a morality. We think, on the contrary, that principles that are too abstract break down when we come to defining action. To take once again the case of that student; by what authority, in the name of what golden rule of morality, do you think he could have decided, in perfect peace of mind, either to abandon his mother or to remain with her? There are no means of judging. The content is always concrete, and therefore unpredictable; it has always to be invented. The one thing that counts, is to know whether the invention is made in the name of freedom.

Let us, for example, examine the two following cases, and you will see how far they are similar in spite of their difference. Let us take *The Mill on the Floss*. We find here a certain young woman, Maggie Tulliver, who is an incarnation of the value of passion and is aware of it. She is in love with a young man, Stephen, who is engaged to another, an insignificant young woman. This Maggie Tulliver, instead of heedlessly seeking her own happiness, chooses in the name of human solidarity to sacrifice herself and to give up the man she loves. On the other hand, La Sanseverina in Stendhal's *Chartreuse de Parme,* believing that it is passion which endows man with his real value, would have declared that a grand passion justifies its sacrifices, and must be preferred to the banality of such conjugal love as would unite Stephen to the little goose he was engaged to marry. It is the latter that she would have chosen to sacrifice in realizing her own happiness, and, as Stendhal shows, she would also sacrifice herself upon the plane of passion if life made that demand upon her. Here we are facing two clearly opposed moralities; but I claim that they are equivalent, seeing that in both cases the overruling aim is freedom. You can imagine two attitudes exactly similar in effect, in that one girl might prefer, in resignation, to give up her lover while the other preferred, in fulfillment of sexual desire, to ignore the prior engagement of the man she loved; and, externally, these two cases might appear the same as the two we have just cited, while being in fact entirely different. The attitude of La Sanseverina is much nearer to that of Maggie Tulliver than to one of careless greed. Thus, you see, the second objection is at once true and false. One can choose anything, but only if it is upon the plane of free commitment.

The third objection, stated by saying, "You take with one hand what you give with the other," means, at bottom, "your values are not serious, since you choose them yourselves." To that I can only say that I am very sorry that it should be so; but if I have excluded God the Father, there must be somebody to invent values. We have to take things as they are. And moreover, to say that we invent values means neither more nor less than this; that there is no sense in life *a priori.* Life is nothing until it is lived; but it is yours to make sense of, and the value of it is nothing else but the sense that you choose. . . .

·   ·   ·

13

FREEDOM AND RESPONSIBILITY

p. h. nowell-smith

I

1

We have now to consider the logic of the language which we use to ascribe responsibility, to award praise and blame, and to justify our moral verdicts. I shall consider five types of moral judgement.

He broke a law or moral rule.	(1)
He could have acted otherwise.	(2)
He deserves censure (or punishment).	(3)
It would be just to censure (or punish) him.	(4)
He is a bad (cruel, mean, dishonest, etc.) man.	(5)

It is clear that all these are logically connected. It is not just a fact about the world that we learn from experience that only bad men deserve blame or that it is only just to blame those who could have acted otherwise. Yet the items cannot all be treated as analytically connected; for we should then find that it was senseless to ask certain questions that obviously do make sense.

. . .

2

The most difficult and important of the items on our list of moral judgements is "He could have acted otherwise" (2). The facts about its logical connections with the others are tolerably clear. It is a necessary condition of all except (1) and it is also a necessary condition of (1) if "He broke a law" is taken to imply that he broke it voluntarily. What is not so clear is what (2) means or why it should be a necessary condition of the other items.

From P. H. Nowell-Smith, *Ethics* (Harmondsworth, England: Penguin Books Ltd., 1954), Chaps. 19, 20, pp. 270–285, 291–297. Reprinted by permission of the publisher.

A man is not considered blameworthy if he could not have acted otherwise; and, although it is often easy to decide in practice whether he could have acted otherwise or not, it is not clear how we do this or why we should think it necessary to do it. Let us first examine the use of "could have" in some nonmoral cases.

"Could have" is a modal phrase, and modal phrases are not normally used to make straightforward, categorical statements. "It might have rained last Thursday" tells you something about the weather, but not in the way that "It rained last Thursday" does. It is sometimes said that it is used to express the speaker's ignorance of the weather; but what it expresses is not just this but his ignorance of any facts that would strongly tend to rule out the truth of "It rained." It would be a natural thing to say in the middle of an English, but not of a Californian summer. But, whatever it does express, what it does *not* express is a belief in a third alternative alongside "it rained" and "it did not rain." Either it rained or it did not; and "it might have rained" does not represent a third alternative which excludes the other two in the way that these exclude each other.

But these modal phrases are also sometimes used in cases in which they cannot express ignorance since they imply a belief that the event concerned did not occur. It would be disingenuous for a rich man to say "I might have been a rich man"; but he could well say "I might have been a poor man" while knowing himself to be rich. The puzzle here arises from the fact that, if he is rich, he cannot be poor. His actual riches preclude his possible poverty in a way that would seem to imply that we could have no use for "He might have been poor." But this is only puzzling so long as we try to treat these modal expressions in a categorical way.

"Would have" and "might have" are clearly suppressed hypotheticals, incomplete without an "if . . ." or an "if . . . not. . . ." Nobody would say "Jones would have won the championship" unless (a) he believed that Jones did not win and (b) he was prepared to add "if he had entered" or "if he had not sprained his ankle" or some such clause.

It is not so obvious that "could have" sentences also express hypotheticals; indeed in some cases they obviously do not. If a man says "It could have been a Morris, but actually it was an Austin," it would be absurd to ask him under what conditions it could or would have been a Morris. "Could have" is here used to concede that, although I happen to know it was an Austin, your guess that it was a Morris was not a bad one. But "could have" also has a use which is more important for our purpose and in which, as I shall try to show, it is equivalent to "would have . . . if. . . ." It refers to a tendency or capacity. Consider the following examples:

(1) He could have read *Emma* in bed last night, though he actually read *Persuasion;* but he could not have read *Werther* because he does not know German.

(2) He could have played the *Appassionata,* though he actually played the *Moonlight;* but he could not have played the *Hammerklavier,* because it is too difficult for him.

These are both statements, since they could be true or false; and to understand their logic we must see how they would be established or rebutted. Neither could be established or rebutted in the way that "He read *Persuasion*" could, by observing what he actually did; and it is partly for this reason that we do not call them categorical. But, although they could not be directly verified or falsified by observation of what he did, this might be relevant evidence. It would be almost conclusive evidence in the first case, since it would be very odd if a man who actually read

Persuasion was incapable of reading *Emma*. On the other hand, his having played the *Moonlight* is only weak evidence that he could have played the *Appassionata,* since the latter is more difficult and also because he might never have learned it.

In each of these cases, in order to establish the "could have" statement we should have to show (a) that he has performed tasks of similar difficulty sufficiently often to preclude the possibility of a fluke, and (b) that nothing prevented him on this occasion. For example we should have to establish that there was a copy of *Emma* in the house.

Statements about capacities, whether of the "can" or of the "could have" kind, contextually imply unspecified conditions under which alone the person might succeed; and "could have" statements can be refuted either by showing that some necessary condition was absent (there was no copy of *Emma*) or by showing that the capacity was absent. The first point could be established directly. How could the second be established? In practice we do this either by appealing to past performances or failures or by asking him to try to do it now. It is clear that neither of these methods could be applied directly to the occasion in question. We know that he did not read *Emma,* and it is nonsense to ask him to try to have read *Emma* last night. And the very fact that evidence for or against "could have" statements must be drawn from occasions other than that to which they refer is enough to show that "He could have acted otherwise" is not a straightforward categorical statement, at least in the type of case we have been considering. Whether it is possible or necessary to interpret it categorically in moral cases is a point which I shall examine in the next section.

·　　·　　·

3

Libertarianism. Before considering why "He could have acted otherwise," interpreted in this hypothetical way, is regarded as relevant to ascriptions of responsibility, it is necessary to examine the theory that, although the hypothetical interpretation is correct in most cases, in the special case of moral choice the phrase must be interpreted in a categorical way. It would indeed be remarkable if modal forms which are normally used in a hypothetical way were used categorically in one type of case alone; and I have already suggested that their logic is partly determined by the method that would be used to support or rebut statements which employ them. The thesis that "he could have acted otherwise" is categorical is equivalent to the thesis that it could be verified or falsified by direct observation of the situation to which it refers.

It is essential to notice that the categorical interpretation is supposed to be necessary only in a very small, but very important part of the whole range of human choice. And this too is remarkable; for it implies that the words "free" and "choose" are logically different in moral and in nonmoral cases. There is a sense of "free" to which I have already alluded in which it is contrasted with "under compulsion"; and in this sense actions are still free when they are completely determined by the agent's tastes and character. For to say that they are determined in this way is not to say that he is a Pawn in the hands of Fate or a Prisoner in the iron grip of Necessity. It is only to say that anyone who knew his tastes and character well enough could predict what he will do. The fact that we can predict with a high degree of probability how Sir Winston Churchill will vote at the next election does not imply that he does not cast his vote freely. To be "free" in this sense is to be free to do what one wants to do, not to be able to act in spite of one's desires.

According to the theory to be examined most of our voluntary actions are "free" only in this sense which implies no breach in causal continuity. I choose what I choose because my desires are what they are; and they have been molded by countless influences from my birth or earlier. But, it is said, *moral* choices are free in a quite different sense, and one that is incompatible with their being predictable. This unpredictability is an essential feature in the categorical interpretation of "he could have acted otherwise"; for, if anyone could predict what I am going to do, I should not really be choosing between genuinely open alternatives, although I might think I was.

> Professor [Charles A.] Campbell puts the contrast in the following way: Free will does not operate in those practical situations in which no conflict arises in the agent's mind between what he conceives to be his "duty" and what he feels to be his "strongest desire." It does not operate here because there is just no occasion for it to operate. There is no reason whatever why the agent should here even contemplate choosing any course other than that prescribed by his strongest desire. In all such situations, therefore, he naturally wills in accordance with his strongest desire. But his "strongest desire" is simply the specific expression of that system of conative and emotive dispositions which we call his "character." In all such situations, therefore, whatever may be the case elsewhere, his will is in effect determined by his character as so far formed. . . .
>
> . . . [On the other hand] in the situation of moral conflict, I, as agent, have before my mind a course of action, X, which I believe to be my duty; and also a course of action, Y, incompatible with X, which I feel to be that which I most strongly desire. Y is, as it is sometimes expressed, "in the line of least resistance" for me—the course which I am aware that I should take, if I let my purely desiring nature operate without hindrance. It is the course towards which I am aware that my *character,* as so far formed, naturally inclines me. Now, as actually engaged in this situation, I find that I cannot help believing that I *can* rise to duty and choose X; the "rising to duty" being affected by what is commonly called "effort of will." And I further find, if I ask myself just what it is I am believing when I believe that I "can" rise to duty, that I cannot help believing that it lies with me, here and now, quite absolutely, which of two genuinely open possibilities I adopt; whether, that is, I make the effort of will and choose X or, on the other hand, let my desiring nature, my character as so far formed, "have its way," and choose Y, the course in the line of least resistance." [1]

Now it is certainly true that many determinists have paid too little attention to the concept of "trying" or "making an effort"; but I think that there are certain difficulties in Professor Campbell's account of moral conflict and, in particular, in his attempt to construe "I could have acted otherwise" in a categorical way. The first point to which I wish to draw attention is the question of method.

[1] *Mind,* 1952, pp. 460–3.

(1) Campbell insists that the question whether choice is "free" in a contra-causal sense must be settled by introspection.[2] But is this so? To doubt the findings of his self-examination may seem impertinent; but the doubt is concerned, not with what he finds, but with the propriety of the language he uses to describe what he finds. The universal negative form of statement ("Nothing caused my decision," "No one could have predicted my decision") does not seem to be a proper vehicle for anything that one could be said to *observe* in self-examination. That I know introspectively what it is like to choose may be true; but I cannot be said to know introspectively that my choice was contra-causal or unpredictable; and this is the point at issue. He represents "I can rise to duty" as a report of a mental event or, perhaps, a state of mind, not as a statement about a capacity, and "I could have . . ." as a statement about a past state of mind or mental event. But, if this is really so, it is at least surprising that, in this one context alone, we use the modal words "can" and "could have" for making categorical reports. The issue between determinists and libertarians is an issue about the way in which expressions such as "choose," "can," and "alternative possibilities" are to be construed; and this is surely an issue which is to be settled not by self-observation but by logical analysis.

There are many other phrases in Campbell's account which give rise to the same doubts about the propriety of the introspective method. The phrase "conative disposition" is embedded in a large and complex mass of psychological theory and its use implies the acceptance of this theory; so that one could hardly be said to know by introspection that one has a conative tendency to do something. And phrases such as "determined," "contra-causal," and even "desiring nature" take us beyond psychology into metaphysics. To say this is not to condemn the phrases; perhaps metaphysics is just what is needed here. But a metaphysician is not a reporter; he is an interpreter of what he "sees"; and it is over the interpretation that the disputes arise.

(2) A more obvious difficulty—and it is one of which libertarians are well aware —is that of distinguishing a "free" action from a random event. The essence of Campbell's account is that the action should not be predictable from a knowledge of the agent's character. But, if this is so, can what he does be called *his* action at all? Is it not rather a *lusus naturae*, an Act of God or a miracle? If a hardened criminal, bent on robbing the poor box, suddenly and *inexplicably* fails to do so, we should not say that he *chose* to resist or deserves *credit* for resisting the temptation; we should say, if we were religious, that he was the recipient of a sudden outpouring of Divine Grace or, if we were irreligious, that his "action" was due to chance, which is another way of saying that it was inexplicable. In either case we should refuse to use the active voice.

The reply to this criticism is that we must distinguish *In*determinism from *Self-*determinism. Choice is a creative act of the "self" and is not only unconstrained by external forces but also unconstrained by desire or character. But the difficulty here is to construe "self-determinism" in such a way that the "self" can be distinguished from the "character" without lapsing into indeterminism.

If we could construe "self-determined" by analogy with other "self"-compounds, such as self-adjusting, self-regulating, self-propelled, self-centered, self-controlled, and self-governing, there would be no difficulty. Some of these words apply to nonhuman

2 Scepticism and Construction, p. 131.

objects, and they never imply that there is a part of the object called the "self" which adjusts, regulates, or controls the rest, though the object does have a special part without which it would not be self-adjusting, etc. I can point to the self-starter of a car, but not to the self that starts the car; to say that a heating system is "self-regulating" is to say that it maintains a constant temperature without anyone watching the dials and turning the knobs. Coming to the human scene, to say that a state is "self-governing" is to say that its inhabitants make their own laws without foreign intervention; and to say that a man is "self-centered" is to say, not that he is always thinking and talking about something called his "self," but that he is always thinking and talking about *his* dinner, *his* golf handicap, the virtues of *his* wife, and the prowess of *his* children. In each case there is a subject and an object; but the "self" is neither subject nor object.

But if we construe "self-determined" in this way, it is clear that being self-determined implies only that a man acts freely in the ordinary sense of "freely" which the libertarian rejects as inadequate in the special case of moral choice. There would be no incompatibility between an action's being "self-determined" and its being predictable or characteristic of the agent; for "self-determined" would mean "determined by *his* motives and character," as opposed to "forced on him by circumstances or other people." But the libertarian regards explanation in terms of character as incompatible with genuine freedom and must therefore draw a contrast between "the self" and "the character." But if "self-determined" is to mean "determined by the self," it is necessary to give some account of what the "self" is. And if the question whether an action was determined by the "self" or not is to be relevant to the ascription of responsibility and the justice of adverse verdicts, we must be able to provide some criterion for deciding whether the self which determined the action is the same self that we are proposing to hold responsible or condemn.

Now the problem of Personal Identity is admittedly a difficult one and the danger of desert island argument is particularly acute here, since Jekyll-and-Hyde cases that a layman would dismiss as flights of fancy have been known to occur. In fact we decide whether the man I met yesterday is the same that I met last year partly by seeing whether he looks the same, partly by observing an identity of characteristic behavior, and partly by discovering what he can remember. And if we are to avoid the rather crude course of defining "same self" in terms of the spatiotemporal continuity of bodily cells, it seems that we must define it in terms of character and memory. But the libertarian's "self" is neither an empirical object nor displayed in characteristic action.

(3) If it is necessary to decide whether or not a man could have acted otherwise before ascribing responsibility, it is necessary that we should have some criterion for deciding this; and on the libertarian theory such a criterion is quite impossible. For, let us suppose that we know a great deal about his character and also that the temptation which he faced seems to be a fairly easy one for such a man to overcome. On the libertarian hypothesis this information will not be sufficient to enable us to conclude that he could have acted otherwise. If he in fact does the wrong thing, there are three alternative conclusions that we might draw. (a) The action was not against his moral principles at all, so that no conflict between "duty" and "inclination" arose. This is what I have called "wickedness"; (b) he knew it was wrong and could have resisted the temptation but did not (moral weakness); (c) he knew it was wrong but the temptation was *too* strong for him; he *could* not overcome it (addiction). Now it

is essential to be able to distinguish case (b) from case (c), since (b) is a culpable state while (c) is not. By treating "He could have acted otherwise" in a hypothetical way, the determinist thesis does provide us with a criterion for distinguishing between these cases; but the categorical interpretation cannot provide one, since no one, not even the man himself, could know whether he could have overcome the temptation or not.

(4) The libertarian theory involves putting a very special construction on the principle that "ought" implies "can," which it is very doubtful whether it can bear. If we take this principle in a common-sense way it is undoubtedly true. It is no longer my duty to keep a promise, if I literally *cannot* do so. But when we say this we have in mind such possibilities as my being detained by the police or having a railway accident or the death of the promisee; and it is possible to discover empirically whether any of these exonerating conditions obtained. But if "cannot" is construed in such a way that it covers my being too dishonest a person or not making the necessary effort, it is no longer obvious that "ought" implies "can." These reasons for failure, so far from exonerating, are just what make a man culpable.

(5) Even if it were possible to discover whether or not a man could have acted otherwise by attending to the actual occasion, as the categorical interpretation insists, why should this be held relevant to the question whether or not he is to blame? I shall try to explain this connection in the next chapter; but on the libertarian hypothesis it will, I think, be necessary to fall back on insight into a relation of fittingness between freedom and culpability.

· · ·

II

1

In the last chapter I tried to show that "could have" sentences in nonmoral contexts can be analyzed in terms of "would have . . . if . . ."; and we must now see whether the application of this analysis to moral cases is consistent with our ordinary use of moral language.

The first question to be considered is the question what sorts of if-clauses are in fact allowed to excuse a man from blame. Clearly "I could not have kept my promise because I was kidnapped" will exculpate me while "I could not have kept my promise because I am by nature a person who takes promises very lightly" will not. Translated into the hypothetical form, these become respectively "I would have kept my promise if I had not been kidnapped" and "I would have kept my promise if I had been a more conscientious person." Again it is clear that the first exculpates while the second does not. The philosophical difficulties, however, are to decide just why some "would . . . ifs" excuse while others do not and to provide a criterion for distinguishing the exculpating from the non-exculpating cases. Forcible seizure exculpates; but do threats or psychological compulsion? And if, as some suggest, desires are internal forces which operate on the will, do they exculpate in the way in which external forces do? The problem of free will is puzzling just because it seems impossible, without indulging in sheer dogmatism, to know just where to stop treating desires as "compelling forces."

Now before tackling this difficulty it will be prudent to examine what goes on in a place where questions of responsibility are settled every day and have been settled daily for hundreds of years, namely a court of law. Lawyers have evolved a terminology of remarkable flexibility, refinement, and precision and, although there may be a difference between moral and legal verdicts, it would be strange if the logic of lawyers' talk about responsibility were very different from our ordinary moral talk.

To establish a verdict of "guilty" in a criminal case it is necessary to establish that the accused did that which is forbidden by the law or, in technical language, committed the *actus reus*, and also that he had what is called *mens rea*. This last phrase is sometimes translated "guilty mind" and in many modern textbooks of jurisprudence it is supposed to consist of two elements, (a) foresight of the consequences and (b) voluntariness. But, whatever the textbooks may say, in actual practice lawyers never look for a positive ingredient called volition or voluntariness. A man is held to have *mens rea,* and therefore to be guilty, if the *actus reus* is proved, *unless* there are certain specific conditions which preclude a verdict of guilty. "What is meant by the mental element in criminal liability (*mens rea*) is only to be understood by considering certain defences or exceptions, such as Mistake of Fact, Accident, Coercion, Duress, Provocation, Insanity, Infancy." [3] The list of pleas that can be put up to rebut criminal liability is different in different cases; but in the case of any given offence there is a restricted list of definite pleas which will preclude a verdict of guilty.

This is not to say that the burden of proof passes to the defence. In some cases, such as murder, it is necessary for the prosecution to show that certain circumstances were not present which would, if present, defeat the accusation. The essential point is that the concept of a "voluntary action" is a negative, not a positive one. To say that a man acted voluntarily is in effect to say that he did something when he was not in one of the conditions specified in the list of conditions which preclude responsibility. The list of pleas is not exhaustive; we could, if we wished, add to it; and in making moral judgments we do so. For example we sometimes allow the fact that a man acted impulsively to exonerate him morally or at least to mitigate his offence in a case in which the law would not allow this. But it remains true that, in deciding whether an action was voluntary or not, we do not look for a positive ingredient but rather for considerations that would preclude its being voluntary and thereby exonerate the agent. In moral cases the most important types of plea that a man can put forward are (a) that he was the victim of certain sorts of ignorance, and (b) that he was the victim of certain sorts of compulsion.

2

Ignorance. A man may be ignorant of many elements in the situation in which he acts. For example he may not know that it was a policeman who told him to stop, that

3 Professor H. L. A. Hart: *Proceedings of the Aristotelian Society,* 1948–9. Aristotle in effect defines "the voluntary" in the same negative way as what is done not under compulsion and not through ignorance.

the stuff he put in the soup was arsenic, that the money he took was not his own. In such cases he would be blamed only if it was thought that he ought to have known or taken the trouble to find out. And his vicious trait of character was not contumacy or callousness or greed or disregard for any moral principle, but carelessness; and carelessness can amount to a vice. Firearms are so notoriously dangerous that the excuse "I didn't know it was loaded" will not do. The reason why he is blamed for carelessness and not for the specific vice for which he would have been blamed if he had done any of these things intentionally is that, although he intended to do what he did, he did not intend to break a moral rule. He intended to take the money, but not to steal. His action was not, therefore, a manifestation of the particular vice that the actions of thieves manifest. Ignorance of fact excuses or reduces the seriousness of an offence; but there is one type of ignorance that never excuses; and that is, in legal contexts, ignorance of the law and, in moral contexts, ignorance of right and wrong.

Now why should ignorance of fact excuse while ignorance of rules does not? Why should a man who takes someone else's money, thinking it to be his own, be guiltless of anything (except possibly carelessness), while a man who takes it, knowing it not to be his own but because he sees nothing wrong in taking other people's money, be held guilty and therefore blameworthy? We are not here concerned with the question why some types of action should be stigmatized as "wrong," but solely with the question why ignorance of what is wrong should not be held to exculpate.

The reason is that while the man who thought the money was his own did not intend to act on the maxim "It is permitted to take other people's money," the thief does act on this maxim. If a man does something because he does not think it wrong he cannot plead that he did not choose to do it, and it is for choosing to do what is *in fact* wrong, whether he knows it or not, that a man is blamed. The situation is exactly analogous to that in which some nonmoral capacity is concerned. "I would have solved the problem, if I had known all the data" would, if substantiated, allow me to get full marks. But "I would have solved the problem if I had known more mathematics" would not. Since competence at mathematics is not a moral trait of character, men are not blamed for lack of it; but they are given low marks and denied prizes.

3

Compulsion. So long as "compulsion" is used in the literal sense it is not difficult to see why it should be held to exonerate. If a man is compelled to do something, he does not choose to do it and his action is not a manifestation of his moral character or principles. Now, since the purpose of blame and punishment is to change a man's character and principles, neither blame nor punishment is called for in such a case. It would be unjust to punish him since the rules for punishing lay down that a man who acts under compulsion is not to be punished; and the rules lay this down because, with due allowance for superstition and stupidity, we do not have pointless rules. Once more we must be careful to avoid the mistake of saying that the justice of a sentence turns on the question whether the accused is likely to be reformed by it. What is at issue here is not our reason for exonerating this accused, but our reason for making a *general* exception in the case of men whose actions are not expressions of their moral character. Physical compulsion is an obvious case where this is so.

But what if the source of compulsion is within the man himself? It is not an accident that we use "compulsion" in a psychological way and exonerate compulsives. There are two questions that are relevant here. In the first place we ask whether the man could have resisted the "compulsion"; and we decide this in the way that we decide all "could have" questions. We look for evidence of his past behavior in this, and also in related matters; for the behavior of the compulsive is usually odd in matters unconnected with his special compulsion; and we compare his case with other known cases. Once the capacity to resist the compulsion is established beyond reasonable doubt we do not allow unsupported sceptical doubts about his capacity to resist it in a particular case to rebut the conclusion that he could have helped it. And we do not allow this because there is no way of establishing or refuting the existence of a capacity except by appeal to general evidence. If the capacity has been established and all the necessary conditions were present, we would not say that, in this case, he was the victim of a compulsion. Indeed a "compulsion" is not something that could be said to operate in a particular case only; for to say that a man has a psychological compulsion is to say something about his behavior over a long period. A compulsion is more like a chronic disorder than like a cold; and it is still less like a sneeze.

It is also relevant to raise the question whether he had any motive for doing what he did. Part of the difference between a kleptomaniac and a thief lies in the fact that the former has no motive for what he does; and he escapes blame because the point of blame is to strengthen some motives and weaken others. We are sometimes inclined to take the psychologists' talk about compulsions too seriously. We think that a man is excused because he has a "compulsion," as if the compulsion could be pointed to in the way that an external object which pushed him could be pointed to. But compulsions are not objects inside us; and we use the word "compulsion," not because we have isolated and identified the object which caused him to do what he did, but because we want to excuse him in the same sort of way that we excuse someone who is literally pushed; and we want to excuse him for the same sort of reason. We know that it will do no good to punish him.

Desires. A man might plead that he would have acted otherwise if he had not had a strong desire to do what he did; but the desire was so strong that, as things were, he could not have acted otherwise. Would this plea be allowed to exonerate him? In some cases it would; for there are, as we have seen, cases of addiction in which we allow that a man is not to blame since his craving was too strong for him. But in most cases it would be considered frivolous to say "I would have done the right thing if I hadn't wanted to do the wrong thing"; for it is just for this that men are blamed.

To distinguish an overwhelming desire from one that the agent could have resisted is not always easy; but the criterion that we in fact use for making the distinction is not difficult to understand. We know from experience that most men can be trained to curb some desires, but not others; and we assume that what is true in most cases is true in a given case unless special reasons are given for doubting this. Now it might seem that, although this evidence enables us to predict that we shall be able to train the man to curb his desire in future, it sheds no light on the question whether he could have curbed it on the occasion in question. I shall say more about this question of moral training later; here I only wish to point out that we have no criterion for deciding whether a man could have resisted a desire on a given occasion other than general evidence of his capacity and the capacity of others like him. We do not, because we cannot, try to answer this question as if it referred solely to the given occasion; we treat it as a question about a capacity.

Character. Finally a man might plead that he could not help doing what he did because that's the sort of man he is. He would not have done it if he had been more honest or less cowardly or less mean and so on. This sort of plea is paradoxical in the same sort of way that the plea of ignorance of moral rules and the plea that he did it because he wanted to are paradoxical. And all three paradoxes stem from the same source, the uncritical extension of "ought implies can" and of the exculpatory force of "he could not have acted otherwise" to cases which they will not cover. We know that these pleas are not in fact accepted; the puzzle is to see why.

• • •

Selected Bibliography for Part V

Baier, Kurt. *The Moral Point of View*. Ithaca, N.Y.: Cornell University Press, 1958.

Brandt, R. B., ed. *Value and Obligation*. New York: Harcourt, Brace, 1961.

Broad, C. D. *Five Types of Ethical Theory*. New York: Humanities Press, 1930.

Dewey, John. *Theory of Moral Life*, ed. Arnold Isenberg. New York: Holt, Rinehart, 1960.

Ewing, A. C. *Ethics*. London: English Universities Press, 1953.

Frankena, William K. *Ethics*. Englewood Cliffs, N.J.: Prentice-Hall, 1963.

Girvetz, Harry K., ed. *Contemporary Moral Issues*. Belmont, Cal.: Wadsworth, 1968.

Hook, Sidney, ed. *Determinism and Freedom: In the Age of Modern Science*. New York: Macmillan, 1958.

Hospers, John. *Human Conduct*. New York: Harcourt, Brace, 1961.

Jones, W. T., *et al.*, eds. *Approaches to Ethics: Representative Selections from Classical Times to the Present*. New York: McGraw-Hill, 1962.

Nietzsche, Friedrich. *Birth of Tragedy;* and *The Genealogy of Morals*, trans. Francis, Golffing. New York: Doubleday, 1956.

Rader, Melvin. *Ethics and the Human Community*. New York: Holt, Rinehart, 1964.

Sellars, Wilfrid, and Hospers, John, eds. *Readings in Ethical Theory*. New York: Appleton-Century-Crofts, 1952.

Sidgwick, Henry. *Outlines of the History of Ethics*. Boston: Beacon, 1960.

———. *The Methods of Ethics*. New York: Dover, 1874.

Stevenson, Charles L. *Ethics and Language*. New Haven: Yale University Press, 1944.

Taylor, Paul W., ed. *Problems of Moral Philosophy: An Introduction to Ethics*. Belmont, Cal.: Dickenson, 1967.

Toulmin, Stephen E. *An Examination of the Place of Reason in Ethics*. Cambridge: Cambridge University Press, 1950.

Warnock, Mary. *Ethics Since 1900*. London: Oxford University Press, 1960.

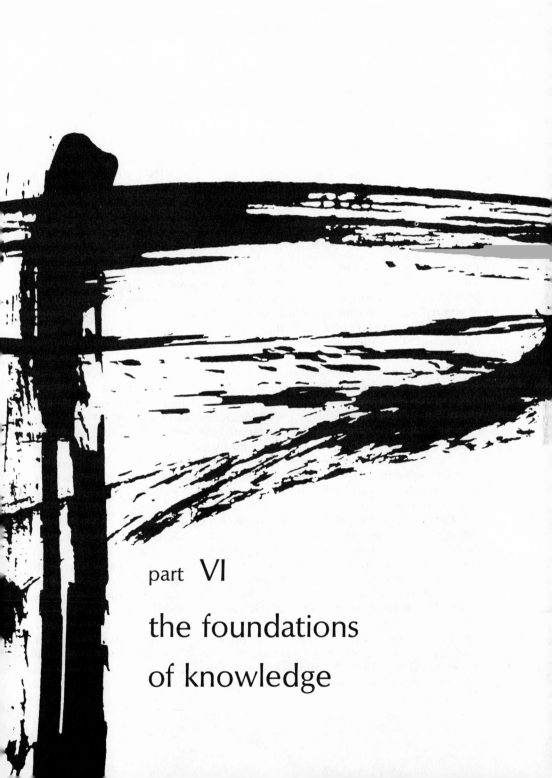

part VI

the foundations
of knowledge

INTRODUCTION

The nature of knowledge

Philosophers have devoted a great deal of attention to questions concerning the nature, extent, and basis of knowledge. Indeed, such problems—which belong to the branch of philosophy known as epistemology, or the theory of knowledge—have been of primary concern to some of the most original and influential of philosophic minds. A few of these thinkers have, with their own distinctive and usually controversial epistemological contributions, revitalized or even transformed the philosophic enterprise.

Philosophers who claim that epistemological questions are fundamental to all other philosophic problems believe it to be virtually self-evident that all that we claim to know—whether that knowledge be of a scientific, matter-of-fact, or philosophic nature—would come to nought if we are unable to support our knowledge claims. Neither a metaphysical doctrine of the self, nor a physical theory of the atom, nor even a simple reference to an ordinary event (such as the assertion that it is raining this very minute outside my study window) may be exempt from the need for justification. We are confronted, then, with the task of explaining how we know what we claim to know and how we may know what we wish to know (or judge someone else's claim to such knowledge).

The epistemologist's obligation, of course, is not to provide a justification for this or that particular knowledge claim, but more significantly, to determine what constitutes justification for *any* knowledge claim. The fundamental epistemological question, then, can be stated as, "What are the justifiable and legitimate grounds for calling something (or anything) knowledge?" The epistemologist's first task, in short, is to attempt to formulate criteria for identifying genuine knowledge. Some philosophers have firmly declared that this task consists strictly of explicating and systematizing generally accepted norms that are implicit in common practice; while others, for various reasons, are equally convinced that these popular norms are far from cogent (and are perhaps even incoherent), and thus cannot serve as standards for what merits being called knowledge. The latter group maintains that a wide chasm separates what is accepted as knowledge from what *truly is* knowledge; and that we must, therefore, revise our notions of what constitutes knowledge. Still other philosophers maintain that it is inherently impossible to formulate any criteria for knowledge, since knowledge, or the act of knowing, cannot be analyzed or rationally understood.

But even if the epistemologist could define knowledge, his task would not be complete. He must secondly demonstrate the reasonableness, superiority, and basal nature of his conception of knowledge over against all other claimants. In the face of this requirement, the scope of the problem increases and the number of questions multiply. Part VI will of course deal with some of these subsidiary, though essential questions—such questions as: What is the meaning of such epistemological terms as "truth," "belief," and "meaningfulness"? Are we justified in maintaining that what we have observed to be true until now will continue to be true tomorrow? (Or, as philosophers are fond of asking, "How do we know that the sun will rise tomorrow just because it has always risen in the past, to the best of our memories?) How far does knowledge extend? For example, are we capable of knowing about the past, the conscious states of other persons, or even the nature of the physical world?)

The initial problem appears to be that of trying to understand the nature of knowledge and to distinguish it from that which is not knowledge (including that which may have been mistaken for knowledge, e.g., "true belief"). As soon as one begins to probe critically into the problem, one will find himself rejecting various superficially adequate definitions of knowledge. A philosopher of a sceptical temperament, in fact, may insist that *any* account or definition of knowledge proposed can be shown to be undermined by its own assumptions, that it cannot be consistently fulfilled or that it may entail unacceptable consequences.

Among the selections on the nature of knowledge, Plato's discussion in the dialogue the *Theaetetus* is a prime example of the value of a critical stance. His apparently successful refutations of a succession of definitions of knowledge (e.g., knowledge as perception, as true belief, as true belief with an account) while yielding, in this dialogue, no positive conclusions, demonstrate the contribution that critical scrutiny may make toward understanding the nature of knowledge.

A. D. Woozley analyzes a number of traditional ways of distinguishing between knowledge and belief and demonstrates why they are unsatisfactory. But, unlike Plato in the *Theaetetus*, Woozley offers concrete and carefully argued suggestions on how we can differentiate between these two types of cognitive claims.

The problem of the nature of knowledge is approached in a somewhat different and less direct manner by those who, unwilling to seek a definition that would pass the critical judgment of the sceptical minded, are quite content to accept as genuine knowledge that which normally passes for such. The problem of knowledge, for some of these individuals, involves ascertaining whether or not there are different kinds of knowledge (i.e., to determine the *limits* of knowledge) and, if there are, to explain how these kinds of knowledge may be obtained (i.e., to determine the *source* of knowledge).

Perhaps the most common view on this question is that there are two basic types of knowledge: rational knowledge and empirical knowledge. Unfortunately very few philosophers have agreed on what constitutes the precise distinction between the two, but, for our purposes, we may broadly define them as they are most generally understood. Rational knowledge, exemplified by mathematical truths (e.g., that 2 plus 2 equals 4), is knowledge achieved through reason without the aid of the senses.

Empirical knowledge, on the other hand, is the knowledge achieved through sense experience, e.g., that snow is white. Now philosophers have been divided on the question of whether reason or sense-perception is the *primary* or *ultimate* source of knowledge (and of the role that each must play in the achievement of knowledge). Those who opt for reason (the so-called rationalists) base their position on the contention that rational knowledge is the only sort that is certain, that is not subject to illusion or alteration: that 2 plus 2 equals 4 is absolutely certain and, for everyone who understands it, cannot be conceived to be otherwise. In other words, the rationalists hold that only rational knowledge fulfills what they take to be the criteria of genuine knowledge. Advocates of sensory knowledge (the empiricists), on the other hand, tend to maintain that knowledge of the external world can be achieved only through the senses, since reason cannot produce original knowledge but only relate those facts that the senses present to it. In short, their concern, unlike that of the rationalists, is not primarily with certainty, but with knowing the actual world.

The rationalistic position is represented (in this book) by G. W. Leibniz, who attempts to prove that "*Being* itself and *truth* are not known wholly through the senses . . ." and that "reasoning requires something else in addition to what is from the senses." If the only source of knowledge were the senses, a number of crucial features of our corpus of knowledge would be inexplicable.

Aside from the entrenched opposition of the rationalist, an empiricist must confront the problems involved in basing what we claim to know about objects and events in the external world upon the data given to the senses. Can we *infer* matters of fact (general or particular) on the basis of what we now perceive or remember having perceived? It is one thing to know that we have such and such an experience of a particular object, but it is quite another thing to claim that from such experiences alone we can have knowledge of the object itself. Bertrand Russell, fully aware of this crucial problem, sketches out an answer to it, which, although it does not take account of the various ramifications or interpretations of the question, is nevertheless a valuable development of the empiricist's position. It is Russell's contention that "if an individual is to know anything beyond his own experiences up to the present moment, his stock of uninferred knowledge must consist not only of matters of fact but also of general laws. . . ." The nature and validity of such laws, of course, present imposing problems.

Definitions of the nature of knowledge have tended, for the most part, to reflect what people ordinarily take to be knowledge. They have served to reassure us that we indeed know the things we always thought we knew. However, there have also been, in the history of thought, radical departures from such views. These departures, often provocative and influential, have stemmed from the rejection of fundamental presuppositions in normal attitudes concerning knowledge. Two of these unorthodox theories are represented in the section of the Nature of Knowledge. One is by Henri Bergson, who contends that if the ultimate purpose of knowledge is to grasp the nature of the "real," then the route that we usually take (through the intellect or the senses, or both) will lead to total failure. Reality, in his view, must be grasped *intuitively*, that is, through a mode of knowing that is nonconceptual and does not artificially represent the real (which Bergson calls the "absolute") by means of preëxisting, abstract concepts. It is a mode of knowing, Bergson says, "which installs itself in that which is moving and adopts the very life of things." Bergson's conception of the nature of authentic knowledge is thus entwined with his unique conception of the nature of reality.

The other radical theory of knowledge in the first section of Part VI is representative of a recent, distinctive philosophic movement known as *phenomenology*, a movement which shares some roots with Bergsonian philosophy (both philosophies are most prevalent in Germany and France). While the advocates of phenomenology reflect diverging interests and have developed theses and ideas that are conspicuously fluid and multifarious, they appear to be agreed on the essentials of what is called the *phenomenological method*—a method for strict philosophical investigation developed by Edmund Husserl, the seminal figure of the phenomenological movement. In the selection included here, Alfred Schutz, a respected phenomenologist and social scientist, sets forth the major tenets of the phenomenological method, and explains the uniqueness of the orientation that it provides toward an understanding of the problems of knowledge.

The concept of truth

One often-mentioned criterion for identifying knowledge is that of *truth*. (The concept in question is that of *factual*, or *empirical*, truth, rather than *formal*, or *mathematical* truth, the latter being irrelevant for the purposes of this discussion.) It may be argued, according to this criterion, that when we claim to know something, it is implicitly understood that this "something" is a true proposition. The judgment, "John knows *p*" (where *p* is a proposition), really means that "John knows that *p* is true." It would seem quite obvious that a person cannot reasonably claim to know something about the world unless he agrees that what he claims to know is true. It follows that if and when what we thought we knew to be true is shown to be false, we are obliged to acknowledge our error and retract our claim.

The acknowledgment of the role that the concept of truth plays in our understanding of the grounds of knowledge impels us to consider the question of the nature of truth. What does it actually mean to say that a proposition, belief, or statement is true? (This question must not be confused with the quite different one of how to justify the assertion that something is true.) It must be noted that we have been employing and shall continue to employ a number of terms (belief, statement, sentence, proposition, judgment, and so forth) to denote the "entity" that is supposed to possess the property of truth or falsehood. In so doing, we largely ignore the question of what sorts of things can properly be said to be true (and whether there should be one or several classes of such entities), judging it to be perhaps a pseudo-question, and, at least, one that is irrelevant to our discussion.

Although we may refer to truth and falsehood as "properties" of statements or propositions or the like, they are not properties in the sense of being inherent in the makeup of such entities. They may be called properties for convenience, because of the fact that we do attribute truth or falsity to a proposition whenever it is clearly warranted by the *relation* of the proposition to some objective state of affairs or merely to "something" that determines its truth. The standard types of so-called Theories of Truth may be differentiated by the manner in which each conceives of the form taken by this relationship (between the proposition and that which warrants its truth).

One may immediately suggest that the relationship between an assertion and that which makes it true is best conceived of as a kind of *correspondence*. It seems obvious that an assertion is true if what it asserts about the world corresponds to what the world is actually like, and is false if there is no such correspondence. What is not obvious, however, or easily defined, is what kind of relationship is meant by the term "correspondence." Every correspondence theory encounters objections to the particular interpretation of "correspondence" inherent in it. These objections either weaken the theory or refute it altogether. For example, it would be extremely difficult to rebut criticisms leveled against the view that a proposition is true if it "resembles" (either in a structural or material sense) some existent object or state of affairs. This sort of correspondence theory tries to explicate the term "correspond" by reducing it to a concept which is far more liable to attack; for what similarities can a proposition (whether defined ideationally or linguistically) have with a physical fact or state of affairs? And if we grant that there can be a resemblance between a proposition and an objective fact, is this resemblance another kind of objective fact? If so, what kind is it? If one claims to know *that* proposition p resembles a fact F (let us call that which is claimed, another proposition h), then this claim in order to be true must resemble another fact F' (i.e., the second order fact that p resembles F); but the resultant claim that h resembles F' (represented by the proposition h') calls for its correspondence to still another new fact F'' and so on, *ad infinitum*.

A proponent of the correspondence view might retort that such criticisms mistakenly presuppose that the contention that p corresponds to F requires the *comparison* of p with F, when, in fact, all that is required is our being able to maintain that *what we say is the case* (the asserting of p) *is indeed the case* (F obtains). The determination that F does really obtain involves the *test* of truth and not the *meaning* of truth (the latter being our chief concern here). Unfortunately this tempting escape route merely brings us back to where we were at the outset. All that has been accomplished is the construction of a circular definition, for "is the case" is simply another way of saying "is true."

Brand Blanshard, in attempting to arrive at a more intelligible and, hopefully, more acceptable theory of truth, rejects the correspondence theory in favor of the concept of *coherence*. A proposition, according to Blanshard, is true insofar as it is entailed by other propositions within a system of beliefs, a system whose members are necessarily accepted as true. It must be stressed that coherence demands more than consistency. A proposition, although it does not contradict the propositions of a given system, nevertheless need not be accepted as a coherent part of that system. Coherence demands a relationship of necessity (the exact nature of which is not always clear and invariable in Blanshard's writings) linking one judgment with another in such a way that if we accept one, we are obliged to accept the other.

There are many unique (and surprising) features in Blanshard's coherence theory of truth, and many difficulties as well. And since there is really no substitute for the philosopher's own words, we shall simply direct the reader to the selection in which Blanshard presents and later defends his position. It would be helpful, however, to point out that Blanshard's coherence theory, in contrast to the correspondence theory, views truth and falsehood neither as absolute properties of propositions nor as being based on external relationships. In other words, a proposition or judgment cannot be said to be absolutely true or absolutely false, but only approximately true or approximately false, depending, not upon a demonstrable relationship with the external world, but upon the extent of our experience, or (what is the same thing) the relative comprehensiveness of the system of beliefs which the proposition is to join. There are more or less coherent systems of beliefs, and the only absolutely true judgment that one can make is that judgment which is coherent with (mutually entails) the whole of experience, i.e., the whole of reality itself. In short, *absolute truth* is identified with *absolute reality*, for the only thing that can be true *without qualification* is a rational system that is "a whole at once coherent and all-embracing." (A perfectly coherent system cannot fail to entail even the most insignificant aspects of reality.) Obviously, no one (except for the most perfect of all minds, i.e., God) can achieve the knowledge of the "one true proposition," for this notion of *absolute truth* and *absolute reality* is the unattainable goal and ultimate standard of human knowledge. Blanshard admits that this conception of the Ideal (that the world is fully intelligible or that the "real is rational") is not a demonstrable conclusion, but a postulate of his philosophy.

The *pragmatic* theory of truth, like the correspondence and coherence theories, has many versions. But the classic version—and the most distinctive one—is that of William James. Truth, according to James, is not based upon a comparison between a proposition and some kind of external, objective fact, or upon the incorporation of propositions into a more or less coherent system of beliefs. The trouble with these opposing views is that their proponents on both sides have posed the wrong question. We should not ask how our ideas or judgments agree with, or relate to, reality, but what makes our ideas or judgments true.

> Grant an idea or belief to be true . . . what concrete difference will its being true make in anyone's actual life? How will the truth be realized? What experiences will be different from those which would obtain if the belief were false? What, in short, is the truth's cash-value in experiential terms?

The truth of an idea is thus constituted by the *practical* difference it makes in our day-to-day experiences, and should not be construed as a static relationship between the idea and an unchanging, fully completed reality; this reality simply makes no sense to James. The term "practical" unfortunately is used in several different ways and it is not immediately obvious how they fit together.

The article by Alfred Tarski represents a different approach to the concept of truth. Tarski foregoes any attempt to develop a comprehensive theory but, rather, restricts himself to the problem of finding a linguistic definition for the term "truth." His goal is to develop a *semantic definition* of a linguistic entity within a given language. Such a definition must be both materially adequate (in the sense of preserving the essential meaning of the term as it is commonly used and allowing one to determine which sentences are true in a given language) and formally correct (in the sense of being free from inconsistencies and paradoxical implications). Although a precise, unambiguous, and unparadoxical definition can only be obtained within a language whose structure is rigorously and exactly specified (i.e., in an artificially constructed, *ideal* language), Tarski would nevertheless maintain that his schema for finding such a definition can be utilized profitably—although not perfectly—in natural languages such as English.

P. F. Strawson attacks the semantic conception of truth in particular and all theories in general that construe truth as a predicate ascribable to sentences, propositions, or beliefs. It is his contention that appending the expression "is true" to an assertion is a superfluous act; to assert that "*p* is true" is not to make an assertion *about p*, but is simply another way of expressing or affirming *p*. Insofar as the expression "true" has a function, it is not a descriptive function but a *performatory* one. One who says that an assertion is true is *assenting* to, *conceding*, or *endorsing* the claim; he is *doing* something, but not describing a property of a sentence. Discussion on the problem of truth may be sharply curtailed in some instances and cleared of confusion in others, Strawson suggests, if misconstruction (such as Tarski's) of the concept of truth is fully recognized as such.

The final selection on truth is J. L. Austin's discussion of what some have labeled a "purified version" of the correspondence theory. Truth, for Austin, must still be understood as basically a relationship of correspondence between a statement and a state of affairs in the external world. However, this relationship should not be construed as being naturally grounded on some kind of similarity between the two members of the relationship—for this would result in the same errors and objections that have already plagued this type of theory. Correspondence must, instead, be taken to mean "a purely conventional correlation" that is much more complex than the concept of similarity. We have thus come full circle; and like a circle, the discussion and debate over the problem of truth seemingly has no end.

The problem of induction

In addition to the truth criterion, a second major assumption maintained nearly uniformly by those who have been occupied with the definition of knowledge is that one cannot have knowledge in the absence of evidence, i.e., that knowledge cannot be based on mere guesswork. In those cases where the evidence for a factual claim is complete (where there are no unexamined cases subsumed under that factual claim), the inference from evidence to the appropriate factual proposition presents no problem whatsoever. If we were to examine every apple in a certain basket and verify that each was rotten, it would follow (assuming that we could trust our senses) without any possibility of error or contradiction, that the general proposition, "every apple in the basket is rotten," would be true. We could confidently claim to know that fact about all the apples in the basket on the basis of the given evidence.

Obviously this type of inference is devoid of uncertainty because, loosely speaking, both the premise and conclusion express the same information or possess the same factual content. It furthermore belongs to that important class of inferences or arguments in which the conclusion cannot be in doubt if the premises are known to be (or accepted as) true. In such inferences we are assured (assuming that they are correctly accomplished and do not violate the principles of logic) that the same conditions or circumstances which render the premises true also, necessarily, render the conclusion true.

In stark contrast to the type of inference described above are those inferences in which the premises of an argument do not provide irrefutable proof of the conclusion, and in which there is, in fact, no assurance that the conclusion is not *false*, even though the premises are undeniably true and the inference is correctly accomplished (i.e., in accordance with accepted rules). When we base the truth of an assertion concerning all the members of a particular class of objects (events, persons, etc.) on evidence concerning only some members of that class, we rely on what is called an inductive inference. But since we cannot claim that what is true of some things ("some apples in that basket are rotten") is necessarily true of all such things, are we justified in claiming even that such evidence warrants one conclusion rather than another? Is the fact that, of the one hundred apples in a basket, the ninety apples that have been examined are rotten, sufficient in itself to justify the conclusion that *all* the apples in the basket are rotten? Or might we be equally justified, on the basis of the same evidence, in maintaining that the ten unexamined apples will turn out *not* to be rotten?

A possible reply, at this point, would be that the correct conclusion is easily determined by the application of an *acceptable* rule of induction. In this case, it would be the basic rule of induction by *simple enumeration,* or what John Stuart Mill called *generalization from experience.* This rule directs us to take to be true of *all* instances of a class that which has been observed to be true of all *given* instances of that same class, *everything else being equal.* But such a reply, rather than solving the problem of induction, focuses our attention on its crux. Can we be *certain* that this rule—or any rule of induction—will be successful? And if not, how can we find such a rule to be acceptable? These questions have been approached by philosophers in various ways, the most important of which are represented in the section on the Problem of Induction.

David Hume, in his admirably lucid and incisive presentation of the problem, sought to show that, in the light of a precise understanding of the problem and a clear conception of the meaning of justification, any suggested solution is rendered either *irrelevant* or *circular.* An inductive argument may be psychologically persuasive, or may have practical value, but no inductive argument has any cognitive value or is justifiable in terms of logic or experience.

Hans Reichenbach recognizes the futility of attempting to combat Hume by a frontal assault. Reichenbach contends that Hume's question ("How can induction be justified?") is stated in an unanswerable form, the dilemma hinging on the construction placed on the term "justification." What Hume required was *validation:* how we can know, or be assured, that what is true of a random sample of a class of objects will also be true of the entire class, or that the prediction of a future event will prove accurate because similar predictions of the same kind of events have been successful in the past. What Hume was asking, then, was whether or not we can *know the future.* Of course the answer is No.

The failure to validate inductive inference (or some rule or method of induction) does not preclude at all, in Reichenbach's estimation, the possibility of *vindicating* induction. The question of justification is not a question of how we *know* that the future will be like the past, or that the unknown will be like the known, but, rather, why we should accept a proposition or draw a particular conclusion *from incomplete evidence,* on the basis of inductive rules which fail to tell us whether the conclusion is true or false. It is Reichenbach's contention that inductive rules of inference are unique in that they are guaranteed (by a formal proof, and assuming a certain theory of probability) to *eventually* (and with repeated use of the same rules) lead the inquirer to true conclusions, *if such exist.* Implicit in this proof is the notion that inductive methods are *self-corrective* (i.e., that we can correct or alter the results of an inductive inference by means of the same inductive procedures and rules); for this is precisely what is meant by claiming that it is by the *repeated use* of inductive rules that success can be achieved. Notice, however, that Reichenbach's elaborate proof depends upon the assumption that *there are true conclusions* (that it is possible to make true statements about the future), an *assumption* no more justified than its converse. Are we then given an empty assurance that inductive methods will lead to success *if success is possible* and no assurance at all that success *is* possible? Reichenbach's reply is that his theory of induction is not intended to show that we are justified in using inductive methods to achieve *knowledge of the future* (for this is impossible, and any alleged justification in this respect is illusory), but, rather, to show that it is *reasonable or practical to act according to rules of induction*. Reichenbach's defense of induction is an argument for relying on induction to achieve those hypotheses or, as Reichenbach calls them), *anticipative posits* that are necessary to deal effectively with an unknown future. His justification of induction is thus a *pragmatic* one.

An alternative solution to the problem of induction is proposed by Max Black, who maintains that inductive arguments can be self-supporting (and thus validated) in a sense that escapes Hume's charge of circularity. An argument is circular, in the most basic and obvious sense, if the conclusion to be established is itself used (even in a different form) as one of the premises. The classic inductive (or *a posteriori*) justification of induction, formulated by John Stuart Mill, is an excellent example of this circularity; for to argue that inductive inferences will be successful in the future because they have been successful in the past, presupposes for its validity the very principle that the argument is trying to establish (i.e., the argument is itself inductive).

Black tries, in an ingenious manner, to build a justificatory argument in a form that escapes any charge of circularity. He rightly contends that if the justificatory argument is governed by a rule that differs in substance from the rule of induction, whose reliability is at issue, there can be no charge of circularity. The question is whether or not Black has succeeded in formulating such an argument.

There is one more approach to the dilemma identified by Hume remaining to be dealt with here (and many others that must be left out). It is the position, represented by P. F. Strawson, that inductive inferences do not require justification or vindication; that, hitherto, philosophers have been unprofitably occupied with a nonexistent problem. Strawson argues that the misunderstanding was based on the erroneous assumption that an inductive inference must meet requirements like those of valid deductive arguments, requirements that it, of its own nature, *cannot meet* and *should not have to meet*. If it were to meet these requirements, in the only ways possible, induction would be transformed into something else. The question of which inductive rule is the proper one in a particular circumstance can be sensibly answered; but if one persists in asking why we should employ any inductive rules or procedures at all, we can only reply that to arrive at non-demonstrative, inductive knowledge, it is rational to use the method that is appropriate.

The theory of meaning

In the prevailing climate of recent Anglo-American philosophy, the single most prominent cluster of problems in the area of epistemology (protruding into nearly every other area as well) centers around the notion of meaning or the meaningfulness of linguistic expressions. (There is, in addition, a great deal of interest in the problem of meaning—especially on the continent—among those who practice non-linguistic types of philosophy, although in these cases the emphasis and mode of approach are naturally different.) This concern with meaning is related to the orientation of many twentieth-century Anglo-American schools—such as logical positivism, logical empiricism, and ordinary language analysis—away from speculative philosophy and toward the analysis of the linguistic medium for philosophic expression.

A major factor contributing to the emergence of this preoccupation with linguistic questions was the realization early in this century that philosophical problems previously deemed significant were in fact illusory, or were fraught with ambiguity and confusion. A number of philosophers, immensely impressed by the contrast between the precision and clarity of scientific discourse and the obscurity and irresoluteness of dominant philosophical approaches to such matters as God, man, and the universe, felt a need for radical reform. They asked why the philosopher could not emulate the scientist by being rigorous, precise, objective, and hardheaded. Such virtues would result in the forthright and unsentimental rejection of those theories or claims—however brilliant or imaginative—which were devoid of empirical meaning. But in order to be able to identify empirically meaningless statements, it would be necessary to analyze language in such a way as to establish criteria for meaningful statements.

Thus, the central problem for the initiators of this twentieth-century revolution in philosophy became that of establishing a comprehensive *theory of meaning;* without it, the intended reforms in philosophy would have no basis. The early positivists generally agreed, perhaps because of their scientific biases, that to be cognitively meaningful, a statement must express either (1) a formal relationship (whose validity depends on the conventions of a symbolic system such as that of logic or mathematics) or (2) an actual or possible observation, or an hypothesis from which such statements can be logically derived. But the articulation of criteria for the statements of the second group (2) presented an especially puzzling and formidable problem.

An early attempt to develop a comprehensive theory of meaning was made by the logical positivists who, along the lines suggested by the philosophy of David Hume, formulated the celebrated *verifiability theory of meaning.* This general criterion of meaning, presented in the selection by A. J. Ayer, asserts essentially that a sentence is empirically meaningful if and only if it is understood to be empirically verifiable. But Ayer and other philosophers sympathetic to this position have unfortunately been unable to arrive at a precise version of the verification principle that would answer all the objections of its countless critics. Ayer himself has been quite aware of many of the difficulties surrounding the principle and has introduced some fairly helpful distinctions. He suggests, for example, that we might consider the merits of interpreting "verification" in the "weak" sense rather than the more commonly known "strong" sense; that is, instead of requiring that a statement be amenable to conclusive verification, we should consider a statement meaningful if we can demonstrate that it may be rendered *probably* true by empirical observation.

One school of analytic philosophers, while rejecting the principle of verification *as the fundamental basis* for the determination of linguistic meaning, nevertheless retains this principle as one of several criteria of meaning. The concept of meaning has become, for these philosophers, multi-faceted. They charge that the theory of language of Ayer and his followers is based on the incorrect assumption that "meanings" are entities of some sort functioning as denotations of linguistic expressions. Gilbert Ryle, in a very lucid discussion, explains the emergence and attractiveness of Ayer's theory of language and presents some criticisms of it. Ryle also puts forth—

but does not attempt to develop or fully defend—his own view that meanings must be understood *contextually,* and not as absolutely determinate referents of a given expression independent of the context in which it appears. The theory of meaning that Ryle presents, in short, maintains that the meaning of an expression is nothing more than its "use," or the role that it performs in a particular language system—a so-called *language game*—for a particular group of participants in that system. Therefore, when confronted with the question of what an expression means, Ryle advises us not to seek its denotation (whether in experience, the mind, or the world), but to examine its use.

Friedrich Waismann, on the other hand, warns against the emerging "cult of ordinary usage and language" and argues that it is a grave mistake to demand that everything conform to the standards of normal usage. Waismann maintains that "language shapes and fashions the frame in which experience is set," that it is a collective instrument or medium of thought that determines our understanding of all that we experience, but that, because language is *also* the product of contingent human experience (i.e., it is a human *achievement*), it is both a deficient and treacherous instrument. Therefore, if we are to advance our knowledge or "convey a new insight not in conformity with the ideas dominant of the time, with ideas, moreover, precipitated in language," we cannot be *bound* to the normal or "correct" usages (and meanings) inherent in our language.

Up to now, the selections have been devoted to the two major analytic approaches to the problem of meaning. It might, therefore, be instructive at this point to examine a totally different conception of what is significant in the problem of meaning. The crux of the problem to Eugene Gendlin is the question of how the dimension of experienced, or "felt," meaning may be related to the logical and objective order of concepts that are used in describing the world. Gendlin is convinced that our understanding of the meaning of the concepts used in everyday life, and in science and other more technical endeavors, will remain on an artificial and arbitrary plane unless attention is paid to the dimension of "concrete" or "preconceptual" experiencing. All that this brief selection by Gendlin can give us is an introductory picture of this subjective realm of meaning, a realm which may have important consequences for our efforts to deal constructively with the many ramifications of the concept of meaning.

The nature of knowledge

1

WHAT KNOWLEDGE IS NOT

plato

• • •

THEAETETUS. . . . It seems to me that one who knows something is perceiving the thing he knows, and, so far as I can see at present, knowledge is nothing but perception.

• • •

SOCRATES. Now suppose you were asked: "When a man sees white or black things or hears high or low tones, what does he see or hear with?" I suppose you would say: "With eyes and ears."

THEAET. Yes, I should.

SOCR. To use words and phrases in an easygoing way without scrutinizing them too curiously is not, in general, a mark of ill-breeding; on the contrary there is something low-bred in being too precise. But sometimes there is no help for it, and this is a case in which I must take exception to the form of your answer. Consider: is it more correct to say that we see and hear *with* our eyes and ears or *through* them?

THEAET. I should say we always perceive through them, rather than with them.

From Plato's *Theaetetus*, Francis Macdonald Cornford, trans., in Francis Macdonald Cornford, *Plato's Theory of Knowledge* (London: Routledge & Kegan Paul Ltd., 1957), pp. 29, 103–157. Reprinted by permission of Routledge & Kegan Paul Ltd. and Humanities Press Inc.

SOCR. Yes; it would surely be strange that there should be a number of senses ensconced inside us, like the warriors in the Trojan horse, and all these things should not converge and meet in some single nature—a mind, or whatever it is to be called —*with* which we perceive all the objects of perception *through* the senses as instruments.

THEAET. Yes, I think that is a better description.

SOCR. My object in being so precise is to know whether there is some part of ourselves, the same in all cases, with which we apprehend black or white through the eyes, and objects of other kinds through the other senses. Can you, if the question is put to you, refer all such acts of apprehension to the body? Perhaps, however, it would be better you should speak for yourself in reply to questions, instead of my taking the words out of your mouth. Tell me: all these instruments through which you perceive what is warm or hard or light or sweet are parts of the body, aren't they?—not of anything else.

THEAET. Of nothing else.

SOCR. Now will you also agree that the objects you perceive through one faculty cannot be perceived through another—objects of hearing, for instance, through sight, or objects of sight through hearing?

THEAET. Of course I will.

SOCR. Then, if you have some thought about both objects at once, you cannot be having a perception including both at once through either the one or the other organ.

THEAET. No.

SOCR. Now take sound and color. Have you not, to begin with, this thought which includes both at once—that they both *exist?*

THEAET. I have.

SOCR. And, further, that each of the two is *different* from the other and the *same* as itself?

THEAET. Naturally.

SOCR. And again, that both together are *two,* and each of them is *one?*

THEAET. Yes.

SOCR. And also you can ask yourself whether they are *unlike* each other or *alike?*

THEAET. No doubt.

SOCR. Then through what organ do you think all this about them both? What is common to them both cannot be apprehended either through hearing or through sight. Besides, here is further evidence for my point. Suppose it were possible to inquire whether sound and color were both brackish or not, no doubt you could tell me what faculty you would use—obviously not sight or hearing, but some other.

THEAET. Of course: the faculty that works through the tongue.

SOCR. Very good. But now, through what organ does that faculty work, which tells you what is common not only to these objects but to all things—what you mean by the words "exists" and "does not exist" and the other terms applied to them in the questions I put a moment ago? What sort of organs can you mention, corresponding to all these terms, through which the perceiving part of us perceives each one of them?

THEAET. You mean existence and nonexistence, likeness and unlikeness, sameness and difference, and also unity and numbers in general as applied to them; and clearly your question covers "even" and "odd" and all that kind of notions. You are asking, through what part of the body our mind perceives these?

SOCR. You follow me most admirably, Theaetetus; that is exactly my question.

THEAET. Really, Socrates, I could not say, except that I think there is no special organ at all for these things, as there is for the others. It is clear to me that the mind in itself is its own instrument for contemplating the common terms that apply to everything.

SOCR. In fact, Theaetetus, you are handsome, not ugly as Theodorus said you were; for in a discussion handsome is that handsome does. And you have treated me more than handsomely in saving me the trouble of a very long argument, if it is clear to you that the mind contemplates some things through its own instrumentality, others through the bodily faculties. That was indeed what I thought myself; but I wanted you to agree.

THEAET. Well, it is clear to me.

·   ·   ·

SOCR. Under which head, then, do you place existence? For that is, above all, a thing that belongs to everything.

THEAET. I should put it among the things that the mind apprehends by itself.

SOCR. And also likeness and unlikeness and sameness and difference?

THEAET. Yes.

SOCR. And how about "honorable" and "dishonorable" and "good" and "bad"?

THEAET. Those again seem to me, above all, to be things whose being is considered, one in comparison with another, by the mind, when it reflects within itself upon the past and the present with an eye to the future.

SOCR. Wait a moment. The hardness of something hard and the softness of something soft will be perceived by the mind through touch, will they not?

THEAET. Yes.

SOCR. But their existence and the fact that they both exist, and their contrariety to one another and again the existence of this contrariety are things which the mind itself undertakes to judge for us, when it reflects upon them and compares one with another.

THEAET. Certainly.

SOCR. Is it not true, then, that whereas all the impressions which penetrate to the mind through the body are things which men and animals alike are naturally constituted to perceive from the moment of birth, reflections about them with respect to their existence and usefulness only come, if they come at all, with difficulty through a long and troublesome process of education?

THEAET. Assuredly.

SOCR. Is it possible, then, to reach truth when one cannot reach existence?

THEAET. It is impossible.

SOCR. But if a man cannot reach the truth of a thing, can he possibly know that thing?

THEAET. No, Socrates, how could he?

SOCR. If that is so, knowledge does not reside in the impressions, but in our reflection upon them. It is there, seemingly, and not in the impressions, that it is possible to grasp existence and truth.

THEAET. Evidently.

SOCR. Then are you going to give the same name to two things which differ so widely?

THEAET. Surely that would not be right.

SOCR. Well then, what name do you give to the first one—to seeing, hearing, smelling, feeling cold and feeling warm?

THEAET. Perceiving. What other name is there for it?

SOCR. Taking it all together, then, you call this perception?

THEAET. Necessarily.

SOCR. A thing which, we agree, has no part in apprehending truth, since it has none in apprehending existence.

THEAET. No, it has none.

SOCR. Nor, consequently, in knowledge either.

THEAET. No.

SOCR. Then, Theaetetus, perception and knowledge cannot possibly be the same thing.

THEAET. Evidently not, Socrates. Indeed, it is now perfectly plain that knowledge is something different from perception.

. . .

SOCR. But when we began our talk it was certainly not our object to find out what knowledge is not, but what it is. Still, we have advanced so far as to see that we must not look for it in sense perception at all, but in what goes on when the mind is occupied with things by itself, whatever name you give to that.

THEAET. Well, Socrates, the name for that, I imagine, is "making judgments."

SOCR. You are right, my friend. Now begin all over again. Blot out all we have been saying, and see if you can get a clearer view from the position you have now reached. Tell us once more what knowledge is.

THEAET. I cannot say it is judgment as a whole, because there is false judgment; but perhaps true judgment is knowledge. You may take that as my answer. If, as we go further, it turns out to be less convincing than it seems now, I will try to find another.

SOCR. Good, Theaetetus; this promptness is much better than hanging back as you did at first. If we go on like this, either we shall find what we are after, or we shall be less inclined to imagine we know something of which we know nothing whatever; and that surely is a reward not to be despised. And now, what is this you say: that there are two sorts of judgment, one true, the other false, and you define knowledge as judgment that is true?

THEAET. Yes; that is the view I have come to now.

. . .

SOCR. Imagine, then, for the sake of argument, that our minds contain a block of wax, which in this or that individual may be larger or smaller, and composed of wax that is comparatively pure or muddy, and harder in some, softer in others, and sometimes of just the right consistency.

THEAET. Very well.

SOCR. Let us call it the gift of the Muses' mother, Memory, and say that whenever we wish to remember something we see or hear or conceive in our own minds, we hold this wax under the perceptions or ideas and imprint them on it as we might stamp the impression of a seal ring. Whatever is so imprinted we remember and know so long as the image remains; whatever is rubbed out or has not succeeded in leaving an impression we have forgotten and do not know.

THEAET. So be it.

SOCR. Now take a man who knows things in this way, and is attending to something that he sees or hears. Is there not here a possibility of his making a false judgment?

THEAET. How?

Socr. By thinking that things he knows are other things he knows, or sometimes things he does not know. We were wrong when we agreed earlier that this was impossible.

.   .   .

Socr. Take things you know: you can suppose them to be other things which you both know and perceive; or to be things you do not know, but do perceive; or you can confuse two things which you both know and perceive.

Theaet. Now I am more in the dark than ever.

Socr. Let me start again, then, and put it in this way. I know Theodorus and have a memory in my mind of what he is like, and the same with Theaetetus. At certain moments I see or touch or hear or otherwise perceive them; at other times, though I have no perception of you and Theodorus, I nevertheless remember you both and have you before my mind. Isn't that so?

Theaet. Certainly.

Socr. That, then, is the first point I want to make clear—that it is possible either to perceive or not to perceive something one is acquainted with.

Theaet. True.

Socr. And it is also possible, when one is not acquainted with a thing, sometimes not to perceive it either, sometimes merely to perceive it and nothing more.

Theaet. That is possible too.

Socr. Well, that is what I was saying: if you know one of two people and also perceive him and if you get the knowledge you have to correspond with the perception of him, you will never think he is another person whom you both know and perceive, if your knowledge of him likewise is got to correspond with the perception. That was so, wasn't it?

Theaet. Yes.

Socr. But there was left over the case I have been describing now, in which we say false judgment does occur: the possibility that you may know both and see or otherwise perceive both, but not get the two imprints to correspond each with its proper perception. Like a bad archer, you may shoot to one side and miss the mark—which is indeed another phrase we use for error.

Theaet. With good reason.

Socr. Also, when a perception is present which belongs to one of the imprints, but none which belongs to the other, and the mind fits to the present perception the imprint belonging to the absent one, in all such cases it is in error. To sum up: in the case of objects one does not know and has never perceived, there is, it seems, no possibility of error or false judgment, if our present account is sound; but it is precisely in the field of objects both known and perceived that judgment turns and twists about and proves false or true—true when it brings impressions straight to their proper imprints; false when it misdirects them crosswise to the wrong imprint.

Theaet. Surely that is a satisfactory account, isn't it, Socrates?

Socr. You will think still better of it when you hear the rest. To judge truly is a fine thing and there is something discreditable in error.

Theaet. Of course.

Socr. Well, they say the differences arise in this way. When a man has in his mind a good thick slab of wax, smooth and kneaded to the right consistency, and the impressions that come through the senses are stamped on these tables of the "heart"—

Homer's word hints at the mind's likeness to wax [1]—then the imprints are clear and deep enough to last a long time. Such people are quick to learn and also have good memories, and besides they do not interchange the imprints of their perceptions but think truly. These imprints being distinct and well spaced are quickly assigned to their several stamps—the "real things" as they are called—and such men are said to be clever. Do you agree?

THEAET. Most emphatically.

SOCR. When a person has what the poet's wisdom commends as a "shaggy heart," or when the block is muddy or made of impure wax, or over soft or hard, the people with soft wax are quick to learn, but forgetful, those with hard wax the reverse. Where it is shaggy or rough, a gritty kind of stuff containing a lot of earth or dirt, the impressions obtained are indistinct; so are they too when the stuff is hard, for they have no depth. Impressions in soft wax also are indistinct, because they melt together and soon become blurred. And if, besides this, they overlap through being crowded together into some wretched little narrow mind, they are still more indistinct. All these types, then, are likely to judge falsely. When they see or hear or think of something, they cannot quickly assign things to their several imprints. Because they are so slow and sort things into the wrong places, they constantly see and hear and think amiss, and we say they are mistaken about things and stupid.

THEAET. Your description could not be better, Socrates.

SOCR. We are to conclude, then, that false judgments do exist in us?

THEAET. Most certainly.

SOCR. And true ones also, I suppose?

THEAET. True ones also.

SOCR. At last, then, we believe we have reached a satisfactory agreement that both these kinds of judgments certainly exist?

THEAET. Most emphatically.

SOCR. It really does seem to be true, Theaetetus, that a garrulous person is a strange and disagreeable creature.

THEAET. Why, what makes you say that?

SOCR. Disgust at my own stupidity. I am indeed garrulous: what else can you call a man who goes on bandying arguments to and fro because he is such a dolt that he cannot make up his mind and is loath to surrender any one of them?

THEAET. But why are you disgusted with yourself?

SOCR. I am not merely disgusted but anxious about the answer I shall make if someone asks: "So, Socrates, you have made a discovery: that false judgment resides, not in our perceptions among themselves nor yet in our thoughts, but in the fitting together of perception and thought?" I suppose I shall say, Yes, and plume myself on this brilliant discovery of ours.

THEAET. I don't see anything to be ashamed of in what you have just pointed out, Socrates.

SOCR. "On the other hand," he will continue, "you also say that we can never imagine that a man whom we merely think of and do not see is a horse which again we do not see or touch but merely think of without perceiving it in any way?" I suppose I shall say, Yes, to that.

THEAET. And rightly.

---

1 The Homeric word for heart (κέαϱ) resembles κηϱός (wax). [Cornford's note.]

SOCR. "On that showing," he will say, "a man could never imagine that 11, which he merely thinks of, is 12, which again he merely thinks of." Come, you must find the answer now.

THEAET. Well, I shall answer that, if he saw or handled eleven things, he might suppose they were twelve; but he will never make that judgment about the 11 and the 12 he has in his thoughts.

SOCR. Well now, does a man ever consider in his own mind 5 and 7—I don't mean five men and seven men or anything of that sort, but just 5 and 7 themselves, which we describe as records in that waxen block of ours, among which there can be no false judgment—does anyone ever take these into consideration and ask himself in his inward conversation how much they amount to; and does one man believe and state that they make 11, another that they make 12, or does everybody agree they make 12?

THEAET. Far from it; many people say 11; and if larger numbers are involved, the more room there is for mistakes; for you are speaking generally of any numbers, I suppose.

SOCR. Yes, that is right. Now consider what happens in this case. Is it not thinking that the 12 itself that is stamped on the waxen block is 11?

THEAET. It seems so.

SOCR. Then haven't we come round again to our first argument? For when this happens to someone, he is thinking that one thing he knows is another thing he knows; and that, we said, was impossible. That was the very ground on which we were led to make out that there could be no such thing as false judgment: it was in order to avoid the conclusion that the same man must at the same time know and not know the same thing.

THEAET. Quite true.

SOCR. If so, we must account for false judgment in some other way than as the misfitting of thought to perception. If it were that, we should never make mistakes among our thoughts themselves. As the case stands now, either there is no such thing as false judgment, or it is possible not to know what one does know. Which alternative do you choose?

THEAET. I see no possible choice, Socrates.

SOCR. But the argument is not going to allow both alternatives. However, we must stick at nothing: suppose we try being quite shameless.

THEAET. In what way?

SOCR. By making up our minds to describe what knowing is like.

THEAET. How is that shameless?

SOCR. You seem to be unaware that our whole conversation from the outset has been an inquiry after the nature of knowledge on the supposition that we did not know what it was.

THEAET. No, I am quite aware of that.

SOCR. Then, doesn't it strike you as shameless to explain what knowing is like, when we don't know what knowledge is? The truth is, Theaetetus, that for some time past there has been a vicious taint in our discussion. Times out of number we have said: "we know," "we do not know," "we have knowledge," "we have no knowledge," as if we could understand each other while we still know nothing about knowledge. At this very moment, if you please, we have once more used the words "know nothing" and "understand," as if we had a right to use them while we are still destitute of knowledge.

THEAET. Well, but how are you going to carry on a discussion, Socrates, if you keep clear of those words?

SOCR. I cannot, being the man I am, though I might if I were an expert in debate. If such a person were here now, he would profess to keep clear of them and rebuke us severely for my use of language. As we are such bunglers, then, shall I be so bold as to describe what knowing is like? I think it might help us.

THEAET. Do so, then, by all means. And if you cannot avoid those words, you shall not be blamed.

SOCR. Well, you have heard what "knowing" is commonly said to be?

THEAET. Possibly; but I don't remember at the moment.

SOCR. They say it is "having knowledge."

THEAET. True.

SOCR. Let us make a slight amendment and say: "possessing knowledge."

THEAET. What difference would you say that makes?

SOCR. None, perhaps; but let me tell you my idea and you shall help me test it.

THEAET. I will if I can.

SOCR. "Having" seems to me different from "possessing." If a man has bought a coat and owns it, but is not wearing it, we should say he possesses it without having it about him.[2]

THEAET. True.

SOCR. Now consider whether knowledge is a thing you can possess in that way without having it about you, like a man who has caught some wild birds—pigeons or what not—and keeps them in an aviary he has made for them at home. In a sense, of course, we might say he "has" them all the time inasmuch as he possesses them, mightn't we?

THEAET. Yes.

SOCR. But in another sense he "has" none of them, though he has got control of them, now that he has made them captive in an enclosure of his own; he can take and have hold of them whenever he likes by catching any bird he chooses, and let them go again; and it is open to him to do that as often as he pleases.

THEAET. That is so.

SOCR. Once more then, just as a while ago we imagined a sort of waxen block in our minds, so now let us suppose that every mind contains a kind of aviary stocked with birds of every sort, some in flocks apart from the rest, some in small groups, and some solitary, flying in any direction among them all.

THEAET. Be it so. What follows?

SOCR. When we are babies we must suppose this receptacle empty, and take the birds to stand for pieces of knowledge. Whenever a person acquires any piece of knowledge and shuts it up in his enclosure, we must say he has learned or discovered the thing of which this is the knowledge, and that is what "knowing" means.

THEAET. Be it so.

SOCR. Now think of him hunting once more for any piece of knowledge that he wants, catching and holding it, and letting it go again. In what terms are we to describe that—the same that we used of the original process of acquisition, or different

2 Ἔχειν is commonly used of "wearing" a garment. It also means "to have hold off"—the phrase used below for holding the bird that has been caught inside the aviary. [Cornford's note.]

ones? An illustration may help you to see what I mean. There is a science you call "arithmetic."

THEAET. Yes.

SOCR. Conceive that, then, as a chase after pieces of knowledge about all the numbers, odd or even.

THEAET. I will.

SOCR. That, I take it, is the science in virtue of which a man has in his control pieces of knowledge about numbers and can hand them over to someone else.

THEAET. Yes.

SOCR. And when he hands them over, we call it "teaching," and when the other takes them from him, that is "learning," and when he has them in the sense of possessing them in that aviary of his, that is "knowing."

THEAET. Certainly.

SOCR. Now observe what follows. The finished arithmetician knows all numbers, doesn't he? There is no number the knowledge of which is not in his mind.

THEAET. Naturally.

SOCR. And such a person may sometimes count either the numbers themselves in his own head or some set of external things that have a number.

THEAET. Of course.

SOCR. And by counting we shall mean simply trying to find out what some particular number amounts to?

THEAET. Yes.

SOCR. It appears, then, that the man who, as we admitted, knows every number, is trying to find out what he knows as if he had no knowledge of it. No doubt you sometimes hear puzzles of that sort debated.

THEAET. Indeed I do.

SOCR. Well, our illustration from hunting pigeons and getting possession of them will enable us to explain that the hunting occurs in two ways: first, before you possess your pigeon in order to have possession of it; secondly, after getting possession of it, in order to catch and hold in your hand what you have already possessed for some time. In the same way, if you have long possessed pieces of knowledge about things you have learned and know, it is still possible to get to know the same things again, by the process of recovering the knowledge of some particular thing and getting hold of it. It is knowledge you have possessed for some time, but you had not got it handy in your mind.

THEAET. True.

SOCR. That, then, was the drift of my question, what terms should be used to describe the arithmetician who sets about counting or the literate person who sets about reading; because it seemed as if, in such a case, the man was setting about learning again from himself what he already knew.

THEAET. That sounds odd, Socrates.

SOCR. Well, but can we say he is going to read or count something he does *not* know, when we have already granted that he knows all the letters or all the numbers?

THEAET. No, that is absurd too.

SOCR. Shall we say, then, that we care nothing about words, if it amuses anyone to turn and twist the expressions "knowing" and "learning"? Having drawn a distinction between possessing knowledge and having it about one, we agree that it is impossible not to possess what one does possess, and so we avoid the result that a man should not know what he does know; but we say that it is possible for him to get hold of a false judgment about it. For he may not have about him the knowledge of that thing, but a different piece of knowledge instead, if it so happens that, in hunting for some particular piece of knowledge, among those that are fluttering about, he misses it and catches hold of a different one. In that case, you see, he mistakes 11 for 12, because he has caught hold of the knowledge of 11 that is inside him, instead of his knowledge of 12, as he might catch a dove in place of a pigeon.

THEAET. That seems reasonable.

SOCR. Whereas, when he catches the piece of knowledge he is trying to catch, he is not mistaken but thinks what is true. In this way both true and false judgments can exist, and the obstacles that were troubling us are removed. You will agree to this, perhaps? Or will you not?

THEAET. I will.

SOCR. Yes; for now we are rid of the contradiction about people not knowing what they do know. That no longer implies our not possessing what we do possess, whether we are mistaken about something or not. But it strikes me that a still stranger consequence is coming in sight.

THEAET. What is that?

SOCR. That the interchange of pieces of knowledge should ever result in a judgment that is false.

THEAET. How do you mean?

SOCR. In the first place, that a man should have knowledge of something and at the same time fail to recognize that very thing, not for want of knowing it but by reason of his own knowledge; and next that he should judge that thing to be something else and *vice versa*—isn't that very unreasonable: that when a piece of knowledge presents itself, the mind should fail to recognize anything and know nothing? On this showing, the presence of ignorance might just as well make us know something, or the presence of blindness make us see—if knowledge can ever make us fail to know.

THEAET. Perhaps, Socrates, we were wrong in making the birds stand for pieces of knowledge only, and we ought to have imagined pieces of ignorance flying about with them in the mind. Then, in chasing them, our man would lay hold sometimes of a piece of knowledge, sometimes of a piece of ignorance; and the ignorance would make him judge falsely, the knowledge truly, about the same thing.

SOCR. It is not easy to disapprove of anything you say, Theaetetus; but think again about your suggestion. Suppose it is as you say; then the man who lays hold of the piece of ignorance will judge falsely. Is that right?

THEAET. Yes.

SOCR. But of course he will not think he is judging falsely.

THEAET. Of course not.

SOCR. No; he will think he is judging truly; and his attitude of mind will be the same as if he knew the thing he is mistaken about.

THEAET. Naturally.

SOCR. So he will imagine that, as a result of his chase, he has got hold of a piece of knowledge, not a piece of ignorance.

THEAET. Clearly.

SOCR. Then we have gone a long way round only to find ourselves confronted once more with our original difficulty. Our destructive critic will laugh at us. "You wonderful people," he will say, "are we to understand that a man knows both a piece of knowledge and a piece of ignorance, and then supposes that one of these things he knows is the other which he also knows? Or does he know neither, and then judge that one of these unknown things is the other? Or does he know only one, and identify this known thing with the unknown one, or the unknown one with the known? Or are you going to tell me that there are yet further pieces of knowledge *about* your pieces of knowledge and ignorance, and that their owner keeps these shut up in yet another of your ridiculous aviaries or waxen blocks, knowing them so long as he possesses them, although he may not have them at hand in his mind? On that showing you will find yourselves perpetually driven round in a circle and never getting any further." What are we to reply to that, Theaetetus?

THEAET. Really, Socrates, I don't know what we are to say.

SOCR. Maybe, my young friend, we have deserved this rebuke, and the argument shows that we were wrong to leave knowledge on one side and look first for an explanation of false judgment. That cannot be understood until we have a satisfactory account of the nature of knowledge.

THEAET. As things now stand, Socrates, one cannot avoid that conclusion.

SOCR. To start all over again, then: what is one to say that knowledge is? For surely we are not going to give up yet.

THEAET. Not unless you do so.

SOCR. Then tell me: what definition can we give with the least risk of contradicting ourselves?

THEAET. The one we tried before, Socrates. I have nothing else to suggest.

SOCR. What was that?

THEAET. That true belief is knowledge. Surely there can at least be no mistake in believing what is true and the consequences are always satisfactory.

SOCR. Try, and you will see, Theaetetus, as the man said when he was asked if the river was too deep to ford. So here, if we go forward on our search, we may stumble upon something that will reveal the thing we are looking for. We shall make nothing out, if we stay where we are.

THEAET. True; let us go forward and see.

SOCR. Well, we need not go far to see this much: you will find a whole profession to prove that true belief is not knowledge.

THEAET. How so? What profession?

SOCR. The profession of those paragons of intellect known as orators and lawyers. There you have men who use their skill to produce conviction, not by instruction, but by making people believe whatever they want them to believe. You can hardly imagine teachers so clever as to be able, in the short time allowed by the clock, to instruct their hearers thoroughly in the true facts of a case of robbery or other violence which those hearers had not witnessed.

THEAET. No, I cannot imagine that; but they can convince them.

SOCR. And by convincing you mean making them believe something.

THEAET. Of course.

SOCR. And when a jury is rightly convinced of facts which can be known only by an eyewitness, then, judging by hearsay and accepting a true belief, they are judging without knowledge, although, if they find the right verdict, their conviction is correct?

THEAET. Certainly.

SOCR. But if true belief and knowledge were the same thing, the best of jurymen could never have a correct belief without knowledge. It now appears that they must be different things.

THEAET. Yes, Socrates, I have heard someone make the distinction. I had forgotten, but now it comes back to me. He said that true belief with the addition of an account (*logos*) was knowledge, while belief without an account was outside its range. Where no account could be given of a thing, it was not "knowable"—that was the word he used—where it could, it was knowable.

SOCR. A good suggestion. But tell me how he distinguished these knowable things from the unknowable. It may turn out that what you were told tallies with something I have heard said.

THEAET. I am not sure if I can recall that; but I think I should recognize it if I heard it stated.

SOCR. If you have had a dream, let me tell you mine in return. I seem to have heard some people say that what might be called the first elements of which we and all other things consist are such that no account can be given of them. Each of them just by itself can only be named; we cannot attribute to it anything further or say that it exists or does not exist; for we should at once be attaching to it existence or nonexistence, whereas we ought to add nothing if we are to express just it alone. We ought not even to add "just" or "it" or "each" or "alone" or "this," or any other of a host of such terms. These terms, running loose about the place, are attached to everything, and they are distinct from the things to which they are applied. If it were possible for an element to be expressed in any formula exclusively belonging to it, no other terms ought to enter into that expression; but in fact there is no formula in which any element can be expressed: it can only be named, for a name is all there is that belongs to it. But when we come to things composed of these elements, then, just as these things are complex, so the names are combined to make a description (*logos*), a description being precisely a combination of names. Accordingly, elements are inexplicable and unknowable, but they can be perceived; while complexes ("syllables") are knowable and explicable, and you can have a true notion of them. So when a man gets hold of the true notion of something without an account, his mind does think truly of it, but he does not know it; for if one cannot give and receive an account of a thing, one has no knowledge of that thing. But when he has also got hold of an account, all this becomes possible to him and he is fully equipped with knowledge.

Does that version represent the dream as you heard it, or not?

THEAET. Perfectly.

SOCR. So this dream finds favor and you hold that a true notion with the addition of an account is knowledge?

THEAET. Precisely.

SOCR. Can it be, Theaetetus, that, all in a moment, we have found out today what so many wise men have grown old in seeking and have not found?

THEAET. I, at any rate, am satisfied with our present statement, Socrates.

SOCR. Yes, the statement just in itself may well be satisfactory; for how can there ever be knowledge without an account and right belief? But there is one point in the theory as stated that does not find favor with me.

THEAET. What is that?

SOCR. What might be considered its most ingenious feature: it says that the elements are unknowable, but whatever is complex ("syllables") can be known.

THEAET. Is not that right?

Socr. We must find out. We hold as a sort of hostage for the theory the illustration in terms of which it was stated.

Theaet. Namely?

Socr. Letters—the elements of writing—and syllables. That and nothing else was the prototype the author of this theory had in mind, don't you think?

Theaet. Yes, it was.

Socr. Let us take up that illustration, then, and put it to the question, or rather put the question to ourselves: did we learn our letters on that principle or not? To begin with: is it true that an account can be given of syllables, but not of letters?

Theaet. It may be so.

Socr. I agree, decidedly. Suppose you are asked about the first syllable of "Socrates": "Explain, Theaetetus; what is SO?" How will you answer?

Theaet. S and O.

Socr. And you have there an account of the syllable?

Theaet. Yes.

Socr. Go on, then; give me a similar account of S.

Theaet. But how can one state the elements of an element? The fact is, of course, Socrates, that S is one of the consonants, nothing but a noise, like a hissing of the tongue; while B not only has no articulate sound but is not even a noise, and the same is true of most of the letters. So they may well be said to be inexplicable, when the clearest of them, the seven vowels themselves, have only a sound, and no sort of account can be given of them.

Socr. So far, then, we have reached a right conclusion about knowledge.

Theaet. Apparently.

Socr. But now, have we been right in declaring that the letter cannot be known, though the syllable can?

Theaet. That seems all right.

Socr. Take the syllable then: do we mean by that both the two letters or (if there are more than two) all the letters? Or do we mean a single entity that comes into existence from the moment when they are put together?

Theaet. I should say we mean all the letters.

Socr. Then take the case of the two letters S and O. The two together are the first syllable of my name. Anyone who knows that syllable knows both the letters, doesn't he?

Theaet. Naturally.

Socr. So he knows the S and the O.

Theaet. Yes.

Socr. But has he, then, no knowledge of *each* letter, so that he knows both without knowing either?

Theaet. That is a monstrous absurdity, Socrates.

Socr. And yet, if it is necessary to know each of two things before one can know both, he simply must know the letters first, if he is ever to know the syllable; and so our fine theory will vanish and leave us in the lurch.

Theaet. With a startling suddenness.

Socr. Yes, because we are not keeping a good watch upon it. Perhaps we ought to have assumed that the syllable was not the letters but a single entity that arises out of them with a unitary character of its own and different from the letters.

THEAET. By all means. Indeed, it may well be so rather than the other way.

SOCR. Let us consider that. We ought not to abandon an imposing theory in this poor-spirited manner.

THEAET. Certainly not.

SOCR. Suppose, then, it is as we say now: the syllable arises as a single entity from any set of letters which can be combined; and that holds of every complex, not only in the case of letters.

THEAET. By all means.

SOCR. In that case, it must have no parts.

THEAET. Why?

SOCR. Because, if a thing has parts, the whole thing must be the same as all the parts. Or do you say that a whole likewise is a single entity that arises out of the parts and is different from the aggregate of the parts?

THEAET. Yes, I do.

SOCR. Then do you regard the sum (τὸ πᾶν) as the same thing as the whole, or are they different?

THEAET. I am not at all clear; but you tell me to answer boldly, so I will take the risk of saying they are different.

SOCR. Your boldness, Theaetetus, is right; whether your answer is so, we shall have to consider.

THEAET. Yes, certainly.

SOCR. Well, then, the whole will be different from the sum, according to our present view.

THEAET. Yes.

SOCR. Well but now, is there any difference between the sum and all the things it includes? For instance, when we say, "one, two, three, four, five, six," or "twice three" or "three times two" or "four and two" or "three and two and one," are we in all these cases expressing the same thing or different things?

THEAET. The same.

SOCR. Just six, and nothing else?

THEAET. Yes.

SOCR. In fact, in each form of expression we have expressed all the six.

THEAET. Yes.

SOCR. But when we express them all, is there no sum that we express?

THEAET. There must be.

SOCR. And is that sum anything else than "six"?

THEAET. No.

SOCR. Then, at any rate in the case of things that consist of a number, the words "sum" and "all the things" denote the same thing.

THEAET. So it seems.

SOCR. Let us put our argument, then, in this way. The number of (square feet in) an acre, and the acre are the same thing, aren't they?

THEAET. Yes.

SOCR. And so too with the number of (feet in) a mile?

THEAET. Yes.

SOCR. And again with the number of (soldiers in) an army and the army, and so on, in all cases. The total number is the same as the total thing in each case.

THEAET. Yes.

SOCR. But the number of (units in) any collection of things cannot be anything but *parts* of that collection?

THEAET. No.

SOCR. Now, anything that has parts consists of parts.

THEAET. Evidently.

SOCR. But all the parts, we have agreed, are the same as the sum, if the total number is to be the same as the total thing.

THEAET. Yes.

SOCR. The whole, then, does not consist of parts; for if it were all the parts it would be a sum.

THEAET. Apparently not.

SOCR. But can a part be a part of anything but its whole?

THEAET. Yes; of the sum.

SOCR. You make a gallant fight of it, Theaetetus. But does not "the sum" mean precisely something from which nothing is missing?

THEAET. Necessarily.

SOCR. And is not a whole exactly the same thing—that from which nothing whatever is missing? Whereas, when something is removed, the thing becomes neither a whole nor a sum: it changes at the same moment from being both to being neither.

THEAET. I think now that there is no difference between a sum and a whole.

SOCR. Well, we were saying—were we not?—that when a thing has parts, the whole or sum will be the same thing as all the parts?

THEAET. Certainly.

SOCR. To go back, then, to the point I was trying to make just now; if the syllable is not the same thing as the letters, does it not follow that it cannot have the letters as parts of itself; otherwise, being the same thing as the letters, it would be neither more nor less knowable than they are?

THEAET. Yes.

SOCR. And it was to avoid that consequence that we supposed the syllable to be different from the letters.

THEAET. Yes.

SOCR. Well, if the letters are not parts of the syllable, can you name any things, other than its letters, that are parts of a syllable?

THEAET. Certainly not, Socrates. If I admitted that it had any parts, it would surely be absurd to set aside the letters and look for parts of any other kind.

SOCR. Then, on the present showing, a syllable will be a thing that is absolutely one and cannot be divided into parts of any sort?

THEAET. Apparently.

SOCR. Do you remember then, my dear Theaetetus, our accepting a short while ago a statement that we thought satisfactory: that no account could be given of the primary things of which other things are composed, because each of them, taken just by itself, was incomposite; and that it was not correct to attribute even "existence" to it, or to call it "this," on the ground that these words expressed different things that were extraneous to it; and this was the ground for making the primary thing inexplicable and unknowable?

THEAET. I remember.

SOCR. Then is not exactly this, and nothing else, the ground of its being simple in nature and indivisible into parts? I can see no other.

THEAET. Evidently there is no other.

SOCR. Then has not the syllable now turned out to be a thing of the same sort, if it has no parts and is a unitary thing?

THEAET. Certainly.

SOCR. To conclude, then: if, on the one hand, the syllable is the same thing as a number of letters and is a whole with the letters as its parts, then the letters must be neither more nor less knowable and explicable than syllables, since we made out that all the parts are the same thing as the whole.

THEAET. True.

SOCR. But if, on the other hand, the syllable is a unity without parts, syllable and letter likewise are equally incapable of explanation and unknowable. The same reason will make them so.

THEAET. I see no way out of that.

SOCR. If so, we must not accept this statement: that the syllable can be known and explained, the letter cannot.

THEAET. No, not if we hold by our argument.

SOCR. And again, would not your own experience in learning your letters rather incline you to accept the opposite view?

THEAET. What view do you mean?

SOCR. This: that all the time you were learning you were doing nothing else but trying to distinguish by sight or hearing each letter by itself, so as not to be confused by any arrangement of them in spoken or written words.

THEAET. That is quite true.

SOCR. And in the music school the height of accomplishment lay precisely in being able to follow each several note and tell which string it belonged to; and notes, as everyone would agree, are the elements of music.

THEAET. Precisely.

SOCR. Then, if we are to argue from our own experience of elements and complexes to other cases, we shall conclude that elements in general yield knowledge that is much clearer than knowledge of the complex and more effective for a complete grasp of anything we seek to know. If anyone tells us that the complex is by its nature knowable, while the element is unknowable, we shall suppose that, whether he intends it or not, he is playing with us.

THEAET. Certainly.

SOCR. Indeed we might, I think, find other arguments to prove that point. But we must not allow them to distract our attention from the question before us, namely, what can really be meant by saying that an account added to true belief yields knowledge in its most perfect form.

． ． ．

SOCR. Then we must not be too ready to charge the author of the definition of knowledge now before us with talking nonsense. Perhaps that is not what he meant. He may have meant: being able to reply to the question, what any given thing is, by enumerating its elements.

THEAET. For example, Socrates?

SOCR. For example, Hesiod says about a wagon, "In a wagon are a hundred pieces of wood." I could not name them all; no more, I imagine, could you. If we were asked what a wagon is, we should be content if we could mention wheels, axle, body, rails, yoke.

THEAET. Certainly.

SOCR. But I dare say he would think us just as ridiculous as if we replied to the question about your own name by telling the syllables. We might think and express ourselves correctly, but we should be absurd if we fancied ourselves to be grammarians and able to give such an account of the name Theaetetus as a grammarian would offer. He would say it is impossible to give a scientific account of anything, short of adding to your true notion a complete catalogue of the elements, as, I think, was said earlier.

THEAET. Yes, it was.

SOCR. In the same way, he would say, we may have a correct notion of the wagon, but the man who can give a complete statement of its nature by going through those hundred parts has thereby added an account to his correct notion and, in place of mere belief, has arrived at a technical knowledge of the wagon's nature, by going through all the elements in the whole.

THEAET. Don't you approve, Socrates?

SOCR. Tell me if you approve, my friend, and whether you accept the view that the complete enumeration of elements is an account of any given thing, whereas description in terms of syllables or of any larger unit still leaves it unaccounted for. Then we can look into the matter further.

THEAET. Well, I do accept that.

SOCR. Do you think, then, that anyone has knowledge of whatever it may be, when he thinks that one and the same thing is a part sometimes of one thing, sometimes of a different thing; or again when he believes now one and now another thing to be part of one and the same thing?

THEAET. Certainly not.

SOCR. Have you forgotten, then, that when you first began learning to read and write, that was what you and your schoolfellows did?

THEAET. Do you mean, when we thought that now one letter and now another was part of the same syllable, and when we put the same letter sometimes into the proper syllable, sometimes into another?

SOCR. That is what I mean.

THEAET. Then I have certainly not forgotten; and I do not think that one has reached knowledge so long as one is in that condition.

SOCR. Well then, if at that stage you are writing "Theaetetus" and you think you ought to write T and H and E and do so, and again when you are trying to write "Theodorus," you think you ought to write T and E and do so, can we say that you know the first syllable of your two names?

THEAET. No; we have just agreed that one has not knowledge so long as one is in that condition.

SOCR. And there is no reason why a person should not be in the same condition with respect to the second, third, and fourth syllables as well?

THEAET. None whatever.

SOCR. Can we, then, say that whenever in writing "Theaetetus" he puts down all the letters in order, then he is in possession of the complete catalogue of elements together with correct belief?

THEAET. Obviously.

SOCR. Being still, as we agree, without knowledge, though his beliefs are correct?

THEAET. Yes.

SOCR. Although he possesses the "account" in addition to right belief. For when he wrote he was in possession of the catalogue of the elements, which we agreed was the "account."

THEAET. True.

SOCR. So, my friend, there is such a thing as right belief together with an account, which is not yet entitled to be called knowledge.

THEAET. I am afraid so.

SOCR. Then, apparently, our idea that we had found the perfectly true definition of knowledge was no better than a golden dream.

•   •   •

KNOWING AND BELIEVING

a. b. woozley

1 Traditional distinction of knowledge and belief

The notion that our cognitive activities can be sharply divided into kinds which are fundamentally different from each other, knowing on the one hand and believing on the other, has a long philosophical history, and has endured a less checkered career than most philosophical notions of its antiquity. According to the traditional view, which derives from Plato, knowledge and belief are mental faculties, each *sui generis*, no more to be defined one in terms of the other than are, say, love and friendship. They are, indeed, allied, as love and friendship are allied, and they are more like each other than either is to, say, doubt or love or desire. They are alike in that what a man knows he will express in the form of an assertion or denial, and that what he believes he will similarly express. Again, from many of a man's statements one cannot tell without further questioning whether what he asserts is something which he claims to know or something which he claims to believe.

If a man is very careful he will say, "I know it is raining" (and perhaps even there he is not being careful enough), or "I believe Black Beauty will win the 2.30." But more often than not he will say, "It is raining," or "Black Beauty will win the 2.30." Knowledge and belief then resemble each other in that what is known or believed is normally expressible in an assertion or denial ("John of Gaunt hasn't a hope against Black Beauty"), which does not contain the words "know" or "believe" or their equivalents. On the other hand, the expression of a doubt (in the sense of not being willing to commit oneself either way) cannot be made without either saying, "I doubt . . ." or without using a phrase which operates in an equivalent way, such as "may or may not," "just possibly," and so on.

But although they are alike in that respect, a respect which might roughly be covered by calling them both judging faculties, knowledge and belief have been held to be otherwise different in kind. We might and do confuse them, for a man can think he knows when he does not, but nevertheless according to this view they are

From A. B. Woozley, *Theory of Knowledge: An Introduction* (New York: Barnes & Noble, Inc., 1966), Chap. VIII, pp. 176–193. Reprinted by permission of the publisher and Hutchinson & Co. Ltd.

not adjacent portions on a single scale, so that one merges into the other across a borderline which may be shadowy, shifting, and conventional. About the exact distinction between them philosophers who have maintained that they are generically different activities have not always been as clear or helpful as could be wished. To say, for instance, that in knowing the mind apprehends facts, but in believing it has propositions for its objects is, as our earlier discussion of facts and propositions should have indicated, totally uninformative, and is merely a more long-winded way of saying that in knowing one knows, but in believing one believes.

Perhaps the distinction which is mainly, although by no means without exception, adhered to is one which again goes back to Plato: that the only things a man may know are necessary truths, such as the truths of mathematics or of logic, while all else can at best be a matter of belief. I may then know that two Euclidean triangles having the same base and between the same parallels are equal in area, and I may know that if A is larger than B and if B is larger than C, then A is larger than C. They, it is held, are necessary truths which could not conceivably be otherwise, which a man has only to understand to perceive that they must be true. On the other hand, most of what commonly passes for knowledge is strictly not knowledge at all—both singular pieces, as that you are now reading a book which I have written, that you had two cups of tea for breakfast this morning, and that in 1950 Easter Sunday falls on April 9; and general pieces, as that bottles thrown out of the window fall downwards, not upwards (or more generally still, that material objects attract each other), that unnecessary pulling of the communication cord on an English railway train renders the offender liable to a fine, and that most cricketers bat right-handed.

These propositions are not the objects of knowledge, not because they are not true (for they well may be, and the theory is not concerned to deny that they are), but because they are contingent truths, which might conceivably be false. They carry no guarantee which provides 100 per cent insurance against their being false; and if they might conceivably be false, however remote the possibility may be, they cannot be the objects of knowledge, for knowledge cannot be wrong. Impressed with the uncertified character of contingent propositions, Descartes attempted by a systematic scrutiny to find some strict knowledge which would underwrite them, valiantly but signally failed, and by his failure led on to Hume's insistence on the uncertain character of all matter of fact beliefs, a form of scepticism which recent preoccupation with problems of perception has done much to perpetuate.

2 Knowledge and belief as dispositions

That this traditional division of cognition into two essentially different kinds, knowledge and belief, is false and rests on a confusion I hope to show in what follows. But there is another mistake which is attributed to the theory, and which I do not propose to discuss, although in a more detailed study it could not be avoided. Knowing and believing have been spoken of above as activities, and that, or something like it, is the way they are normally and perhaps thoughtlessly spoken of. This naturally leads to (or perhaps itself leads from) thinking of knowing something (and correspondingly for belief) as a mental act which has a certain object and which occurs at a certain time. The reason may well be that because "know" is a transitive verb governing an accusative we tend in our thought to assimilate knowing to other acts which are named by transitive verbs governing themselves.

Take the case of hitting, for example. If we hear that *A* has hit *B*, we may want to ask when he hit him, or how long he continued to hit him. Hitting is an event or a process, about which it is sense to ask when it occurred or when it started and how long it lasted. But we cannot ask the corresponding things about knowing. Knowing and believing are not properly to be called acts at all, but are dispositional in character. That is, it does not have to be the case that some event is now going on in my mind, or that I am performing some mental act, for it to be the case that I know (as I do) that six nines are fifty-four, or that a Communist coup succeeded in Czechoslovakia at the end of February 1948. My daughter believes that I am clever at mending things, although she is not now thinking of that. My wife knows that milk boils over easily, although she is not now thinking of it, and although she almost never thinks of it when she is boiling milk.

Nevertheless, to say that knowledge and belief are not activities or states but dispositions is not the whole story, for there is such an occurrence as coming to know and coming to believe ("I suddenly realized . . .," "It was only when she blushed that I believed she was lying," etc.). That is, it is sense to ask questions such as, "When did you first know . . .?" and "When did you cease to believe . . .?" And although they may be interpreted as questions asking when certain dispositions were initiated, these dispositions are initiated by something happening, and by that something happening to the person who thereafter knows or who thereafter no longer believes, e.g., the woman who thought her blouse was white until she saw her neighbor's. Whatever realizing, ceasing to believe, etc., may be, they are certainly events involving minds. And therefore, although it may be, as I think it is, correct to insist on the dispositional nature of knowledge and belief, that does not automatically dispose of the problems which worried philosophers who wrongly thought of knowing and believing as acts of different and special sorts. With that proviso, therefore, and without the need to attempt an analysis of what a disposition is, we may return to our main problem of determining the difference between knowledge and belief.

3 Distinction between a priori and empirical propositions

As already indicated, the traditional insistence on a difference in kind between all knowing and all believing is closely connected with the traditional distinction between *a priori* and empirical propositions, the first being held to be knowable, but the second only believable. The distinction between *a priori* and empirical propositions, and its relevance to the supposed difference in kind between knowledge and belief, can be pointed out in two ways, both emphasizing the necessity of *a priori* propositions and the contingency of empirical propositions. First, there is the difference already referred to, that a true *a priori* proposition could not conceivably be false. The proposition expressed by the sentence "3 + 4 =7" is, as a proposition of pure mathematics, a proposition of this kind; no state of this or any other world is conceivable in which that proposition might be false. We might, of course, alter our symbolism in English so as to use the character "2" where we have hitherto written "4," and thenceforth it would be correct to say "3 + 2 = 7." But what we should then mean by "3 + 2 = 7" would be exactly what we now mean by "3 + 4 = 7," and not what we now mean by "3 + 2 = 7."

Continuing to use our present symbolism, the sentence "3 + 4 = 7" expresses a necessary truth, and that 7 is not the sum of 3 plus 4 is necessarily false. On the other hand, that the earth rotates on its axis from west to east is a hypothesis which might conceivably be false. It is simply a matter of empirical fact that it does spin that way. It is, that is, an exceedingly well established hypothesis, so well established that for practical purposes it can be accepted as a piece of knowledge, but there is no necessity about it. We can easily conceive its spinning from east to west. That is, whereas "3 + 2 = 7" could only be made true by a change in our linguistic usage, and the fact expressed by that sentence would be the same as the fact previously expressed by the sentence "3 + 4 = 7," "The earth spins from east to west" could be made true by a change in the behaviour of the earth.

The second way of emphasizing the difference between a priori and empirical propositions is to point out the difference in our mode of establishing them. Once we grasp the truth of an a priori proposition we do not look for further evidence in its favor, and we do not, indeed, treat fresh instances or applications of it as evidence at all. We would not say that a man's knowledge of 3 + 4 = 7 was in any way improved or better established by his coming across more and more cases of a trio and a quartet adding up to a septet. We may, in fact, learn some a priori truths that way. I am sure, for instance, that I first learned that the angle subtended by the diameter of a circle at any point on the circumference is a right angle by drawing a number of diagrams and measuring (or guessing at) the angle in each case; and that only later did I discover or was I taught the demonstrative proof of that conclusion, making use of already established knowledge of the properties of isosceles triangles. But once it was established by demonstration within the system of Euclid there was no need for me to go on collecting instances; the conclusion being certain, the collection of fresh evidence could do nothing to improve its certainty.

On the other hand, if we take an empirical generalization such as "All horses are herbivorous," we find that it was not only learned inductively, but that it is only to be established or validated inductively, too. The more horses we come across and find to be herbivorous, the more evidence we accumulate in favor of our generalization, and the greater its probability becomes. Our confidence in the truth of an empirical generalization is increased by the addition of further instances or applications of it, in a way in which our confidence in an a priori proposition is not increased by the addition of further instances or applications of it.

4   The corresponding distinction between knowledge and belief is false

Now, how does this affect the issue between knowledge and belief? Simply in this way, that empirical propositions are held not to be objects of knowledge because they are not necessary, and because they are only established as probabilities, of however high a degree. There is always, however remote, a possibility of an empirical proposition being false, and therefore it cannot truthfully be said to be known; for we reserve knowledge for certainties, for what cannot be false. This dubitability, or possibility of being false, infects *all* empirical propositions, and not merely the generalizations such as "All horses are herbivorous," in which one gives a pledge to the future.

It applies equally to statements about the present ("I am now in Oxford") as to statements about the future ("The sun will rise in the east tomorrow"), and to statements about the past ("Rommel suffered from desert sores"). It applies to my supposed presence in Oxford, because however many tests I may apply to determine whether I am in Oxford, there is still the possibility that I am the victim of an elaborate hoax, which my tests have not been sufficient to find out: I *might,* for all I know, have been transported during my sleep last night to another city built exactly like Oxford in all respects. We say we know that Rommel suffered from desert sores, because we have a collection of evidence that he did; but do we know? There is the possibility that although all concerned, including the doctors, believed that he had desert sores, they were wrong, for he had some other very similar complaint; and there are other possibilities which could easily be multiplied.

These illustrations should be enough to show the difference which, it is held, lies between knowledge and belief. Knowledge is, on this view, confined to demonstrative systems, and is a goal at which belief may aim but which, although it may come closer and closer, it can never quite attain. Belief, bound however lightly by the ties of contingency and probability, is different in kind from knowledge, firmly enclosed within the circle of certainty.[1]

Now, as I said earlier, this rigid distinction is false and rests on a confusion, which is none the less a confusion for being easily made. Because knowledge is of what is true, and of what could not possibly be false, and because, in the case of an empirical proposition, there is some possibility of its being false, it is concluded that empirical propositions cannot be known, but can only at best be truly believed. But that argument involves confusing two different notions of possibility. The sense in which a necessary truth could not possibly be false is the sense of logical possibility; it is logically impossible for $3 + 4$ to equal 8, if "$3 + 4 = 8$" is interpreted as an *a priori* proposition. If all horses are herbivorous, and if Brown Jack is a horse, then it is logically impossible for Brown Jack not to be herbivorous. Whether or not we

[1] This *a priori*-empirical view of the antithesis between knowledge and belief is liable to be confused with another, by which all propositions are divided up into incorrigible and corrigible. On this view knowledge will have for its field the province of what is incorrigible, and included in that province will be some empirical propositions, which have been variously referred to as basic, or primitive, or protocol propositions. It has been held, for example, that although I may be wrong in supposing that what I see is a table, I cannot be wrong in supposing that it looks like a table; or, in other terminology, although I may be wrong in supposing that I am perceiving a green material object, I cannot be wrong in supposing that I sense a green sense-datum. Thus some empirical propositions are in a way necessary propositions (although not logically necessary, not *a priori*), and these, but not others, may be known. On this distinction, various theories of knowing, or of knowing of one kind, as being a non-inferential acquaintance, are constructed. I do not discuss them in this chapter because I cannot accept the distinction itself. I may be less likely to make a mistake in supposing that what I see looks like a table than in supposing that it is a table, or in supposing that I am sensing a green sense-datum than in supposing that I perceive a green leaf. But there is nothing especially privileged about the first alternative in either case. I am, of course, very unlikely to be wrong if I play for safety by supposing anything so vague as that a sense-datum is green. But if I am more precise and suppose it to be emerald green or avocado green or leaf green, I can and often do go wrong (and wrong not only about words). And that is a matter of common enough experience to justify passing over here a view about knowledge which depends on denying it.

can know that all horses are herbivorous, we can know that if all horses are herbivorous, and if Brown Jack is a horse, then Brown Jack is herbivorous; and what we there know is as good an *a priori* necessity as what we know in knowing that $3 + 4 = 7$. In that sense of "possible," it is always possible that an empirical proposition is false. It is not logically impossible that the sun will rise in the west tomorrow, or that water freezes at 50 degrees Fahrenheit.

But although there is a logical possibility of an empirical proposition being false—that there is such a possibility is part of what is meant by calling it an *empirical* proposition—there is another sense of "possible," in which it is not possible for some empirical propositions to be false. In this sense there is no possibility that Gandhi was not murdered, that I am not now in Oxford, that the sun will rise in the west tomorrow. Take another instance: you are, you suppose, now sitting in your chair reading this book, and it occurs to you to try doubting whether you are sitting in your chair reading this book. How would you set about clearing up the doubt, removing the possibility of your being wrong? You would do it, of course, by pinching yourself to test whether you were awake, by feeling the chair, by getting up and looking at it, by sitting down in it again, by trying to put your fist through the book and failing, by asking the man opposite if this was a book and that was a chair, and so on, for as long as you like. Can you, after passing all those tests, doubt that this is a book and that that is a chair? If so, it is not a doubt that any empirical tests, however successful and however long continued, will remove; and if it is not that sort of a doubt, what sort of a doubt is it?

The plain fact is that if you, the chair, and the book all pass the above tests (which could be indefinitely extended, although in practice you would be satisfied with far fewer), then there is no possibility of your being mistaken, and you know that you are sitting in the chair reading the book. On the other hand, you only believe that your wife is out playing bridge because, although she is out and although she usually does play bridge on this afternoon in the week, she sometimes goes to the cinema instead; there is, then, a real possibility that she is at the cinema. You know what you are now doing, but you do not know what she is now doing.

5   Knowledge not confined to what is necessarily true

What the view which we are criticizing is asking us to do is to confine the word "know" to *necessary* facts, on the ground that if a fact is not necessary there is some possibility of its not being a fact. But there is no possibility of its not being a fact, and it is absurd to suggest that there might be. Knowledge is certainly of what cannot possibly be other than what it is, but, as I have tried to show, possibility is certainly an ambiguous and, I think, also a vague notion. That you are not now reading this book is logically possible, in that the proposition that you are not now reading this book is not self-contradictory. But there is no possibility that you are not now reading this book, and you know it. There may be a possibility that you will immediately give up reading it, but not that you are not now reading it. When there is no possibility that x is not occurring, then you may know that x is occurring; and although philosophically determining the conditions of the presence or absence of such a possibility may prove difficult, we normally have no difficulty in practice in recognizing its absence or presence. There is, then, no solid case for maintaining that knowing is confined within demonstrative systems.

We can put the matter, if we like, by saying that there is more than one sense of the word "know." But we only make fools of ourselves if we try to pretend that we do not really know such things as that Gandhi was murdered, that World War II ended in 1945, that Frenchmen talk a different language from Englishmen, that airplanes travel faster than snails, and so on. Not merely do we know such facts, and thousands of others like them, but we learned how to use the word "know" precisely with reference to such facts. Extending it to refer to necessary truths comes at a later and normally unnoticed stage, unnoticed because the distinction between necessary and contingent truths is a sophisticated distinction which few men have any occasion to make.

6 Knowledge and belief may have the same objects

So far, then, we have seen that knowledge cannot be distinguished from belief by a difference in their objects. We may distinguish necessary from contingent or empirical truths, but we have no right to say that the latter cannot be objects of knowledge. Again, there seems no solid ground for denying that we can have successively belief and knowledge of the same objects, both in the case of necessary and in the case of contingent truths. During the period when I was drawing my diagrams of the angles subtended by the diameter of a circle at points on the circumference I came to hold the belief that all such angles were right angles; and, later, when I learned the proof, I came to know that all such angles were right angles. I believe there is a house on fire somewhere in the district when I hear the clanging of the fire bells and see the fire engines dash past my window; I know there is a house on fire somewhere in the district when, having pursued the fire engines, I find them outside a blazing house, with the crews pumping water onto the flames. Normally the passage of thought is from belief to knowledge: one starts with belief and later (but not, of course, always) arrives at knowledge. That is, belief, when it is confirmed, becomes knowledge.

Exactly the reverse process is not possible: we cannot say that knowledge, when it is infirmed (i.e., shown not to be certain), becomes belief, because our notion of knowledge (or our usage of "knowledge") prevents us speaking that way. Our notion of knowledge is such that a man does not know something unless what he knows is not only true but certainly true; consequently, if what a man once took to be certainly true is shown not to be certainly true, we would not say that he formerly knew it but now only believed it; we might say that formerly he *thought* he knew, but that he must have been wrong in thinking so, because what he thought he knew is not certainly true, and therefore cannot be said to be known.

Nevertheless, there is a different process by which knowledge can relapse into belief, namely, through forgetfulness or losing the evidence. My geometrical example again will serve: when searching my mind for an instance to illustrate my statement on p. 426 that an *a priori* truth can be learned inductively, I hit on that one. But, because in the last twenty years I have had no occasion to think about angles subtended by diameters, not only had I forgotten how to prove that they were right angles, but I was not even *quite* sure that it was true that they were right angles, although I was strongly inclined to think so. I was, therefore, in the position of believing what I once knew (although I could not at the time of believing it know that I once knew). This belief has now once more been converted into knowledge, by my remembering what I had forgotten, namely, how to prove the theorem. My history with reference to the truth of that theorem, then, is that at one period I believed it, later I knew it, later again I believed it, and now once more I know it. I see no good reason for supposing that my present knowledge will not rapidly lapse into belief.

7   *That one knows is not discovered by introspection*

We tend to talk of knowing and believing as activities or states of mind. But it should now be clear that whether or not one can determine the character of some so-called states of mind by introspection, one cannot tell by introspection whether a given state of mind is one of knowing. If on claiming to know that your wife is in the kitchen your claim is challenged, you cannot tell introspectively (and you are not, in fact, tempted to try finding out that way) whether you really do know. So-called examining your mind to find out whether you do know (except, perhaps, in the case of memory) is most unlike examining your mind to find out whether your present feeling is one of regret or of remorse. You can, perhaps, tell introspectively whether you are sure of something, if being sure consists of having a present feeling of conviction. But even there there is a risk of ambiguity, because normally when you are asked the question "Are you sure?," as you might be when you claimed to know that your wife was in the kitchen, you do not take the question to be an invitation to examine or measure a feeling of conviction, but you take it as invitation to re-examine the proposition which you claimed to know, together with the relevant evidence, to determine whether you are still sure, and whether you would still claim to know.

If, having asserted that it is raining, you are asked whether you are sure, you take the question to be an invitation to look out of the window again, and perhaps more carefully than before. "Are you sure?" has other meanings, too, and may, for instance, be an invitation, not to reëxamine the proposition and the evidence for it, but to express your confidence, e.g., by making a bet. "How sure are you?" is often and correctly answered by saying how much one is prepared to bet on the proposition being true. In short, we can never determine by introspection whether we know, and we seldom try to determine by introspection whether we are sure.

8   *Differences between knowing and being sure*

That, however they may be related, knowing and being sure are different, can be shown by two quite simple considerations. First, one can be sure and be wrong, but one cannot know and be wrong. From the fact that you are sure that it is raining it does not follow that it is raining, but from the fact that you know that it is raining it does follow that it is raining. It does not, of course, follow from the fact that you *say* that you know it is raining; for you may say you know and be wrong about that, for you do not know. If a man says he is sure it is raining (and if we do not suppose that he is lying) and we discover that it is, in fact, not raining, we say that he was sure but he was wrong. But if he said not that he was sure but that he knew that it was raining, and we discovered that it was not raining, then we should say that he *thought* he knew but he was wrong. In the first case, we do not say, "He *thought* he was sure, but he was not sure" [2] (to be contrasted with the fact that we do say, "He *thought* he knew, but he did not know"); and in the second case we do not say, "He knew, but he was wrong" (to be contrasted with the fact that we do say, "He was sure, but he was wrong").

A second difference between knowing and being sure is that to say, "I know that . . ." offers a guarantee in a way in which to say, "I am sure that . . ." does not. Suppose at a party you ask me who is the man talking to our hostess and I reply that it is Dr. Brown, and suppose that in response to further inquiries from you (for you do not know Dr. Brown, but have long been anxious to meet him), I insist that I know it is Dr. Brown. If, on the strength of that, you introduce yourself to him and find that he is not Dr. Brown at all, you would then round on me for unreliability in a way in which you might be less inclined to round on me if I had only said that I was sure that the man was Dr. Brown. Saying that I know both pledges myself in a way that saying I am sure does not, and also emphasizes that what I say that I know is a hard, impersonal fact which is quite independent of me. Saying that I am sure does not offer the same 100 per cent guarantee, and does not insist on the dissociation of the fact from myself.[3] Again, one is ready to qualify sureness ("I'm pretty sure . . . not quite sure . . . almost sure," etc.) in a way in which one is not prepared to qualify knowledge.[4]

Nevertheless, being sure is necessary to knowledge, for it would not be sense to say, "I know that it is raining, but I am not quite sure of it." We may, therefore, say so far that knowing involves:

(i) that what is known is true;
(ii) that the person knowing is sure that it is true.

However, although these are necessary conditions, they are not yet sufficient, for it would not be difficult to think of situations in which both conditions were fulfilled and yet one could not truly be said to know. For instance, Professor Hubble may be sure that the universe is expanding at a speed higher than that of any normal explosion, and he may be right, but he does not know that the universe is expanding at that speed; for the data which he has observed, namely, the shift towards red of the light of remote nebulae, are consistent with alternative hypotheses to his own. Or a pessimist may be sure that it will rain tonight because he is giving a large fireworks

---

[2] We do sometimes say that a man thought he was sure, but he was not sure, but not on the ground that what he was sure of turned out to be false; what he thought he was sure of might indeed even turn out to be true. E.g., a man might say that he was sure that he could perform a certain trick, and yet by the way he tackled the trick show that he was not sure, even though he succeeded in doing it.

[3] This certifying or guaranteeing character of "I know that . . ." is clearly brought out in a discussion by J. L. Austin in *Supplementary Proceedings of the Aristotelian Society*, Vol. XX, pp. 170–4.

[4] The qualification "I almost know . . ." is used, in a way that does not correspond to almost being sure, where the knowledge is knowledge how. An actor may almost know his part, or a small boy his nine times table, in the sense that they can almost recite them without mistakes.

party, and he may turn out to be right, for it does rain tonight, but he would hardly be said to have known that it would rain. On reading a newspaper report of the prosecution's case in a murder trial I may be sure that the defendant will be found guilty, and I may be right (for he is subsequently found guilty), but I certainly do not know that he will be found guilty; for that I should at least require to have heard or to have read a fair summary of the case for the defense, quite apart from questions about the impartiality or the sound judgment of the jury.

9   Conditions of knowledge

If p is the proposition in question, then a man does not know p, even although he is sure of p, and although p is true, in any of the following conditions:

> (a) he has no evidence for p;
> (b) he is wrong about the evidence;
> (c) he is wrong about the relation of the evidence to p.

The pessimist who claims to know that his fireworks party will be spoiled by rain does not know, because he has no evidence for saying that it will be so spoiled; he comes under condition (a). Conditions (b) and (c) concern mistakes about evidence, but mistakes of different kinds. Mistakes under (b) consist of being misinformed about the data which one is using as evidence, e.g., as the sky grows darker, taking it to be due to the piling up of rain clouds, when it is, in fact, due to clouds of smoke from oil storage tanks on fire; I might under that misapprehension unjustifiably predict that rain would spoil my fireworks party tonight. The astronomer would be making a similar mistake if he supposed that the light from the distant nebulae showed a red shift, when actually it did not; and the newspaper reader would be making a similar mistake if he supposed, on reading the heading, "Queen Elizabeth Held Up By Breakdown," that the liner had been delayed, when in fact the train in which the Queen of England was traveling had been held up by a breakdown farther along the line. The astronomer could not, in such circumstances, know that the universe was expanding at the speed of an explosion (even although he was right, and it was); and the newspaper reader could not know that the liner would dock at Southampton behind schedule (even although he was right, and it would).

Mistakes under (c) are probably more common. Here one is wrong not about the evidence itself, but about its function as evidence, about its relation to the conclusion, either because it is not evidence for the conclusion, or because, although it is evidence for the conclusion, it is not sufficient.

An instance of the first would be an accusation of forgery built up on a hasty comparison of two signatures and the supposition that they were written by the same man, when a more careful scrutiny would have shown that they were not. An instance of the second (more common than the first) would be a charge of murder depending on the presence of the defendant's fingerprints on the door handle of the room in which the body was found; the fingerprints are certainly some evidence, but far from sufficient, for several other people might have had occasion to visit the room at about the time of the murder, each with as good a motive for committing the murder as the defendant had; and in order to point suspicion towards the defendant (who certainly did visit the room) the others might have been careful to wear gloves or not to touch the door handle. In each of these two cases the charges might be correct, for the defendants did commit respectively the forgery and the murder, but in neither case could it be known from the facts mentioned above as evidence that the defendants were guilty.

To know, then, a man must

(a) have evidence;

(b) be right about the evidence; and

(c) be right about the relation of the evidence to the conclusion.

He must also be sure that he is right under (b) and (c). It is not necessary to knowing *p* that the man should go through a long and explicit process of self-questioning under (b) and (c). A man's claim to know that Gandhi is dead is legitimate if he *can* now prove it; it is not necessary that he should just *have* proved it.

10   Conditions of belief

We may now turn to belief, supplementing what has so far been said about knowledge; and in the light of the earlier discussion what follows can be put fairly shortly. Believing *p* consists in a combination of the following two points: (i) being prepared to say yes to the question *p?* with varying degrees of conviction; and (ii) having some evidence for *p*. Where an increase in conviction is produced by an increase in the evidence (and evidence can increase in more than one dimension) the belief is rational. We would call irrational the belief that it will rain tonight simply because one has arranged a fireworks party, and rational the belief that it will rain tonight because the official weather forecasts predict rain for tonight. Belief may wander throughout the whole range of rationality and irrationality, according to the extent, nature, and value of the evidence, but I do not think we ever believe, if there is a total absence of anything which one would regard as evidence (even though one might be quite wrong in so regarding it).

One may in some cases have to act as if one believed, e.g., deciding on a batting order of a cricket team, knowing nothing of any of the players' ability; but being prepared to act as if one believes is different from believing, and acting as if one believes is different from acting because one believes. There are, too, cases where one "has a hunch," or when one is blindly confident, but would feel hard put to it to produce any evidence. But here, I think, the feeling of difficulty is due not to consciousness of inability to produce the evidence, but to a consciousness of its comparative or total worthlessness as evidence if produced. One therefore takes refuge in blind hunches or in insisting that "it is my lucky day."

Increase in rational belief may become (and often does become) knowledge, namely, when the evidence increases to the point of becoming conclusive. Whether there is a genuine problem about when evidence in general becomes conclusive, it is not my business to discuss. I am inclined to think there is not, and I am certain that even if there is it cannot be a problem such that until it is solved we have no justification for saying that we have conclusive evidence in particular cases. We do have conclusive evidence for a vast number of empirical propositions, singular, particular, and general, and when we have conclusive evidence for a proposition we know it to be true.

Belief, then, covers the following five cases:

(i) Being sure and being right, on evidence which is not conclusive.

(ii) Being sure and being wrong, on evidence which is not conclusive.

(iii) Being unsure and being right, on evidence which is not conclusive.

(iv) Being unsure and being wrong, on evidence which is not conclusive.

(v) Being unsure and being right, on evidence which is conclusive.

The final case, namely,

(vi) Being sure and being right, on evidence which is conclusive, is the case not of believing, but of knowing. Knowing p, then, will consist of surely believing p where p is true, and of the belief being due to having conclusive evidence for p. Having conclusive evidence for p will consist either in explicitly attending to it and consciously treating it as evidence, inferring p from it, or in being able, if called on, to attend to it explicitly, etc., i.e., in the possibility of inferring p. Knowledge has thus been analyzed, not as something generically different from belief, but as the limiting case of belief, something which belief becomes when the evidence is good enough.

Because I do not know that it is logically impossible (indeed I know that it is logically possible) for the thing in front of me which looks like a telephone not to be a telephone, it does not follow that I do not know that it is a telephone. In fact, I do know that it is a telephone, because it bears the marks by which I have always distinguished my telephone, and because I have just used it as a telephone. If suddenly it *should* vanish or I *should* see standing in its place a radio which I have never seen before, I should be extremely surprised. I should wonder how it could have disappeared, or how a radio could have been substituted for it without my noticing. I might even wonder whether a radio had been substituted for it, or whether it had turned into a radio. But I should not doubt, not have reason to doubt, that what had been there until this minute was a telephone. I know, in fact, that the telephone is not going to play any such tricks on me, but even if I did not know that I should still know that it was a telephone, the evidence being what it is.

From this account it follows that the tests of knowledge and belief are twofold. The first concerns what is known or believed: if that is false, it must be belief; if it is true, the test is indecisive as between knowledge and belief. The second concerns the person involved: if he is unsure, or sure on inconclusive evidence, it must be belief; if he is sure on conclusive evidence, it is knowledge. It is therefore wrong to think of knowledge and belief simply as states of mind. They are partly states of mind (or, preferably, dispositions), but the difference between them may be nonmental, as the object is true or false, or mental as the subject is sure or unsure, or partly mental and partly non-mental as the subject's attitude is due to conclusive or inconclusive evidence. For either knowledge or belief to exist one member out of each of these three pairs of factors must be present. Only when the first member of each pair is present do we have knowledge, and in all other combinations we have belief.

ON THE SUPERSENSIBLE
ELEMENT IN KNOWLEDGE

gottfried wilhelm leibniz

.   .   .

Being itself and *truth* are not known wholly through the senses; for it would not be impossible for a creature to have long and orderly dreams, resembling our *life,* of such a sort that everything which it thought it perceived through the senses would be but mere *appearances.* There must therefore be something beyond the senses, which distinguishes the true from the apparent. But the truth of the demonstrative sciences is exempt from these doubts, and must even serve for judging of the truth of sensible things. For as able philosophers, ancient and modern, have already well remarked: if all that I should think that I see should be but a dream, it would always be true that I who think while dreaming, would be something, and would actually think in many ways, for which there must always be some reason.

Thus what the ancient Platonists have observed is very true, and is very worthy of being considered, that the existence of intelligible things and particularly of the *Ego* which thinks and which is called spirit or soul, is incomparably more sure than the existence of sensible things; and that thus it would not be impossible, speaking with metaphysical rigor, that there should be at bottom only these intelligible substances, and that sensible things should be but appearances. While on the other hand our lack of attention makes us take sensible things for the only true things. It is well also to observe that if I should discover any demonstrative truth, mathematical or other, while dreaming (as might in fact be), it would be just as certain as if I had been awake. This shows us how intelligible truth is independent of the truth or of the existence outside of us of sensible and material things.

This conception of *being* and of *truth* is found therefore in the Ego and in the understanding, rather than in the external senses and in the perception of external objects.

There we find also what it is to affirm, to deny, to doubt, to will, to act. But

From a Letter to Queen Charlotte of Prussia, 1702, in *Leibniz* Selections, Philip P. Wiener, ed., pp. 359–364. Reprinted with the permission of Charles Scribner's Sons. Copyright 1951 Charles Scribner's Sons.

above all we find there the *force of the consequences* of reasoning, which are a part of what is called the *natural light*. For example, from this premise, that *no wise man is wicked,* we may, by reversing the terms, draw this conclusion, that *no wicked man is wise.* Whereas from this sentence, that *every wise man is praiseworthy,* we cannot conclude by converting it, that *every one praiseworthy is wise* but only that *some praiseworthy ones are wise.* Although we may always convert particular affirmative propositions, for example, if *some wise man is rich* it must also be that *some rich men are wise,* this cannot be done in particular negatives. For example, we may say that *there are charitable persons who are not just,* which happens when charity is not sufficiently regulated; but we cannot infer from this that *there are just persons who are not charitable;* for in justice are included at the same time charity and the rule of reason.

It is also by this *natural light* that the *axioms* of mathematics are recognized; for example, that *if from two equal things the same quantity be taken away the things which remain are equal;* likewise that *if in a balance everything is equal on the one side and on the other, neither will incline,* a thing which we foresee without ever having experienced it. It is upon such foundations that we construct arithmetic, geometry, mechanics, and the other demonstrative sciences; in which, in truth, the senses are very necessary, in order to have certain ideas of sensible things, and experiments are necessary to establish certain facts, and even useful to verify reasonings as by a kind of proof. But the force of the demonstrations depends upon intelligible notions and truths, which alone are capable of making us discern what is necessary, and which, in the conjectural sciences, are even capable of determining demonstratively the degree of probability upon certain given suppositions, in order that we may choose rationally among opposite appearances, the one which is greatest. Nevertheless this part of the art of reasoning has not yet been cultivated as much as it ought to be.

But to return to *necessary truths,* it is generally true that we know them only by this natural light, and not at all by the experiences of the senses. For the senses can very well make known, in some sort, what is, but they cannot make known what *ought to be* or could not be otherwise.

For example, although we may have experienced numberless times that every massive body tends toward the centre of the earth and is not sustained in the air, we are not sure that this is necessary as long as we do not understand the reason of it. Thus we could not be sure that the same thing would occur in air at a higher altitude, at a hundred or more leagues above us; and there are philosophers who imagine that the earth is a magnet, and as the ordinary magnet does not attract the needle when a little removed from it, they think that the attractive force of the earth does not extend very far either. I do not say that they are right, but I do say that one cannot go very certainly beyond the experiences one has had, when one is not aided by reason.

This is why the geometricians have always considered that what is only proved by *induction* or by examples, in geometry or in arithmetic, is never perfectly proved. For example, experience teaches us that odd numbers continuously added together produce the square numbers, that is to say, those which come from multiplying a number by itself. Thus 1 and 3 make 4, that is to say 2 times 2. And 1 and 3 and 5 make 9, that is to say 3 times 3. And 1 and 3 and 5 and 7 make 16, that is 4 times 4. And 1 and 3 and 5 and 7 and 9 make 25, that is 5 times 5. And so on.

1	1	1	1
3	3	3	3
—	5	5	5
4	—	7	7
	9	—	9
		16	—
			25
2	3	4	5
x	x	x	x
2	3	4	5
—	—	—	—
4	9	16	25

However, if one should experience it a hundred thousand times, continuing the calculation very far, he may reasonably think that this will always follow; but he does not therefore have absolute certainty of it, unless he learns the demonstrative reason which the mathematicians found out long ago. And it is on this foundation of the uncertainty of inductions, but carried a little too far, that an Englishman has lately wished to maintain that we can avoid death. For (said he) the inference is not good: my father, my grandfather, my great-grandfather are dead and all the others who have lived before us; therefore we shall also die. For their death has no influence on us. The trouble is that we resemble them a little too much in this respect that the causes of their death subsist also in us. For the resemblance would not suffice to draw sure consequences without the consideration of the same reasons.

In truth there are *experiments* which succeed numberless times and ordinarily, and yet it is found in some extraordinary cases that there are *instances* where the experiment does not succeed. For example, if we should have found a hundred thousand times that iron put all alone on the surface of water goes to the bottom, we are not sure that this must always happen. And without recurring to the miracle of the prophet Elisha, who made iron float, we know that an iron pot may be made so hollow that it floats, and that it can even carry besides a considerable weight, as do boats of copper or of tin. And even the abstract sciences like geometry furnish cases in which what ordinarily occurs occurs no longer. For example, we ordinarily find that two lines which continually approach each other finally meet, and many people will almost swear that this could never be otherwise. And nevertheless geometry furnishes us with extraordinary lines, which are for this reason called *asymptotes,* which prolonged *ad infinitum* continually approach each other, and nevertheless never meet.

This consideration shows also that there is a *light born within us.* For since the senses and inductions could never teach us truths which are thoroughly universal, nor that which is absolutely necessary, but only that which is, and that which is found in particular examples; and since we nevertheless know necessary and universal truths of the sciences, a privilege which we have above the brutes; it follows that we have derived these truths in part from what is within us. Thus we may lead a child to these by simple interrogations, after the manner of Socrates, without telling him anything, and without making him experiment at all upon the truth of what is asked him. And this could very easily be practiced in numbers and other similar matters.

I agree, nevertheless, that in the present state the external senses are necessary to us for thinking, and that, if we had none, we could not think. But that which is necessary for something does not for all that constitute its essence. Air is necessary for life, but our life is something else than air. The senses furnish us the matter for reasoning, and we never have thoughts so abstract that something from the senses is not mingled therewith; but reasoning requires something else in addition to what is from the senses.

.   .   .

KNOWLEDGE OF FACTS AND LAWS

bertrand russell

When we examine our beliefs as to matters of fact, we find that they are sometimes based directly on perception or memory, while in other cases they are inferred. To common sense this distinction presents little difficulty: the beliefs that arise immediately from perception appear to it indubitable, and the inferences, though they may sometimes be wrong, are thought, in such cases, to be fairly easily rectified except where peculiarly dubious matters are concerned. I know of the existence of my friend Mr. Jones because I see him frequently: in his presence I know him by perception, and in his absence by memory. I know of the existence of Napoleon because I have heard and read about him, and I have every reason to believe in the veracity of my teachers. I am somewhat less certain about Hengist and Horsa, and much less certain about Zoroaster, but these uncertainties are still on a common-sense level, and do not seem, at first sight, to raise any philosophical issue.

This primitive confidence, however, was lost at a very early stage in philosophical speculation, and was lost for sound reasons. It was found that what I know by perception is less than had been thought, and that the inferences by which I pass from perceived to unperceived facts are open to question. Both these sources of scepticism must be investigated.

There is, to begin with, a difficulty as to what is inferred and what is not. I spoke a moment ago of my belief in Napoleon as an inference from what I have heard and read, but there is an important sense in which this is not quite true. When a child is being taught history, he does not argue: "My teacher is a person of the highest moral character, paid to teach me facts; my teacher says there was such a person as Napoleon; therefore probably there was such a person." If he did, he would retain considerable doubt, since his evidence of the teacher's moral character is likely to be inadequate, and in many countries at many times teachers have been paid to teach the opposite of facts. The child in fact, unless he hates the teacher, spontaneously believes what he is told. When we are told anything emphatically or authoritatively, it is an effort not to believe it, as anyone can experience on April Fools' Day. Nevertheless there is still a distinction, even on a common-sense level, between what we are told and what we know for ourselves. If you say to the child, "How do you know about

From Bertrand Russell, *Human Knowledge: Its Scope and Limits*, Part III, Chap. 1, pp. 165–175. Copyright 1948, by Bertrand Russell. Reprinted by permission of Simon & Schuster, Inc. and George Allen & Unwin Ltd.

Napoleon?" the child may say, "Because my teacher told me." If you say, "How do you know your teacher told you?" the child may say, "Why, of course, because I heard her." If you say, "How do you know you heard her?" he may say, "Because I remember it distinctly." If you say, "How do you know you remember it?" he will either lose his temper or say, "Well, I do remember it." Until you reach this point, he will defend his belief as to a matter of fact by belief in another matter of fact, but in the end he reaches a belief for which he can give no further reason.

There is thus a distinction between beliefs that arise spontaneously and beliefs for which no further reason can be given. It is the latter class of beliefs that are of most importance for theory of knowledge, since they are the indispensable minimum of premises for our knowledge of matters of fact. Such beliefs I shall call "data." In ordinary thinking they are *causes* of other beliefs rather than *premises* from which other beliefs are inferred; but in a critical scrutiny of our beliefs as to matters of fact we must whenever possible translate the causal transitions of primitive thinking into logical transitions, and only accept the derived beliefs to the extent that the character of the transitions seems to justify. For this there is a common-sense reason, namely, that every such transition is found to involve some risk of error, and therefore data are more nearly certain than beliefs derived from them. I am not contending that data are ever completely certain, nor is this contention necessary for their importance in theory of knowledge.

There is a long history of discussions as to what was mistakenly called "scepticism of the senses." Many appearances are deceptive. Things seen in a mirror may be thought to be "real." In certain circumstances, people see double. The rainbow seems to touch the ground at some point, but if you go there you do not find it. Most noteworthy in this connection are dreams: however vivid they may have been, we believe, when we wake up, that the objects which we thought we saw were illusory. But in all these cases the core of data is not illusory, but only the derived beliefs. My visual sensations, when I look in a mirror or see double, are exactly what I think they are. Things at the foot of the rainbow do really look colored. In dreams I have all the experiences that I seem to have; it is only things outside my mind that are not as I believe them to be while I am dreaming. There are in fact no illusions of the senses, but only mistakes in interpreting sensational data as signs of things other than themselves. Or, to speak more exactly, there is no evidence that there are illusions of the senses.

Every sensation which is of a familiar kind brings with it various associated beliefs and expectations. When, say, we see and hear an airplane, we do not merely have the visual sensation and the auditory sensation of a whirring noise; spontaneously and without conscious thought we interpret what we see and hear and fill it out with customary adjuncts. To what an extent we do this becomes obvious when we make a mistake—for example, when what we thought was an airplane turns out to be a bird. I knew a road, along which I used often to go in a car, which had a bend at a certain place, and a white washed wall straight ahead. At night it was very difficult not to see the wall as a road going straight on up a hill. The right interpretation as a house and the wrong interpretation as an uphill road were both, in a sense, inferences from the sensational datum, but they were not inferences in the logical sense, since they occurred without any conscious mental process.

I give the name "animal inference" to the process of spontaneous interpretation of sensations. When a dog hears himself called in tones to which he is accustomed, he looks round and runs in the direction of the sound. He may be deceived, like the dog looking into the gramophone in the advertisement of "His Master's Voice." But since inferences of this sort are generated by the repeated experiences that give rise to habit, his inference must be one which has usually been right in his past life, since otherwise the habit would not have been generated. We thus find ourselves, when we begin to reflect, expecting all sorts of things that in fact happen, although it would be logically possible for them not to happen in spite of the occurrence of the sensations which give rise to the expectations. Thus reflection upon animal inference gives us an initial store of scientific laws, such as "Dogs bark." These initial laws are usually somewhat unreliable, but they help us to take the first steps toward science.

Everyday generalizations, such as "Dogs bark," come to be explicitly believed after habits have been generated which might be described as a pre-verbal form of the same belief. What sort of habit is it that comes to be expressed in the words "Dogs bark"? We do not expect them to bark at all times, but we do expect that *if* they make a noise it will be a bark or a growl. Psychologically, induction does not proceed as it does in the textbooks, where we are supposed to have observed a number of occasions on which dogs barked, and then proceeded consciously to generalize. The fact is that the generalization, in the form of a habit of expectation, occurs at a lower level than that of conscious thought, so that, when we begin to think consciously, we find ourselves believing the generalization, not, explicitly, on the basis of the evidence, but as expressing what is implicit in our habit of expectation. This is a history of the belief, not a justification of it.

Let us make this state of affairs somewhat more explicit. First comes the repeated experience of dogs barking, then comes the habit of expecting a bark, then, by giving verbal expression to the habit, comes belief in the general proposition "Dogs bark." Last comes the logician, who asks not "Why do I believe this?" but "What reason is there for supposing this true?" Clearly the reason, if any, must consist of two parts: first, the facts of perception consisting of the various occasions on which we have heard dogs bark; second, some principle justifying generalization from observed instances to a law. But this logical process comes historically after, not before, our belief in a host of common-sense generalizations.

The translation of animal inferences into verbal generalizations is carried out very inadequately in ordinary thinking, and even in the thinking of many philosophers. In what counts as perception of external objects there is much that consists of habits generated by past experience. Take, for example, our belief in the permanence of objects. When we see a dog or a cat, a chair or a table, we do not suppose that we are seeing something which has a merely momentary existence; we are convinced that what we are seeing has a past and a future of considerable duration. We do not think this about everything that we see; a flash of lightning, a rocket, or a rainbow is expected to disappear quickly. But experience has generated in us the expectation that ordinary solid objects, which can be touched as well as seen, usually persist, and can be seen and touched again on suitable occasions. Science reinforces this belief by explaining away apparent disappearances as transformations into gaseous forms. But the belief in quasi-permanence, except in exceptional cases, antedates the scientific doctrine of the indestructibility of matter, and is itself antedated by the animal expectation that common objects can be seen again if we look in the right place.

The filling out of the sensational core by means of animal inferences, until it becomes what is called "perception," is analogous to the filling out of telegraphic press messages in newspaper offices. The reporter telegraphs the one word "King," and the newspaper prints "His Gracious Majesty King George VI." There is some risk of error in this proceeding, since the reporter may have been relating the doings of Mr. Mackenzie King. It is true that the context would usually reveal such an error, but one can imagine circumstances in which it would not. In dreams, we fill out the bare sensational message wrongly, and only the context of waking life shows us our mistake.

The analogy to abbreviated press telegrams is very close. Suppose, for instance, you see a friend at the window of an incoming train, and a little later you see him coming toward you on the platform. The physical causes of your perceptions (and of your interpretation of them) are certain light signals passing between him and your eyes. All that physics, by itself, entitles you to infer from the receipt of these signals is that, somewhere along the line of sight, light of the appropriate colors has been emitted or reflected or refracted or scattered. It is obvious that the kind of ingenuity which has produced the cinema could cause you to have just these sensations in the absence of your friend, and that in that case you would be deceived. But such sources of deception cannot be frequent, or at least cannot have been frequent hitherto, since, if they were, you would not have formed the habits of expectation and belief in context that you have in fact formed. In the case supposed, you are confident that it is your friend, that he has existed throughout the interval between seeing him at the window and seeing him on the platform, and that he has pursued a continuous path through space from the one to the other. You have no doubt that what you saw was something solid, not an intangible object like a rainbow or a cloud. And so, although the message received by the senses contains (so to speak) only a few key words, your mental and physical habits cause you, spontaneously and without thought, to expand it into a coherent and amply informative dispatch.

This expansion of the sensational core to produce what goes by the somewhat question-begging name of "perception" is obviously only trustworthy in so far as our habits of association run parallel to processes in the external world. Clouds looked down upon from a mountain may look so like the sea or a field of snow that only positive knowledge to the contrary prevents you from so interpreting your visual sensations. If you are not accustomed to the gramophone, you will confidently believe that the voice you hear on the other side of the door proceeds from a person in the room that you are about to enter. There is no obvious limit to the invention of ingenious apparatus capable of deceiving the unwary. We know that the people we see on the screen in the cinema are not really there, although they move and talk and behave in a manner having some resemblance to that of human beings; but if we did not know it, we might at first find it hard to believe. Thus what we seem to know through the senses may be deceptive whenever the environment is different from what our past experience has led us to expect.

From the above considerations it follows that we cannot admit as data all that an uncritical acceptance of common sense would take as given in perception. Only sensations and memories are truly data for our knowledge of the external world. We must exclude from our list of data not only the things that we consciously infer, but all that is obtained by animal inference, such as the imagined hardness of an object seen but not touched. It is true that our "perceptions," in all their fullness, are data for psychology: we do in fact have the experience of believing in such-and-such an object. It is only for knowledge of things outside our own minds that it is necessary to regard only sensations as data. This necessity is a consequence of what we know of physics and physiology. The same external stimulus, reaching the brains of two men with different experiences, will produce different results, and it is only what these different results have in common that can be used in inferring external causes. If it is objected that the truth of physics and physiology is doubtful, the situation is even worse; for if they are false, nothing whatever as to the outer world can be inferred from my experiences. I am, however, throughout this work, assuming that science is broadly speaking true.

If we define "data" as "those matters of fact of which, independently of inference, we have a right to feel most nearly certain," it follows from what has been said that all my data are events that happen to me, and are, in fact, what would commonly be called events in my mind. This is a view which has been characteristic of British empiricism, but has been rejected by most Continental philosophers, and is not now accepted by the followers of Dewey or by most of the logical positivists. As the issue is of considerable importance, I shall set forth the reasons which have convinced me, including a brief repetition of those that have already been given.

There are, first, arguments on the common-sense level, derived from illusions, squinting, reflection, refraction, etc., but above all from dreams. I dreamed last night that I was in Germany, in a house which looked out on a ruined church; in my dream I supposed at first that the church had been bombed during the recent war, but was subsequently informed that its destruction dated from the wars of religion in the sixteenth century. All this, so long as I remained asleep, had all the convincingness of waking life. I did really have the dream, and did really have an experience intrinsically indistinguishable from that of seeing a ruined church when awake. It follows that the experience which I call "seeing a church" is not conclusive evidence that there is a church, since it may occur when there is no such external object as I suppose in my dream. It may be said that, though when dreaming I may *think* that I am awake, when I wake up I *know* that I am awake. But I do not see how we are to have any such certainty; I have frequently dreamed that I woke up; in fact once, after ether, I dreamed it about a hundred times in the course of one dream. We condemn dreams, in fact, because they do not fit into a proper context, but this argument can be made inconclusive, as in Calderon's play *La Vida es Sueño*. I do not believe that I am now dreaming, but I cannot prove that I am not. I am, however, quite certain that I am having certain experiences, whether they be those of a dream or those of waking life.

We come now to another class of arguments, derived from physics and physiology. This class of arguments came into philosophy with Locke, who used it to show that secondary qualities are subjective. This class of arguments is capable of being used to throw doubt on the truth of physics and physiology, but I will first deal with them on the hypothesis that science, in the main, is true.

We experience a visual sensation when light waves reach the eye, and an auditory sensation when sound waves reach the ear. There is no reason to suppose that light waves are at all like the experience which we call seeing something, or sound waves at all like the experience which we call hearing a sound. There is no reason whatever to suppose that the physical sources of light and sound waves have any more resemblance to our experiences than the waves have. If the waves are produced in unusual ways, our experience may lead us to infer subsequent experiences which it turns out that we do not have; this shows that even in normal perception interpretation plays a larger part than common sense supposes, and that interpretation sometimes leads us to entertain false expectations.

Another difficulty is connected with time. We see and hear now, but what (according to common sense) we are seeing and hearing occurred some time ago. When we both see and hear an explosion, we see it first and hear it afterward. Even if we could suppose that the furniture of our room is exactly what it seems, we cannot suppose this of a nebula millions of light-years away, which looks like a speck but is not much smaller than the Milky Way, and of which the light that reaches us now started before human beings began to exist. And the difference between the nebula and the furniture is only one of degree.

Then there are physiological arguments. People who have lost a leg may continue to feel pain in it. Dr. Johnson, disproving Berkeley, thought the pain in his toe when he kicked a stone was evidence for the existence of the stone, but it appears that it was not even evidence for the existence of his toe, since he might have felt it even if his toe had been amputated. Speaking generally, if a nerve is stimulated in a given manner, a certain sensation results, whatever may be the source of the stimulation. Given sufficient skill, it ought to be possible to make a man see the starry heavens by tickling his optic nerve, but the instrument used would bear little resemblance to the august bodies studied by astronomers.

The above arguments, as I remarked before, may be interpreted sceptically, as showing that there is no reason to believe that our sensations have external causes. As this interpretation concedes what I am at present engaged in maintaining—namely, that sensations are the sole data for physics—I shall not, for the moment, consider whether it can be refuted, but shall pass on to a closely similar line of argument which is related to the method of Cartesian doubt. This method consists in searching for data by provisionally rejecting everything that it is found possible to call in question.

Descartes argues that the existence of sensible objects might be uncertain, because it would be possible for a deceitful demon to mislead us. *We* should substitute for a deceitful demon a cinema in technicolor. It is, of course, also possible that we may be dreaming. But he regards the existence of our thoughts as wholly unquestionable. When he says, "I think, therefore I am," the primitive certainties at which he may be supposed to have arrived are particular "thoughts," in the large sense in which he uses the term. His own existence is an inference from his thoughts, an inference whose validity does not at the moment concern us. In the context, what appears certain to him is that there is doubting, but the experience of doubting has no special prerogative over other experiences. When I see a flash of lightning I may, it is maintained, be uncertain as to the physical character of lightning and even as to whether anything external to my self has happened, but I cannot make myself doubt that there has been the occurrence which is called "seeing a flash of lightning," though there may have been no flash outside my seeing.

It is not suggested that I am certain about all my own experiences; this would certainly be false. Many memories are dubious, and so are many faint sensations. What I am saying—and in this I am expounding part of Descartes' argument—is that there are some occurrences that I cannot make myself doubt, and that these are all of the kind that, if we admit a not-self, are part of the life of myself. Not all of them are sensations; some are abstract thoughts, some are memories, some are wishes, some are pleasures or pains. But all are what we should commonly describe as mental events in me.

My own view is that this point of view is in the right in so far as it is concerned with data that are matters of fact. Matters of fact that lie outside my experience can be made to seem doubtful, unless there is an argument showing that their existence follows from matters of fact within my experience together with laws of whose certainty I feel reasonably convinced. But this is a long question, concerning which, at the moment, I wish to say only a few preliminary words.

Hume's scepticism with regard to the world of science resulted from (a) the doctrine that all my data are private to me, together with (b) the discovery that matters of fact, however numerous and well selected, never logically imply any other matter of fact. I do not see any way of escaping from either of these theses. The first I have been arguing; I may say that I attach especial weight in this respect to the argument from the physical causation of sensations. As to the second, it is obvious as a matter of syntax to anyone who has grasped the nature of deductive arguments. A matter of fact which is not contained in the premises must require for its assertion a proper name which does not occur in the premises. But there is only one way in which a new proper name can occur in a deductive argument, and that is when we proceed from the general to the particular, as in "All men are mortal, therefore Socrates is mortal." Now, no collection of assertions of matters of fact is logically equivalent to a general assertion, so that, if our premises concern only matters of fact, this way of introducing a new proper name is not open to us. Hence the thesis follows.

If we are not to deduce Hume's scepticism from the above two premises, there seems to be only one possible way of escape, and that is to maintain that among the premises of our knowledge, there are some general propositions, or there is at least one general proposition, which is not analytically necessary, i.e., the hypothesis of its falsehood is not self-contradictory. A principle justifying the scientific use of induction would have this character. What is needed is some way of giving probability (not certainty) to the inferences from known matters of fact to occurrences which have not yet been, and perhaps never will be, part of the experience of the person making the inference. If an individual is to know anything beyond his own experiences up to the present moment, his stock of uninferred knowledge must consist not only of matters of fact but also of general laws, or at least a law, allowing him to make inferences from matters of fact; and such law or laws must, unlike the principles of deductive logic, be synthetic, i.e., not proved true by their falsehood being self-contradictory. The only alternative to this hypothesis is complete scepticism as to all the inferences of science and common sense, including those which I have called animal inferences.

5

CONCEPTUAL AND INTUITIVE KNOWLEDGE

henri bergson

. . .

I. *There is a reality that is external and yet given immediately to the mind.* Common sense is right on this point, as against the idealism and realism of the philosophers.

II. This reality is mobility. Not *things* made, but things in the making, not self-maintaining *states,* but only changing states, exist. Rest is never more than apparent, or, rather, relative. The consciousness we have of our own self in its continual flux introduces us to the interior of a reality, on the model of which we must represent other realities. *All reality, therefore, is tendency, if we agree to mean by tendency an incipient change of direction.*

III. Our mind, which seeks for solid points of support, has for its main function in the ordinary course of life that of representing *states* and *things.* It takes, at long intervals, almost instantaneous views of the undivided mobility of the real. It thus obtains *sensations* and *ideas.* In this way it substitutes for the continuous the discontinuous, for motion stability, for tendency in process of change, fixed points marking a direction of change and tendency. This substitution is necessary to common sense, to language, to practical life, and even, in a certain sense, which we shall endeavor to determine, to positive science. *Our intellect, when it follows its natural bent, proceeds, on the one hand, by solid perceptions, and, on the other, by stable conceptions.* It starts from the immobile, and only conceives and expresses movement as a function of immobility. It takes up its position in ready-made concepts, and endeavors to catch in them, as in a net, something of the reality which passes. This is certainly not done in order to obtain an internal and metaphysical knowledge of the real, but simply in order to utilize the real, each concept (as also each sensation) being a *practical question* which our activity puts to reality and to which reality replies, as must be done in business, by a Yes or a No. But, in doing that, it lets that which is its very essence escape from the real.

IV. The inherent difficulties of metaphysics, the antinomies which it gives rise to, and the contradictions into which it falls, the division into antagonistic schools, and the irreducible opposition between systems are largely the result of our applying, to the disinterested knowledge of the real, processes which we generally employ for practical ends. They arise from the fact that we place ourselves in the immobile in order to lie in wait for the moving thing as it passes, instead of replacing ourselves in the moving thing itself, in order to traverse with it the immobile positions. They arise from our professing to reconstruct reality—which is tendency and consequently mobility—with percepts and concepts whose function it is to make it stationary. With stoppages, however numerous they may be, we shall never make mobility; whereas, if mobility is given, we can, by means of diminution, obtain from it by thought as many stoppages as we desire. In other words, *it is clear that fixed concepts may be extracted by our thought from mobile reality; but there are no means of reconstructing the mobility of the real with fixed concepts.* Dogmatism, however, in so far as it has been a builder of systems, has always attempted this reconstruction.

V. In this it was bound to fail. It is on this impotence and on this impotence only that the sceptical, idealist, critical doctrines really dwell: in fact, all doctrines that deny to our intelligence the power of attaining the absolute. But because we fail to reconstruct the living reality with stiff and ready-made concepts, it does not follow that we cannot grasp it in some other way. *The demonstrations which have been given of the relativity of our knowledge are therefore tainted with an original vice; they imply, like the dogmatism they attack, that all knowledge must necessarily start from concepts with fixed outlines, in order to clasp with them the reality which flows.*

VI. But the truth is that our intelligence can follow the opposite method. It can place itself within the mobile reality, and adopt its ceaselessly changing direction; in short, can grasp it by means of that *intellectual sympathy* which we call intuition. This is extremely difficult. The mind has to do violence to itself, has to reverse the direction of the operation by which it habitually thinks, has perpetually to revise, or rather to recast, all its categories. But in this way it will attain to fluid concepts, capable of following reality in all its sinuosities and of adopting the very movement of the inward life of things. Only thus will a progressive philosophy be built up, freed from the disputes which arise between the various schools, and able to solve its problems naturally, because it will be released from the artificial expression in terms of which such problems are posited. *To philosophize, therefore, is to invert the habitual direction of the work of thought.*

VII. This inversion has never been practiced in a methodical manner; but a profoundly considered history of human thought would show that we owe to it all that is greatest in the sciences, as well as all that is permanent in metaphysics. The most powerful of the methods of investigation at the disposal of the human mind, the infinitesimal calculus, originated from this very inversion. Modern mathematics is precisely an effort to substitute the *being made* for the *ready-made*, to follow the generation of magnitudes, to grasp motion no longer from without and in its displayed result, but from within and in its tendency to change; in short, to adopt the mobile continuity of the outlines of things. It is true that it is confined to the outline, being only the science of magnitudes. It is true also that it has only been able to achieve its marvelous applications by the invention of certain symbols, and that if the intuition of which we have just spoken lies at the origin of invention, it is the symbol alone which is concerned in the application. But metaphysics, which aims at no application, can and usually must abstain from converting intuition into symbols. Liberated from the obligation of working for practically useful results, it will indefinitely enlarge the domain of its investigations. What it may lose in comparison with science in utility and exactitude, it will regain in range and extension. Though mathematics is only the science of magnitudes, though mathematical processes are applicable only to quantities, it must not be forgotten that quantity is always quality in a nascent state; it is, we might say, the limiting case of equality. It is natural, then, that metaphysics should adopt the generative idea of our mathematics in order to extend it to all qualities; that is, to reality in general. It will not, by doing this, in any way be moving towards universal mathematics, that chimera of modern philosophy. On the contrary, the farther it goes, the more untranslatable into symbols will be the objects it encounters. But it will at least have begun by getting into contact with the continuity and mobility of the real, just where this contact can be most marvelously utilized. It will have contemplated itself in a mirror which reflects an image of itself, much shrunken, no doubt, but for that reason very luminous. It will have seen with greater clearness what the mathematical processes borrow from concrete reality, and it will continue in the direction of concrete reality, and not in that of mathematical processes. Having then discounted beforehand what is too modest, and at the same time too ambitious, in the following formula, we may say that *the object of metaphysics is to perform* qualitative *differentiations and integrations.*

VIII. The reason why this object has been lost sight of, and why science itself has been mistaken in the origin of the processes it employs, is that intuition, once attained, must find a mode of expression and of application which conforms to the habits of our thought, and one which furnishes us, in the shape of well-defined concepts, with the solid points of support which we so greatly need. In that lies the condition of what we call exactitude and precision, and also the condition of the unlimited extension of a general method to particular cases. Now this extension and this work of logical improvement can be continued for centuries, while the act which creates the method lasts but for a moment. That is why we so often take the logical equipment of science for science itself forgetting the metaphysical intuition from which all the rest has sprung.

From the overlooking of this intuition proceeds all that has been said by philosophers and by men of science themselves about the "relativity" of scientific knowledge. *What is relative is the symbolic knowledge by preexisting concepts, which proceeds from the fixed to the moving, and not the intuitive knowledge which installs itself in that which is moving and adopts the very life of things.* This intuition attains the absolute.

Science and metaphysics therefore come together in intuition. A truly intuitive philosophy would realize the much-desired union of science and metaphysics. While it would make of metaphysics a positive science—that is, a progressive and indefinitely perfectible one—it would at the same time lead the positive sciences, properly so called, to become conscious of their true scope, often far greater than they imagine. It would put more science into metaphysics, and more metaphysics into science. It would result in restoring the continuity between the intuitions which the various sciences have obtained here and there in the course of their history, and which they have obtained only by strokes of genius.

IX. That there are not two different ways of knowing things fundamentally, that the various sciences have their root in metaphysics, is what the ancient philosophers generally thought. Their error did not lie there. It consisted in their being always dominated by the belief, so natural to the human mind, that a variation can only be the expression and development of what is invariable. Whence it followed that action was an enfeebled contemplation, duration a deceptive and shifting image of immobile eternity, the Soul a fall from the Idea. The whole of the philosophy which begins with Plato and culminates in Plotinus is the development of a principle which may be formulated thus: "There is more in the immutable than in the moving, and we pass from the stable to the unstable by a mere diminution." Now it is the contrary which is true.

Modern science dates from the day when mobility was set up as an independent reality. It dates from the day when Galileo, setting a ball rolling down an inclined plane, firmly resolved to study this movement from top to bottom for itself, in itself, instead of seeking its principle in the concepts of *high* and *low,* two immobilities by which Aristotle believed he could adequately explain the mobility. And this is not an isolated fact in the history of science. Several of the great discoveries, of those at least which have transformed the positive sciences or which have created new ones, have been so many soundings in the depths of pure duration. The more living the reality touched, the deeper was the sounding.

But the lead line sunk to the sea bottom brings up a fluid mass which the sun's heat quickly dries into solid and discontinuous grains of sand. And the intuition of duration, when it is exposed to the rays of the understanding, in like manner quickly turns into fixed, distinct, and immobile concepts. In the living mobility of things the understanding is bent on marking real or virtual stations, it notes departures and arrivals; for this is all that concerns the thought of man in so far as it is simply human. It is more than human to grasp what is happening in the interval. But philosophy can only be an effort to transcend the human condition.

Men of science have fixed their attention mainly on the concepts with which they have marked out the pathway of intuition. The more they laid stress on these residual products, which have turned into symbols, the more they attributed a symbolic character to every kind of science. And the more they believed in the symbolic character of science, the more did they indeed make science symbolical. Gradually they have blotted out all difference, in positive science, between the natural and the artificial, between the data of immediate intuition, and the enormous work of analysis which the understanding pursues round intuition. Thus they have prepared the way for a doctrine which affirms the relativity of all our knowledge.

But metaphysics has also labored to the same end.

How could the masters of modern philosophy, who have been renovators of science as well as of metaphysics, have had no sense of the moving continuity of reality? How could they have abstained from placing themselves in what we call concrete duration? They have done so to a greater extent than they were aware; above all, much more than they said. If we endeavor to link together, by a continuous connection, the intuitions about which systems have become organized, we find, together with other convergent and divergent lines, one very determinate direction of thought and of feeling. What is this latent thought? How shall we express the feeling? To borrow once more the language of the Platonists, we will say—depriving the words of their psychological sense, and giving the name of Idea to a certain settling down into easy intelligibility, and that of Soul to a certain longing after the restlessness of life—that an invisible current causes modern philosophy to place the Soul above the Idea. It thus tends, like modern science, and even more so than modern science, to advance in an opposite direction to ancient thought.

But this metaphysics, like this science, has enfolded its deeper life in a rich tissue of symbols, forgetting sometimes that, while science needs symbols for its analytical development, the main object of metaphysics is to do away with symbols. Here, again, the understanding has pursued its work of fixing, dividing, and reconstructing. It has pursued this, it is true, under a rather different form. Without insisting on a point which we propose to develop elsewhere, it is enough here to say that the understanding, whose function it is to operate on stable elements, may look for stability either in *relations* or in *things*. In so far as it works on concepts of relations, it culminates in *scientific* symbolism. In so far as it works on concepts of things, it culminates in *metaphysical* symbolism. But in both cases the arrangement comes from the understanding. Hence, it would fain believe itself independent. Rather than recognize at once what it owes to an intuition of the depths of reality, it prefers exposing itself to the danger that its whole work may be looked upon as nothing but an artificial arrangement of symbols. So that if we were to hold on to the letter of what metaphysicians and scientists say, and also to the material aspect of what they do, we might believe that the metaphysicians have dug a deep tunnel beneath reality, that the scientists have thrown an elegant bridge over it, but that the moving stream of things passes between these two artificial constructions without touching them.

One of the principal artifices of the Kantian criticism consisted in taking the metaphysician and the scientist literally, forcing both metaphysics and science to the extreme limit of symbolism to which they could go, and to which, moreover, they make their way of their own accord as soon as the understanding claims an independence full of perils. Having once overlooked the ties that bind science and metaphysics to intellectual intuition, Kant has no difficulty in showing that our science is wholly relative, and our metaphysics entirely artificial. Since he has exaggerated the independence of the understanding in both cases, since he has relieved both metaphysics and science of the intellectual intuition which served them as inward ballast, science with its relations presents to him no more than a film of form, and metaphysics, with its things, no more than a film of matter. Is it surprising that the first, then, reveals to him only frames packed within frames, and the second only phantoms chasing phantoms?

He has struck such telling blows at our science and our metaphysics that they have not even yet quite recovered from their bewilderment. Our mind would readily resign itself to seeing in science a knowledge that is wholly relative, and in metaphysics a speculation that is entirely empty. It seems to us, even at this present date, that the Kantian criticism applies to all metaphysics and to all science. In reality, it applies more especially to the philosophy of the ancients, as also to the form—itself borrowed from the ancients—in which the moderns have most often left their thought. It is valid against a metaphysics which claims to give us a *single* and completed system of things, against a science professing to be a *single* system of relations; in short, against a science and a metaphysics presenting themselves with the architectural simplicity of the Platonic theory of ideas or of a Greek temple. If metaphysics claims to be made up of concepts which were ours before its advent, if it consists in an ingenious arrangement of preexisting ideas which we utilize as building material for an edifice, if, in short, it is anything else but the constant expansion of our mind, the ever-renewed effort to transcend our actual ideas and perhaps also our elementary logic, it is but too evident that, like all the works of pure understanding, it becomes artificial. And if science is wholly and entirely a work of analysis or of conceptual representation, if experience is only to serve therein as a verification for "clear ideas," if, instead of starting from multiple and diverse intuition—which insert themselves in the particular movement of each reality, but do not always dovetail into each other—it professes to be a vast mathematics, a single and closed-in system of relations, imprisoning the whole of reality in a network prepared in advance—it becomes a knowledge purely relative to human understanding. If we look carefully into the *Critique of Pure Reason,* we see that science for Kant did indeed mean this kind of *universal mathematics,* and metaphysics this practically unaltered *Platonism.* In truth, the dream of a universal mathematics is itself but a survival of Platonism. Universal mathematics is what the world of ideas becomes when we suppose that the Idea consists in a relation or in a law, and no longer in a thing. Kant took this dream of a few modern philosophers for a reality; more than this, he believed that all scientific knowledge was only a detached fragment of, or rather a steppingstone to, universal mathematics. Hence the main task of the *Critique* was to lay the foundation of this mathematics—that is, to determine what the intellect must be, and what the object, in order that an uninterrupted mathematics may bind them together. And of necessity, if all possible experience can be made to enter thus into the rigid and already formed framework of our understanding, it is (unless we assume a pre-established harmony) because our understanding itself organizes nature, and finds itself again therein as in a mirror. Hence the possibility of science, which owes all its efficacy to its relativity, and the impossibility of metaphysics, since the latter finds nothing more to do than to parody with phantoms of things the work of conceptual arrangement which science practices seriously on relations. Briefly, *the whole* Critique *of* Pure Reason *ends in establishing that Platonism, illegitimate if Ideas are things, becomes legitimate if Ideas are relations, and that the ready-made idea, once brought down in this way from heaven to earth, is in fact, as Plato held, the common basis alike of thought and of nature. But the whole of the* Critique of Pure Reason *also rests on this postulate, that our intellect is incapable of anything but Platonizing—* that is, of pouring all possible experience into preexisting molds.

On this the whole question depends. If scientific knowledge is indeed what Kant supposed, then there is one simple science, preformed and even preformulated in nature, as Aristotle believed; great discoveries, then, serve only to illuminate, point by point, the already drawn line of this logic, immanent in things, just as on the night of a fete we light up one by one the rows of gas-jets which already outline the shape of some building. And if metaphysical knowledge is really what Kant supposed, it is reduced to a *choice* between two attitudes of the mind before all the great problems, both equally possible; its manifestations are so many arbitrary and always ephemeral choices between two solutions, virtually formulated from all eternity: it lives and dies by antinomies. But the truth is that modern science does not present this unilinear simplicity, nor does modern metaphysics these irreducible oppositions.

Modern science is neither one nor simple. It rests, I freely admit, on ideas which in the end we find clear; but these ideas have gradually become clear through the use made of them; they owe most of their clearness to the light which the facts, and the applications to which they led, have by reflection shed on them—the clearness of a concept being scarcely anything more at bottom than the certainty, at last obtained, of manipulating the concept profitably. At its origin, more than one of these concepts must have appeared obscure, not easily reconcilable with the concepts already admitted into science, and indeed very near the borderline of absurdity. This means that science does not proceed by an orderly dovetailing together of concepts predestined to fit each other exactly. True and fruitful ideas are so many close contacts with currents of reality, which do not necessarily converge on the same point. However, the concepts in which they lodge themselves manage somehow, by rubbing off each other's corners, to settle down well enough together.

On the other hand, modern metaphysics is not made up of solutions so radical that they can culminate in irreducible oppositions. It would be so, no doubt, if there were no means of accepting at the same time and on the same level the thesis and the antithesis of the antinomies. But philosophy consists precisely in this, that by an effort of intuition one places oneself within that concrete reality, of which the *Critique* takes from without the two opposed views, thesis and antithesis. I could never imagine how black and white interpenetrate if I had never seen gray; but once I have seen gray I easily understand how it can be considered from two points of view, that of white and that of black. Doctrines which have a certain basis of intuition escape the Kantian criticism exactly in so far as they are intuitive; and these doctrines are the whole of metaphysics, provided we ignore the metaphysics which is fixed and dead in *theses,* and consider only that which is living in *philosophers.* The divergencies between the schools—that is, broadly speaking, between the groups of disciples formed round a few great masters—are certainly striking. But would we find them as marked between the masters themselves? Something here dominates the diversity of systems, something, we repeat, which is simple and definite like a sounding, about which one feels that it has touched at greater or less depth the bottom of the same ocean, though each time it brings up to the surface very different materials. It is on these materials that the disciples usually work; in this lies the function of analysis. And the master, in so far as he formulates, develops, and translates into abstract ideas what he brings, is already in a way his own disciple. But the simple act which started the analysis, and which conceals itself behind the analysis, proceeds from a faculty quite different from the analytical. This is, by its very definition, intuition.

In conclusion, we may remark that there is nothing mysterious in this faculty. Every one of us has had occasion to exercise it to a certain extent. Any one of us, for instance, who has attempted literary composition, knows that when the subject has been studied at length, the materials all collected, and the notes all made, something more is needed in order to set about the work of composition itself, and that is an often very painful effort to place ourselves directly at the heart of the subject, and to seek as deeply as possible an impulse, after which we need only let ourselves go. This impulse, once received, starts the mind on a path where it rediscovers all the information it had collected, and a thousand other details besides; it develops and analyzes itself into terms which could be enumerated indefinitely. The farther we go, the more terms we discover; we shall never say all that could be said, and yet, if we turn back suddenly upon the impulse that we feel behind us, and try to seize it, it is gone; for it was not a thing, but the direction of a movement, and though indefinitely extensible, it is infinitely simple. Metaphysical intuition seems to be something of the same kind. What corresponds here to the documents and notes of literary composition is the sum of observations and experience gathered together by positive science. For we do not obtain an intuition from reality—that is, an intellectual sympathy with the most intimate part of it—unless we have won its confidence by a long fellowship with its superficial manifestations. And it is not merely a question of assimilating the most conspicuous facts; so immense a mass of facts must be accumulated and fused together, that in this fusion all the preconceived and premature ideas which observers may unwittingly have put into their observations will be certain to neutralize each other. In this way only can the bare materiality of the known facts be exposed to view. Even in the simple and privileged case which we have used as an example, even for the direct contact of the self with the self, the final effort of distinct intuition would be impossible to anyone who had not combined and compared with each other a very large number of psychological analyses. The masters of modern philosophy were men who had assimilated all the scientific knowledge of their time, and the partial eclipse of metaphysics for the last half-century has evidently no other cause than the extraordinary difficulty which the philosopher finds today in getting into touch with positive science, which has become far too specialized. But metaphysical intuition, although it can be obtained only through material knowledge, is quite other than the mere summary or synthesis of that knowledge. It is distinct from these, we repeat, as the motor impulse is distinct from the path traversed by the moving body, as the tension of the spring is distinct from the visible movements of the pendulum. In this sense metaphysics has nothing in common with a generalization of facts, and nevertheless it might be defined as *integral experience*.

6

PHENOMENOLOGICAL ANALYSIS

alfred schutz

. . .

The search for a realm of indubitable truth as a starting point for philosophical thinking is not at all new in modern philosophy. On the contrary, it may be said that modern philosophy starts with the famous Cartesian attempt to attain absolute certainty by systematically casting doubt upon all our experiences which can be put in question. It is hardly necessary to enter into a discussion of the peculiar way taken by Descartes in his *Meditations* in his effort to establish *"Cogito, ergo sum"* as the indubitable certainty that lies at the basis of all our thinking. But it seems advisable to emphasize the importance of his basic thought, his insistence that any philosopher must at least once in his life make the radical effort to examine critically all the seemingly given data of his experiences and of the elements of his stream of thought; must, for this purpose, turn away from the uncritical attitude toward the world he lives in naïvely among his fellowmen, unconcerned whether this world of his daily life has the character of existence or of mere appearance. This fundamental discovery of Descartes opened an avenue of approach for all future philosophical thinking.

Descartes' meditations were the outstanding pattern for Husserl's phenomenology. But Husserl believed that Descartes' analysis was not radical enough. Holding in his hand the key to a great discovery, he hesitated to use it, hesitated to pursue the indispensable consequences. To be sure, he laid bare the indubitable *"ego cogito"* as the origin of all our knowledge, and thus defined the stream of thought as the field of all further philosophical investigation. But he was not aware of the implications hidden in both terms of this *"ego cogito."*

To start with the latter, Descartes handled the cogitations that appear within the stream of thought as isolated entities. Neither was he aware of the through and through interconnectedness of the stream of thought in inner time, nor did he make a sufficiently radical distinction between the act of thinking and the object of thought. The first problem, that of the interconnectedness of the stream of thought, will be dealt with later. The second one found its solution only through the discovery,

From "Some Leading Concepts of Phenomenology," in Alfred Schutz, *Collected Papers,* Maurice Natanson, ed. (The Hague: Martinus Nijhoff, 1962), I: 102–115. Reprinted by permission of the publisher.

by Franz Brentano, Husserl's teacher, of the *intentional* character of all our thinking. Any of our experiences as they appear within our stream of thought, Brentano held, are necessarily referred to the object experienced. There is no such thing as thought, fear, fantasy, remembrance as such; every thought is thought *of,* every fear is fear *of,* every remembrance is remembrance *of* the object that is thought, feared, remembered.

The technical term coined by Husserl to designate this relationship is "intentionality." The intentional character of all our cogitations necessarily involves a sharp distinction between the act [1] of thinking, fearing, remembering, and the objects to which these acts are referred. Husserl considerably deepened the inquiry into the intentional character of cogitations, and he frequently declared the field of intentionality to be the outstanding topic of phenomenological research. It will be necessary to return later to the implications carried by the concept of intentionality; here we are interested only in the fact that the Cartesian concept of the stream of cogitations may be considerably radicalized by pointing out their intentional character.

Another radicalization seems necessary with respect to Descartes' concept of the ego, whose indubitable existence was the outcome of his meditations. As we have seen, the Cartesian method involves an artificial change in the attitude that man observes in his daily life. In daily life we accept the existence of the world naïvely as it is, and only by means of philosophical doubt can the indubitability of the *"ego cogitans"* be reinstated. But after having made the important discovery of the field of transcendental subjectivity as the domain of certainty, Descartes dropped it immediately by identifying this ego with *mens sive animus sive intellectus,* thus substituting the human soul or mind *within* the world for the ego that can be discovered only by detaching from and reflecting upon the world. This is exactly the point where phenomenological criticism sets in, the point where Husserl started a Cartesian meditation all over again. In order to lay bare the pure field of consciousness Husserl developed the famous and frequently misunderstood technique of "phenomenological reduction," which will now be presented in broad outline. It is no more than a radicalized renewal of the Cartesian method.

The phenomenologist does not deny the existence of the outer world, but for his analytical purpose he makes up his mind to suspend belief in its existence—that is, to refrain intentionally and systematically from all judgments related directly or indirectly to the existence of the outer world. Borrowing terms from mathematical technique, Husserl called this procedure "putting the world in brackets" or "performing the phenomenological reduction." There is nothing mysterious in these notions, which are merely names for the technical device of phenomenology for radicalizing the Cartesian method of philosophical doubt, in order to go beyond the natural attitude of man living within the world he accepts, be it reality or mere appearance.

It is an admittedly artificial change from man's attitude in his daily life toward the world and his belief in it to the attitude of the philosopher, who by his very problem is bound to reject any presupposition that does not stand the test of his critical doubt. The purpose of such a technique is only to reach a level of indubitable certainty which lies beyond the realm of mere belief—in other words, to disclose the pure field of consciousness. As will be shown below, this pure field of consciousness

---

1 Husserl defined "acts" not as psychical activities, but as intentional experiences [Natanson's note.]

can be explored and described in its own right, can be analyzed and questioned about its genesis.[2] If this technique succeeds in attaining its goal—and the phenomenologist thinks it does—if it helps really to make possible an investigation within the purified sphere of conscious life, upon which all our beliefs are founded, then we may turn back later on from this aprioristically reduced sphere to the mundane one. Since to each empirical determination within the latter there necessarily corresponds a feature within the former, we may be confident that all our discoveries within the reduced sphere will stand the test also in the mundane sphere of our life within the world.

Although "phenomenological reduction" does not require any magic or mysterious faculty of mind, the technique of bracketing which it suggests is by no means a simple one if applied with the necessary radicalism. What we have to put in brackets is not only the existence of the outer world, along with all the things in it, inanimate and animate, including fellowmen, cultural objects, society and its institutions. Also our belief in the validity of our statements about this world and its content, as conceived within the mundane sphere, has to be suspended. Consequently, not only our practical knowledge of the world but also the propositions of all the sciences dealing with the existence of the world, all natural and social sciences, psychology, logic, and even geometry—all have to be brought within the brackets. This means that none of their truths, tested or not by experiences and proofs within the mundane sphere, can be taken over in the reduced sphere without critical examination. And even more—I, the human being, am also, as a psycho-physiological unit, an element of this world that has to be bracketed, and so is my body and my mind or my soul or whatever name you prefer to give to the scheme of reference to which we relate our experiences of the world. In performing the phenomenological reduction I have to suspend belief also in my mundane existence as a human being within the world. Thus the process of reduction transcends the world in every respect, and the reduced sphere is in the very meaning of the word a transcendental one or, in the well-understood meaning of the word, an aprioristic one.

But a student who is willing to try to perform this suppression of all natural habits of thinking may ask whether this phenomenological reduction does not lead toward an absolute nihilism. If I have annulled, so to speak, not only the world and my beliefs in it, not only all the results of sciences dealing with the world, but also myself as a psycho-physiological unit, what then remains? Is it not the only possible conclusion that nothing can be left outside the brackets when all the aforementioned elements have been bracketed?

The answer is emphatically No. What remains after the performance of the transcendental reduction is nothing less than the universe of our conscious life, the stream of thought in its integrity, with all its activities and with all its cogitations and experiences (both terms being used in the broadest—the Cartesian—sense, which includes not only perceptions, conceptions, judgments, but also acts of will, feelings, dreams, fantasies, etc.).

And now it is useful to remember what was said above with respect to the intentional character of all our cogitations. They are essentially and necessarily cogitations *of* something; they refer to intentional objects. This intentional character of our cogitations has not only been preserved within the reduced sphere; it has even been

---

2 Husserl's term "genesis" refers to the process by which knowledge arises in its "origin-form" of self-givenness, and has nothing to do with the factual process of meanings arising out of a definite historical subjectivity. [Natanson's note.]

purified and made visible. My perception of this chair in the natural attitude corroborates my belief in its existence. Now I perform the transcendental reduction. I refrain from believing in the existence of this chair. Thereafter the chair perceived remains outside the bracketing, but the perception itself is without any doubt an element of my stream of thought. And it is not "perception as such," without any further reference; it remains "perception *of*"—specifically perception *of* this *chair*. I am no longer attaching to this perception, however, any judgment whether this chair is really an existing object in the outer world. It is not the corporeal thing "chair" to which my perception intentionally refers, but the intentional object of my preserved perception is "the chair *as I have perceived it*," the *phenomenon* "chair *as it appears to me*," which may or may not have an equivalent in the bracketed outer world. Thus the whole world is preserved within the reduced sphere in so far, but only in so far, as it is the intentional correlate of my conscious life—with the radical modification, however, that these intentional objects are no longer the things of the outer world as they exist and as they really are, but the phenomena as they appear to me. This difficult distinction requires further comment.

I perceive the blossoming tree in the garden. This, my perceiving of the tree as it appears to me, is an indubitable element of the stream of my thought. And the same is valid for the phenomenon "blossoming-tree-as-it-appears-to-me," which is the intentional object of my perceiving. This phenomenon is independent of the fate of the real tree in the outer world. The tree in the garden may change its colors and shades by the interplay of sun and cloud, it may lose its blossoms, it may be destroyed by fire. The once perceived phenomenon "blossoming-tree-as-it-appears-to-me" remains untouched by all these events, and also remains untouched by the performance of the phenomenological reduction described above. A second perception may refer to the tree as it appears to me at that time, and may or may not be consistent with the first one. If it is, I may perform a synthesis, an identification of the two phenomena (or more correctly, of the second phenomenon actually perceived and the recollected phenomenon caught by the first perception). If the second perception is not consistent with the first, I may doubt either of them, or I may search for an explanation of their apparent inconsistency.

In any case, each act of perceiving and its intentional object are indubitable elements of my stream of thought; and equally certain is the doubt I may have about whether the "tree as it appears to me" has a correlate in the outer world. The foregoing example has illustrated the fact that my cogitations and their intentional objects are elements of my stream of thought which are not influenced by the changes that may happen to their correlates in the outer world. But this does not mean that the cogitations are not subject to modification by events happening within my stream of consciousness. In order to make this clear let us first distinguish between the act of perceiving and the perceived, between the *cogitare* and the *cogitatum* or, to use Husserl's technical term, between the Noesis and the Noema.

There are modifications of the intentional object which are due to activities of the mind and are therefore noetical, and others which originate within the intentional object itself and are therefore noematical. It is impossible, of course, to enter here into a full discussion of these noetical-noematical modifications, the systematic exploration of which constitutes a vast field of phenomenological research. But merely in order to give some idea of the importance of the problems involved, I shall mention a few examples of the implications hidden within the appearing phenomenon itself.

When, for the sake of abbreviation, I used language like "I am perceiving this chair" or "I am perceiving this blossoming cherry tree in the garden," I did not adequately describe what was perceived by those perceptions, but rather the outcome of a very complicated process of interpretation, in which the present perception was connected with previously experienced perceptions (cogitations) of the different aspects of this cherry tree when I walked around it, of this cherry tree as it appeared to me yesterday, of my experiences of cherry trees and of trees in general, of corporeal things and so on. The intentional object of my perceiving is a specific mixture of colors and shapes in a special perspective of distance, and it stands out over against other objects afterward called "my garden," "the heavens," "clouds." Interpretation of this total as "the blossoming cherry tree in my garden as it appears to me" is the outcome of a complicated reference to pre-experienced cogitations. Nevertheless, all these pre-experienced cogitations, referring to corporeal things, have produced a certain "universal style" of interpreting the noematic correlate of my perceiving activity. I may even say that the noema itself, the intentional object perceived, carries along many implications which may be explicated systematically.

Let us for the sake of simplification restrict our examples to the so-called perceptions of corporeal things. What I am perceiving is only one aspect of the thing. Not only when I move around do other aspects appear. In addition, the aspect of the thing caught by my perceiving act suggests other possible aspects: the front side of the house suggests its back, the facade the interior, the roof the unseen foundation and so on. All these moments together may be called the "inner horizon" of the perceived object, and it can be systematically explored by following the intentional indications within the noema itself. But there is an outer horizon too. The tree refers to my garden, the garden to the street, to the city, to the country in which I am living, and finally to the whole universe. Every perception of a "detail" refers to the "thing" to which it pertains, the thing to other things over against which it stands out and which I call its background. There is not an isolated object as such, but a field of perceptions and cogitations with a halo, with a horizon or, to use a term of William James, with fringes relating it to other things. These groups of implications, which we have called the inner and the outer horizon, are concealed within the noema itself, and if I follow its intentional indications the noema itself seems to be modified; whereas the noetical side, the perceiving act, does not change.

From these noematical modifications have to be distinguished, for the purpose of analysis, the noetical modifications that are due to the perceiving activity itself. These are, for instance, the different attitudes peculiar to the perceiving act which in psychology textbooks are handled under the heading of "attention." There is also the important distinction between the originary experience of the experienced thing and such derived experiences as those based upon recollection or retention of previous experiences. (Without entering into this very complicated problem I may add that the distinction just made is very important for the solution of one of the greatest enigmas of all psychology, the problem of evidence: to the phenomenologist, evidence is not a hidden quality inherrent in a specific kind of experience, but the possibility of referring derived experiences to an originary one.) This distinction is based upon the interconnectedness of the stream of thought in inner time: the present cogitation is surrounded by fringes of retentions and protentions connecting it with what just now happened and with what may be expected to happen immediately, and refers to cogitations of the more distant past by recollection and to the future by anticipations.

All this leads to an entirely new theory of memory and experience in inner time, and to the definite overthrow of the psychology of association. In radicalizing the insight into the through and through connectedness of our stream of experiences, phenomenology comes very close to the early writings of William James and to the doctrine of the Gestaltists. But the basic concept of phenomenology leads also to an entirely new interpretation of logic. Before this can be made clear we have to turn for a moment to another topic.

So far this discussion has been deliberately restricted to the phenomenological interpretation of so-called real objects, of things in the outer world. It is now time to introduce Husserl's concept of "ideal objects." These are by no means of metaphysical origin, and have nothing to do with Plato's or Kant's ideas or with any kind of Berkeleyan or Hegelian idealism. An ideal object is, for instance, the concept of number and the whole system of numbers with which arithmetic and algebra deal; or the content of the Pythagorean theorem as a meaningful entity; or the meaning of a sentence or a book; or a notion like "the Hegelian philosophy" or "Calvin's concept of original sin"; or any of the so-called social and cultural objects which are meaningful and can at any time be made intentional objects of our cogitations.

It is the peculiarity of intentional objects that they are *founded* upon so-called "real" objects of the outer world, and that they can be communicated only by signs and symbols which are in turn perceptible things, such as the sound waves of the spoken word, or printed letters. Therefore phenomenology had to develop a very important theory of semantics. It is characteristic of a sign that it suggests another thing which belongs to quite another category. The well known sign for "root" suggests a specific mathematical notion that is entirely independent of the typographical shape of the root sign in different printing styles, and of whether this sign appears printed in a textbook, written with ink or pencil on paper or with chalk on the blackboard, whether I refer to it in speech by the sound sign "Wurzel" or "root" or "racine." And the same holds true for the specific sign system and for all sign systems or languages. They indicate the ideal objects but they are not themselves the ideal objects.

The thing of the outer world which will be interpreted as a sign, its meaning, its meaning within the system of the universe of discourse, its specific meaning within the context at hand—all these have to be sharply distinguished. A glance at the doctrines of certain logicians of our time who are pleased to reduce logic, science, and even philosophy to a pre-given system of semantics shows the full importance of Husserl's distinction. This does not mean, however, that Husserl did not have a full understanding of the genuine problem of the *mathesis universalis*. Indeed, an outstanding contribution of phenomenology toward this problem is one of his *Logical Investigations* called "The Distinction of Independent and Dependent Meanings and the Idea of Pure Grammar."

The theory of ideal objects opens an avenue of approach to another phenomenological insight, the importance of which is not limited, however, to our experiencing of ideal objects. As high school students we all learned to derive the Pythagorean theorem $a^2 + b^2 = c^2$ from certain other geometrical propositions by developing step by step certain conclusions from certain assured premises. This performance of many separate although interconnected mental operations disclosed to us the meaning of the theorem in question, and this meaning has since become our permanent possession. It is not necessary now for us to repeat this mental process of deriving the theorem, in order to understand its meaning. On the contrary, although some of us might have some difficulty if we had to prove why the sum of the squares of the sides of a right triangle must always be equal to the square of the hypotenuse, we do understand the meaning of this proposition, which we find ready at hand within the stock of our experience.

In more general terms, our mind builds up a thought by single operational steps, but in hindsight it is able to look in a single glance at this whole process and its outcome. We can even go a step further: our knowledge of an object, at a certain given moment, is nothing else than the sediment of previous mental processes by which it has been constituted. It has its own history, and this history of its constitution can be found by questioning it. This is done by turning back from the seemingly ready-made object of our thought to the different activities of our mind in which and by which it has been constituted step by step.

This is the kernel of Husserl's theory of constitution, and it gives an insight into one of his great contributions to the interpretation of logic.

Our current school-logic is merely a refinement of the Aristotelian formal logic, which regards concepts as ready-made and works out operational rules for the technique of judgment, of conclusions, of deduction and subsumption and so on. This logic is based upon the assumption of a world in which there are things with qualities, relationships between things, species and genera, all of them representable by well circumscribed notions. The basic assumption of this kind of logic is the principle of predicability, according to the well known formula "S is P."

Phenomenological analysis shows, however, that there is a pre-predicative stratum of our experience, within which the intentional objects and their qualities are not at all well circumscribed; that we do not have original experiences of isolated things and qualities, but that there is rather a field of our experiences within which certain elements are selected by our mental activities as standing out against the background of their spatial and temporal surroundings; that within the through and through connectedness of our stream of consciousness all these selected elements keep their halos, their fringes, their horizons; that an analysis of the mechanism of predicative judgment is warranted only by recourse to the mental processes in which and by which pre-predicative experience has been constituted. Formal logic must therefore be founded upon a logic of the underlying constitutional processes, which can be investigated only within the transcendental field made accessible by the phenomenological reduction.

This, in oversimplified outline, is Husserl's distinction between "Formal and Transcendental Logic." In his book of that name he shows that analyses of this kind lead to entirely new interpretations of certain basic concepts of our current logic, such as evidence, tautology, the principle of the excluded middle, and so on. He shows the presuppositions of formal logic which are derived from certain ontological assumptions; and he starts to investigate the role of intersubjectivity within the field of logic, which refers not to my private world but to the world common to all of us, and which alone explains the problem of intersubjective truth.

It is of course impossible to enter here into a discussion of these very intricate problems. The short catalogue given above can show only that questions of the greatest importance for all the sciences are at stake. I even venture to say that the many great performances in the field of logic for which our generation is indebted to Dewey's operationalism and James' pragmatism can find their justification only by recourse to the field of pre-predicative experience. All the overt and covert ontological assumptions made by these schools have to be carefully analyzed in order to determine the sphere where these theories are legitimately applicable and yet avoid the mistake of considering them as general principles of our thought, which they are not.

Even a short account of the basic methods of Husserl's phenomenology would be incomplete without a mention of the important distinction between the empirical and the eidetical approach. According to Husserl, phenomenology aims to be an eidetical science, dealing not with existence but with essence (*Wesen*). Phenomenological methods can of course be applied with the greatest success within the empirical sphere as well. But only by recourse to the eidetical sphere can the aprioristic character of phenomenology as a *prima philosophia* and even as a phenomenological psychology be assured. I wish strongly to emphasize that the distinction between the empirical and the eidetical approaches has nothing to do with the distinction between the mundane and the reduced sphere, dealt with so far. Within the mundane sphere, too, eidetical science (*Wesenswissenschaft*) is possible.

The unfortunate terms *Wesen* and *Wesensschau* which Husserl chose for characterizing the eidetical approach have created many misunderstandings and have almost prevented readers of good will from studying Husserl's *Ideen*, which starts with an exposition of this method. The term *Wesen* has a metaphysical connotation in philosophical literature; the Greek term "eidetic" induces the reader to identify the "essence" with the Platonic idea; and the term *Wesensschau* suggests a kind of irrational intuition, like certain techniques of revelation accessible only to the mystic in ecstasy, which is used by the phenomenological esoteric in order to gaze at the eternal truths.

Actually, the eidetic approach, like the phenomenological reduction, is no more than another methodological device of investigation. The principle of this method is as follows. Let us assume that on the desk before me, illuminated by the lamp, stands a red wooden cube, of one-inch dimensions. In the natural attitude I perceive this thing as unquestionably real, having the qualities and characteristics I have mentioned. In the phenomenologically reduced sphere the phenomenon-cube—the cube as it appears to me—keeps the same qualities as an intentional object of my perceiving act. But suppose I am interested in finding what are the qualities common to all cubes. I do not want to do so by the method of induction, which not only presupposes the existence of similar objects but also implies certain unwarranted logical assumptions. I have before me only this single concrete object perceived. I am free, however, to transform this perceived object in my fancy, by successively varying its features—its color, its size, the material of which it is made, its perspective, its illumination, its surroundings and background and so on. Thus I may imagine an infinite number of varied cubes. But these variations do not touch on a set of characteristics common to all imaginable cubes, such as rectangularity, limitation to six squares, corporeality. This set of characteristics, unchanged among all the imagined transformations of the concrete thing perceived—the kernel, so to speak, of all possibly imaginable cubes—

I shall call the essential characteristics of the cube or, using a Greek term, the *eidos* of the cube. No cube can be thought of that would not have these essential features. All the other qualities and characteristics of the concrete object under scrutiny are nonessential. (Needless to say, I could use my red wooden cube as point of departure for other imagined variations in order to find the *eidos* of color, of corporeal thing, of object of perception, and so on.)

Thus eidetic investigations do not deal with concrete real things but with possibly imaginable things. It is in this sense that we must understand Husserl's frequently criticized dictum that phenomenology has to do not only with objects perceived but also with objects imagined, and that the latter are of even greater importance for the phenomenological approach.

Again we see that the eidetic approach is merely a methodological device for the solution of a special task. The phenomenologist, we may say, does not have to do with the objects themselves; he is interested in their *meaning*, as it is constituted by the activities of our mind.

The importance of this original method should not be underestimated. It leads to an entirely new theory of induction and association, and also it opens the way to a scientific ontology. Only by the eidetical method may we find, for instance, the real reason for so-called spheres of incompatibility; only by using it may we discover and describe the important relationship of foundation which subsists between certain ontological realms.

.   .   .

The concept of truth

7

THE COHERENCE THEORY

brand blanshard

Coherence as the Nature of Truth

.   .   .

To think is to seek understanding. And to seek understanding is an activity of mind that is marked off from all other activities by a highly distinctive aim. This aim . . . is to achieve systematic vision, so to apprehend what is now unknown to us as to relate it, and relate it necessarily, to what we know already. We think to solve problems; and our method of solving problems is to build a bridge of intelligible relation from the continent of our knowledge to the island we wish to include in it. Sometimes this bridge is causal, as when we try to explain a disease; sometimes teleological, as when we try to fathom the move of an opponent over the chess board; sometimes geometrical, as in Euclid. But it is always systematic; thought in its very nature is the

The first part of this selection is from Brand Blanshard, *The Nature of Thought* (New York: The Macmillan Company, 1941), II: 261–269, 292–294. Reprinted by permission of George Allan & Unwin Ltd. and Humanities Press.
"Coherence and Correspondence" is from a section of the same title in *Philosophical Interrogations*, Sydney and Beatrice Rome, eds., pp. 203–212. Copyright © 1964 by Holt, Rinehart and Winston, Inc. Reprinted by permission of Holt, Rinehart and Winston, Inc.

attempt to bring something unknown or imperfectly known into a sub-system of knowledge, and thus also into that larger system that forms the world of accepted beliefs. That is what explanation is. *Why* is it that thought desires this ordered vision? Why should such a vision give satisfaction when it comes? To these questions there is no answer, and if there were, it would be an answer only because it had succeeded in supplying the characteristic satisfaction to this unique desire.

But may it not be that what satisfies thought fails to conform to the real world? Where is the guarantee that when I have brought my ideas into the form my ideal requires, they should be *true?* . . . In our long struggle with the relation of thought to reality we saw that if thought and things are conceived as related only externally, then knowledge is luck; there is no necessity whatever that what satisfies intelligence should coincide with what really is. It may do so, or it may not; on the principle that there are many misses to one bull's-eye, it more probably does not. But if we get rid of the misleading analogies through which this relation has been conceived, of copy and original, stimulus and organism, lantern and screen, and go to thought itself with the question what reference to an object means, we get a different and more hopeful answer. To think of a thing is to get that thing itself in some degree within the mind. To think of a color or an emotion is to have that within us which if it *were developed and completed,* would identify itself with the object. In short, if we accept its own report, thought is related to reality as the partial to the perfect fulfillment of a purpose. The more adequate its grasp the more nearly does it approximate, the more fully does it realize in itself, the nature and relations of its objects.

•   •   •

. . . We may look at the growth of knowledge, individual or social, either as an attempt by our own minds to return to union with things as they are in their ordered wholeness, or the affirmation through our minds of the ordered whole itself. And if we take this view, our notion of truth is marked out for us. Truth is the approximation of thought to reality. It is thought on its way home. Its measure is the distance thought has travelled, under guidance of its inner compass, toward that intelligible system which unites its ultimate object with its ultimate end. Hence at any given time the degree of truth in our experience as a whole is the degree of system it has achieved. The degree of truth of a particular proposition is to be judged in the first instance by its coherence with experience as a whole, ultimately by its coherence with that further whole, all-comprehensive and fully articulated, in which thought can come to rest.

But it is time we defined more explicitly what coherence means. To be sure, no fully satisfactory definition can be given; and as Dr. Ewing says, "it is wrong to tie down the advocates of the coherence theory to a precise definition. What they are doing is to describe an ideal that has never yet been completely clarified but is none the less immanent in all our thinking." [1] Certainly this ideal goes far beyond mere consistency. Fully coherent knowledge would be knowledge in which every judgment entailed, and was entailed by, the rest of the system. Probably we never find in fact a system where there is so much of interdependence. What it means may be clearer if we take a number of familiar systems and arrange them in a series tending to such coherence as a limit. At the bottom would be a junk-heap, where we could know

---

[1] *Idealism,* 231.

every item but one and still be without any clue as to what that remaining item was. Above this would come a stone-pile, for here you could at least infer that what you would find next would be a stone. A machine would be higher again, since from the remaining parts one could deduce not only the general character of a missing part, but also its special form and function. This is a high degree of coherence, but it is very far short of the highest. You could remove the engine from a motorcar while leaving the other parts intact, and replace it with any one of thousands of other engines, but the thought of such an interchange among human heads or hearts shows at once that the interdependence in a machine is far below that of the body. Do we find then in organic bodies the highest conceivable coherence? Clearly not. Though a human hand, as Aristotle said, would hardly be a hand when detached from the body, still it would be something definite enough; and we can conceive systems in which even this something would be gone. Abstract a number from the number series and it would be a mere unrecognizable x; similarly, the very thought of a straight line involves the thought of the Euclidean space in which it falls. It is perhaps in such systems as Euclidean geometry that we get the most perfect examples of coherence that have been constructed. If any proposition were lacking, it could be supplied from the rest; if any were altered, the repercussions would be felt through the length and breadth of the system. Yet even such a system as this falls short of the ideal system. Its postulates are unproved; they are independent of each other, in the sense that none of them could be derived from any other or even from all the others together; its clear necessity is bought by an abstractness so extreme as to have left out nearly everything that belongs to the character of actual things. A completely satisfactory system would have none of these defects. No proposition would be arbitrary, every proposition would be entailed by the others jointly and even singly, no proposition would stand outside the system. The integration would be so complete that no part could be seen for what it was without seeing its relation to the whole, and the whole itself could be understood only through the contribution of every part.

· · ·

Now if we accept coherence as the test of truth, does that commit us to any conclusions about the *nature* of truth or reality? I think it does, though more clearly about reality than about truth. It is past belief that the fidelity of our thought to reality should be rightly measured by coherence if reality itself were not coherent. To say that the nature of things may be *in*coherent, but we shall approach the truth about it precisely so far as our thoughts become coherent, sounds very much like nonsense. And providing we retained coherence as the test, it would still be nonsense even if truth were conceived as correspondence. On this supposition we should have truth when, our thought having achieved coherence, the correspondence was complete between that thought and its object. But complete correspondence between a coherent thought and an incoherent object seems meaningless. It is hard to see, then, how anyone could consistently take coherence as the test of truth unless he took it also as a character of reality.

Does acceptance of coherence as a test commit us not only to a view about the structure of reality but also to a view about the nature of truth? This is a more difficult question. As we saw at the beginning of the chapter, there have been some highly reputable philosophers who have held that the answer to "What is the test of truth?" is "Coherence," while the answer to "What is the nature or meaning of truth?" is "Correspondence." These questions are plainly distinct. Nor does there seem to be any direct path from the acceptance of coherence as the test of truth to its acceptance as the nature of truth. Nevertheless there is an indirect path. If we accept coherence as our test, we must use it everywhere. We must therefore use it to test the suggestion that truth *is* other than coherence. But if we do, we shall find that we must reject the suggestion as leading to *in*coherence. Coherence is a pertinacious concept and, like the well-known camel, if one lets it get its nose under the edge of the tent, it will shortly walk off with the whole.

Suppose that, accepting coherence as the test, one rejects it as the nature of truth in favor of some alternative; and let us assume, for example, that this alternative is correspondence. This, we have said, is incoherent; why? Because if one holds that truth is correspondence, one cannot intelligibly hold either that it is tested by coherence or that there is any dependable test at all. Consider the first point. Suppose that we construe experience into the most coherent picture possible, remembering that among the elements included will be such secondary qualities as colors, odors, and sounds. Would the mere fact that such elements as these are coherently arranged prove that anything precisely corresponding to them exists "out there"? I cannot see that it would, even if we knew that the two arrangements had closely corresponding patterns. If on one side you have a series of elements a, b, c . . . , and on the other a series of elements α, β, γ . . . , arranged in patterns that correspond, you have no proof as yet that the *natures* of these elements correspond. It is therefore impossible to argue from a high degree of coherence within experience to its correspondence in the same degree with anything outside. And this difficulty is typical. If you place the nature of truth in one sort of character and its test in something quite different, you are pretty certain, sooner or later, to find the two falling apart. In the end, the only test of truth that is not misleading is the special nature or character that is itself constitutive of truth.

Feeling that this is so, the adherents of correspondence sometimes insist that correspondence shall be its own test. But then the second difficulty arises. If truth does consist in correspondence, no test can be sufficient. For in order to know that experience corresponds to fact, we must be able to get at that fact, unadulterated with idea, and compare the two sides with each other. And we have seen . . . that such fact is not accessible. When we try to lay hold of it, what we find in our hands is a judgment which is obviously not itself the indubitable fact we are seeking, and which must be checked by some fact beyond it. To this process there is no end. And even if we did get at the fact directly, rather than through the veil of our ideas, that would be no less fatal to correspondence. This direct seizure of fact presumably gives us truth, but since that truth no longer consists in correspondence of idea with fact, the main theory has been abandoned. In short, if we can know fact only through the medium of our own ideas, the original forever eludes us; if we can get at the facts directly, we have knowledge whose truth is not correspondence. The theory is forced to choose between scepticism and self-contradiction.

Thus the attempt to combine coherence as the test of truth with correspondence as the nature of truth will not pass muster by its own test. The result is *in*coherence. We believe that an application of the test to other theories of truth would lead to a like result. The argument is: Assume coherence as the test, and you will be driven by the incoherence of your alternatives to the conclusion that it is also the nature of truth.

.   .   .

Coherence means more than consistency. It means not only that the various constituents entering into the system of truth are compatible with each other, but also that they necessitate each other. The system assumed is a system ideally perfect, for nothing less than this would satisfy intelligence as stable beyond rectification. In such a system there would be no loose ends. Difference anywhere would be reflected in difference everywhere.

. . .

Now it is obvious that we cannot show *in detail* that a difference anywhere in the system of truth must be reflected everywhere; we do not know enough, nor is it likely we ever shall. But we can do something else that is as near to this as can be reasonably asked. We can show that in the system of truth, *so far as reflected in our knowledge,* such interconnection holds, and that the denial of an apparently isolated judgment does in fact have implications for every other. The argument is as follows: When I say that Bishop Stubbs died in his bed, or indeed when I say anything, I always do so on evidence. This evidence may be hard or easy to bring to light, but it is there invariably; I never simply discharge judgments into the air with no ground or warrant at all. And by the rules of hypothetical argument, to admit the falsity of a judgment is to throw doubt upon its ground. Indeed it is to do more. It is to throw doubt, if I am consistent, upon *all* evidence of this kind and degree. Now the evidence on which it is believed that Bishop Stubbs died a natural death is of the kind and degree that would be accepted without hesitation by any historian or scientist. It is the sort of evidence on which science and history generally rest. Hence if I deny this proposition, and thus call in question the value of this sort of evidence, I must in consistency call in question most science and history also. And that would shatter my world of knowledge. Thus the truth about Bishop Stubbs is anything but isolated. However unimportant practically, it is so entangled with my system of beliefs that its denial would send repercussions throughout the whole.

To some this reply may seem an *ignoratio elenchi*. It is one thing, they may say, to show that the abandonment of a *belief* would logically compel the abandonment of other beliefs; it is another thing to show that in the real world about which these beliefs are held, a change in one fact or event would necessitate that all others be different. Suppose I climb the hill behind my farm house in Vermont and look across at Mount Washington. I am wearing a felt hat at the time. Is it sensible or quite sane to argue that if I had worn a straw hat instead, that fact would have made a difference to Mount Washington?

I not only believe it would, but that the argument for this conclusion is strong almost to demonstration. In outline it is as follows: my putting on this particular hat had causes, which lay in part in the workings of my brain; these workings also had causes, which lay in part in the workings of other bodily organs; these in turn depended upon countless physical factors in the way of food, air, light, and temperature, every one of which had its own conditions. It is plain that before we took many steps in this retreat, we should find ourselves involved in millions of conditions, and that if we were able *per impossibile* to traverse all the diverging branches, there would probably be no region of the universe that would remain unpenetrated. Now if we reject, as I suppose we must, the plurality of causes, and hold that the causal relation is reciprocating, then a denial of the causal consequent will require a denial of its antecedent. A different event, then, from that on which these various lines converge would require differences throughout the range of the countless conditions themselves. Very well; let us assume such a different event to have occurred—my wearing a straw hat instead of a felt one—and having ascended the causal lines, let us now descend them. If the antecedents of the present event were scattered throughout the universe, and we suppose them altered throughout, is there any reason whatever to suppose that the present state of the world would be as we find it? The answer is obvious. The world would not only be different, but so extensively different that we could point neither to Mount Washington nor to anything else and say that it would be exempt from change.

. . .

Coherence and Correspondence

A. C. Ewing: What would be Blanshard's reaction to the proposal to substitute for "coherence" as the test of truth "coherence with experience"? Even granting that we cannot separate what is given from our interpretation of it, it is surely equally true that we cannot have interpretation without some experience to interpret, and must not the truth of interpretation depend at least as much on its conformity with the nature of what is interpreted as on its internal coherence and its coherence with other well-established judgments? Further, can we really say that we believe in the truth of judgments of memory primarily because they cohere? Do we not, in many cases, see them immediately to be true without having first to determine their coherence with anything? These considerations suggest that the criterion of truth should be not coherence alone but coherence as organizing and connecting immediate cognitions. It is true that immediate cognitions could not be *formulated* without a more or less coherent system of concepts; but that is not the same thing as to say that once formulated, the only *evidence for their truth* is coherence with other propositions.

Richard B. Brandt: In holding that "the coherence of judgments within a system is . . . our only test of any truth or fact," Blanshard is, I suggest, setting forth an imperative like this: "Believe all and only the propositions in the set S, in preference to all and only the propositions in S′, if and only if S is a more coherent system than S′, providing however that S contains at least the vast majority of the propositions which seem to express your present experience and your recollections of the past." (Blanshard could not quite accept the final clause, but I wish that he would suggest a reformulation which would make it reasonably acceptable to him.) What is his justification for this view?

Perhaps he has discovered fatal objections to all other possible proposals. But has he refuted, at least by implication, all proposals of imperatives to attribute certainty or antecedent probability to propositions which seem to describe present experiences or recollections?

Blanshard also argues that the coherence principle is the one we actually do follow in reflective moments, whatever we may say about it. But what would Blanshard say to such facts as these, which raise the question whether the intuitive convictions of responsible scientists can be shown to be in agreement with the coherence principle: (1) The widespread reliance on truth-table testing for analyticity does not seem like an appeal to coherence. (2) Is it an appeal to coherence if a scientist thinks a generalization more firmly established by evidence drawn from various fields, rather than by homogeneous instances? (3) Is it appeal to coherence that makes scientists shy away from *ad hoc* hypotheses? (4) Is it an appeal to coherence when scientists prefer the simpler of two theories if the two give results equally in agreement with experimental facts?

Charles Hartshorne: Blanshard has argued that the ideal of knowledge is a system in which all relations are grasped as necessary. But is understanding exclusively the grasp of necessities, or is it not rather the insight into both necessities as such and contingencies as such? Is not the significance of "*p* is necessary, given *q*" dependent upon its being *false* that *p* is necessary given anything whatever, and is not the significance of "*r* is necessary unconditionally" due to its being false that all things are necessary unconditionally? In short, is not all understanding the distinguishing of the necessary and the non-necessary, rather than the effort to collapse this distinction into a mere appearance?

Adolf Grünbaum: In *An Analysis of Knowledge and Valuation,*[2] C. I. Lewis argues that "every empirical supposition, being a contingent statement, is contained in some self-consistent system which is as comprehensive as you please," because whether we start with an empirical belief or statement *p* or its contradictory, one or other of every pair of further empirical statements can be conjoined with *p* to form a self-consistent set, or in the same way with *not-p*. Hence no empirical truth can be determined by the criterion of consistency alone. What reply would Blanshard make to this objection?

Blanshard: A. C. Ewing and Richard B. Brandt make some acute criticisms of coherence as the test of truth. Both think that coherence by itself is not enough. They do not offer the objection so often made against the theory, that a system may be large and logically well knit without being true—for example, some fantastic system of geometry—for they know that defenders of coherence have insisted that the only system providing a warrant of truth is one that includes actual experience. But they are inclined to say that such a qualification surrenders the case for coherence. When one says that the system must include actual experience, is not this really saying that some judgments of perception and memory are true independently of the system? Start with such judgments, and you can build a system around them, but unless you can start with *some* proposition known intuitively to be true, the whole system seems to hang in the air. The mere coherence of judgment A with judgment B will not increase its likelihood unless B is known to be true already. And that means that B's truth must be known on other grounds.

Ewing has argued persuasively for this view in his Hertz lecture on "Reason and Intuition." He agrees that coherence has an important role in the testing of truth, but holds that its office is to develop and organize our intuitions rather than to set itself up in their place as the exclusive authority. He asks whether I should not be ready to go along with this and accept as the test of truth not coherence simply, but "coherence with experience."

Yes, I should. This does seem to me to be the test we actually use. The only question is how it should be interpreted. Would the acceptance of it commit one to

[2] La Salle, Ill.: Open Court Publishing Company, 1947, pp. 338–343.

the correspondence theory of truth for those perceptual judgments which are presumably meant here by "experience"?

Suppose we say, "The table in the next room is round"; how should we test this judgment? No doubt by going to the door and looking. If our judgment "corresponds" with the given fact, we regard it as verified and true; if not, as false. To this the defender of coherence replies that when one talks of given fact, one is talking loosely. Presumably "given" means given in sense. But one cannot sense a fact, for a fact is of the form "that S is P," and what is of this form can be grasped by nothing simpler than judgment. This judgment need not be explicit or expressed; it may be of the lowly type that is commonly present in perception; but it must be the apprehension of at least two terms in relation. In the case in question, what verifies the statement of fact is the perceptual judgment that I make when I open the door and look. But then what verifies the perceptual judgment itself? Is it not the correspondence I discover between the judged roundness of the table and its actually sensed roundness? To which the reply is, as before, that a judgment of fact can be verified only by the sort of apprehension that can present us with a fact, and that this must be a further judgment. And an agreement between judgments is best described not as correspondence, but as coherence.

This is the line I took in *The Nature of Thought*. The most effective criticisms of it seem to me to be two: (1) that facts may after all be given, and (2) that, whether they are or not, at least particular data are given, and that these by themselves may serve to verify judgments. Let us consider these criticisms.

CAN FACTS BE GIVEN? "A is to the left of B." "A came before B." "This is darker than that." "This is a shade of red." These are all statements of fact, in which a relation is alleged between two terms. But is it not possible that the facts to which they refer, and which would serve to verify them, should actually be given, as the correspondence theory holds? If this means given in sense, it still seems to me very questionable. Take the last case above: "This is a shade of red." The relation apprehended here is that of genus and species, and to suppose that we could see or hear or otherwise sense a relation of this kind seems clearly mistaken; some form of apprehension that involves intelligence is at work. "This is darker than that." When we say this, the items compared are both before us, but the activity of comparing them and of placing them higher and lower on a scale is more than a process of sensing. "A came before B." When we grasp this fact, do we sense the passage of time? Kant thought not; at least we seemed to apprehend it in a very different way from that in which we are aware of colors and sounds, a way that he called "pure perception"; and the distinction is surely well taken. "A is to the left of B." Do we have here a sensible fact? We do seem to have a fact that is as clearly imposed upon us, and in that sense given, as any color, sound, or pain. But is the spatial relation *sensed,* as the items that form its terms are sensed? Once more, I think not. In all these cases the relation involved in the fact eludes apprehension by sense; in all of them the fact can be expressed by nothing short of a proposition or judgment. Thus if we seek to verify any of the four judgments above, we must do so by another judgment.

ONE MAY REPLY: "What is important about the fact referred to is not that it is sensed, but that it is given. You have admitted that relations of genus and species, of time and space, are forced upon you, and if you call the apprehension of them judgments, there is at least nothing in these judgments that is uncertain or speculative; facts may be as truly given to intelligence as colors are to vision. And the innocent thesis that the correspondence theory maintains is that what renders such judgments true is their correspondence to these non-sensorily given facts."

I must agree that this is a reasonable way of putting the matter and if to accept it is to accept correspondence, I suppose I am an adherent of that theory. Whether the verification in these cases is by coherence or correspondence would seem to be a matter of words. Should the support given to a judgment by another and perceptual judgment, or, if you will, by a complex non-sensory intuition, be called by the one name or the other? It does not seem important. Still, the advocate of correspondence may say that we are really conceding his case, since coherence now means not coherence within a system, but coherence with given facts of experience. I can only reply that to me it means both. Coherence with fact can stand alone only if the fact as given is stable, in the sense of ultimate and incorrigible; for only then do we have a fixed object with which our judgment may be compared. But no such objects are fixed, and no such facts are incorrigible. For a fact to be given means that it is given to a mind in a context of other experiences; this context is in process of change, and this change does not leave the given unaffected. Could one reasonably say, for example, that the fact reported by "this shade is a color" would be absolutely the same as it presented itself, first, to one of the lower animals, then to a man whose experience of color was confined to red, and finally to a man who experienced a normal range of colors? I very much doubt it. A mind is not put together like a mosaic of hard, exclusive pieces. The pieces themselves change their character, some more, some less, with changes in the whole. Coherence with experience gives a good starting point. But it must be supplemented and corrected by coherence with a wider experience.

DO SENSE DATA VERIFY? The second main criticism of coherence as the test was that in some cases sense data by themselves serve, naked and unashamed, as tests of truth. And when that which actually confirms is a simple, unanalyzable sensory datum, it is idle to say that the test is still coherence within a system of judgments. Suppose I say that in exactly five minutes from now I shall see a bright flash, and I do in fact see it. My prediction has turned out true. Is it not clear that that which verified it was the occurrence of the flash, and that the relation between the prediction and the event was one of correspondence with a sheer brute datum?

Here again, the position seems to me very nearly correct. Nearly correct? But why not completely correct? For this reason: It seems to assume a pure sensory datum as that to which the judgment corresponds. Its defender would probably admit that so far as the datum is not pure, that is, so far as it is a construct molded by the relations or interpretations imposed on it by the perceiving mind, the language of coherence is still plausible, whereas if this ideal molding can be excluded and a pure sensum attained, correspondence is the more appropriate description. And the reason I am not content with correspondence by itself is that, however closely we approach the pure given, we never do in fact reach it. Even when we take correspondence at its best, as in the case of the bright flash, this still seems to be true. The flash that is taken as verifying the judgment has obviously been worked over by what can only be described as thought; its recognition as a flash and as bright puts it in a framework of concepts; it is placed at a particular point in an extended setting of space and time; it is grasped as something that fulfills a prediction, and probably also as produced by a particular kind of cause; its character as experienced may be so bound up with its affective setting—of apprehension, placidity, or terror—that it would lose its identity apart from this. As A. E. Taylor says:

It seems plain on reflection that merely to say "green" with significance is to perform an act of comparison and recognition; interpretation has already begun before we proceed to the implication "here, not there; now, not then." If there ever was a time, as we may fairly doubt, in our own past history when we were purely receptive, the time must have passed before we could so much as name things, and to recapture the condition must be beyond the power of "articulate-speaking men." [3]

The conclusion would appear to be that the correspondence theory is correct so far as the reference in judgment is to a pure given datum, but that in practice we never get either the datum or the reference. What we do get are approximations in various degrees to both. But in saying that the datum is thus an ideal limit rather than an isolable item of experience, I do not want to be taken as belittling its importance. If it is hard to capture in its purity, it is still harder to dispense with. Indeed, escape from it would mean the abandonment of any anchorage not only for common sense, but also for speculative thought, the dancing of an "unearthly ballet of bloodless categories." I trust that all this will make reasonably clear what I mean by saying that the coherence I accept must include Ewing's "coherence with experience."

WHAT SYSTEM IS USED AS THE TEST? I hope this will help, also, to meet a difficulty of Grünbaum's. He asks what I should say about the criticism of coherence as a test of truth offered by C. I. Lewis in *An Analysis of Knowledge and Valuation*.[4] Lewis' main contention is substantially the same as Ewing's, namely, that the system used as the test must not hang in the air, but must at some point rest on experience. But he offers another argument that calls for comment.

As I understand it, it runs as follows: Every empirical statement is contingent or non-necessary; its contradictory is conceivable. Very well; take any consistent set of empirical statements, for example, "the table is brown," "stones are heavy," "water is wet." Of each of these statements the contradictory is conceivable, and these contradictories, like the originals, will be consistent among themselves. This set of statements can be extended just as far as the original set of statements. The two sets or systems, then, will be equally extensive and equally consistent. Hence if mere consistency within a system were all that is required to warrant truth, you could warrant the truth of any empirical statement whatever, or of its contradictory, with equal readiness. By itself the appeal to coherence is thus worthless in distinguishing truth from falsity.

My comments on this are as follows: (1) I agree with Lewis that the system taken as the test cannot be any system taken at random; there must be coherence with experience in the sense explained above. But further, (2) coherence does not mean for me consistency merely, but also mutual entailment, and in this respect the two systems are not parallel. For some empirical statements entail others, while there is no parallel entailment between their contradictories. That this table is brown entails that it is extended; that it is not brown does not entail that it is not extended. I admit that with our present knowledge we can seldom see necessity linking empirical propositions, but I am inclined to think it is there whether we see it or not, and that it must be included within the meaning of coherence. And its presence is more readily

[3] *The Faith of a Moralist* (London: Macmillan & Co., Ltd., 1930), II, 217.
[4] Pp. 338 ff.

discernible in System 1 than in System 2. (3) I take it that according to Lewis, empirical facts and propositions are not only contingent in themselves, but are contingently related; the fact that a billiard ball is moving with a certain velocity when it strikes another is not connected necessarily with that other's motion. Rightly or wrongly, I dissent from this view. All empirical facts are in the end necessitated, I think, by the remaining empirical facts. This view is far more readily acceptable if necessity is seen as implicit in causality. In the first of two systems contemplated above, there is room for causality; in the second, it is virtually excluded. Between the first billiard ball's striking the other with a certain velocity and the other's moving away, it makes sense to say that there is a causal relation; between the first's *not* having a certain velocity and the other's *not* moving away, the assertion of causality would be absurd; a thing's not having a certain property can cause nothing. Thus the systems are again not equivalent from the point of view of coherence as I conceive it. (4) The system that at any time I should use as a test of truth would of course include *a priori* as well as empirical statements, and if the proposed alternative system were to parallel it, it would have to include also the contradictories of these *a priori* statements. But it could not do this. For among the statements that would have to be denied is the law of contradiction, and I suppose it is obvious that if you include within your system the contradictory of this law, you cannot have a system at all. Thus a system consisting of the contradictories of *all* statements composing the present body of knowledge is impossible. (5) It is sometimes suggested that there might be more than one system which included all facts, and therefore that the notion of a single all-inclusive system is arbitrary. On the contrary, it is so far from arbitrary that its alternative —the notion of two or more all-inclusive systems—is unthinkable. For let us suppose that A and B are two systems, each inclusive of all facts, and exclusive of each other. If they are to be thus exclusive, there is one fact at least that will fall outside each of them: the fact that A is all-inclusive will not be included in B, and the fact that B is all-inclusive will not be included in A. But to say that either is all-inclusive while there is some fact lying outside it is self-contradictory. A plurality of all-inclusive systems is impossible.

8

THE PRAGMATIC THEORY

william james

. . .

Truth, as any dictionary will tell you, is a property of certain of our ideas. It means their "agreement," as falsity means their disagreement, with "reality." Pragmatists and intellectualists both accept this definition as a matter of course. They begin to quarrel only after the question is raised as to what may precisely be meant by the term "agreement," and what by the term "reality," when reality is taken as something for our ideas to agree with.

In answering these questions the pragmatists are more analytic and painstaking, the intellectualists more offhand and irreflective. The popular notion is that a true idea must copy its reality. Like other popular views, this one follows the analogy of the most usual experience. Our true ideas of sensible things do indeed copy them. Shut your eyes and think of yonder clock on the wall, and you get just such a true picture or copy of its dial. But your idea of its "works" (unless you are a clock-maker) is much less of a copy, yet it passes muster, for it in no way clashes with the reality. Even though it should shrink to the mere word "works," that word still serves you truly; and when you speak of the "time-keeping function" of the clock, or of its spring's "elasticity," it is hard to see exactly what your ideas can copy.

You perceive that there is a problem here. Where our ideas cannot copy definitely their object, what does agreement with that object mean? Some idealists seem to say that they are true whenever they are what God means that we ought to think about that object. Others hold the copy-view all through, and speak as if our ideas possessed truth just in proportion as they approach to being copies of the Absolute's eternal way of thinking.

These views, you see, invite pragmatistic discussion. But the great assumption of the intellectualists is that truth means essentially an inert static relation. When you've got your true idea of anything, there's an end of the matter. You're in possession; you *know;* you have fulfilled your thinking destiny. You are where you ought to be mentally; you have obeyed your categorical imperative; and nothing more need follow

From William James, *Pragmatism: A New Name for Some Old Ways of Thinking* (New York: Longmans, Green & Co. Ltd., 1907), pp. 198–217.

on that climax of your rational destiny. Epistemologically you are in stable equilibrium.

Pragmatism, on the other hand, asks its usual question. "Grant an idea or belief to be true," it says, "what concrete difference will its being true make in any one's actual life? How will the truth be realized? What experiences will be different from those which would obtain if the belief were false? What, in short, is the truth's cash-value in experiential terms?"

The moment pragmatism asks this question, it sees the answer: *True ideas are those that we can assimilate, validate, corroborate and verify. False ideas are those that we can not.* That is the practical difference it makes to us to have true ideas; that, therefore, is the meaning of truth, for it is all that truth is known as.

This thesis is what I have to defend. The truth of an idea is not a stagnant property inherent in it. Truth *happens* to an idea. It *becomes* true, is *made* true by events. Its verity *is* in fact an event, a process: the process namely of its verifying itself, its veri-*fication*. Its validity is the process of its valid-*ation*.

But what do the words verification and validation themselves pragmatically mean? They again signify certain practical consequences of the verified and validated idea. It is hard to find any one phrase that characterizes these consequences better than the ordinary agreement-formula—just such consequences being what we have in mind whenever we say that our ideas "agree" with reality. They lead us, namely, through the acts and other ideas which they instigate, into or up to, or towards, other parts of experience with which we feel all the while—such feeling being among our potentialities—that the original ideas remain in agreement. The connexions and transitions come to us from point to point as being progressive, harmonious, satisfactory. This function of agreeable leading is what we mean by an idea's verification. Such an account is vague and it sounds at first quite trivial, but it has results which it will take the rest of my hour to explain.

Let me begin by reminding you of the fact that the possession of true thoughts means everywhere the possession of invaluable instruments of action; and that our duty to gain truth, so far from being a blank command from out of the blue, or a "stunt" self-imposed by our intellect, can account for itself by excellent practical reasons.

The importance to human life of having true beliefs about matters of fact is a thing too notorious. We live in a world of realities that can be infinitely useful or infinitely harmful. Ideas that tell us which of them to expect count as the true ideas in all this primary sphere of verification, and the pursuit of such ideas is a primary human duty. The possession of truth, so far from being here an end in itself, is only a preliminary means towards other vital satisfactions. If I am lost in the woods and starved, and find what looks like a cow-path, it is of the utmost importance that I should think of a human habitation at the end of it, for if I do so and follow it, I save myself. The true thought is useful here because the house which is its object is useful. The practical value of true ideas is thus primarily derived from the practical importance of their objects to us. Their objects are, indeed, not important at all times. I may on another occasion have no use for the house; and then my idea of it, however verifiable, will be practically irrelevant, and had better remain latent. Yet since almost any object may some day become temporarily important, the advantage of having a general stock of *extra* truths, of ideas that shall be true of merely possible situations, is obvious. We store such extra truths away in our memories, and with the overflow we fill our books of reference. Whenever such an extra truth becomes practically relevant to one of our emergencies, it passes from cold-storage to do work in the world and our belief in it grows active. You can say of it then either that "it is useful because it is true" or that "it is true because it is useful." Both these phrases mean exactly the same thing, namely that here is an idea that gets fulfilled and can be verified. True is the name for whatever idea starts the verification-process, useful is the name for its completed function in experience. True ideas would never have been singled out as such, would never have acquired a class-name, least of all a name suggesting value, unless they had been useful from the outset in this way.

From this simple cue pragmatism gets her general notion of truth as something essentially bound up with the way in which one moment in our experience may lead us towards other moments which it will be worth while to have been led to. Primarily, and on the common-sense level, the truth of a state of mind means this function of *a leading that is worth while*. When a moment in our experience, of any kind what-ever, inspires us with a thought that is true, that means that sooner or later we dip by that thought's guidance into the particulars of experience again and make ad-vantageous connexion with them. This is a vague enough statement, but I beg you to retain it, for it is essential.

Our experience meanwhile is all shot through with regularities. One bit of it can warn us to get ready for another bit, can "intend" or be "significant of" that remoter object. The object's advent is the significance's verification. Truth, in these cases, meaning nothing but eventual verification, is manifestly incompatible with waywardness on our part. Woe to him whose beliefs play fast and loose with the order which realities follow in his experience; they will lead him nowhere or else make false connexions.

By "realities" or "objects" here, we mean either things of common sense, sensibly present, or else common-sense relations, such as dates, places, distances, kinds, activi-ties. Following our mental image of a house along the cow-path, we actually come to see the house; we get the image's full verification. *Such simply and fully verified leadings are certainly the originals and prototypes of the truth-process.* Experience offers indeed other forms of truth-process, but they are all conceivable as being pri-mary verifications arrested, multiplied or substituted one for another.

Take, for instance, yonder object on the wall. You and I consider it to be a "clock," altho no one of us has seen the hidden works that make it one. We let our notion pass for true without attempting to verify. If truths mean verification-process essentially, ought we then to call such unverified truths as this abortive? No, for they form the overwhelmingly large number of the truths we live by. Indirect as well as direct verifications pass muster. Where circumstantial evidence is sufficient, we can go without eye-witnessing. Just as we here assume Japan to exist without ever having been there, because it *works* to do so, everything we know conspiring with the belief, and nothing interfering, so we assume that thing to be a clock. We *use* it as a clock, regulating the length of our lecture by it. The verification of the assumption here means its leading to no frustration or contradiction. Verifi*ability* of wheels and weights and pendulum is as good as verification. For one truth-process completed there are a million in our lives that function in this state of nascency. They turn us *towards* direct verification; lead us into the *surroundings* of the objects they envisage; and then, if everything runs on harmoniously, we are so sure that verification is possible that we omit it, and are usually justified by all that happens.

Truth lives, in fact, for the most part on a credit system. Our thoughts and beliefs "pass," so long as nothing challenges them, just as bank-notes pass so long as nobody refuses them. But this all points to direct face-to-face verifications somewhere, without which the fabric of truth collapses like a financial system with no cash-basis whatever. You accept my verification of one thing, I yours of another. We trade on each other's truth. But beliefs verified concretely by *somebody* are the posts of the whole superstructure.

.   .   .

Between the coercions of the sensible order and those of the ideal order, our mind is thus wedged tightly. Our ideas must agree with realities, be such realities concrete or abstract, be they facts or be they principles, under penalty of endless inconsistency and frustration.

So far, intellectualists can raise no protest. They can only say that we have barely touched the skin of the matter.

Realities mean, then, either concrete facts, or abstract kinds of thing and relations perceived intuitively between them. They furthermore and thirdly mean, as things that new ideas of ours must no less take account of, the whole body of other truths already in our possession. But what now does "agreement" with such threefold realities mean?—to use again the definition that is current.

Here it is that pragmatism and intellectualism begin to part company. Primarily, no doubt, to agree means to copy, but we saw that the mere word "clock" would do instead of a mental picture of its works, and that of many realities our ideas can only be symbols and not copies. "Past time," "power," "spontaneity,"—how can our mind copy such realities?

To "agree" in the widest sense with a reality *can only mean to be guided either straight up to it or into its surroundings, or to be put into such working touch with it as to handle either it or something connected with it better than if we disagreed.* Better either intellectually or practically! And often agreement will only mean the negative fact that nothing contradictory from the quarter of that reality comes to interfere with the way in which our ideas guide us elsewhere. To copy a reality is, indeed, one very important way of agreeing with it, but it is far from being essential. The essential thing is the process of being guided. Any idea that helps us to *deal,* whether practically or intellectually, with either the reality or its belongings, that doesn't entangle our progress in frustrations, that *fits,* in fact, and adapts our life to the reality's whole setting, will agree sufficiently to meet the requirement. It will hold true of that reality.

.   .   .

Agreement thus turns out to be essentially an affair of leading—leading that is useful because it is into quarters that contain objects that are important. True ideas lead us into useful verbal and conceptual quarters as well as directly up to useful sensible termini. They lead to consistency, stability and flowing human intercourse. They lead away from excentricity and isolation, from foiled and barren thinking. The untrammelled flowing of the leading-process, its general freedom from clash and contradiction, passes for its indirect verification; but all roads lead to Rome, and in the end and eventually, all true processes must lead to the face of directly verifying sensible experiences *somewhere,* which somebody's ideas have copied.

Such is the large loose way in which the pragmatist interprets the word agreement. He treats it altogether practically. He lets it cover any process of conduction from a present idea to a future terminus, provided only it run prosperously. It is only thus that "scientific" ideas, flying as they do beyond common sense, can be said to agree with their realities. It is, as I have already said, *as if* reality were made of ether, atoms or electrons, but we mustn't think so literally. The term "energy" doesn't even pretend to stand for anything "objective." It is only a way of measuring the surface of phenomena so as to string their changes on a simple formula.

Yet in the choice of these man-made formulas we can not be capricious with impunity any more than we can be capricious on the common-sense practical level. We must find a theory that will *work;* and that means something extremely difficult; for our theory must mediate between all previous truths and certain new experiences. It must derange common sense and previous belief as little as possible, and it must lead to some sensible terminus or other that can be verified exactly. To "work" means both these things; and the squeeze is so tight that there is little loose play for any hypothesis. Our theories are wedged and controlled as nothing else is. Yet sometimes alternative theoretic formulas are equally compatible with all the truths we know, and then we choose between them for subjective reasons. We choose the kind of theory to which we are already partial; we follow "elegance" or "economy." Clerk-Maxwell somewhere says it would be "poor scientific taste" to choose the more complicated of two equally well-evidenced conceptions; and you will all agree with him. Truth in science is what gives us the maximum possible sum of satisfactions, taste included, but consistency both with previous truth and with novel fact is always the most imperious claimant.

.   .   .

9

THE SEMANTIC CONCEPTION

alfred tarski

• • •

2. THE EXTENSION OF THE TERM "TRUE." . . . The predicate "true" is sometimes used to refer to psychological phenomena such as judgments or beliefs, sometimes to certain physical objects, namely, linguistic expressions and specifically sentences, and sometimes to certain ideal entities called "propositions." By "sentence" we understand here what is usually meant in grammar by "declarative sentence"; as regards the term "proposition," its meaning is notoriously a subject of lengthy disputations by various philosophers and logicians, and it seems never to have been made quite clear and unambiguous. For several reasons it appears most convenient to *apply the term "true" to sentences,* and we shall follow this course.

Consequently, we must always relate the notion of truth, like that of a sentence, to a specific language; for it is obvious that the same expression which is a true sentence in one language can be false or meaningless in another.

• • •

3. THE MEANING OF THE TERM "TRUE." . . . The word *"true,"* like other words from our everyday language, is certainly not unambiguous. And it does not seem to me that the philosophers who have discussed this concept have helped to diminish its ambiguity. In works and discussions of philosophers we meet many different conceptions of truth and falsity, and we must indicate which conception will be the basis of our discussion.

We should like our definition to do justice to the intuitions which adhere to the *classical Aristotelian conception of truth*—intuitions which find their expression in the well-known words of Aristotle's *Metaphysics:*

> To say of what is that it is not, or of what is not that it is, is false, while
> to say of what is that it is, or of what is not that it is not, is true.

If we wished to adapt ourselves to modern philosophical terminology, we could perhaps express this conception by means of the familiar formula:

From Alfred Tarski, "The Semantic Conception of Truth," in *Philosophy and Phenomenological Research* IV: 342–353. Reprinted by permission.

The truth of a sentence consists in its agreement with (or correspondence to) reality.

(For a theory of truth which is to be based upon the latter formulation the term "correspondence theory" has been suggested.)

If, on the other hand, we should decide to extend the popular usage of the term *"designate"* by applying it not only to names, but also to sentences, and if we agreed to speak of the designata of sentences as "states of affairs," we could possibly use for the same purpose the following phrase:

A sentence is true if it designates an existing state of affairs.

However, all these formulations can lead to various misunderstandings, for none of them is sufficiently precise and clear (though this applies much less to the original Aristotelian formulation than to either of the others); at any rate, none of them can be considered a satisfactory definition of truth. It is up to us to look for a more precise expression of our intuitions.

4. A CRITERION FOR THE MATERIAL ADEQUACY OF THE DEFINITION. Let us start with a concrete example. Consider the sentence *"snow is white."* We ask the question under what conditions this sentence is true or false. It seems clear that if we base ourselves on the classical conception of truth, we shall say that the sentence is true if snow is white, and that it is false if snow is not white. Thus, if the definition of truth is to conform to our conception, it must imply the following equivalence:

The sentence "snow is white" is true if, and only if, snow is white.

Let me point out that the phrase *"snow is white"* occurs on the left side of this equivalence in quotation marks, and on the right without quotation marks. On the right side we have the sentence itself, and on the left the name of the sentence. Employing the medieval logical terminology we could also say that on the right side the words *"snow is white"* occur in *suppositio formalis,* and on the left in *suppositio materialis.* It is hardly necessary to explain why we must have the name of the sentence, and not the sentence itself, on the left side of the equivalence. For, in the first place, from the point of view of the grammar of our language, an expression of the form *"X is true"* will not become a meaningful sentence if we replace in it *"X"* by a sentence or by anything other than a name—since the subject of a sentence may be only a noun or an expression functioning like a noun. And, in the second place, the fundamental conventions regarding the use of any language require that in any utterance we make about an object it is the name of the object which must be employed, and not the object itself. In consequence, if we wish to say something about a sentence, for example, that it is true, we must use the name of this sentence, and not the sentence itself.

It may be added that enclosing a sentence in quotation marks is by no means the only way of forming its name. For instance, by assuming the usual order of letters in our alphabet, we can use the following expression as the name (the description) of the sentence *"snow is white"*:

the sentence constituted by three words, the first of which consists of the 19th, 14th, 15th, and 23rd letters, the second of the 9th and 19th letters, and the third of the 23rd, 8th, 9th, 20th, and 5th letters of the English alphabet.

We shall now generalize the procedure which we have applied above. Let us consider an arbitrary sentence; we shall replace it by the letter *"p."* We form the name of this sentence and we replace it by another letter, say *"X."* We ask now what is the logical relation between the two sentences *"X is true"* and *"p."* It is clear that from the point of view of our basic conception of truth these sentences are equivalent. In other words, the following equivalence holds:

(T) *X is true if, and only if, p.*

We shall call any such equivalence (with *"p"* replaced by any sentence of the language to which the word *"true"* refers, and "X" replaced by a name of this sentence) an *"equivalence of the form* (T)."

Now at last we are able to put into a precise form the conditions under which we will consider the usage and the definition of the term *"true"* as adequate from the material point of view: we wish to use the term *"true"* in such a way that all equivalences of the form (T) can be asserted, and *we shall call a definition of truth "adequate" if all these equivalences follow from it.*

It should be emphasized that neither the expression (T) itself (which is not a sentence, but only a schema of a sentence) nor any particular instance of the form (T) can be regarded as a definition of truth. We can only say that every equivalence of the form (T) obtained by replacing *"p"* by a particular sentence, and "X" by a name of this sentence, may be considered a partial definition of truth, which explains wherein the truth of this one individual sentence consists. The general definition has to be, in a certain sense, a logical conjunction of all these partial definitions.

(The last remark calls for some comments. A language may admit the construction of infinitely many sentences; and thus the number of partial definitions of truth referring to sentences of such a language will also be infinite. Hence to give our remark a precise sense we should have to explain what is meant by a "logical conjunction of infinitely many sentences"; but this would lead us too far into technical problems of modern logic.)

5. TRUTH AS A SEMANTIC CONCEPT. I should like to propose the name *"the semantic conception of truth"* for the conception of truth which has just been discussed.

Semantics is a discipline which, speaking loosely, *deals with certain relations between expressions of a language and the objects* (or "states of affairs") *"referred to" by those expressions.* As typical examples of semantic concepts we may mention the concepts of *designation, satisfaction,* and *definition* as these occur in the following examples:

  the expression "the father of his country" designates (denotes) George Washington;

   snow satisfies the sentential function (the condition) "x is white";

  the equation "2 • x = 1" defines (uniquely determines) the number $\frac{1}{2}$

While the words *"designates," "satisfies,"* and *"defines"* express relations (between certain expressions and the objects "referred to" by these expressions), the word *"true"* is of a different logical nature: it expresses a property (or denotes a class) of certain expressions, viz., of sentences. However, it is easily seen that all the formulations which were given earlier and which aimed to explain the meaning of this word (cf.

Sections 3 and 4) referred not only to sentences themselves, but also to objects "talked about" by these sentences, or possibly to "states of affairs" described by them. And, moreover, it turns out that the simplest and the most natural way of obtaining an exact definition of truth is one which involves the use of other semantic notions, e.g., the notion of satisfaction. It is for these reasons that we count the concept of truth which is discussed here among the concepts of semantics, and the problem of defining truth proves to be closely related to the more general problem of setting up the foundations of theoretical semantics.

· · ·

6. LANGUAGES WITH A SPECIFIED STRUCTURE. Because of the possible occurrence of antinomies, the problem of specifying the formal structure and the vocabulary of a language in which definitions of semantic concepts are to be given becomes especially acute; and we turn now to this problem.

There are certain general conditions under which the structure of a language is regarded as *exactly specified*. Thus, to specify the structure of a language, we must characterize unambiguously the class of those words and expressions which are to be considered *meaningful*. In particular, we must indicate all words which we decide to use without defining them, and which are called *"undefined* (or *primitive) terms"*; and we must give the so-called *rules of definition* for introducing new or *defined terms*. Furthermore, we must set up criteria for distinguishing within the class of expressions those which we call *"sentences."* Finally, we must formulate the conditions under which a sentence of the language can be *asserted*. In particular, we must indicate all *axioms* (or *primitive sentences*), i.e., those sentences which we decide to assert without proof; and we must give the so-called *rules of inference* (or *rules of proof*) by means of which we can deduce new asserted sentences from other sentences which have been previously asserted. Axioms, as well as sentences deduced from them by means of rules of inference, are referred to as *"theorems"* or *"provable sentences."*

If in specifying the structure of a language we refer exclusively to the form of the expressions involved, the language is said to be *formalized*. In such a language theorems are the only sentences which can be asserted.

At the present time the only languages with a specified structure are the formalized languages of various systems of deductive logic, possibly enriched by the introduction of certain nonlogical terms. However, the field of application of these languages is rather comprehensive; we are able, theoretically, to develop in them various branches of science, for instance, mathematics and theoretical physics.

(On the other hand, we can imagine the construction of languages which have an exactly specified structure without being formalized. In such a language the assertability of sentences, for instance, may depend not always on their form, but sometimes on other, non-linguistic factors. It would be interesting and important actually to construct a language of this type, and specifically one which would prove to be sufficient for the development of a comprehensive branch of empirical science; for this would justify the hope that languages with specified structure could finally replace everyday language in scientific discourse.)

The problem of the definition of truth obtains a precise meaning and can be solved in a rigorous way only for those languages whose structure has been exactly specified. For other languages—thus, for all natural, "spoken" languages—the meaning of the problem is more or less vague, and its solution can have only an approximate character. Roughly speaking, the approximation consists in replacing a natural language (or a portion of it in which we are interested) by one whose structure is exactly specified, and which diverges from the given language "as little as possible."

7. THE ANTINOMY OF THE LIAR. In order to discover some of the more specific conditions which must be satisfied by languages in which (or for which) the definition of truth is to be given, it will be advisable to begin with a discussion of that antinomy which directly involves the notion of truth, namely, the antinomy of the liar.

To obtain this antinomy in a perspicuous form, consider the following sentence:

The sentence printed in this paper on p. 483, l. 8, is not true.

For brevity we shall replace the sentence just stated by the letter *"s."*

According to our convention concerning the adequate usage of the term *"true,"* we assert the following equivalence of the form (T):

(1)   *"s" is true if, and only if, the sentence printed in this paper on p. 483, l. 8, is not true.*

On the other hand, keeping in mind the meaning of the symbol *"s,"* we establish empirically the following fact:

(2)   *"s" is identical with the sentence printed in this paper on p. 483, l. 8.*

Now, by a familiar law from the theory of identity (Leibniz's law), it follows from (2) that we may replace (1) the expression *"the sentence printed in this paper on p. 483, l. 8"* by the symbol *" 's.' "* We thus obtain what follows:

(3)   *"s" is true if, and only if, "s" is not true.*

In this way we have arrived at an obvious contradiction.

In my judgment, it would be quite wrong and dangerous from the standpoint of scientific progress to depreciate the importance of this and other antinomies, and to treat them as jokes or sophistries. It is a fact that we are here in the presence of an absurdity, that we have been compelled to assert a false sentence (since (3), as an equivalence between two contradictory sentences, is necessarily false). If we take our work seriously, we cannot be reconciled with this fact. We must discover its cause, that is to say, we must analyze premises upon which the antinomy is based; we must then reject at least one of these premises, and we must investigate the consequences which this has for the whole domain of our research.

It should be emphasized that antinomies have played a preëminent role in establishing the foundations of modern deductive sciences. And just as class-theoretical antinomies, and in particular Russell's antinomy (of the class of all classes that are not members of themselves), were the starting point for the successful attempts at a consistent formalization of logic and mathematics, so the antinomy of the liar and other semantic antinomies give rise to the construction of theoretical semantics.

8. THE INCONSISTENCY OF SEMANTICALLY CLOSED LANGUAGES. If we now analyze the assumptions which lead to the antinomy of the liar, we notice the following:

(I) We have implicitly assumed that the language in which the antinomy is constructed contains, in addition to its expressions, also the names of these expressions, as well as semantic terms such as the term *"true"* referring to sentences of this language; we have also assumed that all sentences which determine the adequate usage of this term can be asserted in the language. A language with these properties will be called *"semantically closed."*

(II) We have assumed that in this language the ordinary laws of logic hold.

(III) We have assumed that we can formulate and assert in our language an empirical premise such as the statement (2) which has occurred in our argument.

It turns out that the assumption (III) is not essential, for it is possible to reconstruct the antinomy of the liar without its help. But the assumptions (I) and (II) prove essential. Since every language which satisfies both of these assumptions is inconsistent, we must reject at least one of them.

It would be superfluous to stress here the consequences of rejecting the assumption (II), that is, of changing our logic (supposing this were possible) even in its more elementary and fundamental parts. We thus consider only the possibility of rejecting the assumption (I). Accordingly, we decide *not to use any language which is semantically closed* in the sense given.

This restriction would of course be unacceptable for those who, for reasons which are not clear to me, believe that there is only one "genuine" language (or, at least, that all "genuine" languages are mutually translatable). However, this restriction does not affect the needs or interests of science in any essential way. The languages (either the formalized languages or—what is more frequently the case—the portions of everyday language) which are used in scientific discourse do not have to be semantically closed. This is obvious in case linguistic phenomena and, in particular, semantic notions do not enter in any way into the subject matter of a science; for in such a case the language of this science does not have to be provided with any semantic terms at all. However, we shall see in the next section how semantically closed languages can be dispensed with even in those scientific discussions in which semantic notions are essentially involved.

The problem arises as to the position of everyday language with regard to this point. At first blush it would seem that this language satisfies both assumptions (I) and (II), and that therefore it must be inconsistent. But actually the case is not so simple. Our everyday language is certainly not one with an exactly specified structure. We do not know precisely which expressions are sentences, and we know even to a smaller degree which sentences are to be taken as assertible. Thus the problem of consistency has no exact meaning with respect to this language. We may at best only risk the guess that a language whose structure has been exactly specified and which resembles our everyday language as closely as possible would be inconsistent.

9. OBJECT-LANGUAGE AND META-LANGUAGE. Since we have agreed not to employ semantically closed languages, we have to use two different languages in discussing the problem of the definition of truth and, more generally, any problems in the field of semantics. The first of these languages is the language which is "talked about" and which is the subject matter of the whole discussion; the definition of truth which we are seeking applies to the sentences of this language. The second is the language in which we "talk about" the first language, and in terms of which we wish, in particular, to construct the definition of truth for the first language. We shall refer to the first language as *"the object-language,"* and to the second as *"the meta-language."*

It should be noticed that these terms "object-language" and "meta-language" have only a relative sense. If, for instance, we become interested in the notion of truth applying to sentences, not of our original object-language, but of its meta-language, the latter becomes automatically the object-language of our discussion; and in order to define truth for this language, we have to go to a new meta-language—so to speak, to a meta-language of a higher level. In this way we arrive at a whole hierarchy of languages.

The vocabulary of the meta-language is to a large extent determined by previously stated conditions under which a definition of truth will be considered materially adequate. This definition, as we recall, has to imply all equivalences of the form (T):

(T) $\qquad\qquad\qquad X$ is true if, and only if, p.

The definition itself and all the equivalences implied by it are to be formulated in the meta-language. On the other hand, the symbol "p" in (T) stands for an arbitrary sentence of our object-language. Hence it follows that every sentence which occurs in the object-language must also occur in the meta-language; in other words, the meta-language must contain the object-language as a part. This is at any rate necessary for the proof of the adequacy of the definition—even though the definition itself can sometimes be formulated in a less comprehensive meta-language which does not satisfy this requirement.

(The requirement in question can be somewhat modified, for it suffices to assume that the object-language can be translated into the meta-language; this necessitates a certain change in the interpretation of the symbol "p" in (T). In all that follows we shall ignore the possibility of this modification.)

Furthermore, the symbol "X" in (T) represents the name of the sentence which "p" stands for. We see therefore that the meta-language must be rich enough to provide possibilities of constructing a name for every sentence of the object-language.

In addition, the meta-language must obviously contain terms of a general logical character, such as the expression "if, and only if."

It is desirable for the meta-language not to contain any undefined terms except such as are involved explicitly or implicitly in the remarks above, i.e.: terms of the object-language; terms referring to the form of the expressions of the object-language, and used in building names for these expressions; and terms of logic. In particular, we desire *semantic terms* (referring to the object-language) *to be introduced into the meta-language only by definition*. For, if this postulate is satisfied, the definition of truth, or of any other semantic concept, will fulfill what we intuitively except from every definition; that is, it will explain the meaning of the term being defined in terms whose meaning appears to be completely clear and unequivocal. And, moreover, we have then a kind of guarantee that the use of semantic concepts will not involve us in any contradictions.

We have no further requirements as to the formal structure of the object-language and the meta-language; we assume that it is similar to that of other formalized languages known at the present time. In particular, we assume that the usual formal rules of definition are observed in the meta-language.

10. CONDITIONS FOR A POSITIVE SOLUTION OF THE MAIN PROBLEM. Now, we have already a clear idea both of the conditions of material adequacy to which the definition of truth is subjected, and of the formal structure of the language in which this definition is to be constructed. Under these circumstances the problem of the definition of truth acquires the character of a definite problem of a purely deductive nature.

The solution of the problem, however, is by no means obvious, and I would not attempt to give it in detail without using the whole machinery of contemporary logic. Here I shall confine myself to a rough outline of the solution and to the discussion of certain points of a more general interest which are involved in it.

The solution turns out to be sometimes positive, sometimes negative. This depends upon some formal relations between the object-language and its meta-language; or, more specifically, upon the fact whether the meta-language in its logical part is "*essentially richer*" than the object-language or not. It is not easy to give a general and precise definition of this notion of "essential richness." If we restrict ourselves to languages based on the logical theory of types, the condition for the meta-language to be "essentially richer" than the object-language is that it contain variables of a higher logical type than those of the object-language.

If the condition of "essential richness" is not satisfied, it can usually be shown that an interpretation of the meta-language in the object-language is possible; that is to say, with any given term of the meta-language a well-determined term of the object-language can be correlated in such a way that the assertible sentences of the one language turn out to be correlated with assertible sentences of the other. As a result of this interpretation, the hypothesis that a satisfactory definition of truth has been formulated in the meta-language turns out to imply the possibility of reconstructing in that language the antinomy of the liar; and this in turn forces us to reject the hypothesis in question.

(The fact that the meta-language, in its nonlogical part, is ordinarily more comprehensive than the object-language does not affect the possibility of interpreting the former in the latter. For example, the names of expressions of the object-language occur in the meta-language, though for the most part they do not occur in the object-language itself; but, nevertheless, it may be possible to interpret these names in terms of the object-language.)

Thus we see that the condition of "essential richness" is necessary for the possibility of a satisfactory definition of truth in the meta-language. If we want to develop the theory of truth in a meta-language which does not satisfy this condition, we must give up the idea of defining truth with the exclusive help of those terms which were indicated above (in Section 8). We have then to include the term "*true*," or some other semantic term, in the list of undefined terms of the meta-language, and to express fundamental properties of the notion of truth in a series of axioms. There is nothing essentially wrong in such an axiomatic procedure, and it may prove useful for various purposes.

It turns out, however, that this procedure can be avoided. For *the condition of the "essential richness" of the meta-language proves to be, not only necessary, but also sufficient for the construction of a satisfactory definition of truth;* i.e., if the meta-language satisfies this condition, the notion of truth can be defined in it. We shall now indicate in general terms how this construction can be carried through.

11. THE CONSTRUCTION (IN OUTLINE) OF THE DEFINITION. A definition of truth can be obtained in a very simple way from that of another semantic notion, namely, of the notion of *satisfaction*.

Satisfaction is a relation between arbitrary objects and certain expressions called "*sentential functions*." These are expressions like "*x is white*," "*x is greater than y*," etc. Their formal structure is analogous to that of sentences; however, they may contain the so-called free variables (like *"x"* and *"y"* in *"x is greater than y"*), which cannot occur in sentences.

In defining the notion of a sentential function in formalized languages, we usually apply what is called a "recursive procedure"; i.e., we first describe sentential functions of the simplest structure (which ordinarily presents no difficulty), and then we indicate the operations by means of which compound functions can be constructed from simpler ones. Such an operation may consist, for instance, in forming the logical disjunction or conjunction of two given functions, i.e., by combining them by the word *"or"* or *"and."* A sentence can now be defined simply as a sentential function which contains no free variables.

As regards the notion of satisfaction, we might try to define it by saying that given objects satisfy a given function if the latter becomes a true sentence when we replace in it free variables by names of given objects. In this sense, for example, snow satisfies the sentential function *"x is white"* since the sentence *"snow is white"* is true. However, apart from other difficulties, this method is not available to us, for we want to use the notion of satisfaction in defining truth.

To obtain a definition of satisfaction we have rather to apply again a recursive procedure. We indicate which objects satisfy the simplest sentential functions; and then we state the conditions under which given objects satisfy a compound function —assuming that we know which objects satisfy the simpler functions from which the compound one has been constructed. Thus, for instance, we say that given numbers satisfy the logical disjunction *"x is greater than y or x is equal to y"* if they satisfy at least one of the functions *"x is greater than y"* or *"x is equal to y."*

Once the general definition of satisfaction is obtained, we notice that it applies automatically also to those special sentential functions which contain no free variables, i.e., to sentences. It turns out that for a sentence only two cases are possible: a sentence is either satisfied by all objects, or by no objects. Hence we arrive at a definition of truth and falsehood simply by saying that *a sentence is true if it is satisfied by all objects, and false otherwise.*

(It may seem strange that we have chosen a roundabout way of defining the truth of a sentence, instead of trying to apply, for instance, a direct recursive procedure. The reason is that compound sentences are constructed from simpler sentential functions, but not always from simpler sentences; hence no general recursive method is known which applies specifically to sentences.)

From this rough outline it is not clear where and how the assumption of the "essential richness" of the meta-language is involved in the discussion; this becomes clear only when the construction is carried through in a detailed and formal way.

·   ·   ·

10

TRUTH

p. f. strawson

. . .

In recent discussions of truth, one or both of two theses are commonly maintained. These are:

First, any sentence beginning "It is true that . . ." does not change its assertive meaning when the phrase "It is true that" is omitted. More generally, to say that an assertion is true is not to make any further assertion at all; it is to make the same assertion. This I shall call Thesis 1.

Second, to say that a statement is true is to make a statement about a sentence of a given language, viz., the language in which the first statement was made. It is (in other and more technical terms) to make a statement in a meta-language ascribing the semantic property of truth (or the semantic predicate "true") to a sentence in an object-language. The object-sentence concerned should strictly be written in inverted commas [i.e., quotation marks] to make it clear that we are talking *about the sentence;* and the phrase "is true" should strictly be followed by some such phrase as "in L," where "L" designates the object-language concerned. This I shall call Thesis 2.

Of these two theses, the first is true, but inadequate; the second is false, but important. The first thesis is right in what it asserts, and wrong in what it suggests. The second thesis is wrong in what it asserts, but right in what it implies. The first thesis is right in asserting that to say that a statement is true is not to make a further statement; but wrong in suggesting that to say that a statement is true is not to do something different from, or additional to, just making the statement. The second thesis is right in implying that to say that a statement is true is to do something different from just making the statement; but wrong in asserting that this "something different" consists in making a further statement, viz., a statement about a sentence.

Although both theses are sometimes maintained by the same philosopher, it is easy to see that they cannot both be correct. For if it is true that to say (1) "Moths fly by night" is to make the same assertion as to say (2) "It is true that moths fly by night," then it is false that to say (2) is to say anything about the English sentence

From P. F. Strawson, "Truth," in *Analysis* 9, no. 6 (June 1949): pp. 83–97. Reprinted by permission of Basil Blackwell & Mott Ltd.

"Moths fly by night"; i.e., false that (2) ought strictly to be written " 'Moths fly by night' is true in English." If to say (2) is to make the same assertion as to say (1), then to say (2) cannot be to say anything about an English sentence; for to say (1) is not to say anything about an English sentence, but is to say something about moths.

Independently of this, one sees how misleading it is to say that the phrase ". . . is true" is used to talk *about sentences,* by comparing it with other phrases which certainly are used to talk about sentences (or words, or phrases). For example, someone says, in French, "Il pleuve"; and someone else corrects him, saying: " 'Il pleuve' is *incorrect* French. 'Il pleut' is the right way of saying it." Or, criticising the style of a passage, someone says: "The sentence '. . . .' is *badly expressed.*" Similarly, one may ask what a sentence *means,* or say that a sentence is *ungrammatical, misspelt, a poor translation.* In all these cases, it is natural to say that one is talking *about a sentence.* If any statement of this kind were correctly translated into any language at all, the sentence which was being discussed would reappear, quoted and untranslated, in the translation of the statement as a whole. Otherwise the translation would be incorrect. But it is perfectly obvious that a correct translation of any statement containing the phrase "is true" (used as it is ordinarily used) never contains a quoted and untranslated sentence to which the phrase "is true" was *applied* in the original sentence. The phrase "is true" is not *applied to* sentences; for it is not *applied to* anything.

Truth is not a property of symbols; for it is not a property.

.   .   .

The best way of showing that Thesis 1 is true is to correct its inadequacy. The best way of correcting its inadequacy is to discover the further reasons which have led to Thesis 2. To bring out those features of the situation which lead to the mistake of saying that the word "true" is used meta-linguistically (to talk about sentences), I want first to compare the use of "true" with that of "Yes." If you and I have been sitting together in silence for some time, and I suddenly say "Yes," you would, perhaps, look at me with surprise and answer "I didn't say anything." Of course, a man may say "Yes" to himself; and this will be a sign that he has resolved a doubt in his own mind, or come to a decision. But the normal use of "Yes" is to answer: and where no question is asked, no answer can be given. Suppose you now ask: "Was Jones there?" and I say "Yes"; there seems no temptation whatever to say that, in so answering, I am *talking about* the English sentence "Was Jones there?" So, in the case of "Yes," we have a word of which the normal use requires some linguistic occasion (a question), without there being any temptation at all to say that it is used to *talk about* the sentence of which the utterance is the occasion for its use. There is indeed a temptation to go further in the opposite direction and say that in answering "Yes" I am not talking *about* anything, not making any assertion, at all; but simply answering. In a way, this is correct; but in a way, it's wrong. For it would be perfectly correct for you, reporting our dialogue, to say of me: "He said Jones was there." So of the ordinary use of "Yes," we may say: first, that it demands a linguistic occasion, namely the asking of a question; second, that it is not used meta-linguistically, to talk about the question, but to answer it; third, that in so far as we are making an assertion at all in using it, the content of the assertion is the same as the content of the question. Now imagine a possible, and perhaps vulgarly current, use of the expression "Ditto." You make an assertion, and I say "Ditto." In so far as I assert anything, talk about anything, I talk about and assert what you talk about and assert. Of course—and this points to the inadequacy of Thesis 1 and the reason for the meta-linguistic error—to say "Ditto" is not *the same as* to make the statement in question; for, whereas I might have made the statement before anyone else had spoken, it would be meaningless for me to say "Ditto" before anyone else had spoken. "Ditto," like "Yes," requires a linguistic occasion. But again, and largely, I think, because the expression "Ditto" does not consist of a grammatical subject and a grammatical predicate, there is absolutely no temptation to say that in thus using "Ditto," I should be talking *about the sentence* you used, and the utterance of which was the linguistic occasion for my use of this expression. I am not talking about what you said (the noise you made, or the sentence you spoke, or the proposition you expressed). I am agreeing with, endorsing, underwriting what you said; and, unless you had said something, I couldn't perform *these* activities, though I could *make the assertion* you made. Now the expression "That's true" sometimes functions in just the way in which I have suggested the expression "Ditto" might function. A says "Jones was there" and B says "That's true"; and C, reporting the conversation, can correctly say: "Both A and B said that Jones was there." But the point is that B couldn't have said that Jones was there in the way he *did* say it (i.e., by the use of the expression "That's true") unless A had previously uttered the *sentence* "Jones was there," or some equivalent sentence. It is, perhaps, *this* fact about the use (*this* use) of the word "true," together with the old prejudice that any indicative sentence must describe (be "about") something, which encourages those who have become chary of saying that truth is a property of propositions to say instead that in using the word "true," we are talking about sentences. (What I have said about the use of "That's true" applies, of course, with suitable alterations, to the use of "That's false").

Now those who assert that "true" is a predicate of sentences have not, in general, considered these simple cases of the use of "true" (and "false"), but the more puzzling cases which lead, or seem to lead, to paradoxes: such as the case where someone utters the isolated sentence "What I am saying now is false," or writes on an otherwise clean blackboard the sentence "Every statement on this blackboard is false." The solution on meta-linquistic lines is to treat these sentences as making statements of the second order to the effect: (1) that there is some statement of the first order written on the blackboard (or said by me now); and (2) that any first-order statement written on the blackboard (or said by me now) is false.

By means of this distinction of orders, the distinction between meta- and object-language, the puzzling sentences are said no longer to engender contradictions: either they are simply false, since the existential part of what they assert is false; or, alternatively, leaving out the existential part of the analysis, and treating them solely as hypotheticals, they are seen to be vacuously true, since no first-order statements occur. This solution is formally successful in avoiding the apparent contradictions. But it seems to me to achieve this success only by repeating the fundamental mistake from which the contradictions themselves arise, and also, and consequently, involving the difficulties mentioned at the beginning of this paper. That is, first, it involves the view that to say that a statement is true (or false) is to make a further, second-order, statement (thus contradicting Thesis 1); and, second, it (usually) involves the unplausibility of saying that this second-order statement is *about* a sentence or sentences. Now the point of the previous discussion of the actual use of "Yes," the possible use of "Ditto" and the actual use of "That's true" is to show that these expedients are unnecessary. When no one has spoken, and I say "Ditto," I am not making a false statement to the effect that something true has been said, nor a true statement to the effect that nothing false has been said. I am not making a statement at all; but producing a pointless utterance. When somebody has made an assertion previously, my saying "Ditto" acquires a point, has an occasion: and, if you like, you may say that I am now making a statement, repeating, in a manner, what the speaker said. But I am not making an additional statement, a meta-statement. It would perhaps be better to say that my utterance is not a statement at all, but a linguistic performance for which in the first case there was not, and in the second case there was, an occasion: so that in the first case it was a spurious, and in the second case a genuine, performance. Similarly, the words "true" and "false" normally require, as an occasion for their significant use, that somebody should have made, be making or be about to make (utter or write), some statement. (The making of the statement need not precede the use of "true": it may follow it as in the case of the expression "It is true that . . . ."—a form of words I shall discuss later.) But in all cases the indicative clause of which the grammatical predicate is the phrase "is true" does not in itself make any kind of statement at all (not even a meta-statement), and *a fortiori* cannot make the statement, the making of which is required as the occasion for the significant use of the words "true" or "false." This is not, as it stands, quite accurate. For an indicative sentence of which the grammatical predicate is the phrase "is true" may sometimes, as I shall shortly show, be used to make an implicit meta-statement. But when this is so, the phrase "is true" plays no part in the making of this meta-statement. The phrase "is true" *never* has a statement-making role. And when this is seen, the paradoxes vanish without the need for the meta-linguistic machinery; or at least without the need for regarding the words "true" and "false" as part of that machinery. The paradoxes arise on the assumption that the words "true" and "false" can be used to make first-order assertions. They are formally solved by the declaration that these words can be used only to make second-order assertions. Both paradoxes and solution disappear on the more radical assumption that they are not used to make assertions of any order, are not used to make assertions at all.

I said, however, that indicative sentences of which the grammatical predicate is the phrase "is true" or the phrase "is false" may be used to make an implicit meta-statement, in the making of which these phrases themselves play no part. To elucidate this, consider the following sentences:

(1) What I am saying now is false.
(2) All statements made in English are false.
(3) What the policeman said is true.

It is certainly not incorrect to regard each of these sentences as implicitly making an *existential* meta-statement, which does not involve the words "true" or "false." The implict meta-statements in these cases might be written as follows:

(1a) I have just made (am about to make) a statement.
(2a) Some statements are made in English.
(3a) The policeman made a statement.

These are all second-order assertive sentences to the effect that there are some first-order assertive sentences, uttered (*a*) by me, (*b*) in English, (*c*) by the policeman.

These second-order assertive sentences we can regard as part of the analysis of the sentences (1), (2), and (3). Obviously they are not the whole of their analysis. The sentence "The policeman made a statement" clearly has not the same use as the sentence "What the policeman said is true." To utter the second is to do something more than to assert the first. What is this additional performance? Consider the circumstances in which we might use the expression "What the policeman said is true." Instead of using this expression, I might have *repeated* the policeman's story. In this case, I shall be said to have *confirmed* what the policeman said. I might, however, have made exactly the same set of statements as I made in repeating his story, but have made them *before* the policeman spoke. In this case, though the assertions I have made are no different, I have not done what I did in the other case, namely, "confirmed his story." So to confirm his story is not to say anything further *about* his story, or the sentences he used in telling it, though it is to do something that cannot be done unless he has told his story. Now, unlike the confirming narrative which I might have told, the sentence "What the policeman said is true" has no use *except* to confirm the policeman's story; [1] but like the confirming narrative, the sentence does not say anything further *about* the policeman's story or the sentences he used in telling it. It is a device for confirming the story without telling it again. So, in general, in using such expressions, we are confirming, underwriting, admitting, agreeing with, what somebody has said; but (except where we are implicitly making an existential meta-statement, in making which the phrase "is true" plays no part), we are not making any assertion additional to theirs; and are *never* using "is true" to talk *about* something which is *what they said,* or the sentences they used in saying it. To complete the analysis, then, of the entire sentence (3) "What the policeman said is true," we have to add, to the existential meta-assertion, a phrase which is not assertive, but (if I may borrow Mr. [J.L.] Austin's word) performatory. We might, e.g., offer, as a complete analysis of one case, the expression: "The policeman made a statement. I confirm it"; where, in uttering the words "I confirm it," I am not describing something I do, but *doing* something. There is, then, a difference between the more complicated cases in which the phrase "is true" is preceded by a descriptive phrase, and the simpler sentences (e.g., "That's true") in which the phrase "is true" is preceded by a demonstrative. The former may be regarded as involving an implicit meta-statement, while the latter are purely confirmatory (or purely "admittive"). But in neither sort of case has the phrase "is true" any assertive (or meta-assertive) function.

·   ·   ·

In philosophical discussion of this whole subject, very little attention has been paid to the actual use of "true." And I want to conclude by distinguishing some of its normal uses in a little more detail. The uses mentioned so far I was tempted to call "performatory." But this is a misnomer. A performatory word, in Austin's sense, I take to be a verb, the use of which, in the first person present indicative, seems to describe some activity of the speaker, but in fact *is* that activity. Clearly the use of "is true" does not seem to describe any activity of the speaker; it *has seemed* to describe a sentence, a proposition, or statement. The point of using Austin's word at all is the fact that the phrase "is true" can sometimes be replaced,[2] without any

---

[1] This needs qualification. Uttered by a witness, the sentence is a *confirmation;* wrung from the culprit it is an *admission*. No doubt there are other cases.

[2] Of course, not *simply* replaced. Other verbal changes would be necessary.

important change in meaning, by some such phrase as "I confirm it," which is performatory in the strict sense. I shall take the substitute performatory word as a title
for each of these cases; and shall speak, e.g., of the "confirmatory" or "admissive"
use of "true." What commends the word as, e.g., a confirmatory device is its economy.
By its means we can confirm without repeating.

The word has other, equally non-descriptive, uses. A familiar one is its use in
sentences which begin with the phrase "It's true that," followed by a clause, followed
by the word "but," followed by another clause. It has been pointed to me that the
words "It's true that . . . but . . ." could, in these sentences, be replaced by the
word "Although"; or, alternatively, by the words "I concede that . . . but . . ." This
use of the phrase, then, is concessive. The inappropriateness of the meta-linguistic
treatment seems peculiarly apparent here.

The purely confirmatory use is probably no more common than other uses which
look much the same, but which are, I think, distinct. A man may make an assertion
to you, not wanting you to confirm it, to remove the doubt of others or his own;
but wanting to know that you share his belief, or his attitude. If, in this case, you
say "That's true," you are not *saying,* but *indicating,* that you do share his belief. It
seems to me natural to describe this simply as "agreeing." Again, it seems to me that
we very often use the phrase "That's true" to express, not only agreement with what
is said, but also our sense of its novelty and force. We register the impact of what is
said, much as we might register it by saying: "I never thought of that." Contrast the
ironical "very true" with which we sometimes rudely greet the obvious. The use of
"true" here is effectively ironical just because we normally use it to express agreement
when our agreement is in doubt, or to register a sense of revelation. Sometimes, in
sentences beginning "Is it true that . . . ?" or "So it's true that . . . ." we could
preserve the expressive quality of the utterance by substituting the adverb "really"
for the quoted phrases, at an appropriate point in the sentence; to convey, as they do,
incredulity or surprise.

No doubt, the word has other functions; but those I have mentioned are probably
as common as any. The important point is that the performance of these functions
(and, I suspect, of all other nontechnical jobs the word may do) does not involve the
use of a meta-linguistic predicate; and that we *could,* with no very great violence to
our language, perform them without the need for any expression which *seems* (as
"is true" seems) to make a statement. For instance, the substitution of "although" for
"It's true that . . . but . . ." is an obvious way of dealing with the concessive use;
an extension of the practice of the inarticulate election-candidate whose speech consisted of "Ditto to Mr. X" might deal with the confirmatory and, partly, with the
expressive uses; and so on. The selection of the substitute-expressions would of
course be governed by the propagandist consideration that they should provide the
minimum encouragement to anyone anxious to mistake them for statement-making
phrases, or descriptive words.

One last point: a suggestion on the reasons why the puzzle about truth has
commonly got entangled with the puzzle about certainty. It is above all when a doubt
has been raised, when mistakes or deceit seem possible; when the need for confirmation is felt; that we tend to make use of those certifying words of which "true" is
one and of which others are "certain," "know," "prove," "establish," "validate," "confirm," "evidence," and so on. So that the question "What is the nature of truth?" leads

naturally to the question "What are the tests for truth?", and this, in its turn, to the question "What are the conditions of certainty?" The historical or judicial search for truth is the search for the evidence which will set doubt at rest. The philosophical endeavor to characterize truth *in general* has tended to become the endeavor to characterize that which *in general* sets doubt at rest; really and finally at rest. Where you find the indubitable, there you find the true. And this metaphysical road branches into different paths, at the end of one of which you find the Atomic Fact, and, at the end of another, the Absolute.

Finally, I will repeat that in saying that the word "true" has not in itself any assertive function, I am not of course saying that a sentence like "His statement is true" is incorrect. Of course the word "statement" may be the grammatical subject of a sentence of which the phrase "is true" is the grammatical predicate. Nor am I recommending that we drop this usage. But for the usage, there would be no problem.

11

TRUTH AS CORRESPONDENCE

j. l. austin

1. "What is truth?" said jesting Pilate, and would not stay for an answer. Pilate was in advance of his time. For "truth" itself is an abstract noun, a camel, that is, of a logical construction, which cannot get past the eye even of a grammarian. We approach it cap and categories in hand: we ask ourselves whether Truth is a substance (the Truth, the Body of Knowledge), or a quality (something like the color red, inhering in truths), or a relation ("correspondence").[1] But philosophers should take something more nearly their own size to strain at. What needs discussing rather is the use, or certain uses, of the word "true." *In vino,* possibly, *"veritas,"* but in a sober symposium *"verum."*

2. What is it that we say is true or is false? Or, how does the phrase "is true" occur in English sentences? The answers appear at first multifarious. We say (or are said to say) that beliefs are true, that descriptions or accounts are true, that propositions or assertions or statements are true, and that words or sentences are true: and this is to mention only a selection of the more obvious candidates. Again, we say (or are said to say) "It is true that the cat is on the mat," or "It is true to say that the cat is on the mat," or " 'The cat is on the mat' is true." We also remark on occasion, when someone else has said something, "Very true" or "That's true" or "True enough."

Most (though not all) of these expressions, and others besides, certainly do occur naturally enough. But it seems reasonable to ask whether there is not some use of "is true" that is primary, or some generic name for that which at bottom we are always saying "is true." Which, if any, of these expressions is to be taken *au pied de la lettre?* To answer this will not take us long, nor, perhaps, far: but in philosophy the foot of the letter is the foot of the ladder.

I suggest that the following are the primary forms of expression:

> It is true (to say) that the cat is on the mat.
> That statement (of his, etc.) is true.
> The statement that the cat is on the mat is true.

This paper, originally entitled "Truth," is reprinted from J. L. Austin's *Philosophical Papers* (Oxford: The Clarendon Press, 1961), pp. 85–101, by permission of the Clarendon Press.

[1] It is sufficiently obvious that "truth" is a substantive, "true" an adjective, and "of" in "true of" a preposition.

But first for the rival candidates:

(a) Some say that "truth is primarily a property of beliefs." But it may be doubted whether the expression "a true belief" is at all common outside philosophy and theology: and it seems clear that a man is said to hold a true belief when, and in the sense that, he believes (in) *something which* is true, or believes that *something which* is true is true. Moreover if, as some also say, a belief is "of the nature of a picture," then it is of the nature of what cannot be true, though it may be, for example, faithful.[2]

(b) True descriptions and true accounts are simply varieties of true statements or of collections of true statements, as are true answers and the like. The same applies to propositions too, in so far as they are genuinely said to be true (and not, as more commonly, sound, tenable, and so on).[3] A proposition in law or in geometry is something portentous, usually a generalization, that we are invited to accept and that has to be recommended by argument: it cannot be a direct report on current observation —if you look and inform me that the cat is on the mat, that is not a proposition though it is a statement. In philosophy, indeed, "proposition" is sometimes used in a special way for "the meaning or sense of a sentence or family of sentences": but whether we think a lot or little of this usage, a proposition in this sense cannot, at any rate, be what we say is true or false. For we never say "The meaning (or sense) of this sentence (or of these words) is true": what we do say is what the judge or jury says, namely that "*The words* taken in this sense, or if we assign to them such and such a meaning, or so interpreted or understood, *are true*."

(c) Words and sentences are indeed said to be true, the former often, the latter rarely. But only in certain senses. Words as discussed by philologists, or by lexicographers, grammarians, linguists, phoneticians, printers, critics (stylistic or textual), and so on, are not true or false: they are wrongly formed, or ambiguous or defective or untranslatable or unpronounceable or misspelled or archaistic or corrupt or what not.[4] Sentences in similar contexts are elliptic or involved or alliterative or ungrammatical. We may, however, genuinely say "His closing words were very true" or "The third sentence on page 5 of his speech is quite false": but here "words" and "sentence" refer, as is shown by the demonstratives (possessive pronouns, temporal verbs, definite descriptions, etc.), which in this usage consistently accompany them, to the words or sentence *as used by a certain person on a certain occasion*. That is, they refer (as does "Many a true word spoken in jest") to *statements*.

A statement is made and its making is an historic event, the utterance by a certain speaker or writer of certain words (a sentence) to an audience with reference to an historic situation, event or what not.[5]

---

[2] A likeness is true *to* life, but not true *of* it. A *word* picture can be true, just because it is *not* a picture.

[3] Predicates applicable also to "arguments," which we likewise do not say are true, but, for example, valid.

[4] Peirce made a beginning by pointing out that there are two (or three) different senses of the word "word," and adumbrated a technique ("counting" words) for deciding what is a "different sense." But his two senses are not well defined, and there are many more—the "vocable" sense, the philologist's sense in which "grammar" is the same word as "glamour," the textual critic's sense in which the "the" in 1. 254 has been written twice, and so on. With all his 66 divisions of signs, Peirce does not, I believe, distinguish between a sentence and a statement.

[5] "Historic" does not, of course, mean that we cannot speak of future or possible statements. A "certain" speaker need not be any definite speaker. "Utterance" need not be public utterance—the audience may be the speaker himself.

A sentence is made *up of* words, a statement is made *in* words. A sentence is not English or not good English, a statement is not in English or not in good English. Statements are made, words or sentences are used. We talk of *my* statement, but of *the English* sentence (if a sentence is mine, I coined it, but I do not coin statements). The *same* sentence is used in making *different* statements (I say "It is mine," you say "It is mine"): it may also be used on two occasions or by two persons in making the *same* statement, but for this the utterance must be made with reference to the same situation or event.[6] We speak of "the statement that 'S,' " but of the "the sentence 'S,' " not of "the sentence that S." [7]

When I say that a statement is what is true, I have no wish to become wedded to one word. "Assertion," for example, will in most contexts do just as well, though perhaps it is slightly wider. Both words share the weakness of being rather solemn (much more so than the more general "what you said" or "your words")—though perhaps we are generally being a little solemn when we discuss the truth of anything. Both have the merit of clearly referring to the historic use of a sentence by an utterer, and of being therefore precisely not equivalent to "sentence." For it is a fashionable mistake to take as primary "(The sentence) 'S' is true (in the English language)." Here the addition of the words "in the English language" serves to emphasize that "sentence" is not being used as equivalent to "statement," so that it precisely is not what can be true or false (and moreover, "true in the English language" is a solecism, mismodelled presumably, and with deplorable effect, on expressions like "true in geometry").

3. When is a statement true? The temptation is to answer (at least if we confine ourselves to "straightforward" statements): "When it corresponds to the facts." And as a piece of standard English this can hardly be wrong. Indeed, I must confess I do not really think it is wrong at all: the theory of truth is a series of truisms. Still, it can at least be misleading.

If there is to be communication of the sort that we achieve by language at all, there must be a stock of symbols of some kind which a communicator ("the speaker") can produce "at will" and which a communicatee ("the audience") can observe: these may be called the "words," though, of course, they need not be anything very like what we should normally call words—they might be signal flags, etc. There must also be something other than the words, which the words are to be used to communicate about: this may be called the "world." There is not reason why the world should not include the words, in every sense except the sense of the actual statement itself which on any particular occasion is being made about the world. Further, the world must exhibit (we must observe) similarities and dissimilarities (there could not be the one

---

6 "The same" does not always mean the same. In fact it has no meaning in the way that an "ordinary" word like "red" or "horse" has a meaning: it is a (the typical) device for establishing and distinguishing the meanings of ordinary words. Like "real," it is part of our apparatus *in* words for fixing and adjusting the semantics *of* words.

7 Inverted commas [i.e., quotation marks] show that the words, though uttered (in writing), are not to be taken as a statement by the utterer. This covers two possible cases, (i) where what is to be discussed is the sentence, (ii) where what is to be discussed is a statement made elsewhen in the words "quoted." Only in case (i) is it correct to say simply that the token is doing duty for the type (and even here it is quite incorrect to say that "The cat is on the mat" is the *name* of an English sentence—though possibly *The Cat is on the Mat* might be the title of a novel, or a bull might be known as *Catta est in matta*). Only in case (ii) is there something true or false, viz., (not the quotation but) the statement made in the words quoted.

without the other): if everything were either absolutely indistinguishable from anything else or completely unlike anything else, there would be nothing to say. And
finally (for present purposes—of course there are other conditions to be satisfied too)
there must be two sets of conventions:

> *Descriptive* conventions correlating the words (= sentences) with the *types* of
> situation, thing, event, etc., to be found in the world.
> *Demonstrative* conventions correlating the words (= statements) with the *historic*
> situations, etc., to be found in the world.[8]

A statement is said to be true when the historic state of affairs to which it is
correlated by the demonstrative conventions (the one to which it "refers") is of a
type [9] with which the sentence used in making it is correlated by the descriptive conventions.[10]

3a. Troubles arise from the use of the word "facts" for the historic situations,
events, etc., and in general, for the world. For "fact" is regularly used in conjunction
with "that" in the sentences "The fact is that S" or "It is a fact that S" and in the
expression "the fact that S," all of which imply that it would be true to say that S.[11]

This may lead us to suppose that

> (i) "fact" is only an alternative expression for "true statement." We note that
> when a detective says "Let's look at the facts" he does not crawl round the
> carpet, but proceeds to utter a string of statements: we even talk of "stating
> the facts";

---

[8] Both sets of conventions may be included together under "semantics." But they differ
greatly.

[9] "Is of a type with which" means "is sufficiently like those standard states of affairs
with which." Thus, for a statement to be true one state of affairs must be *like* certain others,
which is a natural relation, but also *sufficiently* like to merit the same "description," which
is no longer a purely natural relation. To say "This is red" is not the same as to say "This
is like those," nor even as to say "This is like those which were called red." That things
are *similar*, or even "exactly" similar, I may literally see, but that they are the *same* I cannot
literally see—in calling them the same color a convention is involved additional to the
conventional choice of the name to be given to the color which they are said to be.

[10] The trouble is that sentences contain words or verbal devices to serve both descriptive
and demonstrative purposes (not to mention other purposes), often both at once. In philosophy we mistake the descriptive for the demonstrative (theory of universals) or the demonstrative for the descriptive (theory of monads). A sentence as normally distinguished from a
mere word or phrase is characterized by its containing a minimum of verbal demonstrative
devices (Aristotle's "reference to time"); but many demonstrative conventions are nonverbal
(pointing, etc.), and using these we can make a statement in a single word which is not a
"sentence." Thus, "languages" like that of (traffic, etc.) *signs* use quite distinct media for
their descriptive and demonstrative elements (the sign on the post, the site of the post). And
however many verbal demonstrative devices we use as auxiliaries, there must *always* be a
nonverbal *origin* for these coordinates, which is the point of utterance of the statement.

[11] I use the following *abbreviations:*
> S for the cat is on the mat.
> ST for it is true that the cat is on the mat.
> tst for the statement that.

I take tstS as my example throughout and not, say, tst Julius Caesar was bald or tst all
mules are sterile, because these latter are apt in their different ways to make us overlook the
distinction between sentence and statement: we have, apparently, in the one case a sentence
capable of being used to refer to only one historic situation, in the other a statement without
reference to at least (or to any particular) one.

If space permitted other types of statement (existential, general, hypothetical, etc.) should
be dealt with: these raise problems rather of meaning than of truth, though I feel uneasiness
about hypotheticals.

(ii) for every true statement there exists "one" and its own precisely corresponding fact—for every cap the head it fits.

It is (i) which leads to some of the mistakes in "coherence" or formalist theories; (ii) to some of those in "correspondence" theories. Either we suppose that there is nothing there but the true statement itself, nothing to which it corresponds, or else we populate the world with linguistic *Doppelgänger* (and grossly overpopulate it— every nugget of "positive" fact overlaid by a massive concentration of "negative" facts, every tiny detailed fact larded with generous general facts, and so on).

When a statement is true, there is, *of course,* a state of affairs which makes it true and which is *toto mundo* distinct from the true statement about it: but equally of course, we can only *describe* that state of affairs *in words* (either the same or, with luck, others). I can only describe the situation in which it is true to say that I am feeling sick by saying that it is one in which I am feeling sick (or experiencing sensations of nausea): [12] yet between stating, however truly, that I am feeling sick and feeling sick there is a great gulf fixed.[13]

"Fact that" is a phrase designed for use in situations where the distinction between a true statement and the state of affairs about which it is a truth is neglected; as it often is with advantage in ordinary life, though seldom in philosophy—above all in discussing truth, where it is precisely our business to prize the words off the world and keep them off it. To ask "Is the fact that S the true statement that S or that which it is true of?" may beget absurd answers. To take an analogy: although we may sensibly ask "Do we *ride* the word 'elephant' or the animal?" and equally sensibly "Do we *write* the word or the animal?" it is nonsense to ask "Do we *define* the word or the animal?" For defining an elephant (supposing we ever do this) is a compendious description of an operation involving both word and animal (do we focus the image or the battleship?); and so speaking about "the fact that" is a compendious way of speaking about a situation involving both words and world.[14]

3b. "Corresponds" also gives trouble, because it is commonly given too restricted or too colorful a meaning, or one which in this context it cannot bear. The only essential point is this: that the correlation between the words (= sentences) and the type of situation, event, etc., which is to be such that when a statement in those words is made with reference to an historic situation of that type the statement is then true, is *absolutely and purely* conventional. We are absolutely free to appoint *any* symbol to describe *any* type of situation, so far as merely being true goes. In a small one-spade language tst nuts might be true in exactly the same circumstances as the statement in English that the National Liberals are the people's choice.[15] There is no need whatsoever for the words used in making a true statement to "mirror" in any way, however indirect, any feature whatsoever of the situation or event; a statement no more needs, in order to be true, to reproduce the "multiplicity," say, or

12 If this is what was meant by "'It is raining' is true if and only if it is raining," so far so good.

13 It takes two to make a truth. Hence (obviously) there can be no criterion of truth in the sense of some feature detectable in the statement itself which will reveal whether it is true or false. Hence, too, a statement cannot, without absurdity, refer to itself.

14 "It is true that S" and "It is a fact that S" are applicable in the same circumstances; the cap fits when there is a head it fits. Other words can fill the same role as "fact": we say, e.g., "The situation is that S."

15 We could use "nuts" even now as a code word: but a code, as a transformation of a language, is distinguished from a language, and a code word dispatched is not (called) "true."

the "structure" or "form" of the reality, than a word needs to be echoic or writing pictographic. To suppose that it does, is to fall once again into the error of reading back into the world the features of language.

The more rudimentary a language, the more, very often, it will tend to have a "single" word for a highly "complex" type of situation: this has such disadvantages as that the language becomes elaborate to learn and is incapable of dealing with situations which are nonstandard, unforeseen, for which there may just be no word. When we go abroad equipped only with a phrase book, we may spend long hours learning by heart—

$$A^l\text{-moest-fa}^i\text{nd-}^e\text{tschâ}^r\text{woum}^e\text{n,}$$
$$Ma^i\text{hwîl-iz-wau}^r\text{pt (bènt),}$$

and so on and so on, yet faced with the situation where we have the pen of our aunt, find ourselves quite unable to say so. The characteristics of a more developed language (articulation, morphology, syntax, abstractions, etc.), do not make statements in it any more capable of being true or capable of being any more true; they make it more adaptable, more learnable, more comprehensive, more precise, and so on; and *these* aims may no doubt be furthered by making the language (allowance made for the nature of the medium) "mirror" in conventional ways features descried in the world.

Yet even when a language does "mirror" such features very closely (and does it ever?) the truth of statements remains still a matter, as it was with the most rudimentary languages, of the words used being the ones *conventionally appointed* for situations of the type to which that referred to belongs. A picture, a copy, a replica, a photograph—these are *never* true in so far as they are reproductions, produced by natural or mechanical means: a reproduction can be accurate or lifelike (true *to* the original), as a gramophone recording or a transcription may be, but not true (*of*) as a record of proceedings can be. In the same way a (natural) sign *of* something can be infallible or unreliable but only an (artificial) sign *for* something can be right or wrong.[16]

There are many intermediate cases between a true account and a faithful picture, as here somewhat forcibly contrasted, and it is from the study of these (a lengthy matter) that we can get the clearest insight into the contrast. For example, maps: these may be called pictures, yet they are highly conventionalized pictures. If a map can be clear or accurate or misleading, like a statement, why can it not be true or exaggerated? How do the "symbols" used in map-making differ from those used in statement-making? On the other hand, if an air-mosaic is not a map, why is it not? And when does a map become a diagram? These are the really illuminating questions.

4. Some have said that—

To say that an assertion is true is not to make any further assertion at all.

In all sentences of the form "*p* is true" the phrase "is true" is logically superfluous.

To say that a proposition is true is just to assert it, and to say that it is false is just to assert its contradictory.

---

[16] Berkeley confuses these two. There will not be books in the running brooks until the dawn of hydro-semantics.

But wrongly. TstS (except in paradoxical cases of forced and dubious manufacture) refers to the world or any part of it exclusive of tstS, i.e., of itself.[17] TstST refers to the world or any part of it *inclusive* of tstS, though once again exclusive of itself, i.e., of tstST. That is, tstST refers to something to which tstS cannot refer. TstST does not, certainly, include any statement referring to the world exclusive of tstS which is not included already in tstS—more, it seems doubtful whether it does include that statement about the world exclusive of tstS which is made when we state that S. (If I state that tstS is true, should we really agree that I have stated that S? Only "by implication.") [18] But all this does not go any way to show that tstST is not a statement different from tstS. If Mr. Q writes on a notice-board "Mr. W is a burglar," then a trial is held to decide whether Mr. Q's published statement that Mr. W is a burglar is a libel: finding "Mr. Q's statement was true (in substance and in fact)." Thereupon a second trial is held, to decide whether Mr. W is a burglar, in which Mr. Q's statement is no longer under consideration: verdict "Mr. W is a burglar." It is an arduous business to hold a second trial: why is it done if the verdict is the same as the previous findings? [19]

What is felt is that the evidence considered in arriving at the one verdict is the same as that considered in arriving at the other. This is not strictly correct. It is more nearly correct that whenever tstS is true then tstST is also true and conversely, and that whenever tstS is false tstST is also false and conversely.[20] And it is argued that the words "is true" are logically superfluous because it is believed that generally if any two statements are always true together and always false together then they must mean the same. Now whether this is in general a sound view may be doubted: but even if it is, why should it not break down in the case of so obviously "peculiar" a phrase as "is true"? Mistakes in philosophy notoriously arise through thinking that what holds of "ordinary" words like "red" or "growls" must also hold of extraordinary words like "real" or "exists." But that "true" is just such another extraordinary word is obvious.[21]

There is something peculiar about the "fact" which is described by tstST, something which may make us hesitate to call it a "fact" at all; namely, that the relation between tstS and the world which tstST asserts to obtain is a *purely conventional* relation (one which "thinking makes so"). For we are aware that this relation is one which we could alter at will, whereas we like to restrict the word "fact" to *hard* facts, facts which are natural and unalterable, or anyhow not alterable at will. Thus, to take an analogous case, we may not like calling it a fact that the word elephant means what it does, though we can be induced to call it a (soft) fact—and though, of course, we have no hesitation in calling it a fact that contemporary English speakers use the word as they do.

17 A statement may refer to "itself" in the sense, for example, of the sentence used or the utterance uttered in making it ("statement" is not exempt from all ambiguity). But paradox does result if a statement purports to refer to itself in a more full-blooded sense, purports, that is, to state that it itself is true, or to state what it itself refers to ("This statement is about Cato").

18 And "by implication" tstST asserts something about the making of a statement which tstS certainly does not assert.

19 This is not quite fair: there are many legal and personal reasons for holding two trials—which, however, do not affect the point that the issue being tried is not the same.

20 Not *quite* correct, because tstST is only in place at all when tstS is envisaged as made and has been verified.

21 *Umum, verum, bonum*—the old favorites deserve their celebrity. There *is* something odd about each of them. Theoretical theology is a form of onomatolatry.

An important point about this view is that it confuses falsity with negation: for according to it, it is the same thing to say "He is not at home" as to say "It is false that he is at home." (But what if no one has said that he *is* at home? What if he is lying upstairs dead?) Too many philosophers maintain, when anxious to explain away negation, that a negation is just a second-order affirmation (to the effect that a certain first-order affirmation is false), yet, when anxious to explain away falsity, maintain that to assert that a statement is false is just to assert its negation (contradictory). It is impossible to deal with so fundamental a matter here.[22] Let me assert the following merely. Affirmation and negation are exactly on a level, in this sense, that no language can exist which does not contain conventions for both and that both refer to the world equally directly, not to statements about the world: whereas a language can quite well exist without any device to do the work of "true" and "false." Any satisfactory theory of truth must be able to cope equally with falsity: [23] but "is false" can only be maintained to be logically superfluous by making this fundamental confusion.

5. There is another way of coming to see that the phrase "is true" is not logically superfluous, and to appreciate what sort of a statement it is to say that a certain statement is true. There are numerous other adjectives which are in the same class as "true" and "false," which are concerned, that is, with the relations between the words (as uttered with reference to an historic situation) and the world, and which nevertheless no one would dismiss as logically superfluous. We say, for example, that a certain statement is exaggerated or vague or bald, a description somewhat rough or misleading or not very good, an account rather general or too concise. In cases like these it is pointless to insist on deciding in simple terms whether the statement is "true or false." Is it true or false that Belfast is north of London? That the galaxy is the shape of a fried egg? That Beethoven was a drunkard? That Wellington won the battle of Waterloo? There are various *degrees and dimensions* of success in making statements: the statements fit the facts always more or less loosely, in different ways on. different

---

[22] The following two sets of logical axioms are, as Aristotle (though not his successors) makes them, quite distinct:
    (*a*) No statement can be both true and false.
        No statement can be neither true nor false.
    (*b*) Of two contradictory statements—
        Both cannot be true.
        Both cannot be false.
The second set demands a definition of contradictories, and is usually joined with an unconscious postulate that for every statement there is one and only one other statement such that the pair are contradictories. It is doubtful how far any language does or must contain contradictories, however defined, such as to satisfy both this postulate and the set of axioms (*b*).
    Those of the so-called "logical paradoxes" (hardly a genuine class) which concern "true" and "false" are *not* to be reduced to cases of self-contradiction, any more than "S but I do not believe it" is. A statement to the effect that it is itself true is every bit as absurd as one to the effect that it is itself false. There are *other* types of sentence which offend against the fundamental conditions of all communication in ways *distinct from* the way in which "This is red and is not red" offends—e.g., "This does (I do) not exist," or equally absurd "This exists (I exist)." There are more deadly sins than one; nor does the way to salvation lie through any hierarchy.
[23] To be false is (not, of course, to correspond to a non-fact, but) to mis-correspond with a fact. Some have not seen how, then, since the statement which is false does not describe the fact with which it mis-corresponds (but mis-describes it), we know which fact to compare it with: this was because they thought of all linguistic conventions as descriptive—but it is the demonstrative conventions which fix which situation it is to which the statement refers. No statement can state what it itself refers to.

occasions for different intents and purposes. What may score full marks in a general knowledge test may in other circumstances get a gamma. And even the most adroit of languages may fail to "work" in an abnormal situation or to cope, or cope reasonably simply, with novel discoveries: is it true or false that the dog goes round the cow? 24 What, moreover, of the large class of cases where a statement is not so much false (or true) as out of place, *inept* ("All the signs of bread" said when the bread is before us)?

We become obsessed with "truth" when discussing statements, just as we become obsessed with "freedom" when discussing conduct. So long as we think that what has always and alone to be decided is whether a certain action was done freely or was not, we get nowhere: but so soon as we turn instead to the numerous other adverbs used in the same connection ("accidentally," "unwillingly," "inadvertently," etc.), things become easier, and we come to see that no concluding inference of the form "Ergo, it was done freely (or not freely)" is required. Like freedom, truth is a bare minimum or an illusory ideal (the truth, the whole truth and nothing but the truth about, say, the battle of Waterloo or the *Primavera*).

6. Not merely is it jejune to suppose that all a statement aims to be is "true," but it may further be questioned whether every "statement" does aim to be true at all. The principle of Logic, that "Every proposition must be true or false," has too long operated as the simplest, most persuasive and most pervasive form of the descriptive fallacy. Philosohers under its influence have forcibly interpreted all "propositions" on the model of the statement that a certain thing is red, as made when the thing concerned is currently under observation.

Recently, it has come to be realized that many utterances which have been taken to be statements (merely because they are not, on grounds of grammatical form, to be classed as commands, questions, etc.) are not in fact descriptive, nor susceptible of being true or false. When is a statement not a statement? When it is a formula in a calculus; when it is a performatory utterance; when it is a value-judgment; when it is a definition; when it is part of a work of fiction—there are many such suggested answers. It is simply not the business of such utterances to "correspond to the facts" (and even genuine statements have other businesses besides that of so corresponding).

It is a matter for decision how far we should continue to call such masqueraders "statements" at all, and how widely we should be prepared to extend the uses of "true" and "false" in "different senses." My own feeling is that it is better, when once a masquerader has been unmasked, *not* to call it a statement and *not* to say it is true or false. In ordinary life we should not call most of them statements at all, though philosophers and grammarians may have come to do so (or rather, have lumped them all together under the term of art "proposition"). We make a difference between "You said you promised" and "You stated that you promised": the former can mean that you said "I promise," whereas the latter must mean that you said "I promised": the latter, which we say you "stated," is something which is true or false, whereas for the

---

24 Here there is much sense in "coherence" (and pragmatist) theories of truth, despite their failure to appreciate the trite but central point that truth is a matter of the relation between words and world, and despite their wrongheaded *Gleichschaltung* of all varieties of statemental failure under the lone head of "partly true" (thereafter wrongly equated with "part of the truth"). "Correspondence" theorists too often talk as one would who held that every map is either accurate or inaccurate; that accuracy is a single and the sole virtue of a map; that every country can have but one accurate map; that a map on a larger scale or showing different features must be a map of a different country; and so on.

former, which is not true or false, we use the wider verb to "say." Similarly, there is a difference between "You say this is (call this) a good picture" and "You state that this is a good picture." Moreover, it was only so long as the real nature of arithmetical formulae, say, or of geometrical axioms remained unrecognized, and they were thought to record information about the world, that it was reasonable to call them "true" (and perhaps even "statements"—though were they ever so called?): but, once their nature has been recognized, we no longer feel tempted to call them "true" or to dispute about their truth or falsity.

In the cases so far considered, the model "This is red" breaks down because the "statements" assimilated to it are not of a nature to correspond to facts at all—the words are not descriptive words, and so on. But there is also another type of case where the words *are* descriptive words and the "proposition" does in a way have to correspond to facts, but precisely not in the way that "This is red" and similar statements setting up to be true have to do.

In the human predicament, for use in which our language is designed, we may wish to speak about states of affairs which have not been observed or are not currently under observation (the future, for example). And although we *can* state anything "as a fact" (which statement will then be true or false [25]) we need not do so: we need only say "The cat *may be* on the mat." This utterance is quite different from tstS—it is not a statement at all (it is not true or false; it is compatible with "The cat may *not* be on the mat"). In the same way, the situation in which we discuss whether and state that tstS is *true* is different from the situation in which we discuss whether it is *probable* that S. Tst it is probable that S is out of place, inept, in the situation where we can make tstST, and, I think, conversely. It is not our business here to discuss probability: but is worth observing that the phrases "It is true that" and "It is probable that" are in the same line of business,[26] and in so far incompatibles.

7. In a recent article in *Analysis* Mr. Strawson has propounded a view of truth which it will be clear I do not accept. He rejects the "semantic" account of truth on the perfectly correct ground that the phrase "is true" is not used in talking about *sentences,* supporting this with an ingenious hypothesis as to how meaning may have come to be confused with truth: but this will not suffice to show what he wants—that "is true" is not used in talking about (or that "truth is not a property of") *anything.* For it *is* used in talking about *statements* (which in his article he does not distinguish clearly from sentences). Further, he supports the "logical superfluity" view to this extent, that he agrees that to say that ST is not to make any further assertion at all, beyond the assertion that S: but he disagrees with it in so far as he thinks that to say that ST *is* to *do* something more than just to assert that S—it is namely to *confirm* or to *grant* or something of that kind) the assertion, made or taken as made already, that S. It will be clear that and why I do not accept the first part of this: but what of the second part? I agree that to say that ST "is" very often, and according to the all-important linguistic occasion, to confirm tstS, or to grant, it or what not; but this cannot show that to say that ST is not also and at the same time to make an assertion about tstS. To say that I believe you "is" on occasion to accept your statement; that it is also to make an assertion, which is not made by the strictly performatory utterance

---

[25] Though it is not yet in place to call it either. For the same reason, one cannot lie or tell the truth about the future.

[26] Compare the odd behaviors of "was" and "will be" when attached to "true" and to "probable."

"I accept your statement." It is common for quite ordinary statements to have a performatory "aspect": to say that you are a cuckold may be to insult you, but it is also and at the same time to make a statement which is true or false. Mr. Strawson, moreover, seems to confine himself to the case where I *say* "Your statement is true" or something similar—but what of the case where you state that S and I *say* nothing but *"look and see"* that your statement is true? I do not see how this critical case, to which nothing analogous occurs with strictly performatory utterances, could be made to respond to Mr. Strawson's treatment.

One final point: if it is admitted (*if*) that the rather boring yet satisfactory relation between words and world which has here been discussed does genuinely occur, why should the phrase "is true" not be our way of describing it? And if it is not, what else is?

The problem of induction

12

THE PROBLEM OF INDUCTIVE KNOWLEDGE

david hume

All the objects of human reason or enquiry may naturally be divided into two kinds, to wit, *Relations of Ideas,* and *Matters of Fact.* Of the first kind are the sciences of Geometry, Algebra, and Arithmetic; and in short, every affirmation which is either intuitively or demonstratively certain. *That the square of the hypothenuse is equal to the square of the two sides,* is a proposition which expresses a relation between these figures. *That three times five is equal to the half of thirty,* expresses a relation between these numbers. Propositions of this kind are discoverable by the mere operation of thought, without dependence on what is anywhere existent in the universe. Though there never were a circle or triangle in nature, the truths demonstrated by Euclid would for ever retain their certainty and evidence.

Matters of fact, which are the second objects of human reason, are not ascertained in the same manner; nor is our evidence of their truth, however great, of a like nature with the foregoing. The contrary of every matter of fact is still possible; because it can never imply a contradiction, and is conceived by the mind with the same facility and distinctness, as if ever so conformable to reality. *That the sun will not rise*

From *An Enquiry Concerning the Human Understanding,* Sec. IV, Parts I, II, in David Hume, *Enquiries Concerning the Human Understanding and Concerning the Principles of Morals,* 2nd ed., L. A. Selby-Bigge, ed. (Oxford: The Clarendon Press, 1963), pp. 25–39. Reprinted by permission of the Clarendon Press.

tomorrow is no less intelligible a proposition, and implies no more contradiction than the affirmation, *that it will rise*. We should in vain, therefore, attempt to demonstrate its falsehood. Were it demonstratively false, it would imply a contradiction, and could never be distinctly conceived by the mind.

It may, therefore, be a subject worthy of curiosity, to enquire what is the nature of that evidence which assures us of any real existence and matter of fact, beyond the present testimony of our senses, or the records of our memory. This part of philosophy, it is observable, has been little cultivated, either by the ancients or moderns; and therefore our doubts and errors, in the prosecution of so important an enquiry, may be the more excusable; while we march through such difficult paths without any guide or direction. They may even prove useful, by exciting curiosity, and destroying that implicit faith and security, which is the bane of all reasoning and free enquiry. The discovery of defects in the common philosophy, if any such there be, will not, I presume, be a discouragement, but rather an incitement, as is usual, to attempt something more full and satisfactory than has yet been proposed to the public.

All reasonings concerning matter of fact seem to be founded on the relation of *Cause and Effect*. By means of that relation alone we can go beyond the evidence of our memory and senses. If you were to ask a man, why he believes any matter of fact, which is absent; for instance, that his friend is in the country, or in France; he would give you a reason; and this reason would be some other fact; as a letter received from him, or the knowledge of his former resolutions and promises. A man finding a watch or any other machine in a desert island, would conclude that there had once been men in that island. All our reasonings concerning fact are of the same nature. And here it is constantly supposed that there is a connection between the present fact and that which is inferred from it. Were there nothing to bind them together, the inference would be entirely precarious. The hearing of an articulate voice and rational discourse in the dark assures us of the presence of some person: Why? because these are the effects of the human make and fabric, and closely connected with it. If we anatomize all the other reasonings of this nature, we shall find that they are founded on the relation of cause and effect, and that this relation is either near or remote, direct or collateral. Heat and light are collateral effects of fire, and the one effect may justly be inferred from the other.

If we would satisfy ourselves, therefore, concerning the nature of that evidence, which assures us of matters of fact, we must enquire how we arrive at the knowledge of cause and effect.

I shall venture to affirm, as a general proposition, which admits of no exception, that the knowledge of this relation is not, in any instance, attained by reasonings *a priori*; but arises entirely from experience, when we find that any particular objects are constantly conjoined with each other. Let an object be presented to a man of ever so strong natural reason and abilities; if that object be entirely new to him, he will not be able, by the most accurate examination of its sensible qualities, to discover any of its causes or effects. Adam, though his rational faculties be supposed, at the very first, entirely perfect, could not have inferred from the fluidity and transparency of water that it would suffocate him, or from the light and warmth of fire that it would consume him. No object ever discovers, by the qualities which appear to the senses, either the causes which produced it, or the effects which will arise from it; nor can our reason, unassisted by experience, ever draw any inference concerning real existence and matter of fact.

This proposition, *that causes and effects are discoverable, not by reason but by experience,* will readily be admitted with regard to such objects, as we remember to have once been altogether unknown to us; since we must be conscious of the utter inability, which we then lay under, of foretelling what would arise from them. Present two smooth pieces of marble to a man who has no tincture of natural philosophy; he will never discover that they will adhere together in such a manner as to require great force to separate them in a direct line, while they make so small a resistance to a lateral pressure. Such events, as bear little analogy to the common cause of nature, are also readily confessed to be known only by experience; nor does any man imagine that the explosion of gunpowder, or the attraction of a loadstone, could ever be discovered by arguments *a priori.* In like manner, when an effect is supposed to depend upon an intricate machinery or secret structure of parts, we make no difficulty in attributing all our knowledge of it to experience. Who will assert that he can give the ultimate reason, why milk or bread is proper nourishment for a man, not for a lion or a tiger?

But the same truth may not appear, at first sight, to have the same evidence with regard to events, which have become familiar to us from our first appearance in the world, which bear a close analogy to the whole course of nature, and which are supposed to depend on the simple qualities of objects, without any secret structure of parts. We are apt to imagine that we could discover these effects by the mere operation of our reason, without experience. We fancy, that were we brought on a sudden into this world, we could at first have inferred that one Billiard-ball would communicate motion to another upon impulse; and that we needed not to have waited for the event, in order to pronounce with certainty concerning it. Such is the influence of custom, that, where it is strongest, it not only covers our natural ignorance, but even conceals itself, and seems not to take place, merely because it is found in the highest degree.

But to convince us that all the laws of nature, and all the operations of bodies without exception, are known only by experience, the following reflections may, perhaps, suffice. Were any object presented to us, and were we required to pronounce concerning the effect, which will result from it, without consulting past observation; after what manner, I beseech you, must the mind proceed in this operation? It must invent or imagine some event, which it ascribes to the object as its effect; and it is plain that this invention must be entirely arbitrary. The mind can never possibly find the effect in the supposed cause, by the most accurate scrutiny and examination. For the effect is totally different from the cause, and consequently can never be discovered in it. Motion in the second Billiard-ball is a quite distinct event from motion in the first; nor is there anything in the one to suggest the smallest hint of the other. A stone or piece of metal raised into the air, and left without any support, immediately falls: but to consider the matter *a priori,* is there anything we discover in this situation which can beget the idea of a downward, rather than an upward, or any other motion, in the stone or metal?

And as the first imagination or invention of a particular effect, in all natural operations, is arbitrary, where we consult not experience; so must we also esteem the supposed tie or connexion between the cause and effect, which binds them together, and renders it impossible that any other effect could result from the operation of that cause. When I see, for instance, a Billiard-ball moving in a straight line towards another; even suppose motion in the second ball should by accident be suggested to me, as the result of their contact or impulse; may I not conceive, that a hundred different events might as well follow from that cause? May not both these balls remain at absolute rest? May not the first ball return in a straight line, or leap off from the second in any line or direction? All these suppositions are consistent and conceivable. Why then should we give the preference to one, which is no more consistent or conceivable than the rest? All our reasonings *a priori* will never be able to show us any foundation for this preference.

In a word, then, every effect is a distinct event from its cause. It could not, therefore, be discovered in the cause, and the first invention or conception of it, *a priori*, must be entirely arbitrary. And even after it is suggested, the conjunction of it with the cause must appear equally arbitrary; since there are always many other effects, which, to reason, must seem fully as consistent and natural. In vain, therefore, should we pretend to determine any single event, or infer any cause or effect, without the assistance of observation and experience.

.   .   .

But we have not yet attained any tolerable satisfaction with regard to the question first proposed. Each solution still gives rise to a new question as difficult as the foregoing, and leads us on to farther enquiries. When it is asked, *What is the nature of all our reasonings concerning matter of fact?* the proper answer seems to be, that they are founded on the relation of cause and effect. When again it is asked, *What is the foundation of all our reasonings and conclusions concerning that relation?* it may be replied in one word, Experience. But if we still carry on our sifting humour, and ask, *What is the foundation of all conclusions from experience?* this implies a new question, which may be of more difficult solution and explication. Philosophers, that give themselves airs of superior wisdom and sufficiency, have a hard task when they encounter persons of inquisitive dispositions, who push them from every corner to which they retreat, and who are sure at last to bring them to some dangerous dilemma. The best expedient to prevent this confusion, is to be modest in our pretensions; and even to discover the difficulty ourselves before it is objected to us. By this means, we may make a kind of merit of our very ignorance.

I shall content myself, in this section, with an easy task, and shall pretend only to give a negative answer to the question here proposed. I say then, that, even after we have experience of the operations of cause and effect, our conclusions from that experience are *not* founded on reasoning, or any process of the understanding. This answer we must endeavour both to explain and to defend.

It must certainly be allowed, that nature has kept us at a great distance from all her secrets, and has afforded us only the knowledge of a few superficial qualities of objects; while she conceals from us those powers and principles on which the influence of those objects entirely depends. Our senses inform us of the colour, weight, and consistence of bread; but neither sense nor reason can ever inform us of those qualities which fit it for the nourishment and support of a human body. Sight or feeling conveys an idea of the actual motion of bodies; but as to that wonderful force or power, which would carry on a moving body for ever in a continued change of place, and which bodies never lose but by communicating it to others; of this we cannot form the most distant conception. But notwithstanding this ignorance of natural powers and principles, we always presume, when we see like sensible qualities, that they have like secret powers, and expect that effects, similar to those which we have experienced, will follow from them. If a body of like colour and consistence with that

bread, which we have formerly eat, be presented to us, we make no scruple of repeating the experiment, and foresee, with certainty, like nourishment and support. Now
this is a process of the mind or thought, of which I would willingly know the foundation. It is allowed on all hands that there is no known connection between the sensible
qualities and the secret powers; and consequently, that the mind is not led to form
such a conclusion concerning their constant and regular conjunction, by anything
which it knows of their nature. As to past *Experience,* it can be allowed to give *direct*
and *certain* information of those precise objects only, and that precise period of time,
which fell under its cognizance: but why this experience should be extended to future
times, and to other objects, which for aught we know, may be only in appearance
similar; this is the main question on which I would insist. The bread, which I formerly
eat, nourished me; that is, a body of such sensible qualities was, at that time, endued
with such secret powers: but does it follow, that other bread must also nourish me
at another time, and that like sensible qualities must always be attended with like
secret powers? The consequence seems nowise necessary. At least, it must be acknowledged that there is here a consequence drawn by the mind; that there is a certain step
taken; a process of thought, and an inference, which wants to be explained. These two
propositions are far from being the same, *I have found that such an object has always*
been attended with such an effect, and *I foresee, that other objects, which are, in*
appearance, similar, will be attended with similar effects. I shall allow, if you please,
that the one proposition may justly be inferred from the other: I know, in fact, that
it always is inferred. But if you insist that the inference is made by a chain of reasoning, I desire you to produce that reasoning. The connexion between these propositions
is not intuitive. There is required a medium, which may enable the mind to draw such
an inference, if indeed it be drawn by reasoning and argument. What that medium is,
I must confess, passes my comprehension; and it is incumbent on those to produce it,
who assert that it really exists, and is the origin of all our conclusions concerning
matter of fact.

This negative argument must certainly, in process of time, become altogether convincing, if many penetrating and able philosophers shall turn their enquiries this way
and no one be ever able to discover any connecting proposition or intermediate step,
which supports the understanding in this conclusion. But as the question is yet new,
every reader may not trust so far to his own penetration, as to conclude, because an
argument escapes his enquiry, that therefore it does not really exist. For this reason
it may be requisite to venture upon a more difficult task; and enumerating all the
branches of human knowledge, endeavour to show that none of them can afford such
an argument.

All reasonings may be divided into two kinds, namely, demonstrative reasoning,
or that concerning relations of ideas, and moral reasoning, or that concerning matter
of fact and existence. That there are no demonstrative arguments in the case seems
evident; since it implies no contradiction that the course of nature may change, and
that an object, seemingly like those which we have experienced, may be attended with
different or contrary effects. May I not clearly and distinctly conceive that a body,
falling from the clouds, and which, in all other respects, resembles snow, has yet the
taste of salt or feeling of fire? Is there any more intelligible proposition than to affirm,
that all the trees will flourish in December and January, and decay in May and June?
Now whatever is intelligible, and can be distinctly conceived, implies no contradiction,

and can never be proved false by any demonstrative argument or abstract reasoning *a priori.*

If we be, therefore, engaged by arguments to put trust in past experience, and make it the standard of our future judgment, these arguments must be probable only, or such as regard matter of fact and real existence, according to the division above mentioned. But that there is no argument of this kind, must appear, if our explication of that species of reasoning be admitted as solid and satisfactory. We have said that all arguments concerning existence are founded on the relation of cause and effect; that our knowledge of that relation is derived entirely from experience; and that all our experimental conclusions proceed upon the supposition that the future will be conformable to the past. To endeavour, therefore, the proof of this last supposition by probable arguments, or arguments regarding existence, must be evidently going in a circle, and taking that for granted, which is the very point in question.

In reality, all arguments from experience are founded on the similarity which we discover among natural objects, and by which we are induced to expect effects similar to those which we have found to follow from such objects. And though none but a fool or madman will ever pretend to dispute the authority of experience, or to reject that great guide of human life, it may surely be allowed a philosopher to have so much curiosity at least as to examine the principle of human nature, which gives this mighty authority to experience, and makes us draw advantage from that similarity which nature has placed among different objects. From causes which appear *similar* we expect similar effects. This is the sum of all our experimental conclusions. Now it seems evident that, if this conclusion were formed by reason, it would be as perfect at first, and upon one instance, as after ever so long a course of experience. But the case is far otherwise. Nothing so like as eggs; yet no one, on account of this appearing similarity, expects the same taste and relish in all of them. It is only after a long course of uniform experiments in any kind, that we attain a firm reliance and security with regard to a particular event. Now where is that process of reasoning which, from one instance, draws a conclusion, so different from that which it infers from a hundred instances that are nowise different from that single one? This question I propose as much for the sake of information, as with an intention of raising difficulties. I cannot find, I cannot imagine any such reasoning. But I keep my mind still open to instruction, if any one will vouchsafe to bestow it on me.

Should it be said that, from a number of uniform experiments, we *infer* a connexion between the sensible qualities and the secret powers; this, I must confess, seems the same difficulty, couched in different terms. The question still recurs, on what process of argument this *inference* is founded? Where is the medium, the interposing ideas, which join propositions so very wide of each other? It is confessed that the colour, consistence, and other sensible qualities of bread appear not, of themselves, to have any connexion with the secret powers of nourishment and support. For otherwise we could infer these secret powers from the first appearance of these sensible qualities, without the aid of experience; contrary to the sentiment of all philosophers, and contrary to plain matter of fact. Here, then, is our natural state of ignorance with regard to the powers and influence of all objects. How is this remedied by experience? It only shows us a number of uniform effects, resulting from certain objects, and teaches us that those particular objects, at that particular time, were endowed with such powers and forces. When a new object, endowed with similar sensible qualities, is produced, we expect similar powers and forces, and look for a like effect. From a body of like colour and consistence with bread we expect like nourishment and support. But this surely is a step or progress of the mind, which wants to be explained. When a man says, *I have found, in all past instances, such sensible qualities conjoined with such secret powers:* And when he says, *Similar sensible qualities will always be conjoined with similar secret powers,* he is not guilty of a tautology, nor are these propositions in any respect the same. You say that the one proposition is an inference from the other. But you must confess that the inference is not intuitive; neither is it demonstrative: Of what nature is it, then? To say it is experimental, is begging the question. For all inferences from experience suppose, as their foundation, that the future will resemble the past, and that similar powers will be conjoined with similar sensible qualities. If there be any suspicion that the course of nature may change, and that the past may be no rule for the future, all experience becomes useless, and can give rise to no inference or conclusion. It is impossible, therefore, that any arguments from experience can prove this resemblance of the past to the future; since all these arguments are founded on the supposition of that resemblance. Let the course of things be allowed hitherto ever so regular; that alone, without some new argument or inference, proves not that, for the future, it will continue so. In vain do you pretend to have learned the nature of bodies from your past experience. Their secret nature, and consequently all their effects and influence, may change, without any change in their sensible qualities. This happens sometimes, and with regard to some objects: Why may it not happen always, and with regard to all objects? What logic, what process of argument secures you against this supposition? My practice, you say, refutes my doubts. But you mistake the purport of my question. As an agent, I am quite satisfied in the point; but as a philosopher, who has some share of curiosity, I will not say scepticism, I want to learn the foundation of this inference. No reading, no enquiry has yet been able to remove my difficulty, or give me satisfaction in a matter of such importance. Can I do better than propose the difficulty to the public, even though, perhaps, I have small hopes of obtaining a solution? We shall at least, by this means, be sensible of our ignorance, if we do not augment our knowledge.

I must confess that a man is guilty of unpardonable arrogance who concludes, because an argument has escaped his own investigation, that therefore it does not really exist. I must also confess that, though all the learned, for several ages, should have employed themselves in fruitless search upon any subject, it may still, perhaps, be rash to conclude positively that the subject must, therefore, pass all human comprehension. Even though we examine all the sources of our knowledge, and conclude them unfit for such a subject, there may still remain a suspicion, that the enumeration is not complete, or the examination not accurate. But with regard to the present subject, there are some considerations which seem to remove all this accusation of arrogance or suspicion of mistake.

It is certain that the most ignorant and stupid peasants—nay infants, nay even brute beasts—improve by experience, and learn the qualities of natural objects, by observing the effects which result from them. When a child has felt the sensation of pain from touching the flame of a candle, he will be careful not to put his hand near any candle; but will expect a similar effect from a cause which is similar in its sensible qualities and appearance. If you assert, therefore, that the understanding of the child is led into this conclusion by any process of argument or ratiocination, I may justly require you to produce that argument; nor have you any pretence to refuse so equitable a demand. You cannot say that the argument is abstruse, and may possibly escape your enquiry; since you confess that it is obvious to the capacity of a mere infant. If you hesitate, therefore, a moment, or if, after reflection, you produce any intricate or profound argument, you, in a manner, give up the question, and confess that it is not reasoning which engages us to suppose the past resembling the future, and to expect similar effects from causes which are, to appearance, similar. This is the proposition which I intended to enforce in the present section. If I be right, I pretend not to have made any mighty discovery. And if I be wrong, I must acknowledge myself to be indeed a very backward scholar; since I cannot now discover an argument which, it seems, was perfectly familiar to me long before I was out of my cradle.

13

THE VINDICATION OF INDUCTION

hans reichenbach

. . .

The first to criticize the inference of induction by enumeration and to question its legitimacy was David Hume. Ever since his famous criticism, philosophers have regarded the problem of induction as an unsolved riddle precluding the completion of an empiricist theory of knowledge. In Hume's analysis it does not appear as a problem of probability; he includes it, rather, in the problem of causality. We observe, Hume explains, that equal causes are always followed by equal effects. We then infer that the same effects will occur in future. On what grounds do we base this inference? Hume's criticism gave two negative answers to the question:

1. The conclusion of the inductive inference cannot be inferred *a priori*, that is, it does not follow with logical necessity from the premises; or, in modern terminology, it is not tautologically implied by the premises. Hume based this result on the fact that we can at least *imagine* that the same causes will have another effect tomorrow than they had yesterday, though we do not believe it. What is logically impossible cannot be imagined—this psychological criterion was employed by Hume for the establishment of his first thesis.

2. The conclusion of the inductive inference cannot be inferred *a posteriori*, that is, by an argument from experience. Though it is true that the inductive inference has been successful in past experience, we cannot infer that it will be successful in future experience. The very inference would be an inductive inference, and the argument thus would be circular. Its validity presupposes the principle that it claims to prove.

Hume did not see a way out of this dilemma. He regarded the inductive inference as an unjustifiable procedure to which we are conditioned by habit and the apparent cogency of which must be explained as an outcome of habit. The power of habit is so strong that even the clearest insight into the unfounded use of the inductive inference cannot destroy its compelling character. Though this explanation is psy-

From Hans Reichenbach, *The Theory of Probability,* 2nd ed., trans. Ernest H. Hutten and Maria Reichenbach (Berkeley: University of California Press, 1949), Sec. 91, pp. 470–482. Reprinted by permission of the publisher.

chologically true, we cannot admit that it has any bearing on the logical problem. Perhaps the inductive inference is a habit—the logician wants to know whether it is a good habit. The question would call for an answer even if it could be shown that we can never overcome the habit. The logical problem of justification must be carefully distinguished from the question of psychological laws.

Up to our day the problem has subsisted in the sceptical version derived from Hume, in spite of many attempts at its solution. Kant's attempt to solve the problem by regarding the principle of causality as a synthetic judgment *a priori* failed because the concept of the synthetic judgment *a priori* was shown to be untenable. I may add that Kant never attempted to make use of his theory for a detailed analysis of the inductive inference. In the empiricism of our time the problem has come to the fore, overshadowing all other problems of the theory of knowledge. It has held this place persistently without changing the sceptical form that Hume gave it.

· · ·

The frequency theory of probability, with its interpretation of probability statements as posits, makes it possible to give a justification of the rule of induction. The problem will be discussed with respect to the wider form of statistical induction; the results will then include the special case of classical induction. The generalization expressed in the use of statistical induction is relevant because it weakens the inference. Whereas classical induction wishes to establish a rigorous inference that holds for every individual case, statistical induction renounces every assertion about the individual case and makes a prediction only about the whole sequence.

There is another sense in which the statistical version involves a different interpretation of the problem. The classical conception entails the question whether the rule of induction leads to true conclusions, but the statistical version deals only with the question whether the rule of induction leads to a method of approximation, whether it leads to posits that, when repeated, approach the correct result step by step. The answer is that this is so if the sequences under consideration have a limit of the frequency. The inductive posit anticipates the final result and must eventually arrive at the correct value of the limit within an interval of exactness.

The method of anticipation may be illustrated by an example from another field. An airplane flies in the fog to a distant destination. From two ground stations the pilot receives radio messages about his position, ascertained by radio bearings. He then determines the flight direction by means of a map, adjusts the compass to the established course, and flies on, keeping continuously to the direction given by the compass. In the fog he has no other orientation than to follow the adopted course. After a while, however, he inquires again of the ground stations for another determination of his position. It turns out that the airplane was subject to a wind drift that has carried the ship off its course. The pilot, therefore, establishes a new course that he follows thereafter.

This method, repeatedly applied, is a method of approximation. The direction from the position ascertained to the destination is not the most favorable one because of wind currents; but the pilot does not know the changing currents and therefore at first *posits* this direction. He does not believe that he has found the final direction. He knows that only when he is very close to his destination will the straight line be the most favorable flying direction—but he acts as though the coincidence of the most favorable flying direction and a straight-line connection were reached. He thus anticipates the final result. He may do so because he uses this anticipation only in the sense of a posit. By correcting the posit repeatedly, always following the same rule, he must finally come to the correct posit and thus reach his destination.

The analogy with the anticipative method of the rule of induction is obvious. In the analysis of Hume's problem we thus arrive at a preliminary result: if a limit of the frequency exists, positing the persistence of the frequency is justified because this method, applied repeatedly, must finally lead to true statements. We do not maintain the truth of every individual inductive conclusion, but we do not need an assumption of this kind because the application of the rule presupposes only its qualification as a method of approximation.

This consideration bases the justification of induction on the assumption of the existence of a limit of the frequency. It is obvious, however, that for such an assumption no proof can be constructed. When we wish to overcome Hume's scepticism we must eliminate this last assumption from our justification of induction.

The traditional discussion of induction was dominated by the opinion that it is impossible to justify induction without an assumption of this kind, that is, without an assumption stating a general property of the physical world. The supposedly indispensable assumption was formulated as a postulate of the uniformity of nature, expressed, for instance, in the form that similar event patterns repeat themselves. The principle used above, that sequences of events converge toward a limit of the frequency, may be regarded as another and perhaps more precise version of the uniformity postulate. So long as logicians maintained that without a postulate of this kind the inductive inference could not be accounted for, and so long as there was no hope of proving such a postulate true or probable, the theory of induction was condemned to remain an unsolvable puzzle.

The way out of the difficulty is indicated by the following considerations. The insistence on a uniformity postulate derives from an unfortunate attempt to construct the theory of inductive inference by analogy with that of deductive inference—the attempt to supply a premise for the inductive conclusion cannot be asserted as true; but it was hoped to give a demonstrative proof, by the addition of such a premise, for the statement that the conclusion is probable to a certain degree. Such a proof is dispensable because we can assert a statement in the sense of a posit even if we do not know a probability, or weight, for it. If the inductive conclusion is recognized as being asserted, not as a statement maintained as true or probable, but as an anticipative posit, it can be shown that a uniformity postulate is not necessary for the derivation of the inductive conclusion.

We used the assumption of the existence of a limit of the frequency in order to prove that, if no probabilities are known, the anticipative posit is the best posit because it leads to success in a finite number of steps. With respect to the individual act of positing, however, the limit assumption does not supply any sort of information. The posit may be wrong, and we can only say that if it turns out to be wrong we are willing to correct it and to try again. But if the limit assumption is dispensable for every individual posit, it can be omitted for the method of positing as a whole. The omission is required because we have no proof for the assumption. But the absence of proof does not mean that *we know that there is no limit;* it means only that *we do not know whether there is a limit.* In that case we have as much reason to try a posit as in the case that the existence of a limit is known; for, if a limit of the frequency exists, we shall find it by the inductive method if only the acts of positing are continued sufficiently. Inductive positing in the sense of a trial-and-error method is justified so long as it is not known that the attempt is hopeless, that there is no limit of the frequency. Should we have no success, the positing was useless; but why not take our chance?

The phrase "take our chance" is not meant here to state that there is a certain probability of success; it means only that there is a possibility of success in the sense that there is no proof that success is excluded. Furthermore, the suggestion to try predictions by means of the inductive method is not an advice of a trial at random, of trying one's luck, so to speak; it is the proposal of a systematic method of trial so devised that if success is attainable the method will find it.

To make the consideration more precise, some auxiliary concepts may be introduced. The distinction between necessary and sufficient conditions is well known in logic. A statement c is a *necessary* condition of a statement a if $a \supset c$ holds, that is, if a cannot be true without c being true. The statement c will be a *sufficient* condition of a if $c \supset a$ holds. For instance, if a physician says that an operation is a necessary condition to save the patient, he does not say that the operation will save the man; he only says that without the operation the patient will die. The operation would be a sufficient condition to save the man if it is certain that it will lead to success; but a statement of this kind would leave open whether there are other means that would also save him.

These concepts can be applied in the discussion of the anticipative posit. If there is a limit of the frequency, the use of the rule of induction will be a sufficient condition to find the limit to a desired degree of approximation. There may be other methods, but this one, at least, is sufficient. Consequently, when we do not know whether there is a limit, we can say, if there is any way to find a limit, the rule of induction will be such a way. It is, therefore, a necessary condition for the existence of a limit, and thus for the existence of a method to find it, that the aim be attainable by means of the rule of induction.

To clarify these logical relations, we shall formulate them in the logical symbolism. We abbreviate by a the statement, "There exists a limit of the frequency"; by b the statement, "I use the rule of induction in a repeated procedure"; by c the statement, "I shall find the limit of the frequency." We then have the relation

$$a \supset (b \supset c) \tag{1}$$

This means, $b \supset c$ is the *necessary* condition of a, or, in other words, the attainability of the aim by the use of the rule of induction is a necessary condition of the existence of a limit. Furthermore, if a is true, b is a *sufficient* condition of c. This means, if there is a limit of the frequency, the use of the rule of induction is a sufficient instrument to find it.

It is in this relation that I find the justification of the rule of induction. Scientific method pursues the aim of predicting the future; in order to construct a precise formulation for this aim we interpret it as meaning that scientific method is intended to find limits of the frequency. Classical induction and predictions of individual events are included in the general formulation as the special case that the relative frequency is $= 1$. It has been shown that if the aim of scientific method is attainable it will be reached by the inductive method. This result eliminates the last assumption we had to use for the justification of induction. The assumption that there is a limit of the frequency must be true if the inductive procedure is to be successful. But we

need not know whether it is true when we merely ask whether the inductive procedure is justified. It is justified as an attempt at finding the limit. Since we do not
know a sufficient condition to be used for finding a limit, we shall at least make use
of a necessary condition. In positing according to the rule of induction, always
correcting the posit when additional observation shows different results, we prepare
everything so that if there is a limit of the frequency we shall find it. If there is none,
we shall certainly not find one—but then all other methods will break down also.

The answer to Hume's question is thus found. Hume was right in asserting that
the conclusion of the inductive inference cannot be proved to be true; and we may
add that it cannot even be proved to be probable. But Hume was wrong in stating
that the inductive procedure is unjustifiable. It can be justified as an instrument that
realizes the necessary conditions of prediction, to which we resort because sufficient
conditions of prediction are beyond our reach. The justification of induction can be
summarized as follows:

*Thesis θ. The rule of induction is justified as an instrument of positing because
it is a method of which we know that if it is possible to make statements about the
future we shall find them by means of this method.*

This thesis is not meant to say that the inductive rule represents the only method
of the kind described. In [a previous section] were formulated other forms of posits
that also must lead to the limit if there is one. Let us investigate whether the rule
of induction constitutes the *best* method of finding the limit.

In order to answer the question we must divide the possible methods in two
classes. In the first class we put all rules . . . that differ from the rule of induction
only inasmuch as they include a function c_n that is formulated explicitly so as to
converge to 0 with increasing n. In the second class we put all other methods that
will lead to the limit of the frequency. These methods will also converge asymptotically
with the rule of induction; but they differ from the [other] form . . . because they
do not state the convergence explicitly.

As to the first class, it was explained that we cannot prove the rule of induction
to be superior to other methods included in the class. There may be, and in general
will be, forms of the function c_n that are more advantageous than the function
$c_n = 0$. If we knew one of these forms, we should prefer it to the rule of induction.
The method of correction may be regarded as an instrument for finding such forms.
When, on the contrary, we know nothing, we can choose what we like. The rule of
induction has the advantage of being easier to handle, owing to its descriptive simplicity. Since we are considering a choice among methods all of which will lead to
the aim, we may let considerations of a technical nature determine our choice.

In regard to the second class the situation is different. If a method is presented
with the assertion that it is a method of this class, the difficulty arises of how to
prove the assertion. Of course, there may be such a method. Every oracle or soothsayer
maintains that he has found one. Such a method is usually presented in the form of
a prediction of individual events. This is included in our theory as the case in which
the probability, or the frequency limit, is $= 1$. We may, therefore, generalize the
problem so as to concern the prediction of any value of the limit of the frequency.
Assume that a clairvoyant asserts that he is able to predict only the probability of an
event—to predict the limit of the frequency in a sequence. We shall not be willing to

believe him until we have checked his abilities. He might well be following a method that will never lead to the limit of the frequency. Such methods are certainly possible. For instance, if we were to posit that the limit is *outside* the interval $f^n \pm \delta$, we should certainly never reach the limit by continued application of this rule. The inadequacy of the methods of oracles and soothsayers is not so clearly apparent. But how can such methods be tested?

Obviously, there is only one way—to test these methods by means of the rule of induction. We would ask the soothsayer to predict as much as he could, and see whether his predictions finally converged sufficiently with the frequency observed in the continuation of the sequence. Then we would count his success rate. If the latter were sufficiently high, we would infer by the rule of induction that it would remain so, and thus conclude that the man was an able prophet. If the success rate were low, we would refuse to consult him further. It is true that in the latter case the soothsayer may refer us to the future, declaring that on continuation of the sequence his prediction of a limit may still come true. Although clairvoyants favor such an attitude, finally even the most ardent believer no longer places any faith in them. In the end the believer submits his judgment to the rule of induction. He must do so because the rule of induction is a method *of which he knows that it will lead to the aim* if the aim is attainable, whereas *he does not know anything* about the oracle and the clairvoyant.

We see, by the way, that with this subordination to induction the oracle in all its forms loses its mystical glamor. Like other methods of prediction, it is subject to a scientific test. It was explained above that science itself is at work to find methods of better convergence by the construction of a network of inductions in the form of the method of correction. There is no need, therefore, to ask the help of oracles or clairvoyants in order to improve our methods of approximation.

We thus come to the result that the rule of induction can by no means be maintained to be the best method of approximation. But with its help it is possible to find better methods of approximation. Scientific method makes use of this fact to a great extent. The concatenation of empirical results in a scientific system is the way to improve the method of approximation. The rule of induction, or one of its equivalents, is the only method that can be used in the test of other methods of approximation, because it is the only method *of which we know* that it represents a method of approximation.

.   .   .

Some critics have called my justification of induction a weak justification. Such judgments originate from a rationalistic conception of scientific method. In spite of the empiricist trend of modern science, the quest for certainty, a product of the theological orientation of philosophy, still survives in the assertion that some general truths about the future must be known if scientific predictions are to be acceptable. It is hard to see what would be gained by the knowledge of such general truths. As was pointed out earlier, if we knew for certain that sequences of natural events have limits of the frequency, our situation in the face of any individual prediction would not be better than it is without such knowledge, since we would never know whether the observed initial section of the sequence were long enough to supply a satisfactory approximation of the frequency. It is no better with other forms of the uniformity postulate. How does it help to know that similar event patterns repeat themselves, if we do not know whether the pattern under consideration is one of them? In view of our ignorance concerning the individual event expected, all general truths must appear as illusory supports.

The aim of knowing the future is unattainable; there is no demonstrative truth informing us about future happenings. Let us therefore renounce the aim and renounce, too, the critique that measures the attainable in terms of that aim. It is not a weak argument that has been constructed. We can devise a method that will lead to correct predictions if correct predictions can be made—that is ground enough for the application of the method, even if we never know, before the occurrence of the event, whether the prediction is true.

. . .

The justification of induction constructed may, therefore, be called a *pragmatic* justification: it demonstrates the usefulness of the inductive procedure for the purpose of acting. It shows that our actions need not depend on a proof that the sequences under consideration have the limit property. Actions can be made in the sense of trials, and it is sufficient to have a method that will lead to successful trials if success is attainable at all. It is true that this method has no guaranty of success. But who would dare to ask for such a guaranty in the face of the uncertainty of all human planning? The physician who operates on a patient because he knows that the operation will be the only chance to save the patient will be regarded as justified, though he cannot guarantee success. If we cannot base our actions on demonstrative truth, we shall welcome it that we can at least take our chance.

That is a rational argument. But who refers to it when he applies the inductive method in everyday life? If asked why he accepts the inductive rule, he answers that he believes in it, that he is firmly convinced of its validity and simply cannot give up inductive belief. Is there a justification for this belief?

The answer is a definite "No." The belief cannot be justified. As long as such a "No" was averred by a philosophy of scepticism, it constituted a negative judgment on all human planning and acting, which it seemed to prove utterly useless. It is different for the philosophy of logical analysis, which distinguishes between justification of the belief and justification of the action. Actions directed by the rule of induction are legitimate attempts at success; no form of belief is required for the proof. He who wants to act need not believe in success; it is a sufficient reason for action to know how to prepare for success, how to be ready for the case that success is attainable. Belief in success is a personal addition; whoever has it need not give it up. For his actions it is logically irrelevant: whether or not he believes in success, the same actions will follow.

I say "*logically* irrelevant," for I know very well that, psychologically speaking, belief may not be irrelevant. Many a person is not able to act according to his posits unless he believes in their success, since few have the inner strength to take a possible failure into account and yet pursue their aim. Nature seems to have endowed us with the inductive belief as a measure of protection, as it were, facilitating our actions, though without it we would be equally justified, or obliged, to act. It is difficult, indeed, to free oneself from such a belief; and Hume was right when he called the belief in induction an unjustified but ineradicable habit. But since Hume could not show that even without this belief action is justified when it follows the rule of induction, there remained for him only sceptical resignation.

The logician need not share this negative attitude. He can show that we must act according to the rule of induction even if we cannot believe in it. This result may be the reason why it is easier for him to renounce the belief; with the loss of the belief he does not at the same time lose his orientation in the sphere of action. We do not know whether tomorrow the order of the world will not come to an end; tomorrow all known physical laws may be invalidated, the sun may no longer shine, and food no longer nourish us—or at least our own world may come to an end, because we may close our eyes forever. Tomorrow is unknown to us, but this fact need not make any difference in considerations determining our actions. We adjust our actions to the case of a predictable world—if the world is not predictable, very well, then we have acted in vain.

A blind man who has lost his way in the mountains feels a trail with his stick. He does not know where the path will lead him, or whether it may take him so close to the edge of a precipice that he will be plunged into the abyss. Yet he follows the path, groping his way step by step; for if there is any possibility of getting out of the wilderness, it is by feeling his way along the path. As blind men we face the future; but we feel a path. And we know: if we can find a way through the future it is by feeling our way along this path.

14

SELF-SUPPORTING INDUCTIVE ARGUMENTS

max black

The use of inductive rules has often led to true conclusions about matters of fact. Common sense regards this as a good reason for trusting inductive rules in the future, if due precautions are taken against error. Yet an argument from success in the past to probable success in the future itself uses an inductive rule, and therefore seems circular. Nothing would be accomplished by any argument that needed to assume the reliability of an inductive rule in order to establish that rule's reliability.

Suppose that inferences governed by some inductive rule have usually resulted in true conclusions; and let an inference from this fact to the probable reliability of the rule in the future be called a *second-order* inference. So long as the rule by which the second-order inference is governed differs from the rule whose reliability is to be affirmed, there will be no appearance of circularity. But if the second-order inference is governed by the very same rule of inference whose reliability is affirmed in the conclusion, the vicious circularity seems blatant.

Must we, then, reject forthwith every second-order inductive argument purporting to support the very rule of inference by which the argument itself is governed? Contrary to general opinion, a plausible case can be made for saying, No.[1] Properly constructed and interpreted, such "self-supporting" inferences, as I shall continue to call them, can satisfy all the conditions for legitimate inductive inference: when an inductive rule has been reliable (has generated true conclusions from true premises more often than not) in the past, a second-order inductive inference governed by the same rule can show that the rule deserves to be trusted in its next application.

The reasons I have given for this contention have recently been sharply criticized by Professor Wesley C. Salmon.[2] In trying to answer his precisely worded objections, I hope to make clearer the view I have been defending and to dispel some lingering misapprehensions.

Reprinted from the *Journal of Philosophy* LV, no. 17 (August 14, 1958): 718–725, by permission of the author and the *Journal of Philosophy*.
[1] See Max Black, *Problems of Analysis* (Ithaca, N. Y., 1954), chapter 11, and E. B. Braithwaite, *Scientific Explanation* (Cambridge, 1953), chapter 8.
[2] See Wesley C. Salmon, "Should We Attempt to Justify Induction?" *Philosophical Studies,* Vol. VIII, no. 3 (April, 1957), pp. 45–47.

My original example of a legitimate self-supporting inductive argument was the following: [3]

> (a) In most instances of the use of R in arguments with true premises examined in a wide variety of conditions, R has been successful.
> *Hence (probably):*
> In the next instance to be encountered of the use of R in an argument with a true premise, R will be successful.

The rule of inductive inference mentioned in the premise and the conclusion of the above argument is:

> R: To argue from *Most instances of A's examined in a wide variety of conditions have been B* to (probably) *The next A to be encountered will be B.*

Thus the second-order argument (a) uses the rule R in showing that the same rule will be "successful" (will generate a true conclusion from a true premise [4]) in the next encountered instance of its use.

The rule, R, stated above is not intended to be a "supreme rule" of induction, from which all other inductive rules can be derived; nor is it claimed that R, as it stands, is a wholly acceptable rule for inductive inference. The unsolved problem of a satisfactory formulation of canons of inductive inference will arise only incidentally in the present discussion. The rule R and the associated argument (a) are to serve merely to illustrate the logical problems that arise in connection with self-supporting arguments: the considerations to be adduced in defense of (a) could be adapted to fit many other self-supporting arguments.

The proposed exculpation of the self-supporting argument (a) from the charge of vicious circularity is linked to a feature of the corresponding rule R that must be carefully noted. Inductive arguments governed by R vary in "strength" [5] according to the number and variety of the favorable instances reported in the premise. So, although R permits us to assert a certain conclusion categorically, it is to be understood throughout that the strength of the assertion fluctuates with the character of the evidence. If only a small number of instances have been examined and the relative frequency of favorable instances (A's that are B) is little better than a half, the strength of the argument may be close to zero; while a vast predominance of favorable instances in a very large sample of observations justifies a conclusion affirmed with nearly maximal strength. The presence of the word "probably" in the original formulation of R indicates the variability of strength of the corresponding argument; in more refined substitutes for R, provision might be made for some precise measure of the associated degree of strength.

---

[3] See *Problems,* page 197, where the argument is called " (a₂)" and the rule by which it is governed "R_2." At that place, I also presented another self-supporting argument with a more sweeping conclusion of the *general* reliability of the corresponding rule. But since I was unable to accept the premise of that argument, or the reliability of the rule it employed, I shall follow Salmon in discussing only the argument presented above.

[4] Here and throughout this discussion, I assume for simplicity that all the premises of any argument or inference considered have been conjoined into a single statement.

[5] In *Problems,* page 193, I spoke, with the same intention, of the "degree of support" given to the conclusion by the premise. If the latter has the form *m/n A's examined in a wide variety of conditions have been B,* it is natural to suppose that the strength of the argument increases as m increases, and also as m/n increases. A plausible formula for the "strength" of the argument might be $(1 - e^{-m})(2m/n - 1)$.

Variability in strength is an important respect in which inductive arguments differ sharply from deductive ones. If a deductive argument is not valid, it must be *in*valid, no intermediate cases being conceivable; but a legitimate inductive argument, whose conclusion may properly be affirmed on the evidence supplied, may still be very weak. Appraisal of an inductive argument admits of degrees.

Similar remarks apply to inductive rules, as contrasted with deductive ones. A deductive rule is either valid or invalid—*tertium non datur;* but at any time in the history of the employment of an inductive rule, it has what may be called a *degree of reliability* depending upon its ratio of successes in previous applications. A legitimate or correct inductive rule may still be a weak one: appraisal of an inductive rule admits of degrees.

Now in claiming that the second-order argument (a) *supports* the rule R, I am claiming that the argument raises the degree of reliability of the rule, and hence the strength of the arguments in which it will be used; I have no intention of claiming that the self-supporting argument can definitively establish or demonstrate that the rule is correct. Indeed, I do not know what an outright demonstration of the correctness or legitimacy of an inductive rule would be like. My attempted rebuttal of Salmon's objections will turn upon the possibility of raising the degree of reliability of an inductive rule, as already explained.

The contribution made by the second-order argument (a) to strengthening the rule R by which it is governed can be made plain by a hypothetical illustration. Suppose evidence is available that $4/5$ of the A's so far examined have been B, and it is proposed, by an application of the rule R, to draw the inference that the next A to be encountered will be B. For the sake of simplicity the proposed argument may be taken to have a strength of $4/5$.[6] Before accepting the conclusion about the next A, we may wish to consider the available evidence about past successes of the rule R. Suppose, for the sake of argument, that we know R to have been successful in $9/10$ of the cases in which it has been previously used. If so, the second-order argument affirms with strength $9/10$ that R will be successful in the next instance of its use. But the "next instance" is before us, as the argument whose premise is that $4/5$ of the $A's$ have been B. For R to be "successful" in this instance is for the conclusion of the first-order argument to be true; the strength of the second-order argument is therefore immediately transferred to the first-order argument. Before invoking the second-order argument, we were entitled to affirm the conclusion of the first-order argument with a strength of no better than $4/5$, but we are now able to raise the strength to $9/10$. Conversely, if the second-order argument had shown R to have been unsuccessful in less than $4/5$ of its previous uses, our confidence in the proposed conclusion of the first-order argument would have been diminished.

There is no mystery about the transfer of strength from the second-order argument to the first-order argument: the evidence cited in the former amplifies the evidence immediately relevant to the latter. Evidence concerning the proportion of A's found to have been B permits the direct inference, with strength $4/5$, that the next A to be encountered will be B. It is, however, permissible to view the situation in another aspect as concerned with the extrapolation of an already observed statistical association between true premises of a certain sort and a corresponding conclusion.

---

6 This means taking m/n as the measure of strength, rather than some more complicated formula like the one suggested in footnote 5 above. The argument does not depend upon the exact form of the measure of strength.

The evidence takes the form: In 9 cases out of 10, the truth of a statement of the form *m/n X's have been found to be Y's* has been found associated in a wide variety of cases with the truth of the statement *The next X to be encountered was Y*.[7] This is better evidence than that cited in the premise of the original first-order argument: it is therefore to be expected that the strength of the conclusion shall be raised.

It should be noticed that the evidence cited in the second-order argument is not merely greater in amount than the evidence cited in the first-order argument. If *R* has been successfully used for drawing conclusions about fish, neutrons, planets, etc. (the "wide variety of conditions" mentioned in the premise of the second-order argument), it would be illegitimate to coalesce such heterogeneous kinds of objects into a single class for the sake of a more extensive *first-order* argument. Proceeding to "second-order" considerations allows us to combine the results of previous inductive inquiries in a way which would not otherwise be possible.

Nothing in this conception of inductive method requires us to remain satisfied with the second-order argument. If circumstances warrant, and suitable evidence can be found, we might be led to formulate third- or even higher-order arguments. These might conceivably result in lowering the measures of strength we at present attach to certain arguments in which *R* is used. But if this were to happen, we would not have been shown to have been mistaken in previously attaching these measures of strength. Nor is it required that a first-order argument be checked against a corresponding second-order argument before the former can properly be used. If we have no reason to think that *R* is unsuccessful most of the time, or is objectionable on some logical grounds, that is enough to make our employment of it so far reasonable. The function of higher-order arguments in the tangled web of inductive method is to permit us to progress from relatively imprecise and uncritical methods to methods whose degrees of reliability and limits of applicability have themselves been checked by inductive investigations. It is in this way that inductive method becomes self-regulating and, if all goes well, self-supporting.

Salmon's objections to the foregoing conception are summarized by him as follows:

> The so-called self-supporting arguments are . . . circular in the following precise sense: the conclusiveness of the argument cannot be established without assuming the truth of the conclusion. It happens, in this case, that the assumption of the truth of the conclusion is required to establish the correctness of the rules of inference used rather than the truth of the premises, but that makes the argument no less viciously circular. The circularity lies in regarding the facts stated in the premises as *evidence* for the conclusion, rather than as evidence against the conclusion or as no evidence either positive or negative. To regard the facts in the premises as evidence for the conclusion is to assume that the rule of inference used in the argument is a correct one. And this is precisely what is to be proved. If the conclusion is denied, then the facts stated in the premises are no longer evidence for the conclusion.[8]

Comments: (1) Salmon's reference to "conclusiveness" smacks too much of the appraisal of deductive argument. An inductive argument is not required to be "conclusive" if that means that its conclusion is entailed or logically implied by its

---

[7] We might wish to restrict the second-order argument to cases in which the ratio m/n was close to $\frac{4}{5}$. Other refinements readily suggest themselves.

[8] Salmon, *loc. cit.*, p. 47.

premises; it is, of course, required to be correct or legitimate, but that means only that the rule of inductive inference shall be reliable—shall usually lead from true premises to true conclusions. The correctness of an inductive argument could only depend upon the truth of its conclusion if the latter asserted the reliability of the rule by which the argument was governed. But this was not the case in our argument (a). The conclusion there was that R would be successful in the next instance of its use: this might very well prove to be false without impugning the reliability of R. Salmon was plainly mistaken if he thought that the falsity of (a)'s conclusion entails the incorrectness of the rule by which (a) is governed.[9]

(2) Can the *correctness* of argument (a) be "established without assuming the truth of the conclusion" of (a)? Well, if "established" means the same as "proved by a deductive argument," the answer must be that the correctness of (a) cannot be established at all. But again, a correct inductive argument in support of the rule governing (a) can certainly be constructed without assuming (a)'s conclusion. We do not have to assume that R will be successful in the next instance in order to argue correctly that the available evidence supports the reliability of R.

(3) Salmon says: "To regard the facts in the premises as evidence for the conclusion is to assume that the rule of inference used in the argument is a correct one." In using the rule of inference we certainly *treat* it as correct: we would not use it if we had good reasons for suspecting it to be unreliable. If this is what Salmon means, what he says is right, but not damaging to the correctness of (a). But he would be plainly wrong if he maintained that an assertion of the correctness of (a) was an additional premise required by (a), or that an argument to the effect that (a) was correct must precede the legitimate use of (a). For if this last demand were pressed, it would render deductive inference no less than inductive inference logically impossible. If we were never entitled to *use* a correct rule of inference before we had formally argued in support of that rule, the process of inference could never get started.

I shall end by considering an ingenious counter-example provided by Salmon. He asks us to consider the following argument:

(a'): In most instances of the use of R' in arguments with true premises in a wide variety of conditions, R' has been *un*successful.
Hence (probably):
In the next instance to be encountered of the use of R' in an argument with a true premise, R' will be successful.

The relevant rule is the "counter-inductive" one:

R': To argue from *Most instances of A's examined in a wide variety of conditions have not been B* to (probably) *the next A to be encountered will be B*.

Salmon says that while (a') must be regarded as a self-supporting argument by my criteria, the rule here supported, R', is in conflict with R. From the same premises

---

[9] I conjecture that Salmon was led into making this mistake by forgetting the conclusion of the argument that he correctly reproduces at the foot of page 45 of his article. It is a sheer blunder to say "A given inductive rule can be established by a self-supporting argument, according to Black" (p. 45)—if "established" means the same as "proved reliable." The self-supporting argument can *strengthen* the rule, and in this way *"support"* it.

the two rules "will almost always produce contrary conclusions." [10] This must be granted. But Salmon apparently overlooks an important respect in which the "counter-inductive" rule R' must be regarded as illegitimate.

In calling an inductive rule "correct," so that it meets the canons of legitimacy of *inductive* rules of inference, we claim at least that the rule is reliable, in the sense of usually leading from true premises to true conclusions. That is part of what we *mean* by a "correct inductive rule." It can easily be shown that R' must fail to meet this condition.

Suppose we were using R' to predict the terms of a series of 1's and 0's, of which the first three terms were known to be 1's. Then our first two predictions might be as follows (shown by underlining):

$$1 \ 1 \ 1 \ \underline{0} \ \underline{0}$$

At this point, suppose R' has been used successfully in each of the two predictions, so that the series is in fact now observed to be 1 1 1 0 0. Since 1's still predominate, direct application of the rule calls for 0 to be predicted next. On the other hand, the second-order argument shows that R' has been successful each time and therefore demands that it not be trusted next time, i.e., calls for the prediction of 1. So the very definition of R' renders it impossible for the rule to be successful without being *incoherent*.[11] The suggested second-order argument in support of R' could be formulated only if R' were known to be unreliable, and would therefore be worthless. So we have an *a priori* reason for preferring R to its competitor R'. But it is easy to produce any number of alternative rules of inductive inference, none of which suffers from the fatal defect of R'. The choice between such rules, I suggest, has to be made in the light of experience of their use. I have tried to show in outline how such experience can properly be invoked without logical circularity.

[10] Salmon, *loc. cit.*, p. 46.

[11] A parallel situation would arise in the use of R in predicting the members of the 1-0 series only if R were to be predominantly *un*successful. But then we would have the best of reasons for assigning R zero strength, and the second-order argument would be pointless.

15

THE PSEUDO-PROBLEM OF INDUCTION

p. f. strawson

. . .

If someone asked what grounds there were for supposing that deductive reasoning was valid, we might answer that there were in fact no grounds for supposing that deductive reasoning was always valid; sometimes people made valid inferences, and sometimes they were guilty of logical fallacies. If he said that we had misunderstood his question, and that what he wanted to know was what grounds there were for regarding deduction *in general* as a valid method of argument, we should have to answer that his question was without sense, for to say that an argument, or a form or method of argument, was valid or invalid would *imply* that it was deductive; the concepts of validity and invalidity had application only to individual deductive arguments or forms of deductive argument. Similarly, if a man asked what grounds there were for thinking it reasonable to hold beliefs arrived at inductively, one might at first answer that there were good and bad inductive arguments, that sometimes it was reasonable to hold a belief arrived at inductively and sometimes it was not. If he, too, said that his question had been misunderstood, that he wanted to know whether induction in general was a reasonable method of inference, then we might well think his question senseless in the same way as the question whether deduction is in general valid; for to call a particular belief reasonable or unreasonable is to apply inductive standards, just as to call a particular argument valid or invalid is to apply deductive standards. The parallel is not wholly convincing; for words like "reasonable" and "rational" have not so precise and technical a sense as the word "valid." Yet it is sufficiently powerful to make us wonder how the second question could be raised at all, to wonder why, in contrast with the corresponding question about deduction, it should have seemed to constitute a genuine problem.

Suppose that a man is brought up to regard formal logic as the study of the science and art of reasoning. He observes that all inductive processes are, by deductive standards, invalid; the premises never entail the conclusions. Now inductive processes are notoriously important in the formation of beliefs and expectations about everything which lies beyond the observation of available witnesses. But an *invalid* argu-

From P. F. Strawson, *Introduction to Logical Theory* (London: Methuen & Co., Ltd., 1960) Part II, Chap. 9, pp. 249–252, 256–263. Reprinted by permission of the publisher.

ment is an *unsound* argument; an *unsound* argument is one in which *no good reason* is produced for accepting the conclusion. So if inductive processes are invalid, if all the arguments we should produce, if challenged, in support of our beliefs about what lies beyond the observation of available witnesses are unsound, then we have no good reason for any of these beliefs. This conclusion is repugnant. So there arises the demand for a justification, not of this or that particular belief which goes beyond what is entailed by our evidence, but a justification of induction in general. And when the demand arises in this way it is, in effect, the demand that induction shall be shown to be really a kind of deduction; for nothing less will satisfy the doubter when this is the route to his doubts.

Tracing this, the most common route to the general doubt about the reasonableness of induction, shows how the doubt seems to escape the absurdity of a demand that induction in general shall be justified by inductive standards. The demand is that induction should be shown to be a rational process; and this turns out to be the demand that one kind of reasoning should be shown to be another and different kind. Put thus crudely, the demand seems to escape one absurdity only to fall into another. Of course, inductive arguments are not deductively valid; if they were, they would be deductive arguments. Inductive reasoning must be assessed, for soundness, by inductive standards. Nevertheless, fantastic as the wish for induction to be deduction may seem, it is only in terms of it that we can understand some of the attempts that have been made to justify induction.

The kind of attempt I shall consider might be called the search for the supreme premise of inductions. In its primitive form it is quite a crude attempt; and I shall make it cruder by caricature. We have already seen that for a particular inductive step, such as "The kettle has been on the fire for ten minutes, so it will be boiling by now," we can substitute a deductive argument by introducing a generalization (e.g., "A kettle always boils within ten minutes of being put on the fire") as an additional premise. This manoeuvre shifted the emphasis of the problem of inductive support on to the question of how we established such generalizations as these, which rested on grounds by which they were not entailed. But suppose the manoeuvre could be repeated. Suppose we could find one supremely general proposition, which taken in conjunction with the evidence for any accepted generalization of science or daily life (or at least of science) would entail that generalization. Then, so long as the status of the supreme generalization could be satisfactorily explained, we could regard all sound inductions to unqualified general conclusions as, at bottom, valid deductions. The justification would be found, for at least these cases. The most obvious difficulty in this suggestion is that of formulating the supreme general proposition in such a way that it shall be precise enough to yield the desired entailments, and yet not obviously false or arbitrary. Consider, for example, the formula: "For all f, g, wherever n cases of $f \cdot g$, and no cases of $f \cdot \sim g$, are observed, then all cases of f are cases of g." To turn it into a sentence, we have only to replace "n" by some number. But what number? If we take the value of "n" to be 1 or 20 or 500, the resulting statement is obviously false. Moreover, the choice of any number would seem quite arbitrary; there is no privileged number of favorable instances which we take as decisive in establishing a generalization. If, on the other hand, we phrase the proposition vaguely enough to escape these objections—if, for example, we phrase it as "Nature is uniform"—then it becomes too vague to provide the desired entailments. It should be noticed that the impossibility of framing a general proposition of the kind required is really a special case of the impossibility of framing precise rules for the assessment of evidence. If we could frame a rule which would tell us precisely when we had *conclusive* evidence for a generalization, then it would yield just the proposition required as the supreme premise.

Even if these difficulties could be met, the question of the status of the supreme premise would remain. How, if a non-necessary proposition, could it be established? The appeal to experience, to inductive support, is clearly barred on pain of circularity. If, on the other hand, it were a necessary truth and possessed, in conjunction with the evidence for a generalization, the required logical power to entail the generalization (e.g., if the latter were the conclusion of a hypothetical syllogism, of which the hypothetical premise was the necessary truth in question), then the evidence would entail the generalization independently, and the problem would not arise: a conclusion unbearably paradoxical. In practice, the extreme vagueness with which candidates for the role of supreme premise are expressed prevents their acquiring such logical power, and at the same time renders it very difficult to classify them as analytic or synthetic under pressure they may tend to tautology; and, when the pressure is removed, assume an expansively synthetic air.

In theories of the kind which I have here caricatured the ideal of deduction is not usually so blatantly manifest as I have made it. One finds the "Law of the Uniformity of Nature" presented less as the suppressed premise of crypto-deductive inferences than as, say, the "presupposition of the validity of inductive reasoning." . . .

. . .

Let us turn from attempts to justify induction to attempts to show that the demand for a justification is mistaken. We have seen already that what lies behind such a demand is often the absurd wish that induction should be shown to be some kind of deduction—and this wish is clearly traceable in the two attempts at justification which we have examined. What other sense could we give to the demand? Sometimes it is expressed in the form of a request for proof that induction is a *reasonable* or *rational* procedure, that we have *good grounds* for placing reliance upon it. Consider the uses of the phrases "good grounds," "justification," "reasonable," etc. Often we say such things as "He has *every justification* for believing that *p*"; "I have *very good reasons* for believing it"; "There are *good grounds* for the view that *q*"; "There is *good evidence* that *r*." We often talk, in such ways as these, of justification, good grounds or reasons or evidence for certain beliefs. Suppose such a belief were one expressible in the form "Every case of *f* is a case of *g*." And suppose someone were asked what he meant by saying that he had good grounds or reasons for holding it. I think it would be felt to be a satisfactory answer if he replied: "Well, in all my wide and varied experience I've come across innumerable cases of *f* and never a case of *f* which wasn't a case of *g*." In saying this, he is clearly claiming to have *inductive* support, *inductive* evidence, of a certain kind, for his belief; and he is also giving a perfectly proper answer to the question, what he meant by saying that he had ample justification, good grounds, good reasons for his belief. It is an analytic proposition that it is reasonable to have a degree of belief in a statement which is proportional to the strength of the evidence in its favor; and it is an analytic proposition, though not a proposition of mathematics, that, other things being equal, the evidence for a generalization is strong in proportion as the number of favorable instances, and the variety of circumstances in which they have been found, is great. So to ask whether it is reasonable to place reliance on inductive procedures is like asking whether it is reasonable to proportion the degree of one's convictions to the strength of the evidence. Doing this is what "being reasonable" *means* in such a context.

As for the other form in which the doubt may be expressed, viz., "Is induction a justified, or justifiable, procedure?," it emerges in a still less favorable light. No sense has been given to it, though it is easy to see why it seems to have a sense. For it is generally proper to inquire *of a particular belief*, whether its adoption is justified; and, in asking this, we are asking whether there is good, bad, or any, evidence for it. In applying or withholding the epithets "justified," "well founded," etc., in the case of specific beliefs, we are appealing to, and applying, inductive standards. But to what standards are we appealing when we ask whether the application of inductive standards is justified or well grounded? If we cannot answer, then no sense has been given to the question. Compare it with the question: Is the law legal? It makes perfectly good sense to inquire of a particular action, of an administrative regulation, or even, in the case of some states, of a particular enactment of the legislature, whether or not it is legal. The question is answered by an appeal to a legal system, by the application of a set of legal (or constitutional) rules or standards. But it makes no sense to inquire in general whether the law of the land, the legal system as a whole, is or is not legal. For to what legal standards are we appealing?

The only way in which a sense might be given to the question, whether induction is in general a justified or justifiable procedure, is a trival one which we have already noticed. We might interpret it to mean "Are all conclusions, arrived at inductively, justified?" i.e., "Do people always have adequate evidence for the conclusions they draw?" The answer to this question is easy, but uninteresting: it is that sometimes people have adequate evidence, and sometimes they do not.

It seems, however, that this way of showing the request for a general justification of induction to be absurd is sometimes insufficient to allay the worry that produces it. And to point out that "forming rational opinions about the unobserved on the evidence available" and "assessing the evidence by inductive standards" are phrases which describe the same thing, is more apt to produce irritation than relief. The point is felt to be "merely a verbal" one; and though the point of this protest is itself hard to see, it is clear that something more is required. So the question must be pursued further. First, I want to point out that there is something a little odd about talking of "the inductive method," or even "the inductive policy," as if it were just one possible method among others of arguing from the observed to the unobserved, from the available evidence to the facts in question. If one asked a meteorologist what method or methods he used to forecast the weather, one would be surprised if he answered: "Oh, just the inductive method." If one asked a doctor by what means he diagnosed a certain disease, the answer "By induction" would be felt as an impatient evasion, a joke, or a rebuke. The answer one hopes for is an account of the tests made, the signs taken account of, the rules and recipes and general laws applied. When such a specific method of prediction or diagnosis is in question, one can ask whether the method is justified in practice; and here again one is asking whether its employment is inductively justified, whether it commonly gives correct results. This question would normally seem an admissible one. One might be tempted to conclude that, while there are many different specific methods of prediction, diagnosis, etc., appropriate to different subjects of inquiry, all such methods could properly be called "inductive" in the sense that their employment rested on inductive support; and that, hence, the phrase "non-inductive method of finding out about what lies deductively beyond the evidence" was a description without meaning, a phrase to which no sense had been given; so that there could be no question of justifying our selection of one method, called "the inductive," of doing this.

However, someone might object: "Surely it is possible, though it might be foolish, to use methods utterly different from accredited scientific ones. Suppose a man, whenever he wanted to form an opinion about what lay beyond his observation or the observation of available witnesses, simply shut his eyes, asked himself the appropriate question, and accepted the first answer that came into his head. Wouldn't this be a non-inductive method?" Well, let us suppose this. The man is asked: "Do you usually get the right answer by your method?" He might answer: "You've mentioned one of its drawbacks; I never do get the right answer; but it's an extremely easy method." One might then be inclined to think that it was not a method of finding things out at all. But suppose he answered: "Yes, it's usually (always) the right answer." Then we might be willing to call it a method of finding out, though a strange one. But, then, by the very fact of its success, it would be an inductively supported method. For each application of the method would be an application of the general rule, "The first answer that comes into my head is generally (always) the right one"; and for the truth of this generalization there would be the inductive evidence of a long run of favorable instances with no unfavorable ones (if it were "always"), or of a sustained high proportion of successes to trials (if it were "generally").

So every successful method or recipe for finding out about the unobserved must be one which has inductive support; for to say that a recipe is successful is to say that it has been repeatedly applied with success; and repeated successful application of a recipe constitutes just what we mean by inductive evidence in its favor. Pointing out this fact must not be confused with saying that "the inductive method" is justified by its success, justified because it works. This is a mistake, and an important one. I am not seeking to "justify the inductive method," for no meaning has been given to this phrase. A fortiori, I am not saying that induction is justified by its success in finding out about the unobserved. I am saying, rather, that any successful method of finding out about the unobserved is necessarily justified by induction. This is an analytic proposition. The phrase "successful method of finding things out which has no inductive support" is self-contradictory. Having, or acquiring, inductive support is a necessary condition of the success of a method.

Why point this out at all? First, it may have a certain therapeutic force, a power to reassure. Second, it may counteract the tendency to think of "the inductive method" as something on a par with specific methods of diagnosis or prediction and therefore, like them, standing in need of (inductive) justification.

There is one further confusion, perhaps the most powerful of all in producing the doubts, questions, and spurious solutions discussed in this Part. We may approach it by considering the claim that induction is justified by its success in practice. The phrase "success of induction" is by no means clear and perhaps embodies the confusion of induction with some specific method of prediction, etc., appropriate to some particular line of inquiry. But, whatever the phrase may mean, the claim has an obviously circular look. Presumably the suggestion is that we should argue from the past "successes of induction" to the continuance of those successes in the future; from the fact that it has worked hitherto to the conclusion that it will continue to work. Since an argument of this kind is plainly inductive, it will not serve as a justification of induction. One cannot establish a principle of argument by an argument which uses that principle. But let us go a little deeper. The argument rests the justification of induction on a matter of fact (its "past successes"). This is characteristic of nearly all attempts to find a justification. The desired premise of [page 529] was to be some fact about the constitution of the universe which, even if it could not be used as a suppressed premise to give inductive arguments a deductive turn, was at any rate a "presupposition of the validity of induction." . . . I think the source of this general desire to find out some fact about the constitution of the universe which will "justify induction" or "show it to be a rational policy" is the confusion, the running together, of two fundamentally different questions: to one of which the answer is a matter of non-linguistic fact, while to the other it is a matter of meanings.

There is nothing self-contradictory in supposing that all the uniformities in the course of things that we have hitherto observed and come to count on should cease to operate tomorrow; that all our familiar recipes should let us down, and that we should be unable to frame new ones because such regularities as there were were too complex for us to make out. (We may assume that even the expectation that all of us, in such circumstances, would perish, were falsified by someone surviving to observe the new chaos in which, roughly speaking, nothing foreseeable happens.) Of course, we do not believe that this will happen. We believe, on the contrary, that our inductively supported expectation-rules, though some of them will have, no doubt, to be dropped or modified, will continue, on the whole, to serve us fairly well; and that we shall generally be able to replace the rules we abandon with others similarly arrived at. We might give a sense to the phrase "success of induction" by calling this vague belief the belief that induction will continue to be successful. It is certainly a factual belief, not a necessary truth; a belief, one may say, about the constitution of the universe. We might express it as follows, choosing a phraseology which will serve the better to expose the confusion I wish to expose:

I. (The universe is such that) induction will continue to be successful.

I is very vague: it amounts to saying that there are, and will continue to be, natural uniformities and regularities which exhibit a humanly manageable degree of simplicity. But, though it is vague, certain definite things can be said about it. (1) It is not a necessary, but a contingent, statement; for chaos is not a self-contradictory concept. (2) We have good inductive reasons for believing it, good inductive evidence for it. We believe that some of our recipes will continue to hold good because they have held good for so long. We believe that we shall be able to frame new and useful ones, because we have been able to do so repeatdly in the past. Of course, it would be absurd to try to use I to "justify induction," to show that it is a reasonable policy; because I is a conclusion inductively supported.

Consider now the fundamentally different statement:

II. Induction is rational (reasonable).

We have already seen that the rationality of induction, unlike its "successfulness," is not a fact about the constitution of the world. It is a matter of what we mean by the word "rational" in its application to any procedure for forming opinions about what lies outside our observations or that of available witnesses. For to have good reasons for any such opinion is to have good inductive support for it. The chaotic universe just envisaged, therefore, is not one in which induction would cease to be rational; it is simply one in which it would be impossible to form rational expectations to the effect that specific things would happen. It might be said that in such a universe it would at least be rational to refrain from forming specific expectations, to expect nothing but irregularities. Just so. But this is itself a higher-order induction: where irregularity is the rule, expect further irregularities. Learning not to count on things is as much learning an inductive lesson as learning what things to count on.

So it is a contingent, factual matter that it is sometimes possible to form rational opinions concerning what specifically happened or will happen in given circumstances (I); it is a noncontingent, a priori matter that the only ways of doing this must be inductive ways (II). What people have done is to run together, to conflate, the question to which I is answer and the quite different question to which II is an answer; producing the muddled and senseless questions: "Is the universe such that inductive procedures are rational?" or "What must the universe be like in order for inductive procedures to be rational?" It is the attempt to answer these confused questions which leads to statements like "The uniformity of nature is a presupposition of the validity of induction." The statement that nature is uniform might be taken to be a vague way of expressing what we expressed by I; and certainly this fact is a condition of, for it is identical with, the likewise contingent fact that we are, and shall continue to be, able to form rational opinions, of the kind we are most anxious to form, about the unobserved. But neither this fact about the world, nor any other, is a condition of the necessary truth that, if it is possible to form rational opinions of this kind, these will be inductively supported opinions. The discordance of the conflated questions manifests itself in an uncertainty about the status to be accorded to the alleged presupposition of the "validity" of induction. For it was dimly, and correctly, felt that the reasonableness of inductive procedures was not merely a contingent, but a necessary, matter; so any necessary condition of their reasonableness had likewise to be a necessary matter. On the other hand, it was uncomfortably clear that chaos is not a self-contradictory concept; that the fact that some phenomena do exhibit a tolerable degree of simplicity and repetitiveness is not guaranteed by logic, but is a contingent affair. So the presupposition of induction had to be both contingent and necessary: which is absurd. And the absurdity is only lightly veiled by the use of the phrase "synthetic a priori" instead of "contingent necessary."

The theory of meaning

16

THE PRINCIPLE OF VERIFICATION

a. j. ayer

The principle of verification is supposed to furnish a criterion by which it can be determined whether or not a sentence is literally meaningful. A simple way to formulate it would be to say that a sentence had literal meaning if and only if the proposition it expressed was either analytic or empirically verifiable. To this, however, it might be objected that unless a sentence was literally meaningful it would not express a proposition; for it is commonly assumed that every proposition is either true or false, and to say that a sentence expressed what was either true or false would entail saying that it was literally meaningful. Accordingly, if the principle of verification were formulated in this way, it might be argued not only that it was incomplete as a criterion of meaning, since it would not cover the case of sentences which did not express any propositions at all, but also that it was otiose, on the ground that the question which it was designed to answer must already have been answered before the principle could be applied. It will be seen that when I introduce the principle in this book I try to avoid this difficulty by speaking of "putative propositions" and of the proposition which a sentence "purports to express"; but this device is not satis-

From A. J. Ayer, *Language, Truth and Logic* (London: Victor Gollancz Ltd., 1962), Introduction, pp. 5–15. Reprinted by permission of the publisher and Dover Publications, Inc.

factory. For, in the first place, the use of words like "putative" and "purports" seems to bring in psychological considerations into which I do not wish to enter, and secondly, in the case where the "putative proposition" is neither analytic nor empirically verifiable, there would, according to this way of speaking, appear to be nothing that the sentence in question could properly be said to express. But if a sentence expresses nothing there seems to be a contradiction in saying that what it expresses is empirically unverifiable; for even if the sentence is adjudged on this ground to be meaningless, the reference to "what it expresses" appears still to imply that something is expressed.

This is, however, no more than a terminological difficulty, and there are various ways in which it might be met. . . .

. . . .

The solution that I prefer is to introduce a new technical term; and for this purpose I shall make use of the familiar word "statement," though I shall perhaps be using it in a slightly unfamiliar sense. Thus I propose that any form of words that is grammatically significant shall be held to constitute a sentence, and that every indicative sentence, whether it is literally meaningful or not, shall be regarded as expressing a statement. Furthermore, any two sentences which are mutually translatable will be said to express the same statement. The word "proposition," on the other hand, will be reserved for what is expressed by sentences which are literally meaningful. Thus, the class of propositions becomes, in this usage, a subclass of the class of statements, and one way of describing the use of the principle of verification would be to say that it provided a means of determining when an indicative sentence expressed a proposition, or, in other words, of distinguishing the statements that belonged to the class of propositions from those that did not.

Returning now to the principle of verification, we may, for the sake of brevity, apply it directly to statements rather than to the sentences which express them, and we can then reformulate it by saying that a statement is held to be literally meaningful if and only if it is either analytic or empirically verifiable. But what is to be understood in this context by the term "verifiable"? I do indeed attempt to answer this question . . .; but I have to acknowledge that my answer is not very satisfactory.

To begin with, it will be seen that I distinguish between a "strong" and a "weak" sense of the term "verifiable," and that I explain this distinction by saying that "a proposition is said to be verifiable in the strong sense of the term, if and only if its truth could be conclusively established in experience," but that "it is verifiable, in the weak sense, if it is possible for experience to render it probable." And I then give reasons for deciding that it is only the weak sense of the term that is required by my principle of verification. What I seem, however, to have overlooked is that, as I represent them, these are not two genuine alternatives. For I subsequently go on to argue that all empirical propositions are hypotheses which are continually subject to the test of further experience; and from this it would follow not merely that the truth of any such proposition never was conclusively established but that it never could be; for however strong the evidence in its favor, there would never be a point at which it was impossible for further experience to go against it. But this would mean that my "strong" sense of the term "verifiable" had no possible application, and in that case there was no need for me to qualify the other sense of "verifiable" as weak; for on my own showing it was the only sense in which any proposition could conceivably be verified.

If I do not now draw this conclusion, it is because I have come to think that there is a class of empirical propositions of which it is permissible to say that they can be verified conclusively. It is characteristic of these propositions, which I have elsewhere [1] called "basic propositions," that they refer solely to the content of a single experience, and what may be said to verify them conclusively is the occurrence of the experience to which they uniquely refer. Furthermore, I should now agree with those who say that propositions of this kind are "incorrigible," assuming that what is meant by their being incorrigible is that it is impossible to be mistaken about them except in a verbal sense. In a verbal sense, indeed, it is always possible to misdescribe one's experience; but if one intends to do no more than record what is experienced without relating it to anything else, it is not possible to be factually mistaken; and the reason for this is that one is making no claim that any further fact could confute. It is, in short, a case of "nothing venture, nothing lose." It is, however, equally a case of "nothing venture, nothing win," since the mere recording of one's present experience does not serve to convey any information either to any other person or indeed to oneself; for in knowing a basic proposition to be true one obtains no further knowledge than what is already afforded by the occurrence of the relevant experience. Admittedly, the form of words that is used to express a basic proposition may be understood to express something that is informative both to another person and to oneself, but when it is so understood it no longer expresses a basic proposition. . . .

• • •

Whether or not one chooses to include basic statements in the class of empirical propositions, and so to admit that some empirical propositions can be conclusively verified, it will remain true that the vast majority of the propositions that people actually express are neither themselves basic statements, nor deducible from any finite set of basic statements. Consequently, if the principle of verification is to be seriously considered as a criterion of meaning, it must be interpreted in such a way as to admit statements that are not so strongly verifiable as basic statements are supposed to be. But how then is the word "verifiable" to be understood?

It will be seen that, in this book, I begin by suggesting that a statement is "weakly" verifiable, and therefore meaningful, according to my criterion, if "some possible sense experience would be relevant to the determination of its truth or falsehood." But, as I recognize, this itself requires interpretation; for the word "relevant" is uncomfortably vague. Accordingly, I put forward a second version of my principle, which I shall restate here in slightly different terms, using the phrase "observation-statement," in place of "experiential proposition," to designate a statement "which records an actual or possible observation." In this version, then, the principle is that a statement is verifiable, and consequently meaningful, if some observation-statement can be deduced from it in conjunction with certain other premises, without being deducible from those other premises alone.

I say of this criterion that it "seems liberal enough," but in fact it is far too liberal, since it allows meaning to any statement whatsoever. For, given any statement "S" and observation-statement "O," "O" follows from "S" and if S then O" without following from if "S then O" alone. Thus, the statements "the Absolute is lazy" and "if the

[1] "Verification and Experience," *Proceedings of the Aristotelian Society,* Vol. XXXVII; cf. also *The Foundations of Empirical Knowledge,* pp. 80–84.

Absolute is lazy, this is white" jointly entail the observation-statement "this is white," and since "this is white" does not follow from either of these premises, taken by itself, both of them satisfy my criterion of meaning. Furthermore, this would hold good for any other piece of nonsense that one cared to put, as an example, in place of "the Absolute is lazy," provided only that it had the grammatical form of an indicative sentence. But a criterion of meaning that allows such latitude as this is evidently unacceptable.

It may be remarked that the same objection applies to the proposal that we should take the possibility of falsification as our criterion. For, given any statement "S" and any observation-statement "O," "O" will be incompatible with the conjunction of "S" and if "S then not O." We could indeed avoid the difficulty, in either case, by leaving out the stipulation about the other premises. But as this would involve the exclusion of all hypotheticals from the class of empirical propositions, we should escape from making our criteria too liberal only at the cost of making them too stringent.

Another difficulty which I overlooked in my original attempt to formulate the principle of verification is that most empirical propositions are in some degree vague. Thus, as I have remarked elsewhere,[2] what is required to verify a statement about a material thing is never the occurrence of precisely this or precisely that sense-content, but only the occurrence of one or other of the sense-contents that fall within a fairly indefinite range. We do indeed test any such statement by making observations which consist in the occurrence of particular sense-contents; but, for any test that we actually carry out, there is always an indefinite number of other tests, differing to some extent in respect either of their conditions or their results, that would have served the same purpose. And this means that there is never any set of observation-statements of which it can truly be said that precisely they are entailed by any given statement about a material thing.

Nevertheless, it is only by the occurrence of some sense-content, and consequently by the truth of some observation-statement, that any statement about a material thing is actually verified; and from this it follows that every significant statement about a material thing can be represented as entailing a disjunction of observation-statements, although the terms of this disjunction, being infinite, can not be enumerated in detail. Consequently, I do not think that we need be troubled by the difficulty about vagueness, so long as it is understood that when we speak of the "entailment" of observation-statements, what we are considering to be deductible from the premises in question is not any particular observation-statement, but only one or other of a set of such statements, where the defining characteristic of the set is that all its members refer to sense-contents that fall within a certain specifiable range.

There remains the more serious objection that my criterion, as it stands, allows meaning to any indicative statement whatsoever. To meet this, I shall emend it as follows. I propose to say that a statement is directly verifiable if it is either itself an observation-statement, or is such that in conjunction with one or more observation-statements it entails at least one observation-statement which is not deducible from these other premises alone; and I propose to say that a statement is indirectly verifiable if it satisfies the following conditions: first, that in conjunction with certain other premises it entails one or more directly verifiable statements which are not deducible

<hr>

[2] *The Foundations of Empirical Knowledge,* pp. 240–241.

from these other premises alone; and secondly, that these other premises do not include any statement that is not either analytic, or directly verifiable, or capable of being independently established as indirectly verifiable. And I can now reformulate the principle of verification as requiring of a literally meaningful statement, which is not analytic, that it should be either directly or indirectly verifiable, in the foregoing sense.

It may be remarked that in giving my account of the conditions in which a statement is to be considered indirectly verifiable, I have explicitly put in the proviso that the "other premises" may include analytic statements; and my reason for doing this is that I intend in this way to allow for the case of scientific theories which are expressed in terms that do not themselves designate anything observable. For while the statements that contain these terms may not appear to describe anything that anyone could ever observe, a "dictionary" may be provided by means of which they can be transformed into statements that are verifiable; and the statements which constitute the dictionary can be regarded as analytic. Were this not so, there would be nothing to choose between such scientific theories and those that I should dismiss as metaphysical; but I take it to be characteristic of the metaphysician, in my somewhat pejorative sense of the term, not only that his statements do not describe anything that is capable, even in principle, of being observed, but also that no dictionary is provided by means of which they can be transformed into statements that are directly or indirectly verifiable.

·   ·   ·

It has sometimes been assumed by my critics that I take the principle of verification to imply that no statement can be evidence for another unless it is a part of its meaning; but this is not the case. Thus, to make use of a simple illustration, the statement that I have blood on my coat may, in certain circumstances, confirm the hypothesis that I have committed a murder, but it is not part of the meaning of the statement that I have committed a murder that I should have blood upon my coat, nor, as I understand it, does the principle of verification imply that it is. For one statement may be evidence for another, and still neither itself express a necessary condition of the truth of this other statement, nor belong to any set of statements which determines a range within which such a necessary condition falls; and it is only these cases that the principle of verification yields the conclusion that the one statement is part of the meaning of the other. Thus, from the fact that it is only by the making of some observation that any statement about a material thing can be directly verified it follows, according to the principle of verification, that every such statement contains some observation-statement or other as part of its meaning, and it follows also that, although its generality may prevent any finite set of observation-statements from exhausting its meaning, it does not contain anything as part of its meaning that cannot be represented as an observation-statement; but there may still be many observation-statements that are relevant to its truth or falsehood without being part of its meaning at all. Again, a person who affirms the existence of a deity may try to support his contention by appealing to the facts of religious experience; but it does not follow from this that the factual meaning of his statement is wholly contained in the propositions by which these religious experiences are described. For there may be other empirical facts that he would also consider to be relevant; and it is possible that the descriptions of these other empirical facts can more properly be regarded as containing the factual meaning of his statement than the descriptions of the religious experiences.

At the same time, if one accepts the principle of verification, one must hold that his statement does not have any other factual meaning than what is contained in at least some of the relevant empirical propositions; and that if it is so interpreted that no possible experience could go to verify it, it does not have any factual meaning at all.

.   .   .

17

THE THEORY OF MEANING

gilbert ryle

We can all use the notion of *meaning*. From the moment we being to learn to translate English into French and French into English, we realize that one expression does or does not mean the same as another. But we use the notion of meaning even earlier than that. When we read or hear something in our own language which we do not understand, we wonder what it means and ask to have its meaning explained to us. The ideas of understanding, misunderstanding, and failing to understand what is said already contain the notion of expressions having and lacking specifiable meanings.

It is, however, one thing to ask, as a child might ask, What, if anything, is meant by "vitamin," or "abracadabra" or "$(a + b)^2 = a^2 + b^2 + 2ab$?" It is quite another sort of thing to ask What are meanings? It is, in the same way, one thing to ask, as a child might ask, What can I buy for this shilling? and quite another sort of thing to ask What is purchasing power? or What are exchange values?

. . .

Now answers to this highly abstract question, What are meanings? have, in recent decades, bulked large in philosophical and logical discussions. Preoccupation with the theory of meaning could be described as the occupational disease of twentieth-century Anglo-Saxon and Austrian philosophy. We need not worry whether or not it is a disease. But it might be useful to survey the motives and the major results of this preoccupation.

. . .

For our purposes it is near enough true to say that the first influential discussion of the notion of meaning given by a modern logician was that with which John Stuart Mill opens his *System of Logic* (1843). He acknowledges debts both to Hobbes and to the Schoolmen, but we need not trace these borrowings in detail.

. . .

Mill, following Hobbes's lead, starts off his account of the notion of meaning by considering single words. As we have to learn the alphabet before we can begin to

From Gilbert Ryle "The Theory of Meaning," in *British Philosophy in Mid-Century*, C. A. Mace, ed. (London: George Allen & Unwin Ltd., 1957), pp. 239–257. Reprinted by permission of the publisher.

spell, so it seemed natural to suppose that the meanings of sentences are compounds of the components, which are the meanings of their ingredient words. Word-meanings are atoms, sentence-meanings are molecules. I say that it seemed natural, but I hope soon to satisfy you that it was a tragically false start. Next Mill, again following Hobbes's lead, takes it for granted that all words, or nearly all words, are names, and this, at first, sounds very tempting. We know what it is for "Fido" to be the name of a particular dog, and for "London" to be the name of a particular town. There, in front of us, is the dog or the town which has the name, so here, one feels, there is no mystery. We have just the familiar relation between a thing and its name. The assimilation of all or most other single words to names gives us, accordingly, a cozy feeling. We fancy that we know where we are. The dog in front of us is what the word "Fido" stands for, the town we visited yesterday is what the word "London" stands for. So the classification of all or most single words as names makes us feel that what a word means is in all cases some manageable thing that that word is the name of. Meanings, at least word-meanings, are nothing abstruse or remote, they are, *prima facie,* ordinary things and happenings like dogs and towns and battles.

Mill goes further. Sometimes the grammatical subject of a sentence is not a single word but a many-worded phrase, like "the present Prime Minister" or "the first man to stand on the summit of Mt. Everest." Mill has no qualms in classifying complex expressions like these also as names, what he calls "many-worded names." There do not exist proper names for everything we want to talk about; and sometimes we want to talk about something or somebody whose proper name, though it exists, is unknown to us. So descriptive phrases are coined by us to do duty for proper names. But they are still, according to Mill, names, though the tempting and in fact prevailing interpretation of this assertion differs importantly from what Mill usually wanted to convey. For, when Mill calls a word or phrase a "name," he is using "name" not, or not always, quite in the ordinary way. Sometimes he says that for an expression to be a name it must be able to be used as the subject or the predicate of a subject-predicate sentence—which lets in, e.g., adjectives as names. Sometimes his requirements are more stringent. A name is an expression which can be the subject of a subject-predicate sentence—which leaves only nouns, pronouns, and substantial phrases. "Name," for him, does not mean merely "proper name." He often resisted temptations to which he subjected his successors.

Before going any further, I want to make you at least suspect that this initially congenial equation of words and descriptive phrases with names is from the outset a monstrous howler—if, like some of Mill's successors, though unlike Mill himself, we do systematically construe "name" on the model of "proper name." The assumption of the truth of this equation has been responsible for a large number of radical absurdities in philosophy in general and the philosophy of logic in particular. It was a fetter round the ankles of Meinong, from which he never freed himself. It was a fetter round the ankles of Frege, Moore, and Russell, who all, sooner or later, saw that without some big emendations, the assumption led inevitably to fatal impasses. It was, as he himself says in his new book, a fetter round the ankles of Wittgenstein in the *Tractatus,* though in that same book he had found not only the need but the way to cut himself partially loose from it.

I am still not quite sure why it seems so natural to assume that all words are names, and even that every possible grammatical subject of a sentence, one-worded or many-worded, stands to something as the proper name "Fido" stands to the dog Fido, and, what is a further point, that the thing it stands for is what the expression means. Even Plato had had to fight his way out of the same assumption. But he at least had a special excuse. The Greek language had only the one word ὄνομα where we have the three words "word," "name," and "noun." It was hard in Greek even to say that the Greek counterpart to our verb "is" was a word but not a noun. Greek provided Plato with no label for verbs, or for adverbs, conjunctions, etc. That "is" is a word, but is not a name or even a noun was a tricky thing to say in Greek where ὄνομα did duty both for our word "word," for our word "name," and, eventually, for our word "noun." But even without this excuse people still find it natural to assimilate all words to names, and the meanings of words to the bearers of those alleged names. Yet the assumption is easy to demolish.

First, if every single word were a name, then a sentence composed of five words, say "three is a prime number" would be a list of the five objects named by those five words. But a list, like "Plato, Aristotle, Aquinas, Locke, Berkeley" is not a sentence. It says nothing, true or false. A sentence, on the contrary, may say something—some one thing—which is true or false. So the words combined into a sentence at least do something jointly which is different from their severally naming the several things that they name, if they do name any things. What a sentence means is not decomposable into the set of things which the words in it stand for, if they do stand for things. So the notion of *having meaning* is at least partly different from the notion of *standing for*.

More than this. I can use the two descriptive phrases "the Morning Star" and "the Evening Star," as different ways of referring to Venus. But it is quite clear that the two phrases are different in meaning. It would be incorrect to translate into French the phrase "the Morning Star" by *"l'Étoile du Soir."* But if the two phrases have different meanings, then Venus, the planet which we describe by these two different descriptions, cannot be what these descriptive phrases mean. For she, Venus, is one and the same, but what the two phrases signify are different. As we shall see in a moment Mill candidly acknowledges this point and makes an important allowance for it.

Moreover it is easy to coin descriptive phrases to which nothing at all answers. The phrase "the third man to stand on the top of Mt. Everest" cannot, at present, be used to refer to anybody. There exists as yet no one whom it fits and perhaps there never will. Yet it is certainly a significant phrase, and could be translated into French or German. We know, we have to know, what it means when we say that it fits no living mountaineer. It means *something,* but it does not designate *somebody.* What it means cannot, therefore, be equated with a particular mountaineer. Nor can the meaning conveyed by the phrase "the first person to stand on the top of Mt. Everest" be equated with Hillary, though, we gather, it fits him and does not fit anyone else. We can understand the question, and even entertain Nepalese doubts about the answer to the question "Is Hillary the first person to conquer Mt. Everest?" where we could not understand the question "Is Hillary Hillary?"

We could reach the same conclusion even more directly. If Hillary was, *per impossible,* identified with what is meant by the phrase "the first man to stand on the top of Mt. Everest," it would follow that the meaning of at least one phrase was born in New Zealand, has breathed through an oxygen mask and has been decorated by Her Majesty. But this is patent nonsense. Meanings of phrases are not New Zealand citizens; what is expressed by a particular English phrase, as well as by any paraphrase or translation of it, is not something with lungs, a surname, long legs, and a sunburnt face. People are born and die and sometimes wear boots; meanings are not born and do not die and they never wear boots—or go barefoot either. The Queen does not decorate meanings. The phrase "the first man to stand on the top of Mt. Everest" will not lose its meaning when Hillary dies. Nor was it meaningless before he reached the summit.

Finally, we should notice that most words are not nouns; they are, e.g., adverbs or verbs or adjectives or prepositions or conjunctions or pronouns. But to classify as a name a word which is not even a noun strikes one as intolerable the moment one considers the point. How could "ran" or "often" or "and" or "pretty" be the name of anything? It could not even be the grammatical subject of a sentence. I may ask what a certain economic condition, moral quality, or day of the week is called and get the answer "inflation," "punctiliousness," or "Saturday." We do use the word "name" for what something is called, whether it be what a person or river is called, or what a species, a quality, an action, or a condition is called. But the answer to the question "What is it called?" must be a noun or have the grammar of a noun. No such question could be answered by giving the tense of a verb, an adverb, a conjunction, or an adjective.

Mill himself allowed that some words like "is," "often," "not," "of," and "the" are not names, even in his hospitable use of "name." They cannot by themselves function as the grammatical subjects of sentences. Their function, as he erroneously described it, is to subserve, in one way or another, the construction of many-worded names. They do not name extra things but are ancillaries to the multi-verbal naming of things. Yet they certainly have meanings. "And" and "or" have different meanings, and "or" and the Latin "aut" have the same meaning. Mill realized that it is not always the case that for a word to mean something, it must denote somebody or some thing. But most of his successors did not notice how impotrant this point was.

Even more to Mill's credit was the fact that he noticed and did partial justice to the point, which I made a little while back, that two different descriptive phrases may both fit the same thing or person, so that the thing or person which they both fit or which, in his unhappy parlance, they both name is not to be equated with either (or of course both) of the significations of the two descriptions. The two phrases "the previous Prime Minister" and "the father of Randolph Churchill" both fit Sir Winston Churchill, and fit only him; but they do not have the same meaning. A French translation of the one would not be a translation of the other. One might know or believe that the one description fitted Sir Winston Churchill while still questioning whether the other did so too. From just knowing that Sir Winston was Prime Minister one could not infer that Randolph Churchill is his son, or vice versa. Either might have been true without the other being true. The two phrases cannot, therefore, carry the same information.

Mill, in effect, met this point with his famous theory of denotation and connotation. Most words and descriptive phrases, according to him, do two things at once. They denote the things or persons that they are, as he unhappily puts it, all the names of. But they also connote, or signify, the simple or complex attributes by possessing which the thing or person denoted is fitted by the description. Mill's word "connote" was a very unhappily chosen word and has misled not only Mill's successors but Mill himself. His word "denote" was used by him in a far from uniform way, which left him uncommitted to consequences from which some of his successors, who used it less equivocally, could not extricate themselves. For Mill, proper names denote their bearers, but predicate-expressions also denote what they are truly predicable of. Fido is denoted by "Fido" and by "dog" and by "four-legged."

So to ask for the function of an expression is, on Mill's showing, to ask a double question. It is to ask Which person or persons, thing or things the expression denotes? in one or other of Mill's uses of this verb—Sir Winston Churchill, perhaps—but it is also to ask What are the properties or characteristics by which the thing or person is described?—say that of having begotten Randolph Churchill. As a thing or person can be described in various ways, the various descriptions given will differ in connotation, while still being identical in denotation. They characterize in different ways, even though their denotation is identical. They carry different bits of information or misinformation about the same thing, person, or event.

Mill himself virtually says that according to our ordinary natural notion of meaning, it would not be proper to say that, e.g., Sir Winston Churchill is the meaning of a word or phrase. We ordinarily understand by "meaning" not the thing denoted but only what is connoted. That is, Mill virtually reaches the correct conclusions that the meaning of an expression is never the thing or person referred to by means of it; and that descriptive phrases and, with one exception, single words are never names, in the sense of "proper names." The exception is just those relatively few words which really are proper names, i.e., words like "Fido," and "London," the words which do not appear in dictionaries.

Mill got a further important point right about these genuine proper names. He said that while most words and descriptive phrases both denote, or name, and connote, proper names only denote and do not connote. A dog may be called "Fido," but the word "Fido" conveys no information or misinformation about the dog's qualities, career, or whereabouts, etc. There is, to enlarge this point, no question of the word "Fido" being paraphrased, or correctly or incorrectly translated into French. Dictionaries do not tell us what proper names mean—for the simple reason that they do not mean anything. The word "Fido" names or denotes a particular dog, since it is what he is called. But there is no room for anyone who hears the word "Fido" to understand it or misunderstand it or fail to understand it. There is nothing for which he can require an elucidation or a definition. From the information that Sir Winston Churchill was Prime Minister, a number of consequences follow, such as that he was the leader of the majority party in Parliament. But from the fact that yonder dog is Fido, no other truth about him follows at all. No information is provided for anything to follow from. Using a proper name is not committing oneself to any further assertions whatsoever. Proper names are appellations and not descriptions; and descriptions are descriptions and not appellations. Sir Winston Churchill *is* the father of Randolph Churchill. He is not *called* and was not christened "the father of Randolph Churchill." He is called "Winston Churchill." The Lady Mayoress of Liverpool can give the name *Mauretania* to a ship which thenceforward has that name. But if she called Sir Winston Churchill "the father of Sir Herbert Morrison" this would be a funny sort of christening, but it would not make it true that Morrison is the son of Sir Winston Churchill. Descriptions carry truths or falsehoods and are not just arbitrary bestowals. Proper names are arbitrary bestowals, and convey nothing true and nothing false, for they convey nothing at all.

Chinese astronomers give the planets, stars, and constellations names quite different from those we give. But it does not follow that a single proposition of Western astronomy is rejected by them, or that a single astronomical proposition rejected by us is accepted by them. Stellar nomenclature carries with it no astronomical truths or falsehoods. Calling a star by a certain name is not saying anything about it, and saying something true or false about a star is not naming it. Saying is not naming and naming is not saying.

This brings out a most important fact. Considering the meaning (or Mill's "connotation") of an expression is considering what can be said with it, i.e., said truly or said falsely, as well as asked, commanded, advised, or any other sort of saying. In this, which is the normal sense of "meaning," the meaning of a sub-expression like a word or phrase, is a functional factor of a range of possible assertions, questions, commands, and the rest. It is tributary to sayings. It is a distinguishable common locus of a range of possible tellings, askings, advisings, etc. This precisely inverts the natural assumption with which, as I said earlier, Mill and most of us start, the assumption namely that the meanings of words and phrases can be learned, discussed, and classified before consideration begins of entire sayings, such as sentences. Word-meanings do not stand to sentence-meanings as atoms to molecules or as letters of the alphabet to the spellings of words, but more nearly as the tennis racket stands to the strokes which are or may be made with it. This point, which Mill's successors and predecessors half-recognized to hold for such little words as "if," "or," "the," and "not," holds good for all significant words alike. Their significances are their roles inside actual and possible sayings. Mill's two-way doctrine, that nearly all words and phrases both denote, or are names, and connote, i.e., have significance, was therefore, in effect, though unwittingly, a coalition between an atomistic and a functionalist view of words. By the irony of fate, it was his atomistic view which was, in most quarters, accepted as gospel truth for the next fifty or seventy years. Indeed, it was more than accepted, it was accepted without the important safeguard which Mill himself provided when he said that the thing or person denoted by a name was not to be identified with what that name meant. Mill said that to mean is to connote. His successors said that to mean is to denote, or, more rarely, both to denote and to connote. Frege was for a long time alone in seeing the crucial importance of Mill's argument that two or more descriptive phrases with different senses may apply to the same planet or person. This person or planet is not, therefore, what those phrases mean. Their different senses are not their common denotation. Russell early realized the point which Mill did not very explicitly make, though Plato had made it, that a sentence is not a list. It says one thing; it is not just an inventory of a lot of things. But only much later, if at all, did Russell see the full implications of this.

I surmise that the reason why Mill's doctrine of denotation, without its safeguards, caught on, while his truths about connotation failed to do so, were two. First, the word "connote" naturally suggests what we express by "imply," which is not what is wanted. What the phrase "the previous Prime Minister of the United Kingdom" signifies is not to be equated with any or all of the consequences which can be inferred from the statement that Churchill is the previous Prime Minister. Deducing is not translating. But more important was the fact that Mill himself rapidly diluted his doctrine of connotation with such a mass of irrelevant and false sensationalist and associationist psychology, that his successors felt forced to ignore the doctrine in order to keep clear of its accretions.

Let me briefly mention some of the consequences which successors of Mill actually drew from the view, which was not Mill's, that to mean is to denote, in the toughest sense, namely that all significant expressions are proper names, and what they are the names of are what the expressions signify.

First, it is obvious that the vast majority of words are unlike the words "Fido" and "London" in this respect, namely, that they are general. "Fido" stands for a particular dog, but the noun "dog" covers this dog Fido, and all other dogs past, present, and future, dogs in novels, dogs in dog breeders' plans for the future, and so on indefinitely. So the word "dog," if assumed to denote in the way in which "Fido" denotes Fido, must denote something which we do not hear barking, namely either the set or class of all actual and imaginable dogs, or the set of canine properties which they all share. Either would be a very out-of-the-way sort of entity. Next, most words are not even nouns, but adjectives, verbs, prepositions, conjunctions, and so on. If these are assumed to denote in the way in which "Fido" denotes Fido, we shall have a still larger and queerer set of nominees or *denotata* on our hands, namely nominees whose names could not even function as the grammatical subjects of sentences. (Incidentally it is not true even that all ordinary general nouns can function by themselves as subjects of sentences. I can talk about *this* dog, or *a* dog, or *the* dog which . . . ; or about *dogs, all* dogs, or *most* dogs, and so on. But I cannot make the singular noun "dog" by itself the grammatical subject of a sentence, save inside quotes, though I can do this with nouns like "grass," "hydrogen," and "Man.") Finally, since complexes of words, like descriptive and other phrases, and entire clauses and sentences have unitary meanings, then these too will have to be construed as denoting complex entities of very surprising sorts. Now Meinong in Austria and Frege in Germany, as well as Moore and Russell in this country, in their early days, accepted some or most of these consequences. Consistently with the assumed equation of signifying with naming, they maintained the objective existence or being of all sorts of abstract and fictional *entia rationis*.

Whenever we construct a sentence, in which we can distinguish a grammatical subject and a verb, the grammatical subject, be it a single word or a more or less complex phrase, must be significant if the sentence is to say something true or false. But if this nominative word or phrase is significant, it must, according to the assumption, denote something which is there to be named. So not only Fido and London, but also centaurs, round squares, the present King of France, the class of albino Cypriots, the first moment of time, and the nonexistence of a first moment of time must all be credited with some sort of reality. They must *be*, else we could not say true or false things of them. We could not truly say that round squares do not exist, unless in some sense of "exist" there exist round squares for us, in another sense, to deny existence of. Sentences can begin with abstract nouns like "equality" or "justice" or "murder" so all Plato's Forms or Universals must be accepted as entities. Sentences can contain mentions of creatures of fiction, like centaurs and Mr. Pickwick, so all conceivable creatures of fiction must be genuine entities too. Next, we can say that propositions are true or false, or that they entail or are incompatible with other propositions, so any significant "that"-clause, like "that three is a prime number" or "that four is a prime number," must also denote existent or subsistent objects. It was accordingly, for a time, supposed that if I know or believe that three is a prime number, my knowing or believing this is a special relation holding between me on the one hand and the truth or fact, on the other, denoted by the sentence "three is a prime number." If I weave or follow a romance, my imagining centaurs or Mr. Pickwick is a special relation holding between me and these centaurs or that portly old gentleman. I could not imagine him unless he had enough being to stand as the correlate-term in this postulated relation of being imagined by me.

Lastly, to consider briefly what turned out, unexpectedly, to be a crucial case, there must exist or subsist classes, namely appropriate *denotata* for such collectively employed plural descriptive phrases as "the elephants in Burma" or "the men in the moon." It is just of such classes or sets that we say that they number 3000, say, in the one case, and 0 in the other. For the results of counting to be true or false, there must be entities submitting to numerical predicates; and for the propositions of arithmetic to be true or false there must exist or subsist an infinite range of such classes.

At the very beginning of this century Russell was detecting some local unplausibilities in the full-fledged doctrine that to every significant grammatical subject there must correspond an appropriate *denotatum* in the way in which Fido answers to the name "Fido." The true proposition "round squares do not exist" surely cannot require us to assert that there really do subsist round squares. The proposition that it is false that four is a prime number is a true one, but its truth surely cannot force us to fill the Universe up with an endless population of objectively existing falsehoods.

But it was classes that first engendered not mere unplausibilities but seemingly disastrous logical contradictions—not merely peripheral logical contradictions but contradictions at the heart of the very principles on which Russell and Frege had taken mathematics to depend. We can collect into classes not only ordinary objects like playing cards and bachelors, but also such things as classes themselves. I can ask how many shoes there are in a room and also how many pairs of shoes, and a pair of shoes is already a class. So now suppose I construct a class of all the classes that are not, as anyhow most classes are not, members of themselves. Will this class be one of its own members or not? If it embraces itself, this disqualifies it from being one of the things it is characterized as embracing; if it is not one of the things it embraces, this is just what qualifies it to be one among its own members.

So simple logic itself forbids certain ostensibly denoting expressions to denote. It is at least unplausible to say that there exist objects denoted by the phrase "round squares"; there is self-contradiction in saying that there exists a class which is a member of itself on condition that it is not, and *vice versa*.

Russell had already found himself forced to say of some expressions which had previously been supposed to name or denote, that they had to be given exceptional treatment. They were not names but what he called "incomplete symbols," expressions, that is, which have no meaning, in the sense of denotation, by themselves; their business was to be auxiliary to expressions which do, as a whole, denote. (This was what Mill had said of the syncategorematic words.) The very treatment which had since the Middle Ages been given to such little words as "and," "not," "the," "some," and "is" was now given to some other kinds of expressions as well. In effect, though not explicitly, Russell was saying that, e.g., descriptive phrases were as syncategorematic as "not," "and," and "is" had always been allowed to be. Here Russell was on the brink of allowing that the meanings or significations of many kinds of expressions are matters not of *naming* things, but of *saying* things. But he was, I think, still held up by the idea that saying is itself just another variety of naming, i.e., naming a complex or an "objective" or a proposition or a fact—some sort of postulated *Fido rationis*.

He took a new and most important further step to cope with the paradoxes, like that of the class of classes that are not members of themselves. For he now wielded a distinction, which Mill had seen but left inert, the distinction between sentences which are either true or false on the one hand, and on the other hand sentences which, though proper in vocabulary and syntax, are none the less nonsensical, meaningless, or absurd; and therefore neither true nor false. To assert them and to deny them are to assert and deny nothing. For reasons of a sort which are the proper concern of logic, certain sorts of concatenations of words and phrases into sentences produce things which cannot be significantly said. For example, the very question Is the class of all classes which are not members of themselves a member of itself or not? has no answer. Russell's famous "Theory of Types" was an attempt to formulate the reasons of logic which make it an improper question. We need not consider whether he was successful. What matters for us, and what made the big difference to subsequent philosophy, is the fact that at long last the notion of meaning was realized to be, at least in certain crucial contexts, the obverse of the notion of the nonsensical—what can be said, truly or falsely, is at last contrasted with what cannot be significantly said. The notion of meaning had been, at long last, partly detached from the notion of naming and reattached to the notion of saying. It was recognized to belong to, or even to constitute the domain which had always been the province of logic; and as it is at least part of the official business of logic to establish and codify rules, the notion of meaning came now to be seen as somehow compact of rules. To know what an expression means involves knowing what can (logically) be said with it and what cannot (logically) be said with it. It involves knowing a set of bans, fiats, and obligations, or, in a word, it is to know the rules of the employment of that expression.

It was, however, not Russell but Wittgenstein who first generalized or half-generalized this crucial point. In the *Tractatus Logico-Philosophicus,* which could be described as the first book to be written on the philosophy of logic, Wittgenstein still had one foot in the denotationist camp, but his other foot was already free. He saw and said, not only what had been said before, that the little words, the so-called logical constants, "not," "is," "and," and the rest, do not stand for objects, but also, what Plato had also said before, that sentences are not names. Saying is not naming. He realized, as Frege had done, that logicians' questions are not questions about the properties or relations of the *denotata,* if any, of the expressions which enter into the sentences whose logic is under examination. He saw, too, that all the words and phrases that can enter into sentences are governed by the rules of what he called, slightly metaphorically, "logical syntax" or "logical grammar." These rules are what are broken by such concatenations of words and phrases as result in nonsense. Logic is or includes the study of these rules. Husserl had at the beginning of the century employed much the same notion of "logical grammar."

It was only later still that Wittgenstein consciously and deliberately withdrew his remaining foot from the denotationist camp. When he said "Don't ask for the meaning, ask for the use," he was imparting a lesson which he had had to teach to himself after he had finished with the *Tractatus.* The use of an expression, or the concept it expresses, is the role it is employed to perform, not any thing or person or event for which it might be supposed to stand. Nor is the purchasing power of a coin to be equated with this book or that car ride which might be bought with it. The purchasing power of a coin has not got pages or a terminus. Even more instructive is the analogy which Wittgenstein now came to draw between significant expressions and pieces with which are played games like chess. The significance of an expression and the powers or functions in chess of a pawn, a knight, or the queen have much in common. To know what the knight can and cannot do, one must know the rules of chess, as well as be familiar with various kinds of chess situations which may arise. What the knight may do cannot be read out of the material or shape of the piece of ivory or boxwood or tin of which this knight may be made. Similarly to know what an expression means is to know how it may and may not be employed, and the rules governing its employment can be the same for expressions of very different physical compositions. The word "horse" is not a bit like the word "*cheval*"; but the way of wielding them is the same. They have the same role, the same sense. Each is a translation of the other. Certainly the rules of the uses of expressions are unlike the rules of games in some important respects. We can be taught the rules of chess up to a point before we begin to play. There are manuals of chess, where there are not manuals of significance. The rules of chess, again, are completely definite and inelastic. Questions of whether a rule has been broken or not are decidable without debate. Moreover we opt to play chess and can stop when we like, where we do not opt to talk and think and cannot opt to break off. Chess is a diversion. Speech and thought are not only diversions. But still the partial assimilation of the meanings of expressions to the powers or the values of the pieces with which a game is played is enormously revealing. There is no temptation to suppose that a knight is proxy for anything, or that learning what a knight may or may not do is learning that it is a deputy for some ulterior entity. We could not learn to play the knight correctly without having learned to play the other pieces, nor can we learn to play a word by itself, but only in combination with other words and phrases.

Besides this, there is a further point which the assimilation brings out. There are six different kinds of chess-pieces, with their six different kinds of roles in the game. We can imagine more complex games involving twenty or two hundred kinds of pieces. So it is with languages. In contrast with the denotationist assumption that almost all words, all phrases, and even all sentences are alike in having the one role of naming, the assimilation of language to chess reminds us of what we knew *ambulando* all along, the fact that there are indefinitely many kinds of words, kinds of phrases, and kinds of sentences—that there is an indefinitely large variety of kinds of roles performed by the expressions we use in saying things. Adjectives do not do what adverbs do, nor do all adjectives do the same sort of thing as one another. Some nouns are proper names, but most are not. The sorts of things that we do with sentences are different from the sorts of things that we do with most single words—and some sorts of things that we can significantly do with some sorts of sentences, we cannot significantly do with others. And so on.

There is not one basic mold, such as the "Fido"-Fido mold, into which all significant expressions are to be forced. On the contrary, there is an endless variety of categories of sense or meaning. Even the *prima facie* simple notion of naming or denoting itself turns out on examination to be full of internal variegations. Pronouns are used to denote people and things, but not in the way in which proper names do so. No one is *called* "he" or "she." "Saturday" is a proper name, but not in the same way as "Fido" is a proper name—and neither is used in the way in which the fictional proper name "Mr. Pickwick" is used. The notion of denotation, so far from providing the final explanation of the notion of meaning, turns out itself to be just one special branch or twig on the tree of signification. Expressions do not mean because they denote things; some expressions denote things, in one or another of several different manners, because they are significant. Meanings are not things, not even very queer things. Learning the meaning of an expression is more like learning a piece of drill than like coming across a previously unencountered object. It is learning to operate correctly with an expression and with any other expression equivalent to it.

.   .   .

18

A CRITIQUE OF ORDINARY LANGUAGE

friedrich waismann

Language is always changing. That is a commonplace, yet, oddly enough, one not enough heeded by those who are clamoring for "the ordinary use of language," quite prepared, it seems, to damn everything out of hand—in philosophy—if it fails to conform to its standards. While appreciating the service done to clear thinking by the insistence on the normal use, I feel that the time has come to say a word of warning against the cult of it, for such it has almost become. Like any cult, while it is likely to protect its votaries from certain dangers—getting trapped in the vagaries of speech —it is apt to make them blind to the obvious narrowness of such a view, particularly when it is just on the point of becoming one of the major influences of our time. It tends to instil, in the faithful and in the not-so-faithful alike, a belief, a complacent one, in the adequacy of language which is far from the truth. In actual fact, language is a deficient instrument, and treacherous in many ways. As this opens a subject of vast dimensions I shall confine myself to a few scattered observations.

First, I shall try to argue that a departure from the beaten track need not only not be anathematized, but may be the *very thing* to be strived for—in poetry, science, and in philosophy. My second point is that language, far from serving merely to report facts, is a collective instrument of thought that enters experience itself, shaping and molding the whole apprehension of phenomena (such as color and luster, e.g.) in a certain definite way, and, who knows, giving to them just that subtle bias which makes all the difference. How curiously different, for instance, must the world of color have appeared to the Romans who had in their language no word for grey, brown, nor any *generic* word for blue (though they had a number of words to denote particular shades of this color). How curiously different, it would seem, must human action appear when seen through the filter of Eskimo language where, owing to the lack of transitive verbs, it is likely to be perceived as a sort of happening without an active element in it. (In Greenlandic one cannot say "I kill him," "I shoot the arrow," but only "He dies to me," "The arrow is flying away from me," just as "I hear" is expressed by "me-sound-is.") Eskimo philosophers, if there were any, would be likely to say that what we call action is "really" a pattern, or gestalt, of succeeding impressions. Just as

From Friedrich Waismann, "Analytic—Synthetic" V, in *Analysis* 13 (October 1952): 1–14. Reprinted by permission of the author's estate and Basil Blackwell & Mott Ltd.

Greenlandic assimilates action to impression—which strikes us as strange—so our language tends to bias us in just the opposite way: it makes us assimilate perception to action. We say not only "I cut the tree," but also "I see the tree": the use of the same construction makes it appear as if the "I" was the *subject* from which issued the seeing, and as if the seeing was a sort of action directed at the tree; nor are we any better off if we use the passive voice "The tree is seen by me"—for now it almost looks as if something *happened* to the tree, as if it had to undergo or suffer my seeing it. Following the clues of speech, we are led to interpret the world of experience one-sidedly, just as "owing to the common philosophy of grammar," as Nietzsche put it, i.e., "owing to the unconscious domination and guidance of similar grammatical functions the way seems barred against certain other possibilities of world-interpretation." In other words, every language contains, deep-sunken in it, certain molds, designs, forms to apprehend phenomena, human action, etc. It is hardly going too far to say that a whole world picture is wedded to the use of the transitive verb and the actor-action scheme that goes with it—that if we spoke a different language we would perceive a different world. By growing up in a certain language, by thinking in its semantic and syntactical grooves, we acquire a certain more or less uniform outlook on the world—an outlook we are scarcely aware of until (say) by coming across a language of a totally different structure we are shocked into seeing the oddity of the obvious, or what seemed to be obvious. Finally, I want to say that philosophy *begins* with distrusting language—that medium that pervades, and warps, our very thought. But this is perhaps too strong an expression. I do not mean to say that language *falsifies* experience, twists it into something else; the point is that it supplies us with certain categorial forms without which the formation of a coherent system of experience, a world picture, would be impossible. In this sense, language shapes and fashions the frame in which experience is set, and different languages achieve this in different ways. A philosopher, more than others, should be sensitive to this sort of influence, alive to the dangers that lie dormant in the forms of expression—the very thing, that is, which, so misguidedly, has been raised to the standard in philosophical controversy.

When I spoke of the change of language I was not thinking of those cases which delight the heart of a philologist—umlaut, ablaut, and the like. Nor was I referring to changes in meaning and vocabulary—what was originally stupid, wanton, Latin *nescius,* becomes "nice"; a horse that is well-fed and grows a smooth, shiny coat is "glad"—*glatt* in German; what is now silly was formerly "sely" corresponding to German *selig* —happy, blessed; for while such changes are instructive in many ways, they are hardly such as to deserve the philosopher's attention. Neither was I thinking of those more subtle changes in the *valeurs* of a word which—as in the case of "romantic"—are significant of a change in the tone of thought of a whole period—of a half-conscious awakening of new ways of feeling and responses to nature, so elusive and yet, to the historian, so important. What I had in mind were cases which are best illustrated by a few examples.

Nothing is so opposed as day and night; yet there is a sense, as when we speak of a "three days' journey," in which "day" includes night. "Man" is used in contrast to woman, but occasionally as a term including woman; and a similar shift of sense is perceptible in "he" and "she"—as an arguer, also woman is "he." We say of a child that he is two years "old," not two years "young," just as we inquire "How *long* (not how *short*) will you stay?" or "How far (not how *near*) is it from here to the station?" The word "quality," while for the most part used indifferently, is sometimes uttered in a peculiar tone—as when we say "He has quality." White and black are commonly contrasted with colors in the strict and proper sense ("illustrations in color" *versus* "illustrations in black and white"), yet in certain contexts we are inclined to reckon them among the colors; as when we say "Look round you—everything you see has some color or other," thinking, perhaps, that even air and vapor, or glass and water are possessed by some very pale, some very pearly tone. Thus "color" tends to absorb into its meaning all shades, even black and white, the otherwise "colorless" hues. But these are instances betraying a deeper drift. In the ordinary sense, motion is opposed to rest, speed to slowness, size to littleness, numerous to a few, depth to shallowness, strength to weakness, value to worthlessness, just as far is opposed to near, hot to cold, dry to wet, dark to bright, heavy to light, and true to false. And this was, roughly, the way in which Greek philosophers regarded such contrasts. "Up" for them was simply "not-down," "soft" "not-hard," "dry" "not-wet," and so on. The fact that two polar terms were in use may have played a role in underpinning the belief that things which are hot and cold, or hard and soft, etc., are different, not in degree, but in kind—a fateful belief, for on it hinged their understanding—no, their lack of understanding of change. They signally failed to penetrate it. The Greeks never mastered the problem of motion—which is but the simplest case—they never evolved a science of dynamics, which is surprising enough in view of their genius for mathematics. They give the impression that they somehow got started on the wrong track— for them heavenly and terrestrial motion were entirely different, the one governed by law, eternal and unchanging, the other lawless, corrupt, confused; if faced with a change, such as a thing getting heated, they thought that one quality must be destroyed to let the opposite quality take its place. Thus they were, perhaps as a consequence of their quaint ideas, mightily impeded in coming to grips with the problem of change.

In science a language has come into use in which those contrasted terms are looked upon as degrees of one and the same quality—darkness as light intensity of illumination, slowness as the lower range of speed, rest as the limiting case of motion; there is a scale only of hardness, not of softness, only a physical theory of heat, not a theory of coldness; what we measure is the strength of a rope, a current, etc., not its weakness, what we count is number, not fewness; the air has a degree of moisture, not of dryness; and everything has weight and mass, even an electron. Again, we speak of health irrespective of whether it is good or bad health, and of the value of things which are of no value. Under the influence of such examples, it would seem, a term like "truth-value" has been coined to cover both truth and falsity of a statement, just as "verification" is, prevalently, used to include falsification. "Distance," "width," "wealth," "intelligence" are further nouns which had the same career; though the same is not so true of the adjectives—"distant," "wealthy," "intelligent" are not yet relativized, any more than "hard," "hot," "speedy," "weighty" are, of "healthy," "valuable" and "worthy"; on the contrary, they retain the original sense. Adjectives, it would appear, have a much tougher life than nouns, and not only in English. But that only in passing.

Here we see a whole array of terms shifting in a parallel way, and in a way which is of far-reaching consequence: for the construction of modern science is bound up with it and would not have been possible without it. The change-over from the static view—where the adjective is seen as the expression of permanent quality—to a dynamical which apprehends quality as a variable degree within a certain scale made possible "functional thinking" (I use the word as mathematicians do), the kind of thinking that can cope with change and the conceptual difficulties it presents. What happened was obviously this: one term of a pair of contraries had a tendency to swallow up the other and stand for the whole range of variation. Whether this tendency can be traced to the rationalizing influence of science, or whether it is prior to science and has itself given an impetus to that revolution of thought is a question still undecided. It is in this context, perhaps, not without significance that Latin and Greek were lacking in all the finer means to express continuous change and functional dependence: in Latin, for instance, there are no *general* terms to express the relation "the more—the less"; the phrases used for "the more—the more" are confined to simple *proportionality*, the analogue to *statics*. Nor has any classical language an equivalent for "to become" (*devenir* in French, *devenire* in medieval Latin) so essential to our way of describing a change in quality, for neither *fieri* nor γίγνεσθαι can be used in the same way to express the idea of *continuous* change. There are no uses of intransitive verbs such as "to soften," (*rubesco* is inceptive), etc.

The new idiom, which sprang up first in the vernacular about the 14th century, has not entirely displaced the older one (as can still be seen from the adjectives cited above). Both exist side by side. Though the use of "moisture" for dry as well as wet (as in meteorology), or of "truth-value" in logic still has the ring of jargon, in other instances the new idiom has become completely naturalized—as with "distance" for near and far, "age" for young and old, "size" for big and small, "density" for thick and thin. Yet even so, we can use any such term in two distinct ways—we may ask "*Is* he old?" "or *How* old is he?"; and so in the other cases.

At the time of Nicole Oresme, Bishop of Lisieux, when a new way of looking at change was growing up, and with it a new way of speaking of qualities, this must have been felt as a shocking departure from the ordinary use, supported and sanctioned as it was by old tradition. How the cloisters of the schoolmen must have resounded with "*intensio et remissio formarum*"—the disputes as to whether a quality might have degrees and, in changing, could yet remain the same, or whether this was patent nonsense. One may imagine the indignant outcries of the purists of the time, their loathing of what must have appeared to them as "new-fangled ways of speaking" and as a "complete perversion" of grammar. The latter, more even than the vocabulary, embodies a good deal of the conservatism of mankind, and progress had often to be made in the teeth of the enormous resistance offered by its structure to ways of thinking which do not, or not smoothly, fit its grooves. (See what has been said in the foregoing on Greek language and absence of dynamics.) Grammar draws a *cordon sanitaire* against any rebellious ideas that dare to crop up.

The importance of functional correlation can, moreover, be seen in a different domain: in perspective, and the enthusiasm with which it was universally greeted when it was discovered—another coincidence?—at the very time when new aspects of thought and feeling were just about to take shape: Duccio's Maesta and Giotto's wall paintings in the Capella degli Scrovegni in Padua both belong to the early fourteenth century. The "strange fascination which perspective had for the Renaissance mind cannot be accounted for exclusively by a craving for verisimilitude," as Panofsky [1] observes. A sensibility to functional relation is apparent in this, and the interest in perspective—so alien to the Greeks—is almost symbolic of the time. A reflex of it can

[1] E. Panofsky, *Albrecht Dürer*, 1945, I: 260.

still be caught from the writings of Leonardo da Vinci and Dürer. As perspective rests essentially on a clear understanding of the way in which two variables, the apparent size of an object and its distance from the beholder, are connected, Leonardo saw in painting a "science." He certainly must have been struck by the affinity between this "science" and the philosophical speculations on dynamics of the schoolmen of which he was fully aware (he even employed their ideas in his theory of painting).

If those pedantic schoolmen and masters had had their way, there would today be no science and no dynamics; but, for consolation, "correct" grammar. To look at any departure from the norm as a crime is nothing but a blind prejudice; and a fateful one at that as it tends to drain the lifeblood of any independent inquiry. Language is an instrument that must, as occasion requires, be bent to one's purpose. To stick to language as it is can only lead to a sort of Philistinism which insists on the observance of the *cliché* and will end up with a harakiri of living thought. Indeed, the guardian of language who jealously watches over its "correctness" is in the long run bound to turn into a reactionary who looks askance at any innovation. Correctness is a useful, but a negative virtue. Follow those prophets, and you will soon find yourself imprisoned in a language cage, clean, disinfected, and unpleasant like a sanatorium room.

Understandably enough, there is an instinctive prejudice against neologisms, in part springing from a wholesome fear that novelty of speech may screen poverty of thought. We all dislike new words. And yet there is another and perfectly proper urge to give expression to meanings so far unexpressed, or, in the present language, indeed inexpressible. When Freud, for instance, says *der Patient erinnert den Vorfall* he is using the verb *erinnern* in a novel manner; in the ordinary way, the verb is used reflexively, *sich an etwas erinnern*. Why has Freud (who wrote a very good style) diverged at this point? There is a queer way in which a neurotic person who is under treatment may suddenly remember long-forgotten scenes of his early life which, as Freud puts it, have been "repressed" and are now being relived. What has been inaccessible to the patient, however hard he may have tried, breaks, in a violent storm of emotion, through to consciousness. In order to set apart this kind of remembrance from the ordinary one where we remember at will, Freud uses the verb transitively, in a way no one has done before; and with this syntactical innovation goes a semantic change. By this use Freud has enriched the German language. Such stray deviations, hit upon in a lucky hour and accepted by custom, these little, yet expressive departures from the beaten track, have not only a vividness, a sparkle of their own, but they sharpen the tools of thought and keep language from going blunt. So why cavil at them?

What those sticklers for correctness prefer not to see is that we are living in a *changing world,* and that language is always lagging behind these changes. To cite only one sort of examples out of a great many parallel ones—in psychological experiments one constantly comes across situations which call for new ways of describing. If Maxwell disks, for instance, are rotated, one sees, so long as the movement is slow, several color sectors, and when the disk is spinning rapidly, a uniform color, the result of fusion, but in between there is a certain point where a flicker is seen. There are cases in which the color itself is seen flickering, and others, as when the disk is watched through a small screen-hole, which are more aptly described by saying that there is a flickering *across* the disk or *before* it in space, or again that the disk's surface is seen *behind* the flicker. These modes of expression, though perfectly natural and instantly understood by every one, yet digress from the norm. For "before" and "be-

hind," while clearly denoting spatial relations, are used in such a way that it makes
no longer sense to ask, "Exactly how many millimeters before the disk is the flickering?" Here we have a sense of "before" which admits of no distance. To cite a few
similar cases—if we look at a metal its color seems to lie *behind* its surface, just as its
glitter appears *in front of*, or *superimposed* on it; the glow of a piece of red-hot iron
is seen not simply as color that lies on its surface but as *extending back* into the
object. Again, it has been said that, when a person is speaking with someone in
complete darkness, the voice of the other sounds distinctly *behind* the darkness,
not *in* the darkness. In some cases an object is seen as "desurfaced," with a filmy,
fluffy sort of outline, a bit unreal perhaps. Queer idioms which say what cannot
quite be said by anything else: but condemn them on account of that? Notice
with what unerring instinct language contrives to say, at the cost of a slight departure, what would be unsayable if we moved along the rigid grooves of speech.
Indeed, how should one describe such phenomena if not by breaking away from the
clichés? Is there anything objectionable in that? If so, language could never keep
pace with life. Yet new situations, unforeseen, arise, and with them the need of describing them; it can only be met by adjusting language—either by coining new
words, or, as the word-creating faculty is scanty, by pressing old ones into new services,
in this way cutting through the dead mass of convention. It is precisely because speech
runs so much in ready-made molds that an occasional anomaly, a happy flouting of the
laws of grammar, an uncommon phrasing, arouses our attention and lends luster to
the point we want to bring out. It is in this way, by *transgressing*, that language
manages to achieve what it is meant to achieve, and that it grows. Why, then, the
squeamishness?

Not only should the scientist be free to deviate from common language, where
the need arises, but he is bound to do so if he is to convey a new insight not in conformity with the ideas dominant of the time, with ideas, moreover, precipitated in
language. The classical example of this is Einstein. When he was groping his way,
there was, in his own words, "a feeling of direction," of going toward something he
didn't quite know—which centered more and more on a suspicion that all was not
well with the idea of simultaneity. He could at first not say what was wrong with it,
and yet felt that here, if anywhere, was the key to all the dark puzzles that troubled
the physicists at that time. Had be been brought up as a pupil of G. E. Moore, imbued
with a belief in the infallibility of the ordinary modes of expression, he could never
have made his discovery, clogged as he would have been by the dead weight of usage.
As it was, he paid no respect to common sense, let alone the common speech. He insisted on asking himself, Do I *really* understand what I mean when I say that two
events are simultaneous? Once the question was brought into sharp focus, he came to
see, gradually perhaps and to his surprise, that there was a gap in his understanding.
For the sense in which we speak of two events happening at the same time, when they
are in the same place, or nearby, cannot be applied to events in distant places. It
would be *blind*, he felt, to apply the familiar meaning of "simultaneous" to these
other cases—it would only land us in perplexities beyond resolve. Einstein saw that
the term "simultaneous" had first to be *defined* for the case of distant events, and
defined in such a way that the definition supplies us with a method to decide experi-
mentally whether or not two events are simultaneous. This "seeing" of a crucial point
in the meaning of "simultaneous" has *absolutely nothing* to do with the way the word
is actually used in language. It is as well to remind you that in 1905, when Einstein's

first essay appeared, there was only *one* use, not two uses of "simultaneous," and that it would be absurd to pretend that, when Einstein found a difference in meaning, he was making a *linguistic* discovery. (A sidelight on how wrong the philosophical equation meaning = use is.) On the contrary, anyone who had taken ordinary language, or common sense, for his guide, and had been asked whether he understood what "simultaneous" meant, would have replied with a decided Yes—no matter whether he could, or could not, specify a method for finding out. He would have said that the meaning of the word is clear in itself and needs no further explanation. In fact, no one before Einstein, whether a plain man, a scientist, or a philosopher, doubted for a minute that the concept was clear to him, so clear that he need not trouble. That's precisely what made people slur over the decisive point. Einstein *saw*: that is how he freed himself from the the the thought-habits imposed on us by speech, radically so. By following the lead of language, or of the common-sense philosophers one would have barred oneself from the spark of insight which was to be the dawn of a new era in physics.

These facts speak for themselves. That science cannot live under the tutelage of any ideas on "correctness," will perhaps be conceded. . . .

·   ·   ·

Poets and literary critics feel, today perhaps more keenly than ever before, that there is something disquieting about language. If I correctly read the signs, there is a susceptibility to the perils of words, a growing one, and a suspicion that language comes between us and the things we want to say. "In speaking one always says more than one intends to" observes Sartre; and T. S. Eliot, having noticed the vanity of words to express what is unique in experience, says "The particular has no language." Philosophers, on the other hand, are on the whole more likely to be found in the opposite camp—"debunking" all this talk as "pseudo-complaints which masquerade as genuine." [2] I think that this is a mistaken attitude for a number of reasons, and this is perhaps the place to set out some of them.

First, to talk of *the* ordinary use of language is, as I have already hinted in a previous article, unrealistic. Though I would not go so far as Ezra Pound in saying that our whole speech is "churning and chugging" today, the fact remains that language is in a state of flux. But, it will be said, that is the concern of the historian of language, not of the philosopher. All the philosopher needs to know is the *stock* use of a word or phrase, as it is employed at present, in contrast with its non-stock uses.[3] This answer is unsatisfactory. Though it would be silly to pretend that one did not know the stock use of "cat" or "shut the door," there are other cases where one would feel less sure. Is a "taste of onions" the stock use and a "taste for history" derived, secondary, figurative? (But it is not *felt* as a metaphor!) Is only a "brilliant sunshine" standard use and a "brilliant style" non-standard? Is "day" as opposed to night, or as including night the norm? What about speaking of a "wild laughter," a "brooding silence," or saying that a "recollection of this experience moved in his eyes?" It is easy to see that the "stock use" shifts with the context, and shifts in time. What was stock use may become obsolete and fall into the limbo of silence, just as new uses may spring up and may, in their turn, become standard language; but where is

[2] Alice Ambrose, "The Problems of Linguistic Inadequacy," *Philosophical Analysis*, Max Black, ed., Cornell University Press, 1950.
[3] I am indebted here to Prof. G. Ryle for letting me read an article of his in which such distinctions are discussed.

one to draw the line? It is well to remember that almost all expressions which refer to the mental are derived from others whose primary sense was sensuous and that this is a process which goes on to the present day; just as a good many words, under the influence of science, philosophy, or something still more elusive, have only in fairly recent times undergone a change in meaning—e.g., "organic," "nervous," "unconscious," "original," "creative," "objective," "curiosity," "to entail," etc. There is continuous change and continuous creation in language. Finally, there is such a thing as ambiguity which—except in exceptional cases—mars any attempt to single out one use as the stock one. Exactly how many standard uses has "nature"? What about "in," "on," "about," etc.? "The English prepositions," says Empson, "from being used in so many ways and in combination with so many verbs, have acquired not so much a number of meanings as a body of meaning continuous in several dimensions." [4] If so, or if the uses shade off into one another imperceptibly, how can one peel off and throw away all the non-stock uses and retain the stock ones? Yes, this view *is* unrealistic.

Next, and this raises a bigger issue, even if there was such a thing as a stock use, it need not matter much to the philosopher. I mean, he need not be *bound* to this use; I should even go further and say that, sooner or later, he is bound to commit the crime and depart from it—that is, if he has something new to say. In this respect, his position is not altogether different from that of the poet or the scientist, and for similar reasons. He, too, may have come to see something which, in the ordinary way, cannot quite be said. I shall argue later that this is a characteristic feature of some philosophizing. To mention here just one small point, the English language has been enriched by many words coined by philosophers who were sensitive to gaps in our vocabulary. "Optimism," for instance, is due to Leibniz, and was borrowed from him by Voltaire. "Impression" in its modern sense was introduced by Hume, "intuition" by De Quincey, "intuitionism" by Sidgwick, "intuitionist" by H. Spencer. "Scientist" is an invention of Whewell, "aesthetic" one of Baumgarten, and so on. That even the laws of grammar can be flouted with salubrious effect can be seen from Lichtenberg's remark that one should say "It thinks in me."

My third point is that certain features of one's own language are noticed and appreciated in their full significance only when it is compared with other languages— with German (verbal way of expressing color), Greenlandic (dominance of the impression verb), Latin (absence of words for blue, grey, and brown), etc. Is, then, the philosopher to go to the Eskimos to learn his trade? Not exactly; yet the mere *awareness* of other possibilities is, philosophically, of the utmost importance: it makes us see in a flash other ways of world-interpretation of which we are unaware, and thus drives home what is conventional in our outlook. The technique of the ordinary-use philosophers has suffered from the fact that they restricted themselves to the study of one language to the exclusion of any other—with the result that they became blind to those ubiquitous features of their own language on which their whole mode of thinking, indeed their world picture, depends.

Connected with this is another large point—the misleadingness of our speechforms. That language, "the embodied and articulated Spirit of the Race," as Coleridge put it, is in many ways inadequate can, I take it, by no one be doubted. In particular, it is the syntax and the field of analogies embedded in language which, unperceived, hold our thought in thrall, or push it along perilous lines. . . .

4 Seven Types of Ambiguity, p. 5.

But there are still more reasons for guarding against this official doctrine. The one is that its champions pay heed only to the actual use of language not to its gaps, revealing as they are. Suppose, for instance, that I say "I ought to do so-and-so"; when I say that it is obvious that the "I" is here only a pseudo-subject from which the ought seems to proceed, whereas in fact it is more a *point d'appui* to which it is directed. We regard a rule of ethics, politeness, etc., as something outside ourselves which applies to us as objects. We are rather in a passive (obedient) frame of mind, and what is active is, at most, the consent we give to that duty. "I am under an obligation," "it is my duty" are therefore phrases which are more appropriate. That "ought" does not refer to an occult activity betrays itself in a number of features; thus we do not say "I will ought," "I choose (decide) to ought," any more than we say "I ought to ought," or "I am resolved upon oughting." There is no such thing as a "will to ought." The complete absence of these idioms *is* revealing. That philosophers have concentrated on the use, and neglected the nonuse of expressions is a further weakness of their technique.

·   ·   ·

19

THE SIGNIFICANCE OF FELT MEANING

eugene t. gendlin

Besides the logical dimension and the operational dimension of knowledge, there is also a directly felt, experiential dimension. *Meaning* is not only *about things* and it is not only a certain *logical* structure, but it also involves *felt* experiencing. Any concept, thing, or behavior is meaningful only as some noise, thing, or event interacts with felt experiencing. Meanings are formed and had through an interaction between experiencing and symbols or things.

In the past, meaning has been analyzed very largely in terms of things (objective reference, sense perception) and in terms of logical structure. Of course, meanings were viewed as concerning experience, but "experience" was usually construed as a logical scheme that organizes sense perceptions or as a logical construct that intervenes to relate and predict observations of behavior.

Today, however, we can no longer construe "experience" so narrowly. Besides logical schemes and sense perception we have come to recognize that there is also a powerful *felt* dimension of experience that is prelogical, and that functions importantly in what we think, what we perceive, and how we behave.

The task at hand is to examine the relationships between this felt dimension of experience and the logical and objective orders. How can logical symbolizations and operational definitions be related to felt experiencing? Or, to reverse the question: What are the functions of felt experiencing in our conceptual operations and in our observable behavior?

One group of modern thinkers (Bergson, Sartre) have especially pointed out this concrete affective side of experience and its central importance in human life. They have also pointed out how difficult is the application of logic and concepts to experience as actually lived and felt. They have said that only "intuition" or actual living can grasp it adequately, while concepts and definitions can distort and deaden it. The attempt to define, they say, can turn living experience into abstractions or into dead objects of study. Thus, despite its crucial importance, felt experience has been conceptualized only vaguely, and only as it occurs at a few crucial junctures of life (for

From Eugene T. Gendlin, *Experiencing and the Creation of Meaning*, Introduction, pp. 1–16, 24. Reprinted by permission of The Macmillan Company. © by the Free Press of Glencoe, a Division of The Macmillan Company, 1962.

example, "encounter," "commitment"), rather than as the ever-present and ever-powerful factor it is.

These views in modern thought lead to the problem of effectively studying directly felt experience, of employing its meanings in science and life, of making thought concerning it possible for more than a few initiates—in short, the problem of *relating* concepts to felt experience without distorting or deadening it.

The other side of modern thought (pragmatism, logical positivism) has emphasized the logical and empirical requirements of science and meaning. Precise logical definitions and empirical testing are necessary to advance science, and only on the basis of these can we continue to work for the unbiased type of truth that makes men free and permits any man, if his findings can be objectively defined and tested, to question or disprove accepted tenets.

However, to remain only within current concepts and methods of science and logic imposes severe limitations. This side of modern thought leads to the problem of *extending* science to human behavior—without distorting or diluting logical precision and objective empirical criteria.

These two sides of modern thought really define the basic task as it is posed today. For we cannot really be content to lose either side or to leave both as they are. Current scientific methods need to be not only analyzed as they are now, but extended. Nor can we indefinitely leave the ever present concrete sense of "experience" in a vague no-man's land. It functions importantly in human behavior. The study of human behavior can be guided and aided if we can learn what kind of concept *can* relate to felt experience and how concepts of this kind can, in turn, relate to objective concepts and measurements.

In order to embark upon this task, we shall have to be clear that we require more than a logical scheme of "experience." We must be concerned not only with what is already logical, but with experience before it is logically ordered. We must be concerned with experience as it functions in the *formation* of meaning and logical orders. We must investigate prelogical, "preconceptual" experience as it *functions together with* logical symbols, but not substitute one for the other. Our remaining entirely on the logical level cannot reveal how experience functions together with logic. Thus we cannot consider experience to be a logically schematic construct, no matter how complex. At best we can have a scheme of how experience and logic can relate. Even then, experience must be referred to directly—it must be thought of as that partly unformed stream of feeling that we have every moment. I shall call it "experiencing," using that term for the flow of feeling, concretely, to which you can every moment attend inwardly, if you wish.

Experiencing plays basic roles in behavior and in the formation of meaning. If logical schemes are not considered in relation to these roles of experiencing, then logical schemes are empty.

·   ·   ·

Heretofore, either it was assumed that meaning lies in felt experiencing—and logic distorts it, or it was assumed that meaning lies in logic and feeling is a chaotic morass to be avoided. It is not so. Meaning is formed in the interaction of experiencing and something that functions as a symbol. This fact has been viewed as a troublesome chaos instead of as the basic source of order in human behavior. For, when symbolized meanings occur in interaction with experiencing, they change. And when one employs symbols to attend to a felt meaning, it changes. The effort is vain merely to "observe" feeling and then say what it means. We need to understand and systematically employ what happens in an interaction between symbols (selective attention is already a "symbolic" process) and experiencing. So long as we only exclaim: "But everything changes!" we view as merely troublesome the human functioning in which meaning and order are formed.

• • •

The "meanings" of experiencing as such are "preconceptual." We can investigate the orderly changes occurring when the "preconceptual" interacts with symbols (words, objects, behaviors, persons), and we can employ that interaction.

• • •

What, then, is this "concrete" or "preconceptual" experiencing? We cannot talk about it without the use of symbols. Even to pay attention to it is a symbolic process. Yet there are many *different* ways in which symbols and concrete experiencing can function together. And we require experiencing to move from one to another of these ways of using symbols. Thought as we actually have it always requires experiencing; thought is really a functional relationship between symbols and experiencing.

In my first rough descriptions of experiencing, I will chiefly employ a use of symbols which I term "direct reference." I will ask you to let my symbols refer directly to your experiencing.

I use the word "experienc*ing*" to denote *concrete* experience, because the phenomenon I refer to is the *raw*, present, ongoing *functioning* (in us) of what is usually called experience. Let me describe it.

It is something so simple, so easily available to every person, that at first its very simplicity makes it hard to point to. Another term for it is "felt meaning," or "feeling." However, "feeling" is a word usually used for specific contents—for this or that feeling, emotion, or tone, for feeling good, or bad, or blue, or pretty fair. But regardless of the many changes in *what* we feel—that is to say, really, *how* we feel—there always is the concretely present flow of feeling. At any moment we can individually and privately direct our attention inward, and when we do that, there it is. Of course, we have this or that specific idea, wish, emotion, perception, word, or thought, but we *always* have concrete feeling, an inward sensing whose nature is broader. It is a concrete mass in the sense that it is "there" for us. It is not at all vague in its being there. It may be vague only in that we may not know what it is. We can put only a few aspects of it into words. The mass itself is always something there, no matter what we say "it is." Our definitions, our knowing "what it is," are symbols that specify aspects of it, "parts" of it, as we say. Whether we name it, divide it, or not, there it is.

Let me give a few very simple examples, just to point your attention toward experiencing. In each example I will be using symbols that will specify some specific aspect of experiencing. Yet I would like you not so much to think of the specific aspect I refer to as to notice where you are inwardly looking.

First, feel your body. Your body can, of course, be looked at from the outside, but I am asking you to feel it from the inside. There you are. There, as simply put as possible, is your experiencing of this moment, now. But we need not remain with that global feel of your body. Let us "divide" it a bit, although no hard and fast division into parts is really possible. Let us create a few aspects of it. We do this with symbols. The symbols will be my sentences, below:

Perhaps you feel some tension, or perhaps you feel ease. These words ("tension," "ease") give certain qualities and specify certain aspects of your present experiencing. Let us fashion another, different sort of aspect: how does your chest feel when you inhale?

Nor need we remain with entirely present descriptions. You will have an equally present felt meaning (aspect of experiencing), in the sense that you will have the felt meaning now, if I ask you: how do you generally feel before a meal when you haven't eaten for a long time? (You feel hunger—using the word to refer to your inward sense of it.) Or recall the way you feel after you have filled your stomach, the heavy satiation. Boredom, that strained impatient deadness which hurts in quite an alive way, often is another aspect you can specify in experiencing.

But I am sure you are beginning to notice that I am each time asking you to attend inwardly to some aspect of feeling. All the thousands of different kinds of feeling and feeling tones, felt meanings, and so on are aspects of feeling, of "inner sense," a location, a referent of your inward attention. This inward referent (always this or that concrete aspect you attend to) is what I term "experiencing."

Notice, it is always there for you. It may not always be clearly definable. In fact, when you pay attention you can notice that it is really never just any given definable quality or tone or content. It can always be further differentiated and further aspects of it can be specified. A concrete aspect of experiencing accompanies every description, every meaningful thing you say. Above and beyond the symbols there is always also the feeling referent itself. Always it is concretely and definitely there, present for you, an inward sensing.

Let us move from these very simple examples to more complex ones. Consider a sentence: "What is the law of supply and demand?" In what way do you have *your* meaning of the sentence? Of course, the sentence is objective, spoken or written. But for *you,* how do you have its meaning—what it is to you? You have it in your experiencing. Let us say you have read the sentence. Does it have meaning for you or not? If it is in a language you know and makes sense, then you have an experiential sense of its meaning. Where do you find such an experiential sense of meaning? Again, it is in the same location, with the same inward reference of attention to the ever present feeling mass, that you find meaning. The sentence, of course, consists of the verbal noises (or auditory images of noises). But their meaning? It is *felt* by you. If you must now say what this sentence means (using your own words), you must refer your attention to this *felt* meaning—that is to say to your experiencing. You must refer to that aspect of your experiencing which constitutes the meaning of the sentence for you. We could say that it is a "part" of your inward body sense, for it is located within this bodily, felt, inward sense. However, it is obviously a quite specific aspect of your total body feeling that your attention specifies. We say you are "concentrating" on it. Concentrating on *your* meaning, your attention is focused inwardly on this aspect of your felt experiencing.

A situation in which you are and behave appropriately usually does not require your telling yourself in words what it is all about. For example, you walk across the room and sit down. You may not need words, at least not the thousands and thousands of words that would be necessary to verbalize everything the situation means to you —everything it must mean to you if you are to walk across the room correctly and sit down in a chair. You do not need to have all these many, many meanings explicit and separated. The felt experiencing of the moment interacts with *things* and *events,* and enables you to respond properly. Your response most often springs from the inwardly felt experiencing without *verbal* symbolization.

Notice that, depending upon what you need, you can focus on a very general, broad aspect of experiencing, such as feeling joyful or tense, or you may focus on a very, very specific and finely determined aspect, such as, "What is the law of supply and demand?" Either way, you refer to an experiential felt sense, and either way you have something concrete and definitely present to you, though its meaning may be vague.

Perhaps now you know where I wish to point your attention when I say "experiencing." Perhaps you can appreciate the ubiquity, the constant presence to you, to me, and to anyone, of this concrete feeling datum: experiencing.

Now, if it is the case that we are really dealing with *experiencing* whenever we feel something, whenever we mean something, whenever we live in a situation, whenever we think, then experiencing is obviously so ubiquitous and so basic that we must take it to be a very fundamental phenomenon.

Experiencing is an aspect of human living that is constant, like body life, metabolism, sensory input. In this constancy it differs from the intermittent aspects of life, such as looking, moving the legs, thinking, speaking, and sleeping, for we do the latter only sometimes. Thus experiencing underlies every moment's special occurrences of living. In a theoretical way we could consider it as the inward receptivity of a living body, although we must take care not to forget that one can "specify" highly detailed aspects of it, each of which can be referred to very specifically by our attention, and each of which can be employed to give rise to very many specific meanings. Experiencing is a constant, ever present, underlying phenomenon of inwardly sentient living, and therefore there is an experiential side of anything, no matter how specifically detailed and finely specified, no matter whether it is a concept, an observed act, an inwardly felt behavior, or a sense of a situation.

We can be very modest, or very grandiose, about experiencing. In a modest way we can say: experiencing is simply feeling, as it concretely exists for us inwardly, and as it accompanies every lived aspect of what we are and mean and perceive. Or we can be grandiose about it and say that for the sake of (this or that aspect of) experiencing mankind do all they do in a lifespan. Within experiencing lie the mysteries of all that we are. For the sake of our experiential sense of what we observe, we react as we do. From out of it we create what we create. And, because of its puzzles, and for the desperation of some of its puzzles, we overthrow good sense, obviousness, and reality, if need be. The speaker who has temporarily lost his inward datum of what he is about to say, cannot continue to speak. He is lost, pauses, searches to "remember" —that is, he searches with his attention inward to find again that concrete and definite *feeling* of what he wants to say, so that his words may pour out again. If he cannot find it, he is lost. Similarly, if our direct touch with our own personally important experiencing becomes too clouded, narrowed, or lost, we go to any length to regain it; we go to a friend, to a therapist, or to the desert. For nothing is as debilitating as a confused or distant functioning of experiencing. And the chief malaise of our society is perhaps that it allows so little pause and gives so little specifying response and interpersonal communion to our experiencing, so that we must much of the time pretend that we are only what we seem externally, and that our meanings are only the objective references and the logical meanings of our words.

I want to emphasize one vital characteristic of experiencing: any datum of experiencing—any aspect of it, no matter how finely specified—can be symbolized and interpreted *further and further,* so that it can guide us to many, many more symbolizations. We can endlessly "differentiate" it further. We can synthesize endless numbers of meanings in it.

Given a sentence or situation, an observation or behavior, a person or a moment's speech by a person, or anything, we can focus on our experiencing of it, and we can say what it means in a sentence, in a paragraph, or in a book. It does not have only one meaning but, depending upon the symbols we apply, the behaviors and events that occur, it can be differentiated and symbolized in the formation of very many meanings.

•   •   •

This "preconceptual" character of experiencing has not been appreciated; consequently the application of logical and scientific order to organize observations of man has lagged.

Science must use logically defined concepts that mean the same whenever they occur. These logically defined concepts have what I call "logical order." Without them we cannot have science. However, we require propositions that can be tested successfully by applying to the actual order of observed events. Only when the order of concepts and propositions bears some relation to the actual order of events (and when variables are isolated and defined in accordance with the order of events) can predictions be verified. Thus we must take account of the kinds of relations that logical order can have to the preconceptual. . . .

•   •   •

SELECTED BIBLIOGRAPHY FOR PART VI

The nature of knowledge

Ackermann, Robert. *Theories of Knowledge: A Critical Introduction.* New York: McGraw-Hill, 1965.

Ayer, A. J. *The Problem of Knowledge.* Harmondsworth, Eng.: Penguin, 1956.

Canfield, John V., and Donnell, Franklin H. Jr., eds. *Readings in the Theory of Knowledge.* New York: Appleton-Century-Crofts, 1964. Part 1.

Chisholm, Roderick M. *Theory of Knowledge.* Englewood Cliffs, N.J.: Prentice-Hall, 1966.

Dewey, John. *The Quest for Certainty.* New York: Minton, Balch, 1929.

Ewing, A. C. *Idealism.* London: Methuen, 1934.

Grene, Marjorie. *The Knower and the Known.* London: Faber, 1966.

Griffiths, A. Phillips, ed. *Knowledge and Belief.* London: Oxford University Press, 1967.

Hill, Thomas E. *Contemporary Theories of Knowledge.* New York: Ronald Press, 1961.

Husserl, Edmund. *Cartesian Meditations: An Introduction to Phenomenology,* trans. Dorion Cairns. The Hague: Martinus Nijhoff, 1960.

———. *Ideas: General Introduction to Pure Phenomenology,* trans. W. R. Boyce Gibson. London: Allen and Unwin, 1931.

Lewis, C. I. *Mind and the World Order.* New York: Dover, 1929.

Malcolm, Norman. *Knowledge and Certainty.* Englewood Cliffs, N.J.: Prentice-Hall, 1963.

Montague, William P. *The Ways of Knowing.* London: Allen and Unwin, 1925.

Moore, G. E. *Some Main Problems of Philosophy.* London: Allen and Unwin, 1953. Chaps. 4, 5, and 6.

Nagel, Ernest, and Brandt, Richard B. *Meaning and Knowledge: Systematic Readings in Epistemology.* New York: Harcourt, Brace, 1965.

Pasch, Alan. *Experience and the Analytic.* Chicago: University of Chicago Press, 1958.

Prichard, H. A. *Knowledge and Perception.* Oxford: Clarendon Press, 1950. Pp. 71–103.

Quinton, Anthony. "The Foundations of Knowledge," in *British Analytical Philosophy,* Bernard Williams and Alan Montefiore, eds. New York: Humanities Press, 1966.

Ryle, Gilbert. *The Concept of Mind.* New York: Barnes and Noble, 1949.

Stroll, Avrum, ed. *Epistemology: New Essays in the Theory of Knowledge.* New York: Harper and Row, 1967.

Thévenaz, Pierre. *What is Phenomenology? And Other Essays,* ed. James M. Edie, trans. James M. Edie, Charles Courtney, and Paul Brockelman. Chicago: Quadrangle, 1962.

Urban, W. H. *Beyond Realism and Idealism.* London: Allen and Unwin, 1949.

Walsh, W. H. *Reason and Experience.* Oxford: Clarendon Press, 1947.

Weigel, Gustav E., and Madden, Arthur. *Knowledge: Its Value and Limits.* Englewood Cliffs, N.J.: Prentice-Hall, 1961.

The concept of truth

Ayer, A. J. *The Concept of a Person and Other Essays.* New York: St. Martin's, 1963. Chap. 6.

Black, Max. "The Semantic Definition of Truth," in *Language and Philosophy.* Ithaca, N.Y.: Cornell University Press, 1949.

Bradley, F. H. *Appearance and Reality: A Metaphysical Essay,* 2nd ed. Oxford: Clarendon Press, 1897. Chaps. 15 and 24.

———. *Essays on Truth and Reality.* London: Oxford University Press, 1914. Chaps. 5, 7, and 8.

Brentano, Franz. *The True and The Evident,* ed. Oscar Kraus, trans. Roderick Chisholm, Ilse Politzer, and Kurt R. Fischer. New York: Humanities Press, 1966.

Dummet, Michael. "Truth," "*Proceedings of the Aristotelian Society,* 59 (1958–59).

Joachim, H. H. *The Nature of Truth*. Oxford: Clarendon Press, 1906.

Pitcher, George, ed. *Truth*. Englewood Cliffs, N.J.: Prentice-Hall, 1964.

Royce, Josiah. "The Nature of Truth," in *The Idealist Tradition*, A. C. Ewing, ed. New York: Macmillan, 1957.

Russell, Bertrand. *Philosophical Essays*. New York: Simon and Schuster, 1966. Chaps. 5, 6, and 7.

————. *The Problems of Philosophy*. London: Oxford University Press, 1912.

Sellars, Wilfred. "Truth and Correspondence," *Journal of Philosophy*, 59 (1962).

Strawson, P. F. "Truth," *Proceedings of the Aristotelian Society*, Supplementary vol. 24 (1950).

Warnock, G. J. "Truth and Correspondence," in *Knowledge and Experience*, C. D. Rollins, ed. Pittsburgh: University of Pittsburgh Press, 1966.

Woozley, A. D. *Theory of Knowledge*. New York: Barnes and Noble, 1966. Chaps. 6 and 7.

The problem of induction

Ambrose, Alice. "The Problem of Justifying Inductive Inference," *Journal of Philosophy*, vol. 44, no. 10 (May 8, 1947).

Barker, Stephen F. *Induction and Hypothesis*. Ithaca, N.Y.: Cornell University Press, 1957. Chaps. 8 and 9.

Black, Max. *Language and Philosophy*. Ithaca, N.Y.: Cornell University Press, 1949. Chap. 3.

————. *Models and Metaphors*. Ithaca, N.Y.: Cornell University Press, 1962. Chaps. 11 and 12.

————. *Problems of Analysis*. Ithaca, N.Y.: Cornell University Press, 1954. Part 3.

Braithwaite, R. B. *Scientific Explanation*. Cambridge: Cambridge University Press, 1953. Chap. 8.

Foster, Marguerite H., and Martin, Michael L., eds. *Probability, Confirmation, and Simplicity*. New York: Odyssey Press, 1966. Part 4.

Katz, Jerrold J. *The Problem of Induction and Its Solution*. Chicago: University of Chicago Press, 1962.

Keynes, J. M. *A Treatise on Probability*. London: Macmillan, 1921. Part 3.

Kneale, W. *Probability and Induction*. Oxford: Clarendon Press, 1949.

Madden, Edward H., ed. *The Structure of Scientific Thought*. Boston: Houghton Mifflin, 1960. Part 6.

Russell, Bertrand. *Human Knowledge: Its Scope and Limits*. New York: Simon and Schuster, 1948. Part 5.

Salmon, Wesley C. *The Foundations of Scientific Inference*. Pittsburgh: University of Pittsburgh Press, 1967.

Skyrms, Brian. *Choice and Chance: An Introduction to Inductive Logic*. Belmont, Cal.: Dickenson, 1966. Chap. 2.

The theory of meaning

Alston, William P. *The Philosophy of Language*. Englewood Cliffs, N.J.: Prentice-Hall, 1964.

Ayer, A. J., ed. *Logical Positivism*. New York: Free Press, 1959.

Blanshard, Brand. *Reason and Analysis*. La Salle, Ill.: Open Court, 1962.

Caton, Charles E., ed. *Philosophy and Ordinary Language*. Urbana, Ill.: University of Illinois Press, 1963.

Chappell, V. C., ed. *Ordinary Language*. Englewood Cliffs, N.J.: Prentice-Hall, 1964.

Feiblemann, J. K. *Inside the Great Mirror: A Critical Examination of Russell, Wittgenstein, and Their Followers*. The Hague: Martinus Nijhoff, 1958.

Feigl, Herbert, and Sellars, Wilfred, eds. *Readings in Philosophical Analysis*. New York: Appleton-Century-Crofts, 1949. Parts 1 and 2.

Gellner, Ernest A. *Words and Things: A Critical Account of Linguistic Philosophy and a Study of Ideology*. Boston: Beacon, 1960.

Hempel, C. G. "The Concept of Cognitive Significance: A Reconsideration," *Proceedings of the American Academy of Arts and Sciences*, 80 (1951).

Katz, Jerrold J. *The Philosophy of Language*. New York: Harper and Row, 1966.

Lewis, C. I. *Analysis of Knowledge and Valuation*. La Salle, Ill.: Open Court, 1946. Chaps. 3, 4, and 6.

Lewis, H. D., ed. *Clarity is Not Enough: Essays in Criticism of Linguistic Philosophy.* New York: Humanities Press, 1963.

Price, H. H. *Thinking and Experience*. London: Hutchinson, 1953.

Roty, Richard, ed. *The Linguistic Turn*. Chicago: University of Chicago Press, 1967.

Urmson, J. O. *Philosophical Analysis: Its Development Between the Two World Wars*. Oxford: Clarendon Press, 1956.

Waismann, F. *The Principles of Linguistic Philosophy*. London: Macmillan, 1965.

Wittgenstein, Ludwig. *Philosophical Investigations,* trans. G. E. M. Anscombe. New York: Macmillan, 1953.

———. *Tractatus Logico-Philosophicus,* trans. D. F. Pears and B. F. McGuinness. London: Routledge, 1961.

part VII what is philosophy?

INTRODUCTION

Throughout the past twenty-five centuries, philosophers of the Western world have given a variety of answers to the question "What is philosophy?" Yet none of these answers has gained universal acceptance; philosophers still disagree. This disagreement is due to the fact that each definition of philosophy has its foundation in the general philosophical position of its author. And, no agreement has been reached concerning which philosophical position is correct. In other words, when one asks a question concerning the nature or function of philosophy, he is asking a philosophical question; in answering such a question, he actually philosophizes and takes a philosophical position.

Although it is difficult to formally define philosophy, those who read and reflect upon the ideas of philosophers naturally develop a conception of what philosophy is. Upon the assumption that the question "What is philosophy" can best be dealt with by those who have already been exposed to philosophical writings, our consideration of this question has been placed last.

One way to approach the question "What is philosophy?" is through the etymology of the word. "Philosophy" is derived from two Greek words—*philein,* the verb for love, and *sophia,* the noun for wisdom. Hence "philosophy" means "love of wisdom." For the Greeks, then, the philosopher was a seeker of wisdom. And wisdom included both organized knowledge of the world—which we now call science—and knowledge of how men ought to live.

Not everyone, however, would accept the etymological definition as a satisfactory definition of philosophy. One obvious reason for this is that many aspects of the study of the universe that were included in the Greek notion of wisdom—such as astronomy, physics, and zoology—are no longer considered branches of philosophy. Therefore, it may be helpful to observe which of the interests of ancient philosophers have been most consistently shared by their modern counterparts.

Most philosophers have been primarily concerned with a basic set of questions about man, his nature, his values, and his place in the cosmos. Three of the most basic questions, as we have seen in earlier parts of this book, are "What is real?" "What is knowledge?" and "What is good?" But before viewing philosophy as the discipline that seeks to answer these basic questions, one should note the following provisos. First, the above list of questions is incomplete. Many problems, some general and some specific, have not been mentioned. Secondly, a particular philosophical problem cannot be considered in isolation. An answer to any of the basic questions has consequences for the rest. Philosophy is like a mobile in that an adjustment to any part causes an adjustment throughout the entire structure.

In answering the basic questions, most philosophers have tried to give men a comprehensive picture of the universe. Plato, Aristotle, Aquinas, Descartes, Berkeley, Kant, and Blanshard are among the philosophers who have sought this goal. The philosophies of such men are generally arrived at by reflecting upon and synthesizing all available knowledge, including that derived from common sense, the sciences, and the insights of aesthetic and religious experiences. The result of such reflection and speculation is usually a general scheme that can be used by men as their philosophy of life. It answers their basic questions and establishes goals that they should seek to realize, both individually and collectively. In other words, it provides them with an intellectual basis that can be used in making judgments about the great issues of life.

"Speculative philosophy" is the label usually applied to the efforts of those philosophers who seek to provide comprehensive answers to the basic questions of men. René Descartes is an excellent example of a speculative philosopher. He, like the majority of philosophers in the Western tradition, views philosophy as the quest for wisdom. Descartes follows the Greeks by defining wisdom as "not only . . . prudence in affairs, but also a perfect knowledge of all things that man can know. . . ." Descartes first seeks a self-evident principle from which all other knowledge can be deduced. The principle that he selects is "cogito ergo sum," which is usually translated as "I think, therefore I am." Beginning with this basic principle, Descartes proceeds to deduce the existence of God and the world. Descartes believed that by a similar deduction, he and his successors could deduce knowledge in all areas, including the realms of science and value. Upon completion of the required deductions, man would have a comprehensive view of the universe.

Many philosophers have questioned the traditional concept of philosophy because they seek a discipline that is scientifically respectable. And, clearly, some of the goals and methods of traditional speculative philosophy are beyond the scope of contemporary science. These critics of speculative philosophy point out that a comprehensive world view is, at best, very difficult to produce and that, to date, none of the suggested philosophies has attained universal acceptance.

Along with such criticism, there has developed a new concept of philosophy, which is usually referred to as critical philosophy. In contrast to speculative philosophy, critical philosophy is primarily concerned with the meanings of concepts and the evaluation of beliefs. The critical philosopher studies and analyzes our concepts in order to provide the clearest possible understanding of their meaning. Moritz Schlick, one of the most influential critical philosophers writes:

> Socrates' philosophy consists of what we may call the "Pursuit of Meaning." He tried to clarify thought by analyzing the meaning of our expressions and the real sense of our propositions. Here then we find a definite contrast between this philosophic method, which has for its object the discovery of meaning, and the method of the sciences, which have for their object the discovery of truth. . . . Science should be defined as the "pursuit of truth" and

philosophy as the "pursuit of meaning." Socrates has set the example of the true philosophic method for all times.[1]

In evaluating our beliefs, the critical philosopher examines the assumptions on which they rest, and the methods by which they were derived. Among the beliefs investigated are those of the individual, those of common sense, and those of the sciences.

A. J. Ayer presents the classic statement of the critical philosopher's position. In sharp contrast to Descartes, Ayer maintains that it is not the business of the philosopher to posit first principles and then deduce from them a picture of reality. Such theories, he argues, cannot be verified. Rather, the philosopher's role is entirely critical, and more specifically, entirely analytic. The philosopher analyzes the meaning of the words in our language, while the scientist deals with empirical facts. Ayer maintains that every philosophical problem can either (1) be resolved by the analysis of language; (2) be seen to deal with scientific facts, and, hence to be non-philosophical; or (3) be seen to be meaningless in that it is open to neither philosophic nor scientific approaches.

John Wisdom is generally considered an analyst and as such he, too, stresses the importance of language analysis in solving philosophical problems. However, he also argues that linguistic treatment by itself is often inadequate to solve a philosophical dispute. Its inadequacy stems from the fact that there is also a psychological element —"an echo from the heart"—that must be considered.

Like Ayer and Wisdom, Alfred North Whitehead thinks in terms of critical and speculative philosophy. However, unlike them, he stresses the importance of "speculative philosophy," which he defines as "the endeavor to frame a coherent, logical, necessary system of general ideas in terms of which every element of our experience can be interpreted." [2] In seeking his goal, Whitehead presents "working hypotheses" that reflect the total of human experience. By thinking of speculative philosophy as a system of hypotheses, Whitehead produces what could be called a "scientific speculative philosophy," which avoids the dogmatic certainty claimed by such philosophers as Descartes.

Unlike those who advocate either the analysis of language or speculative theories of the cosmos, Karl Jaspers presents an existential view of philosophy. He conceives of philosophy as the path by which an individual can become a total human being. Communication plays a particularly important role, since it is only by communication with other men concerning the human situation—with such essential elements as love, death, and anxiety—that one can transcend the level of empirical thought. Like the critical philosophers, Jaspers sees philosophy as a method, rather than as a set of doctrines. But for him, the doctrines of science, theology and traditional philosophy are all veils that are likely to hide from man his own true nature.

John Dewey, like the critical philosophers and the existentialists, is critical of the traditional conception of philosophy. It is to undermine this traditional conception that he presents his view of the social and emotional foundations of philosophy. Dewey hopes that upon recognizing philosophy's origins and its true nature, philosophers will proceed to illuminate and resolve the social and moral conflicts of their day. In presenting his pragmatic conception of philosophy, Dewey argues that philosophy should be useful to men.

[1] *Publications in Philosophy*, The College of the Pacific, Stockton, California, 1932.
[2] *Adventures of Ideas* (New York: Macmillan Co., 1933), p. 285.

Finally, Bertrand Russell, in the course of asserting the value of philosophy, provides us with an insight into his conception of its nature. He observes that although philosophy seeks knowledge, irrefutable answers to the basic philosophic questions have not been found and are not likely to be found. It is philosophy's effect on the lives of those who study it, rather than any knowledge that it yields, that makes philosophy valuable. Philosophy shows an individual a variety of answers to each important question and by so doing frees him from the narrow limits of common sense and traditional beliefs. The result is that the individual becomes less selfish and less dogmatic; he becomes more open-minded and more objective. Thus, while Dewey sees philosophy contributing to our society by resolving its problems, Russell sees philosophy making its contribution to our culture by changing individuals, and by making their minds great.

Although each of the philosophers mentioned above has his own conception of the nature and function of philosophy, most, but not all, philosophers agree on the following interrelated points. 1) Philosophy is a rational enterprise. The philosopher depends on reason, either as the source of knowledge or as the tool for ordering human experience. The philosopher does not choose his philosophy subjectively; he chooses the position that he thinks is founded upon the soundest rational arguments. 2) Philosophy, in contrast to most disciplines, has no particular subject matter of its own. It deals with virtually everything, in one way or another. Hence, in his search, the philosopher freely crosses the boundaries of various disciplines. 3) Philosophy is an unusually persistent search. The philosopher does not stop his inquiry where others would; he pushes beyond. The critical philosopher carries his analysis of the meaning of our concepts beyond the point at which most men are satisfied. For example, we frequently use the word "cause" and think we know what it means; but the philosopher seeks its precise meaning. In like manner, the critical philosopher carefully evaluates the beliefs that are ordinarily assumed to be true. The traditional philosopher presses beyond ordinary thought in his attempt to synthesize all knowledge into one consistent picture of the universe. 4) Philosophy is a continuing activity. We can undoubtedly learn much from the great philosophers of the past and present; but the philosopher's task is never completed. He continues to analyze concepts and evaluate beliefs. He continues to provide contemporary answers to the perennial questions of philosophy. R. G. Collingwood's analogy of the ship is appropriate. He writes: "If the philosopher is no pilot, neither is he a mere spectator, watching the ship from his study window. He is one of the crew. . . ." [3] The philosopher today is no pilot; he cannot give us certain guidance because he does not have demonstrable answers to the problems that confront us. Neither is the philosopher a passive spectator, who merely stands idle while civilization progresses. Rather, the philosopher continues to make his contribution to the content and direction of our culture.

3 "The Present Need of a Philosophy," *Philosophy* 9 (1934): 263.

PHILOSOPHY—QUEST FOR WISDOM

rené descartes

SIR,

The version of my Principles which you have taken the trouble to make is so polished and well-finished that it causes me to hope that the work may be read by more persons in French than in Latin, and that it will be better understood. My only apprehension is that the title may repel certain people who have not been nourished upon letters, or else who hold philosophy in evil esteem, because that which has been taught them has not satisfied them; and this makes me think that it would be a good thing to add a preface which would expound the subject matter of the book, the design I had in writing it, and the use to be derived from it. But although it should be my business to write this preface because I ought to know these things better than anyone else, I can on my own account promise nothing but a summary of the principal points which seem to me as though they ought to be treated of in it; and I leave it to your discretion to communicate to the public whatever you deem desirable.

I should have first of all desired to explain in it what philosophy is, beginning with the most ordinary matters, such as that this word "philosophy" signifies the study of wisdom, and that by wisdom we not only understand prudence in affairs, but also a perfect knowledge of all things that man can know, both for the conduct of his life and for the conservation of his health and the invention of all the arts; and that in order that this knowledge should subserve these ends, it is essential that it should be derived from first causes, so that in order to study to acquire it (which is properly termed philosophizing), we must begin with the investigation of these first causes, i.e., of the Principles. It is also necessary that these Principles should have two conditions attached to them; first of all they should be so clear and evident that the mind of man cannot doubt their truth when it attentively applies itself to consider them: in the second place it is on them that the knowledge of other things depends,

This selection consists of all but one paragraph of Descartes' letter to the Abbé Claude Picot, the translator of Descartes' *Principles of Philosophy* from the original Latin into French. Reprinted from *The Philosophical Works of Descartes*, trans. Elizabeth S. Haldane and G. R. T. Ross (New York: Dover Publications, Inc., 1955), I: 203–215, by permission of the publisher and the Cambridge University Press.

so that the Principles can be known without these last, but the other things cannot reciprocally be known without the Principles. We must accordingly try to so deduce from these Principles the knowledge of the things that depend on them, that there shall be nothing in the whole series of the deductions made from them which shall not be perfectly manifest. It is really only God alone who has Perfect Wisdom, that is to say, who has a complete knowledge of the truth of all things; but it may be said that men have more wisdom or less according as they have more or less knowledge of the most important truths. And I think that in this there is nothing regarding which all the learned do not concur.

I should in the next place have caused the utility of this philosophy to be considered, and shown that since it extends over the whole range of human knowledge, we are entitled to hold that it alone is what distinguishes us from savages and barbarians, and that the civilization and refinement of each nation is proportionate to the superiority of its philosophy. In this way a state can have no greater good than the possession of true philosophy. And, in addition, it would have been pointed out that as regards the individual, it is not only useful to live with those who apply themselves to this study, but it is incomparably better to set about it oneself; just as it is doubtless much better to avail oneself of one's own eyes for the direction of one's steps, and by the same means to enjoy the beauty of color and light, than to close these eyes and trust to the guidance of another. But this last is better than to hold them closed, and not have any but oneself to act as guide. Speaking accurately, living without philosophy is just having the eyes closed without trying to open them; and the pleasure of seeing everything that is revealed to our sight, is not comparable to the satisfaction which is given by the knowledge of those things which are opened up to us by philosophy. And finally, this study is more necessary for the regulation of our manners and for our conduct in life, than is the use of our eyes in the guidance of our steps. The brute beasts who have only their bodies to preserve, devote their constant attention to the search for the sources of their nourishment; but men, in whom the principal part is the mind, ought to make their principal care the search after wisdom, which is its true source of nutriment. And I am likewise able to assure myself that there are many who would not fail to make the search if they had any hope of success in so doing, and knew to what an extent they were capable of it. There does not exist the soul so ignoble, so firmly attached to objects of sense, that it does not sometimes turn away from these to aspire after some other greater good, even although it is frequently ignorant as to wherein that good consists. Those most favored by fortune, those who have abundance of health, honor, and riches, are not exempt from this desire any more than others; on the contrary, I am persuaded that it is those very people who yearn most ardently after another good more perfect and supreme than all those that they possess already. And this sovereign good, considered by the natural reason without the light of faith, is none other than the knowledge of the truth through its first causes, i.e., the wisdom whose study is philosophy. And because all these things are absolutely true, it would not be difficult to persuade men of them, were they well argued and expressed.

But since we are prevented from believing these doctrines by experience, which shows us that those who profess to be philosophers are frequently less wise and reasonable than others who have never applied themselves to the study, I should here have succinctly explained in what all the knowledge we now possess consists, and to what degrees of wisdom we have attained. The first of these contains only notions which are of themselves so clear that they may be acquired without any meditation. The second comprehends all that which the experience of the senses shows us. The third, what the conversation of other men teaches us. And for the fourth we may add to this the reading, not of all books, but especially of those which have been written by persons who are capable of conveying good instruction to us, for this is a species of conversation held with their authors. And it seems to me that all the wisdom that we usually possess is acquired by these four means only; for I do not place divine revelation in the same rank, because it does not lead us by degrees, but raises us at a stroke to an infallible belief. There have indeed from all time been great men who have tried to find a fifth road by which to arrive at wisdom, incomparably more elevated and assured than these other four. That road is to seek out the first causes and the true principles from which reasons may be deduced for all that which we are capable of knowing; and it is those who have made this their special work who have been called philosophers. At the same time I do not know that up to the present day there have been any in whose case this plan has succeeded. The first and principal whose writings we possess, are Plato and Aristotle, between whom the only difference that exists is that the former, following the steps of his master Socrates, ingenuously confessed that he had never yet been able to discover anything for certain, and was content to set down the things that seemed to him to be probable, for this end adopting certain principles whereby he tried to account for other things. Aristotle, on the other hand, had less candor, and although he had been Plato's disciple for twenty years, and possessed no other principles than his master's, he entirely changed the method of stating them, and proposed them as true and certain although there was no appearance of his having ever held them to be such. But these two men had great minds and much wisdom acquired by the four methods mentioned before, and this gave them great authority, so that those who succeeded them were more bent on following their opinions than in forming better ones of their own. The main dispute between their disciples was as to whether every thing should be doubted, or whether there were some things which were certain. And this carried them, both on the one side and on the other, into extravagant errors; for certain of those who argued for doubt, extended it even to the actions of life, so that they omitted to exercise ordinary prudence in its conduct; and those who supported the doctrine of certainty, supposing it to depend on the senses, trusted to them entirely. To such a point was this carried that it is said that Epicurus ventured to affirm, contrary to all the reasonings of the astronomers, that the sun is no larger than it appears. A fault which may be observed in most disputes is that since the truth is a mean between the two opinions which are maintained, each disputant removes himself so much the farther from it the greater his desire to contradict. But the error of those who tended too much to the side of doubt, was not followed for long, and that of the others has been in some degree corrected by the recognition of the fact that in many instances the senses deceive us. At the same time I do not know that it has been entirely removed by showing that certainty is not in the senses, but only in the understanding, when it has evident perceptions; and that while we only possess the knowledge which is acquired by the first four degrees of wisdom, we should not doubt those things that appear to be true in what concerns the conduct of life, while yet we should not hold them to be so certain that we may not change our minds regarding them when obliged to do so by the evidence of reason. From lack of having known this truth, or else, if there be those who have known it, from neglecting it, the greater part of those in later times who aspired to be philosophers, have blindly followed Aristotle, so that frequently they have corrupted the sense of his writings, attributing diverse opinions to him which he would not recognize as his, were he to return to this world; and those who have not followed him (amongst whom many of the best minds are to be found) have yet been imbued with his teaching in their youth, for it forms the sole teaching in the Schools; and these minds were so much occupied with this, that they were incapable of attaining to a knowledge of true Principles. And although I respect them all and would never wish to incur the odium of denouncing them, I can give a proof of my assertion which I do not think any one of them will gainsay, and this is that all have taken for granted some particular principle which they have not perfectly understood. For example I have known none of them who did not presuppose weight in terrestrial bodies, but although experiment proves to us very clearly that the bodies we call weighty descend towards the centre of the earth, we do not for all that know the nature of what is called gravity, that is, the reason or principle which causes bodies to descend thus, and we must derive it from elsewhere. The same may be said of the vacuum and of atoms, of heat and cold, of dryness and damp, and of salt, sulphur, mercury, and all other similar things which have been adopted as their principles by some. And none of the conclusions deduced from a principle which is not evident can be evident even though they are deduced from them in a manner which is evident and valid, and from this it follows that none of the reasonings which they rested on principles such as these could give them any certain knowledge of anything, nor in consequence cause them to advance one step in the search after wisdom. And if they have discovered any truth this has only come to pass by means of certain of the four methods above mentioned. All the same I do not desire one whit to detract from the honor to which each of them may aspire, I am only obliged to say for the consolation of those who have never studied, that just as in traveling while we turn our backs on the place to which we desire to go, the longer and quicker we walk the further we recede from the place we are making for, so that though we are afterwards put back into the right way, we cannot arrive at our destination as soon as if we had not walked in the wrong direction before; so when our principles are bad, the more we cultivate them and the more carefully we apply ourselves to derive from them various consequences, thinking that we are philosophizing very well, the further we are moving from the knowledge of the truth and from wisdom. From this we must conclude that those who have learned least about all that which has hitherto been named philosophy, are the most capable of apprehending the truth.

After having made these matters very clear, I should have desired to set forth the reasons which serve to prove that the true principles by which we may arrive at that highest point of wisdom in which the sovereign good of the life of man consists, are those which I have put forward in this book. And only two are requisite for that, the first that the principles must be very clear, and the second that from them we may deduce all other things; for there are but these two conditions that are essential in true principles. And I can easily prove that they are very clear, first of all by the manner in which I have found them, i.e., by rejecting all those propositions in respect to which I could find the slightest occasion for doubt; for it is certain that those which could not be rejected in this way when application was made to their consideration, are the most evident and clear of all that the human mind can know. Thus in considering that he who would doubt all things cannot yet doubt that he exists while he doubts, and that what reasons so in being unable to doubt of itself and yet doubting all else, is not what we call our body but what we call our soul or thought, I have taken the being or existence of this thought as the first principle from which I have very clearly deduced the following: viz., that there is a God who is the author of all that is in the world, or who, being the source of all truth, has not created in us an understanding liable to be deceived in the judgments that it forms on matters of which it has a very and distinct perception. These comprise the whole of the principles of which I make use respecting immaterial or metaphysical things, from which I very clearly deduce those of corporeal or physical things, to wit, that there are bodies extended in length, breadth and depth, which have diverse figures and move in diverse ways. These, in sum, are all the principles from which I deduce the truth of other things. The other reason which proves the clearness of the principles is that they have been known from all time, and even received as true and indubitable by all men, with the sole exception of the existence of God, which has been placed in doubt by certain people because they have ascribed too much to the perceptions of the senses, and because God can neither be seen nor touched. But although all the truths which I place in my Principles have been known from all time and by all men, nevertheless there has never yet been any one, as far as I know, who has recognized them as the principles of philosophy, that is to say, as principles from which may be derived a knowledge of all things that are in the world: that is why it here remains to me to prove that they are such. And it appears to me that I cannot do better than cause this to be established by experience, that is to say, by inviting my readers to peruse this book. For although I have not treated of everything, and although this is impossible, I consider that I have so explained all those matters with which I have had occasion to deal, that those who read them with attention will have reason to persuade themselves that there is no need to seek other principles than those I have brought forward, in order to arrive at all the most exalted knowledge of which the human mind is capable. And this will more especially be the case if, after having read my works, they take the trouble to consider how many diverse questions are therein explained, and if, perusing also the works of others, they observe how few are the probable reasons that can be given to explain the same questions by principles differing from mine. And in order that they may undertake this with greater ease, I should have been able to say to them that those who are imbued with my doctrines have much less trouble in understanding the works of others and in recognizing their true value than those who are not so imbued; and this is diametrically opposite to what I have just said of those who commenced with the ancient philosophy, i.e., that the more they have studied it the less are they fitted rightly to apprehend the truth.

I should also have here added a word of advice as regards the method of reading this book, which is that I should desire that it may first of all be run through in its entirety like a novel, without forcing the attention unduly upon it, or stopping at difficulties which may be met with, so that a general knowledge may be arrived at of the matters of which I have treated; and after that, if it is found that they deserve to be examined more carefully, and if the reader has the curiosity to inquire about their causes, it may be read a second time in order to notice the sequence of my reasoning. But though the reader cannot follow the argument adequately throughout, or understand the whole of its bearing, he must not therefore immediately cast it aside. It is only necessary to mark with a pen the places where difficulty is found, and continue to read without interruption to the end. Then if the book is taken up for a third time, I venture to say that he will discover the solution of the greater part of the difficulties which have formerly been marked, and that if certain still remain, their solution will be discovered on a further perusal.

I have noticed on examining the nature of many different minds, that there are almost none of them so dull or slow of understanding that they are incapable of high feelings, and even of attaining to all the profoundest sciences, were they trained in the right way. And that may also be proved by reason. For since the principles are clear and nothing must be deduced from them but by very evident reasoning, we have all sufficient intelligence to comprehend the conclusions that depend on them. But in addition to the drawbacks of prejudice from which no one is entirely exempt, although it is those who have studied the false sciences most deeply whom they harm the most, it almost always happens that those of moderate intelligence neglect to study because they do not consider themselves capable of doing so, and that the others who are more eager, hasten on too quickly. And from this it comes that they often accept principles which are not really evident, and from them derive consequences which are uncertain. That is why I desire to assure those who too greatly disparage their powers, that there is nothing in my writings which they are not capable of completely understanding if they take the trouble to examine them; while I also warn the others that even the most superior understanding will require much time and attention to comprehend all the matters which I have designed to embrace in them.

Following on this, and in order to make very clear the end I have had in view in publishing them, I would like to explain here what seems to me to be the order which should be followed in our self-instruction. To begin with, a man who as yet has merely the common and imperfect knowledge which may be acquired by the four methods before mentioned, should above all try to form for himself a code of morals sufficient to regulate the actions of his life, because this does not brook any delay, and we ought above all other things to endeavor to live well. After that he should likewise study logic—not that of the Schools, because it properly speaking is only a dialectic which teaches how to make the things that we know understood by others, or even to repeat, without forming any judgment on them, many words respecting those that we do not know, thus corrupting rather than increasing good sense—but the logic that teaches us how best to direct our reason in order to discover those truths of which we are ignorant. And since this is very dependent on custom, it is good for him to practice the rules for a long time on easy and simple questions such as those of mathematics. Then when he has acquired a certain skill in discovering the truth in these questions he should begin seriously to apply himself to the true philosophy, the first part of which is metaphysics, which contains the principles of knowledge, amongst which is the explanation of the principal attributes of God, of the immateriality of our souls, and of all the clear and simple notions which are in us. The second is physics in which, after having found the true principles of material things, we examine generally how the whole universe is composed, and then in particular what is the nature of this earth and of all the bodies which are most commonly found in connection with it, like air, water, and fire, the loadstone and other minerals. It is thereafter necessary to inquire individually into the nature of plants, animals, and above all of man, so that we may afterwards be able to discover the other sciences which are useful to man. Thus philosophy as a whole is like a tree whose roots are metaphysics, whose trunk is physics, and whose branches, which issue from this trunk, are all the other sciences. These reduce themselves to three principal ones, viz., medicine, mechanics, and morals—I mean the highest and most perfect moral science which, presupposing a complete knowledge of the other sciences, is the last degree of wisdom.

But just as it is not from the roots or the trunk of the trees that one culls the fruit, but only from the extremities of their branches, so the main use of philosophy is dependent on those of its parts that we cannot learn till the end. Although, however, I am ignorant of almost all of these, the zeal which I have always shown in trying to render service to the public is the reason of my causing to be printed ten or twelve years ago certain essays on things which I appeared to have learned. The first part of these essays was a *Discourse on the Method of rightly conducting one's Reason and seeking Truth in the Sciences,* where I summarized the principal rules of logic and of an imperfect system of morals which may be followed provisionally while we still know none better. The other parts were three Treatises: the first *Of the Dioptric;* the second *Of Meteors,* and the last *Of Geometry.* In the *Dioptric* I intended it to be shown that we could make sufficient progress in philosophy to attain by its means a knowledge of those arts which are useful to life, because the invention of the telescope, which I there described, is one of the most difficult ever attempted. In the treatise on *Meteors* I endeavored to make clear the difference which exists between the philosophy which I cultivate and that taught in the Schools, where the same subject is usually treated. Finally in the *Geometry* I professed to show that I had found certain matters of which men were previously ignorant, and thus to afford occasion for believing that many more may yet be discovered, in order by this means to incite all men to the search after truth. From this time onwards, foreseeing the difficulty which would be felt by many in understanding the foundations of metaphysics, I tried to explain the principal points in a book of *Meditations* which is not very large, but whose volume has been increased, and whose matter has been much illuminated, by the Objections which many very learned persons have sent me in their regard, and by the replies which I have made to them. Then, finally, when it appeared to me that these preceding treatises had sufficiently prepared the mind of readers to accept the *Principles of Philosophy,* I likewise published them, and I divided the book containing them into four parts, the first of which contains the principles of knowledge, which is what may be called the First Philosophy or Metaphysics. That is why it is better to read beforehand the Meditations which I have written on the same subject, in order that it may be properly understood. The other three parts contain all that is most general in Physics, i.e., and explanation of the first laws or principles of nature, the manner in which the heavens and fixed stars, the planets, the comets, and generally all the universe is composed. Then the nature of this earth, and of the air, water, fire, and the loadstone, is dealt with more particularly, for these are the bodies which may most commonly be found everywhere about it, as also all the qualities observed in these bodies, such as light, heat, weight, and such like. By this means I believe myself to have commenced to expound the whole of philosophy in its order without having omitted anything which ought to precede the last of which I have written. But in order to carry this plan to a conclusion, I should afterwards in the same way explain in further detail the nature of each of the other bodies which are on the earth, i.e., minerals, plants, animals, and above all man; then finally treat exactly of medicine, morals, and mechanics. All this I should have to do in order to give to mankind a body of philosophy which is complete; and I do not feel myself to be so old, I do not so much despair of my strength, I do not find myself so far removed from a knowledge of what remains, that I should not venture to endeavor to achieve this design, were I possessed of the means of making all the experiments necessary to me in order to support and justify my reasoning. But seeing that for this end great expense is requisite to which the resources of an individual like myself could not attain were he not given assistance by the public, and not seeing that I can expect that aid, I conceive it to be henceforward my duty to content myself with studying for my own private instruction, trusting that posterity will pardon me if I fail henceforward to work for its good.

In order, however, to show in how far I believe myself to have already been of service to my fellowmen, I shall here state what are the fruits which I believe may be culled from my Principles. The first is the satisfaction which we must derive from discovering in them certain truths of which we have hitherto been ignorant; for although frequently the truth does not so much affect our imagination as does falsity and pretence, because it seems less wonderful and more simple, yet the satisfaction which it brings is always more lasting and solid. The second fruit is that in studying these Principles, we shall little by little accustom ourselves to judge better of all things with which we come in contact, and thus to become wiser. In this regard they will have an effect contrary to that of the ordinary philosophy, for it may easily be observed in those who are known as pedants, that it renders them less capable of reasoning than they would have been had they never learned it at all. The third fruit is that the truths which they contain, being perfectly clear and certain, will remove all subjects of dispute, and thus dispose men's minds to gentleness and concord. On the other hand the controversies of the Schools, by insensibly making those who practice themselves in them more captious and self-sufficient, are possibly the chief causes of the heresies and dissensions which now exercise the world. The last and principal fruit of these Principles is that by cultivating them we may discover many truths which I have not expounded, and thus, passing little by little from one to the other, acquire in time a perfect knowledge of the whole of philosophy and attain to the highest degree of wisdom. For in all the arts we perceive how, although at the first they are rude and imperfect, yet because they contain something that is true and whose effect is revealed by experience, they come little by little to perfection through practice. So, when we have true principles in philosophy we cannot fail, by following them, occasionally to meet with other truths; and there is no way in which we can better prove the falsity of those of Aristotle, than by pointing out that no progress has been attained by their means in all the centuries in which they have been followed.

·   ·   ·

I well know likewise that many centuries may pass until all the truths which may be deduced from these principles are so deduced, because the greater part of those which remain to be discoverd depend on certain particular experiments which chance circumstances will never bring about, but which should be investigated with care and expense by the most intelligent of men, and because it will be unlikely that the same people who have the capacity of availing themselves of them will have the means of contriving them, and also because the majority of the best minds have formed such a bad conception of philosophy as a whole, owing to the defects which they have observed in that which has hitherto been in vogue, that they will not be able to discover a better. But finally, if the difference which is observable between these principles and those of all other men, and the great array of truths which may be deduced from them, causes them to perceive how important it is to continue in the search after these truths, and to observe to what a degree of wisdom, to what perfection of life, to what happiness they may lead us, I am convinced that no one will be found who will not attempt to occupy himself with so profitable a study, or at least will not favor and endeavor to assist with all his might those who employ themselves in this way with success. I trust that posterity may behold its happy issue.

THE FUNCTION OF PHILOSOPHY

a. j. ayer

Among the superstitions from which we are freed by the abandonment of metaphysics is the view that it is the business of the philosopher to construct a deductive system. In rejecting this view we are not, of course, suggesting that the philosopher can dispense with deductive reasoning. We are simply contesting his right to posit certain first principles, and then offer them with their consequences as a complete picture of reality. To discredit this procedure, one has only to show that there can be no first principles of the kind it requires.

As it is the function of these first principles to provide a certain basis for our knowledge, it is clear that they are not to be found among the so-called laws of nature. For we shall see that the "laws of nature," if they are not mere definitions, are simply hypotheses which may be confuted by experience. And, indeed, it has never been the practice of the system-builders in philosophy to choose inductive generalizations for their premises. Rightly regarding such generalizations as being merely probable, they subordinate them to principles which they believe to be logically certain.

This is illustrated most clearly in the system of Descartes. It is commonly said that Descartes attempted to derive all human knowledge from premises whose truth was intuitively certain: but this interpretation puts an undue stress on the element of psychology in his system. I think he realized well enough that a mere appeal to intuition was insufficient for his purpose, since men are not all equally credulous, and that what he was really trying to do was to base all our knowledge on propositions which it would be self-contradictory to deny. He thought he had found such a proposition in *"cogito,"* which must not here be understood in its ordinary sense of "I think," but rather as meaning "there is a thought now." In fact he was wrong, because *"non cogito"* would be self-contradictory only if it negated itself: and this no significant proposition can do. But even if it were true that such a proposition as "there is a thought now" was logically certain, it still would not serve Descartes' purpose. For if *"cogito"* is taken in this sense, his initial principle, *"cogito ergo sum,"* is false. "I exist" does not follow from "there is a thought now." The fact that a thought occurs at a given moment does not entail that any other thought has occurred at any other

From A. J. Ayer, *Language, Truth and Logic* (London: Victor Gollancz Ltd., 1960), Chap. II, pp. 46–59. Reprinted by permission of the publisher and Dover Publications, Inc.

moment, still less that there has occurred a series of thoughts sufficient to constitute a single self. As Hume conclusively showed, no one event intrinsically points to any other. We infer the existence of events which we are not actually observing, with the help of general principles. But these principles must be obtained inductively. By mere deduction from what is immediately given we cannot advance a single step beyond. And, consequently, any attempt to base a deductive system on propositions which describe what is immediately given is bound to be a failure.

The only other course open to one who wished to deduce all our knowledge from "first principles," without indulging in metaphysics, would be to take for his premises a set of *a priori* truths. But, as we have already mentioned, and shall later show, an *a priori* truth is a tautology. And from a set of tautologies, taken by themselves, only further tautologies can be validly deduced. But it would be absurd to put forward a system of tautologies as constituting the whole truth about the universe. And thus we may conclude that it is not possible to deduce all our knowledge from "first principles"; so that those who hold that it is the function of philosophy to carry out such a deduction are denying its claim to be a genuine branch of knowledge.

The belief that it is the business of the philosopher to search for first principles is bound up with the familiar conception of philosophy as the study of reality as a whole. And this conception is one which it is difficult to criticize, because it is so vague. If it is taken to imply, as it sometimes is, that the philosopher somehow projects himself outside the world, and takes a bird's-eye view of it, then it is plainly a metaphysical conception. And it is also metaphysical to assert, as some do, that "reality as a whole" is somehow generically different from the reality which is investigated piecemeal by the special sciences. But if the assertion that philosophy studies reality as a whole is understood to imply merely that the philosopher is equally concerned with the content of every science, then we may accept it, not indeed as an adequate definition of philosophy, but as a truth about it. For we shall find, when we come to discuss the relationship of philosophy to science, that it is not, in principle, related to any one science more closely than to any other.

In saying that philosophy is concerned with each of the sciences, . . . we mean also to rule out the supposition that philosophy can be ranged alongside the existing sciences, as a special department of speculative knowledge. Those who make this supposition cherish the belief that there are some things in the world which are possible objects of speculative knowledge and yet lie beyond the scope of empirical science. But this belief is a delusion. There is no field of experience which cannot, in principle, be brought under some form of scientific law, and no type of speculative knowledge about the world which it is, in principle, beyond the power of science to give. We have already gone some way to substantiate this proposition by demolishing metaphysics; and we shall justify it to the full in the course of this book.

With this we complete the overthrow of speculative philosophy. We are now in a position to see that the function of philosophy is wholly critical. In what exactly does its critical activity consist?

One way of answering this question is to say that it is the philosopher's business to test the validity of our scientific hypotheses and everyday assumptions. But this view, though very widely held, is mistaken. If a man chooses to doubt the truth of all the propositions he ordinarily believes, it is not in the power of philosophy to reassure him. The most that philosophy can do, apart from seeing whether his beliefs are self-consistent, is to show what are the criteria which are used to determine the truth or falsehood of any given proposition: and then, when the sceptic realizes that certain observations would verify his propositions, he may also realize that he could make those observations, and so consider his original beliefs to be justified. But in such a case one cannot say that it is philosophy which justifies his beliefs. Philosophy merely shows him that experience can justify them. We may look to the philosopher to show us what we accept as constituting sufficient evidence for the truth of any given empirical proposition. But whether the evidence is forthcoming or not is in every case a purely empirical question.

·   ·   ·

It should now be sufficiently clear that if the philosopher is to uphold his claim to make a special contribution to the stock of our knowledge, he must not attempt to formulate speculative truths, or to look for first principles, or to make *a priori* judgments about the validity of our empirical beliefs. He must, in fact, confine himself to works of clarification and analysis of a sort which we shall presently describe.

In saying that the activity of philosophizing is essentially anayltic, we are not, of course, maintaining that all those who are commonly called philosophers have actually been engaged in carrying out analyses. On the contrary, we have been at pains to show that a great deal of what is commonly called philosophy is metaphysical in character. What we have been in search of, in inquiring into the function of philosophy, is a definition of philosophy which should accord to some extent with the practice of those who are commonly called philsophers, and at the same time be consistent with the common assumption that philosophy is a special branch of knowledge. It is because metaphysics fails to satisfy this second condition that we distinguish it from philosophy, in spite of the fact that it is commonly referred to as philosophy. And our justification for making this distinction is that it is necessitated by our original postulate that philosophy is a special branch of knowledge, and our demonstration that metaphysics is not.

Although this procedure is logically unassailable, it will perhaps be attacked on the ground that it is inexpedient. It will be said that the "history of philosophy" is, almost entirely, a history of metaphysics; and, consequently, that although there is no actual fallacy involved in our using the word "philosophy" in the sense in which philosophy is incompatible with metaphysics, it is dangerously misleading. For all our care in defining the term will not prevent people from confusing the activities which we call philosophical with the metaphysical activities of those whom they have been taught to regard as philosophers. And therefore it would surely be advisable for us to abandon the term "philosophy" altogether, as a name for a distinctive branch of knowledge, and invent some new description for the activity which we were minded to call the activity of philosophizing.

Our answer to this is that it is not the case that the "history of philosophy" is almost entirely a history of metaphysics. That it contains some metaphysics is undeniable. But I think it can be shown that the majority of those who are commonly supposed to have been great philosophers were primarily not metaphysicians but analysts. For example, I do not see how anyone who follows the account which we shall give of the nature of philosophical analysis and then turns to Locke's *Essay Concerning Human Understanding* can fail to conclude that it is essentially an analytic work. Locke is generally regarded as being one who, like G. E. Moore at the present time, puts forward a philosophy of common sense.[1] But he does not, any more than Moore, attempt to give an *a priori* justification of our common-sense beliefs. Rather does he appear to have seen that it was not his business as a philosopher to affirm or deny the validity of any empirical propositions, but only to analyze them. For he is content, in his own words, "to be employed as an under-laborer in clearing the ground a little, and removing some of the rubbish that lies in the way of knowledge"; and so devotes himself to the purely analytic tasks of defining knowledge, and classifying propositions, and displaying the nature of material things. And the small portion of his work which is not philosophical, in our sense, is not given over to metaphysics, but to psychology.

Nor is it fair to regard Berkeley as a metaphysician. For he did not, in fact, deny the reality of material things, as we are still too commonly told. What he denied was the adequacy of Locke's analysis of the notion of a material thing. He maintained that to say of various "ideas of sensation" that they belonged to a single material thing was not, as Locke thought, to say that they were related to a single unobservable underlying "somewhat," but rather that they stood in certain relations to one another. And in this he was right. Admittedly he made the mistake of supposing that what was immediately given in sensation was necessarily mental; and the use, by him and by Locke, of the word "idea" to denote an element in that which is sensibly given is objectionable, because it suggests this false view. Accordingly we replace the word "idea" in this usage by the neutral word "sense-content," which we shall use to refer to the immediate data not merely of "outer" but also of "introspective" sensation, and say that what Berkeley discovered was that material things must be definable in terms of sense-contents. We shall see, when we come finally to settle the conflict between idealism and realism, that his actual conception of the relationship between material things and sense-contents was not altogether accurate. It led him to some notoriously paradoxical conclusions, which a slight emendation will enable us to avoid. But the fact that he failed to give a completely correct account of the way in which material things are constituted out of sense-contents does not invalidate his contention that they are so constituted. On the contrary, we know that it must be possible to define material things in terms of sense-contents, because it is only by the occurrence of certain sense-contents that the existence of any material thing can ever be in the least degree verified. And thus we see that we have not to enquire whether a phenomenalist "theory of perception" or some other sort of theory is correct, but only what form of phenomenalist theory is correct. For the fact that all causal and representative theories of perception treat material things as if they were unobservable entities entitles us, as Berkeley saw, to rule them out *a priori*. The unfortunate thing is that, in spite of this, he found it necessary to postulate God as an unobservable cause of our "ideas"; and he must be criticized also for failing to see that the argument which he uses to dispose of Locke's analysis of a material thing is fatal to his own conception of the nature of the self, a point which was effectively seized upon by Hume.

Of Hume we may say not merely that he was not in practice a metaphysician, but that he explicitly rejected metaphysics. We find the strongest evidence of this in the passage with which he concludes his *Enquiry Concering Human Understanding*. "If," he says, "we take in our hand any volume; of divinity, or school metaphysics, for in-

---

[1] Vide G. E. Moore, "A Defence of Common Sense," *Contemporary British Philosophy*, Vol. II.

stance; let us ask, Does it contain any abstract reasoning concerning quantity or number? No. Does it contain any experimental reasoning concerning matter of fact and existence? No. Commit it then to the flames. For it can contain nothing but sophistry and illusion." What is this but a rhetorical version of our own thesis that a sentence which does not express either a formally true proposition or an empirical hypothesis is devoid of literal significance? It is true that Hume does not, so far as I know, actually put forward any view concerning the nature of philosophical propositions themselves, but those of his works which are commonly accounted philosophical are, apart from certain passages which deal with questions of psychology, works of analysis. If this is not universally conceded, it is because his treatment of causation, which is the main feature of his philosophical work, is often misinterpreted. He has been accused of denying causation, whereas in fact he was concerned only with defining it. So far is he from asserting that no causal propositions are true that he is himself at pains to give rules for judging of the existence of causes and effects.[2] He realized well enough that the question whether a given causal proposition was true or false was not one that could be settled a priori, and accordingly confined himself to discussing the analytic question, What is it that we are asserting when we assert that one event is causally connected with another? And in answering this question he showed, I think conclusively, first that the relation of cause and effect was not logical in character, since any proposition asserting a causal connection could be denied without self-contradiction, secondly that causal laws were not analytically derived from experience, since they were not deducible from any finite number of experiential propositions, and, thirdly, that it was a mistake to analyze propositions asserting causal connections in terms of a relation of necessitation which held between particular events, since it was impossible to conceive of any observations which would have the slightest tendency to establish the existence of such a relation. He thus laid the way open for the view, which we adopt, that every assertion of a particular causal connection involves the assertion of a causal law, and that every general proposition of the form "C causes E" is equivalent to a proposition of the form "whenever C, then E," where the symbol "whenever" must be taken to refer, not to a finite number of actual instances of C, but to the infinite number of possible instances. He himself defines a cause as "an object, followed by another, and where all the objects similar to the first are followed by objects similar to the second," or, alternatively, as "an object followed by another, and whose appearance always conveys the thought to that other"; [3] but neither of these definitions is acceptable as it stands. For, even if it is true that we should not, according to our standards of rationality, have good reason to believe that an event C was the cause of an event E unless we had observed a constant conjunction of events like C with events like E, still there is no self-contradiction involved in asserting the proposition "C is the cause of E" and at the same time denying that any events like C or like E ever have been observed; and this would be self-contradictory if the first of the definitions quoted was correct. Nor is it inconceivable, as the second definition implies, that there should be causal laws which have never yet been thought of. But although we are obliged, for these reasons, to reject Hume's actual definitions of a cause, our view of the nature of causation remains substantially the same as his. And we agree with him that there can be no other justification for inductive reasoning than its success in practice, while insisting more strongly than he did that no better

[2] Vide A Treatise of Human Nature, Book I, Part III, section 15.
[3] An Enquiry Concerning Human Understanding, section 7.

justification is required. For it is his failure to make this second point clear that has given his views the air of paradox which has caused them to be so much undervalued and misunderstood.

When we consider, also, that Hobbes and Bentham were chiefly occupied in giving definitions, and that the best part of John Stuart Mill's work consists in a development of the analyses carried out by Hume, we may fairly claim that in holding that the activity of philosophizing is essentially analytic we are adopting a standpoint which has always been implicit in English empiricism. Not that the practice of philosophical analysis has been confined to members of this school. But it is with them that we have the closest historical affinity.

If I refrain from discussing these questions in detail, and make no attempt to furnish a complete list of all the "great philosophers" whose work is predominantly analytic—a list which would certainly include Plato and Aristotle and Kant—it is because the point to which this discussion is relevant is one of minor importance in our inquiry. We have been maintaining that much of "traditional philosophy" is genuinely philosophical, by our standards, in order to defend ourselves against the charge that our retention of the word "philosophy" is misleading. But even if it were the case that none of those who are commonly called philosophers had ever been engaged in what we call the activity of philosophizing, it would not follow that our definition of philosophy was erroneous, given our initial postulates. We may admit that our retention of the word "philosophy" is causally dependent on our belief in the historical propositions set forth above. But the validity of these historical propositions has no logical bearing on the validity of our definition of philosophy, nor on the validity of the distinction between philosophy, in our sense and metaphysics.

It is advisable to stress the point that philosophy, as we understand it, is wholly independent of metaphysics, inasmuch as the analytic method is commonly supposed by its critics to have a metaphysical basis. Being misled by the associations of the word "analysis," they assume that philosophical analysis is an activity of dissection; that it consists in "breaking up" objects into their constituent parts, until the whole universe is ultimately exhibited as an aggregate of "bare particulars," united by external relations. If this were really so, the most effective way of attacking the method would be to show that its basic presupposition was nonsensical. For to say that the universe was an aggregate of bare particulars would be as senseless as to say that it was Fire or Water or Experience. It is plain that no possible observation would enable one to verify such an assertion. But, so far as I know, this line of criticism is in fact never adopted. The critics content themselves with pointing out that few, if any, of the complex objects in the world are simply the sum of their parts. They have a structure, an organic unity, which distinguishes them, as genuine wholes, from mere aggregates. But the analyst, so it is said, is obliged by his atomistic metaphysics to regard an object consisting of parts a, b, c, and d in a distinctive configuration as being simply $a + b + c + d$, and thus gives an entirely false account of its nature.

If we follow the Gestalt psychologists, who of all men talk most constantly about genuine wholes, in defining such a whole as one in which the properties of every part depend to some extent on its positions in the whole, then we may accept it as an empirical fact that there exist genuine, or organic, wholes. And if the analytic method involved a denial of this fact, it would indeed be a faulty method. But, actually, the validity of the analytic method is not dependent on any empirical, much less any metaphysical, presupposition about the nature of things. For the philosopher, as an analyst, is not directly concerned with the physical properties of things. He is concerned only with the way in which we speak about them.

In other words, the propositions of philosophy are not factual, but linguistic in character—that is, they do not describe the behavior of physical, or even mental, objects; they express definitions, or the formal consequences of definitions. Accordingly, we may say that philosophy is a department of logic. For we shall see that the characteristic mark of a purely logical inquiry is that it is concerned with the formal consequences of our definitions and not with questions of empirical fact.

It follows that philosophy does not in any way compete with science. The difference in type between philosophical and scientific propositions is such that they cannot conceivably contradict one another. And this makes it clear that the possibility of philosophical analysis is independent of any empirical assumptions. That it is independent of any metaphysical assumptions should be even more obvious still. For it is absurd to suppose that the provision of definitions, and the study of their formal consequences, involves the nonsensical assertion that the world is composed of bare particulars, or any other metaphysical dogma.

What has contributed as much as anything to the prevalent misunderstanding of the nature of philosophical analysis is the fact that propositions and questions which are really linguistic are often expressed in such a way that they appear to be factual. A striking instance of this is provided by the proposition that a material thing cannot be in two places at once. This looks like an empirical proposition, and is constantly invoked by those who desire to prove that it is possible for an empirical proposition to be logically certain. But a more critical inspection shows that it is not empirical at all, but linguistic. It simply records the fact that, as the result of certain verbal conventions, the proposition that two sense-contents occur in the same visual or tactual sense-field is incompatible with the proposition that they belong to the same material thing. And this is indeed a necessary fact. But it has not the least tendency to show that we have certain knowledge about the empirical properties of objects. For it is necessary only because we happen to use the relevant words in a particular way. There is no logical reason why we should not so alter our definitions that the sentence "A thing cannot be in two places at once" comes to express a self-contradiction instead of a necessary truth.

Another good example of a linguistically necessary proposition which appears to be a record of empirical fact is the proposition, "Relations are not particulars, but universals." One might suppose that this was a proposition of the same order as, "Armenians are not Mohammedans, but Christians": but one would be mistaken. For, whereas the latter proposition is an empirical hypothesis relating to the religious practices of a certain group of people, the former is not a proposition about "things" at all, but simply about words. It records the fact that relation-symbols belong by definition to the class of symbols for characters, and not to the class of symbols for things.

The assertion that relations are universals provokes the question, "What is a universal?"; and this question is not, as it has traditionally been regarded, a question about the character of certain real objects, but a request for a definition of a certain term. Philosophy, as it is written, is full of questions like this, which seem to be factual but are not. Thus, to ask what is the nature of a material object is to ask for a definition of "material object," and this . . . is to ask how propositions about material objects are to be translated into propositions about sense-contents. Similarly, to ask what is a number is to ask some such question as whether it is possible to translate propositions about the natural numbers into propositions about classes. And the same thing applies to all the other philosophical questions of the form, "What is an x?" or, "What is the nature of x?" They are all requests for definitions, and, as we shall see, for definitions of a peculiar sort.

Although it is misleading to write about linguistic questions in "factual" language, it is often convenient for the sake of brevity. And we shall not always avoid doing it ourselves. But it is important that no one should be deceived by this practice into supposing that the philosopher is engaged on an empirical or a metaphysical enquiry. We may speak loosely of him as analyzing facts, or notions, or even things. But we must make it clear that these are simply ways of saying that he is concerned with the definition of the corresponding words.

PHILOSOPHY AND PSYCHOANALYSIS

john wisdom

1 Philosophical conflict

Wittgenstein once said that he *"holds no opinions in philosophy"* and, again that he tries to remove *"a feeling of puzzlement, to cure a sort of mental cramp."* This emphasizes much more what evil philosophy removes than what good it brings. Nevertheless, all who have felt the old philosophical puzzles know the cramp Wittgenstein refers to. Indeed if one thinks of a philosopher one thinks of a man who talks like this, for example: *"We fancy we sometimes know what other creatures are thinking and how they are feeling. But all we really know is how they nod and smile at this, bark and frown at that. No reasoning from such information will justify a conclusion about how they think and feel; it won't even tell us that they think and feel at all, much less will it tell us what goes on in the souls behind their faces. True we can infer from the faces of clocks what goes on within. But that is different. For some of us have sometimes noted a clock's face and quickly looked within. None of us has ever noted a friend's face and then quickly look within. Maybe we have looked within his body and found a decayed tooth or other sand in the transmission. But not in the happiest days have we ever viewed the landscapes he alone can view. And yet though it seems we* can't *know how others think and feel surely we often* do *know."*

The trouble spreads. The philosopher soon finds himself saying: *"Not only do I not know how or whether anything else thinks or feels but also I cannot really know what is happening in any place hidden from me, in the inside of a clock, for example, or beyond the horizon. I can open some clocks quickly but none quickly enough. On Tuesday at 2 p.m., I know only what is happening near me, within the walls of my room, in my own little ark. For what is happening far away on the waste of waters or in the roaring Strand, I am obliged to rely on doves and telephones. However fast I hurry to the place I'm always late. The dove brings a leaf perhaps, but by the time I reach the distant Spring the leaves are turning or it's full Summer. For, if not, it wasn't Spring but still Winter when I started. Finding fallen leaves in November I may say I was right when in April, in Germany, I thought it was Spring in England. But the fallen leaves are not the Spring of which I dreamed in April. That is now*

From John Wisdom, *Philosophy and Psycho-Analysis* (Oxford: Basil Blackwell, 1957), *"Polemic No. 4,"* pp. 169–181. Reprinted by permission of the author and the publisher.

forever in the past. Even that I don't really know, obliged as I am to rely for all knowledge of the past upon dead leaves, bones, stones, documents and the faded photos in the family album and my memory. Nor do I know the future. For even if I knew what had happened this wouldn't guarantee what will happen.

"And now if I know nothing of the past and nothing of the future then all I seem to see and hear may have no more substance than a dream. For just as a phoenix is not a phoenix unless it renews itself in its own ashes so bread that comes down from Heaven isn't bread but manna, and a dagger that vanishes is not a dagger but an image.

"Further, even if I knew the future and could with perfect propriety predict to all eternity the pattern of my sensations, would this give substance to the shadows in a mirror that mirrors nothing?

"And yet, surely, I do know these things it seems I can't know? I do know that where there's smoke there's fire, that the stone I kick is real, that the friend who speaks with me is not a talking doll."

So spreads and swings the philosophic hesitation. Driven by a caricature of curiosity which is kept for ever hungry by an inexorable desire to be logically perfect and factually infallible the philosopher diminishes his claims to knowledge; agnosticism about the minds of others becomes agnosticism about all things but his own thought as he thinks it—in other words Solipsism. And Solipsism soon becomes Scepticism, the "claim" that we know nothing. For when the philosopher become Solipsist fancies himself about to reap the reward of his logical purity in perfect knowledge, limited indeed but invulnerable, just then the statement he had hoped to make dwindles to the senseless whimper of an elderly infant in the mansions of the dead. I don't mean, of course, that all philosophers in the end become Sceptics and find peace in death. On the contrary, no philosopher becomes really a Sceptic; because if a man really feels what the Sceptic says he feels then he is said to have "a sense of unreality" and is removed to a home. In fact the sceptical philosopher never succeeds in killing his primitive credulities which, as Hume says, reassert themselves the moment he takes up the affairs of life and ceases to murmur the incantations which generate his philosophic doubt. More than that, most philosophers refuse to be Sceptics even in their philosophic moments; these travellers on the road to Nothing mostly look back and would return whence they have come, but cannot. In this sad case, some talk of trans-sensual spheres glimpsed by a trans-sensual awareness, an apprehension of Reality mediated by, but not limited to, the sights and sounds, the headaches and the heartaches to which we seem confined; others, the Realists, pretend that nothing's happened, that everything's all right, that finespun argument can never shake the common sense they had and hold; others, the Phenomenalists, say that everything's all right because the ideal of knowledge of reality beyond appearance is only unattainable because it's unintelligible; others hurry agitatedly from one cult to another; others stand poised *"betwixt a world destroyed and world restored,"* paralyzed in the cramp of conflict.

We have come upon these people before—in other difficulties; indeed they are ourselves. And none of them is at ease. This comes out plainly in those who say they are not. But even those who have erected a temple for tranquillity have often a hidden fear of its falling about their ears. The Transcendentalist must constantly defend himself against the Sceptic and even against the Realist, who are the more menacing because they are not only outside him but also within. The realist must keep forgetting the philosophic qualms which though crammed down into Tartarus are not dead—the confidence he professes is never what it was before he ate of the forbidden tree. The phenomenalist protests too much that there was no baby in the bath water he threw away. None of them is easy—or if he is, he shouldn't be. This last qualification reminds us of the incompleteness in the description of the proper philosopher as one who tries to cure uneasiness. He may set himself to disturb complacency. So may a psychoanalyst. We may recognize this without forgetting how much philosophy and analytic work by patient and analyst is conflict and the cure of it.

2   *Philosophical and obsessional doubt*

I have used words with a clinical flavor in the sketch of philosophers which I have just given because I want to bring out likenesses, connections, between states of philosophical stress and other states of stress arising from internal sources as opposed to states of stress arising from external sources. A general or a businessman who has to decide what to do in a complicated situation may go over the many relevant considerations carefully and may do so many times. A judge considers carefully, even anxiously, the arguments of contending counsel. But the general, the business man, and the judge may consider their problems very patiently and still be very different from the neurotic. The neurotic may discuss his problems—he may indeed—but he never means business; the discussion is not a means to action, to something other than itself; on the contrary, after a while we get the impression that in spite of his evident unhappiness and desire to come from hesitation to decision he also desires the discussion never to end and dreads its ending. Have you not quite often had this impression with philosophers?—philosophers other than ourselves, for we, of course, are never neurotic. I once discussed with a man in a mental hospital whether he should continue to starve himself and study the Scriptures or take more nourishment and lend a hand at home. He put the matter well and with an admirable impartiality, but some months later I learned that he had died in the hospital, still, I believe, unable to settle the issue. And we have all read of the man who cannot be sure that he has turned off the tap or the light. He must go again to make sure, and then perhaps he must go again because though he knows the light's turned off he yet can't *feel* sure. He is obsessed by a chronic doubt. Has he done what he ought about the light or the tap? Perhaps his doubt is less limited, perhaps he is constantly questioning himself as to whether he has done what he ought. Such a man will often want rules of life to save him from continual conflict. Or again, his doubt may be less a matter of whether he has done this or that, or what he ought, and more a doubt as to what is happening where he can't see. He has slammed his front door, he hasn't much time to catch his train, but still he turns back because he wants to feel perfectly sure that things are all right behind the door—to which fortunately he has a key. At least he has a key until, like a philosopher, he wishes to see behind the door without opening it. Instantly it becomes *"a veil past which I cannot see"* and in the darkness of the cave one cannot tell whether She smiles or frowns. If we are watching shadows on a wall and want to know whether the shadows are telling the truth about what is going on behind our backs we can turn our heads and look; we aren't like an infant who, helpless in his cradle, cannot turn his head and cries when his mother goes out of sight; nor like philosophers who perpetually feel they don't know what's going on behind their backs, and who, still like the child, dread to know, cling to their ignorance. God or the gods know what really is so, what goes on among "objective realities," but we know only what goes on among our own toys, copies of real things. The gods know but they never tell us anything, as James Forsythe continually complained when age now instead of youth confined him to his bed. The gods know but they tell us nothing—a conspiracy of silence among the arch-deceivers.

Yesterday a man just beginning philosophy told me that he had said to a friend: *"Some philosophers don't believe in material things and I am now not sure that I do."* His friend said, taking hold of the table, *"You don't believe there's a table here? You're mad."*

I said *"Your friend's right. There is something very odd about the situation when a philosopher says* 'I don't believe there's a table here' *or* 'I doubt whether there's a table here.' *It's not that his question is odd, I mean it's not simply his uttering these words* 'I'm not sure whether there's a table here' *which strikes us as odd. If when you are seeking water in the desert someone gazes at what looks like water in the distance and says* 'I doubt whether there's really water there,' *you don't think him absurd. But the philosopher says* 'I am not sure' *while he's drinking the water; he says it when no one would, or when no one but a madman would, or when no one but a madman or a philosopher would. And then also he is queer in that he doesn't act, doesn't feel, doesn't anticipate the future in the way his words suggest. In this he is at once more and less queer than a madman. The madman says, perhaps,* 'I shouldn't open that door' *and his eyes widen in almost furious terror. You say* 'Why not?' *and continue to walk towards the door. He clutches your arm and says, softly,* 'There's a tiger in there.' *You say* 'Nonsense, I've only just been in the room. You don't suppose a furniture firm has just driven up outside, erected a ladder, and slipped a tiger in through the window, do you?' 'Ah!' *the madman says,* 'He hides' *or* 'You can't see him.' "

This is the psychotic and he is different from the neurotic who says that he must make sure that he hasn't left the lights on but that, of course, it's all nonsense and that he really knows he has turned them off, or that he must make quite sure that his hands are quite clean although it is true he has only just washed them. The neurotic, we might say, doesn't believe what he says. Still he does go back at the risk of losing his train to make sure that the lights are off. The philosopher doesn't. His acts and feelings are even less in accordance with his words than are the acts and feelings of the neurotic. He, even more than the neurotic and much more than the psychotic, doesn't believe what he says, doesn't doubt when he says he's not sure. (Compare wishes when he says he doesn't, i.e., unconsciously wishes.) But if we say that the philosopher doesn't believe what he says, that he's only pretending to doubt, then we must remember that he's very different from someone who, wishing to deceive us, pretends. The philosopher isn't one who merely makes it seem to others that he is in doubt; he also seems to himself to doubt. In other words, although many of his acts and feelings are unsuitable to his words, some are suitable and, in particular, as he speaks he has much of the feeling characteristic of doubt. When he says *"Perhaps it's all in my mind,"* he feels something of the relief or disappointment of one who fearing this, hoping that, says *"Maybe it's all a dream."*

But now what is it that makes philosophers go on in the way they do?

3   The philosopher is different

There is a big difference between the philosopher and both the psychotic and the obsessional neurotic. It lies in the flow of justificatory talk, of rationalization, which the philosopher produces when asked why he takes the extraordinary line he does. It is true that both the psychotic and neurotic listen to reason and defend themselves. The philosopher defends himself more elaborately. But this is not the point. The point is, aren't his rationalizations reasons?

When we call justifying talk "rationalization" we hint that we are not impressed by it and do not expect others to be. But we are impressed by the philosopher's talk, it has a universal effect, reluctantly we are impressed by it. The trouble is that it doesn't impress us quite enough to make us satisfied with his conclusions while yet it impresses us; the reasons seem not quite good enough and not quite bad enough and—connected fact—it seems the same with the reasons for opposing conclusions. At the same time the position is not what it is in science or crime where some evidence lends probability to one hypothesis and other evidence lends probability to another and we may contentedly wait for more evidence to tip the scales. For the philosopher's proofs profess to be *proofs* or nothing. And yet, too, we cannot, as in mathematics or logic, bring the conflict to an end by finding the slip in one of the calculations which purport to demonstrate the conflicting conclusions. There's something queer about philosophical reasons and the reasoning goes on too long.

4   First as to the queerness of philosophical reasons and conflict

Contrast a logical conflict. Lately it was reported in the Press that a railway official upon being asked the cause of a recent run of accidents replied, *"Well, the men are tired, the rolling stock a little the worse for wear, but it's not so much that as the working out of the law of averages."* This explanation is based on the logical doctrine that the longer a die has been thrown without a six the more probable is a six on the next throw, and we may imagine someone who argues for this as follows: When a die is about to be thrown 100 times the probability of at least one six being thrown is very great, namely .999999988 approximately. It may happen, however, that no six has appeared in the first 25 throws. In such a case unless a six appears in the next 75 throws there will have been 100 throws without a six and this, as we have seen, is improbable to the degree .000000012. Therefore it is improbable to the degree .000000012 that no six will appear in the next 75 throws. Again, if it should happen that no six appears in the first 99 throws then unless a six appears in the next throw there will have been 100 throws without a six and this is improbable to the degree .000000012. Therefore it is then improbable to the degree .000000012 that there will not be a six on the next throw while before the throws started this was not improbable but probable to the degree $\frac{5}{6}$.

This reasoning may temporarily impress us but we soon reply: The probability of a six after a long run of anything but sixes is still one in six if we assume that the die is not loaded, while if we do not assume this the probability of a six, so far from having increased as you suggest, has decreased, for the long run of throws without a six suggests that there is something about the die which prevents its falling six uppermost. Your reasoning in favor of the increasing probability of a six is tempting but it's fallacious. When you say *"It may happen that no six has appeared in the first 25 throws—in such a case, unless a six appears in the next 75 throws there will have been 100 throws without a six and this, as we have seen, is improbable to the degree .000000012"*—do you mean that we have seen that given only that a die is about to be thrown 100 times then it is improbable to a degree .000000012 that there will be no sixes? Or do you mean that we have seen that given that a die has been thrown 25 times without a six and that it will be thrown another 75 times, then it is improbable to a degree .000000012 that at the end there will have been no six thrown? The former is true, the latter is false. For given that a die has been thrown 25 times without a six and that it will be thrown another 75 times, the improbability that at the end of the 100 throws no six will have been thrown is the improbability of throwing a six in the next 75 throws, that is $1-(\frac{5}{6})^{75}$. And when 99 throws have been made and another is about to be made, the improbability of this series of 100 throws not including a six, is the improbability of not throwing a six in the next throw, that is $\frac{5}{6}$.

Here the difficulty is cleared up; one proof is definitely mistaken and the mistake is found; the other proof is sound and the matter is settled. So much for the Monte Carlo fallacy.

It may seem a pity that philosophy cannot be conducted on these lines. But it cannot. A philosophical conflict is like a logical or arithmetical conflict. But it's different too. The peculiarity of philosophical conflicts has only lately been grasped. Philosophical theories such as *"Matter (or Mind) does not exist"* are neither theories nor theorems; they are what they sound like—paradoxes; and philosophical questions are not questions (scientific) nor problems (logic)—but are more like riddles such as *"Can one man do what another does? Surely he can. And yet surely it can't be that he can. For suppose A scratches his head. Then if B scratches his head he doesn't do what A does since it's not B's head but A's that A scratches. But if B scratches A's head then again he doesn't do what A does since A scratches his own head and B scratches someone else's.* But here drinks are served all round. For now nobody cares whether we say *"No man can do what another man does,"* or say *"If a man, A, scratches his head and a man, B, also scratches his, B's, head then each does what the other does,"* or say *"If a man, A, scratches his head and a man, B, also scratches A's head then each does what the other does."* And now that nobody cares, the original paradox *"No man can do what another does"* cannot be mistaken for a theory about human powers like *"No man can play billiards like Lindrum."* And, what is more, now that everybody understands, now that everybody has explained his reasons, the doctrine *"No man can do what another does"* can no longer be mistaken for a theorem like *"No man can draw isosceles triangles with the angles at the base unequal."* In fact the paradox now appears as a paradox though in doing so it ceases to be one. For it now appears that one who says *"No man can do what another does"* cuts a caper and encourages us to do likewise, not pointlessly but in order to reveal a concealed curiosity, namely that one man does what another does only when he does something different. One who says *"No man can do what another does"* introduces a new logic to show up a hidden feature of the old, uses language oddly in order to show up an oddity in our usual use. And one who says *"No man can know the mind of another as he does his own"* or *"No one can really know the mind of another"* does the same sort of thing. His statement doesn't come out of experience in the way *"No one can know what a Red man feels"* comes out of experience; and it doesn't come out of ordinary language in the way *"No one can know what a good poker player is thinking"* or *"No one can marry his widow's sister"* does. It is not a statement of fact nor of logic. It comes out of language and out of experience—but in its own way—like *"Tyger, tyger! burning bright."* It comes from extraordinary experience of the ordinary calling for extraordinary use of ordinary language. And to burst this way the bonds of habitual modes of projection is no more extraordinary than a caricature, or a picture that is not a photograph.

The consequence is that paradoxes are not established by experiment and statistics and cannot be proved by conclusive-deductive reasoning. They can be supported by inconclusive-deductive reasoning. The reasoning cannot be conclusive for, if it were, then the opposite of the paradox could not also be supported, and if its opposite could not be supported it would not be a paradox. And the reasoning will not be effective unless it leads to or comes from a new apprehension of the familiar—without that it will be dead words, for after all tigers don't burn, even in forests at night.

A paradox is a flag which declares a discovery—not a new continent nor a cure for pneumonia but a discovery in the familiar—but often it is also the Blue Peter of a new voyage. For often we don't properly understand a paradox until, beginning by regarding it literally, we have noted objections to it and held to it because of the reasons for it, and again noted objections and again held to it, and have come by this route to a state where we are no longer driven to assert it or to deny it. There's no short cut to this; for if *before* treating a paradox and its denial as incompatible and arguing for a win we say *"No doubt there's much in both"* this leaves us entirely vague as to what is in either. No, the journey to the new freedom is mostly long and arduous, the work of bringing to light and setting in order with respect to one another what drives us to accept, and what forces us to deny, a paradox, what makes it so fascinating, so attractive and so repugnant, may fairly take a long time. But it can take too long.

5 *Philosophical dispute can go on too long*

It may fairly take a woman a long time to decide which of two men is the right one for her to marry and it may take a man a long time to decide which of two professions is the right one for him to take up. But again in each case it may take too long. At first, as we review with our friend the many considerations that bear on the issue, we accompany him with interest, later with patience, but, at last, with irritation. For, in time, we feel that the difficulty is no longer a matter of coming to know his own mind, but of making up his mind. He still represents himself as ignorant of what would suit him and in this way conceals his incapacity to choose. *"Win or a place, win or a place"* shout those who quote the possible investments, but still he hesitates. And why can't he decide? Not merely because the considerations are so balanced. There's often nothing to choose on looks, form, breeding, and price between one horse and another, but this doesn't prevent people deciding, before the flags go down, which one to back. No, his chronic indecision, whether it takes the form of enthusiastic oscillation or melancholy inactivity, is due to the fact that besides the reasons revealed in the course of talking the matter over there are others which remain hidden. Family disputes are often very interminable and often have an unpleasant sweetness because they are conducted wholly in terms of what is "right" or "reasonable" while each disputant knows that forces quite other than those mentioned are at work and often knows the other knows. It is not that the things mentioned, the things brought up in the discussion, are not at work but that other things unmentioned and unmentionable are also at work and being unmentioned do not work themselves out, so the disputes get their character—unpleasantly sweet and interminable.

The man I mentioned earlier who died in hospital discussing with himself an issue between altruism and the development of the true self, analyzed himself in vain. Had he overweighted this? Had he neglected that? We struggle to pass from conflict into harmony, to find, as Aristotle said, the proper point between opposites. But unlike Aristotle we cannot face the prospect of choices without end and feel we must have rules to live by. To represent a difficult choice as ignorance of our duty in the situation we are in enables us to escape from facing the hidden sources of our hesitation. How much more can we escape into the wider inquiries of what acts, in general, are right and what, in general, makes good things good. Here we may wander for ever and, when darkness begins to fall, still build an altar to an unknown god.

When earlier I introduced the Monte Carlo fallacy I did so because I thought of it as one which arises purely from linguistic sources, as one which can be removed by turning the light on to linguistic confusion. And it is true that this trouble is more completely curable by linguistic treatment than are more philosophical troubles where the relevant facts of language form such a labyrinth that pressed in one quarter one may always take cover in another. But now it strikes me how very persistent and how very prevalent is even the simple Monte Carlo fallacy. One constantly hears people say *"Ah! that was too good to last"* or *"When we were having all the fine weather I thought we should have to pay for it"* or again, after a run of misadventures, *"Something will turn up. The luck must turn."* Of course, to expect specially bad weather after specially good is not irrational if records show that, regularly, soon after specially good weather, specially bad weather comes. But so far as I know there are no such records and so far as the people who use this argument know there are no such records. What they rely upon is *"the laws of chance working themselves out"*; what they rely upon is their feeling that though they don't know what card Fate will next deal them they do know what pack she holds so that if till now there have been no aces there'll be a lot of them soon to make up. True, there are people who, when all has gone well for a long time, feel more confident than ever; *they* feel that this just shows that Fate is with them. But there are others who begin to feel that they've had more than they deserve and that Fate will soon remind them that they are mortals, Polycrates and Amasis. And this last feeling finds expression, "justification," rationalization, in talk about the laws of chance—confused talk because without the confusion it wouldn't express the way they feel. It's the same when things go badly; some fall into despair, others feel that they have been punished enough and that even the most implacable Fate will now be prepared to "give them a break." So it appears how even this very purely logical paradox is not purely logical. It is true that the reasoning which leads to it, though fallacious, is plausible, it impresses us, and it does so partly because we have not a very firm and adequate understanding of the use of our linguistic tools in many discussions about probabilities; *but it does so also because the resulting paradox suits many people and suits something in most of us.* Gambling has a peculiar and half-secret fascination for many people; so also for many has the most theoretical talk about probability and chance. I submit that though the logical or linguistic explanation of the Monte Carlo fallacy is very adequate, we would have a still more adequate explanation were we able to bring out not only the features of language that make for the committing of that fallacy, but also other causes hidden beneath the flow of talk. And *if this is true of the Monte Carlo fallacy, it is much more true of the philosophical paradoxes.*

Chance and Necessity, Freedom and Deity, Mind and Matter, Space and Time— these words have in them the detachment of the intellect but also echoes from the heart, and the fascination of them is not confined to professional philosophers. I remember how years ago one night in the "Elephant" a gentleman who, it was plain, had already been there some time took me aside in order to explain to me something of the connection between Mind and Matter. The big words of metaphysics have an appeal which is wide and deep and old, and we cannot fully understand and resolve the riddles they present without understanding that appeal. In this sketch of philosophers I have been hinting at this. I have been hinting at connections with what psychoanalysts try to bring into the light. True, philosophy has never been merely a psychogenic disorder; nor is the new philosophical technique merely a therapy. There's a difference. Philosophers reason for and against their doctrines, and in doing so show us not new things but old things anew. Nevertheless, having recognized how different is philosophy from therapy it is worth noticing the connections: (*a*) how philosophical discussion is the bringing out of latent opposing forces like arriving at a decision and not like learning what is behind a closed door or whether $235 \times 6 = 1420$; (*b*) how, often, when the reasoning is done we find that besides the latent linguistic sources there are others non-linguistic and much more hidden which subtly cooperate with the features of language to produce philosophies; (*c*) how, in consequence, a purely linguistic treatment of philosophical conflicts is often inadequate; (*d*) how the non-linguistic sources are the same as those that trouble us elsewhere in our lives, so that the riddles written on the veil of appearance are indeed riddles of the Sphinx.

THE AIM OF PHILOSOPHY

alfred north whitehead

The task of a University is the creation of the future, so far as rational thought and civilized modes of appreciation can affect the issue. The future is big with every possibility of achievement and of tragedy.

Amid this scene of creative action, What is the special function of philosophy?

In order to answer this question, we must first decide what constitutes the philosophic character of any particular doctrine. What makes a doctrine philosophical? No one truth, thoroughly understood in all the infinitude of its bearings, is more or less philosophical than any other truth. The pursuit of philosophy is the one avocation denied to omniscience.

Philosophy is an attitude of mind towards doctrines ignorantly entertained. By the phrase "ignorantly entertained" I mean that the full meaning of the doctrine in respect to the infinitude of circumstances to which it is relevant, is not understood. The philosophic attitude is a resolute attempt to enlarge the understanding of the scope of application of every notion which enters into our current thought. The philosophic attempt takes every word, and every phrase, in the verbal expression of thought, and asks, What does it mean? It refuses to be satisfied by the conventional presupposition that every sensible person knows the answer. As soon as you rest satisfied with primitive ideas, and with primitive propositions, you have ceased to be a philosopher.

Of course you have got to start somewhere for the purposes of discourse. But the philosopher, as he argues from his premises, has already marked down every word and phrase in them as topics for future inquiry. No philosopher is satisfied with the concurrence of sensible people, whether they be his colleagues, or even his own previous self. He is always assaulting the boundaries of finitude.

The scientist is also enlarging knowledge. He starts with a group of primitive notions and of primitive relations between these notions, which defines the scope of his science. For example, Newtonian dynamics assumes Euclidean space, massive matter, motion, stresses and strains, and the more general notion of force. There are

This selection, the Epilogue to Whitehead's *Modes of Thought,* is reprinted by permission of The Macmillan Company. Copyright 1938 by The Macmillan Company, renewed 1966 by T. North Whitehead.

also the laws of motion, and a few other concepts added later. The science consisted in the deduction of consequences, presupposing the applicability of these ideas.

In respect to Newtonian Dynamics, the scientist and the philosopher face in opposite directions. The scientist asks for the consequences, and seeks to observe the realization of such consequences in the universe. The philosopher asks for the meaning of these ideas in terms of the welter of characterizations which infest the world.

It is evident that scientists and philosophers can help each other. For the scientist sometimes wants a new idea, and the philosopher is enlightened as to meanings by the study of the scientific consequences. Their usual mode of intercommunication is by sharing in the current habits of cultivated thought.

There is an insistent presupposition continually sterilizing philosophic thought. It is the belief, the very natural belief, that mankind has consciously entertained all the fundamental ideas which are applicable to its experience. Further it is held that human language, in single words or in phrases, explicitly expresses these ideas. I will term this presupposition, The Fallacy of the Perfect Dictionary.

It is here that the philosopher, as such, parts company with the scholar. The scholar investigates human thought and human achievement, armed with a dictionary. He is the main support of civilized thought. Apart from scholarship, you may be moral, religious, and delightful. But you are not wholly civilized. You will lack power of delicate accuracy of expression.

It is obvious that the philosopher needs scholarship, just as he needs science. But both science and scholarship are subsidiary weapons for philosophy.

The Fallacy of the Perfect Dictionary divides philosophers into two schools, namely, the "Critical School" which repudiates speculative philosophy, and the "Speculative School" which includes it. The critical school confines itself to verbal analysis within the limits of the dictionary. The speculative school appeals to direct insight, and endeavors to indicate its meanings by further appeal to situations which promote such specific insights. It then enlarges the dictionary. The divergence between the schools is the quarrel between safety and adventure.

The strength of the critical school lies in the fact that the doctrine of evolution never entered, in any radical sense, into ancient scholarship. Thus there arises the presupposition of a fixed specification of the human mind; and the blueprint of this specification is the dictionary.

I appeal to two great moments in the history of philosophy. Socrates spent his life in analyzing the current presuppositions of the Athenian world. He explicitly recognized that his philosophy was an attitude in the face of ignorance. He was critical and yet constructive.

Harvard is justly proud of the great period of its philosophic department about thirty years ago. Josiah Royce, William James, Santayana, George Herbert Palmer, Münsterberg, constitute a group to be proud of. Among them Palmer's achievements center chiefly in literature and in his brilliance as a lecturer. The group is a group of men individually great. But as a group they are greater still. It is a group of adventure, of speculation, of search for new ideas. To be a philosopher is to make some humble approach to the main characteristic of this group of men.

The use of philosophy is to maintain an active novelty of fundamental ideas illuminating the social system. It reverses the slow descent of accepted thought towards the inactive commonplace. If you like to phrase it so, philosophy is mystical. For mysticism is direct insight into depths as yet unspoken. But the purpose of philosophy is to rationalize mysticism: not by explaining it away, but by the introduction of novel verbal characterizations, rationally coordinated.

Philosophy is akin to poetry, and both of them seek to express that ultimate good sense which we term civilization. In each case there is reference to form beyond the direct meanings of words. Poetry allies itself to meter, philosophy to mathematic pattern.

5

EXISTENTIAL PHILOSOPHY

karl jaspers

. . .

1. *What is science?* In my youth I sought philosophy as knowledge. The doctrines which I heard and read seemed to meet this claim. They reasoned, proved, refuted; they were analogous with all other knowledge; yet they aimed at the whole rather than at single subjects.

I soon found out that most philosophical and many scientific doctrines failed to yield certainty. My doubting did not become absolute and radical. It was not doubt in the style of Descartes; such doubt, which I encountered later, I did not entertain in reality, but only as a kind of game. Commencing at first with the sciences, my doubt questioned single assertions, each doubt being by way of an experiment.

It shook my faith in the representatives of science, though not in science itself, to discover that famous scientists propounded many things in their textbooks which they passed off as the results of scientific investigation although they were by no means proven. I perceived the endless babble, the supposed "knowledge." In school already I was astonished, rightly or wrongly, when the teachers' answers to objections remained unsatisfactory. The parson proved the existence of God from the failure of the stars to collide and paid no heed to the objection that the stars' great distance from each other makes the probability of a collision small, or that maybe there are collisions which we do not observe because they have not yet involved us. I observed the pathos of historians when they conclude a series of explications with the words "Now things necessarily had to happen in this way," while actually this statement was merely suggestive *ex post facto,* but not at all convincing in itself: alternatives seemed equally possible, and there was always the element of chance. As a physician and psychiatrist I saw the precarious foundation of so many statements and actions, and beheld the reign of imagined insights, e.g., the causation of all mental illnesses by brain processes (I called all this talk about the brain, as it was fashionable then, brain mythology; it was succeeded later by the mythology of psychoanalysis), and realized with horror how, in our expert opinions, we based ourselves on positions which were far from

From Karl Jaspers, "On My Philosophy," Felix Kaufmann, trans., in *Existentialism: From Dostoevsky to Sartre,* Walter Kaufmann, ed. (Cleveland: Meridian Books, 1956), pp. 142–155. Reprinted with the kind permission of Frau Jaspers.

certain, because we had always to come to a conclusion, even when we did not know, in order that science might provide a cover, however unproved, for decisions the state found necessary. I was surprised that so much of medical advice and the majority of prescriptions were based, not on rational knowledge, but merely on the patient's wish for treatment.

From these experiences the basic question emerged: What is science? What can it do? Where are its limits? It became clear that science, to deserve its name, must be cogent and universally valid. Self-discipline in making assertions is necessary above everything to maintain the sharpest criticism, the clearest consciousness of method, the knowledge in which way, for what reasons, and with what certainty, I know in each case. Neither sceptically to surrender everything, nor to seize something dogmatically as a conclusion in advance, but rather to retain the attitude of the researcher, accepting knowledge only on the way, with its reasons, and relative to its viewpoints and methods, turned out to be far from easy. This attitude of mind is attainable only with an ever-active intellectual conscience. As a consequence of this procedure, it appeared that cogent validity does indeed exist and that it is a great privilege of man to be able to grasp it with clear judgment. It appeared, however, that such scientific knowledge is always particularized, that it does not embrace the totality of Being but only a specific subject, that it affords no aim to life, has no answer to the essential problems that move man, that it cannot even furnish a compelling insight into its own importance and significance. Man is reduced to a condition of perplexity by confusing the knowledge that he can prove with the convictions by which he lives.

If science, with its limitation to cogent and universally valid knowledge, can do so little, failing as it does in the essentials, in the eternal problems: why then science at all?

Firstly, there is an irrepressible urge to know the knowable, to view the facts as they are, to learn about the events that happen to us: for example, mental illnesses —how they manifest themselves in association with those that harbor them, or how mental illness might be connected with mental creativity. The force of the original quest for knowledge disappears in the grand anticipatory gestures of seeming total knowledge and increases in mastering what is concretely knowable.

Secondly, science has had tremendously far-reaching effects. The state of our whole world, especially for the last one hundred years, is conditioned by science and its technical consequences: the inner attitude of all humanity is determined by the way and content of its knowledge. I can grasp the fate of the world only if I can grasp science. There is a fundamental question: Why, although there is rationalism and intellectualization wherever there are humans, has science emerged only in the Occident, taking former worlds off their hinges in its consequences and forcing humanity to obey it or perish? Only through science and face-to-face with science can I acquire an intensified consciousness of the historical situation, can I truly live in the spiritual situation of my time.

Thirdly, I have to turn to science in order to learn what it is, in all science, that impels and guides, without itself being cogent knowledge. The ideas that master infinity, the selection of what is essential, the comprehension of knowledge in the totality of the sciences—all this is not scientific insight, but reaches clear consciousness only through the pursuit of the sciences. Only by way of the sciences can I free myself from the bondage of a limited, dogmatic view of the world in order to arrive at the totality of the world and its reality.

The experience of the indispensability and compelling power of science caused me to regard throughout my life the following demands as valid for all philosophizing: There must be freedom for all sciences, so that there may be freedom from scientific superstition, i.e., from false absolutes and pseudo-knowledge. By freely espousing the sciences I become receptive to that which is beyond science but which can only become clear by way of it. Although I should pursue one science thoroughly, I should nevertheless turn to all the others as well; not in order to amass encyclopedic knowledge, but rather in order to become familiar with the fundamental possibilities, principles of knowledge, and the multiplicity of methods. The ultimate objective is to work out a methodology, which arises from the ground of a universal consciousness of Being and points up and illuminates Being.

Above all, the sciences are to be employed as a tool of philosophy. Philosophy is not to be ranged alongside them as merely another science. For even though it is linked to science and never occurs without it, philosophy is wholly different from science. Philosophy is the thinking by which I become aware of Being itself through inner action; or rather it is the thinking which prepares the ascent to Transcendence, remembers it, and in an exalted moment accomplishes the ascent itself as a thinking act of the whole human being.

2. *How is communication possible?* I do not know which impulse was stronger in me when I began to think: the original thirst for knowledge or the urge to communicate with man. Knowledge attains its full meaning only through the bond that unites men; however, the urge to achieve agreement with another human being was so hard to satisfy. I was shocked by the lack of understanding, paralyzed, as it were, by every reconciliation in which what had gone before was not fully cleared up. Early in my life and then later again and again I was perplexed by people's rigid inaccessibility and their failure to listen to reasons, their disregard of facts, their indifference which prohibited discussion, their defensive attitude which kept you at a distance and at the decisive moment buried any possibility of a close approach, and finally their shamelessness, that bares its own soul without reserve, as though no one were present. When ready assent occurred I remained unsatisfied, because it was not based on true insight but on yielding to persuasion; because it was the consequence of friendly cooperation, not a meeting of two selves. True, I knew the glory of friendship (in common studies, in the cordial atmosphere of home or countryside). But then came the moments of strangeness, as if human beings lived in different worlds. Steadily the consciousness of loneliness grew upon me in my youth, yet nothing seemed more pernicious to me than loneliness, especially the loneliness in the midst of social intercourse that deceives itself in a multitude of friendships. No urge seemed stronger to me than that for communication with others. If the never-completed movement of communication succeeds with but a single human being, everything is achieved. It is a criterion of this success that there be a readiness to communicate with every human being encountered and that grief is felt whenever communication fails. Not merely an exchange of words, nor friendliness and sociability, but only the constant urge towards total revelation reaches the path of communication.

The painful stimulus that was philosophically decisive was the question how I was myself to blame for the insufficiency of communication. The insufficiency was indubitable fact. But the fault could not lie only with the others. I, too, am human like them. The same sources of inhibition of communication exist in me as in them. The inner action, by which I train myself, had to illumine my self-concealment, arbitrariness, and obstinacy, and to compel me to strive toward a revelation that can never be completed. The philosophical insight became possible precisely through my own failure. We can only recognize that evil which is in ourselves. What we cannot *be* at all, we cannot *understand* either.

The philosophical mood arose from the experience of insufficiency in communication. Occupation with mere objects which does not lead somehow to communication seemed wrong to me. Solitary devotion to nature—this deep experience of the universe in the landscape and in the physical nearness to its shapes and elements, this source of strength for the soul—could seem like a wrong done to other human beings, if it became a means of avoiding them, and like a wrong done to myself, if it tempted me to a secluded self-sufficiency in nature. Solitude in nature can indeed be a wonderful source of *self-being;* but whoever remains solitary in nature is liable to impoverish his self-being and to lose it in the end. To be near to nature in the beautiful world around me therefore became questionable when it did not lead back to community with humanity and serve this community as background and as language. Subsequently the question "What do they mean for communication?" passed through my philosophizing with respect to all thought, all experience, and all subject-matters. Are they apt to promote communication or to impede it? Are they tempters to solitude or heralds of communication?

This led to the basic philosophical questions: How is communication possible? What forms of communication can be accomplished? What is their relation to each other? In what sense are solitude and the strength to be able to be alone sources of communication? The answers are given, especially in the second volume of my *Philosophy,* in terms of concrete representations—by psychological means—and their principles will be treated in my *Logic.*

The thesis of my philosophizing is: The individual cannot become human by himself. Self-being is only real in communication with another self-being. Alone, I sink into gloomy isolation—only in community with others can I be revealed in the act of mutual discovery. My own freedom can only exist if the other is also free. Isolated or self-isolating Being remains mere potentiality or disappears into nothingness. All institutions that maintain soothing contact between men under unexpressed conditions and within unadmitted limits are certainly indispensable for communal existence; but beyond that they are pernicious, because they veil the truth in the manifestation of human Existenz with illusory contentment.

3. *What is truth?* The limits of science and the urge toward communication both point to a truth that is more than a possession of the intellect.

The cogent correctness of the sciences is but a small part of truth. This correctness, in its universal validity, does not unite us completely as real human beings, but only as intellectual beings. It unites us in the object that is understood, in the particular, but not in the totality. Admittedly, men can be true friends through scientific research, by means of the ideas that are realized in this process, and the impulses towards Existenz that make their appearance in it. But the correctness of scientific knowledge unites all intellectual beings in their equality, as it were, as replaceable points, not, in its essence, as human beings.

To the intellect all else, in comparison with what is correct, counts only as feeling, subjectivity, instinct. In this division, apart from the bright world of the intellect, there is only the irrational, in which is lumped together, according to the point of view, what is despised or desired. The impulse which pursues real truth by thought springs from the dissatisfaction with what is merely correct. The division, spoken of previously, paralyzes this impulse; it causes man to oscillate between the dogmatism of the intellect that transcends its limits and, as it were, the rapture of the vital, the chance of the moment, life. The soul becomes impoverished in all the multiplicity of disparate experience. Then truth disappears from the field of vision and is replaced by a variety of opinions which are hung on the skeleton of a supposedly rational pattern. Truth is infinitely *more* than scientific correctness.

Communication, too, points to this *"more."* Communication is the path to truth in all its forms. Thus the intellect finds clarity only in discussion. How man as an existent, as spirit, as Existenz, is or can be in communication—that is what allows all other truth to appear. The truth that makes itself felt at the boundary of science is the same that is felt in this movement of communication. The question arises what kind of truth it is.

We call the source of this truth the *Encompassing,* to distinguish it from the objective, the determinate, and particular forms in which beings confront us. This concept is by no means familiar and by no means self-evident. We may clarify the Encompassing philosophically, but we cannot know it objectively.

At this point the decision is made whether we can attain philosophizing or whether we fall back again at the boundary where the *leap to transcending thinking* must be made. If such words as feeling, instinct, heart, drives, and affections, which are suggestive of psychological analysis, are claimed as sources of truth, then we merely name the basis of our life, but it remains in darkness, causing us to slip down into supposedly comprehensible psychology, while actually everything depends on reaching the bright region of truly philosophical thought.

The methods of transcending are the bases of all philosophy. It is impossible to anticipate briefly what they accomplish. Perhaps a few words may *suggest,* even if not *explain,* what is meant.

Everything that becomes an *object* to me approaches me, as it were, from the dark background of Being. Every object is a determinate being (as *this* confronting me in a subject-object division), but never all Being. No being known as an object is *the* Being.

Does not the sum of all objects form the totality of Being? No. As the horizon encompasses all things in a landscape, so all objects are encompassed by that in which they are. As we move towards the horizon in the world of space without ever reaching it, because the horizon moves with us and reëstablishes itself ever anew as the Encompassing at each moment, so objective research moves towards totalities at each moment which never become total and real Being, but must be passed through towards new vistas. Only if all horizons met in one closed whole, so that they formed a finite multiplicity, could we attain, by moving through all the horizons, the one closed Being. Being, however, is not closed for us and the horizons are not finite. On all sides we are impelled towards the Infinite.

We inquire after the Being which, with the manifestation of all encountered appearance in object and horizon, yet recedes itself. This Being we call the Encompassing. The Encompassing, then, is that which always makes its presence known, which does not appear itself, but from which everything comes to us.

With this fundamental philosophical thought we must think beyond all determinate beings to the Encompassing in which we are and to the Encompassing which we are ourselves. It is a thought that turns us round, as it were, because it frees us from the shackles of determinate Being; yet the thought of the Encompassing is only a first approach. In its brevity it is still a purely formal concept. With further elaboration, modes of the Encompassing soon emerge (the Being of the Encompassing as such is world and Transcendence; the Being of the Encompassing that we are is an existent, consciousness in general, spirit, Existenz). Thus arises the task of clarifying all modes of the Encompassing. We become aware of truth in its total possibilities, its extent, its width and depth, only with the modes of the Encompassing.

The clarification of all the Encompassing derives its motive from our Reason and Existenz.

The impulses in which we open ourselves without limit, in which we want to give language to everything that is, embrace, as it were, all that is most strange and most distant, seeking a relation with everything, denying communication to nothing, these we call *reason*. This word, to be distinguished radically from *intellect*, meets the condition of truth as it can emerge from all modes of the Encompassing. Philosophical logic is the self-comprehension of reason.

Truth in this comprehensive sense, in which the truth of the intellect (and that of the sciences with it) is but an element, is founded in the *Existenz* that we can become. What matters is that our life is guided by something unconditional which can only spring from the *decision*. Decision makes Existenz real, forms life and changes it in inner action, which, through clarification, keeps us soaring upward. When it is founded on decision, love is no longer an unreliably moving passion, but the fulfillment to which alone real Being reveals itself.

What must be done in thinking of life is to be served by a philosophizing that discovers truth by retrospection and by anticipation. This philosophizing has no meaning unless a reality of the thinker complements the thought. This reality is not profession or application of a doctrine, but the practice of being human which propels itself forward in the echo of the thought. It is a movement, an upward soaring on two wings, as it were. Both wings, the thinking and the reality, must support the flight. Mere thinking would be an empty moving of possibilities, mere reality would remain a dull unconsciousness without self-comprehension, and therefore without unfolding.

This philosophizing emerged for me from psychology, which had to change and became Existenz Clarification. Existenz Clarification in its turn pointed to Philosophical World Orientation and to Metaphysics. Finally, the sense of this thinking understands itself in a Philosophical Logic that considers not only the intellect and its products (judgment and conclusion), but discovers the foundation of truth, in its complete range, in the Encompassing. Being is not the sum of objects; rather objects extend, as it were, toward our intellect in the subject-object division, from the Encompassing of Being itself, which is beyond objective comprehension, but from which nevertheless all separate, determinate objective knowledge derives its limits and its meaning and from which it derives the mood that comes out of the totality in which it has significance.

4. *What is man?*   As a living being among others man is the subject of anthropology. In his inner aspect he is a subject for psychology; in his objective structures, that is in communal life, a subject for sociology. Man, in his empirical reality, can be a subject of research in many directions; but man is always more than he knows or can know about himself.

As something knowable man appears in his manifold empirical aspects. As a being that is known he is always divided up into whatever he will reveal himself to be according to the methods of research employed. He is never a unity and a whole, never man himself, once he has become the subject of knowledge.

If I want to reassure myself philosophically about being human I cannot, therefore, stop at the knowable aspects of empirical man in the world. Man, in a way, is everything (as Aristotle says about the soul). Becoming aware of man's being means becoming aware of Being in time as a whole. Man is the Encompassing that we are; yet even as the Encompassing, man is split. As I said before, we become aware of the Encompassing that we are in a number of ways: as an existent, as consciousness generally, as spirit, as Existenz. Man lives in his world as an existent. As thinking consciousness generally he is searchingly oriented towards objects. As spirit he shapes the idea of a whole in his world existence. As possible Existenz he is related to Transcendence through which he knows himself as given to himself in his freedom. How man achieves unity is a problem, infinite in time and insoluble; but it is nevertheless the path to his search. Man is less certain of himself than ever.

In philosophizing man is not a species of particular existent beside other existents, but he becomes clear to himself as something unique, something all-enclosing, something completely open, as the greatest potentiality and the greatest danger in the world, as being the exception of Being, as the communication of scattered Being, which in him reveals itself to itself.

5. *What is Transcendence?* Man is for us the most interesting being in the world. We, as human beings ourselves, want to know what we are and can be; but a constant occupation with man causes surfeit. It seems as if, in that occupation, the essential was missed. For man cannot be comprehended on the basis of himself, and as we confront man's being there is disclosed the other through which he exists. For man as possible Existenz that [other] is Transcendence, but while man is in the world as a perceptive reality, Transcendence is, as if it were not there. Nor is it fathomable. Its being itself is doubtful. And yet all philosophizing is directed toward the goal of achieving certainty about Transcendence.

It may be objected that philosophy is mistakenly trying to achieve what only religion can achieve. In the cult religion offers the bodily presence, or at least experience, of Transcendence. It founds man on God's revelation. It points paths of faith in revealed reality, in mercy and salvation, and it gives guarantees. Philosophy can achieve none of that.

If philosophizing is a revolving round Transcendence, it must therefore have a relation to religion. The manner in which philosophy and religion react to each other is indeed an expression of their self-comprehension and of the depth of their realization. Historically we see this relation in the form of struggle, of subordination, of exclusion. A final and unchanging relation is not possible. Here a boundary shows itself. Where the problem is not merely grasped by insight but is actually solved, man has become narrow. When religion is excluded by philosophy or philosophy by religion, when one side asserts dominance over the other, by claiming to be the sole and most exalted authority, then man loses his openness to Being and his own potentiality in order to obtain a final closing of knowledge, but even this remains closed to him. He becomes, whether he limits himself to religion or to philosophy, dogmatic, fanatical, and, finally, with failure, nihilistic. To remain truthful religion needs the conscience of philosophy. To retain a significant content philosophy needs the substance of religion; yet any formula, such as this, is too simple; for it obscures the fact that there is more than one original truth in man. All that is possible is to avoid mistaking one for the other. Philosophy, from its side, cannot wish to fight religion. It must acknowledge it, albeit as its polar opposite, yet related to it through this polarity. Religion must always interest it because philosophy is constantly stirred up, prodded, and addressed by it. Philosophy cannot wish to replace religion, compete with it, nor make propaganda on its own behalf against it. On the contrary: philosophy will have to affirm religion at least as the reality to which it, too, owes its existence. If religion were not the life of mankind, there would be no philosophy either.

Philosophy as such, however, cannot look for Transcendence in the guarantee of revelation, but must approach Being in the self-disclosures of the Encompassing that are present in man as man (not in the proofs of the intellect or in the insights which the intellect, as such, might obtain) and through the historicity of the language of Transcendence.

The question "What is Transcendence?" is not answered, therefore, by a knowledge of Transcendence. The answer comes indirectly by a clarification of the incompleteness of the world, the imperfectibility of man, the impossibility of a permanently valid world order, the universal failure—bearing in mind at the same time that there is not nothing, but that in nature, history, and human existence, the magnificent is as real as the terrible. The decisive alternative in all philosophizing is whether my thinking leads me to the point where I am certain that the "from outside" of Transcendence is the source of the "from inside," or whether I remain in Immanence with the negative certainty that there is no outside that is the basis and goal of everything—the world as well as what I am myself.

No proof of God succeeds in philosophy if it attempts to provide compelling knowledge; but it is possible for "proofs" of God to succeed as ways of transcending thought. Rational thinking can transcend the categories of all that is thinkable to the point where opposites coincide; it can go beyond them in the individual category, e.g., that of sufficient cause or purpose—to the, in fact, untenable thought of a last cause and a final purpose. In that way, the necessity of seeking is understood in the baselessness of our merely factual existence and our soul is kept open to the Origin. The representation of the fragmentation of Being and the radical contradictoriness present in every form demonstrates that nothing we can know endures through itself.

Part of the externality of Transcendence is its unkowability; its internality is the code message of all things. In view of the fact that the limit and the basis of all things can be made tangible, it is possible to perceive everywhere the thread of light which connects them with Transcendence. Even though Transcendence is thus immanent, it is so only in an unlimited ambiguity and cannot be grasped with any finality. Philosophizing merely establishes the general right to trust in that which seems to speak to me as the light of Transcendence.

How I understand this language, however, is based on what I really am myself. What I am myself is based on my original relations to Transcendence: in defiance and in surrender, in falling away and in soaring up, in obedience to the law of day and in the passion of night. When I philosophize I clarify and remember and prepare how, through these relations, I can experience Eternity in Time. The experience itself cannot be forced and cannot be proved: it is the fulfilled historicity of my Existenz.

Philosophy can further demonstrate the consequences that appear when the interpretation of Being wishes to restrict itself to pure immanence. It can lift the veils that threaten at all times to wrap man in untruth. It accomplishes this with unprovable propositions of the intellect, with supposed knowledge of the world as a whole, and with results seemingly scientific. But in doing away with pseudo-knowledge philosophy does not establish a positive knowledge of Transcendence comparable to scientific knowledge.

Philosophy can clarify our conscience; it can show how we experience the demand of a universal law that we recognize as inevitable. At the boundary it can show the real failure even of obedience to this law, and cause the individual to feel anew the demand for unconditional obedience which addresses him in his historicity—though without universality or universal validity; and here again philosophy can show the boundary and the failure in Time.

On all paths it is essential to reach the Source where in highest consciousness the demand becomes audible in the world which, in spite of failing to be realized in the world, yet produces the true Being through obedience to it.

Philosophy can clarify that such a Source is possible; yet what the Source is and what it speaks it cannot anticipate. For reality is historical and awaits every individual that arises anew in this world. Everything that philosophy says in substance and remembers in history remains relative, in so far as it is utterable, and has to be translated and appropriated in order to become a path to one's own original comprehension of the Unconditional.

In thinking along these lines, philosophy employs a twofold presupposition that is objectively unprovable but accomplishable in practice. First, man is autonomous in the face of all the authorities of the world: the individual, reared by authority, at the end of the process of his maturation decides in his immediacy and responsibility before Transcendence what is unconditionally true. Second, man is a datum of Transcendence: to obey Transcendence in that unconditional decision leads man to his own Being.

How I can succeed in reading the code message in the fullness of beings, in existing concretely in my relations with Transcendence, in gaining my own Being in historically formed obedience to Transcendence; all this is conjoined to the fundamental question how the One is in the many, what it is, and how I can become certain of the One.

. . .

6

CHANGING CONCEPTS OF PHILOSOPHY

john dewey

Man differs from the lower animals because he preserves his past experiences. What happened in the past is lived again in memory. About what goes on today hangs a cloud of thoughts concerning similar things undergone in bygone days. With the animals, an experience perishes as it happens, and each new doing or suffering stands alone. But man lives in a world where each occurrence is charged with echoes and reminiscences of what has gone before, where each event is a reminder of other things. Hence he lives not, like the beasts of the field, in a world of merely physical things but in a world of signs and symbols. A stone is not merely hard, a thing into which one bumps; but it is a monument of a deceased ancestor. A flame is not merely something which warms or burns, but is a symbol of the enduring life of the household, of the abiding source of cheer, nourishment, and shelter to which man returns from his casual wanderings. Instead of being a quick fork of fire which may sting and hurt, it is the hearth at which one worships and for which one fights. And all this which marks the difference between bestiality and humanity, between culture and merely physical nature, is because man remembers, preserving and recording his experiences.

The revivals of memory are, however, rarely literal. We naturally remember what interests us and because it interests us. The past is recalled not because of itself but because of what it adds to the present. Thus the primary life of memory is emotional rather than intellectual and practical. Savage man recalled yesterday's struggle with an animal not in order to study in a scientific way the qualities of the animal or for the sake of calculating how better to fight tomorrow, but to escape from the tedium of today by regaining the thrill of yesterday. The memory has all the excitement of the combat without its danger and anxiety. To revive it and revel in it is to enhance the present moment with a new meaning, a meaning different from that which actually belongs either to it or to the past. Memory is vicarious experience in which there is all the emotional values of actual experience without its strains, vicissitudes and troubles. The triumph of battle is even more poignant in the memorial war dance than at the moment of victory; the conscious and truly human experience of the chase comes when it is talked over and reënacted by the camp fire. At the time, attention is taken up with practical details and with the strain of uncertainty. Only later do the details compose into a story and fuse into a whole of meaning. At the time of practical experience man exists from moment to moment, preoccupied with the task of the moment. As he resurveys all the moments in thought, a drama emerges with a beginning, a middle, and a movement toward the climax of achievement or defeat.

Since man revives his past experience because of the interest added to what would otherwise be the emptiness of present leisure, the primitive life of memory is one of fancy and imagination, rather than of accurate recollection. After all, it is the story, the drama, which counts. Only those incidents are selected which have a present emotional value, to intensify the present tale as it is rehearsed in imagination or told to an admiring listener. What does not add to the thrill of combat or contribute to the goal of success or failure is dropped. Incidents are rearranged till they fit into the temper of the tale. Thus early man, when left to himself, when not actually engaged in the struggle for existence, lived in a world of memories which was a world of suggestions. A suggestion differs from a recollection in that no attempt is made to test its correctness. Its correctness is a matter of relative indifference. The cloud suggests a camel or a man's face. It could not suggest these things unless some time there had been an actual, literal experience of camel and face. But the real likeness is of no account. The main thing is the emotional interest in tracing the camel or following the fortunes of the face as it forms and dissolves.

Students of the primitive history of mankind tell of the enormous part played by animal tales, myths, and cults. Sometimes a mystery is made out of this historical fact, as if it indicated that primitive man was moved by a different psychology from that which now animates humanity. But the explanation is, I think, simple. Until agriculture and the higher industrial arts were developed, long periods of empty leisure alternated with comparatively short periods of energy put forth to secure food or safety from attack. Because of our own habits, we tend to think of people as busy or occupied, if not with doing at least with thinking and planning. But then men were busy only when engaged in the hunt or fishing or fighting expedition. Yet the mind when awake must have some filling; it cannot remain literally vacant because the body is idle. And what thoughts should crowd into the human mind except experiences with animals, experiences transformed under the influence of dramatic interest to make more vivid and coherent the events typical of the chase? As men in fancy dramatically relived the interesting parts of their actual lives, animals inevitably became themselves dramatized.

They were true dramatis personae and as such assumed the traits of persons. They too had desires, hopes, and fears, a life of affections, loves, and hates, triumphs and defeats. Moreover, since they were essential to the support of the community, their activities and sufferings made them, in the imagination which dramatically revived the past, true sharers in the life of the community. Although they were hunted, yet they permitted themselves after all to be caught, and hence they were friends and allies. They devoted themselves, quite literally, to the sustenance and well-being of the community group to which they belonged. Thus were produced not merely the multitude of tales and legends dwelling affectionately upon the activities and features of animals, but also those elaborate rites and cults which made animals ancestors, heroes, tribal figureheads, and divinities.

I hope that I do not seem to you to have gone too far afield from my topic, the origin of philosophies. For it seems to me that the historic source of philosophies cannot be understood except as we dwell, at even greater length and in more detail, upon such considerations as these. We need to recognize that the ordinary consciousness of the ordinary man left to himself is a creature of desires rather than of intellectual study, inquiry, or speculation. Man ceases to be primarily actuated by hopes and fears, loves and hates, only when he is subjected to a discipline which is foreign to human nature, which is, from the standpoint of natural man, artificial. Naturally our books, our scientific and philosophical books, are written by men who have subjected themselves in a superior degree to intellectual discipline and culture. Their thoughts are habitually reasonable. They have learned to check their fancies by facts, and to organize their ideas logically rather than emotionally and dramatically. When they do indulge in reverie and daydreaming—which is probably more of the time than is conventionally acknowledged—they are aware of what they are doing. They label these excursions, and do not confuse their results with objective experiences. We tend to judge others by ourselves, and because scientific and philosophic books are composed by men in whom the reasonable, logical, and objective habit of mind predominates, a similar rationality has been attributed by them to the average and ordinary man. It is then overlooked that both rationality and irrationality are largely irrelevant and episodical in undisciplined human nature; that men are governed by memory rather than by thought, and that memory is not a remembering of actual facts, but is association, suggestion, dramatic fancy. The standard used to measure the value of the suggestions that spring up in the mind is not congruity with fact but emotional congeniality. Do they stimulate and reinforce feeling, and fit into the dramatic tale? Are they consonant with the prevailing mood, and can they be rendered into the traditional hopes and fears of the community? If we are willing to take the word "dreams" with a certain liberality, it is hardly too much to say that man, save in his occasional times of actual work and struggle, lives in a world of dreams, rather than of facts, and a world of dreams that is organized about desires whose success and frustration form its stuff.

To treat the early beliefs and traditions of mankind as if they were attempts at scientific explanation of the world, only erroneous and absurd attempts, is thus to be guilty of a great mistake. The material out of which philosophy finally emerges is irrelevant to science and to explanation. It is figurative, symbolic of fears and hopes, made of imaginations and suggestions, not significant of a world of objective fact intellectually confronted. It is poetry and drama, rather than science, and is apart from scientific truth and falsity, rationality or absurdity of fact, in the same way in which poetry is independent of these things.

This original material has, however, to pass through at least two stages before it becomes philosophy proper. One is the stage in which stories and legends and their accompanying dramatizations are consolidated. At first the emotionalized records of experiences are largely casual and transitory. Events that excite the emotions of an individual are seized upon and lived over in tale and pantomime. But some experiences are so frequent and recurrent that they concern the group as a whole. They are socially generalized. The piecemeal adventure of the single individual is built out till it becomes representative and typical of the emotional life of the tribe. Certain incidents affect the weal and woe of the group in its entirety and thereby get an exceptional emphasis and elevation. A certain texture of tradition is built up; the story becomes a social heritage and possession; the pantomime develops into the stated rite. Tradition thus formed becomes a kind of norm to which individual fancy and suggestion conform. An abiding framework of imagination is constructed. A communal way of conceiving life grows up into which individuals are inducted by education. Both unconsciously and by definite social requirement individual memories are assimilated to group memory or tradition, and individual fancies are accommodated to the body of beliefs characteristic of a community. Poetry becomes fixated and systematized. The story becomes a social norm. The original drama which reënacts an emotionally important experience is institutionalized into a cult. Suggestions previously free are hardened into doctrines.

The systematic and obligatory nature of such doctrines is hastened and confirmed through conquests and political consolidation. As the area of a government is extended, there is a definite motive for systematizing and unifying beliefs once free and floating. Aside from natural accommodation and assimilation springing from the fact of intercourse and the needs of common understanding, there is often political necessity which leads the ruler to centralize traditions and beliefs in order to extend and strengthen his prestige and authority. Judea, Greece, Rome, and, I presume, all other countries having a long history, present records of a continual working over of earlier local rites and doctrines in the interests of a wider social unity and a more extensive political power. I shall ask you to assume with me that in this way the larger cosmogonies and cosmologies of the race as well as the larger ethical traditions have arisen. Whether this is literally so or not, it is not necessary to inquire, much less to demonstrate. It is enough for our purposes that under social influences there took place a fixing and organizing of doctrines and cults which gave general traits to the imagination and general rules to conduct, and that such a consolidation was a necessary antecedent to the formation of any philosophy as we understand that term.

Although a necessary antecedent, this organization and generalization of ideas and principles of belief is not the sole and sufficient generator of philosophy. There is still lacking the motive for logical system and intellectual proof. This we may suppose to be furnished by the need of reconciling the moral rules and ideals embodied in the traditional code with the matter of fact positivistic knowledge which gradually grows up. . . .

· · ·

Out of this situation emerged, if I mistake not, the entire tradition regarding the function and office of philosophy which till very recently has controlled the systematic and constructive philosophies of the Western world. If I am right in my main thesis that the origin of philosophy lay in an attempt to reconcile the two different types of mental product, then the key is in our hands as to the main traits of subsequent philosophy so far as that was not of a negative and heterodox kind. In the first place, philosophy did not develop in an unbiased way from an open and unprejudiced origin. It had its task cut out for it from the start. It had a mission to perform, and it was sworn in advance to that mission. It had to extract the essential moral kernel out of the threatened traditional beliefs of the past. So far so good; the work was critical and in the interests of the only true conservatism—that which will conserve and not waste the values wrought out by humanity. But it was also precommitted to extracting this moral essence in a spirit congenial to the spirit of past beliefs. The association with imagination and with social authority was too intimate to be deeply disturbed. It was not possible to conceive of the content of social institutions in any form radically different from that in which they had existed in the past. It became the work of philosophy to justify on rational grounds the spirit, though not the form, of accepted beliefs and traditional customs.

The resulting philosophy seemed radical enough and even dangerous to the average Athenian because of the difference of form and method. In the sense of pruning away excrescences and eliminating factors which to the average citizen were all one with the basic beliefs, it was radical. But looked at in the perspective of history and in contrast with different types of thought which developed later in different social environments, it is now easy to see how profoundly, after all, Plato and Aristotle reflected the meaning of Greek tradition and habit, so that their writings remain, with the writings of the great dramatists, the best introduction of a student into the innermost ideals and aspirations of distinctively Greek life. Without Greek religion, Greek art, Greek civic life, their philosophy would have been impossible; while the effect of that science upon which the philosophers most prided themselves turns out to have been superficial and negligible. This apologetic spirit of philosophy is even more apparent when Medieval Christianity about the twelfth century sought for a systematic rational presentation of itself and made use of classic philosophy, especially that of Aristotle, to justify itself to reason. A not unsimilar occurrence characterizes the chief philosophic systems of Germany in the early nineteenth century, when Hegel assumed the task of justifying in the name of rational idealism the doctrines and institutions which were menaced by the new spirit of science and popular government. The result has been that the great systems have not been free from party spirit exercised in behalf of preconceived beliefs. Since they have at the same time professed complete intellectual independence and rationality, the result has been too often to impart to philosophy an element of insincerity, all the more insidious because wholly unconscious on the part of those who sustained philosophy.

And this brings us to a second trait of philosophy springing from its origin. Since it aimed at a rational justification of things that had been previously accepted because of their emotional congeniality and social prestige, it had to make much of the apparatus of reason and proof. Because of the lack of intrinsic rationality in the matters with which it dealt, it leaned over backward, so to speak, in parade of logical form. In dealing with matters of fact, simpler and rougher ways of demonstration may be resorted to. It is enough, so to say, to produce the fact in question and point to it— the fundamental form of all demonstration. But when it comes to convincing men of the truth of doctrines which are no longer to be accepted upon the say-so of custom and social authority, but which also are not capable of empirical verification, there is no recourse save to magnify the signs of rigorous thought and rigid demonstration. Thus arises that appearance of abstract definition and ultra-scientific argumentation which repels so many from philosophy but which has been one of its chief attractions to its devotees.

At the worst, this has reduced philosophy to a show of elaborate terminology, a hair-splitting logic, and a fictitious devotion to the mere external forms of comprehensive and minute demonstration. Even at the best, it has tended to produce an overdeveloped attachment to system for its own sake, and an over-pretentious claim to certainty. Bishop Butler declared that probability is the guide of life; but few philosophers have been courageous enough to avow that philosophy can be satisfied with anything that is merely probable. The customs dictated by tradition and desire had claimed finality and immutability. They had claimed to give certain and unvarying laws of conduct. Very early in its history philosophy made pretension to a similar conclusiveness, and something of this temper has clung to classic philosophies ever since. They have insisted that they were more scientific than the sciences —that, indeed, philosophy was necessary because, after all, the special sciences fail in attaining final and complete truth. There have been a few dissenters who have ventured to assert, as did William James, that "philosophy is vision" and that its chief function is to free men's minds from bias and prejudice and to enlarge their perceptions of the world about them. But, in the main, philosophy has set up much more ambitious pretensions. To say frankly that philosophy can proffer nothing but hypotheses, and that these hypotheses are of value only as they render men's minds more sensitive to life about them, would seem like a negation of philosophy itself.

In the third place, the body of beliefs dictated by desire and imagination and developed under the influence of communal authority into an authoritative tradition, was pervasive and comprehensive. It was, so to speak, omnipresent in all the details of the group life. Its pressure was unremitting and its influence universal. It was then probably inevitable that the rival principle, reflective thought, should aim at a similar universality and comprehensiveness. It would be as inclusive and far-reaching metaphysically as tradition had been socially. Now there was just one way in which this pretension could be accomplished in conjunction with a claim of complete logical system and certainty.

All philosophies of the classic type have made a fixed and fundamental distinction between two realms of existence. One of these corresponds to the religious and supernatural world of popular tradition, which in its metaphysical rendering became the world of highest and ultimate reality. Since the final source and sanction of all important truths and rules of conduct in community life had been found in superior and unquestioned religious beliefs, so the absolute and supreme reality of philosophy afforded the only sure guaranty of truth about empirical matters, and the sole rational guide to proper social institutions and individual behavior. Over against this absolute and noumenal reality which could be apprehended only by the systematic discipline of philosophy itself stood the ordinary empirical, relatively real, phenomenal world of everyday experience. It was with this world that the practical affairs and utilities of men were connected. It was to this imperfect and perishing world that matter-of-fact, positivistic science referred.

This is the trait which, in my opinion, has affected most deeply the classic notion about the nature of philosophy. Philosophy has arrogated to itself the office of demonstrating the existence of a transcendent, absolute, or inner reality and of revealing to man the nature and features of this ultimate and higher reality. It has therefore claimed that it was in possession of a higher organ of knowledge than is employed by positive science and ordinary practical experience, and that it is marked by a superior dignity and importance—a claim which is undeniable *if* philosophy leads man to proof and intuition of a Reality beyond that open to day-by-day life and the special sciences.

This claim has, of course, been denied by various philosophers from time to time. But for the most part these denials have been agnostic and sceptical. They have contented themselves with asserting that absolute and ultimate reality is beyond human ken. But they have not ventured to deny that such Reality would be the appropriate sphere for the exercise of philosophic knowledge provided only it were within the reach of human intelligence. Only comparatively recently has another conception of the proper office of philosophy arisen. . . . It is implied in the account which has been given of the origin of philosophy out of the background of an authoritative tradition; a tradition originally dictated by man's imagination working under the influence of love and hate and in the interest of emotional excitement and satisfaction. Common frankness requires that it be stated that this account of the origin of philosophies claiming to deal with absolute Being in a systematic way has been given with malice prepense. It seems to me that this genetic method of approach is a more effective way of undermining this type of philosophic theorizing than any attempt at logical refutation could be.

If this lecture succeeds in leaving in your minds as a reasonable hypothesis the idea that philosophy originated not out of intellectual material, but out of social and emotional material, it will also succeed in leaving with you a changed attitude toward traditional philosophies. They will be viewed from a new angle and placed in a new light. New questions about them will be aroused and new standards for judging them will be suggested.

If anyone will commence without mental reservations to study the history of philosophy not as an isolated thing but as a chapter in the development of civilization and culture; if one will connect the story of philosophy with a study of anthropology, primitive life, the history of religion, literature, and social institutions, it is confidently asserted that he will reach his own independent judgment as to the worth of the account which has been presented today. Considered in this way, the history of philosophy will take on a new significance. What is lost from the standpoint of would-be science is regained from the standpoint of humanity. Instead of the disputes of rivals about the nature of reality, we have the scene of human clash of social purpose and aspirations. Instead of impossible attempts to transcend experience, we have the significant record of the efforts of men to formulate the things of experience to which they are most deeply and passionately attached. Instead of impersonal and purely speculative endeavors to contemplate as remote beholders the nature of absolute things-in-themselves, we have a living picture of the choice of thoughtful men about what they would have life to be, and to what ends they would have men shape their intelligent activities.

Any one of you who arrives at such a view of past philosophy will of necessity be led to entertain a quite definite conception of the scope and aim of future philosophizing. He will inevitably be committed to the notion that what philosophy has been unconsciously, without knowing or intending it, and, so to speak, under cover, it must henceforth be openly and deliberately. When it is acknowledged that under disguise of dealing with ultimate reality, philosophy has been occupied with the precious values embedded in social traditions, that it has sprung from a clash of social ends and from a conflict of inherited institutions with incompatible contemporary tendencies, it will be seen that the task of future philosophy is to clarify men's ideas as to the social and moral strifes of their own day. Its aim is to become so far as is humanly possible an organ for dealing with these conflicts. That which may be pretentiously unreal when it is formulated in metaphysical distinctions becomes intensely significant when connected with the drama of the struggle of social beliefs and ideals. Philosophy which surrenders its somewhat barren monopoly of dealings with Ultimate and Absolute Reality will find a compensation in enlightening the moral forces which move mankind and in contributing to the aspirations of men to attain to a more ordered and intelligent happiness.

.   .   .

7

THE VALUE OF PHILOSOPHY

bertrand russell

Having now come to the end of our brief and very incomplete review of the problems of philosophy, it will be well to consider, in conclusion, what is the value of philosophy and why it ought to be studied. It is the more necessary to consider this question, in view of the fact that many men, under the influence of science or of practical affairs, are inclined to doubt whether philosophy is anything better than innocent but useless trifling, hairsplitting distinctions, and controversies on matters concerning which knowledge is impossible.

This view of philosophy appears to result, partly from a wrong conception of the ends of life, partly from a wrong conception of the kind of goods which philosophy strives to achieve. Physical science, through the medium of inventions, is useful to innumerable people who are wholly ignorant of it; thus the study of physical science is to be recommended, not only, or primarily, because of the effect on the student, but rather because of the effect on mankind in general. Thus utility does not belong to philosophy. If the study of philosophy has any value at all for others than students of philosophy, it must be only indirectly, through its effects upon the lives of those who study it. It is in these effects, therefore, if anywhere, that the value of philosophy must be primarily sought.

But further, if we are not to fail in our endeavor to determine the value of philosophy, we must first free our minds from the prejudices of what are wrongly called "practical" men. The "practical" man, as this word is often used, is one who recognizes only material needs, who realizes that men must have food for the body, but is oblivious of the necessity of providing food for the mind. If all men were well off, if poverty and disease had been reduced to their lowest possible point, there would still remain much to be done to produce a valuable society; and even in the existing world the goods of the mind are at least as important as the goods of the body. It is exclusively among the goods of the mind that the value of philosophy is to be found; and only those who are not indifferent to these goods can be persuaded that the study of philosophy is not a waste of time.

Philosophy, like all other studies, aims primarily at knowledge. The knowledge it aims at is the kind of knowledge which gives unity and system to the body of the

From Bertrand Russell, *The Problems of Philosophy* (London: Oxford University Press, 1912), Chap. XV, pp. 153–161. Reprinted by permission.

sciences, and the kind which results from a critical examination of the grounds of our convictions, prejudices, and beliefs. But it cannot be maintained that philosophy has had any very great measure of success in its attempts to provide definite answers to its questions. If you ask a mathematician, a mineralogist, a historian, or any other man of learning, what definite body of truths has been ascertained by his science, his answer will last as long as you are willing to listen. But if you put the same question to a philosopher, he will, if he is candid, have to confess that his study has not achieved positive results such as have been achieved by other sciences. It is true that this is partly accounted for by the fact that, as soon as definite knowledge concerning any subject becomes possible, this subject ceases to be called philosophy, and becomes a separate science. The whole study of the heavens, which now belongs to astronomy, was once included in philosophy; Newton's great work was called "the mathematical principles of natural philosophy." Similarly, the study of the human mind, which was a part of philosophy, has now been separated from philosophy and has become the science of psychology. Thus, to a great extent, the uncertainty of philosophy is more apparent than real: those questions which are already capable of definite answers are placed in the sciences, while those only to which, at present, no definite answer can be given, remain to form the residue which is called philosophy.

This is, however, only a part of the truth concerning the uncertainty of philosophy. There are many questions—and among them those that are of the profoundest interest to our spiritual life—which, so far as we can see, must remain insoluble to the human intellect unless its powers become of quite a different order from what they are now. Has the universe any unity of plan or purpose, or is it a fortuitous concourse of atoms? Is consciousness a permanent part of the universe, giving hope of indefinite growth in wisdom, or is it a transitory accident on a small planet on which life must ultimately become impossible? Are good and evil of importance to the universe or only to man? Such questions are asked by philosophy, and variously answered by various philosophers. But it would seem that, whether answers be otherwise discoverable or not, the answers suggested by philosophy are none of them demonstrably true. Yet, however slight may be the hope of discovering an answer, it is part of the business of philosophy to continue the consideration of such questions, to make us aware of their importance, to examine all the approaches to them, and to keep alive that speculative interest in the universe which is apt to be killed by confining ourselves to definitely ascertainable knowledge.

Many philosophers, it is true, have held that philosophy could establish the truth of certain answers to such fundamental questions. They have supposed that what is of most importance in religious beliefs could be proved by strict demonstration to be true. In order to judge of such attempts, it is necessary to take a survey of human knowledge, and to form an opinion as to its methods and its limitations. On such a subject it would be unwise to pronounce dogmatically; but if the investigations of our previous chapters have not led us astray, we shall be compelled to renounce the hope of finding philosophical proofs of religious beliefs. We cannot, therefore, include as part of the value of philosophy any definite set of answers to such questions. Hence, once more, the value of philosophy must not depend upon any supposed body of definitely ascertainable knowledge to be acquired by those who study it.

The value of philosophy is, in fact, to be sought largely in its very uncertainty. The man who has no tincture of philosophy goes through life imprisoned in the prejudices derived from common sense, from the habitual beliefs of his age or his

nation, and from convictions which have grown up in his mind without the cooperation or consent of his deliberate reason. To such a man the world tends to become
definite, finite, obvious; common objects rouse no questions, and unfamiliar possibilities
are contemptuously rejected. As soon as we begin to philosophize, on the contrary, we
find, as we saw in our opening chapters, that even the most everyday things lead to
problems to which only very incomplete answers can be given. Philosophy, though
unable to tell us with certainty what is the true answer to the doubts which it raises,
is able to suggest many possibilities which enlarge our thoughts and free them from
the tyranny of custom. Thus, while diminishing our feeling of certainty as to what
things are, it greatly increases our knowledge as to what they may be; it removes the
somewhat arrogant dogmatism of those who have never traveled into the region of
liberating doubt, and it keeps alive our sense of wonder by showing familiar things
in an unfamiliar aspect.

Apart from its utility in showing unsuspected possibilities, philosophy has a value
—perhaps its chief value—through the greatness of the objects which it contemplates,
and the freedom from narrow and personal aims resulting from this contemplation.
The life of the instinctive man is shut up within the circle of his private interests:
family and friends may be included, but the outer world is not regarded except as it
may help or hinder what comes within the circle of instinctive wishes. In such a life
there is something feverish and confined, in comparison with which the philosophic
life is calm and free. The private world of instinctive interests is a small one, set in
the midst of a great and powerful world which must, sooner or later, lay our private
world in ruins. Unless we can so enlarge our interests as to include the whole outer
world, we remain like a garrison in a beleagured fortress, knowing that the enemy
prevents escape and that ultimate surrender is inevitable. In such a life there is no
peace, but a constant strife between the insistence of desire and the powerlessness of
will. In one way or another, if our life is to be great and free, we must escape this
prison and this strife.

One way of escape is by philosophic contemplation. Philosophic contemplation
does not, in its widest survey, divide the universe into two hostile camps—friends and
foes, helpful and hostile, good and bad—it views the whole impartially. Philosophic
contemplation, when it is unalloyed, does not aim at proving that the rest of the
universe is akin to man. All acquisition of knowledge is an enlargement of the Self,
but this enlargement is best attained when it is not directly sought. It is obtained when
the desire for knowledge is alone operative, by a study which does not wish in advance
that its objects should have this or that character, but adapts the Self to the characters
which it finds in its objects. This enlargement of Self is not obtained when, taking
the Self as it is, we try to show that the world is so similar to this Self that knowledge
of it is possible without any admission of what seems alien. The desire to prove this is
a form of self-assertion and, like all self-assertion, it is an obstacle to the growth of Self
which it desires, and of which the Self knows that it is capable. Self-assertion, in
philosophic speculation as elsewhere, views the world as a means to its own ends; thus
it makes the world of less account than Self, and the Self sets bounds to the greatness
of its goods. In contemplation, on the contrary, we start from the not-Self, and through
its greatness the boundaries of Self are enlarged; through the infinity of the universe
the mind which contemplates it achieves some share in infinity.

For this reason greatness of soul is not fostered by those philosophies which assimilate the universe to Man. Knowledge is a form of union of Self and not-Self; like

all union, it is impaired by dominion, and therefore by any attempt to force the universe into conformity with what we find in ourselves. There is a widespread philosophical tendency toward the view which tells us that Man is the measure of all things, that truth is man-made, that space and time and the world of universals are properties of the mind, and that, if there be anything not created by the mind, it is unknowable and of no account for us. This view, if our previous discussions were correct, is untrue; but in addition to being untrue, it has the effect of robbing philosophic contemplation of all that gives it value, since it fetters contemplation to Self. What it calls knowledge is not a union with the not-Self, but a set of prejudices, habits, and desires, making an impenetrable veil between us and the world beyond. The man who finds pleasure in such a theory of knowledge is like the man who never leaves the domestic circle for fear his word might not be law.

The true philosophic contemplation, on the contrary, finds its satisfaction in every enlargement of the not-Self, in everything that magnifies the objects contemplated, and thereby the subject contemplating. Everything, in contemplation, that is personal or private, everything that depends upon habit, self-interest, or desire, distorts the object, and hence impairs the union which the intellect seeks. By thus making a barrier between subject and object, such personal and private things become a prison to the intellect. The free intellect will see as God might see, without a *here* and *now,* without hopes and fears, without the trammels of customary beliefs and traditional prejudices, calmly, dispassionately, in the sole and exclusive desire of knowledge—knowledge as impersonal, as purely contemplative, as it is possible for man to attain. Hence also the free intellect will value more the abstract and universal knowledge into which the accidents of private history do not enter, than the knowledge brought by the senses, and dependent, as such knowledge must be, upon an exclusive and personal point of view and a body whose sense organs distort as much as they reveal.

The mind which has become accustomed to the freedom and impartiality of philosophic contemplation will preserve something of the same freedom and impartiality in the world of action and emotion. It will view its purposes and desires as parts of the whole, with the absence of insistence that results from seeing them as infinitesimal fragments in a world of which all the rest is unaffected by any one man's deeds. The impartiality which, in contemplation, is the unalloyed desire for truth, is the very same quality of mind which, in action, is justice, and in emotion is that universal love which can be given to all, and not only to those who are judged useful or admirable. Thus contemplation enlarges not only the objects of our thoughts, but also the objects of our actions and our affections: it makes us citizens of the universe, not only of one walled city at war with all the rest. In this citizenship of the universe consists man's true freedom, and his liberation from the thralldom of narrow hopes and fears.

Thus, to sum up our discussion of the value of philosophy: Philosophy is to be studied, not for the sake of any definite answers to its questions, since no definite answers can, as a rule, be known to be true, but rather for the sake of the questions themselves; because these questions enlarge our conception of what is possible, enrich our intellectual imagination and diminish the dogmatic assurance which closes the mind against speculation; but above all because, through the greatness of the universe which philosophy contemplates, the mind also is rendered great, and becomes capable of that union with the universe which constitutes its highest good.

Selected Bibliography for Part VII

Aristotle. *Metaphysics,* ed. W. Jaeger. London: Oxford University Press, 1957.

Ayer, A. J. *Language, Truth and Logic.* London: Gollancz, 1936.

————, ed. *Logical Positivism.* New York: Free Press, 1958.

Bergson, Henri. *An Introduction to Metaphysics,* trans. T. E. Hulme. New York: Bobbs-Merrill, 1949.

Blanshard, Brand. *Reason and Analysis.* La Salle, Ill.: Open Court, 1962.

Bradley, F. H. *Appearance and Reality: A Metaphysical Essay.* London: Oxford University Press, 1930.

Ducasse, Curt J. *Philosophy as a Science.* New York: Stechert, 1941.

Heidegger, Martin. *What is Philosophy?* New York: Twayne, 1958.

Husserl, Edmund. *The Idea of Phenomenology,* trans. W. P. Alston and G. Nakhnikian. The Hague: Martinus Nijhoff, 1964.

James, William. *Some Problems of Philosophy.* New York: Longmans-Green, 1911.

Johnstone, Henry W., ed. *What is Philosophy?* New York: Macmillan, 1965.

Maritain, Jacques. *A Preface to Metaphysics.* New York: New American Library, 1939.

Merleau-Ponty, Maurice. *In Praise of Philosophy,* trans. John Wild and James M. Edie. Evanston, Ill.: Northwestern University Press, 1963.

Plato. *The Republic,* trans. F. M. Cornford. London: Oxford University Press, 1941.

Ryle, Gilbert. *Philosophical Arguments.* London: Oxford University Press, 1945.

Sartre, Jean-Paul. *Being and Nothingness,* trans. Hazel E. Barnes. New York: Philosophical Library, 1956.

Taylor, Richard. *Metaphysics.* Englewood Cliffs, N.J.: Prentice-Hall, 1963.

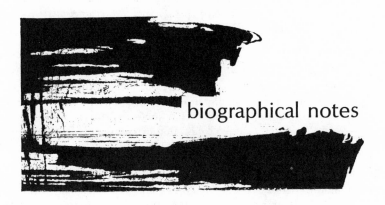

biographical notes

ST. ANSELM OF CANTERBURY (1033–1109) was one of the most important figures of medieval philosophy. He entered the Benedictine order as a young man and eventually became Prior and then Abbot of Bec. In 1093, he was appointed Archbishop of Canterbury by William Rufus, and, in this capacity, vigorously defended the rights of the church against the crown. Anselm is known primarily for the ontological argument for the existence of God, which was presented in his *Proslogium* (1078). Also of considerable interest, however, is the *Monologium* (1077), in which Anselm moves through degrees of perfection to a study of God as the absolute of perfection.

ST. THOMAS AQUINAS (1225–1274) was perhaps the greatest of medieval philosophers. At the age of five, he began his studies under the Benedictine monks of Monte Cassino. In 1244, he entered the Dominican order, and subsequently continued his studies, first at Paris and then under Albertus Magnus at Cologne. His career as a teacher was spent at the University of Paris, at various Dominican monasteries near Rome, and at Naples. Aquinas' work represents the crowning effort of medieval thought to reconcile faith and reason, Christianity and Aristotelianism. His writings comprise some thirty or more volumes. Among his most famous works are the *Summa Theologica* and the *Summa Contra Gentiles*.

ARISTOTLE (384–322 B.C.) was born in Stagira, a Greek colony on the northwestern shore of the Aegean. When he was about seventeen he entered Plato's Academy, where he remaind until Plato's death in 347. In 342, he was called to the court of Philip of Macedon to tutor the young Alexander. After Alexander's accession, Aristotle returned to Athens (335) where he founded a new school, the Lyceum. Following the death of Alexander (323), Aristotle was accused of impiety by the anti-Macedonian party. Mindful of the fate of Socrates, he fled to Chalcis, where he died at the age of sixty-two. Aristotle's writings cover nearly every branch of knowledge known in his day. Among the most famous are *De Anima, Metaphysics, Physics, Posterior Analytics, Nicomachean Ethics, Politics, Rhetoric,* and *Poetics.*

J. L. AUSTIN (1911–1960) was, from 1952 until his death, White's Professor of Moral Philosophy at Oxford and Fellow of Corpus Christi College. He—more than any of his contemporaries—set the tone of the Oxonian linguistic school which has dominated British philosophy since World War II. His unique conception of philosophical analysis (labeled "ordinary language analysis") and his special style of philosophizing were imparted to his colleagues and students more through lectures and discussions than through published writings. In fact, two of his most significant books, *How to Do Things with Words* (1962) and *Sense and Sensibilia* (1962) consist of lectures posthumously edited and reconstructed from Austin's notes. Also published after Austin's death was *Philosophical Papers* (1961).

A. J. AYER (1910–   ). After his graduation from Oxford in 1932, Ayer studied briefly at the University of Vienna, where he was introduced to the Vienna Circle and a "revolutionary" movement in philosophy known as logical positivism. His first book, *Language, Truth and Logic,* which appeared in 1936, is regarded as the most effective, lucid, and uncompromising exposition of that philosophy to the English-speaking world. The fundamental argument of the book is for a *principle of verification* with which to judge the cognitive meaningfulness of assertions in any field of knowledge. Some of Ayer's other prominent works are *The Foundations of Empirical Knowledge* (1940), *Philosophical Essays* (1954), *The Problem of Knowledge* (1956), and *The Concept of a Person and Other Essays* (1963). He has been Wykeham Professor of Logic at Oxford since 1959.

HENRI BERGSON (1859–1941) was born in Paris of Irish-Jewish parents. In 1900, after having held various teaching positions, he became Professor of Philosophy at the Collège de France, where he remained until his retirement. Bergson gained an international reputation through his philosophical writings and his post-World War I activities on behalf of international cooperation, and, in 1927, was awarded the Nobel Prize for literature. During the German occupation of France, the aged and eminent Bergson refused an exemption from the Nazi "Jewish laws." He died in Paris within a few months of the occupation. Bergson's concept of "creative evolution" was formulated to refute mechanistic and materialist explanations of the history of life. His many writings include *Time and Free Will* (1889), *Matter and Memory* (1896), *An Introduction to Metaphysics* (1903), *Creative Evolution* (1907), and *Two Sources of Morality and Religion* (1932).

GEORGE BERKELEY (1685–1753), was born at Kilkenny, in Ireland, of English stock. He was educated at Kilkenny School and at Trinity College, Dublin, where he became a fellow in 1707. In 1724, he became Dean of Derry and immediately immersed himself in a project for establishing a college in Bermuda for American colonists and Indians. In connection with this venture he went to Newport, Rhode Island, where he remained for three years (1728–1731), until it became apparent that the promised grant for his project would not be delivered. In 1734, he became Bishop of Cloyne. Berkeley's famous rejection of the existence of matter reflects his dissatisfaction with Locke's and with Descartes' dualism and, presumably, his desire to buttress his religious orthodoxy by ascribing to God a new and essential role (as the source of ideas). His most important philosophic works are *An Essay Towards a New Theory of Vision* (1709), *A Treatise Concerning the Principles of Human Knowledge* (1710), *Three Dialogues Between Hylas and Philonous* (1713), and *Alciphron* (1732).

MAX BLACK (1909–   ), a Russian-born analytic philosopher, is Professor of Philosophy at Cornell University and an editor of *The Philosophical Review*. He received degrees from Cambridge University and from the University of London, where he subsequently taught. He has written a great deal on logic, the philosophy of language, and the philosophy of science. Among his more notable books are *Language and Philosophy* (1949), *Problems of Analysis: Philosophical Essays* (1954), and *Models and Metaphors* (1962).

BRAND BLANSHARD (1892–   ) is Professor Emeritus at Yale and one of the most distinguished contemporary American philosophers. His two-volume work, *The Nature of Thought* (1939), marked him as the leading contemporary American proponent of idealistic metaphysics and epistemological rationalism. His study of contemporary British philosophy, *Reason and Analysis* (1962), includes a restatement of his epistemological and metaphysical views. Blanshard's ethical views are set forth in *Reason and Goodness* (1961). He is a past president of the American Theological Society, and of the Eastern Division of the

American Philosophical Association, and a Fellow of the British Academy.

RENÉ DESCARTES (1596–1650) is generally considered the founder of modern philosophy, and, more specifically, of modern epistemology. He was born at La Haye, in Touraine, France and educated at the Jesuit College at La Flèche in Anjou. In his twenty-third year, he dreamt that he was destined to unify science. In search of this unity, he invented analytic geometry and made contributions to theoretical physics, the science of optics, and the theory of music, in addition to helping lay the foundations of modern philosophy. Descartes' major philosophical works are: *Discourse on Method* (1637), *Meditations on First Philosophy* (1641), and *Principles of Philosophy* (1644). In 1649, Descartes journeyed to Sweden to instruct Queen Christina. Required to give lessons at 5:00 A.M. on icy mornings, Descartes soon caught a chill, and two weeks later, on February 11, 1650, died of pneumonia.

JOHN DEWEY (1859–1952), philosopher, psychologist, educator, and social critic, was born in Burlington, Vermont. He graduated from the University of Vermont in 1879, and taught school for three years before beginning graduate work at the newly organized Johns Hopkins University. As a student, he found pragmatism, Hegelianism, Kantianism, and psychology particularly interesting. After completing his doctorate, he joined the faculty of the University of Michigan in 1884, where he worked with G. H. Mead. Ten years later Dewey was appointed chairman of the Department of Philosophy, Psychology and Pedagogy at the University of Chicago. There he established a laboratory school which gave him an opportunity to test and develop his psychological and educational theories. In 1904, Dewey left Chicago to accept a position at Columbia University which he held until his retirement in 1930. During this period, Dewey lectured throughout the world and wrote prolifically. His most popular book, *Reconstruction in Philosophy* (1920), was based on lectures that he gave at the Imperial University of Japan. Other important works include *The Quest for Certainty* (1929), *Art as Experience* (1934), *Logic, The Theory of Inquiry* (1938), and *Problems of Men* (1946).

EPICURUS (c. 342–270 B.C.), from whom Epicureanism received its name, was born of Athenian parents on the island of Samos. He began the study of philosophy at an early age, and before long attracted a loyal following with his own ethical teachings. In about 306 B.C., he established in Athens an Epicurean school and community, The Garden, in which he taught until his death. This community included women—quite a radical feature for its time—and consequently was the subject of scandalous rumors. After the death of its founder, Epicureanism spread rapidly throughout the Greek-speaking world and continued to be popular for some five hundred years. The philosophy's most famous Roman exponent was Lucretius. Epicurus' two most famous surviving texts are the letter *To Menoeceus,* and the *Kuriai Doxai (Cardinal Tenets).*

EUGENE T. GENDLIN (1926–   ) was born in Vienna, Austria, and studied at the University of Chicago, where he is now a member of the Department of Psychology. In addition to his book, *Experiencing and the Creation of Meaning* (1962), he has published articles dealing with psychotherapy.

R. M. HARE (1919–   ) is White's Professor of Moral Philosophy at Oxford and Fellow of Corpus Christi College. He was educated at Rugby and at Balliol College, Oxford, where he was later a fellow and tutor in philosophy. His chief publications are *The Language of Morals* (1952), one of the most significant books on ethics of the postwar period, and *Freedom and Reason* (1963).

THOMAS HOBBES (1588–1679) was born at Westport, Wiltshire, England and educated at Magdalen Hall, Oxford. Upon receiving the bachelor's degree in 1608, he became a tutor, an occupation whereby he earned his living most of his adult life. As a tutor, he was able to travel to the continent, where, on his first visit, in 1610, he was inspired with a desire to become a classical scholar. During his second visit, in 1629, Hobbes became interested in geometry. The methods of geometry became the foundation of his materialistic philosophy. Hobbes' political beliefs were first presented in the *Elements of Law, Natural and Politic* (circulated in 1640), which expressed a conviction that the basis of social order is the controlling power of undivided sovereignty. Coming in the midst of England's political strife, this work antagonized both contending factions. Fearing for his safety, Hobbes fled to the continent, where, chiefly in Paris, he spent eleven productive years. In 1651, he returned to England, where he spent his remaining twenty-eight years. His most famous works are *On the Citizen* (1642), *Human Nature* and *De Corpore Politico* (the two parts of the *Elements of Law,* as published in 1650), *Leviathan* (1651), *On Body* (1655), and *On Man* (1658). Hobbes also produced English translations of the *Iliad,* the *Odyssey,* and Thucydides' history of the Peloponnesian War.

JOHN HOSPERS (1918–   ), a native of Iowa, is Director of the School of Philosophy at the University of Southern California and editor of *The Personalist.* His interests center in ethics and aesthetics. Hospers' major publications include *Meaning and Truth in the Arts* (1946) and *Introduction to Philosophical Analysis* (1953).

DAVID HUME (1711–1776), the third and last of the great British Empiricists (following Locke and Berkeley), was born and educated in Edinburgh. In 1739 and 1740, he published the three volumes of *A Treatise of Human Nature*. It was received with only neglect and mockery, much to Hume's disappointment. Later, he recast the *Treatise* and published its Books as separate works. The two most famous of these are an *Enquiry Concerning the Human Understanding* (1748) and an *Enquiry Concerning the Principles of Morals* (1751). Despite his growing success, Hume was unable to get a chair of philosophy at either Edinburgh or Glasgow because of the accusations of atheism leveled against him. However, in 1752, he became keeper of the Advocates' Library, in Edinburgh, and while there wrote his *History of England* (six volumes, 1754–62). Later he was secretary to the British ambassador in Paris and then, after returning to England, served as undersecretary of state for the Northern Department. Before his death, Hume arranged for the posthumous publication of his *Dialogues Concerning Natural Religion* (1779), whose publication during his lifetime would have provided fuel for the charges of atheism.

THOMAS HUXLEY (1825–1895), the eminent British biologist and educator, was born in London and received his medical training at Charing Cross Hospital. From 1846 to 1850, he was assistant surgeon on H.M.S. *Rattlesnake* while it conducted surveying operations in Australian waters. While on the *Rattlesnake,* Huxley examined marine organisms and described his results in a series of papers, on the basis of which he was elected a fellow of the Royal Society. Huxley spent the next four decades as one of the intellectual leaders of England. He supported and popularized Darwin's theory of evolution, argued for agnosticism and the independence of science from theology, and urged extension of scientific education and improvement of instruction in the humanistic disciplines. His views on metaphysics, epistemology, science, evolution, and religion are to be found in *Man's Place in Nature* (1864), *Collected Essays* (1894–1903), and *Scientific Memoirs* (1898–1903).

WILLIAM JAMES (1842–1910), a philosopher and psychologist, was instrumental in founding American pragmatism. Born in New York City, he received his early education in the United States, England, France, Switzerland, and Germany. He also studied science and medicine at Harvard and, from 1865 to 1866, accompanied Louis Agassiz, the great Swiss-American zoologist and geologist, on a scientific expedition to the Amazon. James completed his medical studies in 1869, and, in 1873, began teaching anatomy and physiology at Harvard. In 1875, he began teaching psychology, and in 1879, philosophy. His philosophic views are presented in *Principles of Psychology* (1890), *The Will to Believe and Other Essays in Popular Philosophy* (1897), *The Varieties of Religious Experience* (1902), *Pragmatism: A New Name for Some Old Ways of Thinking* (1907), and *Essays in Radical Empiricism* (1912).

KARL JASPERS (1883–1969), one of the architects of contemporary existentialism, was born in Oldenburg, Germany. After studying both law and medicine at various institutions, he received his M.D. degree from Heidelberg in 1909. While working at Heidelberg in psychiatry and psychology, he published two important works, *General Psychopathology* (1913) and *Psychology of World Views* (1919). In 1921, he accepted a professorship in philosophy at Heidelberg. While at Heidelberg, he published his greatest work, the three volume *Philosophie* (1932), in which he developed his concepts of transcendence and *existenz*. Jaspers was dismissed from his post by the Nazis in 1937, and reinstated in 1945. In 1948, he became Professor of Philosophy at the University of Basel in Switzerland. Jaspers' thought was particularly influenced by Kant, Kierkegaard, Nietzsche, and Husserl.

IMMANUEL KANT (1724–1804) was born in Königsberg in East Prussia, where he spent his entire life; he never ventured to visit even other parts of Prussia. He completed his doctorate in 1755, and then accepted a position as Privatdozent, teaching physics, mathematics, physical geography, and philosophy at the University of Königsberg. He remained in this position for fifteen years, although he had ample opportunities for professional appointments elsewhere, and although his applications for a professorship at Königsberg were twiced refused. Finally, in 1770, he was appointed to the chair of logic and metaphysics at Königsberg. Kant published his greatest work, *The Critique of Pure Reason,* in 1781. This long-awaited work produced great controversy. As a result, Kant wrote his *Prolegomena to Any Future Metaphysics* (1783) in an effort to clear up misunderstanding. Kant continued to write, and in the years that followed he published the *Foundations of the Metaphysics of Morals* (1785), the *Critique of Practical Reason* (1788), the *Critique of Judgment* (1790), and *Religion Within the Bounds of Reason Alone* (1792–1793).

SØREN KIERKEGAARD (1813–1855), the Danish philosopher and religious thinker, is generally considered the founder of modern existentialism. He was born and educated in Copenhagen, where he studied theology for ten years. The two decisive events in Kierkegaard's life were the death of his father, in 1838, and his termination of his engagement to Regine Olsen, in 1841. The latter event served as a catalyst to his authorship and is reflected in his writing. Kierkegaard attacked the established church in Denmark as a mockery of Christianity. Much of his voluminous work, including his chief philosophical works, *Philosophical Fragments* (1844), and *Concluding Unscientific*

Postscript (1846), was published under pseudonyms. In these works, Kierkegaard sets forth his own subjective position and sharply criticizes the systematizing of the prevailing Hegelian philosophy.

GOTTFRIED WILHELM LEIBNIZ (1646–1716), inventor, advisor to monarchs, philosopher, and co-discoverer (along with Newton) of the differential and integral calculus, was not recognized in his lifetime for his original work on symbolic logic and his insights on the foundations of the physical sciences. This was largely because his most important manuscripts were left unpublished and lay buried in the Royal Library of Hanover until this century. Consequently, he was represented by his early commentators as a rationalistic metaphysician in the tradition of Descartes and Spinoza. The son of a Professor of Moral Philosophy at the University of Leipzig, Leibniz began the study of Greek, logic, and scholastic philosophy at the age of twelve, and entered the university when he was fifteen. In 1663, he went to Jena where he spent a summer studying mathematics and then three years studying jurisprudence. After declining a professorship at Altdorf, Leibniz entered the service of the elector of Mainz. In 1673, he entered the service of the House of Brunswick (at Hanover), with whom he remained until his death. Leibniz's duties at Hanover, like those at Mainz, included the application of his intellect to the support of the political designs of his patrons. He died in a state of total neglect, ignored by his royal patrons, by the Berlin Academy, of which he was the founder and first president, and by the Royal Society of London, of which he was a fellow. Among his most important works were *Essays in Theodicy* (1710), *Principles of Nature and Grace* (written in 1714, published in 1718), *Monadology* (written in 1714, published in 1721), and *New Essays on Human Understanding* (written in 1704, published in 1765).

JOHN LOCKE (1632–1704), student of science, physician, political theorist, and philosopher, exercised considerable and lasting influence in two branches of thought—epistemology and political theory. His *Essay Concerning Human Understanding* (1689) initiated the philosophical tradition known as modern British empiricism. In that comprehensive work on the origin, nature, and extent of knowledge, Locke attempted to refute the rationalistic thesis of innate ideas by demonstrating that all of our knowledge is originally derived from sense perception and reflection (in the sense of introspection). Sense perception and reflection are not themselves knowledge, but they provide the mind with "ideas," which, for Locke, are the "materials of knowledge." His *Two Treatises of Government* (1689) and *Letters Concerning Toleration* (1689), both of which he published anonymously, contain ideas—on democracy, religious freedom, natural rights, and the status and structure of government—that inspired the founders of the American republic and influenced the political philosophy of the French encyclopedists.

GEORGE HERBERT MEAD (1863–1931), a social psychologist and philosophical pragmatist, was born in South Hadley, Massachusetts, and studied at Harvard. He taught at the University of Michigan and the University of Chicago. Mead published relatively few papers during his lifetime and no books, but as a teacher he had a strong influence upon psychologists and social scientists. After his death, his students edited (from stenographic recordings, notes on his lectures, and unpublished papers) a four-volume compilation of Mead's ideas: *The Philosophy of the Present* (1932), *Mind, Self, and Society* (1934), *Movements of Thought in the Nineteenth Century* (1936), and *The Philosophy of Act* (1938).

MAURICE MERLEAU-PONTY (1908–1961), one of the most original and important figures of the phenomenological movement, was born in Rochefort-sur-Mer, France, and studied at the École Normale Supérieure. During the thirties, he taught in *lycées* and continued his own philosophical studies. After serving in the French Resistance during the Occupation, Merleau-Ponty refused the Legion of Honor. Following the war, he published *The Phenomenology of Perception* and *The Structure of Behavior,* both in 1945, and founded, with Jean-Paul Sartre the journal *Les Temps Modernes,* in which he frequently presented his political observations. In 1952, Merleau-Ponty accepted the chair of philosophy formerly held by Bergson at the Collège de France. He was the youngest man ever appointed to that post.

JOHN STUART MILL (1806–1873), the most influential nineteenth-century British philosopher, was born in London and educated by his father, James Mill, the Utilitarian philosopher and economist. John was reading Greek at the age of three, studying Latin, Euclid, and algebra at eight, and logic at twelve. In 1823, he became a clerk in the East India Company, where he continued to work for twenty-five years —during which period he published articles and his major systematic works on logic and political economy. In 1865, Mill was elected to Parliament for Westminster although he refused to canvass, answer questions concerning his religious beliefs, or commit himself to support the special interests of the borough. As a philosopher, Mill is best known for his reformulation of British Empiricism and of Bentham's Utilitarianism, and for his monumental work in logic. His liberal view of man and society is reflected in his ethics and social philosophy. Mill's major works include: *The System of Logic* (1843), *The Principles of Political Economy* (1848), *On Liberty* (1859), and *Utilitarianism* (1861).

G. E. MOORE (1873–1958) was born in London and educated at Dulwich College and at Trinity College, Cambridge. He began studying classics at Cambridge, but, largely on the advise of his fellow student, Bertrand Russell, turned his attention to philosophy. In 1898, he was elected to a prize fellowship in philosophy at Trinity. From 1925 to 1939, he was Professor of Philosophy at Cambridge. He edited the journal *Mind* from 1921 to 1947. Although his specific theories were not generally accepted, Moore had an enormous impact—through his method of analysis, his vigorous attack on Idealism, and his defense of the merits of common sense—on the orientation of subsequent British and American philosophy. His writings on ethics and epistemology have been especially influential. His most important works are "The Refutation of Idealism" (1903), *Principia Ethica* (1903), *Ethics* (1912), *Philosophical Studies* (1922), *Some Main Problems of Philosophy* (1953), and *Philosophical Papers* (1959).

ERNEST NAGEL (1901–   ) was born in Novemesto, Czechoslovakia, and studied at the City College of New York and at Columbia, where he is now University Professor of Philosophy. He is noted primarily for his writings on the philosophy of science. Nagel's chief publications are *Principles of the Theory of Probability* (1939), *Sovereign Reason* (1954), *Logic Without Metaphysics* (1956), and *The Structure of Science* (1961).

P. H. NOWELL-SMITH (1914–   ), educated at Winchester, at New College, Oxford, and at Harvard, where he was a Commonwealth Fellow, is Professor of Philosophy at the University of Kent. His chief publication is *Ethics* (1954).

PLATO (428/27–348/47 B.C.), the son of an aristocratic Athenian family, was, throughout his early years, attracted by public service, the traditional calling of his family. Ultimately, however—partly, no doubt, in reaction to the trial and execution of his teacher, Socrates, by the Athenian democracy—he chose to devote himself to the pursuit of the knowledge without which no one could govern justly, and to the education of his fellow men. These efforts—although they failed to bring into existence the ideal state which Plato had envisioned—resulted in a body of great philosophical writings and in the Academy, the school which Plato founded in Athens, and which endured until the sixth century A.D. The legacy of Plato's philosophic achievements and unique literary style is preserved in the Platonic dialogues, the best known of which are: the *Apology, Crito, Protagoras, Meno, Gorgias, Symposium, Phaedo, Republic, Phaedrus, Theaetetus, Parmenides, Sophist, Politicus, Timaeus,* and the *Laws.*

HANS REICHENBACH (1891–1953) was born in Hamburg, Germany, and after attending the Universities of Berlin, Munich, and Göttingen, received his doctorate from the University of Erlangen. He taught at the Universities of Stuttgart and Berlin until Hitler came to power in 1933, and then became Professor of Philosophy at the University of Istanbul. In 1938, he became Professor of Philosophy at the University of California at Los Angeles. Reichenbach was closely associated with the development of the movement known as logical positivism (although he stressed the points of disagreement between himself and the positivists, and called himself a logical empiricist). With Rudolph Carnap, he edited *Erkenntnis* (later the *Journal of Unified Science*), the official journal of logical positivism. Reichenbach is esteemed as one of the outstanding philosophers of science of this century. His writings include *The Rise of Scientific Philosophy* (1951), *Experience and Prediction* (1938), *Modern Philosophy of Science* (1959), *The Theory of Relativity and A Priori Knowledge* (1965), *Philosophic Foundations of Quantum Mechanics* (1944), and many other books and articles.

W. D. ROSS (1877–   ), a distinguished moral philosopher and Aristotelian scholar was born at Thurso, in Caithness, Scotland, and was educated at the Royal High School, Edinburgh, Edinburgh University, and Balliol College, Oxford. He was a fellow and tutor of Oriel College, Oxford, and later was elected Provost of Oriel, a post which he held from 1929 to 1947. Ross was awarded the Order of the British Empire for his service during World War I, and has performed many public services since, including membership on various governmental tribunals and commissions. In addition to many other positions in learned societies, he has been President of the British Academy and, since 1940, chairman of the Council of the Royal Institute of Philosophy. Ross' most famous scholarly achievements are the Oxford Translations of Aristotle (1908–31), which he edited, and which include his own translations of the *Metaphysics* (1908) and the *Ethics* (1925). In the field of moral philosophy, he is the author of two outstanding books, *The Right and the Good* (1930) and *Foundations of Ethics* (1939).

JOSIAH ROYCE (1855–1916) was born in California and studied at Johns Hopkins, Leipzig, and Göttingen. In 1878, he became an instructor in English at the University of California. Four years later, he was invited to teach at Harvard, where, in 1885, he received a regular appointment. Royce is the best American representative of absolute idealism. His thought is revealed in *The Religious Aspect of Philosophy* (1885), *The Conception of God* (1897), *The World and the Individual* (two volumes, 1900–1901), *Philosophy of Loyalty* (1908), and *The Problem of Christianity* (two volumes, 1913).

BERTRAND RUSSELL (1872–   ), the grandson of Lord John Russell, a prime minister under Queen Victoria, was born in Wales. He studied mathematics and philosophy at Trinity College, Cambridge from 1890 to 1894. He was a fellow at Trinity from 1895 to 1901, and a lecturer in philosophy there from 1910 to 1916. In 1916, Russell was dismissed from his position because of his pacifist activities. Then, in 1918, he was sentenced to six months in prison because of an allegedly libelous article in which he expressed his opposition to World War I and his desire for peace. Russell is a fellow of the Royal Society, an honorary fellow of the British Academy, and a recipient of the Order of Merit. He was awarded the Nobel Prize for literature in 1950. In the area of logic, Russell has written *Principles of Mathematics* (1903), *Principia Mathematica* (with A. N. Whitehead; three volumes, 1910–13), and *Introduction to Mathematical Philosophy* (1919). His works in epistemology and metaphysics include *Our Knowledge of the External World* (1914), *The Analysis of Matter* (1927), and *Human Knowledge, Its Scope and Limits* (1948). Among his books on social issues are *Marriage and Morals* (1929), and *Education and the Social Order* (1932).

GILBERT RYLE (1900–   ), editor of the journal *Mind,* and former Waynflete Professor of Metaphysical Philosophy at Oxford, is a leading figure in the brand of linguistic philosophy inspired by the Ludwig Wittgenstein of the *Philosophical Investigations* and dominant in England after the Second World War. Ryle is best known for his work on the problem of meaning and on philosophical methodology. He has maintained that the sole task of philosophy is to remove conceptual confusion and elucidate the hidden logical form of linguistic expressions. Ryle is the author of *The Concept of Mind* (1949), *Dilemmas* (1954), and many important articles. His latest book is *Plato's Progress* (1966).

JEAN-PAUL SARTRE (1905–   ), a leading figure in the intellectual life of the twentieth century, was born in Paris and studied at the École Normale Supérieure (1924–28). He then taught philosophy in a number of *lycées.* As research student in Berlin and Freiburg (1933–35) he studied Heidegger and Husserl, who greatly influenced his thought. In 1936, Sartre published his first philosophical work, and, in 1938, his first novel, *Nausea.* At the outbreak of World War II, he was called to serve in the French Army, was captured, and returned to Paris, where he took part in the resistance movement and wrote his major philosophical work, *Being and Nothingness* (1943). At the end of the war, Sartre became the most widely known figure in the existentialist movement. Recently, he has taken an active role in politics and in ideological controversies. In his *Critique of Dialectical Reason* (1960), he attempts to demonstrate the basic harmony between Marxism and existentialism.

Other philosophical works by Sartre include *The Transcendence of the Ego* (1936), *The Psychology of the Imagination* (1940), *Existentialism and Humanism* (1946), and *The Problem of Method* (1960). In addition to his philosophical writings he has won distinction with his novels, plays, literary and psychological studies, and his autobiographical *The Words* (1964). In 1964, he won the Nobel Prize for literature, which he refused to accept.

ALFRED SCHUTZ (1899–1959) was born in Vienna, where, at the university, he studied law and the social sciences. In his search for the philosophical foundations of the methodology of the social sciences, Schutz came under the influence of the writings of Edmund Husserl. His understanding of Husserl's phenomenology, and the skill with which he applied it to the foundational studies of sociology, so impressed Husserl that he invited Schutz to become his assistant. Schutz declined the offer for personal reasons. He left Austria in advance of the German occupation and, after spending a year in Paris, emigrated to the United States (1939). In 1943, he joined the Graduate Faculty of Political and Social Science at the New School for Social Research. Schutz is recognized as one of the foremost philosophers of social science. His most important works are *The Phenomenology of the Social World* (1932) and the three-volume *Collected Papers* (1962–66).

J. J. C. SMART (1920–   ), a British philosopher who received degrees from the University of Glasgow and from Oxford, is Hughes Professor of Philosophy at the University of Adelaide, in Australia. His writings include *An Outline of a System of Utilitarian Ethics* (1961), *Philosophy and Scientific Realism* (1963), *Problems of Space and Time* (1964), and *Between Science and Philosophy* (1968).

W. T. STACE (1886–1967), an Anglo-American empirical philosopher, was born in London and studied at Trinity College, Dublin. From 1910 to 1932 he served in the British civil service in Ceylon. While in Ceylon, he published *A Critical History of Greek Philosophy* (1920) and *The Philosophy of Hegel* (1924). In 1932, he resigned from the civil service and accepted a teaching position at Princeton University, where he remained until his retirement in 1955. His other works include *The Theory of Knowledge and Existence* (1932), *The Concept of Morals* (1937), *Time and Eternity* (1952), and *Mysticism and Philosophy* (1960).

P. F. STRAWSON (1919–   ) is a fellow of University College, Oxford and a notable British ordinary language philosopher. Strawson has been concerned with the need of linguistic philosophy to transcend its narrow critical function and become more constructive. This concern is evidenced by his development and advocacy of a task which he calls "descriptive metaphysics." As described in Strawson's influential book, *Individuals* (1959), this task involves the demonstration and explanation of those categories and principles that necessarily underlie our language and thought. Strawson is also known as a significant and effective critic of the formalistic, reformative linguistic philosophy that has been prevalent in America. In addition to *Individuals*, he has written *Introduction to Logical Theory* (1952), *The Bounds of Sense* (1966), and several important articles.

ALFRED TARSKI (1902–   ), who received his doctorate in mathematics from the University of Warsaw in 1924, was a member of the Lwow-Warsaw school of Polish analytical philosophy, under the leadership of Kazimierz Twardowski. He taught mathematics at the University of Warsaw until 1939, when he emigrated to the United States. He was appointed lecturer in mathematics at the University of California at Berkeley in 1942, and has been a professor of mathematics at the same institution since 1946. Tarski has made important contributions to the study of the foundations of mathematics and the development of mathematical logic. He was largely responsible for the emergence of the study of *metamathematics,* or the theory of proof. His major papers on these subjects, written between 1923 and 1938, are collected in his book *Logic, Semantics, Metamathematics* (1956). Tarski's other works include *A Decision Method for Elementary Algebra and Geometry* (1948) and *Undecidable Theories* (with A. Mostowski and R. M. Robinson, 1953).

PAUL TILLICH (1886–1965), an eminent German-American theologian and philosopher, was born in Starzeddel, in Brandenburg. He was ordained in the Evangelical Lutheran church in 1912, and served as a chaplain in the German army during World War I. After the war, he taught at the Universities of Berlin, Marburg, Dresden, and Frankfurt. When Hitler became Chancellor in 1933, Tillich was dismissed from his position at Frankfurt, because of his political views. He emigrated to the United States, where he spent the remainder of his life teaching at Union Theological Seminary, at Harvard, and at the University of Chicago. Tillich's major writings, which reflect the strong influence of existentialism, include *Systematic Theology* (3 volumes, 1951–63), *The Courage to Be* (1952), and *Biblical Religion and the Search for Ultimate Reality* (1955).

FRIEDRICH WAISMANN (1896–1959), born in Vienna and trained as a mathematician and philosopher, was an original member of the "Vienna Circle," the famous group of philosophers and scientists who met under the leadership of Moritz Schlick. After the death of Schlick

(1936) and the subsequent disbanding of the Vienna Circle, Waismann went to England. He taught for two years at Cambridge before becoming Reader in the Philosophy of Science at Oxford, a position which he held until his death. In addition to many papers and articles, he wrote *Introduction to Mathematical Thinking* (1951) and *The Principles of Linguistic Philosophy* (1965).

ALFRED NORTH WHITEHEAD (1861–1947), an outstanding mathematician, philosopher of science, and metaphysician, was born at Ramsgate, on the Isle of Thanet, Kent. He studied mathematics at Trinity College, Cambridge, where he became a fellow. From 1900 to 1911, he collaborated with Bertrand Russell, his most distinguished former pupil, to produce *Principia Mathematica* (1910–13), a landmark in the development of mathematical logic. In 1910, Whitehead moved to London, where he taught at London University and, then, at the Imperial College of Science and Technology. In 1924, he accepted a chair in philosophy at Harvard University. While at Harvard, he developed his philosophy of science into a comprehensive metaphysical system. In addition to the *Principia Mathematica,* Whitehead's chief works include *The Concept of Nature* (1920), *Science and the Modern World* (1925), *Process and Reality* (1929), and *Adventures of Ideas* (1933).

JOHN WISDOM (1904–   ) is a British analytic philosopher who was closely associated with Ludwig Wittgenstein and who has held Wittgenstein's chair in philosophy at Cambridge. At present, he is Professor of Philosophy at the University of Oregon. Wisdom has written widely on the nature of philosophy. His major works are *Interpretation and Analysis* (1931), *Problems of Mind and Matter* (1934), *Other Minds* (1952), *Philosophy and Psycho-analysis* (1953), and *Paradox and Discovery* (1965).

A. D. WOOZLEY (1912–   ) was educated at Haileybury College and at Queen's College, Oxford. He was, for several years, Professor of Moral Philosophy at the University of St. Andrews, and is now Professor of Philosophy at the University of Virginia. A frequent contributor to philosophic journals, he is known mainly for his work in epistemology. His publications include *The Theory of Knowledge* (1949), *Plato's Republic: A Philosophical Commentary* (with R. C. Cross, 1964), and an edition of John Locke's *Essay Concerning Human Understanding* (1964).

INDEX

INDEX

Experience (cont.)
  as felt dimension, 561 ff.; see also "Experiencing"
  generalization from, 401
  and ideas, 42
  initial, of child, 41–44
  and knowledge, 2
  past, 510
  perceptual, 4 f.
  and reason, 508 f.
  See also Knowledge from experience
"Experiencing," definition, 563 ff.
Explicative judgment and sensation, 41
Extension, 77, 89

Facts, vs. sense, 261
  and truth, 499 f.
Faith, 204
  and Catholic Church, 244
  definition, 229
  and emotions, 245–246
  justification, 231 ff.
  and knowledge, 242 ff.
  meaning, 242–244
  and Protestant Church, 245
  and temptation, 299
Falsity, 502; see also Truth
Feeling, and body-mind relation, 135
  and existence of God, 261
  and meaning, 563 ff.
Feelings, word, 31–33
Feigl, H., 140, 140 n., 141
First cause, 214, 215, 218
First matter; see Substance and accidents
Forms, 69, 71
Forsythe, James, 596
"Free," definition, 275
Freedom, meaning, 357–368
  and responsibility, 382–392
  of will, 369–381
    problem of, 175
Free will, 234, 369–381; see also Freedom; Indeterminism
Frege, Gottlob, 542, 546–549
Freud, Sigmund, 266, 267, 358, 359
Future, and induction, 512
  knowledge of, 520
  See also Induction

Gaunilo, 203, 207
Gendlin, Eugene, 404
  biography, 631
Gestalt psychology, 60, 162, 165, 590
God, attributes of, 249
  conception of, 277
  existence of, 14–15, 67, 202–267
  and expectations of, 255
  duty toward, 301–303
  and good, 215
  good of, 285
  idea of, 249
  and idealism, 157
  and moral judgment, 274
  proofs of existence; see Motion, argument from; Ontological argument
  and reality, 208 f.
  as ultimate concern, 248 f.
  See also Agnosticism; Atheism; Deism; Existentialism; Idealism; Naturalism; Pantheism; Theism
Good, 223, 272, 273, 278, 289–297
  as adjective, 348–356
  and virtue, 314–322
  will, 304–313
  See also Duty for good
Governance of the world (Acquinas), 215
Gradation in things (Aquinas), 215
Greatest Happiness Principle, 281, 284
Green, T. H., 43
Gruenbaum, Adolf, 469, 472

Hallucination, 162; see also Illusions
Happiness, 276–279, 281 ff.
  as criteria of morality, 286
Happiness principle, 287
Hare, R. M., 275
  biography, 631
"Hard Data," 18, 19
Hard determinism, 275
Hartshorne, Charles, 469
Hedonism, 336 f.
  egoistic, 276–279
  ethical, 273
Hedonistic utilitarianism, 337
Hegel, Georg Wilhelm Friedrich, 298, 299, 301
Hegelian philosophy, 301